February 14, 2019

Dear Lisa,

Thank you very much for years of friendship and comraderie. I have learned much, and I am honored to share and build our community together.

Warmly,

Michael

SHADOW NETWORKS

Shadow Networks

Financial Disorder and the System that Caused Crisis

FRANCISCO LOUÇÃ
AND MICHAEL ASH

OXFORD
UNIVERSITY PRESS

OXFORD
UNIVERSITY PRESS

Great Clarendon Street, Oxford, OX2 6DP,
United Kingdom

Oxford University Press is a department of the University of Oxford. It furthers the University's objective of excellence in research, scholarship, and education by publishing worldwide. Oxford is a registered trade mark of Oxford University Press in the UK and in certain other countries

First Edition published in 2018
Impression: 1

Published in the United States of America by Oxford University Press
198 Madison Avenue, New York, NY 10016, United States of America

British Library Cataloguing in Publication Data
Data available

Library of Congress Control Number: 2018937601

ISBN 978–0–19–882821–1

Printed and bound in Great Britain by
Clays Ltd, Elcograf S.p.A.

In memory of Christopher Freeman—F.L.
For Alison, Larry, Marshall, and Roberta—M.A.

Acknowledgments

In the preparation of the book, assistance from Eugenia Pires is gratefully acknowledged. Her research was crucial for drafting the first chapters describing the functioning of the shadow banking system. The work of Adriano Campos and Nuno Moniz was essential for the compilation of data on the revolving door between politics and business. Katherine Gabriele, Scott Keating, Shannon Kelly, Zhe Liu, Taylor Smith, and Anna Watzker of the University of Massachusetts Amherst provided invaluable research assistance, compiling micro-biographies of center-liberal party and government people in a dozen developed economies for further analysis of the revolving door. R. Bruce Harper and Roberta Garner provided thoughtful feedback at many stages. Gerald Friedman and Robert Pollin reviewed the full manuscript, and we thank them for careful reading and helpful suggestions. In two different seminars held in Lisbon and Arrábida, Portugal, our colleagues Tanya Araújo, Ricardo Cabral, Helder Coelho, Samuel Eleutério, Gerald Epstein, Larry King, and Kevin Young provided important comments and a fruitful discussion. João Ferreira do Amaral and Mariana Mortágua also commented on previous versions of the book and we appreciate their careful and critical assessment, as well as the suggestions of some anonymous referees for OUP.

Contents

List of Figures and Tables

FIGURES

TABLES

Introduction

This book investigates two questions, how did finance become hegemonic in the capitalist system; and what are the social consequences of the rise of finance? We do not dwell on other topics, such as the evolution of the mode of production or the development of class conflict over the longer run. Our theme is not the genesis, history, dynamics, or contradictions of capitalism but, instead, we address the rise of financialization beginning in the last quarter of the twentieth century and continuing into the twenty-first century. Therefore, we investigate the transnationalization of the circuits and processes of capital accumulation that originated the expansion and financialization of the mechanisms of production, social reproduction, and hegemony, including the ideology, the functioning of the states, and the political decision making. We do not discuss the prevailing neoliberalism as an ideology, although we pay attention to the creation and diffusion of ideas, since we sketch an overview of the process of global restructuring of production and finance leading to the prevalence of the shadow economy.

Shadow finance, or the non-regulated part of the financial system, is a crucial part of the operation of big banks and financial agencies and lives in their orbit, notwithstanding the impressive value it manages. It is a form of economic power. We explore the mechanisms of reproduction of the power of finance and observe that the fundamental characteristics and successes of finance, with its reliance on shadow finance, have been projected into an entire shadow economic system.

Beginning with finance, we discuss how the shadow system was developed, how it recruits its personnel, how it reproduces its ideas and organizations, how it dominates political decision, how it conditions choices, and how its power grows in the world of volatile financial markets.

We will thus discuss the shadow system and some of the tensions and dangers it creates. The threats are always political, but at the end of the second decade of the twenty-first century, we face a combination of dangerous politics and dangerous economics. The imminent perils are Trump and his administration, the speculative bubble generated by the massive injections of liquidity by the central banks, the mountain of debt in China, and the continued fragility of the euro.

But market indicators—"the numbers"—seem to indicate otherwise: during the first half of 2017, the FTSE index for banking registered spectacular growth of 24 percent, especially for the US banks and in some cases for the European banks. By the end of 2017, the S&P500 index reached a historical maximum and peaked at 82 percent above its 2007 finish. The European stock market has been exuberant under the ECB and Mario Draghi's stimuli, and a comfortable wealth effect among the owners of financial assets stimulated new housing bubbles. Business seems once again to be back on its feet.

Indeed, confidence abounds. During 2017, the anticipated payouts to shareholders of the major banks over the next year may disburse nearly all bank earnings. Some banks even doubled the dividends. The mammoth Citigroup has set its total dividend at a higher value than its likely earnings. Since 2007 and all through the long recession, the larger Eurozone banks paid dividends in excess of 40 percent of total earnings.[1] The big bankers meanwhile protest against regulation that would impose a substantial capital reserve, asking for a return to the glorious and highly leveraged era before the subprime crisis. In his 2016 letter to shareholders, Jamie Dimon of Morgan Chase criticizes the increased capital requirements; as did Blankfein from Goldman Sachs.[2] Unfazed by their near-death experience, big banks are back in business. Their business is not traditional banking, it is the shadows.

Throughout this book we argue that a dangerous illusion underpins this euphoria. Over the past post-crisis decade the factors of a new crisis have accumulated. Just as those factors that led to the previous recession emerged from disturbances in a small niche of the financial market, the current process is being repeated, under the impulse of deregulation and new waves of growth of shadow finance. The Eurozone, the speculative bubbles in the stock market or in real estate, political conflicts, disarrangements in international trade, collapses in confidence, different factors may ignite a new crash or a major crisis. Zhou Xiaochuan, the governor of the central bank of China for 15 years, until the end of 2017, decided to leave office with a solemn warning: a "Minsky moment" may be coming—as we shall see in the following pages, that means a major financial crash.[3] Furthermore, other facts threaten stability and confidence: the successive cases demonstrating the loss of legitimacy of political systems, if not their collapse, extending from the coups in Brazil, Egypt, and Turkey, to the waves of victorious populism in India, Hungary, and Poland, and to evidence of political fragility of the traditional parties in other countries, such as Spain, Italy, France, and even Germany.

We will show that finance is a structured power and a mode of social organization. Finance manages its own reproduction through sophisticated means mobilizing ideology, universities, think tanks, lobbies, recruitment and indoctrination centers, institutional connections, education of decision makers, and the naturalization of markets as the center of the economy and life of people. Our investigation of this civilizational transformation under late capitalism can make sense of Trump's election and other recent disruptions of the political systems that prevailed between the Second World War and the Great Recession. The greatest shock of this disruption is the convergence of neoliberal politics with authoritarian solutions, as unmoored populist discontent has mobilized for alternatives without shedding a strict market ideology.

DO IDEAS MOVE THE WORLD?

We document the emergence of the shadow economy and the role of deliberations and actions by central bankers, regulators, government officials, and other decision

[1] *The Economist*, 1 July 2017, 6 May 2017.
[2] The letters to the shareholders are available: Dimon (2017) and Blankfein (2016).
[3] *Financial Times*, 19 October 2017.

makers. We establish the coherence of their campaign for deregulation, liberalization, and globalization processes and the dominance of this position in the world economy since the turn of the 1980s.

So are ideas or material conditions at the core? Some of our colleagues in sociology and economics argue that economic doctrines and creeds move the world. Noting "Economics formatting the market" or emphasizing "the role of economics as a discipline, in the broad sense of the term, in the formatting of calculative agencies," Michel Callon defined a research program on how "economics performs, shapes and formats the economy, rather than observing how [the economy] functions."[4]

We take the position that rather than simply describing how the economy functions or directly shaping the economy, economics describes struggles for power that develop independently of interpretation. For example, the major turn represented by 1980–1—Margaret Thatcher's defeat of the miners' strike and push for a large privatization plan, Ronald Reagan's dismissal of the striking air traffic controllers' union, and Deng Xiaoping's consolidation—represented the culmination of previous dislocations among the relationships of forces. The turn reversed conditions for the development of socially oriented policies and instead promoted neoliberal and privatization strategies.[5]

At an earlier point and at the more micro level of an industry and its leading firms, the electrical-power industry in the US took shape as Thomas Edison and J.P. Morgan, the entrepreneurial inventor and the banker, struggled for control of the standards and regulations defining the industry. There was little role for theories, models, or economic ideas. Sheer greed motivated the quarrel, and raw power determined its outcome. The victors triumphed through their capacity to influence the institutions and to create the markets, more by force than by persuasive ideas. So bitter and thoroughgoing was the fight that it successfully locked the United States into an inefficient technology for more than a century.[6]

Economics also has at times a performative dimension. Take the case of Milton Friedman, someone whose work and career we will discuss in great detail. Friedman was a marginal economist outside the scope of the great synthesis defining macroeconomics after the Second World War and often the object of derision—until the turn in politics and economics imposed by the stagflation recession of 1973–4. He then quickly rose in conjunction with a political movement to launch a neoliberal reconstruction of the social contract and the relationship among the different social classes. The major turn in social relations and economic strategies called for Friedman and rescued his ideas from oblivion. Three decades later, the rise of his radical ideas would be heralded as the "Age of Friedman."

The notion that economists make, or at least influence, markets deserves some attention, in any case.[7] Social facts and economic processes are the prime movers, but there is a relevant and creative role of ideas in the formation of networks of social cohesion and in patterns of decision. The power of recognized experts and the mimetic behavior of different universities, think tanks, governments, and

[4] Callon (1998), pp. 23, 46.

[5] Mason (2009), Cowie (2010), J. Stein (2010), Madrick (2011), Frank (2012), and Galbraith (2015), are among the analyses that document the turn.

[6] Granovetter and McGuire (1998).

[7] MacKenzie, Muniesa, and Siu (2007); Kennedy (2016).

institutions are robust processes for the definition of social norms, of established ideas, of public opinion, and even of electoral majorities. Ideas did not create the world, but they are part of it; they do not invent changes, but can justify them, and justifications are indeed necessary. The acceleration of capital accumulation and the vast increase in social inequality was hard for the broader public to swallow. Acceptance of the new social and economic order required convincing arguments presented by a coherent ideological apparatus and a demonstration of consensus by leading social institutions.

As we shall see in the following chapters, as shadow finance and the shadow economy imposed their rules, the new regime called for armies of imaginative deregulators, fearless liberalizers, independent central bankers arguing for their liberation from democratically established norms, professors of economics planning the indoctrination of the university students from the richest families, cooperating think tanks following what they called "good economics," and networks of firms and different institutions financing, defining, and applying the new law of the land.

A TIME OF LIVING DANGEROUSLY

On November 8, 2016, Donald J. Trump was, to the surprise of many, including the authors, elected President of the United States. US electoral rules enabled Trump's election with substantially fewer votes than his Democratic opponent Hillary Clinton.[8]

During the same electoral campaign, a left insurgency in the Democratic Party led by Senators Bernie Sanders and Elizabeth Warren, both northeastern politicians identified with advocacy for expanded social protections and with opposition to financial interests, threatened but ultimately failed to topple the Clintonian neoliberal hold on their Party.

The result of this election has led to a dangerous turn in world politics. Trump's public positions during the campaign represented a noteworthy departure from the neoliberal doctrine that was shared by dominant actors within both major US political parties. Trump declared his opposition to immigration and to free trade (with no comment on the free movement of capital). His opposition to immigration was expressed with xenophobic and racist clarity. Trump's opposition to free trade broke thoroughly with established economic doctrine. Trump blamed trade deals for the loss of good jobs in the United States and promised to tear up the North American Free Trade Agreement and to scuttle the rapidly advancing Trans-Pacific Partnership. These promises apparently attracted many voters in the de-industrializing states of the northern midwest, the states that carried Trump to victory.

In an additional break with orthodoxy in the Republican Party, Trump expressed openness to deficits, declaring himself the King of Debt. Trump's economic

[8] In the popular election, Hillary Clinton got 2,868,691 more votes than did Donald Trump (CNN, 2017).

proposal also includes enormous tax cuts for the wealthy with appeal to the potential for job creation and trickle-down benefits. While Republican delivery of this standard proposal typically uses accounting gimmicks to mask the effect on deficits, which traditional Republicans claim to deplore, Trump evinced less concern about the effect on fiscal balance. Trump also promised infrastructure investment—adding a xenophobic spin, the most heralded infrastructure project was a wall on the US-Mexico border to keep out "illegal immigrants," a favorite scapegoat of the populist wing of the Republican Party. The promise of jobs building infrastructure was undoubtedly a key element of Trump's electoral success in traditionally Democratic rustbelt states. Wisconsin had last voted for a Republican in Reagan's 1984 landslide, and neither Michigan nor Pennsylvania had voted Republican since 1988.

Neoliberal scolds associated with the Democratic Party emphasized the fiscal irresponsibility of the Trump proposals but failed to create an alternative vision of developing infrastructure, providing good jobs, or improving the distribution of income with redistributive fiscal policy.[9]

Trumponomics is a puzzle from which coherence has yet to emerge. Some elements, in particular trade skepticism and infrastructure spending, represent a break with the neoliberal consensus. Other portions, including continued free rein given to finance, the reduction of social protections, and the likelihood that any infrastructure spending that does emerge will be carried out in the form of public-private partnerships, conforms more closely to the neoliberal model.

There is no question that Trumpism carries some of the trappings of populism and right-wing extremism, including, per Robert O. Paxton's definition, an "obsessive preoccupation with community decline, humiliation, or victimhood and by compensatory cults of unity, energy and purity . . . "[10] Yet it is not clear that a really distinct model will emerge.

The greatest long-term dangers of Trumponomics are military spending (including a domestic security state) and denial of climate change. With respect to the military, Trump has turned heavily to hawks for positions in his cabinet and has already seeded conflict with China with an ostentatious and provocative dalliance with Taiwan. Military expenditure has historically proven a reliable means of generating bipartisan support for public spending and fiscal stimulus without the usual concern for balanced budgets. Trump is additionally committed to an overhaul of US nuclear capabilities, to leaning on allies to purchase American-made military hardware, and to wiping out Islamist insurgencies in southwest Asia. Although the stimulative capacity of military spending is less than that of domestic spending,[11] military Keynesianism remains a potent economic force. The risk of escalating conflict that accompanies increased military spending is substantial.

[9] During the campaign, Trump was evasive on the subject of worker protections. At her speech at the Republican Convention, Trump's daughter Ivanka, a close confidant and adviser, suggested support for paid family leave for new parents—a longstanding gap in social protection in the United States. Trump also expressed support for an increase in the minimum wage to $10 per hour from the current $7.25 per hour which has prevailed since 2009. At the same time, Trump campaigned against the Obama health care reforms which extended health insurance coverage to tens of millions of Americans.

[10] Paxton (2007). [11] Pollin and Garrett-Peltier (2009).

With respect to climate change, Trump has surrounded himself with climate-change deniers and executives of fossil-fuel companies. Chasing key votes in depressed mining states, Trump promised to restore the US coal industry by lifting regulations that he blamed for the decline of coal employment. A difficulty for Trump is that market forces, in particular, the rapid reduction in the price of electricity thanks to new technologies in both natural gas and in renewables, have likely placed the coal industry beyond the help of deregulation. But coal can still do enormous climate damage on its way out the door. The consequences of inaction on climate change are grave and cumulative.

For our analysis, does Trump fit into the shadow economy? In terms of personnel, Trump's cabinet is drawn from the elite nomenklatura of the shadow economy, complete with MBAs from the best schools, with C-suite experience, and with long engagement in the financialized economy, especially at Goldman Sachs. Trump's men (overwhelmingly) are coarser and cruder than the operatives whom they displace. They come from an uglier, xenophobic and racist, part of the shadows. Trump's working-class supporters expect their candidate to do something. But it is hard to picture Trump's men significantly intervening in the flows of labor, goods, and capital, the system of tubes that carry wealth for the one percent.

In terms of consequences, the outcomes are harder to predict. The failure to reckon fully with the crash of 2007–8 and to acknowledge and remedy the broad decay of working class wellbeing for a generation has sown seeds of which Trump's election is but one sprout.

At one of the magic moments of his electoral run, Donald Trump chastened finance as "a global power structure that is responsible for the economic decisions that have robbed our working class, stripped our country of its wealth, and put that money into the pockets of a handful of large corporations."[12]

In short, money still rules Washington. The enshrinement of Goldman Sachs in the Trump administration signals the maturity and resilience of a political and economic force unequaled since the House of Morgan, the empire of the

[12] The *New York Times* quoted this speech and noted the contradiction, as the nominees for the new administration were presented and the "elite was embraced" (30 November 2016). Beginning with the election, Trump rapidly and fully aligned with the most anti-worker wing of the Republican Party. The first nominee for Secretary of Labor, an executive of the fast-food industry, the sector of the economy most dependent on low wages, held such a long and flamboyant record of opposition to the minimum wage, overtime, and other worker protections that he was ultimately forced to withdraw from consideration. The commitment to overturning the Obama health care reforms indicates that the populist rhetoric of the campaign can find no place in Trump's government.

As the Trump administration took shape, the financiers emerged and took office as possibly the richest government in history. Trump named Wilbur L. Ross, Jr., an investor in distressed assets, as Secretary of Commerce and billionaire Betsy DeVos, to head the Department of Education. Elaine Chao, the Secretary of Transportation, joins the government directly from the board of Murdoch's News Corporation and also enjoyed experience at Wells Fargo Bank.

Perhaps most striking is the reliance on veterans of Goldman Sachs. Steven Mnuchin, a co-investor of George Soros and ex Goldman Sachs man, serves as the powerful Secretary of the Treasury. Steve Bannon, whose interregnum between Goldman Sachs and the White House, was marked by management of the right-wing media site Breitbart.com, was special adviser to the President. While Goldman was merely a stop on Mnuchin's and Bannon's circuits through power, Gary Cohn, a longtime and senior Sachs executive served as National Economic Adviser. Three months after Trump's election, shares of Goldman Sachs were up by 36 % (*The Economist*, March 18, 2017).

banker J.P. Morgan (1837–1913). President Trump built his unexpected triumph on a declaration of war against Wall Street and Washington. Trump even singled out Goldman Sachs by name, first in attacks on his Republican rival Senator Ted Cruz, whose wife is a Goldman Sachs executive, then on his Democratic rival Hillary Clinton whose paid confidential speeches to it and other banks deflated Democratic support and convinced undecided voters of the insincerity of her more populist stances, and finally in a thinly veiled appeal to anti-Semitic stereotypes about secret leagues of Jewish bankers seeking to control the world.[13]

Throughout the campaign, Trump dabbled in economic populism, promising a return to Glass-Steagall as a symbol of a once-great America led by industry not finance, in spite of the fact that his aides promised to annihilate the Volcker Rule regulating banking. Yet immediately upon his victory, Trump wholeheartedly embraced these creatures from the financial swamp. As a matter of fact, Trump's campaign and, even more so, his cabinet picks rejected financial regulation. As a consequence, a repeal or substantial diminishment of the Dodd-Frank Act, the relatively mild financial reform law passed in the wake of the scandals and crash of 2007–8, seems likely. Trump's dance with finance reflects a longstanding tension on the right between a populist tendency and a fundamental alignment with the goals of elites.

"He can speak their language," explained Gary Kaminsky, a former vice chairman of J.P. Morgan Stanley, defending Mnuchin's appointment.[14] Precisely.

To understand the arrival of the Trump era and what has and has not changed, we explore the language, social behavior, and rules and organization of the financialized economy and its shadows.

THE INTERPRETERS OF THE SHADOW ECONOMY

The shadow economy is moved by economic powers, by social groups, and by a community of thought.[15] One important component of the shadow economy is that network of practitioners and academics—often without sharp delineation between the two—whose authoritative claims to policy-relevant knowledge have reshaped the rules, regulations, and practices of many domestic economies and the global economy over the past four decades. But beyond expertise and competence, the shadow economy comprises one or more concrete networks with access to political and economic power—the ability to shape and make decisions. The shadow economy is distinct because of its capacity to put ideas into practice.

In an article-length obituary in the *Journal of Economic Literature*, Andrei Shleifer refers to this community as he declares the past half-century to be the *Age of Friedman*.[16] Milton Friedman resides at the intellectual core of the shadow economy. Other key intellectual figures include Friedrich Hayek, James Buchanan,

[13] Marshall (2016). [14] *Washington Post*, 30 November 2016.

[15] Haas (1992), p. 3, defined an epistemic community as "a network of professionals with recognized expertise and competence in a particular domain and an authoritative claim to policy relevant knowledge within that domain or issue-area."

[16] Shleifer (2009).

and Eugene Fama. The contributions of the latter to finance and the concomitant centrality of finance are key components of the neoliberal drive. It would also be a mistake to omit Ayn Rand for the *joie d'esprit* that she brought to the enterprise and her influence on acolytes such as Alan Greenspan and legions of admiring fans in the quotidian world of practicing finance. Rand, a prime mover of the Cold War spirit among US intellectuals, contributed to building an edifice of social difference as the anchor of social life: as Ludwig von Mises, a renowned and influential neoliberal economist, put it in a letter to her about the novel *Atlas Shrugged*, "you have the courage to tell the masses what no politician told them: you are inferior and all improvements in your conditions which you simply take for granted you owe to the efforts of men that are better than you."[17]

As a network involving influential individual agents, the shadow economy is certainly not a conspiracy—it is supported and interpreted by a powerful intellectual movement, but also by social and economic forces that emerge from globalization and capital accumulation. They are the subject of this book.

FEATURES OF THE SHADOW INTELLECTUAL MOVEMENT

An important feature of an economic system is resilience, its ability to avert crises and to recover from crises when they do occur. In the case of the shadow economy, the resilience manifested in the undaunted response of the true believers to the crash of 2008. The resilience which demonstrates significant resistance to criticism and a thick skin in the face of obvious disasters. To pronounce, "What bubble? What crisis?" in 2009, 2010, and 2011 required extraordinary cheek. Yet Eugene Fama, another Nobel laureate, known for his neoliberal indoctrination in the field of finance, was able to hold the line. Immediately after the crash, some of his followers could even speak of expansionary austerity with a straight face.

Another important feature of an intellectual system is that it provides methodological completeness and comprehensiveness in its capacity to address new problems. As we will discuss in the course of the next chapters, Friedman, Buchanan, Fama, and Greenspan peddled both values and analysis that gave guidance on what had happened and what to do next. Their success was the creation of ideas, tools, and the will to apply them as part of a reconfiguration of the dominant forces of capital.

The success of this movement also required three other characteristics. It should be capable of disciplining membership, defining the boundaries that can exclude or marginalize deviators, even high-profile defectors such as James K. Galbraith, Joseph Stiglitz, Paul Krugman, and Richard Posner. It should be able to translate between intellectual and wealth-generating worlds, so that ideas can become policies and the desired policies be communicated to academia to become research

[17] From a 23 January 1958 letter by Von Mises to Rand, reprinted in the *Journal of Libertarian Studies* (Winter 2007, p. 11). The novel ends with a train crash, not attributable to negligence but to the very social characteristics of the victims: one was the beneficiary of public money, another was a public regulator, another used to scorn businessmen, as quoted by Frank (2012, p. 147).

agendas. Thirdly, it requires the capacity to mobilize at multiple levels, from palace intrigue and domination of intra-party politics within the center left to electoral success, the control of media, and the production of common sense as hegemony.

Universities, institutes, and think-tank networks, central banks, the selection of professionals and decision makers, networks in private, wealth-generating activity, especially finance, will be the protagonists of this book. This is precisely the construction we will verify in the making, as we investigate the university consensus, the education and reproduction of elites, the weight of the powerful institutions, and the revolving door between politics and business.

SHADOW BANKING *IS* BANKING

We have adopted the term "shadow economy" as an explicit parallel to the concept of shadow banking. Shadow banking builds from the fundamental contradiction of banking. Banking must be conservative. As David Graeber has noted, "We must pay our debts" is at the heart of banking.[18]

In old banking, banks make money on the interest-rate spread, low inflation, and presumptions of repayment. Bankers seek the assistance of the state in keeping inflation low lest inflation erode the real interest rate. Bankers also seek the assistance of the state in collecting debts. Therefore, old style banks were supposed to manage risk and competition in a prudent way; deviation from the creed was not unheard of but remained deviant.

Instead banks today make big money by not being conservative. Bankers make money by making many deals and by collecting service fees. Three deals are better than two and so on. The traditional intermediation of a lender depositing funds in the bank and the bank lending funds to a qualified borrower provides a single interest-rate spread and, at most, two opportunities for fees. But an extended chain of a lender providing funds to a money market fund, a money market fund providing funds to a bank, for example, by a reverse repo, a bank financing (and perhaps operating) a mortgage company, and the mortgage company providing funds to a borrower seeking to buy a new house offers five opportunities for fees with complex formal and informal agreements for sharing the fees among the dealmakers. Bankers maintain these lucrative arrangements by specializing in private and innovative, or "over-the-counter," deals that are not easily subjected to competition by other banks.

Bankers also make money by making leveraged deals that maximize profits with minimal outlay by the bankers themselves. Both fees for service and leveraging up proved high-profit activities for bankers who for many years had to content themselves with collecting the spread between their depositor and borrower interest rates.

But the new banking creates new systemic risks. The additional deals in the lending chain constitute a proliferation of interconnections, a multiplication of counterparty risk, and opportunities for informational asymmetries, exercises of

[18] Graeber (2011).

power, and confidence about probabilities that diverges from actual risks. The deals themselves create streams of fees. The risks are often structured so that success generates high private returns for the parties to the transaction while failure can be spread to the unwitting. Therefore, instead of risks for individual banks (and their customers), systemic risk emerges as the most dangerous form of uncertainty.

By making leveraged deals, banks create a high risk for their own capital and the capital of their funders, a fundamental contradiction. Shadow banking, or non-regulated banking agencies, is a means of extending the chain and extending the leverage beyond what regulated and insured banking is allowed to do.

As we shall discuss, shadow finance is a more complex and certainly more profound system than that evoked by a mere change of mentalities and business practices at the desk of the bank. As a consequence, networks of finance and networks of political power lie at the center of our analysis. In no endeavor has the network become more central than in finance. Indeed, for this, shadow banking has been defined as network finance with the network as their central and defining feature.[19] The power and danger of network finance became clear in the meltdown of 2007–8, but the map has not changed since then. The first part of this book will be dedicated to these events, describing the tsunami of the financial crash.

CAPITALISM AND FINANCE

Capitalism needs to know what "capital is worth." This knowledge is fundamental for decision making, for example, whether to invest and in what to invest.

But "what capital is worth" is probably unknowable. The heated controversies among economists in the 1960s showed disagreements over what capital is and whether it can be valued or not. If every piece of physical capital has ambiguous value because it has a vintage and embedded technology, is itself embedded in firms and other institutions, and can be revalued very quickly if the environment or the embedding institution changes, then it does not make sense to talk about the value of capital. The reasons might be Marxian or Sraffian—the value of capital depends on the rate of profit and the rate of profit is determined in a social rather than technical process—or the reasons might be contextual or environmental. But in any case, "the value of a unit of capital" has limited microeconomic and macroeconomic meaning.

Yet liberal financial markets seem to offer an opportunity to resolve the problem. If financial markets can assign value to capital in real time then "what is capital worth" is saved.

The q theory of investment draws from this faith in financial markets to evaluate capital. In q theory, firms assess the opportunity for capital investment by comparing the financial valuation that financial markets will make concerning the investment to the real concrete price of the new capital. If the financial market valuation of the benefit exceeds the real value of the cost, then the firm is in a profitable investment environment and the acquisition of the asset is warranted. If

[19] Guttmann (2015).

not, then the firm should hold or even disinvest. But this decision making rubric is viable only if financial markets are accurate about the value the firm will derive from the physical capital in question. If and only if financial markets are right, then capitalism is OK. Without reliable valuation of capital, the fundamental arguments about efficiency fall apart.

Deregulated financial markets are supposed to be able to do this, i.e., to accurately value capital, because of incentives to be right and the large numbers of independent guesses. Financial markets are the original crowd-sourcing institutions, indeed the source of the metaphor, with reference to the wisdom of the crowd.

Yet the fundamental problems for the simplistic narrative are correlation and uncertainty. With respect to correlation, both the harsh macro facts, i.e., the shared macroeconomic environment of all of the market participants, and the behavioral problems—mostly herding, from spurs of optimism or pessimism—render the guesses irrevocably dependent rather than independent. All of the practical wisdom of modern finance, in particular the capacity to diversify away idiosyncratic risk, goes out the window when global markets go down the toilet. What the financial crashes prove is that the liberal theory is worthless.

RADICAL UNCERTAINTY

Finance and market transactions need legitimacy. A key part of legitimacy is that it should always be clear who will get—and by extension, deserve—what. Contracts and the legal system give the impression of rationalizing and ordering and thereby allaying potential conflict. According to the contract, the party of the first part will receive this portion and the party of the second part will receive that portion. Good contracts spell out the allocation in contingencies, with excellent contracts virtually airtight against complicated contingencies and conflict. Poor contracts fail to account for contingencies.

The reverence in which contracts are held can be seen in the extent to which they protect even workers in a capitalist system. Failure to pay a contracted wage is a grave offense for a capitalist. In the US, such a failure is punished with treble damages—and this in a system not known for its generosity to workers. (Exploitation is to happen by surplus extraction, not primitive accumulation.) Again, the point is that contracts are expected to spell out what is going to happen to whom.

In the financial sphere, complex contracts are the order of the day. Both vanilla market contracts and over-the-counter contracts specify highly complex contingencies. Consider tranched obligations and credit default swaps.

But the reality of finance is much messier and stickier. When push comes to shove, not all contingencies are provided for. Katharina Pistor of Columbia University argues, indeed, that contracts simply cannot provide for all possible contingencies.[20] The dissolution of one of the parties to the contract, for example, is by definition outside the terms of the contract.

[20] Pistor (2013).

Thus, the relevant financial and legal institutions must be able to determine whose claims will be honored in the breach. Pistor invokes the concept of "Elasticity of Law" in her work towards a Legal Theory of Finance (contrasted explicitly with the liberal "Law and Finance" approach). Not all claims will be honored and not all claims will be honored equally in financial crises. The determination of which claims are and which claims are not fully honored delimits the Elasticity of Law in this case. Pistor writes: "at the apex where the very survival of the system is at stake, law tends to be more elastic by design and/or because the system's ultimate backstop abrogates the discretionary power to do what it takes to rescue the system."[21]

In a distant past already facing financial crises, the British journalist Walter Bagehot enunciated the principle of providing complete liquidity for the solvent and letting the insolvent fall. The contemporary extraordinary extension of liquidity even to insolvent financial institutions that did not qualify under Bagehot's principle constituted a clear stretching of the bounds and rules. This was elasticity in action.

The selection of the beneficiaries of elastic largesse was defended on the basis of systemic necessity. Banks too big to fail or, in the new parlance, too interconnected to fail, received significant assistance and allowances, in the United States and Europe. Even among banks, however, there was differential indulgence, sometimes at random and sometimes via webs of power. Bear Stearns received a bailout in March 2008. Lehman Brothers was permitted to fail that September. In retrospect these decisions appear arbitrary.

Elasticity is not randomly distributed but is dished out according to connectedness and power. No elasticity was available for the poorer peripheral polities of Europe during the European sovereign debt crisis while much slack was paid out to the large banks headquartered in the core.

But, if neither divine nor genetic inscription motivates our inclination toward capital accumulation, why do money, finance, and greed dominate our lives? This book provides a possible answer, discussing how shadow finance became a shadow power in our societies.

SHADOWS EVERYWHERE

As we shall see through the book, shadow finance dominates the developed economies. Its rise has immense consequences and is shattering our world. It is not a consequence of any behavioral constant or human essence imposing greed as the pattern of life under the Sun. It is rather the outcome of the interplay of institutional choices, economic forces, and ideological impositions—three facets of power. The dominance of the shadow economy and finance is part of the logic of capital even if its particular form and evolution were not predetermined.

We will focus on the networks guaranteeing this result over a long period of time. The first great network is that of firms, in particular the financial industry,

[21] Pistor (2013).

connecting giant banks to the domains of unregulated credit and intermediation. The financial industry created the wonders of securitization, security being an ironic name for products that delivered massive insecurity to financial markets. But these firms transformed through the process of deregulation: the balance sheets of banks are typically lies, since they hide their shadow agencies. Regulation became not only a farce but also a pricey one, given the amount of public bailout operations since the subprime crash.[22]

Finance constitutes by itself a dense network. It is capable of mobilizing at different levels, such as through palace intrigue (we will investigate the battle of Lawrence Summers, a US Treasury Secretary, against Brooksley Born, the leader of a regulatory agency who dared to propose to regulate the derivatives); ideological authority (one telling case being the argument for "expansive austerity" in Europe); intellectual comprehensiveness (the central bankers' connection is an example, namely that of the Friedmanite disciples, from Greenspan to Bernanke at the US Federal Reserve), and disciplinary capacity imposing hegemony. To do so, it requires a second network, that of indoctrination and selection of cadre, a network of professionals with common notions, recognized expertise and shared language, active in business and government alike, bridging over differences and establishing cohesion in ruling.

It is remarkable in any case how the neoliberal and financial paradigm survived its first ten years of severe failure basically unscathed. The strength of these networks gives clues to the solution of one historical enigma: why were neoliberal ideas and action replaced by another economic paradigm after the 1929 crisis, and why instead did they come out of the 2008 crash and recession defiant and apparently reinforced? But the wheel is still in spin. Trump's electoral success in the US is among the most prominent signs of the ongoing crisis.

The resilience of failure may surprise someone inattentive to the configuration of the central banks, the rating agencies, the regulators, the governments, and the universities forming the ideas and the personnel for the new world. The access to political and social power by finance is a characteristic part of its dominance of the shadow economy.

THE PLAN OF THE BOOK

Part I tells the story of what happened during the financial crash of 2007–8 and the crisis that followed (the global recession, the 2011 European euro and debt crisis, then the 2014 crisis in many emerging economies). It compiles the definitions, types of structures, and measurements of shadow finance. Finally, we investigate family and traditional businesses, seeking to detect their immense relevance, and

[22] Markets and firms have been in tension since the early days of capitalism. In the late nineteenth century, the balance shifted to the firm with the rise of industrial giants, as documented by Chandler and theorized by Coase. More recently, finance has enshrined the market over the firm both on its own turf, with market finance supplanting bank finance and perhaps as or more importantly in every industrial and service domain as well.

discuss how they intertwine with shadow finance, to discover how small our world is.

Part II describes how changes in policy, from deregulation to central bank management, made the tsunami possible. Shadow finance showed remarkable resilience. After the 2007–8 crash, the shadow banking system, the epicenter responsible for the fall, regrouped, pivoted, resisted criticism, and avoided attempts at a new regulation. The shadow banking system disciplined its tentacles and proved capable of mobilizing through both palace intrigues (defeating the rationalizers of the financial system) and hegemonic moves (imposing austerity in Europe).

Part III investigates how this power was constituted and how it framed the consensus, the ideas, and the system of connections between business and politics. A survey of these connections is presented in order to investigate this global network of ideas, managed by the policymakers and financiers that rule the world. This manufacturing of consent proved capable of resisting and recomposing itself after the global crisis.

Part IV examines the frauds, the institutions, and the practices that created the crash, and introduces the web of power, asking how powerful finance is.

Finally, Part V discusses what comes next. Long depression, secular stagnation, new crashes, or a comfortable recovery? Fairness or inequality, convergence among economies or divergence among societies? Do banks need to be regulated, socialized, or abolished? Global conflicts and local empires? If these are relevant democratic questions, they should be studied and thoroughly discussed. That is our aim.

Part I

The World of Shadow Finance

1

Greed and the Adventures of *Homo economicus*

"Greed moves mountains," "The world is for the winners." You have heard different versions of this speech, always emphasizing that greed is the driving force in modern economies and that everyone benefits from such attitudes. In this chapter, we proceed to a short survey of these justifications, which define the ideology and represent the beginning of finance.

GREED MAKES THE WORLD GO ROUND

Where runaway greed is concerned, there is a fine line between cautionary tale and braggadocio. Gordon Gekko, Michael Douglas's Oscar-winning characterization in Oliver Stone's *Wall Street*, earned notoriety for his flamboyant speech about the goodness of greed. The year was 1987, and greed illuminated the cinema screen and the era. (A significant crash was only months away, but Gekko would be long gone.) Both in manhandling the demoralized workers and well-meaning managerial capitalists of the firm that he would acquire, loot, and discard and in enticing the junk-bond speculators who financed his pillaging, Gekko's message was the same: *Greed rules the world, I'll take what's mine*, just as J.R. Ewing, the oil baron in *Dallas* would have said a decade before.

Entrepreneurship was the banner, accumulation the aim, and wealth the measure. *Wall Street* explored the uncertain frontier between illegal action and creative finance in the culture of plunder. Even though Gekko, an obvious villain, got his just deserts, his tale nonetheless illustrated the narrative that one could easily become very rich very quickly. Reality overshadowed even the exaggerated fiction, as proved by the rapid growth in profits, bonuses, and handsome gifts, and—when they were caught—the feeble penalties imposed on the dominant players in this world.[1] Some moviegoers were confused about whether they were witnessing a critique of or an homage to the power of greed.[2]

[1] The only banker to be punished in Britain immediately after the 2008 crash was an executive of the Royal Bank of Scotland who was stripped of his knighthood (C. Ferguson, 2012, p. 92). About a decade later, four Barclays executives were fined US $400 million by the UK Serious Fraud Office for corruption in Qatar, and five senior executives of Novacaixagalicia, from Spain, were jailed for fraud.

[2] Anthony Scaramucci is one example: he wrote a book, *Goodbye Gordon Gekko* (Scaramucci, 2010), on the culture of greed. Before his fifteen minutes of fame as the communications director of Trump,

In 1985, Michael Lewis, then a 25-years-old university graduate with a degree in English literature, took a job at Salomon Brothers. After three years, Lewis left to tell his tale in *Liar's Poker*, an insider's account disparaging finance. Lewis, whose ongoing career in journalism includes writing in the *New York Times* and editing *Vanity Fair*, devotes his attention to uncovering the secrets and excesses of finance. (In the same vein he also wrote the book adapted into the 2015 film *The Big Short*.)

Salomon was a small firm at the time. In 1985, it managed US $68 billion in assets, and CEO Gutfreund got US $3.2 million, small change by today's standards. Dimon, Blankfein, and Thain would get ten to twenty or thirty times that sum before—and after—the 2007 crash. In 1990, all the top executives and traders of Salomon split US $10 million; nine years later, a single executive of Citigroup would get ten times that much.

Yet Lewis still expresses surprise at the reception of the first book: his exposé of the robber barons was taken by some readers as a paean to the "king of Wall Street" or the "not-so-benevolent king of Wall Street,"[3] Salomon's CEO John Gutfreund. Some readers even took the book as career advice on an exciting journey into financial speculation. Lewis's account of his disillusionment in the short-lived magazine *Portfolio* is worth reading:

> I thought I was writing a period piece about the 1980s in America. Not for a moment did I suspect that the financial 1980s would last two full decades longer or that the difference in degree between Wall Street and ordinary life would swell into a difference in kind. I expected readers of the future to be outraged that back in 1986, the CEO of Salomon Brothers, John Gutfreund, was paid $3.1 million; I expected them to gape in horror when I reported that one of our traders, Howie Rubin, had moved to Merrill Lynch, where he lost $250 million; I assumed they'd be shocked to learn that a Wall Street CEO had only the vaguest idea of the risks his traders were running. What I didn't expect was that any future reader would look on my experience and say, "How quaint."
>
> I had no great agenda, apart from telling what I took to be a remarkable tale, but if you got a few drinks in me and then asked what effect I thought my book would have on the world, I might have said something like, "I hope that college students trying to figure out what to do with their lives will read it and decide that it's silly to phony it up and abandon their passions to become financiers." I hoped that some bright kid at, say, Ohio State University who really wanted to be an oceanographer would read my book, spurn the offer from Morgan Stanley, and set out to sea.
>
> Somehow that message failed to come across. Six months after *Liar's Poker* was published, I was knee-deep in letters from students at Ohio State who wanted to know if I had any other secrets to share about Wall Street. They'd read my book as a how-to manual. In the two decades since then, I had been waiting for the end of Wall Street. The outrageous bonuses, the slender returns to shareholders, the never-ending scandals, the bursting of the internet bubble, the crisis following the collapse of

and before the White House, Scaramucci had a career at Goldman Sachs, from 1989 to 1996, even becoming a vice president in the private wealth management area in 1993. He made his fortune convincing Vikram Pandit, CEO of Citigroup, to sell him the bank's portfolio of hedge funds (Navidi, 2017, 54). He was also notorious for having paid 100 thousand dollars for a participation of 15 seconds in Oliver Stone's *Wall Street: Money Never Sleeps*. In an interview for *Harvard Law Today* (Greenfield, 2010), Scaramucci argues "greed is fundamentally bad," since "it causes people to make short term expedient decisions that are harmful in the long run. That is the fundamental point of the book."

[3] *Time*, 15 February 1999; *Business Week*, 9 December 1985.

> Long-Term Capital Management: over and over again, the big Wall Street investment banks would be, in some narrow way, discredited. Yet they just kept on growing, along with the sums of money that they doled out to 26-year-olds to perform tasks of no obvious social utility. The rebellion by American youth against the money culture never happened. Why bother to overturn your parents' world when you can buy it, slice it up into tranches, and sell off the pieces?
>
> At some point, I gave up waiting for the end. There was no scandal or reversal, I assumed, that could sink the system.[4]

While Upton Sinclair remarked ruefully about his book *The Jungle*, "I aimed for the public's heart and by accident hit it in the stomach," Michael Lewis and Oliver Stone aimed for the public's heart and hit some itchy palms.

The doomed future Lewis was accurately foreseeing would be much brighter for the beneficiaries of "outrageous bonuses" than for the rest of us. With but a few exceptions, the protagonists of the 2007–8 financial meltdown continue to live safely and comfortably. For them, finance was, and is, the avenue that leads to riches and power, and the age of globalization is the perfect epoch for daring enterprises. In 1982, not a single person on the *Forbes* list of the world's fifty richest people was a banker or financier; by 2012, financiers accounted for eleven out of the top fifty,[5] and in 2015 the number increased to thirteen.[6] A global bank may register profits surpassing the GDP of the hundred poorest countries, and a significant number of successful bankers may bring home eight figures. The rise of finance is a dominant feature of our time.

It was not always thus. In 1975, the top American bankers were making less than US $1.5 million per year (in today's dollars, accounting for inflation), including salary, bonuses, director's fees, and deferred compensation (column 1 of Table 1.1).[7] (The then-exotic concept of stock options was not included in the accounting.) These chief bankers also had long terms of service in their banks. The newest member of the top bankers club, Gabriel Hauge of Manufacturers Hanover, had a mere 16 years of service.

Compare the pay for bankers at the leading commercial banks today (see column 2 of Table 1.1).

With all ten earning more than US $10 million and some approaching US $30 million,[8] American bankers have truly entered the realm of Masters of the Universe. And the European bankers are not far behind.[9]

The tale is old enough to have its own anthems. "Money makes the world go around," sang Liza Minnelli on her way to an Oscar in Bob Fosse's 1972 film *Cabaret*. The film, set in the Berlin of the 1930s, showed the darkness that had descended upon the city after an orgy of speculation and collapse. For the two generations that were raised after the narrow defeat of that dreadful shadow

[4] Lewis (2015).

[5] As noted in spring 2013 by fund manager Dylan Grice of Edelweiss Holdings in the ZeroHedge blog (Grice, 2013).

[6] Forbes (2017). [7] Brua (1975).

[8] Tor and Arif (2014); CBInsight (2015), and Equilar (2016). According to Equilar, in 2016, the median pay level of the CEOs of the S&P 500, a sample of large, publicly traded firms, was US $10.8 million; A telling story is that of Henrique de Castro, hired by Marissa Mayer to be the second in charge at Yahoo and then fired one year later with severance pay of US $60 million (Luckerson (2015)).

[9] Spoerry and Arif (2014).

Table 1.1. Pay of top US bankers, 1975 and 2014

Bank	CEO remuneration 1975 (millions)	Bank	CEO remuneration 2014 (millions)
Citicorp	$1.9	J.P. Morgan Chase	$27.7
First Chicago	1.9	Wells Fargo	21.4
Mfrs Hanover	1.4	Capital One	19.6
Chase Manhattan	1.4	U.S. Bancorp	19.4
J.P. Morgan	1.3	State Street	18.8
Harris Bankcorp	1.3	Bank of America	15.3
Nortrust Corp	1.2	Citigroup	14.5
Wachovia Corp	1.2	BB&T	14.4
Chemical	1.1	TCF Financial	13.0

Notes and sources: The table reports the compensation of the nine highest paid bank CEOs for each year in millions of 2014 CPI-inflation-adjusted dollars. Total remuneration for 1975 includes salary, bonuses, director's fees, and deferred compensation but not stock options (Brua, 1975). Total compensation for 2014 includes salary, bonuses, incentives, stock awards, stock options, change in pension value, and other compensation (Tor and Arif, 2014).

world, the business of avarice was synonymous with sociopathic behavior. A major cultural reversal was required to change that perception and the norms encapsulating it.

GREED AND MARKETS

"For the love of money is the root of all evil: which while some coveted after, they have erred from the faith, and pierced themselves through with many sorrows" warns St. Paul in his first epistle to Timothy in the New Testament (*King James Version* 1 Timothy 6:10). Matthew 6:24 observes starkly, "Ye cannot serve God and Mammon." Mammon, or Plutus for the Greeks, appears in Luke 16:9, 16:11, and 16:13, with that verse repeated in Matthew 6:24. Mammon, a prince from Hell, carried by (or sometimes embodying) a wolf, represents greed and wealth. His curse has continued across the centuries. Almost a millennium afterwards, Thomas Aquinas, in his *Summa Theologica* (written in 1265–74), describes avarice as "Mammon being carried up from Hell by a wolf, coming to inflame the human heart with Greed." Similarly, for Dante Alighieri, in the *Divine Comedy*, Mammon was the wolf-like demon of wealth, and greed was indicted as a dangerous form of malice. For the Florentine poet, Mammon represented the bankers of the city, who, because they imposed high rates of interest on desperate people, were relegated to an even lower circle of Hell than thieves. The Italian poet from the thirteenth century proposed a benevolent universal ruler to tame the demons and eradicate the corruption of avarice and greed, but to no avail. Niccolò Machiavelli, another Florentine, responded two centuries later with the figure of the Prince, a despotic ruler who ignored benevolence and instead concentrated on the effective power of money and the sword. Neither writer could imagine the despotic heights of late twentieth-century finance.

Mephistopheles in Goethe's *Faust* (1808) saves the Emperor and the Empire—by introducing paper money. His Majesty learns that, in a society moved by greed, knowledge of greed is power. Both drama and satire, Goethe's play mocks the tortuous emergence of paper money in Europe in the era of the French Revolution. With the emergence of modernity, the Machiavellian Prince can grasp immense power only by understanding human attitudes toward money.

As modern markets came to shape the world, different writers and movements voiced their nostalgic and utopian opposition to Mammon. "The Gospel of Mammonism," a chapter in Thomas Carlyle's *Past and Present* (1843), decries nineteenth-century industry and its materialism. Carlyle, a conservative, fears the loss of civilization under Mammon's curse, as the prince from Hell personifies the winds of modernity in his account of the Industrial Revolution.

KINDNESS AS A SOCIAL FABRIC

In spite of Biblical injunctions and cultural condemnations, Mammon was not cast out. This book investigates how, on the contrary, the beast has come to dominate the world and to change its cultures, economies, and politics.

As modern industry and finance transformed both economy and society, the condemnation of greed and of the new creed of accumulation converged in skirmishes and sorrows. Charles Dickens, one of the most celebrated writers of the epoch, acutely described the Industrial Revolution and the tides of change it unleashed. The antisocial life course of Ebenezer Scrooge, the protagonist of Dickens's *A Christmas Carol*, represents the somber threat of greed. Led by a spirit through the stages of his life,

> Scrooge saw himself. He was older now; a man in the prime of life. His face had not the harsh and rigid lines of later years; but it had begun to wear the signs of care and avarice. There was an eager, greedy, restless motion in the eye, which showed the passion that had taken root, and where the shadow of the growing tree would fall.

In 1843, and at the beginning of the new era, Scrooge's relentless pursuit of profit marks him as deviant, and alienates him from social relations. He loses love, relatives, and faithful employees, and would be on his way to a lonely death were it not for a nearly divine intervention that leads him to change his ways. Dickens condemns Scrooge, but gives him one last chance. Money did not protect him; instead it was his condemnation. But what remained of his human soul could save him.

In a later book, *Dombey and Son*, Charles Dickens questions the power of money: Paul Dombey, owner of a shipping company, states that money rules everything, but his son, Paul the younger, asks his father why money had been unable to save his mother, who died in childbirth. The author's critique of remorseless capitalism also acknowledges both the success and the frailty of the Midas touch, and life and riches are contrasted, as was frequent in the works of Dickens, who wrote most eloquently about human resilience.

Across the Channel, the French naturalists simultaneously painted the decay of a society that had fallen under the spell of money: Balzac's *Père Goriot* (1834), a tale of a fortune amassed during the recent revolution and of the misfortunes of social ascension, served as a key text for Piketty's 2014 exploration of modern wealth. Gustave Flaubert depicted the savage collision of bourgeois dreams and bourgeois reality in *Madame Bovary* (1857). In *Bel-Ami* (1885), Guy de Maupassant recounted the corruption of a young "arriviste," and, in *L'Argent* (1891), Emile Zola described the entanglement and eventual collapse of a bank. These literary cries of indignation and fear showed a society changing rapidly with the emergence of finance and the concomitant concentration of power, and discussed the role of money.[10]

By the twentieth century, the die was cast. In F. Scott Fitzgerald's *The Great Gatsby*, a dark morality tale carefully disguised as a frivolous and ephemeral idyll, Mammon's cruelty lurks behind shining success: "They were careless people, Tom and Daisy—they smashed up things and creatures and then retreated back into their money or their vast carelessness, or whatever it was that kept them together, and let other people clean up the mess they had made."[11] In the end, Gatsby and his fellow nouveau-riche strivers are destroyed by their pursuits, but the real wealth lives on.

"GREED IS GOOD"

Gekko's "Greed is good," channeled Milton Friedman and his disciples. Friedman, whose popular 1980 documentary *Free to Choose* aired not on one of the US private networks but on the Public Broadcasting System (PBS), had recently received the Nobel Prize in economics for the development of his vision of liberated markets.[12] In fact, what Friedman achieved was an elegant encapsulation of the old myths of a certain species, *Homo economicus*, later known as the *econ*.[13] "Greed is good" (and Gekko is its prophet) is a motivational anthem for the market activities of

[10] In previous critiques of merchant societies, the extinction of money was presented as the essential feature of a utopia. In the *Utopia* of Thomas More (1478–1535), absence of money eradicated social conflict. As Freud noted, there is no money in the unconscious. More recently, Habermas described money as "noise" in society's communication system (Jameson (2005), p. 18). Marx, who appreciated Balzac, prepared his magnum opus, *Capital*, as an exploration of the storm of modernization under the violent accumulation of capital. The agonizing novelists and the radical Marx witnessed a century-long ascendance of capital.

[11] *The Great Gatsby*, New York: Scribner, 2004, p. 279.

[12] R. Friedman and M. Friedman (1979). An interesting contrast to Milton Friedman is Kenneth Arrow. Equally brilliant, highly mathematical, dedicated to general equilibrium, Arrow nevertheless proposed an Impossibility Theorem suggesting the inconsistency of the research program. Indeed, some interpreted the highly specific list of axioms required for General Equilibrium to constitute a Pareto optimum as a critique of the possibilities of the free market, whereas no market can exhibit full contractibility in all cases; that could have been the case of the Arrow-Debreu securities, treating the conditions to achieve optimality as a parody. However, the satire was lost on many readers. Arrow did not aggressively pursue a political agenda and he did not leave ideological children in the same way as Friedman did—maybe more successfully than any other academic has ever done.

[13] University of Chicago economist and 2017 recipient of the Nobel Prize Richard Thaler coined this term.

maximizing agents, endowed with perfect insight or complete information, or at least the relevant information about prices, and fighting for their own benefit.

Friedman and the fictional Gekko did not pioneer the idea. It has a long lineage. One of the founding moments, Bernard Mandeville's *The Fable of the Bees* (1705), is a satire suggesting selfishness as the prime mover of the coordination and emergence of social life. Quoting this fable, devotees have presented greed as an anthropological constant, as the very nature of human beings.

Always greed? Not so fast. Neither in economics nor in cultural life was greed accepted as the expression of human nature: scientific explorations on social and individual behavior suggest otherwise, evoking complex and varied motivations and choices, and so do some literary monuments of our epoch. Perhaps no modern writer more fully investigated the depths of the soul in terms of greed and solitude than Fyodor Dostoyevsky, who presented the darkest picture: "The world says: 'You have needs—satisfy them. You have as much right as the rich and the mighty. Don't hesitate to satisfy your needs; indeed, expand your needs and demand more.' This is the worldly doctrine of today. And they believe that this is freedom. The result for the rich is isolation and suicide, for the poor, envy and murder." Envy, isolation, and murder—these are the shadows of greed in his great book, *The Brothers Karamazov* (1880).

In the same book, Dostoyevsky proposed a parable on selfishness to explain both the root and the consequence of this foolish desire to get everything:

> Once upon a time there was a woman, and she was wicked as wicked could be, and she died. And not one good deed was left behind her. The devils took her and threw her into the lake of fire. And her guardian angel stood thinking: what good deed of hers can I remember to tell God? Then he remembered and said to God: once she pulled up an onion and gave it to a beggar woman. And God answered: take now that same onion, hold it out to her in the lake, let her take hold of it and pull, and if you pull her out of the lake, she can go to paradise. The angel ran to the woman and held out the onion to her: here, woman, he said, take hold of it and I'll pull. And he began pulling carefully, and had almost pulled her all of the way out, when other sinners in the lake saw her being pulled out and all began holding on to her so as to be pulled out with her. But the woman was wicked as wicked could be, and she began to kick them with her feet: "It's me who's getting pulled out, not you; it's my onion, not yours." No sooner did she say it than the onion broke. And the woman fell back into the lake and is burning there to this day. And the angel wept and went away.

For Dostoyevsky, selfishness, the egoistic *Homo economicus*, would lead to a despondent mood or even to social destruction. Contrary to Mandeville's optimistic fable, the Russian writer saw neither coordination nor common welfare emerging from egoism, only crime and self-destruction.

In the same tone, Philip K. Dick, the prolific science-fiction writer, best known for providing the outline of the screenplay for Ridley Scott's film *Blade Runner*, wrote, in 1963, the fantasy of *Dr. Bloodmoney*. Dr. Bruno Bluthgeld, nicknamed Dr. Bloodmoney, resembles Edward Teller, the father of the American hydrogen bomb and one of the various inspirations for Stanley Kubrick's *Dr. Strangelove* (1964). While in the Kubrick film, Dr. Strangelove is simply a Cold War maniac launching an atomic catastrophe, Dick's deranged Bluthgeld is empowered with magical abilities by the very nuclear Armageddon he has ignited, motivated by his hatred of Humanity and eager to wreak havoc. A portentous doomsayer, Dr. Bloodmoney is Mammon again. Greed, immoderate greed,[14] makes the world go round?

ECONOMICS FEARING GREED

Milton Friedman's instrumental eulogy of greed contrasted with testimonies of life as suggested by both popular and high culture. But, furthermore, it did not respect the tradition of his science and, indeed, it represented a major shift that was not unperceived by his contemporaries and was praised by his disciples.

In *Free to Choose,* the major popularization of Friedman's doctrine, Milton and Rose Friedman presented their argument as a sequence of a startling intuition by Adam Smith, the founder of modern economics: "It was a startling idea then (with Adam Smith), and it remains one today, that economic order can emerge as the unintended consequence of many people, each seeking his own interest."[15] Again, this is the *Fable of the Bees*: if you excel in greed, everyone benefits and society prospers. Order emerges from greed.

Smith certainly admired and favored the economic initiative leading to the accumulation of profits through competition and social division of labor. From this point of view, he advocated open markets and fought the remnants of feudal and absolutist regimes. But reductionist Smithism ignores how he expressed fear of the social disruption caused by greed and essentially his concern on how wealth accumulation could destroy competition as a social norm. In his *Theory of Moral Sentiments* (1759), Smith held it up as a warning against social differences corrupting the essence of our lives: "The disposition to admire, and almost to worship, the rich and the powerful, and to despise, or, at least, to neglect persons of poor and mean condition, though necessary both to establish and to maintain the distinction of ranks and the order of society, is, at the same time, the great and most universal cause of the corruption of our moral sentiments."[16]

Some rare modern defenders and followers of Friedman seem to share, from time to time, this sense of fear of the consequences of a society dominated by the rules of greedy pursuers of riches. Greenspan, the most powerful of the central bankers in the most powerful of the economies, a man whose thoughts and deeds we will discuss in this book, was one such reverent disciple but in a testimony to the US Senate he warned: "An infectious greed seemed to grip much of our business community [...]. It is not that humans have become any more greedy than in generations past. It is that the avenues to express greed had grown so enormously."[17] This was five years before the crash and Greenspan himself was a

[14] Shakespeare used the adjective "moderate" for love, in Portia's monologue in the *Merchant of Venice*: "O love be *moderate*, allay thy ecstasy. In measure rein thy joy. Scant this excess. I feel too much thy blessing. Make it less. For fear I surfeit" *(Merchant of Venice*, by William Shakespeare, Act 3, Scene 2). One could say that the light of modernity is the contrasting immoderate greed, according to the dominant economists' account.

[15] R. Friedman and M. Friedman (1979), pp. 13–14.

[16] Smith (1759), Section III, chapter 2.

[17] Greenspan (2002).

major player favoring deregulation and thus the conditions for these "avenues" for "infectious greed" to invade the social body.

Of course, greed may act in different ways: in *The Big Short*, Adam McKay's 2015 Oscar-nominated fictionalized adaptation of the book by Michael Lewis, the sole persistent underdog brokers who bet against the market are handsomely rewarded in the end, when the collapse of subprime credit provokes the failure of the collateralized debt obligations and other financial products. The movie was substantially more critical than the book. The book heralds only the financial rewards of the contrarian impulses of the band of shorting brothers: they were rational in contrast to the fever of rational speculation. But the movie exposes the full grotesqueness of the entire structure, including the very success of the shorters' gambles. What kind of order emerges out of the singular actions of economic agents? Does it benefit those generating confidence in the market or those betting on its fall? In either case, calamity looms and no order protects the general population.

GREED IN THE LABORATORY

The predominance of the Friedmanite dogma on greed is a peculiar feature of modern economics, to the point that one of the proselytizers of this idea of selfishness directing human choices found it everywhere and at all times: "Tales of the adventures of *Homo economicus* in unlikely places are beginning to accumulate, in nineteenth-century India, for example, or medieval Europe, or declining Rome," wrote McCloskey triumphantly.[18] Amidst the fervor, McCloskey simply restated the predominant view in economics: greed underlies the structure of society and this is forever true. Greed inspired the vision of mankind that dominates economic science and its theories, models, and machines of computation. As we shall see through this book, without this cultural shift in accepting Friedman's views, the emergence of global finance would not have had its supporters, or they would not have been placed in the highest positions of decision making.

Yet, in a more dispassionate vein, recent economic research suggests that Friedman's insistence on greed is positively wrong, even disregarding the old moral debates on the matter. Greed is not the lone mover of the world. Altruism as well as egoism shape the social patterns of everyday life.

This is why some social psychologists are puzzled when they are first confronted with the code of economics. Daniel Kahneman, a psychologist who nonetheless won the Nobel Prize in Economics (2002), voiced his surprise in the following terms:

> I can still recite the first sentence: "The agent of economic theory is rational, selfish, and his tastes do not change". I was astonished. My economist colleagues worked in

[18] McCloskey (1978, p. 21). By the same token, other economists took this pretense of human essence as the core of economics-explaining-all. Thus, the principles of maximization of the *Homo economicus* were extensively used by Buchanan (1991) in his approach to constitutional order, by Edlund and Korn (2002) in their economics of prostitution, by Barro (2007) in his extravagant account of "work ethic" explained by "belief in God," and throughout by Levitt and Dubner (2005).

> the building next door, but I had not appreciated the profound difference between our intellectual worlds. To a psychologist, it is self-evident that people are neither fully rational nor completely selfish, and that their tastes are anything but stable. Our two disciplines seemed to be studying different species, which the behavioral economist Richard Thaler dubbed *Econs* and *Humans*.[19]

He added: "Rationality is logical coherence—reasonable or not. *Econs* are rational by this definition, but there is overwhelming evidence that Humans cannot be."[20] Not rational in the sense of not having all the information, not seeking to maximize their individual utility or wealth, or not having the means to do so. Greed, therefore, cannot be rational. Could it be emotional, just some kind of fever?

One compelling example is the Prisoner's Dilemma, a classical experiment dating from the 1950s, which constituted one of the first major successes of game theory. The well-known metaphor posits a pair of partners in crime, who have been arrested and are being questioned, with each choosing privately either to cooperate with his partner and remain silent or to defect and inculpate his partner, in order to be rewarded. Ignorant of the other's choice, each must choose a strategy of either cooperation or defection. If both maintain their silence, then both receive modest prison sentences. Betraying one's partner earns a reduced sentence at the expense of the partner—unless the partner similarly engages in betrayal, in which case both are punished severely. Only when the two strategies are revealed do the erstwhile partners find out the outcome of their own option.

Given the structure of the rewards, the best collective solution is to cooperate and the best individual solution is to defect. The game is typically used to exemplify the contrast between the advantage of social cooperation and the impulse to adopt egoistic solutions. The pursuit of rational self-interest is damaging, and cooperation yields substantial rewards. Yet if either agent suspects the other of being egoistic, defection or non-cooperative behavior will emerge as the dominant strategy.

As the game was first formulated, two scientists were recruited to play it and to record their comments on each of 100 rounds of the game. One was the neoclassical economist Armen Alchian and the other the mathematician Merryl Flood, and the written notes of their game are enlightening. The economist, a devotee of the greed maximization principle, frequently opted for egoism, leading to a poor collective result (he did so 78 times out of 100). Instead, the mathematician, free of such ideological chains, obviously understood from the rules of the game that cooperation was beneficial for both and tried to promote the maximization of overall gain through unilateral cooperation, only retaliating against the egoistic play of his partner, when attacked (yet he cooperated 68 times out of 100). As Flood wrote, he was "completely confused" about Alchian's intentions.[21] As a matter of fact, the large experiment conducted some decades later by Anatol Rapoport and summarized by Axelrod found that the best strategy would be "tit-for-tat," or just cooperating unless the other player defects, and defecting if he does.[22]

[19] Kahneman (2011, p. 269). [20] Ibid., p. 411.
[21] A wonderful account of this story is presented by Poundstone (1992).
[22] Axelrod (1984, 1980a,b).

Half a century later, the popular British game show *Golden Balls* turned the Prisoner's Dilemma into entertainment; previously unacquainted contestants sat face to face, communicated with promises and entreaties, and played three rounds. Scientists reviewed 222 rounds on *Golden Balls* and found strong evidence for unilateral cooperation, with 55 percent choosing to cooperate even at the risk of losing substantial sums to an egoist. Even in the final round, bilateral cooperation occurred frequently if it was preceded by previous rounds of successful cooperation. As the stakes grew higher, however, cooperation became less likely. One really must see it to believe it.[23] [No spoilers: watch it, and then listen to the debriefing (RadioLab, 2014).]

Discussing this type of evidence, Kahneman and his late co-author Amos Tversky reviewed hundreds of studies and conducted their own experiments, leading to a detailed account of motivations and choices for actual "economic agents." Others followed the same path. A paper published by the Federal Reserve Bank of Boston shows that higher incentives do not necessarily lead to better performance. Observations of real-life behavior of subjects ranged from taxi drivers in New York City to parents arriving late for pick-up at preschool in Israel. Experiments conducted on subjects ranging from undergraduates at elite US universities to farmworkers in rural India[24] reinforce Kahneman's interpretation: humans are motivated not only or even firstly by greed but also by cooperation and coordination and that is the root of the social community, its rules and forms of living. Indeed, the evidence is substantial enough to question the gentle idea of *The Fable of the Bees* or Gekko's creed.

There is also evidence that studying contemporary economics at university actually makes people behave more like the *Homo economicus*. Nor is this simply a matter of selection, i.e., that people predisposed to selfishness or greed choose to study economics; quasi-random experiments suggest that the effect of studying economics on self-interested behavior is truly causal. Students exposed at random to the tenets of contemporary economics behave more greedily and opportunistically in games of cooperation and defection. Contemporary economics pedagogy also instills certitude about the effects of the minimum wage, rent control, professional licensure, and other matters of economistic "common sense." We surmise that the intellectual edifice of contemporary economics, which enshrines greed as a future and inculcates it in our young, enables the current policy regime.

THE MISER AND THE SPENDTHRIFT

In "The Miser and the Spendthrift," sociologist and flaneur Georg Simmel describes the creation of modern personality types in relation to the money economy, the contemporary matches for a moderate Mammon. For the miser the potential of money is the source of pleasure. For the spendthrift the joy from the act of spending

[23] The final round of 2008 went viral (Golden Balls, 2008). Just as telling is the perverse Golden Balls (2012).

[24] Ariely et al. (2009), Camerer et al. (1997).

is greater than the use of the purchased object. The miser and the spendthrift have analogues in the realm of monetary policy: the gold bug and the wildcat banker.

The wildcat banker is ambitious but frustrated. The wildcat banker understands the opportunities and possibilities of the leveraged boom. The lucky break will finally let him get ahead. The frustration emerges because the big boys—in the American context—back east on New York City's Wall Street keep the little guy from getting ahead with their tough rules and tight money. The eastern banks smack of privilege and monopoly. Set free with enough loose credit and plentiful land, the wildcat banker has a world to win. The wildcat banker is associated with the era of Free Banking in the US after Andrew Jackson had defeated the Second Bank of the United States in the 1830s. Elaborate credit chains and riskily or shadily financed investment booms, in land, canals, and railroads emerged from this era, with frequent crashes punctuating the booms.

There is a grain of truth to the wildcat banker's complaints of the monopoly domination of finance, the easy life of the rentier, and the hardness of hard money for farmers, workers, and other debtors. Yet the free banking solution has brought chaos and ruin. But the opposite of tightfisted rentier plutocracy is not a freewheeling free for all.

The gold bug, who takes the name of a mystery story by Edgar Allen Poe, is a disillusioned product of these nineteenth-century booms and busts. The gold bug rails against fiat currency and fractional reserve banking, the stuff of wildcat banking. The gold bug advocates the gold standard, in principle the hardest of hard money policies, as the antidote to the chains of dreams and leverage that generate booms and busts. The gold bug argues that if only money were hard enough and the fraud of fractional reserve banking were banned, then the type of speculative excess that leads to booms and busts would not be possible.

There is a grain of truth to the gold bug's criticisms of highly leveraged credit chains. But the opposite of soft money is not necessarily hard money. And the dream of the gold bugs, that sufficiently hardened currency and a ban on bank lending can tame the capitalist economy, is a conception of cranks; the proposal ignores the creativity of financiers in creating money and leverage when desired and forgoes useful tools to manage a modern economy.

We point out that the wildcat banker and the gold bug are not in fact opposites but both are the likely (inevitable?) products of an economic system based on finance for profit. The gold bug's dream of mechanically (or elementally) generated stability is neither desirable nor possible. The wildcat's dream of an infinitely long lever of wealth delivered in an accelerating spiral is neither possible nor desirable.

As progressives we seek neither hard money nor soft money but rather money and banking that is democratic, regulated, and functional, not directed at wealth accumulation but at social needs. Democratic banking would crack down on speculation and endogenously stoked booms and finance socially useful activity. Democratic monetary policy would respond to recessions and liquidity crises. Money should be subservient to human needs.

Gold bugs and their rants about fractional reserve banking and fiat money are not preferable to free banking. Indeed they are the other side of the same coin, constantly flipped between heads you win and tails we lose. What we really want is democratic management of money and banks in the public interest. Public spirited management would have both hard and soft elements, a crackdown on speculation and endogenously fed booms, but also following the guidance of Bagehot, Mill, Keynes, Wicksell, and even—to be kinder than he perhaps deserves—Friedman himself with his helicopter money in order to stimulate aggregate demand while in a recession. In this framework, central banks must play an important role in the management of the macroeconomy and the effective management of money and banks.

CONCLUSION

Is greed the mysterious driver, the invisible hand of modern societies? Some of our colleagues have argued that we live in the "age of greed", as the contemporary economic and social instability expresses the triumph of finance and therefore the short-term vision of accumulation of power and riches,[25] whereas others had envisioned a catastrophic halt to that process with the meltdown of 2007 and 2008.[26] In spite of a widespread claim that neoliberalism was bankrupted, as it emerged indicted by the subprime collapse, the fact is that greed is again, after a short decade, the proud conductor of the capital bandwagon. The following chapters discuss how this recovery proceeded and how this power has been established so strongly that it could resist the waves of the general crisis and recession.

[25] Madrick (2011). [26] Mason (2009).

2

Shadows in Times of Crash

In five months, from March to September 2008, eight of the largest financial institutions in the US collapsed: venerable trading houses Bear Stearns and Lehman Brothers; the newly diversified entrant AIG; scrappy upstarts IndyMac, Washington Mutual, and Wachovia; and quasi-public entities Fannie Mae and Freddie Mac. Six of the crashes came in September.[1] In the collapse, Bear Stearns was rescued and sold to J.P. Morgan Chase,[2] Lehman Brothers went bankrupt, and Merrill Lynch was delivered to the Bank of America.[3] Washington Mutual's bankruptcy became the largest ever. It was resolved by the Federal Deposit Insurance Corporation, the US agency responsible for guaranteeing the protection of deposits, and most of WaMu's assets were sold to Morgan Chase. Wachovia, the fourth largest bank in the US, was acquired by Wells Fargo, the sixth largest.[4] Investment banks Goldman Sachs and Morgan Stanley were redefined as "bank holding companies" to qualify for public money. Citigroup and Bank of America were bailed out by the public authorities, as were General Motors and Chrysler. Some US $16 trillion were destroyed in the US crash.[5]

Of the survivors, most have recovered as major players in the world economy. The survivors have even repaid their nominal debts to the public entities. Much is made in the popular press of this repayment, but the survival of these banks in the breach was strictly at public discretion—and at public expense, since the authorities bought the toxic debt at inflated prices in order to save the banks.[6]

[1] Paulson (2010), pp. 435–6. Of the five largest independent broker-dealers, one went bankrupt, two were incorporated into banks, and two were transformed into bank holding companies. Adrian and Ashcraft (2012), p. 18.

[2] Morgan Chase bought Bear Stearns for US $1,500 million (the bank was valued at US $20 billion in January 2007, and the headquarters building alone was worth US $1.4 billion). From 2009 on, it was expected to provide a return of US $1 billion a year to the new shareholders.

[3] Merrill Lynch was sold to the Bank of America for US $29 per share. The market price that day was 17, but it had reached 75 only year before.

[4] Wells Fargo represents a quarter of the American mortgages market and a third of the home loans market.

[5] Frank (2012).

[6] In 2007, before the crash, the list of the ten largest banks according to Banks Daily was Royal Bank of Scotland, Deutsche Bank, BNP Paribas, Barclays, Crédit Agricole, UBS, Société Generale, ABN AMRO, ING Bank, the Bank of Tokyo-Mitsubishi UFJ. BanksDaily (2017a); After the crash, in 2012, Industrial and Commercial Bank of China (ICBC), HSBC Holdings, Crédit Agricole, Deutsche Bank, Mitsubishi UFJ Financial Group (MUFG), BNP Paribas, Japan Post Bank, Barclays, J.P. Morgan Chase, and Bank of America (BoA). BanksDaily (2017b), According to Tier 1, the largest in 2007 were HSBC, Citigroup, Royal Bank of Scotland, J.P. Morgan Chase, Bank of America, Mitsubishi Financial, Crédit

As a consequence of the bailout, the US fiscal deficit rose from 2.7 percent in 2007 to 13 percent in 2009.[7]

In the UK, at the same time, the government nationalized the Bradford & Bingley bank in 2008 (and then sold it to Santander). In October of that same year, the Royal Bank of Scotland (RBS), Lloyds, and the Halifax Bank of Scotland (HBOS) received a public injection amounting to the equivalent of US $64 billion, leading to an effective nationalization. The process of bankruptcies and concentrations continued, as Lloyds bought HBOS in January 2009.

In continental Europe, October 2008 also saw the nationalization of the Fortis Bank, as previously noted, through an injection of €16 billion from the combined efforts of the Belgian and Dutch governments; its Belgian operation was then sold to BNP Paribas and its Dutch operation to ABN Amaro. Dexia, a Franco-Belgian bank, received €6 billion at the same time; after the bailout, the remaining Belgian operation was transformed into another bank, Belfius.

In Europe and in particular in Ireland, Greece, Portugal, Spain, Italy, and Cyprus, the ensuing debt crisis unleashed a new wave of bank restructurings and bailouts. These were the cases of Dexia in Belgium and France (2012), Bankia (2012) and then Banco Popular (2017) in Spain, NKBM in Slovenia (2012), SNS Reaal in Holland (2013), Laïki and Bank of Cyprus in Cyprus (2013), Espirito Santo (2014) and Banif (2015) in Portugal, Monte dei Paschi, Banca delle Marche, Banca Popolare dell'Etruria e del Lazio, and Carife in Italy (2014–15), and *Hypo* Alpe Adria in Austria (2014–15), among others. Then came the Italian restructuring and bailout of banks: the Monte dei Paschi di Siena for €6.6 billion and then, at the end of 2017, the colossal sum of €17 billion for Banca Popolare di Vicenza and Veneto Banca.

THE CRASH, AS SOME SOLID THINGS MELT INTO AIR

Any physicist will tell you that small initial events may lead to a large collapse in a highly interconnected and unstable system. The butterfly effect evokes a discrete wing movement of the insect in Berlin that may lead to a tornado in Texas. The largest convulsion of the world economy since the mid-twentieth century is currently (and controversially) interpreted as one such case: the financial crash was ignited by small losses in a small market, that of subprime mortgages in the US, and not by initial large shocks.[8]

Agricole, Industrial and Commercial Bank of China, Santander, Bank of China. After the crash, at the end of 2012, Tier 1 listed: Industrial and Commercial Bank of China, J.P. Morgan, Bank of America, HSBC, China Construction Bank, Citi, Mitsubishi, Wells Fargo, Bank of China, Agricultural Bank of China (*The Economist*, September 14, 2013).

[7] Eichengreen (2015), p. 54.

[8] The US Financial Crisis Inquiry Commission (2011), pp. 228–9, set up by the US Congress noted in its Final Report that "overall, for 2005 to 2007, (among) vintage tranches of mortgage-backed securities originally rated triple-A, despite the mass downgrades, only about 10% of Alt-A and 4% of subprime securities had been 'materially impaired'—meaning that losses were imminent or had already been suffered—by the end of 2009"; see also Gorton and Ordoñez (2014); A part of the 2004–7 subprime loans, 13%, was in fact owned by *de facto* unregulated bank affiliates, Kregel (2014), but even this level

By a curious coincidence, the 2007 crash occurred a century after another credit crisis, which was described by a contemporary economist and politician as "the most extensive and prolonged breakdown of the country's credit mechanism which has occurred since the establishment of the national banking system."[9]

One century later, a century that encompassed an even greater breakdown, a long-lasting repair, and the erosion of that repair, the financial system was deeply exposed and the effect of the crash was immense. Bernanke, the head of the Federal Reserve, the US central bank, testified in 2008: of the "thirteen of the most important financial institutions in the US, twelve were at risk of failure within a period of a week or two."[10] The same would soon happen all over the world. Was this a butterfly effect, or something more? This question, the crisis, and the subsequent events, are the theme of this book, and we will find a much more complex system than the simple impact of light wings and unintended consequences; we will discover the dense economic interconnections, the web of power, and the force of will and deliberate choice, accounting for the formatting of the modern world.

In human affairs, the flutter of the wing is of less interest than the construction of the complex and tightly coupled system that enables the catastrophe.[11] For this reason, we start by discussing the emergence of the shadow system.

A TSUNAMI

In August 2007 David Viniar, a top manager at Goldman Sachs, a financial giant that is a major player in the narrative of this book, detected some strange perturbations in the stock market. Viniar was not a simple risk analyst: he was the executive vice president and Chief Financial Officer for 14 years (1999–2013) and, after retiring from financial control of the operations of the firm, remained a member of the Goldman board. He had already experienced many financial crashes and crises when he detected the strange movements that summer 2007, but he could find no comparable cases. Indeed, for several days, the oscillations in the prices of some stocks were so great that they were not measurable with the crude seismograph provided by the experienced statistical analysts of the financial

of risk does not explain the contagion effect, which will be discussed through this chapter: it can only be explained by the structure of shadow finance.

9 Andrew (1908a), p. 290; Abram Piatt Andrew, who was shortly thereafter appointed director of the Mint (1909–10) and then sub-secretary of Treasury (1910–12), had already noted: "The closing months of 1907 . . . were marked by an outburst of fright as wide-spread and unreasoning as that of fifty or seventy years before," Andrew (1908b), p. 497.

10 Bernanke's testimony to the US Financial Crisis Inquiry Commission (2011), p. 354.

11 Charles Perrow's elegant *Normal Accidents: Living with High-Risk Technologies*, 2011, posits that catastrophic failures are most likely in systems that are both complex and tightly coupled. The nuclear power plant—and note that the book was written after Three Mile Island but before Chernobyl—is the archetypal case. A university is complex but not tightly coupled: a failure or conflict in the English Department is unlikely to bring down the History Department. A traditional assembly line is tightly coupled but not complex: a line stoppage may back up production but is unlikely to generate catastrophic failure. Finance, although not treated explicitly in Perrow, has both necessary properties for catastrophic vulnerability, high complexity and tight coupling.

firms. One of the firm's hedge funds lost 27 percent of its value in a matter of days, and Goldman immediately injected the fund with US $2 billion of its own capital. In defense of this dramatic action, Viniar explained: "We were seeing things that were 25-standard deviation moves, several days in a row."[12] This 25-Sigma speculative earthquake certainly surprised Viniar, and he was one of the few detecting the danger.

Indeed, under the normal, or bell, curve probability distribution that most financial firms assumed in those days, the chances of a 25-Sigma event occurring two days in a row are the same as those of winning the lottery in the UK forty-two times in succession.[13] A quite desirable prize, yet an implausible, if not a threatening event, one may reckon.

Following Viniar's observation, Goldman Sachs began selling stocks in order to shed its risk. But not all financial agents, and certainly not the majority, did the same. If everyone had acted at once, the catastrophic effect would only have arrived that much earlier. Soon the full collapse came, and it was a tsunami. Large banks and hundred-year-old financial firms went out of business, governments stepped in with huge amounts of cash, and converted enormous private debt into enormous public debt. The United Kingdom had its fourth largest increase in public debt since 1700, surpassed only by the Napoleonic Wars and the two World Wars.[14] The financial disease rapidly spread to the real sector ("from Wall Street to Main Street" in American parlance). Total world output shrank in 2009 for the first time since the Second World War.

It was not the first crisis to have taken place over the last few decades, but it was the first great quake at the core of the global economy: the fixed-rate regime of Bretton Woods, which had underpinned *les Trente Glorieuses*, the thirty golden years of high growth since the end of the Second World War, collapsed in the early 1970s.[15] Since then we have had the debt crisis in Latin America in the 1980s; the US Savings and Loans crisis in 1987–8; the prolonged crisis in Japan through the 1990s; the Mexican crisis of 1994 followed by crises in the Southern Cone of South America, Brazil in 1998–9 and Argentina in 2000–1; the Asian crisis in 1997–8 (Thailand followed by Indonesia, Malaysia, the Philippines, Hong Kong, Taiwan,

[12] Larsen (2007).

[13] "To put this in perspective, a 2-standard deviation loss event should occur only approximately 2.5% of the time, or roughly once every 44 days; a 5-standard deviation event should occur only once every 13,932 years; a 10-standard deviation event only once every 525 quadrillion millennia (the universe, incidentally, is estimated to be between 12 and 14 billion years old); and a 25-standard deviation event should occur roughly once every 1.309 x 10^{136} years. Thus, the expected time between two 25-standard deviation events has more millennia than the universe has number of particles. And yet, according to Viniar, it occurred day after day, in August of 2007, well before the fire sale of Bear Stearns, the collapse of Lehman Brothers, or the bailout of the financial sector, with all the associated market upheaval that followed. Thus, the VaR models Viniar and others used to explain such 25-standard deviation moves, day after day, were not only wrong; they were catastrophically wrong," Conti-Brown (2010), p. 1465; Dowd et al. (2008), also see Wolf (2014), p. 167.

[14] Eichengreen (2015).

[15] The creation of the Eurocurrency markets, then of money market instruments and the network of transnational banks with their systems of payment, changed the banking system, allowing for transfers of funds for offshore and, for what matters to this book, was part of the creation of shadow banking. As Guttmann (2016), noted, "the Euromarket brought down the fixed-rate regime of Bretton Woods in a series of devastating attacks on the dollar (March 1968, August 1971, March 1973)."

Singapore, and South Korea); the collapse of the Long-term Capital Management hedge fund in 1998 followed closely by the Russian debt restructuring; and the dot-com bubble and bust in the United States.

But not all was equal when "we" had crises: booms and busts in the core were modulated by swift and thorough liquidity-extension by the central banks of the developed economies. Indeed, so effective were the central banks, especially the US Federal Reserve, in preventing contagion from financial mishaps to the real economy, that the period came to be known—just before it ended—as The Great Moderation. Not so for the other "we": financial busts in the periphery engulfed real activity. Global finance and its collection agency, the International Monetary Fund, demanded painful structural adjustment to qualify for loan restructuring and life support.

Then came the global shocks of the financial crisis (2007–9) and the euro crisis (2011–13), and these were immediately universal, engulfing the entire global economy, even massive and independent China, in the whirlpool.

The crisis in the financial markets rivaled that of 1929, with the fall in the stock markets even more rapid than that associated with the ticker-tape and images of bankers threatening to leap from New York City's new 1920s skyline. The social devastation was more restrained. Important counter-measures were in place that had not existed in the 1930s, including unemployment benefits and deposit insurance. The political and economic powers in the developed economies were willing to undertake a huge public bailout of the financial institutions on an unprecedented scale. As we will discuss, there might have been other ways to execute the rescue without the massive upward transfer of wealth, but the bailouts unquestionably limited the transmission of financial damage into the real economy. US real output fell by 15 percent between 1929 and 1932 but only by 1 percent from 2008 to 2009. By 2011, the pre-crisis level of GDP had recovered in the US, which pursued aggressive bank bailouts, moderate fiscal stimulus, and unprecedented bond-market intervention, but not in Europe, which aggravated its economic problems with start-stop monetary policy and outright austerity in the fiscal domain.[16]

Even with the various shock absorbers, the consequences were frightening. In 2007 the US experienced a bank run to the doors of Countrywide, one of the largest home mortgage lenders; Great Britain witnessed its first bank run in a century and a half, at Northern Rock, and UK taxpayers spent two billion pounds to cushion the banks. The 2008 bankruptcy of Lehman Brothers, with its debts of US $613 billion for US $700 billion of assets, was until then the largest in US history. Spain had its run on Bankia, overextended both in real estate and in complex financial products, in 2012, Portugal a run on Banif, a small bank, at the end of 2015, and Russia a run on the Otkritie Bank, the fourth in the country, in 2017, leading to the largest rescue in the history of the country.[17]

Lehman was particularly exposed to the subprime mortgage market, not because it was the largest lender—in fact it was only the eleventh largest subprime lender in the US—but because it underwrote more mortgage-backed securities than any other financial institution. In spite of a risk department with 400 people, including

[16] Eichengreen (2015), pp. 57, 281. [17] Bloomberg, 29 August 2017.

former regulators, its structure, like that of many similar firms, was a labyrinth with 7,000 legal entities, 209 of which were registered subsidiaries.[18] Its managers could not even understand, let alone prevent, its exposure to the domino effect of the crash.

In any case, most definitely a tsunami, as Viniar had rightly intuited.

MODERATION EVERYWHERE

The effects were shockingly universal and devastating, and almost nobody, except for a single manager, had sensed a tremor?[19] Although this will be a major topic for the rest of this book, an initial assessment is in order, insofar as most of the financial world itself and the major players in public policy did not notice the danger.

In the mid-2000s, financial firms had few reasons to question their ongoing recipe for success. The assessment of risk was assured by overpaid and pliant rating agencies and gurus, who all used the same type of accounting techniques and were present in the same markets, dealing with the same providers of insurances and guarantees. Their results all coincided with one another: business as usual was thriving. Over the previous years, a cornucopia of new opportunities had been presented, either as new products to be sold or new methods that were available for securitizing, dispersing, or selling risky assets. Only a handful of die-hard "bears," at the time labeled cranks, could imagine the end of this bonanza.

The specialists also confirmed that this was the right course of action. We had entered the new epoch of "Great Moderation," trumpeted some economists, arguing that twenty years of low volatility in US production—despite occasional financial mishaps—constituted near proof that there would be no more annoyingly large business cycles.[20] In 2004, Ben Bernanke, then a member of the Board of Governors of the Federal Reserve and still to be the Bush-appointed Chairman of the US Fed, and a well-known scholar of the history of US monetary policy, was confident enough to proclaim this "Great Moderation," a singular period in economic history. He wrote:

> The Great Moderation, the substantial decline in macroeconomic volatility over the past twenty years, is a striking economic development. Whether the dominant cause of the Great Moderation is structural change, improved monetary policy, or simply good luck is an important question about which no consensus has yet formed. I have argued today that improved monetary policy has likely made an important contribution not only to the reduced volatility of inflation (which is not particularly controversial) but to the reduced volatility of output as well.[21]

[18] Eichengreen (2015), p. 201; A former British Member of Parliament and an expert in regulation, O. McDonald (2015), provided a detailed account of the failure of Lehman Brothers.

[19] Indeed, the analyst was not alone. Keep in mind the alert by several savvy academics, such as Dean Baker, James Crotty, to some extent Robert Shiller, as well as the acute perception of the rare but successful players described by Lewis in his book (the inspiration for the Oscar-awarded film) *The Big Short*.

[20] Bernanke's 2004 speech on the "Great Moderation" is available at the Fed site, Bernanke (2004); Stock and Watson (2003), had coined the term a couple of years before Bernanke used it.

[21] Bernanke (2004).

However, some words of caution were also voiced: shortly before taking office as chair, Bernanke had noticed the possibility of a savings glut, something a general equilibrium approach would not consider to be possible. He observed that should savings exceed investment, free capital circulation would permit a potentially massive credit expansion, low interest rates, high stock values, and the possibility of bubbles both in the housing industry and in the stock market.[22]

While Bernanke detected the problem without anticipating the full systemic danger, others did in fact perceive more ominous precursors. In 2005 Raghuram Rajan, from the University of Chicago, then chief economist at the IMF and later Governor of the Bank of India, provoked a scandal at the annual Federal Reserve Conference for central bankers and distinguished financial specialists at the lovely mountain resort in Jackson Hole, Wyoming. The 2005 Jackson Hole sessions honored Greenspan before his retirement. Out of step with the songs being played at the festivities, Rajan asked "Has financial development made the world riskier?" He concluded affirmatively and did not mince his words: "disaster might loom" because managers have "the incentive to take risk that is concealed from investors." [23] These risks, at low probability but potentially high damage, are known as augmenting "tail risk."

A barrage of indignation followed from his colleagues, exactly what one might expect from telling a rude joke about the boss at his retirement dinner. Former US Secretary of the Treasury and President of Harvard University Lawrence Summers, one of the architects of the Financial Modernization Act of 1998, famously replied that Rajan was a "Luddite" and presented a "misguided" and anti-innovative view.[24] Invective usually reserved for outsiders or wild-eyed radicals was in this case heaped on Rajan, a well-respected and thoroughly mainstream economist, for expressing deep-seated concern about the broad course.[25]

Anyway, Rajan's crude remark was heard but dismissed. The IMF itself ignored the presentiments of its chief economist: a 2006 report announced that the financial system was more resilient than ever thanks to the dispersion of credit risk, and added that "growing recognition" supported this conclusion.[26] "Dispersion" of credit risk referred precisely to the technique of securitization, which generated the pile of debt that would be revealed by the crash.

In March 2007, well past the peak of the housing bubble and with foreclosures growing rapidly, University of Chicago Professor of Economics Austan Goolsbee, who would soon become the economic adviser for Obama's Presidential campaign and later the Chair of the Council of Economic Advisers, could still bring himself to remark—in an opinion piece in the *New York Times*—"the mortgage market has become more perfect, not more irresponsible."[27]

Heavy hitters in academia, Eugene Fama of Chicago (who modeled the efficient market hypothesis) and Michael Jensen of Harvard (who demonstrated how to

[22] Bernanke (2005). [23] Rajan (2005).

[24] "Luddite" refers to the workers who destroyed employment-threatening machines at the beginning of the nineteenth century in Northwestern England under the leadership and inspiration of Ned Ludd.

[25] Since 1994 Rajan considered Glass-Steagall inadequate and wrong since its inception Mirowski (2013), pp. 164f, 180.

[26] World Economic and Financial Surveys (2006a). [27] Goolsbee (2007).

maximize shareholder value) were both honored by their profession for their impressive achievements in enthroning the rationality of capital markets. (We will return to this point again later, when discussing the academic justification for the changes in finance.) As a consequence, the firms' own interests, the views of the regulators, and the vision of the academics all converged to reach a single conclusion: the accepted wisdom was to proceed with financialization, liberalization, and deregulation, free of regulations, and free of the state's mistrust and inefficiency.

It is not surprising that these economists were so innocent of the history of the economies or of that of their discipline, since the ideology of equilibrium and optimization provided for a parallel world of comfortable justification and praise. Had they read the classic work of Charles Kindleberger on *Manias, Panics and Crashes*, they would have noticed that bubbles emerge as "new opportunities for profits are seized, and overdone, in ways so closely resembling irrationality as to constitute a mania." Furthermore, they would have met that old phantom, greed: "It seems clear from the historical record that swindles are a response to the greedy appetite for wealth stimulated by the boom. And as the monetary system gets stretched, institutions lose liquidity, and unsuccessful swindles are about to be revealed, the temptation becomes virtually irresistible to take the money and run."[28] As Kenneth Rogoff and Carmen Reinhart put it, boosters and economists both annoyingly repeat, after each business cycle or financial crisis, that the lesson has been learned and the painful event will be avoided in the future. But each "this time is different."[29] As a prelude to the crash of 2007–8, the inflation of the dot-com bubble of 1996–2000 was accompanied by a multitude of "this time is different" formulations, covering everything from methods for stock valuation (forget Price-to-Earnings ratio when there are no earnings, use Price-Growth instead) to outlandish revenue projections for centuries-old ideas infused with the words dot-com (e.g., home delivery of groceries).

Greenspan's "New economy"[30] was the tune, and almost every number—including the eventual crash—came from the this-time-it's-different songbook.

IT WAS ANNOUNCED

Few people joined Rajan in daring to disagree with those predicting prosperity forever. Warnings came from the skeptical, dangerous neighborhoods of the economics profession such as James Crotty of the University of Massachusetts Amherst and Dean Baker of the iconoclastic Center for Economic Policy Research (CEPR, Washington, D.C., not to be confused with the orthodox CEPR of Europe). Only a handful in the mainstream, in particular, Robert Shiller of Yale University,[31]

[28] Kindleberger and Aliber (2005), pp. 5, 10.

[29] Reinhart and Rogoff (2009). A substantial literature criticizing the standard view in economics as regards the business cycle and, in particular, the subprime crash, has been produced in recent years. Through this book we will cite some of these works. For the moment, it suffices to mention the work of Taibbi (2010b), on the bubble; of Engel and McCoy (2016), on the subprime "virus" and "reckless credit"; of Buckley (2011), on the causes of the financial crisis; and of Duarte (2011), on the theoretical underpinnings of the action of the central banks leading to the crisis.

[30] Greenspan (1996b). [31] Case and Shiller (2003).

perceived the risk early. "The worldwide rise in house prices is the biggest in history. Prepare for the economic pain when it pops," wrote *The Economist* in June 2005.

Proclaiming a bubble in house prices was not in itself controversial: residential real estate prices in the US rose by 125 percent from 1997 to 2006, while the equivalent rises for Spain and Ireland were 175 percent and 260 percent respectively. As prices rose and the interest rate was low, credit boomed. Some gigantic firms emerged in this enlarged market: Countrywide Credit was one of them at the center of the housing market in the US, and Fannie Mae, a semi-public Federal agency, bought more than 70 percent of the mortgages it issued.[32] Although this was not the first housing bubble,[33] it was the first to sweep the entire US simultaneously; previous bubbles had been confined to regional markets, for example in Florida and Boston in recent years. But in addition to its national scope, something new happened this time: the financial system used housing assets to create a spiral in the transmission of debt.[34] Mortgages were securitized, and the whole financial system joined the spiral of confidence and credit that securitization generated. The feedback loop between housing and finance, amplified with new instruments in the system of shadow finance, was a true innovation as we shall see. But Shiller was not heeded. As the pile of private debt grew, so too did the danger lying ahead.

There were already reasons for caution, and there had been some experience of similar surprises: with the 1998 Russian crash, six of the top ten lenders in the subprime mortgage market in the US had gone bankrupt, including ContiMortgage, Amresco, and First Plus.[35] Other misadventures had already occurred with risky financial securities, such as the 1994 bankruptcy of Orange County, California, and the collapse of Long Term Capital Management (LTCM) both after huge investments in derivatives.[36] In any case, these events were regarded as the result of local errors and exogenous perturbations affecting unwise and overconfident individual managers, from Robert Citron of Orange County, California (leading to the largest municipal bankruptcy in the history of the US), to the certified geniuses associated with LTCM, Robert Merton and Myron Scholes, who merited the Nobel Prize in 1997 for unveiling a "new method to determine the value of derivatives" and then, as members of the LTCM board, saw their method applied to great effect.

Ten years later, the tsunami proved individual excuses to be wrong: 4 million of the 60 million US homeowners with mortgages had defaulted in their payments by

[32] Eichengreen (2015), pp. 64, 76, 82, 89.

[33] Previous US property bubbles include the amazing boom of Chicago property values in 1830–41 (an increase of 40775%), that of Los Angeles in the 1880s (900%), and New York between 1920 and 1933 (around 80%) E. L. Glaeser (2013), and more recently Boston in the late 1980s.

[34] Prior to the 2007 crash, "the large amounts of credit intermediation provided by the SB system contributed to the asset price appreciation in residential and commercial real estate markets prior to the financial crisis," Pozsar et al. (2013), p. 4.

[35] Cassidy (2009), p. 255.

[36] LTCM was a hedge fund founded by a previous vice president of Salomon Brothers, John Meriwether, and its board included two economists awarded the Nobel Prize, Myron Scholes and Robert Merton. It was rescued in September 1998 by a syndicate of 16 banks, which bought 90% of the fund for US $3.6 billion, under the guidance of the Federal Reserve Bank of New York, ibid., p. 230.

2009, and another 10 to 15 million had mortgage debts far larger than the market value of their homes, or "under water," endangering the future of many families.[37] As a consequence, major parts of the financial system, sitting on this huge amount of debt, made colossal losses and will probably go on making losses. The worst loss was that of confidence, as the disordered retreat amplified these effects. The world entered recession in 2008.

GIVE ME A LEVER AND I WILL MOVE THE WORLD

Walter Bagehot (1826–77) was a journalist and prolific essayist, who became famous as the editor-in-chief of the London-based *The Economist* for seventeen years, beginning in 1860. In 1873, he gathered together his insights on the financial market into a book, *Lombard Street: A Description of the Money Market*, combining his observations on the role of the Bank of England and his perspicacious view of the functioning of the City, the heart of finance in England. It is one of the most impressive descriptions of the emergence of modern finance and the role of the monetary authorities. Bagehot is still honored by his profession to this day.

One of his most intriguing insights in *Lombard Street* is Bagehot's comment on the function of credit and the importance of the interest rate in defining leverage and the distribution of profits. His argument on leverage is illustrated by an example:

> But though these occasional loans to new enterprises and foreign States are the most conspicuous instances of the power of Lombard Street, they are not by any means the most remarkable or the most important use of that power. English trade is carried on upon borrowed capital to an extent of which few foreigners have an idea, and none of our ancestors could have conceived. In every district small traders have arisen, who "discount their bills" largely, and with the capital so borrowed, harass and press upon, if they do not eradicate, the old capitalist. The new trader has obviously an immense advantage in the struggle of trade. If a merchant has 50,000 pounds all his own, to gain 10 percent on it he must make 5,000 pounds a year, and must charge for his goods accordingly; but if another has only 10,000 pounds, and borrows 40,000 pounds by discount (no extreme instance in our modern trade), he has the same capital of 50,000 pounds to use, and can sell much cheaper. If the rate at which he borrows be 5 percent, he will have to pay 2,000 pounds a year; and if, like the old trader, he makes 5,000 pounds a year, he will still, after paying his interest, obtain 3,000 pounds a year, or 30 percent, on his own 10,000 pounds. As most merchants are content with much less than 30 percent, he will be able, if he wishes, to forego some of that profit, lower the price of the commodity, and drive the old-fashioned trader—the man who trades on his own capital—out of the market. In modern English business, owing to the certainty of obtaining loans on discount of bills or otherwise at a moderate rate of interest, there is a steady bounty on trading with borrowed capital, and a constant discouragement to confine yourself solely or mainly to your own capital.[38]

Tripling the rate of profit, with a fifth of equity capital, and furthermore driving the competitor out of the market, is a handsome result elucidated by Bagehot. The key to success is trading with borrowed capital. Indeed, in a period of an abundance of

[37] Eichengreen (2015), p. 316.

[38] Bagehot (1873), p. 8.

savings and therefore of low interest rates, access to easy credit encourages the use of debt as leverage. The secret is the lever.

A lever has been a prestigious tool since ancient times, when Archimedes presented it as a world-mover, and certainly many diligent workers before and after him used it for very practical purposes. When it comes to modern finance, the lever transfigures itself into an obscure, if not fictitious, method of multiplying value, which was ultimately responsible for the dimension of the financial meltdown caused by the subprime crash.

The lever, or leverage as it is known in the financial milieu, is the value of a firm's total assets compared to its own capital.[39] "Its own capital" sounds benign, even responsible. On the way up, its own capital—the smaller the better—is the denominator of profit. But on the way down, its own capital is the firm's only buffer against losing everything. Leverage was central in the 2008 bankruptcy of Lehman Brothers and the collapse of Bear Stearns: in both cases, immense leverage (30:1 and 33:1)[40] became a virtual guarantee of collapse. A mere 3 percent drop in market value wiped out all of the capital of each firm and forced them to realize their losses. As leverage mounts, even small marginal effects caused by minor changes act like the wings of the metaphorical butterfly, causing a hurricane in the financial balance of the firms.

If the ratio of total assets to the value of equity capital was so large, a very small reduction in the value of the operation would immediately imply its collapse. The owners of the capital would be unable to pay from their own pockets or by borrowing, in the absence of a bailout. Leverage augments the ability to attract funds when expectations are high and amplifies gains, but it also amplifies the losses and the inability to pay for them when the business goes wrong.

One case that has been identified in the Netherlands is that of a Special Purpose Entity, a mysterious name for a firm devoted to creating, managing, or hiding debt, which issued €50 million in securities and operated with a leverage of 2770:1, meaning that a loss of just 0.00036 percent would imply the end of the operation.[41] How did we come to this?

One answer to this question is that increased leverage was the intended outcome of crucial policy decisions. In the UK the share of the bank balance sheets, i.e., assets, in the economy had remained stable throughout the twentieth century through 1970, amounting to some 50 percent of GDP. Bank balances suddenly rose to 200 percent of GDP by 1980 and to 500 percent by 2007, on the eve of the crisis. Average leverage soared spectacularly from 20:1 to 50:1 in the years preceding the crisis, much to the delight of the supervisory authorities, who faced multiple pressures to stimulate a "competitive" banking system.

But the consequence of increased leverage was that small declines in the valuation of banks' assets, e.g., by 2 percent, could easily topple firms into bankruptcy.[42] The same situation was to be found in the US, as the Securities and Exchange Commission (SEC) relaxed the minimum capital requirements for broker-dealers

[39] A popular self-help guide to leverage is 1997's dreadful *Rich Dad, Poor Dad: What The Rich Teach Their Kids About Money That the Poor and Middle Class Do Not!* (Kiyosaki and Lechter, 1997).

[40] Johnson and Kwak (2011), p. 140; Cassidy (2009), p. 313.

[41] Brinkhuis and Eldonk (2008), cited in Thiemann (2014).

[42] See Wolf (2014), pp. 168, 286; and Figure 5.4 in Vickers (2011).

in 2004, falling in line with the EU. Until then, the rules had limited broker-dealers to a leverage ratio of 12:1, while in Europe it was 20:1. After the new ruling, these firms were allowed to increase leverage. As significantly, they were now permitted to estimate their own risk themselves. The new ruling, in fact, meant that firms could do whatever they wanted.[43]

With a capital requirement ratio of 20:1, there would be a capital cushion of only 5 percent against losses in European banks. Less than strict application of the rule meant that anything could go. As European banks tended to be more highly leveraged than their US counterparts, the danger was imminent. On the eve of the crash, Deutsche Bank was leveraged at 40:1, as was the French-Belgian Dexia bank. The balance sheets of Dexia and the Belgian Fortis bank (both of which were eventually nationalized in the wake of the crash) exceeded the GDP of their home countries.[44]

The subprime crash confirmed the dangers of the lever and that leverage makers constitute a social danger. In fact, the subprime market itself was small: the value of all outstanding US mortgages was US $12 trillion and the subprime sector accounted for just US $1 trillion. As the whole US stock market represented around US $18 trillion, even if half of the subprime mortgages were lost—a higher rate than ultimately realized even in the worst of the crisis—this would account for no more than 3 percent of the stock market.[45]

The meltdown occurred only because of the lever: the successive securitizations of these debts; their rehypothecation, or use as collateral in repeated transactions; and the construction of complex derivatives from the securitized debts. This thorough embedding of this small but dangerous asset created a critical mass through the financial system when just a marginal number of the indebted families ceased their payments.

Now, what was the fulcrum of the lever? The answer is: the shadow banking system.

THE NEW MACHINES CREATING DEBT

The mechanism allowing for the transmission of debts was responsible for the butterfly effect, a small shock creating a huge effect. How this became possible is the topic of this section.

[43] Eichengreen (2015), p. 74. In the same sense, the British Independent Commission on Banking concluded that the ratio of risk-weighted assets to non-weighted assets for the four largest banks in the UK fell from 55% in 2004 to 35% in 2008, meaning that, according to their own computations, they considered it to be safer, Wolf (2014), p. 166.

[44] Eichengreen (2015), p. 74, 97, 215.

[45] Cassidy (2009), pp. 301, 306; although small, subprime loans grew rapidly, since they had a 15% margin, instead of the typical 1 or 2% margin on other loans. As a consequence, there was an incentive for promoting bad credit. Only in 2009, after the crash, did the Federal Reserve Board forbid payments to mortgage brokers based on the interest rate charged, Eichengreen (2015), p. 80; Amromin and A. L. Paulson (2010). The data are presented in a study of the Federal Reserve Bank of Chicago; Gorton (2008), pp. 134, 141 indicates that subprime and Alt-A mortgages represented about one quarter of the total market by early 2007.

The first part of the machine was a rapid and resourceful financial innovation. This generated the creatures that pivoted around this lever, attracting savings to be transformed into capital.

In 1971, two hitherto unsuccessful New York consultants, Harry Brown and Bruce Bent, created the Reserve Fund, the very first money market mutual fund. Lying outside the scope of regulation, free of capital requirements, and neither encumbered nor protected by deposit insurance, the Reserve Fund—with no attachment to the US Federal Reserve despite the name—invested in essentially default-proof Treasury Bills, plus some generally safe commercial paper and loans, including securitized mortgages, and offered the mixed cocktail as a reward for the depositors. Returns were higher than the still-regulated interest rate on bank accounts with a presumably (and truly at that time) tiny increase in risk and assurance of liquidity apparently (and truly at that time) as great as a checking account. Paul Samuelson enthusiastically claimed that Brown and Bent should have been given a Nobel Prize,[46] high praise, to be sure, from one of the first recipients of the award.

Brown was less bombastic: "I wish I could say that our 'invention' resulted from any brilliance on our part, but it was actually a combination of the threat of starvation and pure greed that drove us"[47]—greed moving the world, again. In any case, the future of the money funds was now set.

Other products emerged from the innovation machine driven by starvation and greed: in 1983, Salomon Brothers created Collateralized Mortgage Obligations, a debt security backed by house mortgages, for Freddie Mac, an invention immortalized in Lewis's book *Liar's Poker*; Collateralized Debt Obligations were created in 1987, pooling different assets, such as mortgages, bonds, and loans, and selling them to investors.

Citigroup created the first Structured Investment Vehicle in 1988, a type of entity designed to benefit from the credit spread between holding long-term assets and issuing short-term liabilities. In 2001, Fannie Mae patented the repurchase agreement, or *repo*, a money market instrument designed for borrowing, dealing in short-term securities that were sold one day and bought again the next day.[48]

Each of these innovations had a perfectly excellent rationale at the time of introduction. Money market funds offered more attractive rates of return without loss of liquidity for households and small businesses while enabling investors to work with large, quickly raised pools of cash. Securitized debts more rapidly renewed liquidity for front-line lenders by moving their loans off their books and also solved the thorny problem of badly timed prepayments. Special investment vehicles reduced friction and seemingly irrational spreads in markets. And each of these innovations generated generous service fees that staved off the threat of starvation and sated pure greed. And each of these innovations pushed the edge of the envelope beyond the secure world of insured deposits and regulated bank activity. And each of these innovations moved the nexus of financial activity from institutions and firms to functions and markets. As we will see, money funds, collateralized debt obligations, special investment vehicles, and *repos* were just the tip of the iceberg.

[46] Eichengreen (2015), p. 67. [47] Weber (2008). [48] Adrian and Ashcraft (2012).

By the 2000s, the shadow-banking machine operated a huge part of the savings available at a worldwide level. From roughly 5 percent of credit creation occurring in pure market form in 1945, shadow banking constituted more than 60 percent of credit transformation by 2008 when the wings of the crisis began to spread.[49] The main supplier of credit shifted from the traditional banks to the shadow system. Physical investment on the real side of the economy had previously relied on retained earnings and equity; now negotiating with debt became the more typical form of finance, as big firms became net lenders aside from their traditional business. The world's five largest carmakers have financial operations worth US $600 billion in assets, and the world's *non*financial firms together hold US $9 trillion of currency derivatives.[50]

Some small fraction of this financial activity in the real economy is directly relevant to the core operation of the firms, e.g., General Motors providing auto loans to consumers to purchase new cars or a hypothetical textile maker hedging against the risk of appreciation of the currency of a cotton-producing country. Most of the activity is pure speculation because the returns can far exceed what is possible in the mundane world of production for sale.

But the impenetrable forest of instruments, vehicles, and products of the shadow banking system is prone to many dangers. The shadow banking system is insensitive to information and incentives. Instead it generates successive lack of transparency through the securitization process. In long marketized chains of lending and borrowing, agents do not and cannot seek relevant information on the financial health of issuers. Markets, which are supposed to bring transparency relative to the murky dealings inside the firm, in fact, necessarily generate opacity by separating agents and introducing asymmetric information.[51] The securitization and collateral intermediation processes are therefore risky because it is in the interest of the issuer to understate the real risk. Opacity builds value because monopolistic pricing of financial services in over-the-counter transactions is an important source of profit. Furthermore, the shadow system is regulation averse because small advantages in returns (amplified with leverage) often depend on being absolved from obeisance to regulations. Attempts to regulate one product push debt creation onto another product. Shadow banking involves the private, largely unrestricted creation of money through credit to meet the liquidity needs of institutional cash investors, a process that tends to be pro-cyclical and cycle-amplifying. The additional pro-cyclical elasticity of credit creation accentuates the volatility of the financial markets and indeed the global economy.[52]

[49] Ibid., p. 4.

[50] There are ups and downs in this business adventure of nonfinancial firms: In 2015 General Electric decided to sell most of its financial arm, which was at the time the seventh largest bank in the US with assets of US $500 billion and was at one point the largest private issuer of short-term debt with a balance sheet close to that of Goldman Sachs. General Electric is a defining example of a "closet bank," the financialization of previously nonfinancial corporation (*The Economist*, April 18, 2015). The creation of credit by nonfinancial firms exposes them to the danger of default by their clients. For example, Nokia and Motorola lost US $3 billion in Turkey in 2001 (*New York Times*, April 10, 2015).

[51] Gorton (2008); Gorton, Lewellen, and Metrick (2012).

[52] "The emergence of shadow banking thus shifted the systemic risk-return trade-off toward cheaper credit intermediation during booms, at the cost of more severe crises and more expensive intermediation during downturns," Pozsar et al. (2013), p. 2.

The dangers culminate, according to a report submitted to the Federal Reserve Bank of New York, in a shadow system "prone to excessive lowering of underwriting standards and to overly aggressive structuring of securities" and "prone to runs." Worse still, the shadow banking system tends to accumulate "liquidity and capital shortcomings," among other severe agency problems that lead to its collapse. And because of the unobserved connections among the nodes in the network, systemic assessment of shadow banking tends to "underestimate the aggregate risk." As a result, "the confidence that underpinned the stability of the shadow banking system vanished" rapidly in the meltdown of 2007–8.[53] As a matter of fact, "it was the run on the shadow banking system in 2008 that transformed the nonprime mortgage securities meltdown into a full-blown global financial crisis."[54] The run began in the summer of 2007.

SHADOW BANKING IN THE 2007–8 FINANCIAL CRISIS

In the summer of 2007, after a long period of "great moderation," as previously mentioned, coupled with a rapid growth of the stock markets and financial leverage, several major events generated a spectacular change of mood. David Viniar, the powerful CFO at Goldman Sachs, whose exploits were mentioned in the first lines of this chapter, was indeed late in his analysis for August. Two months before, Bear Stearns had announced that it would be halting redemptions in two hedge funds.[55] As Bear Stearns had refused to take part in a joint effort by banks to rescue Long-Term Capital Management (LTCM) in 1998, the firm was not very popular among competitors and one may presume that its difficulties did not meet with much sympathy. But it was not alone. Indeed, on August 9, BNP Paribas, with heavy losses in the subprime market, suspended redemptions in three of its investment funds with American securities. Together, their value was just €1.6 billion; nevertheless the same day the European Central Bank announced that €95 billion would be made available in emergency credit for those funds requiring it.

Rumors of a bailout were almost as anxiety-inducing as rumors of no bailout. Suspicion began to reach the money markets, and the refusal to refinance trading became more widespread. The assets in the shadow banking system reappeared in the balance sheets of banks. There was a run on the shadow banking system.[56]

The US Federal Reserve acted promptly and directly bought commercial paper, securitized mortgages, and related assets, and guaranteed the liabilities of money funds—liabilities that were heretofore explicitly without guarantee—thus, in effect, bailing out these firms. In spite of that prompt action, the interlinkages and leverage

[53] Pozsar et al. (2013), pp. 3, 13. [54] Taub (2013), p. 447.

[55] A detailed chronology, such as that provided by Gorton, indicates how some signals were already apparent in the financial markets: by December 2006, Ownit Mortgage Solutions went bankrupt; by March 13, 2007, the Mortgage Association noticed that late or missed payments had risen to 13.3% in the subprime segment of the market; by April 2, New Century Financial, specialized in mortgages, bankrupted; by May 3, UBS closed the hedge fund Dillon Read Capital Management and, by June and July, there was a massive downgrading of subprime bonds, Gorton (2008), p. 238.

[56] Gorton and Metrick (2010); Thiemann (2014).

at work in shadow banking permitted the subprime crisis to infect the markets of short-term funding, the hedge funds, and then the market for asset-backed commercial paper (in August 2007, this asset-based commercial paper represented more than US $1.2 trillion of outstanding commercial paper, more than all of the outstanding US Treasury Bills put together). The interbank lending system froze.

The 2007–8 financial crisis has shed light on the perverse effects of financial and economic expansion based on what had been previously thought to be safe money, such as short-term financing. A systemic event materialized through a run on several of the market instruments intrinsic to the practice of shadow banking—the epicenter being the repo market, in which short-term borrowing is provided, typically in exchange for a security to be bought back again—but then extended to asset-backed commercial paper and shares in money market mutual funds.[57] The immediate cause was a shock in house prices, which penalized subprime mortgages and other products[58] and led to a selling off of mortgage-backed securities. The shock initiated in mortgage-backed securities rapidly spread to other financial assets because the originators and the arrangers of securitization deals relied on short-term financing to set up their deals and were unable to roll over their short-term debt.

In fact, by August 2007, securitizers, the finance companies that specialized in mortgages, could no longer rely on the traditional short-term funding to raise money, turning to their bank sponsors in their search for liquidity and activating their credit lines.[59]

The banks were then obliged to absorb the losses of subprime assets, and concerns about their ability to repay the cash lent through repos led to an increase in repo haircuts, the difference between the collateral provided and the amount lent.[60] Consequently, in order to avoid insolvency, banks were forced to compensate for the withdrawal of short-term finance either by increasing their equity, by borrowing funds from capital markets, or by deleveraging, i.e., by calling in their funds from other markets. The first two alternatives soon ceased to exist, obliging banks to sell their assets in a bear market. Thus, the subprime crisis had spread to other financial assets.

Between the summer of 2007 and the summer of 2008, a run on the money market, such as the abrupt withdrawal of repo funding by Bear Stearns in March 2008 and Lehman Brothers in September 2008, led to the collapse of many financial institutions' investment banks and hedge funds.[61]

For instance, two highly leveraged subprime hedge funds operated by Bear Stearns had lost nearly half of their value by July 16, 2007, and failed to meet repo margin calls on July 31. On March 5, 2008, the Carlyle Capital Corporation

[57] Gorton (2009b); Gorton and Metrick (2010).

[58] This was the case in the US with Alt-A products, which were mortgages considered to be riskier than prime products, but still less risky than subprime ones.

[59] US Financial Crisis Inquiry Commission (2011); A key moment came on August 9, 2007, when BNP publicly disclosed that, "regardless of its quality or credit rating," it was not able to value subprime assets in three money market mutual funds and so brought a halt to any fund withdrawals. These three funds represented less than 0.5% of the money managed by the bank, Associated Press (2007); yet the crisis was on. The repercussions proved immense. BNP joined Bear Stearns and Union Investment Management GmnH in stopping fund redemptions, S. Boyd (2007).

[60] Gorton (2009b), p. 4.

[61] Copeland, Martin, and Walker (2010).

failed to meet its margin call. The runs on these funds were mainly conducted by institutional investors holding massive cash positions. These runs forced funds to stop the rollover of other financial products and to sell their assets at the peak of the crisis.

In the US, and all around the world, authorities made unprecedented interventions, bailing out the financial system. A critical feature of the bailout was that authorities extended the conventional banking safety nets to the shadow banking system, a system that was previously defined by operating outside the safety net.

Bear Stearns toppled, first slowly, then quickly. In fall 2007 Bear Stearns had raised one billion from a Chinese investment firm,[62] but the teetering leverage from subprime was powerful enough to threaten the firm in spite of the fall infusion. On March 17, 2008, to prevent the collapse of Bear Stearns, the Federal Reserve lent for the first time ever to investment banks through its new Primary Dealer Credit Facility, an overnight loan facility backed by tri-party-eligible collateral. These special lending facilities were later extended to the whole financial system, including money market funds' holdings of commercial paper. Likewise, limits were increased on deposit insurance and a Temporary Liquidity Guarantee Program was created to give the state a personal guarantee of unsecured debt issued by both banks and shadow banks. The US Treasury also created a Temporary Guarantee Program for Money Market Funds, an insurance scheme designed to protect these funds, and reserved part of the funds' Troubled Asset Relief Program to provide capital injections to both banks and shadow banks, buying assets, half of this being mortgage securities. Then the most important shadow banks were transformed into bank holdings, through the Capital Purchase Program, in order to get convenient legal protection. At this juncture, the Fed doubled its balance to over US $2 trillion as a response to the crash.

The bankruptcy of Lehman Brothers, in September 2008, forced the money fund Reserve Primary, which had invested heavily in Lehman, to reprice its shares (thereby "breaking the buck," or being unable to keep the net asset value of a shares at one dollar, a longstanding target, albeit, significantly, not a formal guarantee by money market funds to their depositors). The investment adviser managing the fund was not able to find the financial resources required to support the fund.[63] Concerns about the ability to preserve the net asset value of its shares at around one dollar induced investors to withdraw their saving pools from this and other funds, i.e., investors began a run on Reserve Primary and the rest of the money-market system.

The US authorities also acted to prevent contagion from these events. But the intervention was non-neutral and in fact directly favored large well-connected firms. On September 16, 2008, the government rescued AIG, the world's largest insurer, which had bet heavily against mortgage defaults as a seller of Credit Default Swaps, a form of default insurance. The rescued AIG was then able to repay its creditors, Goldman Sachs, Merrill Lynch, Bank of America, Citigroup, Wachovia, Morgan Stanley, and J.P. Morgan Chase, all of which had heavy exposure to AIG as a counterparty and would have received much less if AIG had been allowed

[62] Cassidy (2009), p. 313. [63] Waggoner (2008).

to go bankrupt.[64] The first response of the different governments, first the US and then European, was to provide "access to backstop liquidity" to the shadow banking system, in order to shield it from the imminence of collapse and catalyze private sector lending. But as the 2007 crisis deepened and the liquidity provided by the private sector dried up, the guarantees were assumed by the public sector,[65] generating enormous deficits.

A BANKING AND POLICY-INDUCED CRISIS IN EUROPE

The crisis originated in the US in the shadow banking system. Through an unplanned but nonetheless concrete network of finance the crisis was transmitted throughout the financial systems. In Europe it exploded as a banking crisis. This outcome is explained by two major differences between the US and Europe. First, Europe was more bank-based than the US, where shadow financing was prevalent. The US banks directly owned only 30 percent of mortgage lending and 30 percent of corporate funding while in Europe banks held 80 percent and 90 percent respectively. Second, larger European banks tend to include shadow activities in their own balances because, without the Rooseveltian Glass-Steagall Act, no distinction between traditional and investment banking was required, that is, the European banks were formally universal rather than *de facto* universal like the American banks with their long shadows.[66]

As the crisis centered on banks, the European Central Bank (ECB) should have intervened, in spite of the limits of its mandate, concentrated on the objective of price stability—yet the financial crisis called for special action. But nothing of the sort happened. The ECB injected money into the financial markets in order to assure liquidity, but could not restore confidence or the opening of huge holes in the balance sheets. The ECB raised the reference interest rate in July 2007 and again, even as the crash was mounting, in April 2008. ECB reduced the rate in May 2009 and then raised it in 2011 before reducing it again to unprecedented historically low levels for several years. The ECB, responsible for monetary policy and financial stability, was able to manage neither, and it failed to avert a decade-long European crisis.

Following the same yo-yo pattern, the European Union authorities first reacted to the recession with a fiscal stimulus package in 2009. This concentrated on bailing out the banks and allowing for an increase in government spending, temporarily easing the Maastricht restrictions, to counter the reduction in aggregate demand. From the middle to the end of 2009, public spending to support finance amounted to 18 percent of Eurozone GDP, but 74 percent for the UK.[67] Huge public deficits

[64] Acemoglu et al. (2016), The public authorities acquired a shareholding of 79.9% in AIG, lending US $85 billion by September 16.

[65] Pozsar et al. (2013), p. 3.

[66] *The Economist*, December 15, 2012.

[67] Alessandri and Haldane (2009). The figures for the US are quite different according to the sources and obviously to what is being measured: by March 2011 the IMF computed the direct cost of the public programs at 12.7% of GDP or US $1.9 trillion, while the Inspector General of TARP, in 2009, had estimated the potential exposure from the financial rescue at 160% of GDP, or US $24 trillion (official data available from the April 2012 summary, The Financial Crisis Response in Charts, US Treasury).

resulted from this choice[68]—further aggravated by the decrease in GDP, generated by the subsequent recessionary measures.

The initial impact of the stimulus was significantly positive. By September 2009, the ten-year yields of Greek and Irish public bonds were lower than at the beginning of the crisis.[69] Merkel and Sarkozy, meeting at an emergency summit in Deauville, France, in October 2010, were even bolder and concluded that in a crisis of the sort that southern Europe was then suffering, governments should force a debt restructuring program on creditors, as a response to the obstacles encountered by the Greek government in negotiations with their private creditors. They also agreed that restructuring should be mandatory albeit delayed until 2013. They then retracted their declaration, with no explanation for the change.[70] With the withdrawal of support by the core of the EU, the debt crisis spread from Greece to Ireland, then to Portugal and Spain, and, finally exploded in Cyprus.[71]

The same option for austerity was imposed by the international institutions. Despite the extraordinary circumstances of crisis management under which the governments of the developed nations had taken on these large deficits, at the 2010 Toronto Summit, the G20 governments agreed to halve their deficits within three years. Considering that total public debt, let alone deficits, had doubled in some of these countries over the three years since the crisis, the deficit-reduction target was too much and too soon, a mistake that led to austerity policies that have prolonged the crisis, as effective global demand collapsed and investment was dragged down.[72] But the priority was to restore confidence in the financial system, no matter what were the economic and social consequences of these instrumental decisions.

In Europe and during this period, the European Central Bank was the key operator in the rescue and austerity plans. A provisional European Fund for Financial Stability was set up in May 2010 with a lending capacity of €440 billion, and then the European Mechanism of Financial Stabilization was instituted. In December 2011, this launched a large-scale operation of €1 trillion for the long-term refinancing of firms.[73] A permanent European Mechanism of Stability

[68] European Central Bank (2015), The direct impact of the different measures on public debt was nevertheless quite unequal: until early 2012 it was 38.5% in Ireland and 3.2% in the US. The ECB published a report in 2015 confirming this assessment of the impact in Europe.

[69] Nevertheless, as the exposure of the German banks and private sector to the Greek debt was large (€25 billion), the authorities were pressed to bail out these creditors as soon as possible. And so they did, Eichengreen (2015), pp. 342, 346.

[70] Eichengreen (2015), pp. 350–1. Later, the IMF concluded it had proceeded wrongly in accepting the austerity programs for Greece without an upfront restructuring of Greek public debt, International Monetary Fund Country Report 13/156 (2013), p. 28.

[71] Portugal received an emergency loan of €78 billion in 2011, Spain one of €100 billion the next year. In the case of Cyprus, the ECB conducted an operation that imposed heavy losses on some depositors in May 2013, including 100% losses for deposits larger than €100 thousand and the closure of Laiki Bank, and 60% losses for deposits over €100 thousand in the largest bank. The larger depositors were forced to bail-in, i.e., formally accept some of the losses of, the banks.

[72] Koo (2014), p. 141.

[73] This was challenged in the German Supreme Court, which, in February 2014, established that this program was in conflict with the German Constitution. Although it consequently did not rule out the illegality of the Outright Monetary Transactions program, the German Court asked for a European Court to rule on this matter.

was introduced in October 2012, with a lending capacity to bailed-out states of €500 billion. If it had been endowed with a banking license, with the commonly accepted (although dangerous) leverage of 20:1, it would have become the largest bank in the world, but such a notion was rejected.

Finally, the 2015 Draghi Plan proposed the creation of an influx of more than €1 trillion into the financial markets from early 2015 until 2016 as part of a program to stave off deflation (it was then extended to September 2018), to permit the euro to depreciate and to create more credit for investment. Although the Draghi Plan protected the euro from speculative pressures, it also fed a new stock bubble and offered scanty results with respect to promoting of investment and aggregate demand. As this new policy for monetizing part of the debt went on, the ECB was able to momentarily stabilize the financial system, at the cost of creating new influxes of speculative capital to the stock markets.

The Eurozone represents the worst of both worlds for managing a common currency: there is neither Federal fiscal support nor capacity for national action. Eichengreen does not mince his words: as an "awful marriage" and a "disaster," the euro increases the danger of devastating budgetary crises. According to him, "the single greatest failure to learn appropriate lessons from this earlier history was surely the decision to adopt the euro."[74]

CONCLUSION

The butterfly effect is nothing more than a naïve and naturalistic narrative inspired by the unpredictable effects of small perturbations in unstable systems. It is difficult to apply this tale of physical wildness to the financial system because the force of states, the pull of international conventions and institutions, the push of social interests and strategies, and the prowess, ingenuity, and cupidity of financial innovation are not natural forces. In this case, the perturbation was created deep in the bowels of the economic fabric: a spiral of debt was the result of the shadow system, and debt was susceptible to a run on the non-traditional banks when the mood turned from ebullience to despondence.

The public authorities in the US and Europe decided to cushion the losses of the financial sector, and imposed austerity policies in order to repay the large deficits generated by this move. In particular, Europe became the apex of austerity. As the historian Barry Eichengreen has noted, the emergency measures taken throughout this crisis have proved that the financial system is indeed the back door of the state.[75]

[74] Eichengreen (2015), pp. 96, 113, 215, 341, 382; Blanchard (2007). Olivier Blanchard, the chiefeconomist of the IMF during most of this period of recession, situates the origin of the problems of the European periphery in the euro, given the fall in interest rates and decline of savings, leading to rising current account imbalances since there were large capital inflows and an overvaluation of the real exchange rate.

[75] Eichengreen (2015), p. 29; Pistor (2013). This interpretation is close to what Pistor called the "elasticity of law."

In other words, the choice of solutions to the financial crash and the ensuing recession was led solely by the interests of the financial sector itself, although they provided just a temporary relief: the toxic danger was not over after years of recession or mediocre recovery and huge payments to the banking and shadow banking industry.[76]

Given this conclusion, in the next chapter and appendix we will investigate the shadow system, its size and its institutions, in order to then discuss how it rose to such power.

[76] In 2007, the Royal Bank of Scotland, with Santander and Fortis, bought ABN and then "went bust, proving that two dogs do not make a tiger" (*The Economist*, March 7, 2015). Also Fortis collapsed, and ABN was nationalized in 2009. The capitalization of Bank of America fell to half its 2005 value. Citigroup floundered with its market capitalization down by 90%, well below book value, and cut its workforce by one third. Bailed out at the time, Citigroup would find itself in trouble again in 2015.

3

The Whole Alphabet Soup

At first encounter, the shadow economy might be presumed to denote the hidden and dishonest corner of society, vice, contraband, smuggling, counterfeiting, and trafficking. To the surprise of many, the shadow also grew in plain sight, not on streetcorners or the docks but in the corridors of power, just down the hall from cabinet ministers, managed by graduate-educated economists. The shadow economy came to dominate the world of finance and was responsible for the major breakdown of the world economy with the 2007–8 crash. We suffered a major run on these parts of the financial (but non-banking) system and, as a consequence, a decline in world output on a scale not seen since the Second World War.

In this chapter, we will look at the current definitions and major interpretations of shadow finance, registering its rise and fall, and then the bright rebirth of the Phoenix from the ashes.

THE INFORMAL SECTOR: SHADOWS IN A DARK CORNER

If the reader peruses a newspaper, magazine, or an economics journal from, say, twenty years ago, the only reference to be found to the shadow economy would be to informal or even illegal activities, untaxed payments for services, tax evasion large and small. Small shops, street sales, local plumbing services, non tax-paying contracts for picking fruit in the summer, or the darker activities of drug trafficking and smuggling, theft and fencing, and for-profit crime in general—this is what would come to mind. Rich people might engage in vice in their leisure time, in illegal hiring to ease access to household help, or in tax evasion at the encouragement of aggressive accountants, and being caught would entail embarrassment.

Of course, readers familiar with less developed countries know that these dimensions of the informal economy often exceed the formal economy, and certainly represent a more important segment of economic life than does the informal economy in Manchester or Munich, Los Angeles or Lyon. The International Labour Organization (ILO) estimated in 2000 that, even excluding agriculture, 82 percent of employment in South Asia, 65 percent in East and Southeast Asia, 66 percent in sub-Saharan Africa, and 51 percent in Latin America occurs in the informal sector.

But, as the ILO developed more sophisticated statistical methods for measuring informal employment,[1] it came to the conclusion that informality was not limited to lower-income economies. In the late 1990s in Mexico, 36 percent of gross value added was generated in the informal economy, while at the same time Italian GDP would have increased 41 percent if the non-observed economy were considered. Informal employment was and is to be found everywhere.

The ILO notes the difficulty in detecting and measuring informal activities, jobs, and income since part of their purpose is the evasion of public control and taxation. Furthermore, the non-registered economy includes another impulse for escaping the oversight of the state: namely crime, ranging from robbery and smuggling to drug trafficking and other offenses. As the "gross criminal product" may be high, ignorance of its income, employment, and social impact reduces the accuracy of national accounts.

Large sectors of both less and more developed economies remain distinct from the formal, tax-paying economy but with permeable membranes separating the two, permitting the passage of people and capital as circumstances warrant. Indeed, periods of havoc, such as the Great Recession, often witness increases in informal jobs and transactions, as desperate people confront unemployment and deprivation.

In the last few decades the noteworthy changes in the shadow economy have not been in local market informal arrangements and outright illegal activities, but in the world of finance, an informalization at the core, not the margins, of the global economy.

Indeed, a large part of this informal economy is in fact rather formal. It involves diligent institutions and sophisticated schemes for managing large flows of illicit funds, of dirty money, including earnings from vice, bribes, tax evasion, and illegal capital flight. The OECD estimates a global flow of US$ 1 trillion per year in bribes, and an unaccounted value of other illicit transfers through the financial system, mostly from developing countries to bank accounts in developed countries or tax havens. The results of efforts to tame the beast are uncertain: for 2010–12 the OECD countries, including all the more developed economies of the world, recovered only US $147 million and have frozen US $1.4 billion of stolen assets.[2]

Spring 2016 witnessed the announcement by a consortium of international journalists of the existence of the Panama Papers, a trove of documentation from a single Panama-based law firm that specializes in hiding the wealth of the wealthy from taxing authorities through a complex system of transfers, beards, and shell corporations.

Global Financial Integrity is a Washington-based think tank that produces a yearly report on the dimension and magnitude of illicit funds from developing countries, investigating these flows that benefit both the owners of the dirty money and the financiers in the developed countries. Their computation is based on discrepancies in trade statistics, for example in trade-invoice discrepancies if the value of goods leaving a country is less than the reported value on arrival, and other leakages in the balance of payments. Global Financial Integrity concludes that the transferred value of money for laundering, crime, corruption, and tax

[1] World Bank (2017b). [2] OECD (2013).

evasion from developing and emergent countries represents more than the sum of direct investment and foreign aid to these countries.

For the period 2004–13, Global Financial Integrity estimates US \$7.8 trillion of illicit financial flows from developing countries, increasing each year at twice the rate of total output. Almost half of this comes from China, which is responsible for five times as much as the next country in the list, Mexico. But Europe's share has been increasing, too, since 2007, now amounting to almost one quarter. For each year after 2010, the sum exceeds US \$1 trillion—it is as if a sum equivalent to the whole Spanish economy had vanished in the darkness of illicit trade.[3]

Another dimension, and not the least relevant, is the export of capital from poor countries—from profits or bribery, from disinvestment or robbery, legal or illegal. In the case of the thirty-three countries of one of the poorest parts of the world, sub-Saharan Africa, a recent investigation contrasted the value of the increase in foreign debt between 1970 and 2008 (from less than US \$50 billion to more than quadruple the amount, at constant dollars, thus excluding the effect of prices and exchange rates), while capital flight amounted to US \$735 billion; in other words, Africa is handsomely financing the financial centers of the world.[4]

This ever more abundant flow of dirty funds (or legal but unequal and resulting in the impoverishment of trade) is part of the growth of the deregulated global financial system. It is managed from the bright shining skyscrapers and exclusive clubs, and it may favor the most prestigious members of our communities. But these flows are just a part, and we reckon it remains a small share, of the less visible networks of the financial system. Since data are limited and this is not the theme of this book, we will mostly ignore it in the following sections, concentrating instead on the measurable movements of capital and their transformation, but not without first issuing a prior warning to the reader about this hidden part of the world we live in.

Instead we examine the new shadow economy, concentrating on its visible part, on its finesse and social power, and not on the old informal economy or even on the intersection of the old informal economy with the brave new world. The new shadow economy becomes our focus in this chapter and in Appendix A, which is somewhat more technical than the rest of the book.

THE RISE OF SHADOW BANKING

Banking was a solid business, having been developed in many cases by dynasties of powerful and respected people. Being essentially conservative and protective of fortunes already made, banks used to make money on the interest-rate spread. After the series of misadventures that led to the Great Depression in 1929, the predominant idea in the era of embedded liberalism was that banks, in exchange for reliable profits and professional salaries, should obey the rules of a central bank, acting as the public issuer of money, and controlling and insuring finance.

[3] Kar and Spanjers (2015). [4] Boyce and Ndikumana (2011).

Confidence is central to banks' effectiveness. Banks are allowed to function in a state of what would be considered technical bankruptcy in any other economic activity, because banks' own capital constitutes only a very small fraction of their assets and liabilities. To be effective, banks cannot be forced to redeem debt at short notice. In the event of serious losses, the state undertakes to repay most creditors, in particular households. Therefore, confidence is the currency of this trade and stodginess the desired personality trait.

For decades after the 1929 crisis, banks operated at the core of the financial system, governed by the New Deal's systemic response to the Great Crash and Depression. Traditional intermediation through banks and a handful of other solid financial institutions was considered the only acceptable way forward in the 1940s through the 1960s, an era characterized as "Boring Banking."[5]

Yet banks operate in a changing world and they change that world. As a consequence, over the last quarter of the twentieth century this world was transformed beyond recognition: Democratic and Republican governments in the US alike gutted the Rooseveltian rules and deregulation proceeded apace in Europe as well. By 2007, on the eve of the grand crash triggered by the subprime crisis, bank intermediation had been reduced to 40 percent of credit; even in recovery and under a broadened definition of "bank," the bank share has scarcely risen above 47 percent of all credit.[6] Banks form a smaller part of a financial system which abandoned traditional spread-based banking and transformed into a casino, making money from deals and service fees, proliferating connections and adventures, building leverage, and risking as much as possible.

The IMF, an institution designed to protect the international economy from systemic threats, justified the emergence of shadow finance as an escape from "strict banking regulations." In a Panglossian mood and advocating for the new financial intermediation, the IMF argued that large institutional demand for assets, namely from insurance companies and pension funds, and large cash pools held outside traditional banks by global investors warranted the introduction of new financial applications to connect the new savers and the new borrowers.[7]

In the neoliberal era, financial functions have diversified and financial institutions have converged. A growing number of non-bank institutions perform traditional banking operations, while banks now provide a broader range of services. The deregulation of financial markets, initiated gently in the 1960s with the relaxation of interest-rate caps and credit limits, accelerated in the 1970s with the liberalization of financial flows. New loans to developing countries in the global South brought a global dimension to capital markets. It crystallized in the Washington Consensus,[8] which consolidated financial liberalization reforms by waiving or eliminating capital controls, promoting the privatization of state

[5] Epstein (2016). [6] Adrian and Ashcraft (2012), p. 3.

[7] World Economic and Financial Surveys (2014).

[8] The "Washington Consensus" is the expression used to describe the set of rules and prescriptions established by the dominant international organizations, from the IMF to the US Treasury, including deregulation, privatization and stabilization measures. It was first coined in 1989 by John Williamson, an economist working for the Institute for International Economics, a think tank.

companies, and channeling private savings into capital markets through pension funds and insurance requirements.

The shadow banking system emerged within this context. Policy change in the mid-1970s provided both pressure and means. Deregulation and the emergence of money funds whose attractive interest rates above the regulated norm ended the quiet life of profitable oligopoly that had benefited commercial banks and created pressure to find higher returns to attract household deposits. Deregulation also gave these banks the means to pursue more roaring forms of finance.[9]

Money market mutual funds finance themselves with commercial paper and repos (large very short-run loans disguised as repurchase agreements for selling a security and then buying it back again)[10] and invest in low-risk assets, albeit ones that are not subject to mark-to-market accounting but to accrual basis accounting. The money funds marked the birth of the modern shadow banking system, which now broadly covers the set of highly leveraged non-bank institutions, which carry out credit intermediation and transformation but have access neither to insured deposits nor to the discount window of central banks. This segment, which expanded rapidly in the 1980s and 1990s and exploded—in every sense—in the first decade of the new century, encompasses large independent investment banks or broker-dealers, hedge funds, investment funds, private equity funds, the multiple special investment vehicles, pension funds, and insurance companies. All are vulnerable to runs.[11]

Jane D'Arista and Tom Schlesinger noted with alarm the rise of an "unregulated parallel banking system" as early as 1993. They warned, "Over the last two decades, the US system has been reshaped by the spread of multifunctional financial conglomerates and the emergence of an unregulated parallel banking system. Along with other powerful trends like securitization, these events have broken down the carefully compartmentalized credit and capital marketplace established in New Deal legislation."[12]

Acknowledging the tide of financial and institutional innovation, Paul McCulley of PIMCO, a California-based investment firm, later coined the term "shadow

[9] Money Market Mutual Funds, which date from the 1970s as one of the earliest financial innovations of the new era, attract large sums from depository institutions and individual account holders to finance deals with short-term maturities. Their safety is presumed to lie in this short maturity, and these mutual funds imply (but do not actually promise) liquidity equivalent to that of an insured deposit account for individual depositors. Money market funds hold some 20% of US household cash balances and are typically treated by households as if they were checking accounts in insured banks. The two largest visible components of the shadow system are money market funds (MMFs) and repurchase agreements ("repos").

[10] Repos are short-term loans masquerading as sales, in which the seller (borrower) sells securities at a discount on their face value (the haircut) to a buyer (lender), while agreeing to buy them back, i.e. repurchase them, for a somewhat larger amount (effectively amounting to added interest) at a future date. The key parameters in a repo are the haircut, which is the face value of the securities less the cash provided and represents skepticism regarding the likelihood of repayment, and the interest rate.

[11] Taub suggests a description of the shadow system including "investment banks, off-balance-sheet entities, money market funds, and hedge funds, as well as some affiliates of traditional banks," indicating that some still add insurance companies and Freddie Mac and Fannie Mae, plus some financialized non-financial companies, such as General Electric and General Motors Taub (2013), p. 449, Hedge funds numbered roughly 500 in 1990 with US $40 billion under management; by the end of 2015 there were nine thousand managing three trillion dollars *The Economist*, 20 February 2016.

[12] D'Arista and Schlesinger (1993b), p. 2.

banking" to capture "the whole alphabet soup of levered-up non-bank investment conduits, vehicles, and structures," in an address to the 2007 Jackson Hole Symposium of the Federal Reserve Bank of Kansas City.[13] The name was sexy, and suggestively dark enough to capture the imagination of the media and public opinion. Shadow banking it became, in spite of mild protests from several princes of the shadows at first, and then of late opposition by the White House's Department of Treasury.[14]

Yet the emphasis on non-banks is misleading because banks appear at the core of non-bank banking, as both owners and coordinators. Even now, years after the subprime crash which wracked the shadow banking system, each of the five largest US bank holding companies have an average of 1,500 shadow subsidiaries with one surpassing 3,000.[15] These bank holding companies control 38 percent of the assets of the largest insurance companies, 41 percent of the total of money market funds assets, and 93 percent of the assets of the largest brokers and dealers. In fact, the ability to intertwine different segments and institutions is the power—and vulnerability—of the financial system.

In the next sections, we will briefly go into the history of the darkness, examining how we came to this point, while also discussing how to measure the shadow system and seeing how it functions.

BULL FIRMS FOR BULL MARKETS

Two major explanations tend to emerge for the growth of shadow finance in the US and both of them deal with the history of banking, arguing in favor of the inevitability and usefulness of the new cohorts of firms and products.

The first goes like this: money and banking have always been contested in the United States. The first era of centralized banking gave way to the free banking era (1837–62) when local banks issued paper money and credit. A gold-based hard-money regime in the late nineteenth century prevented neither booms nor busts and generated large-scale political discontent. A partially managed monetary regime after the creation of the Fed in 1913 still permitted the Great Crash and Depression. The regulated period (1933–99) beginning with the New Deal through the repeal of Glass-Steagall[16] ran into profit squeeze and pressure to free

[13] McCulley (2007), Since 2000, PIMCO has been part of Allianz, a giant German financial firm, and is well-established as a Washington insider: it recruited Greenspan as a senior advisor after he left the Federal Reserve, and in 2015 it did the same with Bernanke.

[14] Secretary of the Treasury Steve Mnuchin issued an October 2017 report, "Financial System That Creates Economic Opportunities—Asset Management and Insurance", stating that "Treasury recommends that the FSB transition away from using the term 'shadow banking' in its monitoring of credit intermediation outside of the regular banking sector," Mnuchin (2017), p. 63.

[15] Adrian and Ashcraft (2012), p. 17.

[16] During the free banking era, different legislation tried to impose order in the financial sector (the National Banking Acts of 1863 and 1864 determined the replacement of bank notes by national currency backed by the deposit of US bonds). The constitution of the Federal Reserve in 1913, after a financial panic, would be the next step for public regulation of the financial system, but it was only with the institution of the federal deposit insurance, in 1933, with the great depression, that the Federal Reserve became the lender of last resort and therefore obtained effective tools for controlling the system (Adrian and Ashcraft, 2012: 10).

the money with deregulation, in order to open new avenues for innovation in credit and financial products enabling capitalists to seek profitable opportunities. As deregulation reigned, shadow banking liabilities grew as substitutes for high-powered money, and business created business.

The second explanation exemplifies the "market strikes back" mentality. Strict regulation of banks creates opportunities for capital, tax, and accounting arbitrage. Banks are not permitted to pursue these opportunities under the regulatory regime—indeed the entire point of the rules is to prevent dangerous anti-social behavior or to encourage pro-social behavior. But as regulation required banks to comply with strict rules, thereby creating juicy arbitrage opportunities, banks created new entities under the revealing name of vehicles—getaway cars come to mind—to escape the supervision of the central banks and to proceed with non-regulated business.

The system has earlier antecedents. The first case of securitization, the pooling of debt to be sold as bonds, dates back to the 1920s in the US and was conducted by government-sponsored enterprises, constituting the Federal Home Loan Banks in 1932, then Fannie Mae in 1938, and Freddie Mac in 1970.[17] Yet these examples do not come close to resembling the system created in the early years of the twenty-first century. The rise in values of the financial markets brooks no comparison with the past: while, in the case of the US, the financial sector's profits rose, in general, in a similar fashion to those of industry from the 1930s until 1980, and thereafter from 1980 until 2005, their real growth was, in fact, 800 percent, three times that of the general economy. The total assets of commercial banks, plus securities firms, evolved from 55 percent to 95 percent of US GDP between 1980 and 2000. They went on climbing the mountain and, two years after the subprime crash, the assets of Citigroup Bank of America and Morgan Chase alone were comparable to half of US GDP.[18] Every cloud has a silver lining.

For the US, this transformation took only a short break to relaunch after the subprime crash. There are only two periods in history during which American stocks rose as quickly as after 2009: 1923–9 (on the eve of the Great Crash) and 1993–9 (when deregulation blossomed and the dot-com bubble flourished).[19] This enthusiastic and bullish finance is not only the result of product innovation and new markets, it is also the effect of a deep and far-reaching social transformation. The next sections will be dedicated to discussing what this transformation is all about.

SHADOW BANKING IN THE MAKING

Early definitions of shadow banking sought to classify entities, juxtaposing bank and non-bank financial institutions such as asset managers, investment funds, pension funds, hedge funds, and money market funds, or focusing on the regulatory

[17] The shadow banking system includes a subsystem of government-sponsored corporations—Freddie Mac and Fannie Mae were the original cases—internal to the traditional banks (with securitization techniques increasing the leverage), and an "external" subsystem (with credit intermediation through brokers and dealers, non-bank specialist intermediaries, and credit risk repositories), Adrian and Ashcraft (2012), pp. 14,19; Pozsar et al. (2013), p. 7.

[18] Johnson and Kwak (2011), pp. 12, 59, 60, 85.

[19] *The Economist*, March 21, 2015.

jurisdiction, in this case juxtaposing risk-based or prudentially regulated financial intermediation and finance without capital requirements, deposit insurance, or access to the lender of last resort. More recently, a functional conceptualization has emerged. By being more focused on the new forms of credit intermediation, it seems to fine-tune the intrinsic complexity inherited with the deregulation and liberalization of the financial system. It further broadens the scope of the definition by opposing deposit-based banking to non-traditional means of gathering funds in the security markets, through asset-backed commercial paper, long-term securitization, and repo and security collateralized lending.

The institutional conceptualization tends to set the focus on the regulatory framework and the legal requirements applied to shadow banking, considering that those regulations that apply to shadow banking are less demanding than the ones applied to banks.[20] In that sense, the Financial Stability Board, an international body established by a G20 Summit in 2009 (it is the successor to the Financial Stability Forum, created in order to research and make recommendations on the management of finance), simply states that the shadow system emerges when credit intermediation proceeds outside the traditional and regulated channels, albeit warning about the close connections between non-bank and bank activities.[21]

A research team well versed in financial markets, including a senior advisor to the US Treasury, a top manager of the Federal Reserve Bank of New York and a vice chair of the Bank of America Merrill Lynch, defined shadow banks as "financial intermediaries that conduct maturity, credit, and liquidity transformation without explicit access to central bank liquidity or public-sector credit guarantees."[22] These authors also emphasize that this system of getting short-term deposits to fund long-term loans or using liquid instruments to fund illiquid assets, in other ways than through traditional banking, transfers risks not to a single balance sheet but to a chain of balances. Contrary to the traditional banking model, intermediation does not occur in a single institution, implying the potential for increased systemic risk.

In any case, shadow banks are those institutions that are able to provide credit outside the traditional banking requirements and protections, the pillars of a regulated banking market. *De facto* regulation was supposed to be provided by credit-rating agencies and counterparty vigilance.[23]

[20] McCulley (2010); Gorton and Metrick (2010); Financial Stability Board (2011b).

[21] The FSB uses two definitions, the broad one being: "the system of credit intermediation that involves entities and activities outside the regular banking system." This is, however, still limited in scope to "credit intermediation" (both on-balance sheet and off-balance sheet) meaning that "only entities and activities involved in extending credit (either directly or as part of a chain of credit intermediation) or involved in facilitating its intermediation are included," but equity trading and foreign currency transactions should be excluded. The narrow definition considers shadow banking as "a system of credit intermediation that involves entities and activities outside the regular banking system, and raises (i) systemic risk concerns, in particular by maturity/liquidity transformation, leverage and flawed credit risk transfer, and/or (ii) regulatory arbitrage concerns" Financial Stability Board (2011b), pp. 2, 4.

[22] Pozsar et al. (2013).

[23] "Shadow banking needed some seal of approval, so that providers of short-dated funding could convince themselves that their claims were de facto 'just as good' as deposits at banks with access to the government's liquidity safety nets. Conveniently, the friendly faces at the rating agencies, paid by the shadow bankers, stood at the ready to provide such seals of approval" McCulley (2009), p. 9; Lapavitsas (2014), pp. 307–327.

For that reason, some authors call for leveling up regulation, extending equally demanding prudential and licensing requirements and public obligations to both types of institutions. In the same sense, McCulley stresses that the focus should not be on the formal regulatory borders, but on the functions actually performed: "what an institution does, not what it is called, should determine how it is regulated."[24]

Defenders of the shadow banking system challenge this view,[25] emphasizing that shadow banking institutions are in fact regulated; shadow banks' dealings in paper are subject to securities regulation, and when the shadow entity is held by a bank, it is also subject to prudential regulation at the consolidated level of the entire bank balance sheet.

We disagree, since this has proved to be ineffective. Banking regulation is risk-based, focuses on the linkages between the payment system and the interbank lending markets, and limits the bank's risk exposure at every moment (to credit risk and interest-rate risk and disaggregated by asset class, security, and counterparty). In contrast, securities regulation only requires the disclosure of the material risks but does not limit risk, either in terms of quantity or domain of intervention. In parallel, rating agencies and counterparty vigilance have proved to be part of the problem and not a solution.

Investigation of shadow banking can shed light on new forms of market-based credit intermediation and uncover its complex ramifications. Studying the intertwining of "shadow banking institutions" and chartered banks exposes how banks in fact make their credit intermediation activity fully reliant upon market-based mechanisms.

Although shadow banking is frequently portrayed as competing with the regulated banking system, the reality is that banks sit atop financial holdings, promoting the expansion of these new non-banking financial institutions through bank credit creation, and backing them up when things go wrong. At the same time, they recycle themselves into new roles and create new sources of profit by developing new financing methods. Banks' provision of "backup credit lines" for finance companies maintains confidence in these profitable non-banking intermediaries while thoroughly entangling banks with their ostensible rivals.[26] This is why the symbiotic connections between the two systems are emphasized as the "New Wall Street System,"[27] while others designate shadow banking as "off-balance banking" (as opposed to on-balance sheet banking),[28] referring to the mix of securitization and repo, arguing that while securitization aims at moving the assets of traditional banks off their balance sheets, repo promotes the use of securitized bonds as money. Both activities are considered fundamental for investment bank financing, while commercial banks also increasingly rely on them. Indeed, this is also referred to as "unstable banking,"[29] identifying securitization and repo as the culprits of universal banking instability.

[24] D'Arista and Schlesinger (1993b), p. 5; McCulley (2009), p. 11.

[25] See, for example, E. Murphy (2013), p. 13; other authors defend shadow banks as promoters of disintermediation, increasing the competition with banks J. H. Boyd and Gertler (1993).

[26] D'Arista and Schlesinger (1993a).

[27] Gowan (2009). [28] Gorton (2009c), p. 24.

[29] Shleifer and Vishny (2010); Some call the hedge funds "the Galapagos Islands of finance" Meyer (2014); Lo (2017).

Since "securitized-banking activities were central to the operations of firms formerly known as 'investment banks' (e.g., Bear Stearns, Lehman Brothers, Morgan Stanley, and Merrill Lynch), but they also play a role at commercial banks, as a supplement to traditional banking activities of firms like Citigroup, J.P. Morgan, and Bank of America," and furthermore "the (former) top US investment banks funded roughly half of their assets using repo markets, with additional exposure due to off-balance sheet financing of their customers,"[30] it is obvious that shadow activities became a dominant feature of both traditional and non-traditional banking.

VALUES AND THEIR DERIVATIVES

Two major changes will be investigated through this part of the book, and one was invoked in the previous paragraphs: the transformation of credit through financial innovation, aggravating risk and uncertainty. The second implication will be summarized in what follows, and it is not a minor feature of the modern capital movements: the creation of money, as "securities have replaced loans as the principal form of credit, with their issue increasingly tied to the process of money creation."[31]

Derivatives, the first letter of the alphabet soup of the shadows, are at the core of this innovation process and money creation. They have been around for ages: the first derivatives can be traced back to the nineteenth century or even earlier, such as those issued at the Dojima Rice Exchange in Osaka, Japan, eventually the first registered futures-exchange market, from 1730, and the Chicago Board of Trade on futures-contracts, operating since 1864. More recently, the Chicago market for futures-exchanges traded currencies has been active since 1972, and has included Treasury bonds since 1975.[32] But in recent years these contracts have expanded as the basis of the new shadow world.

They are based on the value of some underlying asset or entity, either interest rate or future production.[33] So much have derivatives expanded as the favored financial contract that they nearly play the role of money—although unlike money, derivative contracts do not reliably measure or store value. The flexibility of the contracts for derivatives explains the rise of "synthetic finance," or speculation without owning the required debt instruments, as in the "naked Credit Default Swaps," which constitute insurance against a default on a debt which can be held as a hedge by the creditor but also as pure speculation by someone not involved in the debt.

Derivatives are therefore riskier credit operations off the books of traditional finance, as regulation-evading techniques became the standard of the banking industry and different funds became the primary vehicle for savings in lieu of bank

[30] Gorton and Metrick (2012), p. 2; Hördahl and M. R. King (2008), p. 39.

[31] Guttmann (2015). [32] Bryan and Rafferty (2006), p. 109.

[33] They can be option-derivatives, buying a certain item at a fixed price in the future, or exchange-rate swaps derivatives, providing for the exchange of cash flows over a certain time, or insurance contracts, or still something else.

deposits. As a consequence of their prevalence, derivative trading is the epitome of the concentration of financial assets, "the speculative heart of capital," as one author calls it.[34]

There are complementary explanations for the rush towards finance in the new century. David Kotz points to a continued or renewed crisis of accumulation proceeding as the neoliberal model began to run aground.[35] It is also possible that it was simply innovative creativity in chasing profits. In any case, an enormous mobilization of savings, of pension and other funds was channeled into derivatives, raising the demand for financial assets, increasing prices, shortening the period of circulation, and ultimately increasing the propensity for bubbles, despite the veneer of low risk. Everything could become the asset for such a contract, including the weather.[36]

UNSTABLE CONNECTIONS

The shadow banking system is a co-evolved rather than a parallel system because it lies at the heart of banking, providing new forms of financial intermediation.[37] This is why the new form of banking intermediation, the fruit of the growing financialization of entities other than banks, is commonly referred to as "market-based banking" or "network banking." Finally, this does not represent a deviant mood in the financial system, it is instead the development of its core business, and it would be a mistake to understate this trend of adaptation: "the relative decline of commercial banks has been perceived by mainstream economists as marginalization, or 'disintermediation' often in conjunction with the rise of direct finance through open markets. But commercial banks have also transformed themselves, while 'shadow' financial institutions are often dependent on banks for funding. Commercial banks have remained the pivotal institution of the financial system even in the US, as became apparent in the gigantic crisis that broke out in 2007."[38]

The emergence of non-banking financial institutions is, above all, the outcome of the new roles intermediated by banks in the context of financialization: risk pooling for savers, the storage of savings in financial assets other than bank deposits, the trading of these assets in capital markets, and provision of personal credit to households. Although changes in the business practices of non-financial corporations, as well as non-banking financial institutions, contribute to the spread of financialization across society, banks play a fundamental role both in promoting the adoption of these practices by the non-banking institutions and in adopting themselves in order to maximize their profits through leverage.

The symbiotic perspective is now broadly acknowledged. The Financial Stability Board employed a narrowly tailored legal definition of shadow banking—"the system of credit intermediation that involves entities and activities outside the

[34] Norfield (2012). [35] Kotz (2015).

[36] On pricing weather derivatives see Hull (2009); on financial inflation, the reference is Toporowski (2002); Das (2006) provides a general overview of derivatives.

[37] Jeffers and Plihon (2014); M. Friedman (1962), p. 21. [38] Lapavitsas (2014), p. 209.

regular banking system"—but the FSB report, while omitting equity trading and foreign-currency transactions, for the most part recognized the web of connections between bank and non-bank activity.[39]

On the other hand, Daniel Tarullo, a member of the board of governors of the US Federal Reserve, also considers that shadow banking "refers to credit intermediation involving leverage and maturity transformation that is partly or wholly outside the traditional banking system."[40] Nevertheless, the Green Paper submitted to the European Economic and Social Committee simply states that "there are many ways in which shadow banks replicate traditional banks, and some shadow banks are part of traditional banks."[41]

The conceptual limitations underpinning the distinction between banking and non-banking activities have been thoroughly discussed,[42] since many of the activities intermediated by "illuminated banking" also fit within the definition of shadow banking. An institutional concept would oppose "illuminated" banks to "shadow" banks; instead, a functional concept, opposing credit intermediation based on depository banking to credit intermediation that relies on security markets to fund loans, seems more realistic. As banks benefit from market-based banking (because the risk that was once concentrated on a single balance sheet is now spread across a chain of balance sheets, although banks still hold a relevant part of it), only the close study of the banks' balance sheet may uncover the implications of the new mechanism underpinning credit intermediation.[43]

The functional approach allows for a more in-depth analysis of reality, focusing on the actors, the intermediation mechanisms, and the motivations or transmission channels. Such an analysis focuses on the recent transformations observed in credit intermediation, specifically the accrued reliance on market-based credit intermediation, as opposed to deposit-based credit intermediation, as well as both the opening up of credit intermediation to other non-bank financial institutions and the growing reliance upon these methods by banks, while also promoting balance-sheet leverage.

Under this approach, the literature considers the main actors involved in shadow banking activities, the multiple mechanisms underpinning non-deposit credit intermediation, and the contribution of shadow banking to the financial meltdown initiated in 2007. Indeed, in addition to the key role played by banks, we have witnessed the opening up of credit intermediation exclusivity to other non-bank financial institutions, such as money market mutual funds, finance companies, and the designated "cash-pool" institutions. Another relevant element in the fragmented map of credit intermediation consists of non-financial corporations. On the other hand, traditional deposit-based intermediation has given way to

[39] Financial Stability Board (2011a), p. 2. Indeed, the FSB also states, "although shadow banking may be conducted by a single entity that intermediates between end-suppliers and end-borrowers of funds, it often involves multiple entities and activities forming a chain of credit intermediation. In the latter case, one or more of the entities in the chain might be a bank or a bank-owned entity. Banks might also be exposed to the shadow banking system through temporary exposures (warehousing), through the provision of finance or through contingent credit lines. In addition, there may also be important links on the liabilities side, as banks may be funded by entities which form part of the shadow banking system (e.g. money market funds)" Financial Stability Board (2011b), p. 3.

[40] Tarullo (2012).

[41] European Economic and Social Committee (EESC) (2012).

[42] E. Murphy (2013); M. Friedman (1962) p. 23.

[43] Jeffers and Plihon (2014), p. 4.

market-based credit intermediation, more specifically securitization, and collateralized credit, among which the most relevant forms are repo lending, security lending, and asset-backed commercial lending by non-financial corporations.

CONCLUSION

Informal and non-taxed activities have always permeated all mercantile societies. They have risen nowadays to higher ground, since their darkest corners, those of dirty money, have grown exponentially, as deregulation, offshoring, and hidden or anonymously numbered accounts are now freely available in the market place.

But, as summarized in this chapter, the shadow economy, and mostly shadow finance, are not to be compared either to the exploits of crime or to petty business. Just the opposite, they constitute the core of normal finance, although sometimes dealing in the obscure provinces of speculation. The shadow financial system, that "whole alphabet soup" of institutions, securities, accounts, and products, has spread its wings and now comprises most of the pools of cash and credit in the global economy. As money makes the world go round, this is power, even if the adoption of these shadow banking practices contributed to the recent financial meltdown.

How much money? That is the theme of Appendix A. How was this imposed through the destruction of effective regulation? As we shall discuss in Part II of the book, the force of the shadows is beyond the pale of explanations of economics alone, since it refers to a social process of the concentration of power that has marked the beginning of our century.

APPENDIX A

The Realm of Shadow Finance: How and How Much

Is it twice the size of world output? Probably much more. The size of the shadow banking system is not rigorously computed; perhaps it is not even computable, given the obscure dimensions, indefinite boundaries, hidden values, artificially priced assets, and enormous divergence between notional and actual values contained within a labyrinth of institutions and products. In any case, this mountain of capital and debt is the most important iceberg in the world of financialization.

What is loosely called "financialization" is a forest of changes going from deregulation of the financial sector, freeing capital flows, to new financial products, to the emergence of market-based intermediation replacing traditional credit systems, elevating institutional investors as big players, favoring boom and bust in asset markets, imposing social norms of shareholder value dominance or, as one author puts it, "financialization means the increasing role of financial motives, financial markets, financial actors, and financial institutions in the operation of the domestic and international economies."[1]

This appendix gathers together the evidence and the arguments explaining who is involved in the realm of financialization, in particular through shadow finance, how it came into being, and how much it is worth, listing and discussing first the main actors and secondly the mechanisms of this system.

When the Future was so Bright

Until 2007, the year of the Great Crash, shadow finance had been riding high. According to the post-crash inquests of the G20's Financial Stability Board and the IMF, shadow banking assets had grown from US $27 trillion to US $60 trillion (from twice to quadruple the value of US GDP, or more than total world output, or twice the assets of US pension funds) in only five years.[2] Other estimates suggested a smaller universe for shadow finance: the US Financial Crisis Inquiry Commission estimated shadow assets at a mere US $20 trillion on the eve of the financial panic in 2008,[3] and the Federal Reserve Bank of New York provided a similar estimate.[4] Even based on the more conservative count, assets in the shadow system were twice the value of those managed by traditional banking.[5]

Already by 1995, the shadow banking system was managing more liabilities than traditional banking.[6] But the crash of 2008, which amounted to a run on this parallel banking system, brought substantial public attention to the situation as well as causing a significant

[1] Epstein (2005a), p. 3; Stockhammer (2008), p. 2.

[2] Errico et al. (2014); Other authors agree with this estimate: according to Jeffers and Plihon (2014), p. 3, based on European statistics, the assets of the shadow banking system (included under the category of OFI, "other financial intermediaries") amounted in 2002 to US $26 trillion, in 2007 to US $62 trillion, and again in 2011 to US $67 trillion (of which US $23 trillion were to be found in the US, where they were higher than those of traditional banking, with another US $22 trillion in the Eurozone, and US $9 trillion in the UK alone).

[3] US Financial Crisis Inquiry Commission (2011). [4] Pozsar et al. (2013).

[5] According to some estimates for the US, money market funds grew from US $1,000 million in 1973 to almost US $4 trillion by 2008, and, at the same time, repos represented an additional US $4 trillion worth of assets, Taub (2013), p. 449, Other estimates put the value even higher.

[6] Pozsar et al. (2013), No. 458.

reduction in its assets. Between 2008 and 2010, the shadow system shrank to a smaller size than the traditional banking system, but it has since recovered and flourished.

Using alternative definitions of shadow banking, both the IMF and the FSB have produced impressive figures in estimating the size and scope of the post-crash renaissance. By 2011, the assets of shadow banking again exceeded world GDP and the majority of the system's activity was taking place outside the US.[7] To monitor the universe of non-bank financial intermediation (MUNFI), the FSB uses alternative definitions of shadow banking. Under the broad definition that includes the category Other Financial Institutions, FSB estimates total assets at US $75 trillion in 2013, mostly managed by investment funds and broker-dealers. Under a narrower definition that excludes the assets involved in non-bank intermediation, prudentially consolidated in banks, or those with no risk in terms of their maturity and liquidity transformation the system represents a mere US $35-trillion market.[8] The Eurozone and the US represent roughly equal shares of the market, with the United Kingdom trailing close behind.[9]

In Europe, exposure to the shadow banking system was a major factor in transforming the financial crash into an economic recession. Most countries, especially those on the Germanic model, never had an equivalent to the US Glass-Steagall restriction on bank activity. European banks have generally been "universal" with substantial flexibility to hold alternative asset classes and to offer a range of financial services. Indeed, universal banking with banks holding industrial equities over the long term was held up as a socially responsible alternative to American shareholder capitalism with its churning stock market and short-term focus on quarterly profit reports.

But this beneficent universalism had a shadowy side as well. Universal banks are free to do as they wish in the shadow universe. And they have indeed been operating in the shadows. While pyramidal securitization was more prevalent in the US, risky investments in financial markets were the preferred outlet for European banks.

Different national regulations and motivations delayed and fragmented the financial integration process in Europe compared to the US—as we verify through this appendix, national regulations matter indeed. Over time Europe created a centralized but fragile system for managing money and credit. The 1970 Werner Report sketched the contours of monetary integration, proposing a 1980 completion date, but the European Monetary System emerged only by 1979, and it was a failure. In 1983 the European Commission again proposed a path to financial integration: the Single European Act was approved by 1986 with directives on free movement of capital coming into force in 1990. The Maastricht Treaty followed in 1992, and in January 1999, after thirty years of proclamations, the euro came into being.

The 2007–8 crash hit both the US and European financial systems severely. Their growth had been heralded with the promise of a bright future nourished by adequate funds for investment. In the following sections, we will describe the evolution of this structure.

Credit Intermediation: Leaving the Banks in the Shadows

A fundamental distinction of shadow banking is that credit intermediation takes place in financial markets rather than within banks. Credit intermediation outside traditional

[7] S. Claessens et al. (2012), estimates US $65 trillion in assets in 2011, two-thirds of which were outside the US.

[8] The value of hedge funds is underestimated because offshore funds are not considered (only US $0.1 trillion are declared, while the US SEC reports US $5 trillion). Insurance companies and pension funds are similarly not included, although these were managing assets worth around US $55 trillion in 2013. Financial Stability Board (2014), pp. 7, 10, 19.

[9] Shadow banking was worth US $9 trillion in the UK in 2013, 348% of GDP. For the Netherlands, the value of shadow assets was 760% of the country's GDP, ibid., p. 9.

banking increases both leverage and risk. Savers and borrowers, and a chain of market makers, rather than bank bureaucrats operating within a regulated institutional structure, determine the scale and scope of financial activity.

From the postwar period through to the 1970s, commercial banks were the exclusive institutions that intermediated between savers and borrowers, gathering together the savings of common folk and providing credit to corporations for physical investment. Many corporations did not even go as far as the bank but relied exclusively on their own retained earnings for physical investment.

The liberalization of the financial system, however, replaced retained earnings or the direct link through banks from savers to borrowers with long, complex chains. The range of players and their roles have multiplied.

Multinational corporations have become more sophisticated, relying on capital markets for their financing, thereby shaving basis points off the interest rates on their physical investment borrowing. And these large firms now play both sides of the market. What began for large corporations as dabbling in the role of lender, for example, General Motors providing credit specifically to car buyers, has expanded enormously as firms seek to maximize financial earnings, letting no pot of cash sit idle. This expansion of financial markets and the emergence of multiple financial roles for formerly non-financial corporations that previously only borrowed money have financialized the entire economy.

Working households have been both pulled and pushed into the shadow system. Household savings were previously the source of loanable funds for banks. But new instruments, such as the money market mutual fund both appeared to be equally as safe as and to offer returns higher than boring banks. Middle-class households were handed both the responsibility and seeming opportunity to manage retirement savings as pension plans were shifted from guaranteed annuities managed by employer and the state to individual accounts.

As borrowers, working households relied on credit markets only for occasional big purchases of homes and perhaps automobiles. But with the decay of the labor movement and wage stagnation and with inequality increasing pressure to demonstrate status through consumption, working households have become more dependent on credit to meet the requirements for subsistence, broadly defined as it has been transformed over time.[10] A host of offerings, from credit cards to home-equity loans, are available to meet these new real and perceived needs.[11]

For the intermediaries, the shadow system offers various advantages. At the crudest level, more links in the chain mean more service fees; the greater the specialization and diversification, the greater the opportunity for monopoly profits. The chain also offers opportunities to build leverage. The mixing of own and borrowed funds increases the potential return at each link. Finally, the chain offers opportunities for unadulterated zero-sum gambling for profit.

The financial products have become more fragmented as a consequence, within the framework of larger institutions and gigantic banks and shadow banks. The direct chain is now broken down into partial steps, with multiple financial intermediaries taking on new and highly specific functions. For instance, instead of becoming a bank deposit, household savings may instead be applied in the acquisition of shares in money market mutual funds. The managers of the money market mutual fund devote part of this capital to the acquisition of short-term low-risk securities, use another part for security lending, and lend a third part to an investment bank by taking a long position on a repurchase agreement.

The investment bank, in turn, uses borrowed funds to buy long-term higher-interest assets, such as asset-backed securities (securities backed by a pool of credits that generate a

[10] Kotz (2013). [11] Kotz (2015).

regular stream of income such as home mortgages, automobile loans, and credit card debt) that were sold by a finance company to a special purpose vehicle, a conduit specifically created to issue these bankruptcy-protected securities. Finally, the finance company, using the liquidity generated by the funds from the special purchase vehicle, provides credit to consumers or to small and medium-sized enterprises, thus closing the loop. In summary, a direct chain involving zero or one intermediaries has given way to at least five partial steps involving at least four financial intermediaries (see Figure A.1 and the following description of the different institutions).

The realm of shadow finance thus constitutes innovative forms of credit intermediated through a wide range of securitization techniques. At the same time, the extended chains and complex instruments augment the problem of asymmetric information: all parties, that is, lenders, investors, servicers, savers, and borrowers, are less acquainted with their counterparts, and the techniques and risks involved in their operations. As these risks are either ignored or shifted, the fragility of the system grows.

Main Actors Involved in Shadow Banking Activities

Shadow banking dates back to the mid-1970s and, in some limited cases, to even before then, but its imposing rise was the consequence of deregulation in the US, Europe, and elsewhere, which paved the way for the emergence of highly leveraged non-bank institutions, which are afforded more freewheeling opportunities to raise funds than banks. Credit intermediation was subsequently opened up to non-banking financial intermediaries, such as insurance companies, and money market mutual funds were introduced. This segment expanded in the 1980s and 1990s, and has exploded in the last decade. Since then, we have witnessed the emergence of myriad new non-banking financial institutions devoted to financial intermediation: large independent investment banks (the broker-dealers) that combine intermediation with own-account speculation, insurance companies offering a variety of investment and financial-insurance instruments, hedge funds, investment funds, private equity funds, pension funds, and special investment vehicles. These new financial institutions share a vulnerability to runs, a vulnerability that is inherent in their incentives, structure, and functions, and which was borne out empirically by the Great Crash.

The five main actors—finance companies, money market mutual funds, international cash pools, investment banks, and the external agents—are briefly surveyed in the following.

Financial Companies

Financial companies are unregulated credit intermediaries that lend to households, to businesses, and sometimes to other financial institutions, with funds being gathered through bank loans, bonds, promissory notes, or commercial paper. The window for borrowers, i.e., how the financial company lends, looks very much like a bank. The window for savers, i.e., how the financial company borrows, is quite different. Offering multiple types of credit (consumer, commercial, acceptance, independent, and captive), finance companies are in some cases owned by banks, but also by industrial corporations or by non-bank multi-functional financial conglomerates, where the financial company may act as the in-house bank.

A specialized variant among financial companies is that of residential mortgage originators, who provide home mortgage loans, including subprime and Alt-A products.[12] The business model of mortgage originators is based on pooling their mortgages and selling them to an arranger (usually an investment bank in charge of setting up the special purpose

[12] Alt-A products are mortgages not considered to be subprime, but which are still not prime, or ones that have a worse evaluation of risk.

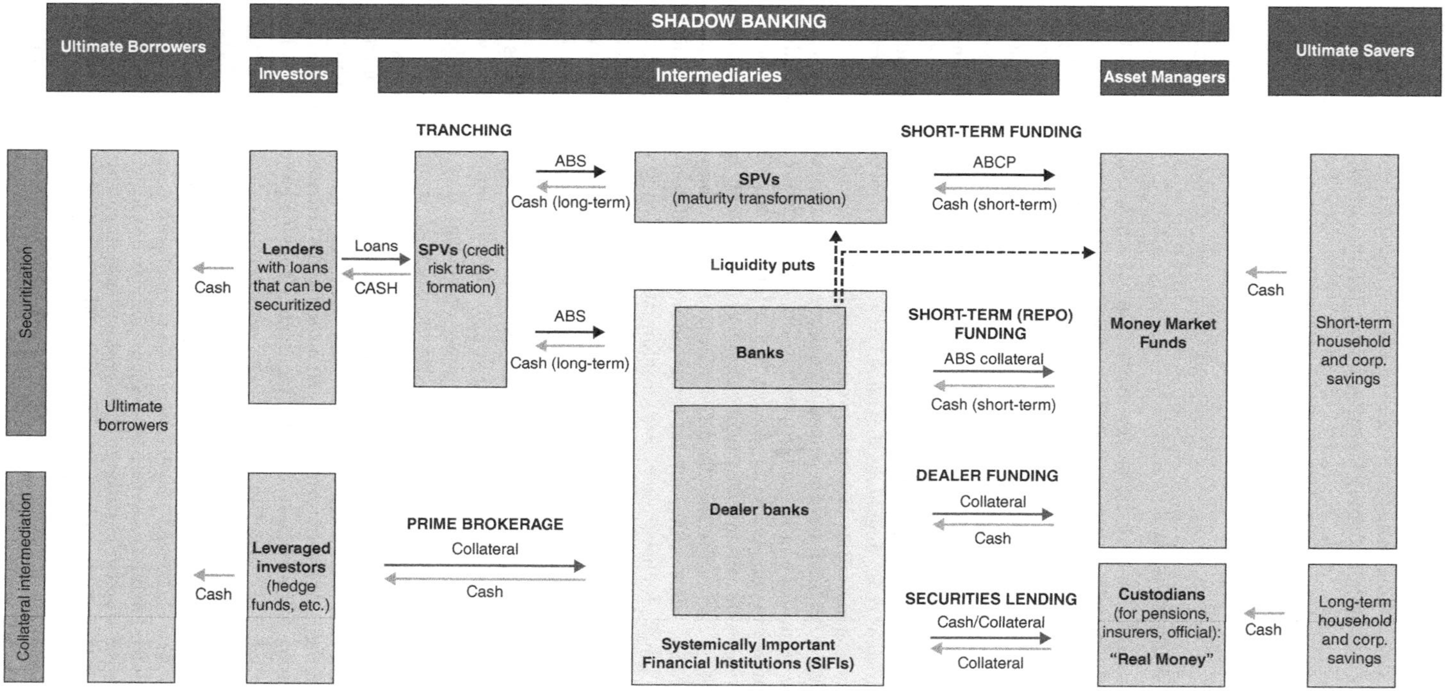

Notes: ABS = asset-backed securities; ABCP = asset-backed commercial paper, SPV = special purpose vehicle

Figure A.1. Market-based credit intermediation through shadow banking

Source: Claessens et al. (2012), p. 20.

vehicle that will sell the asset-backed securities). The originators advance only a small fraction of the required funds and the remainder is funded through repos.[13]

One example, described in detail in the Financial Crisis Inquiry Commission report is the New Century deal of the Citigroup Mortgage Loan Trust, Inc., which in 2006 advanced US $12 million of its own funds, of which US $3 million were in the form of commercial paper, to finance a securitization deal of nearly US $1 billion.[14] The leverage permitted the firm to rapidly pocket US $24 million, a premium of only 2.5 percent in the overall deal, but a comfortable 100 percent return for Citigroup.

Money Market Mutual Funds

On the borrowing side, we have the money market mutual funds, collective investment vehicles created in the early 1970s during the first wave of liberalization. These funds compete directly with banks in seeking household funds for safekeeping, liquidity, and modest returns, but rather than collect deposits, they sell shares. In this case, the window for savers, i.e., how the money funds borrow, looks very much like a bank (minus the insured-deposit sign, to be sure!). But the window for borrowers, i.e., how the finance company lends, looks quite different. The funds do not provide retail credit. Instead, their funds are invested in (presumably) low-risk, high-liquidity instruments: in the past, the money market mutual funds parked money in bank certificates of deposit, but have now gravitated towards repos, highly-rated commercial paper, and short-term government securities, with typical maturities varying between 30 and 270 days.

The US money market funds have benefited from uneven regulatory requirements under the watch of the Securities and Exchange Commission, the regulation agency. Although banks were permitted to compete for funds with higher interest rates after the removal of Regulation Q interest rate caps in 1986 (Regulation Q was imposed on deposits other than demand deposits, as part of the New Deal Glass-Steagall rules),[15] they continued to face reserve requirements, while money market funds did not. In addition to this regulatory advantage, these funds also have lower costs for information gathering and infrastructure and avoid the expense of deposit insurance premia. All in all, these lower regulatory costs enabled the money market mutual funds to generate higher returns for fund owners while providing higher yields to savers and lower costs to borrowers (for instance, in the commercial paper market).

The funds benefited from the widespread perception that they were as safe as bank deposits because they were supposedly invested in high-quality short-term assets, whose net asset value was targeted to remain slightly above one dollar. They also provided the trappings of a demand deposit account with checkbooks and ready liquidity.

Yet these funds are not as safe as they appear. (The fine print in the prospectus really does matter.) They do not have access to the central bank discount windows for emergency liquidity in case of individual or systemic crisis, and savers' deposits are not guaranteed. Although they are subject to tight regulations with respect to the instruments in which they may invest (contrary to other more freewheeling shadow banking entities such as hedge

[13] As previously indicated, repos, or repurchase agreements, are deposit-like instruments in the sense that the asset that is sold with the promise to be bought back (at a higher price) resembles a collateral advance made in order to obtain funds. The difference in the prices of sale and purchase represents the interest paid for holding funds for a specific period of time. The difference in the maturity of the repo and the underlying assets is prone to market and credit risk and maturity mismatch.

[14] The report, US Financial Crisis Inquiry Commission (2011), is controversial; see, for example, p. 116; Mirowski (2013), p. 321, remarks on its "impudence and breezy style."

[15] The partial abolition of Regulation Q has been introduced since the 1960s, when some interest rates became unregulated. In the UK, this change proceeded through the introduction of the Competition and Credit Control legislation in the 1970s, dismantling regulations, Lapavitsas (2014), p. 311.

funds), money funds are not subject to prudential supervision; moreover, their investments are not subject to reserve requirements or quantitative limits.

Money market funds have a propensity for runs that make them a vulnerable point in shadow banking intermediation and a source of inherent instability in the financial system. As early as 1992, long before the Great Crash of 2007–8, money market funds were involved in the "November Nightmare," when access to funds was cut because of mismanagement of their loans portfolio or problems at parent companies. The resulting downgrade of their credit ratings further increased their funding costs as commercial paper and the availability of backup credit lines were withdrawn. Over six days in November 1992 three of the biggest finance corporations experienced losses large enough to lead to their liquidation.[16]

Money market funds also marked the explosion of 2008 with a full-fledged run in the aftermath of the collapse of Lehman Brothers. Unsure of the reliability of its counterparties, or bluntly put, whether it could recover the money which it had invested in short-term assets, the Reserve Primary fund had to reprice its shares, falling below the targeted one dollar net asset value. The shortfall was the first since 1994.[17] Coupled with financial turmoil in the market for asset-backed commercial paper issued by structured investment vehicles with heavy exposure to faltering subprime mortgages, this betrayal of confidence led to a wider run on money market funds. Withdrawals targeted institutional funds and drained liquidity from these funds' traditional sources of cheap funding, commercial paper and repos.

The US Treasury was induced to take unprecedented action: the US Treasury insured the funds' investors and created an extraordinary liquidity facility that extended the safety net of the lender of last resort to a purely shadow finance institution.[18] It had looked like a bank to the hapless depositors; so it had better be bailed out like one.

Institutional Cash Pools

The shadow banking literature tends to emphasize the supply-side view of the financial system, considering the emergence of shadow banking to be due to bank funding preferences, regulatory arbitrage, and financial innovation. An alternative account emphasizes the demand for large pools of "private money" at short notice from international institutional cash investors.[19] These investors hold large pools (typically above US $1 billion) of short-term cash balances for financial speculation, for example, the daily fixing of foreign exchange pegs, for the safe-keeping of corporate cash balances, or for providing liquidity to complex asset management based on derivatives and security lending.[20] Such investors prioritize principal safety and portfolio diversification over yield and avoid taking on large, unsecured exposure to banks with deposits that would be well outside the range of individual depositor insurance. As the supply of short-term government-guaranteed securities is not large enough for these purposes, they turn instead to the shadow banking system, which offers apparently safe, short-term, and liquid instruments.[21]

While cash pools are distinct from money market funds, they take on large positions in these funds. Four sources of institutional cash pools have been identified:[22] first, the liquid

[16] Dymski, Epstein, and Pollin (1993).

[17] Waggoner (2008), ever ready to forget past unpleasantness, the breaking of the buck was widely depicted as the first time ever. Who could have known?.

[18] Taub (2013), p. 463; E. Murphy (2013). [19] Pozsar (2013).

[20] Derivatives include forwards (a contract to buy something at a later date), futures (standardized contracts as to the quantity), options (transacting the right, but not obligation, to buy or sell at a future date at a specified price), and swaps (exchanging the cash flows anticipated from different securities, e.g., interest rates).

[21] Pozsar (2013), estimates that between 2003 and 2008 the supply of this instrument increased by US $1.5 trillion.

[22] Pozsar (2014), p. 24.

portion of foreign exchange reserves, which increases as more foreign exchange regimes become pegged to the dollar; second, cash balances held by multinational corporations, which reflect the increase in profit as a share of national income, the availability of larger cash holdings due to profit retention not designated for physical investment, and the decision to defer or avoid taxes by stashing cash in foreign subsidiaries; third, cash balances of institutional investors and asset managers, explained by the centralization of liquidity management of funds, and the consolidation among asset managers; and finally reinvestment of the cash collateral received in security lending.

These sources of cash pools are related to long-term trends that reflect global macro-imbalances in income distribution: between countries with current account deficits and surpluses; between capital income and workers' wages; and by the centralization of cash management among a shrinking number of asset managers.[23]

Investment Banks

Broker-dealers, like investment banks, were essential for the promotion of market-based credit intermediation as both originators and underwriters of securities, as arrangers of commercial paper issuance and securitization, and as brokers and dealers of repo and security lending. These are the protagonists of shadow banking.[24]

Moreover, in the expansion of their business, investment banks have themselves relied heavily on repo financing. As dealers, they use repos to maximize leverage—and profits. US investment bank reliance on leverage through repos, with the repo share of financing approaching half of total assets,[25] created fragility and vulnerability that came undone in the Great Crash. The actual assets providing collateral for investment banks in the repo market were primarily structured securities, such as private label mortgage-based securities and collateralized debt obligations, which were rated highly (in a deeply flawed rating system), and less well-rated collateral such as high-yield, or junk bonds. Leverage through repos was not an accident, but rather the business plan. Furthermore, investment banks actively managed their operations, taking into consideration prices and measured risk to generate profits. This active management induced an unfortunate systemic byproduct: pro-cyclical leverage.[26]

Investment bank leverage is pro-cyclical as a structural matter, a near-natural consequence of unregulated profit-seeking behavior: "during booms, banks increase their liabilities by more than their assets have risen, thus raising their leverage. During troughs, they reduce their liabilities more sharply than their assets have declined, thus lowering their leverage,"[27] with significant potential for macroeconomic destabilization. Indeed, the highly leveraged, positive-feedback repo market was a key location of financial contagion, both among financial institutions and in spreading the problem to the real economy. Shadow finance spreads because it is profitable.

Commercial banks, not to be outdone by their unregulated cousins, turned increasingly to off-balance sheet financing, transforming themselves into shadow banks, an ironic inversion of the usual metamorphosis.[28]

[23] Ibid., p. 61.

[24] "Although broker-dealers have traditionally played market-making and underwriting roles in securities markets, their importance in the supply of credit has increased in step with securitization," Adrian and Shin (2010), p. 605.

[25] Hördahl and M. R. King (2008), pp. 45–6.

[26] Adrian and Shin (2007, 2008).

[27] Or, "the banks respond to a rise in assets by taking on more liability in the form of repurchase agreements" Adrian and Shin (2008), p. 3, Assets = Liabilities + Net Worth is an accounting identity, but banks have discretion in whether they raise the bridge or lower the river. As we think ahead towards policy, it should be clear that the public will need to regulate actively how banks manage the accounting identity.

[28] Gorton and Metrick (2012); Adrian and Shin (2010).

External Sector

The articulation and integration of international capital markets with national financial systems proves that shadow banking is clearly implicated in the build-up of international interconnectedness.

While there is variation in the build-up of leverage among domestic dealers (investment banks substantially increased leverage while the broker-dealer sector compressed it from 1987 to 2007), foreign dealers operating in the US have both increased their foothold there and have increased the leverage associated with their presence, quadrupling it between 1994 and 2008.[29] Another area of increased connection between US and European finance relates to pledged collateral and rehypothecation rights. Rehypothecation applies to whether or not the same collateral can be used in a chain of transactions. The first borrower pledges an asset as collateral to its lender; that lender then becomes a borrower in a second transaction, pledging the first borrower's pledged collateral to its lender. A single asset can thus serve as collateral in a sequence of financial transactions with a notional value that is far beyond that of the actual asset. US hedge funds have shopped in Europe and, in particular, in the UK for laxer regulations because US SEC Rule 15c3–3 limits rehypothecation to a mere 140 percent of the underlying asset value while the EU has no such cap. EU law permits the parties to strike their own bargain as to how much collateral may hold rights of reuse: "Leverage levels at many UK hedge funds, banks and financial affiliates have been higher, as the United Kingdom does not have a similar cap. Thus, prime brokers and banks would rehypothecate their customers' assets along with their own proprietary assets as collateral for funding from the global financial system."[30] Rehypothecation, which even under the best circumstances lengthens financial chains and increases fragility, also provided an opportunity for forum-shopping and increased US-Europe financial interdependencies. The same thing happened in other regions of the planet.

Market-based Credit Intermediation Mechanisms

Some of the main actors have just been listed. This section will deal with their various proceedings, including securitization, the issuance of commercial debt, repurchase agreements, and other forms of credit intermediation.

Within the literature on shadow banking, a major branch is dedicated to the enlargement of the process of securitization and its impact on the financial crisis.[31] Indeed, some juxtapose traditional banking and securitized banking, the "business of packaging and reselling loans"[32] and conclude that securitized banking magnified the expansion of the real estate bubble and bears responsibility for the subsequent financial meltdown. This literature seeks to identify market failures in the process of securitization. Therefore, it has been devoted to highlighting the fragilities underpinning the short-term funding of securitization,[33] the problems underpinning regulatory arbitrage,[34] and the mismanagement of risk or incomplete risk transfer by banks.[35]

29 Adrian and Shin (2010). 30 M. Singh and Aitken (2010), p. 4.

31 For a description of the process and identification of the transmission mechanisms, see US Financial Crisis Inquiry Commission (2011), p. 113.

32 Gorton and Metrick (2012). 33 J. C. Stein (2010); Gorton and Metrick (2012).

34 Banks securitize assets in order to circumvent capital requirements. This literature considers that regulatory arbitrage stems from faulty regulatory design and a lack of foresight by authorities or the replacement of sensible business models with less sensible ones. See Acharya and Richardson (2008); Acharya, Schnabl, and G. Suarez (2013).

35 Adrian and Shin (2009); Shin (2009); Alessandri and A. G. Haldane (2009); Acharya, Schnabl, and G. Suarez (2013); Lapavitsas and Dos Santos (2008). For an alternative to the mainstream literature about the loss in banks' capacity to collect information and assess risk on a relational basis that underpins securitization and has driven down lending standards, see, for instance, Lapavitsas and Dos Santos (2008).

A key question is whether the liabilities of shadow banks can be counted as money because they are convertible on demand at par—at least when times are good.[36] According to some analysts, holders of large pools of cash, unable to find sufficient quantities of short-term government securities or insured deposit opportunities, demand "private money," assets understood as safe, liquid, and with a fully guaranteed principal. Shadow banking is thus connected to a reasonable financial motivation of international institutional investors.[37] But the explanation based on the demand for private money understates the risks involved in this form of money creation. The misperception of shadow banking as low-risk investment led to the reduction, or even the elimination, of bankruptcy insurance premiums, the excessive issuance of asset-backed securities, and ultimately the unstable expansion of leverage.[38]

As rehypothecation extended liquidity, and as it increased leverage and jurisdictional arbitrage, the foundations had been laid for wholesale repo-based bank panic.[39] Financial innovation, the *alma mater* of shadow banking, further exacerbated the risk and finally led to the crash.

The four mechanisms, securitization, issuing commercial paper, repos, and security lending, will be briefly examined in the following.

Securitization

Securitization emerged in the 1970s as a way of moving assets off the balance sheet by assembling illiquid contractual debts of long and variable duration and selling them as collateralized tradable securities. It is the centerpiece of market-based credit intermediation.[40] The positive case for securitization is that, by moving loans off the balance sheet, securitization frees up the capital of front-line lenders to consumers or to firms and permits these lenders, with their specialized knowledge of customer needs and capacities, to lend again. The negative case is evident in the crash.

In this shadow universe, any stream of income can be transformed into a collateralized debt obligation, although mortgage-backed securities are the most popular, with other assets being aggregated into the generic category of asset-backed securities. Securities sold through the process of securitization are typically long-term assets, such as mortgage or student debt. Yet, it is possible to create short-term collateralized instruments, such as asset-backed commercial paper (these processes are depicted in Figure A.2). Its relevance to the expansion of shadow banking justifies its separate analysis.

Securitization has become popular among originators, especially among banks subject to prudential supervision, because securitization reduces capital requirements and balance-sheet impact, frees up cash flows for immediate reinvestment, and creates financial products with variable fine-tuned risk and return. As the trust that issues the securities, the special

[36] Pozsar (2014); Gorton and Metrick (2012); J. C. Stein (2010); Gabor (2016).

[37] Pozsar (2014); Greenwood, Hanson, and J. C. Stein (2015); Gorton, Lewellen, and Metrick (2012).

[38] Gorton and Metrick (2010); Gennaioli, Shleifer, and Vishny (2012); Geanakoplos (2010).

[39] See M. Singh and Aitken (2010); Adrian and Shin (2009); Shin (2009); Gorton (2009a,b,c); Martin, Skeie, and Von Thadden (2014), When the collateral received in a repo by a client (e.g., a hedge fund) is used as collateral in an unrelated repo by the broker-dealer for its own purposes. This practice is common among hedge funds, which pay lower fees in exchange for signing a general account agreement.

[40] Or, "securitization is the process by which traditionally illiquid loans are packaged and sold into the capital markets. This is accomplished by selling large portfolios of loans to special purpose vehicles (SPVs), which are legal entities that in turn issue rated securities linked to the loan portfolios... The whole process thus takes loans that traditionally would have been held on the balance sheet of the originating firm and creates from them marketable securities that can be sold and traded via the off-balance-sheet SPV," Gorton and Metrick (2010), p. 270.

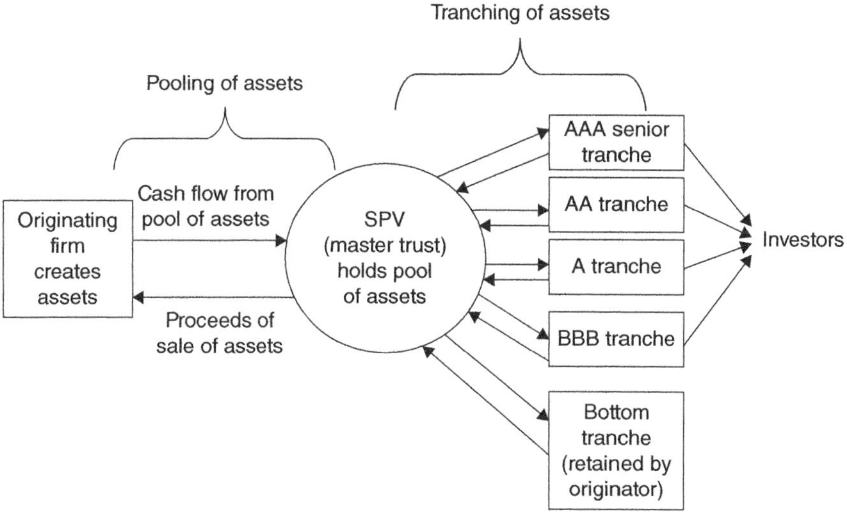

Figure A.2. The securitization process
Source: Gorton and Metrick (2010), p. 271.

purpose vehicle is shielded against bankruptcy; the insolvency of an originator has no impact on the special vehicle. In the event of the pool of assets failing to generate enough income to pay interest, asset-backed securities do not formally trigger a default event, but merely an early amortization event anticipating the redemption of principal. Securitization thus represents a cheap funding alternative with the additional advantage of no questions asked.

The special vehicles portfolios were considered transparent, and they allowed for the "customization of risk," the provision of financial products with fine-tuned adjustable risk and return. Very safe assets were a particular demand of many investors, e.g., pension funds and local governments. Through aggregation and risk tranching and exploiting statistically reliable rates of early payment and default, broker-dealers could provide securities that were perceived by these prudent investors as safe—that was the story, ignoring the hidden risks. This perception of safety satisfied oversight bodies and reduced or even eliminated bankruptcy premia.[41] Unfortunately, the system is built in such a way that investors misunderstand the risks intrinsic to financial innovation.[42] Therefore, mortgage-based securities and collateral debt obligations were perceived as good substitutes for traditional securities and public bonds. These assets became more popular and were used more nonchalantly as collateral than their actual risk warranted. The more obscure products had the additional advantage of providing monopoly rents to their creators.

The financial crisis exposed these underlying risks, their moral hazard, their regulatory costs, and their systemic integration. The preference for off-balance-sheet financing promoted leverage, encouraged strategic and profitable risk-taking through balance-sheet management by credit intermediaries, and fueled systemic risk.[43]

Mortgage-backed securities represent one of the most important segments in the securitization market. For many years, the mortgage segment in the US was dominated by the government enterprises Fannie Mae and Freddie Mac. But regulations limited those firms to

[41] Gorton and Metrick (2010). [42] Gennaioli, Shleifer, and Vishny (2012).
[43] Adrian and Shin (2007, 2008); Gorton and Metrick (2010).

the purchase of high-quality, or "prime" loans, which opened the subprime sector to private-label securitization. The Alt-A and subprime mortgages that lay at the heart of the 2007–9 financial crisis had been rapidly integrated into the world of repurchase agreements and other off-balance-sheet financing mechanisms.[44]

Commercial Paper and Asset-backed Commercial Paper

Commercial paper is a type of uncollateralized borrowing represented by a short-term promissory note issued directly by the borrower or through a broker. In terms of regulatory requirements, such notes were excluded in the US from the Securities Act of 1933 because their buyers were supposedly "sophisticated investors," capable of interpreting the determinations of the credit rating agencies.[45]

In the 1980s and 1990s, commercial paper was an important transmission channel in developing the symbiotic relationship between money market mutual funds and finance companies.[46] Asset-backed commercial paper, or short-term debt securities backed by commercial loans, were introduced in order to broaden the universe of issuers in commercial paper, which had previously been restricted to top-quality issuers. Relying on very short maturities,[47] these programs are often backed up by a standby facility (from a consortium of banks) in case of a withdrawal of market liquidity. This instrument has been used by both bank and non-bank holdings, for instance a bank selling its credit-card loans or an auto-financing company selling its auto-loan repayments. Yet before the crash it was particularly popular among originators specializing in subprime mortgages.

The 2007 credit crunch represents the long-run consequences of credit intermediation based on commercial paper and repos. In August 2007, when vehicles reliant on raising funds through their commercial-debt programs ran into difficulty in those markets, they turned to their bank sponsors searching for liquidity and a way of activating their collateralized backstop credit lines. The banks that had been previously shielded from moderate losses in the subprime sector were now obliged, by these longstanding agreements, to absorb the losses of subprime assets.[48] The special purpose vehicles proved to be closer than they

[44] The Financial Crisis Inquiry Commission report describes the process of securitization of residential mortgages into mortgage-based securities and identifies the relationship of transmission mechanisms with the rest of the financial system: "The origination and securitization of these mortgages also relied on short-term financing from the shadow banking system. Unlike banks and thrifts with access to deposits, investment banks relied more on money market funds and other investors for cash; commercial paper and repo loans were the main sources," US Financial Crisis Inquiry Commission (2011), p. 113.

[45] For a critical overview of the (ir)relevance of this concept, see Taub (2011).

[46] They meet money funds' short-term needs by issuing commercial paper, instead of contracting bank loans. Indeed, according to D'Arista and Schlesinger (1993a), pp. 11–12, finance institutions represented more than half of the commercial paper issued in the 1980s and early 1990s in the US, and an enormous surge that has occurred since then.

[47] Covitz, Liang, and G. A. Suarez (2009), p. 7, concluded: "more than half of ABCP daily issuance has maturities of 1 to 4 days—referred to as 'overnight'—and the average maturity of outstanding paper is about 30 days."

[48] "Commercial banks used commercial paper, in part, for regulatory arbitrage. When banks kept mortgages on their balance sheets, regulators required them to hold 4% in capital to protect against loss. When banks put mortgages into off-balance-sheet entities such as commercial paper programs, there was no capital charge (a minor charge was imposed in 2004). But to make the deals work for investors, banks had to provide liquidity support to these programs, for which they earned a fee. This liquidity support meant that the bank would purchase, at a previously set price, any commercial paper that investors were unwilling to buy when it came up for renewal. During the financial crisis these promises had to be kept, eventually putting substantial pressure on banks' balance sheets," US Financial Crisis Inquiry Commission (2011), p. 114.

appeared. A profitable and seemingly costless guarantee became a frightening link in the chain of panic.

Repurchase Agreements

Repurchase agreements (known as *repos*) are another major feature of the market-based intermediation undertaken within the shadow banking system. Repurchase agreements are, as indicated, deposit-like instruments created in order to obtain funds, benefiting from the maturity mismatch between the use of short-term (mainly overnight) funding, or unstable debt, and illiquid long-term assets to be financed. The buyers are typically pension and mutual funds, or brokers seeking to cover short-term positions, and the sellers are brokers or banks. As they are formally "sales" and "resales" rather than borrowing and repayment, these agreements "can be used to mask debt";[49] indeed, this is their actual function.

Repos are not deposits and are not covered by deposit insurance. But repos do have a special status under the US Bankruptcy Code: they are not subject to automatic stay.[50] Large depositors have mistakenly felt comfortable assuming they would get their money back no matter what, i.e., as if they were insured demand deposits, or as if this was just another form of regular loan with standard collateral and not a highly volatile system of credit. Non-bank institutions with no access to the lender of last resort have also relied on repos as a guaranteed investment. In addition to their role as deposit-like instruments, repos are used to hedge derivative and primary market positions, neutralize arbitrage, take short positions, or even for building leverage. This was common practice among hedge funds and investment banks, as was made dramatically evident in the cases of Lehman Brothers and Bear Stearns.[51]

Afterwards the risks taken become obvious. Traditional banks, too, borrow from depositors for short terms—because the funds are liquid and could in principle be withdrawn at any time—at low rates while loaning the borrowed funds for a longer term and higher yield. But for traditional banks safety nets are in place to protect the socially valuable transformation of term, liquidity, and risk: reserve requirements and oversight of asset valuation provide day-to-day protection with deposit insurance and borrowing rights from the lender of last resort as failsafes in case of emergency. Repos lack these protections and handle large sums, i.e., the exposure is very large, for very short periods, which increases the risk involved in transformation.[52] Indeed, among investment banks, the balance-sheet growth funded by repos has primarily been achieved through overnight repos.[53] Repos doubled between 1994 and 2009 while overnight repos increased sevenfold from the mid-1990s through March 2008.[54]

In any case, the financial crisis of 2007–8 exposed the vulnerability of the repo market to two distinct types of runs. One type of run emerges from doubts about the quality of the

[49] Taub (2013), p. 449.

[50] Taub (2010b); Gorton and Metrick (2010), p. 277, The 1984 amendment to the Bankruptcy Code had provided special exemptions for repos based on Treasury and agency securities, bank certificates of deposit, and bankers' acceptances, making it clear that these repos were not subject to automatic stay, but without clarifying what would happen to repos based on other forms of collateral. The Bankruptcy Reform Act, in 2005, clarified the definition of a repo, expanding it to include any stock, bond, or other security, including mortgage loans, interest on mortgage-related securities, and foreign sovereign debt, and freeing it from automatic stay.

[51] M. Singh and Aitken (2010), show that, when rehypothecation is taken into consideration, the shadow banking system (the sum of primary dealers' repos, financial sector commercial paper, and asset-backed commercial paper) in the US was at least 50% larger than had been documented until then, while the churning of collateral (the ratio of re-use of collateral) for the US and the main European brokers had been around a factor of 4 at the end of 2007, declining thereafter.

[52] Investment banks have financed 50% of the assets in the repo market, Taub (2013), p. 461.

[53] Brunnermeier (2009), p. 80 and see also Adrian and Shin (2009).

[54] Adrian and Shin (2009), p. 607.

collateral, with increasing haircuts being demanded by cash lenders, which ultimately oblige financial institutions to deleverage their balance sheets.[55] The other type of run emerges from doubts about the creditworthiness of the repo counterparty.[56] In this case, cash lenders refuse to roll over the repo altogether, forcing financial institutions that are heavily reliant on short-term debt rollover, such as Lehman Brothers and Bear Stearns, into bankruptcy. The second type of run has an all-or-nothing quality that may not be reflected in slowly growing haircuts. The results are more dramatic as the abrupt withdrawal of funds leaves targeted institutions without the time to seek alternative sources.[57]

Security Lending

Like repos, security lending represents another type of collateralized money market instrument, and the two are closely intertwined. While, in a repurchase agreement, the purpose of the operation is the lending and borrowing of cash, usually exchanged against general collateral, in security lending the purpose is to lend and borrow a specific security, which tends to be done against cash,[58] but can, in fact, accommodate an exchange against other securities. Security lending in equities is a frequently used instrument to set up short-selling trades, especially in equity, to hedge derivative risk, to meet a failing delivery, or to arbitrage the repo rate. Asset holders, such as pension funds, money market funds, hedge funds, and insurance companies, are the main lenders in the security-lending market. In addition to clearing and custodian banks, hedge funds, asset managers, option traders, and security dealers with market-making obligations, are the main borrowers.

Custodian banks are very active in security lending and represent a crucial link in the chain between repos and security lending. These banks and money market funds are significant cash lenders in repo markets as the cash received as collateral is reinvested in general collateral repos. Their security lending positions are open, remaining subject to continued overnight rollover until one of the parties decides to close the position.

The widespread deleveraging that occurred during the 2007–9 crisis imposed significant losses upon security lenders because they were obliged to return cash collateral to security borrowers, while receiving securities that, if sold in the market, would result in massive losses. As in many crises, the question of whether asset value should (or indeed would) be marked to market during a sharp downturn loomed large.

The case of AIG is a telling example. AIG's business model was based on heavy engagement in open-loan security lending, using its cash pool as collateral to invest in lucrative long-term illiquid assets (mainly residential mortgage securities); it was thus performing massive liquidity transformation that was subject to an enormous, yet unaccounted liquidity risk. In September 2008 (see Chapter 2), in order to prevent its failure in the aftermath of Lehman Brothers' collapse, and given the imminent danger of insolvency, the Federal Reserve bailed out AIG with US $85 billion and, at the same time, acquired 80 percent of its equity, creating a credit line to alleviate capital and liquidity pressure associated with the AIG security lending portfolio (as well as a second credit line associated with the AIG credit derivatives contracts).

Conclusion

If our readers have successfully made their way through this technical exposition, they will have gained an overview of the spread of the financial sector into new areas. New products, sometimes masquerading as sales, sometimes as credit and debt instruments, allowed for the creation of a chain for the transmission of value, a chain of speculation and leverage

[55] Gorton (2009b); Gorton and Metrick (2010).
[56] Adrian, Brian, et al. (2013); Copeland, Martin, and Walker (2010).
[57] Copeland, Martin, and Walker (2010).
[58] In this case, the lender of the security is obliged to reinvest the cash and share a portion of its return with the borrower.

augmentation that was based on trust and good profits. After deregulation, the shadow banking system rapidly became a giant in the world economy: the largest fund manager, BlackRock, manages more assets, US $5.4 trillion as of spring 2017,[59] than does the world's largest bank, the Industrial & Commercial Bank of China with total year-end 2017 assets calculated at US $3.6 trillion.[60]

The bond market was long the largest source of non-bank financing, and shadow system lending grew to represent a relevant part of all financial assets, although many of its firms, as pointed out in this and the previous chapters, are arms of the traditional banks. As a consequence, our argument is not that finance built a separate world but instead that banking extended to new dimensions and promoted deregulation and offshoring for the sake of profit, as financial innovation allowed for higher levels of debt-financed spending and higher risks.

Financial innovation is not comparable to industrial innovation. Industrial innovation requires large sunk costs and embodies technology in physical assets. Financial innovation is, in contrast, an acceleration of contractual arrangements. It typically generates no new physical property—the buildings and equipment that constitute a society's production base—and is limited to the first-comer advantage. Consequently, opacity and customization are desirable features for the purveyor.[61] The danger of financial innovation was forcefully demonstrated in the 2007–8 crash.

The following chapters discuss the gearing of this process, looking at how crucial decisions were made and seeing who made them, as well as studying the impacts, perceptions, and social forces that were moving these shadows.

[59] BlackRock (2017). [60] Bratton and Chaudhary (2016). [61] Guttmann (2015).

Part II

Who Decides? Deregulation and Deregulators

4

Big Business and Family Business

Until now, we have described and investigated the financial system and its shadows. The usual suspects in our case—central bankers, financiers, and deregulators (politicians will enter this narrative later on)—are well-known. While their acts, laws and rules, and the consequences of their deeds, are both predicted and predictable, the players, well paid though they be, do not, in fact, own the game. Before we discuss their deed and strategies, we turn in this chapter to the proprietors of capital, to the empires of money and power that rule the world. We will consequently encounter the family businesses, including the giant firms, and also the faceless forms of capital power in the shadow finance system.

THE TOP AND THE BOTTOM

Oxfam, a prestigious non-governmental organization, times the publication of its annual report to coincide with the meeting at Davos, Switzerland, of the wealthiest and most powerful people on the planet. The ritual is consistent: the world's financiers and political power brokers meet at this sophisticated resort, and Oxfam publishes its inquiry into inequality. The 2015 Oxfam Report shows that the world's eighty wealthiest people own as much as half of the population of the planet put together; the 2016 Report reduced that figure to sixty-two. The previous four years increased their net wealth by more than 50 percent:[1] a global crisis for most of the population was a joyous period for the Davos people. But in early 2017 Oxfam reported to the Davos conference that the number of billionaires required to match the resources of half of the world had fallen to just eight people. Oxfam added: "None of them has earned his fortune through talent or hard work, but by inheritance or accumulation through industries which are prone to corruption and cronyism."[2]

In the US, inequality is increasing sharply. The specialists Saez and Zucman show that, with 22 percent of the country's total wealth, the wealthiest 0.1 percent (only 160,000 families) own just as much as the bottom 90 percent (100 million families)[3] The richest 0.01 percent of the US population (16,000 families) enjoy an average

[1] According to the Oxfam Report, Hardoon, Fuentes-Nieva, Ayele (2016) which draws on data from Davies, Lluberas, and Shorrocks (2016), in 2010, 388 ultrabillionaires would be required to match the possessions of the poorer half of the population; in 2011, the number fell to 177, in 2012 to 159, in 2013 to 92 and, in 2014, to 80.

[2] Hardoon (2017). [3] Saez and Zucman (2016).

net worth of US $371 million, together holding 11.2 percent of total wealth, a share that this group last held in 1916.

The history is relevant. After the Great Depression and the Second World War, this 0.1 percent share of the population lost much of their wealth, an economic recalibration that also reset the social and political scales. Since the 1980s, the situation has reversed. In three decades, the share of the wealthiest 0.1 percent rose from 7 to 22 percent of the country's total wealth. The concentration has accelerated. With rising debt, the housing crisis, and the bursting of speculative bubbles taking a bite from the wealth of normal households, the economic power of the very rich has increased yet again. The financial crisis was the crowning moment for a century of regression in terms of inequality.

For the wealthiest of the wealthiest, the picture is even starker. Eight US tycoons, six Waltons and two Kochs, own as much as 44 percent of the US population. The Waltons hold US $149 billion—the GDP of a medium-size developed country—in shares (a 54 percent stake) in their massive Wal-Mart retail chain. The dynasty is half a century old: Wal-Mart was created in 1962 and rapidly grew to become the world's largest retailer. The Waltons have limited their direct political engagement, dabbling primarily in right-wing causes, such as hostility to public education.

The Koch fortune originated in 1925, when Fred Koch founded what is now the second largest privately owned company in the US. The two sons now in charge, David and Charles, bought out their brothers, Frederick, Jr., and Bill, in 1983, and developed the business to the point where their wealth is greater than the value of IBM or Honda. They own oil and petrochemical industries, excelling in fracking, with extensive interests in manufacturing, extraction equipment, chemical production, ethanol, and other investments, having doubled their earnings every half a dozen years.

While the US ruling class has generally appreciated, and occasionally supported, the services of right-wing think tanks, close engagement has been frowned on as being overly political and out of keeping with apolitical American norms. Not so with the Kochs. The family has long mixed its fortune with politics. The founder of the dynasty, Fred Koch, was an early supporter of the John Birch Society, a private Cold War network, consisting primarily of members of the petite bourgeoisie with the occasional, politicized leading industrialist, created in 1957 at the height of McCarthyism to persecute communists and expose supposed communist conspiracies. The sons fund the radical free-market Cato Institute, created in 1977. (See Chapter 7 on the role of these think tanks in indoctrination and the production of ideology.) They engage in direct political activism. In 1980, David was the vice Presidential candidate of the fringe Libertarian Party. More recently, the Kochs have reoriented their efforts toward the mainstream right by funding Republican Party candidates, including those associated with the Tea Party, as part of a concerted effort to pull US politics rightward. They finally entered the hall of fame as supporters of Trump's campaign, namely through their close friends, Mike Pence (the Vice President) and DeVos (Secretary of Education).[4]

[4] *The Guardian*, December 7, 2016. In spite of this choice, Charles Koch, the intellectual of the family, a supporter of Ludwig von Mises, the mentor of Hayek in London, appears not to appreciate Trump. The heart and personal interest are not always aligned.

This process of close connection between politics and business extends to other countries as well, as we shall see.

FAMILY BUSINESS

Early capitalism emerged from family businesses and their ownership. Gigantic movements in capital markets have taken center stage in the world economy, but many of these enormous pools have their origins in the capital of family businesses striving to coordinate their activities with one another in annual general meetings of large stockholders. Much of their money converges to finance the big family businesses, which represent a large part of the economic world.

Patterns of ownership vary according to the history of capital accumulation, and family businesses are today less prevalent in developed countries than in other parts of the world. But, even at the world's economic core, family fortunes remain impressively present in the largest companies. In Western Europe as a whole, 44 percent of firms are family controlled.[5] According to the Boston Consulting Group, families control a full 40 percent of large-sized firms in France and Germany. One third of American companies with revenue of more than US $1 billion are family businesses.

In a study on the subject, *The Economist* quotes some of the legendary examples of the lengthy survival of family firms:[6] one is that of the Italian firearm manufacturer Beretta, born in 1526 when Bartolomeo Beretta fulfilled an order for the production of arms placed with him by the Venetian government. Rothschild, Barings, Ford, Daimler-Benz, Ferrari, Versace, Dow, Gucci, Proctor, Walgreens, Guinness, Hess, Johnson and Johnson, Hewlett and Packard, Kroger, and Ferrero, are other examples of famous family names that are inseparable from the firm itself. Suzuki, Hermès, and Porsche gave their names to firms and products. In some cases, the names are more discreet, but still discernible: the Walton family owns Wal-Mart; the Toyoda family owns Toyota. Carl Benz and Gottlieb Daimler pioneered the development of the internal combustion engine in Central Europe, first competing, and then later merging their dominant car companies. Barings Bank was founded in 1762 by German merchants and was managed by successive generations of the family as the oldest merchant bank in London until its collapse and sale to the Dutch ING bank for one pound, in 1995. The Ferrero family created Nutella, more recently absorbing Kinder and other brands, but use the dynasty's name for its Ferrero Rocher chocolates.

Mayer Amschel Bauer (1743–1812), later Rothschild, dispatched his sons to different countries in order to create banks in Britain (Nathan), Austria (Salomon), France (James), and Italy (Karl) and to lead the Frankfurt branch (Anselm). In the early nineteenth century, Rothschild financial power was an important factor behind the forces mobilized to fight against Napoleon.

[5] Faccio and Lang (2002), There are other famous firms of even older vintage: Kongo Gumi, a construction firm in Japan, was founded in 578 (but went out of business in 2006).

[6] *The Economist*, April 18, 2015.

Family business is also a history of inheritance. A curious piece of research by two investigators of the Banca d'Italia on tax data of Florence in 1427 highlighted that, as far as one can tell following the lead of surnames, the richer families had a significantly higher probability of their apparent descendants being favored by fortune in 2011, or almost six hundred years afterwards, than the other citizens. The authors hypothesize a "long lasting effect of ancestors' socioeconomic status."[7] Family names may have an effect, at least in modern times: investigating 1.8 million small contemporary European firms, it was found that around 20 percent are named after the founder and largest stockholder, and that this is connected to larger returns on assets.[8]

DYNASTIES

Family names indicate continuity, although financialization may constitute an autonomous development, eventually distinct from the family's property and control. Such is the case with Ferrari. Enzo Ferrari created the automobile company, later led by his son Piero. Fiat-Chrysler, owned in large part by the even larger family fortune of the Agnellis, the richest family in Italy, ultimately acquired the majority of shares in Ferrari, in a compromise accepted by the two dynasties.

The Agnelli family dominates a full 10 percent of the Italian stock market. Although a large share by European standards, this is not unheard of in the ecosystem of capital. It is quite common to find powerful dynasties in charge of large parts of the economy. In Asia, dynasties are even more prevalent: the top fifteen families of Hong Kong have wealth equal to 84 percent of GDP; the equivalent figures are 76 percent in Malaysia, 48 percent in Singapore, and 47 percent in the Philippines. In Europe, the top ten families in Portugal controlled 34 percent of the market capitalization (until the 2014 collapse of the Espírito Santo financial group, owned by one of the most powerful of these families); the figure for the top ten families in France and Switzerland is 29 percent in both cases. In Germany, the Quandts are the major stockholders of BMW, Mini, and Rolls Royce.

The two largest Swedish groups owned 63 percent of the value of all listed firms at the end of the last century. The dominant group, the Wallenberg family, represents by itself almost half of the capitalization of the Swedish stock market and has spread its fortune into shares in Ericsson (20 percent), SAS, Nasdaq, ABB, SAAB (40 percent), Electrolux (30 percent), Atlas Copco, AstraZeneca the drug maker, Café Ritazza, and dozens of other companies. The group sprang from a bank created 160 years ago, the Stockholms Enskilda Bank, leading to the development of diversified investments, always under the *dictum* of the family, "Esse non videri," to be, not to be seen.[9]

[7] Barone and Mocetti (2016). [8] Belenzon, Chatterji, and Daley (2017), p. 1653.
[9] *Financial Times* (2015b); Marlow (2014).

The story holds all the more in developing countries. In Ecuador, the Noboa family owns the production of bananas (the Bonita brand, the world's fifth largest producer), and 40 percent of national exports. After a fierce battle with the other heirs, a common feature of these processes, Alvaro Noboa took control of the firm.

In India, the Tata, Birla, and Hinduja families bestride the world like colossi. The Tata empire began in 1858, when a local firm expanded abroad. In addition to its massive domestic investments in iron, steel, automobiles, luxury hotels, and hydroelectric power, Tata, until recently a very stable organization (with only six chairmen since 1868), owns substantial assets in the former colonial metropolis: Tetley Tea, Jaguar, Land Rover, and the biggest steel producer in Britain, although this was shutdown in 2016, destroyed by Chinese competition. By the end of 2016, the Tata group was threatened by the conflict between its patriarch, Ratan Tata, who owns the majority share through distinct charities, and his appointed successor, Cyrus Mistry, whose family owns a fifth of the shares. Families and alliances may not last forever.

The Birla family began in the 1890s with a cotton business and jute manufacturing, growing to form a conglomerate by the 1910s. More than a century later, they are still there.[10] The Hinduja empire was founded in 1914, moved its headquarters to Iran until 1979, and then relocated to London as a diversified conglomerate investing in oil, media, manufacturing, health, and banking. Four scions in the second generation lead the group: the brothers Srichand and Gopichand, possibly the richest men in England, Prakash (in Geneva, taking care of the financial part of the group), and Ashok (in India).

Other Indian magnates, including the three wealthiest businesspeople in India, Mukesh Ambani, Dilip Shanghvi, and Azim Premji, connect through families and networks based in the home province of Narendra Modi, the populist prime minister of India since 2014.

In Argentina, one third of the country's largest groups are controlled by the sons of the founder, another third by the grandsons, and yet another by the great-grandsons.[11] In France, cosmetics giant L'Oréal, linked to an investigation on funds received by the candidacy of former President Nicolas Sarkozy, is led by the third generation, a succession not without œdipal litigation: Liliane Bettencourt, the daughter of 1907 founder Eugène Schueller, was sued by her own daughter who wrested control of the 40-billion-euro business. In South Korea, the largest conglomerates are all family-owned. That is the case of Samsung, Hyundai, LG, CJ, Hanwha, Lotte, Hanjin, and the GS Group.

These stories do not always imply successful evolution for family businesses. The overall picture is rather grim. In large families, inheritance can disperse power. If we take the universe of family business, only 30 percent of heirs continue to manage in the second generation, 12 percent in the third, and 3 percent in the fourth and beyond.[12] The failure rate is high and, after a few generations (usually no more than four), most dynasties collapse. But in exceptional cases,

[10] Lockwood (2012), p. 132; On the relationship of the great Indian industrial families to the Planning Commission and the protection of the post-independence governments, see Chibber (2003).

[11] Fracchia, Mesquita, and Quiroga (2010).

[12] The US-based Family Business Institute (2017), documents the challenges facing these micro-dynasties.

decision making hierarchies can survive the widespread distribution of assets among family members.

Indeed, the numbers of heirs can rise over time to enormous proportions. In the Mulliez family (owners of the French retail, clothing, carpets, and electrical appliances brands Auchan, Decathlon, and Leroy-Merlin Boulanger), more than 600 family members have stakes in the parent holding company, and all adhere to a strict internal pact, assuring cohesion of the company leadership. The French Wendel family employs more than one thousand family members in their Saint Gobain and Nippon Oil Pump concerns. Until the collapse of its GES financial group and the BES bank, the Portuguese Espírito Santo family employed more than 400 family members, including many in rank-and-file positions as well as in senior management.

According to a *Forbes* study on dynastic wealth,[13] in the US we can find the Rockefellers, 200 people holding US $8.5 billion in wealth, the Mellons with 100 people holding US $10 billion, and the Du Ponts, with 300 holding US $12 billion; France has the Michelin family with 400 people holding US $1.2 billion; Germany has the Porsche and Piech (Volkswagen) families, with 50 holding US $10 billion, the Boehringer family, with 12 holding US $10.2 billion, the Merck family, with 100 holding US $4 billion; in Canada, we find the Bombardier family, with seven people holding US $2.7 billion; and, throughout Europe and the US, the Rothschild family consists of 10 people holding US $1.5 billion.

In China, no less than 103 descendants of the "eight immortals" of the Mao Zedong revolution held ruling positions in state-owned firms.[14] Three of them run firms with combined assets amounting to one fifth of the Chinese economy.[15] In the giant firm Dalian Wanda, operating in real estate—it claims to have "120 times more employees than the Vatican" and owns properties in Beverly Hills, the AMC Theatres, and 20 percent of the Spanish football club Atletico Madrid—stakes are reserved for the elder sister of President Xi Jinping and the daughter of former prime minister Wen Jiabao.[16]

The history of Hainan Airlines and the HNA Group demonstrates the importance of this pattern of connections. The co-chairmen of the firm, Cheng Feng and Wang Jian, used family networks to control the different firms in this giant conglomerate, which in addition to running airlines, sells other transportation, software, computers, seafood, Cuban cigars, advertising, and financial services, and owns one tenth of Deutsche Bank, a stake in Hilton Hotels, and valuable property in London and New York.[17] With a hundred billion dollars of yearly revenue, the conglomerate is under the control of the founders, with the brother and son of Feng and the wife and brother of Jian. In spite of depending on leverage and credit and political support, the HNA Group is further proof that, in China as well as in other countries, when it comes to direct control of a giant financial firm, family matters.

[13] *Forbes*, February 28, 2002.

[14] The eight are Deng Xiaoping, Wang Zhen, Chen Yun, Li Xiannian, Peng Zhen, Song Renqiong, Yang Shangkun, and Bo Ybo.

[15] Oster et al. (2012), in Bloomberg News. The rise of China and Asia, as we will discuss in Chapter 12, favors the rapid growth of wealth and capital. Nevertheless, Chinese millionaires are still a small part, some 10%, of those from the US and Europe.

[16] *New York Times*, April 29, 2015. [17] *New York Times*, July 18, 2017.

INHERITANCE AND SELF-MADE BILLIONAIRES

Caroline Freund, former chief economist of the World Bank, studied the rise of tycoons, and in particular the proportions of inherited fortunes and self-made fortunes. The research is based on the *Forbes* list of billionaires, that in 2004 included 587 names, in 2014 1,645 and in 2015 1,826, with a rising proportion of those coming from the "emerging" economies (from 20 percent to 40 percent, mostly from China).

Freund found that the proportion of billionaires owing their advantage to inheritance is declining through time, although still very large: taking the *Forbes* world list of billionaires, in two decades it declined from more than half (55 percent) in 1996 to less than one third (30.4 percent) in 2014. Nevertheless, in the richest economies it surpasses the average, amounting to one third of those in the US and slightly more than half in Europe.

A possible explanation is that the median age of companies is twenty years older in Europe, and that billionaires tend to concentrate their riches in traditional economic sectors in Europe and in finance and high tech in the US, therefore leading to a quicker turnover of opportunities. But, if the share of self-made fortunes is stable at around 60 percent for the whole developed world, in the emerging economies it changed rapidly and mounted from 57 percent (1996) to 79 percent (2014). The author explains this feature as the success of "Schumpeterian" innovators, social exceptions of developers able to create new ideas and products or organizations. Those would be the cases of Terry Gou, from Taiwan, who founded the electronics giant Foxconn and who is China's largest exporter, with one million employees; of Zhou Qunfei, the world's richest self-made woman, who owns Lens Technology; of the two internet giants, Jack Ma (Alibaba) and Robin Li (Baidu); or of the largest drugmaker from India, Dilip Shanghvi, owner of Sun Pharmaceutical.[18]

Although family business dominates in several economies, many of the fortunes are new ventures: according to *Forbes*, 840 of the world's 1,226 ultrabillionaires are self-made people. In some cases, such as that of Italy, tradition and new entrepreneurs are juxtaposed with one another: in the *Forbes* 2015 list of the world's billionaires, among the first two thousand are five Pradas, the oldest family in business, four Benettons, one Dolce, one Gabbana, and one Armani, the newcomers. We note in passing that in some cases these Schumpeterian success stories owe much to favor and political connections.

PYRAMID ORGANIZATION

Families use pyramidal organization of interlocking directorates, cross-ownership of shares, and chains of holding companies to keep control of conglomerates, even when they are listed on the stock market and, consequently, stocks are

[18] Freund and Oliver (2016); Dolan and Kroll (2015), describes the *Forbes* list, which includes people with over US $1 billion in net worth.

openly bought and sold. Stock ownership in these enormous companies clearly denotes wealth but control over operations and accumulation is a more precious commodity.

Investigating business groups with two or more listed firms under common control, a study of twenty-seven developed countries (using a minimum 20 percent stake as its definition of control) found that 54 percent of firms are part of pyramidal organizations, of which two-thirds are family businesses.[19] Other researchers have found the same pattern: in Brazil, Portugal, Mexico, Argentina, Greece, Turkey, Italy, Malaysia, Indonesia, India, the Philippines, Taiwan, and Thailand, the top ten business entities are predominantly pyramid groups.[20]

One example was to be found in Canada. The Bronfman family, which, by the mid-1990s owned more than 500 corporations, managed its control through Imperial Windsor, with a stake of only 0.03 percent, through a chain comprising

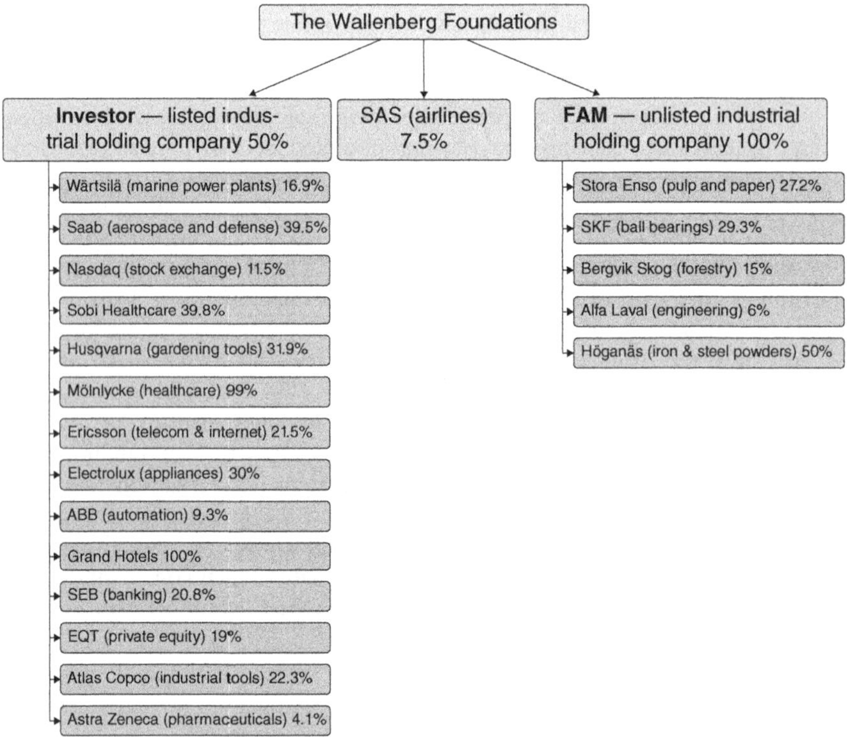

Figure 4.1. The Wallenberg network of companies
Source: Financial Times, 5 June 2015.

[19] Porta, López-de-Silanes, and Shleifer (1999). See also Almeida and Wolfenzon (2006).

[20] This power of control decreased after 2000. Perkins, Morck, and Yeung (2014), pp. 311–12; Almeida and Wolfenzon (2006). Investigations on the structure of pyramidal ownership have been an important part of research on conglomerates, for instance, Franks and Mayer (2001), for the case of Germany, Morck Randall, Stangeland, and Yeung (2000), for Canada, Morck and Nakamura (1999), for Japan, Barca and Becht (2001), for Europe.

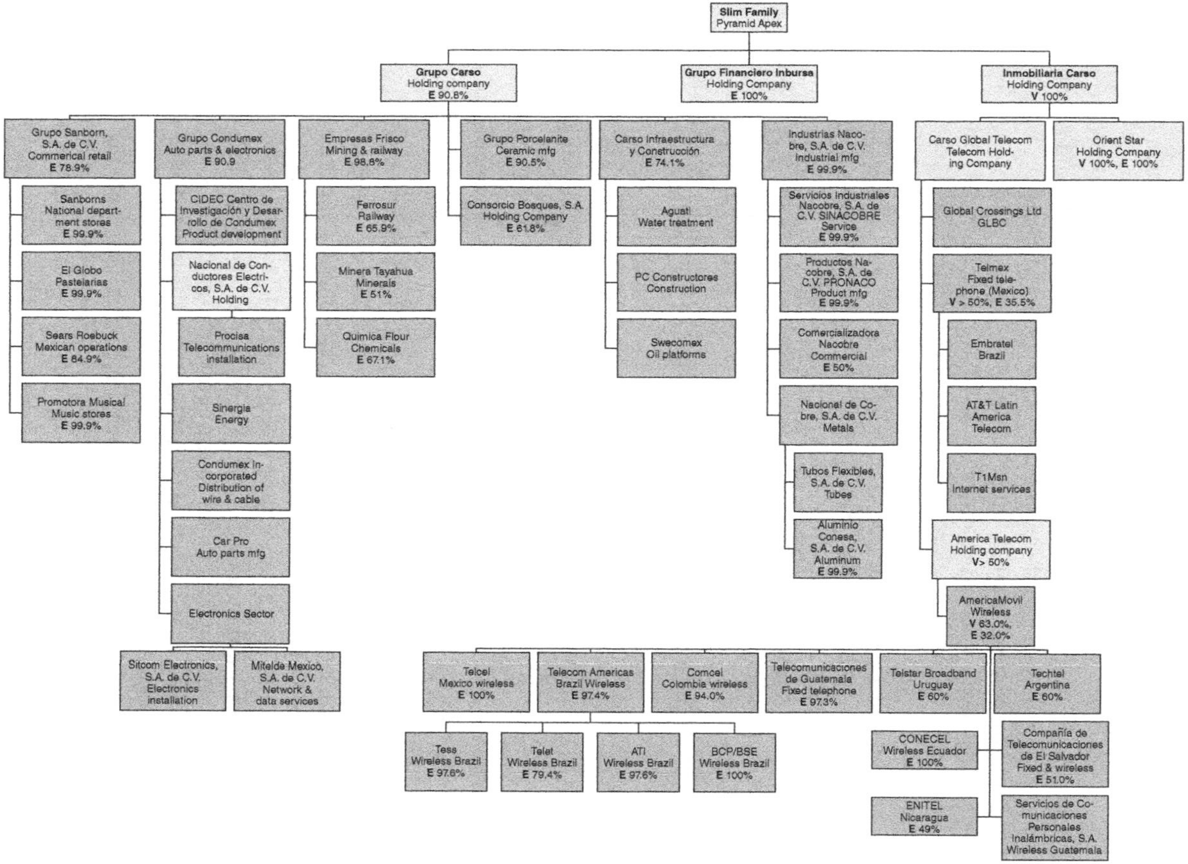

Figure 4.2. Carlos Slim's pyramid organization

Source: Perkins, Morck, and Yeung (2014).

sixteen tiers of controlling firms, culminating at the apex in family trusts.[21] As a consequence, a "one million dollar drop in the value of Imperial Windsor would cost its controlling family about $300."[22] Their power was so effective that someone noted "the family secured a temporary 1991 change in federal tax policy effective around the dates when tax would have become due on a $2.2 billion capital gain in their family trust. A subsequent federal tax deferral of over $2.1 billion for the family also raised eyebrows among tax economists."[23]

This is also the case in Sweden. The Wallenberg family, introduced in the previous section, with just a 0.5 percent holding of direct shares, and a further 22 percent held through a trust, controls Investor, the apex of the group. Figure 4.1 portrays the Wallenberg pyramid.[24]

Mark Zuckerberg, with 28 percent of the stock, controls Facebook. The Carlos Slim case in Mexico is even more impressive. With a fortune of US $60 billion according to the authorized lists of fortunes, Carlos Slim is the world's second richest billionaire. (If he spent one million dollars a day, he would take around 220 years to use up his fortune.) Slim benefited from the political connections that conceded him the privatization of telecommunications in Mexico, and then he added investments in health care, airlines, media, sports, the retail trade, and other businesses. He is famously the largest individual shareholder in the *New York Times*.

Figure 4.2 shows how this pyramid of shares and voting rights has been built up. Ingenious, isn't it?

THE POWER OF THE RIGHT CONNECTIONS

The cases of the Bronfmans and of Carlos Slim are not isolated examples of the power of tycoons. In several other cases, if not in most cases, the ruling families cultivate a careful network with political decision making.

Also in Canada, Arthur Meighen, the head of the largest pyramid group in the 1920s, Canada General Investment, was twice the country's prime minister. In more recent times, Alvaro Noboa has run several times for the Presidency of Ecuador, unsuccessfully to date; he retains unelected distinction as the richest man in Ecuador. The Birla family in India early established close connections with the Congress Party (marked by tragedy when Gandhi was assassinated while residing on their estate). And, as has already been noted, the billionaire Koch brothers conspicuously intervene in the choice of Republican candidates in the US, favoring the most conservative alternatives.

Family continuity is not nurtured only by business, but also by politics. History has provided us with many examples of political dynasties, such as the Kennedy and Bush families in the US, the Trudeaus in Canada, the Fujimoris in Peru (the daughter of the previous President was defeated in the Presidential race of 2011 and again in 2016), the Bhuttos in Pakistan, the Nehru-Gandhis in India, the Le Pens

[21] Tian (2006). [22] Hogfeldt (2005), p. 8. [23] Morck and Yeung (2006), p. 307.
[24] Hogfeldt (2005).

in France, the Papandreou and Karamanlis dynasties in Greece, and the Aylwins, Allesandris, and Freis in Chile. In Singapore, the prime minister Lee Hsien Loong is the son of Lee Kuan Yew who governed for thirty-one years.

As the *New York Times* documented for the US, being born in a palace provides a good ticket in American politics, especially in regional politics, since the son of a senator is 8,500 times more likely to become a senator than is the son of anyone else.[25]

Two particular intersections of politics and business are relevant for this book, because they represent the workings of the shadow system. The first is the direct involvement of political ruling families in business: firms representing 8 percent of the world market capitalization in 2003 were run by relatives of their countries' political leaders.[26] As this evidence will be discussed later on in more detail and new data will also be added about the close connections between politics and business, it is sufficient for the time being to mention here how a decision maker can favor, or be put in the position of eventually favoring, the particular interests of his own kind—and how many such people actually use that power.

Take the case of India. In 2012, the *Forbes* world list of billionaires included forty-six people from the country, and almost half of them operated in rent-seeking sectors, such as real estate, construction, cement, media, infrastructure, and mining. That was the case of Mukesh Ambani, the richest person in the country.[27]

Other cases of politically connected billionaires are conspicuous in the list: in Nigeria, Folorunsho Alakija got her fortune from the oil license granted by the government; Igor Makarov, from Russia (although the company is registered in Cyprus) got his from a joint venture with the state oil company; and Denis O'Brien, from Ireland, obtained his fortune from a mobile phone license, obtained through the notorious intercession of a politician. In South Africa, the close connections between President Jacob Zuma and his wealthy benefactors, the Gupta family, have been scrutinized, as one of the President's wives, a son, and a daughter worked for firms owned by this family of Indian businesspeople and there were claims on their political influence on government. A twice minister of finance for Zuma, Pravin Gordhan, accused his former boss and his associates at different state-owned firms of looting around $11 to $15 billion. At the end of his term, Zuma supported his ex-wife, Dlamini-Zuma, for leadership of the ANC and presumptive candidacy in the next Presidential election, but an insurgency in the ANC rejected the plan.[28]

Cesar Mata Pires, from Brazil, who also shines in the list of world billionaires, got lucky with the public contracts for the stadiums for the 2014 World Cup and the 2016 Olympic Games (he is the son-in-law of the late Antonio Carlos Magalhães, the powerful supporter of the military dictatorship and governor of the State of Bahia, who was nicknamed "Toninho Malvadeza," or "Evil Tony," by the popular press).[29] In the same country, the revelation of lists of payments to politicians by one of the largest construction firms, Odebrecht, by the public petroleum company, Petrobrás, and by the world's largest meat exporter Joesley Batista, initiated a major turmoil that led to a national crisis.

[25] Stephens-Davidowitz (2015). [26] Faccio (2006). [27] Gandhi and Walton (2012).

[28] *Financial Times*, March 8, 2016; *Wall Street Journal*, March 16, 2016; *BBC*, November 2, 2016; *The Economist*, December 9, 2017; *Financial Times*, November 30, 2017.

[29] West (2014); Freund and Oliver (2016), p. 17, 24.

Notwithstanding these legal implications and the major disruption of the political system they created, the protection by the Brazilian State was not always sufficient to maintain financial empires. Eike Batista was listed in 2012 as the twelfth richest man in the world, but in 2015 he was bankrupt. Generous credit from a public bank and, eventually, different favors in public procurement did not avoid the collapse of his empire. Yet other empires were lastingly built on the advantages of public concessions, such as the Globo network of Roberto Marinho, a TV mogul. Edir Macedo, a lottery agent turned bishop of a church he created, IURD, became a billionaire and benefited from the inattention of the fiscal authorities, as Alex Cuadros, a journalist, proves in his *Brazillionaires: The Godfathers of Modern Brazil.*[30] Macedo's nephew, Marcelo Crivella, was elected mayor of Rio de Janeiro, thanks to the support of the church.

And take the case of Jack Ma, the owner of Alibaba, which benefited from the largest initial public offering ever in the US market. Ma is sheltered by the Chinese government from competition in the home market and is a partner of the national social security and sovereign funds in one payments firm that initiated his financial career.[31] Friends matter indeed.

The second intersection with the shadows is to be noted in the way that governments favor the constitution of financial powers and the setting up of industrial and financial groups, or simply support the accumulation of wealth by their allies.

In some ways, cronyism is nothing new. But two recent extreme examples are telling, and they indicate such large changes in quantity as to imply changes in quality. The first is the emergence of the Russian oligarchy, empowered by Presidents Boris Yeltsin and Vladimir Putin.

Yeltsin's election initiated a first phase of mass privatization. From 1992 to 1994, the ownership of 70 percent of medium and large-sized public enterprises was transferred, ostensibly to the general population through the issue of vouchers, which were rapidly accumulated by the wealthiest. From 1994 to 1997, the government borrowed heavily from banks, offering the ownership of large firms as collateral, in what came to be known as the loans-for-shares agreements. In practice, this meant that a handful of oligarchs were selected to manage the firms involved in mineral extraction and export.

Large international banks financed this process. The Deutsche Bank, J.P. Morgan, Crédit Suisse, and Citigroup, among others, counseled or financed the enterprise and benefited from service fees. The Russian people did not benefit: by 1998, the ruble had collapsed and the state was forced to restructure public and private debt and take control of national banks. The country suffered a 42 percent decline in total output, widespread impoverishment, and a concomitant social impact that had disastrous effects on morale, wealth, public services, and even health, as life expectancy plummeted.

Yet the oligarchs prospered amidst the havoc. The major mining and oil firms were transferred into private hands, delivering extraction exports into the hands of the robber barons, to use the adequate US expression for the early capitalist

[30] Cuadros (2016).

[31] *The Economist*, May 7, 2016. Alibaba has developed powerful international connections as well: SoftBank, the Japanese telecom group, owns 28% of its shares.

adventurers. Paul Klebnikov, a senior editor of *Forbes*, aptly called this "the theft of the century."[32]

Klebnikov, who was murdered on a Moscow street in 2004, had investigated and described this process of rapid and efficient looting of the public resources of Russia: in the first phase of privatizations, the directors, or the nomenclature, bought the firms benefiting from embezzlement, and were able to take control of the riches of the country; then the financial and production system was concentrated in the hands of the few oligarchs.

By comparing the voucher auction prices of the first phase of privatization (1993–4) with the stock market prices for the same firms in August 1997, the dimension of the theft can be assessed: Gazprom, the largest gas producer and distributor, increased in value by a factor of 162, from US $250 million to US $40.483 billion; Unified Energy Services, a provider of electricity, increased its value 19 times; Lukoil, Yukos, and Surgutneftegas, oil producers, respectively increased their value 22, 18, and 84 times.[33] The profits were immense.

After the first wave of privatizations, more sophisticated instruments were used to accumulate capital and to transfer wealth between sectors and to safer havens. Two hundred thousand public firms were privatized—roughly 20 times the number privatized by Thatcher in the UK—providing immense opportunities for looting.

One of the oligarchs, Boris Berezovsky, used an ingenious scheme for privatizing the profits of Aeroflot, the state airline company. An external firm, owned by Berezovsky, was contracted to pay for the foreign accounts of Aeroflot, including the orders of oil, repairs, and other expenses required for the airline's normal operations, but it charged Aeroflot an interesting interest rate of 50 percent; then a second firm, registered in Ireland, charged another 30 percent interest from the first; finally, Aeroflot itself paid an interest rate of 95 percent. All in all, the chain neatly transferred the value of Aeroflot to Berezovsky, simply by paying exorbitant prices to his own external firms.

Boris Berezovsky and Roman Abramovich, both close associates of President Yeltsin, acquired Sibfnet, a major oil producer, following the loans-for-shares agreement. They paid a sum of US $100 million for a company worth US $2.7 billion, a tidy profit. Abramovich later acknowledged giving bribes to government officials and gangsters to ease the acquisition. He eventually fought his partner, suing and winning single-handed control of the firm. Berezovsky committed suicide in his mansion in England.

Other oligarchs have also benefited from the mineral resources of Russia: Vladimir Potanin (nickel, oil), Mikhail Fridman (oil), Alisher Usmanov (metals), Viktor Vekselberg (aluminum), and Mikhail Prokhorov (mining), are some of the richest men in the country (and the world). Vagit Alekporov was the 1990 deputy minister for oil and gas and in 1991 he became the head of privatized Lukoil, the largest company in the sector.

Igor Sechin, a close ally of President Putin, leads Rosneft and developed a partnership with ExxonMobil, then under Rex Tillerson who now serves as Trump's Secretary of State. Like Putin, a former member of the security

[32] Klebnikov (2002). [33] Ibid.

services, Sechin benefited from his political alliances, as a major competitor, Mikhail Khodorkovsky, was arrested and his firm, Yukos, dismantled and swallowed by Rosneft. As a result of moves like this, the *Forbes* list of billionaires (total worth US $5.4 trillion) shows the Russian contingent owning almost one tenth of the pot (US $427 billion, or thrice the GDP of a medium-size developed country in Europe).[34]

The Angolan case provides yet another example of oil-soaked crony capitalism. José Eduardo dos Santos, President for near forty years, and his daughter Isabel own one of the largest fortunes in Africa, given the family's control of national oil production. A court of followers benefits from the oil income and uses the capital to invest in property or business: banking, oil distribution, telecommunications, and other sectors, or simply luxurious goods.[35] As the President presented the case in parliament: "The primitive accumulation of capital in the western countries occurred hundreds of years ago and by that time the rules of the game were different. The primitive accumulation of capital taking place now in Africa must be adequate to our reality. This has nothing to do with corruption or the use of public resources for personal benefit."[36]

By the same time, the official newspaper celebrated the inclusion of Isabel dos Santos, the daughter of the President, in the list of *Forbes* billionaires: "The Angolan entrepreneur Isabel dos Santos was classified as the richest woman in Africa by the US magazine Forbes." And the editorial of the newspaper developed the story: "As we do our best for an Angola without poverty, we commemorate the fact that Isabel dos Santos is a reference for world finance. This is good for Angola and the Angolans are proud. After all, our golden dream is that all human beings be rich, in whatever part of the planet."[37] All humans rich, that is certainly an overstatement for Angola, a country with so many resources and whose population is largely living in poverty.

SOCIAL POWER

Although the construction of social legitimacy supporting the exercise of effective power results from the juxtaposition of different and complex processes, and some will be discussed in the chapter on indoctrination and selection of the elites, one should be quoted now, since we presented some evidence for the capture of public resources by the victors of globalization. It is the capture of the public imagination

[34] *Forbes* (2017); This recent accumulation of wealth favors social exhibition: the daughter of Dmitry Ryblovlev, the king of potash and the largest shareholder of the Bank of Cyprus, bought Skorpios, an island in Greece previously owned by the late magnate Aristotle Onassis, for approximately US $150 million. Some 111 billionaires hold 19% of Russian wealth, Credit Suisse Research (2014), and *The Economist* computes that the wealth of crony-capitalists in Russia is around 17% of the national GDP (*The Economist*, May 7, 2016).

[35] Costa, Lopes, and Louçã (2014), One of the authors of this book was part of a team that undertook a detailed investigation of the wealth of the Angolan Presidential family.

[36] Speech of José Eduardo dos Santos in the Angolan parliament, October 16, 2013.

[37] *Jornal de Angola*, January 25, 2013.

and the factories of consensus, namely those provided by sport and its rituals of consecration.

Some of the billionaires previously mentioned understood the opportunity and invested in it. Those are the cases of Carlos Slim, who owns the Club Deportivo Guadalajara, and, more importantly, of Roman Abramovic, who bought Chelsea in London, of Prokhorov, who acquired the Brooklyn Nets, a major team in the US NBA, of Dmitry Ryblovlev, the owner of Monaco, of Wang Jianlin, who got part of Atletico Madrid, or of Zhang Jindong, the leader of the Chinese group Suning, who bought Inter Milan, a major football team in Italy. Other football teams were partially purchased by Chinese capital, such as Espanyol (Rastar Group), Manchester City (China Media Capital), and West Bromwich Albion (Guachuam Lai). In other cases, Chinese firms took total control of the teams: Aston Villa (Tony Xia), Granada (Jiang Lizhang), AC Milan (Sino Europe Sports), Wolverhampton Wanderers (Fosun), and Birmingham City (Trillion Trophy Asia). China Everbright proposed to buy Liverpool.[38] Following the same drive to match fortune and football, Isabel dos Santos, the billionaire daughter of José Eduardo dos Santos, bought the Atlético Petróleos de Luanda, one of the top football clubs in the country. The Secretary of Commerce for the Trump administration, the billionaire Wilbur L. Ross, owns the Chicago Cubs baseball team.

Control of symbolic power and the expression of ideas is thus part of the game. Therefore, it is not irrelevant that some of the registered billionaires are media empires: the *Forbes* 2016 list includes, near the top, two owners of financial news agencies, Michael Bloomberg (owner of the Bloomberg agency, ex-New York mayor) and David Thomson (Reuters).

Near the top of the same list, other moguls are to be found: Charles Ergen (satellite TV, who made a fortune from junk bonds), Samuel and Donald Newhouse (*Vanity Fair*, *New Yorker*, and other publications), among others. The most prominent public personality in the list is Silvio Berlusconi. The ex-premier of Italy is the owner of TV channels and a publishing empire, Mondadori, and built his political career from these dominant positions in the Italian media.

THE WORLD'S CORPORATE ELITE

Up to this point, this chapter has explored the relevance of family business. This is perhaps a surprising turn in a book that is ultimately about structure, not personality or moral versus immoral choice, as the key to understanding the contemporary economy. Yet structure needs a stage and actors. Family business remains the core of some of the most important firms in the world economy, including the most developed countries, the birthplace of managerial, shareholder-based, and financialized capitalism, all of which were supposed to have eclipsed traditional old-style capitalism. We close this chapter by establishing some connections back from the juicy tales of family capitalism to the matter of structure in the contemporary capitalist economy.

As conglomerates diversified their activity, the professionalization of management created complex networks of managers who share with the capital owners

[38] *The Economist*, August 27, 2016.

both the drive and capacity to accumulate power. In some cases, the owners continue to manage the company: perhaps the record holder is Horst Brandstatter, the owner and boss of Playmobil, who managed the firm for no less than fifty-four years. But in any case he was not alone, and family management requires a professional staff of high-ranking experts, who constitute the corporate elite.

Carroll and Sapinski, researchers at the University of Victoria in Canada, investigated the directors listed in the *Fortune* list of the world's most dominant firms, including the 400 largest industrial and commercial and the 100 largest financial companies. Not surprisingly, a pattern emerged of cross responsibilities among the managers or shareholders' representatives in many different firms.

Considering the period from 1996 to 2006, the total number of board members across all of the firms in the sample decreased by 35 percent from 7,921 to 5,248. Considering only those sitting on two or more boards, the number started out much smaller and decreased by 20 percent from 757 to 611. Both changes indicate the rise of insiders, who combine different responsibilities in separate major firms, not necessarily related to the same conglomerate. In fact, a consolidation and concentration process is at work. The leadership of dominant firms is an increasingly centralized network.

This study also cross-referenced board membership with the leadership of eleven major transnational policy boards, such as the International Chamber of Commerce, the Trilateral Commission, Council on Foreign Relations, World Economic Forum, and European Round Table of Industrialists.[39] Between 1996 and 2006, the overlap grew from 419 to 650. Based on the most powerful board members, these eleven institutions, and their interlinkages, the authors identify a "corporate-policy elite" of 887 people in 2006.[40]

This "inner circle," as these authors term it, is simultaneously dominant in the corporations themselves and in major policy-coordination institutions. They certify, support, define, legislate or influence legislation, and match the brokers of different business associations and enterprises.

Some examples are illustrative. Former Mexican President Ernesto Zedillo sits on two US-based corporate boards and three policymaking transnational institutions. Klaus Kleinfeld, the CEO of Siemens, is also a director at Bayer and Alcoa, and participates in the Trilateral Commission, the Transatlantic Business Dialogue, and the powerful European Round Table of Industrialists. Bertrand Collomb, whose curriculum vitae includes being chair of Lafarge and director of Unilever, is a leading member of the Trilateral Commission, the Transatlantic Business Dialogue, the World Business Council for Sustainable Development, the European

[39] The eleven institutions are: International Chamber of Commerce, Bilderberg Conferences, Trilateral Commission, World Economic Forum, International Advisory Board of the Council of Foreign Relations, World Business Council for Sustainable Development, UN Global Compact, European Round Table of Industrialists, EU-Japan Business Round Table, Transatlantic Business Dialogue, and North American Competitive Council (Carroll and Sapinski, 2010).

[40] Carroll and Sapinski (2010), p. 514; Other studies concur: Coates and Kraakman (2007), investigating CEO tenure in S&P500 Companies for 1992–2004, noticed that the longevity of the top managers in the largest firms is longer than in ordinary companies: they average 13.4 years, against 5.5 in other companies.

Round Table of Industrialists, and the EU-Japan Business Round Table, as well as being regularly present at the Bilderberg meetings. Mark Moody-Stuart, the CEO of Shell and director of HSBC and Accenture, is a leading member of the Trilateral Commission and the World Business Council for Sustainable Development. Jorma Ollila, the chair of Nokia and Shell and a director of Ford, is part of the European Round Table of Industrialists and the EU-Japan Business Round Table. Andrew Liveris, the CEO of Dow Chemicals and a director of Citigroup, is an influential member of the Transatlantic Business Dialogue and the World Business Council for Sustainable Development.

This world elite and its network of organizations form an ecology of connections and social relations. Among so many possible examples, Sandra Navidi described her attendance at a marriage and the company she found in the tent:

> Soros's wedding to business consultant Tamiko Bolton in 2013 was even more extravagant. Since the event had been scheduled to take place on the weekend preceding the United Nations General Assembly and the Clinton Global Initiative, many world leaders were in New York. The festivities were held at the Caramoor Estate near Katonah, New York, an hour's drive from the city, and I looked forward to attending. Approaching the venue, we joined a long convoy of black limousines and were greeted by the Budapest Festival Orchestra playing a composition created solely for the occasion. In a splendiferous tent, at the center of which loomed a life-sized sculpture of a hot air balloon made entirely of flowers, a microcosm of the financial elite mingled. IMF chief Christine Lagarde; World Bank President Jim Yong Kim; former UN Secretary-General Kofi Annan; House minority leader Nancy Pelosi; Senator Chuck Schumer; Iceland's President, Ólafur Ragnar Grímsson; Estonian President Toomas Hendrik Ilves; Liberian President Ellen Johnson Sirleaf; Albania's prime minister Edi Rama; Italian foreign minister Emma Bonino; former Greek prime minister George Papandreou; hedge fund titans Paul Tudor Jones, Julian Robertson, and Stan Druckenmiller; Lord Adair Turner; Baron Mark Malloch-Brown . . . .[41]

These people, among others, compose the restricted inner circles of the world's dominant firms. The policy institutions are not themselves dominant organizations; their actual power is limited to influence, to insinuate, to lobby. But they provide a site for coordination and communication, and this generates or supports power.

CONCENTRATION, ACQUISITIONS, AND MERGERS

The growth of the financial institutions proceeds through three main channels: privatizations, direct public support to finance and banking, and the concentration and merger of different institutions. The first two were abundantly discussed in the previous pages and chapters.

Privatizations, as in the Russian and Mexican examples, generate opportunities for looting: oil, gas, coal, timber, defense, information and communication, banking, infrastructure, casinos, energy, ports, airports, real estate and construction, health and education, and other social services are among the most important

[41] Navidi (2017), p. 54.

assets to be transferred to private ownership. Some are natural monopolies and others are simply claims on future fees to be paid by contributors.

The direct support of finance has been a historically unrivaled transfer to the wealthy and powerful. As *The Economist* bluntly noted on the post-subprime crash, "the bailing out of banks has involved the transfer of a great deal of wealth to financiers."[42]

But the third process, concentration by merger and acquisition, is also important, if not determinant, for the financial institutions. The acquisitions and fusions of banks and other firms in the banking industry are indeed impressive.

In the US, the recent financial crises led to increased concentration. During this period of vertigo, NationsBank bought Boatmen's Bancshares in 1996, the Barnett Bank in 1997, and Bank of America in 1998. California-based Bank of America had bought the investment bank Robertson Stephens in 1997, and, in 2004 it bought the Fleet Boston (itself the result of a merger of three banks on the East Coast).

J.P. Morgan Chase, one of the largest banks, results from a long and complex lineage. It emerged from the merger of the Chemical Bank and Manufacturers Hanover in 1991, the First Chicago and National Bank of Detroit in 1995, the Chemical and Chase Manhattan in 1996, Bank One and First Chicago in 1998, J.P. Morgan and Chase Manhattan in 2000, and J.P. Morgan and Bank One in 2004. Then it bought Bear Stearns, the unhappy victim of the subprime recession, for the value of its building; the CEO of J.P. Morgan, Jamie Dimon, sat at the time on the board of the New York Federal Reserve Bank, which conducted the sale, and this eventual conflict of interest provoked speculation.[43]

Wells Fargo bought First Interstate in 1996 and merged with Norwest in 1998. Then it bought Wachovia in 2008, itself a merger of First Union, CoreStates, and Wachovia since 1998. Commercial Credit bought Primerica in 1988, Travelers Insurance in 1993, Salomon Brothers in 1997, and merged with Citigroup in 1998.

At the same time, these venerable banks acquired shadow finance firms as part of their expansion plans: NationsBank bought Hambrecht and Quist in 1999; Credit Suisse bought First Boston in 1988 and Donaldson, Lufkin and Jenrette in 2000; the Swiss Bank Corporation, lately part of UBS, bought Dillon in 1997; and the Deutsche Bank bought Bankers Trust in 1998. A similar process occurred in Europe and in other parts of the world.

BIG BUSINESS

As a consequence, giant banks dominate the economies and influence the political maps. They are not alone and, indeed, globalization was originally moved by other international organizations: the first champions were the multinationals dominating more than half of international trade. Yet some of these champions are in retreat, such as Kentucky Fried Chicken and McDonald's, once shining stars of the global markets, the forerunners of the wave of investments in Moscow and Beijing, whose shares fell from 2012 to 2017 by 20 and 29 percent respectively.

[42] *The Economist*, March 15, 2014.

[43] Johnson and Kwak (2011), 84 ff, 159.

For the other multinationals, prospects are also dim. The company providing FTSE, the British stock index, computed a fall of one quarter of the profits of the 700 multinationals for the same period, 2012–17. Although this is partially explained by the reduction of the price of oil, given the weight of the oil producers in this list, evidence shows that alternatives are stronger now and national brands are competing with the food giants, as well as in other industries. Nevertheless, the power of the global firms is still dominant. Even if their returns go down, they are moving from production to intellectual property: the top fifty US firms, in the last decade, improved their foreign profits from 35 to 65 percent of the total, mostly in technology, drug patents, and finance. And, as we noted in the introduction, the euphoria in stock markets during the year 2017 represented major gains for the financial industry, which garnered more power everywhere and strong allies where it matters most, such as Trump.

GIANTS IN THE SHADOWS

With economic globalization, new giants have emerged. Concentration is the major driver of globalization: Google and Apple provide 90 percent of the operating systems of all smartphones and Google manages 69 percent of all word web search activities—it has become the largest publicity agency in the world.

One widely recognized, but nonetheless amazing, fact of modern times is how globalization and financialization have prevailed, to an extent never before witnessed: in 2015, Facebook, which bought Instagram and WhatsApp, was worth five times the market value of General Motors, or more than General Electric or J.P. Morgan Chase or Wal-Mart; and Apple's value was larger than the combined value of General Electric, General Motors, Wal-Mart, and MacDonalds. Proving the same point, it is noted that George Soros has been able to extract more profit than Warren Buffet plus Walt Disney plus Apple since 2010.[44]

This growth has generated a faceless power, unlike the firms we have been citing until now. BlackRock, the biggest investor in the world, has a portfolio of US $4.1 trillion of directly controlled assets, as well as overseeing a further US $11 trillion of 170 pension funds. This is approximately 7 percent of all world shares, loans, and bonds, or the entire US economy. All the private equity and hedge funds on the planet, put together, would scarcely match BlackRock, which is, as a matter of fact, the largest shareholder in half of the world's largest thirty corporations. This includes around (or more than) 5 percent of shares in such firms as Shell, Procter and Gamble, Wells Fargo, J.P. Morgan Chase, Chevron, General Electric, Johnson and Johnson, Petrochina, Microsoft, Berkshire Hathaway, Google, Exxon Mobile, and Apple, but also relevant stakes in Toyota, Nestlé, Wal-Mart, Roche, Novartis, and ICBC. BlackRock is also the largest shareholder of *The Economist*, which published these data.[45]

[44] Yet Soros's fortune, composed of hedge funds, is worth as much as Phil Knight's (Nike shoes) and one third of that of Bill Gates. Freeland (2014), p. 195.

[45] *The Economist*, December 7, 2013.

Created by Larry Fink in 1998, the firm itself claims no exposure to the financial market; only its clients face risk. BlackRock is a powerful management firm, mostly of institutional and corporate clients. In the period after the crisis, it thrived as a reservoir of confidence. Since the subprime crash, BlackRock has acquired part of Merrill Lynch and Barclays' asset management, and grown fourfold.

This giant of the shadow finance system is also a major player in the traditional banking system, as well as in other firms in the same business. Shadow firms dominate as the top five shareholders of the largest US banks are listed: BlackRock is the first, Vanguard the second, and State Street the third shareholder in the major banks (J.P. Morgan Chase, Bank of America, Citigroup) and BlackRock is second and Vanguard is third in the other largest bank (Wells Fargo). BlackRock, Vanguard, and State Street, taken together, are the largest shareholder in 40 percent of listed US firms, which represent 80 percent of that economy.[46] By itself, Vanguard owns around 5 percent of every US public company and 1 percent of every one abroad.[47]

As BlackRock can be compared in size to the largest economy in the world, other financial institutions also compare to the entire economy of their home countries: BNP Paribas is approximately the size of the French economy, and HSBC is the size of the British economy.

The largest private equity firms, KKR, Blackstone, Carlyle, Apollo, are also giants in this world of finance. The Carlyle portfolio includes 275 companies, with 725,000 employees, and KKR includes 115 companies and 720,000 employees: they are the biggest employers in the US, more than any listed company except Wal-Mart. By 2013, some years after the crash, private equity backed companies represented 23 percent of all medium-sized US firms (this share tripled from 2000 to 2013) and 11 percent of the large companies (this share increased fivefold for the same period).[48]

Finance owns the world.

CONCLUSION

A recounting of the recent history of the most important US financial institutions reads like the food chain in the musical *Jamaica*:

> Man, he eat de Barracuda,
> Barracuda eat de bass.
> Bass eat de little flounder,
> 'Cause de flounder lower class.
>
> Little flounder eat de sardine,
> It's nature's plan;
> Sardine eat de little worm,
> Little worm eat de man.[49]

[46] Azar, Raina, and Schmalz (2016).
[47] *The Economist*, June 11, 2016.
[48] *The Economist*, October 22, 2016.
[49] Arlen and Harburg, 1957.

Except the success of the worm has not yet been established, although it involves more of the world as time goes by.

In this chain, family business was the beginning. Then it combined with the power of banks, mobilizing savings and intertwining with financial firms in order to expand capital accumulation. If shadow finance came to dominate the economy, it emerges out of this combination of different owners of accumulation, from recognizable family business to impersonal management of pension funds.

The consequences of this process of change will be discussed in the next parts of this book.

5

The Liberalizers: Justifying Free-Market Finance

Following our discussion of big firms and the enduring power of economic dynasties, we turn now to another form of power that explains financialization: the thought and action of the liberalizers.

"When the rest of the world is mad, we must imitate them in some measure," is attributed to a rueful banker caught in the 1720 South Sea Bubble. Charles MacKay recounts this observation on herd behavior in his 1841 *Extraordinary Popular Delusions and the Madness of Crowds.*[1] In this vein, we consider whether the 2007–8 crash and the following recession was just another period of madness and collective replication of "popular delusions," or if it was a foreseeable outcome of the imbalances generated in a complex world of conflicting interests and the dominance of rent-seeking behavior. As we will see, despite its failures in 2007–8, the financial oligarchy is stronger since the crisis.

This chapter investigates the process by which advocates justified the changes that led to a regime of systemic financial control of the world's economies. Some of the theoreticians of perfect financial markets are presented, as they rationalized the *blitzkrieg* of deregulation, stalwart in the face of opposition, emergent contradictions, occasional setbacks, and even the Great Crash.

We initiate our discussion of the forces leading towards liberalization and deregulation with the justifiers and their justifications not because we overestimate the afflictions of their quest for pure theory, nor because we ignore the misinterpretations, hesitations, and contradictions of their disciples in government. In some cases, the ideas come first, well before they are propelled by the winds of power.

EVERYONE SO WRONG

The *Wall Street Journal,* the leading business newspaper in the United States, regularly publishes the economic predictions of dozens of the most recognized analysts. Prediction naturally reflects both the condition of the economy and the mood of these gurus of finance. But reality and mood often diverge substantially. That became obvious in 2009, when the editor of the *Wall Street Journal* reviewed

[1] Cassidy (2009), p. 180.

the past predictions of fifty-one of the most renowned US economists. Only one had predicted the ongoing recession, and even this prescient analyst did not anticipate an increase in unemployment.[2] Indeed, almost every prediction was wrong.

But then why should these prognosticators have suspected that something was rotten? Well-honed financial and economic theories precluded the possibility of grotesque mis-valuations of financial assets. The leaders of the governing institutions expressed certainty that lessons of the past had been understood and that the tragedies of the business cycle would wane into oblivion.

Enjoying and coming to believe in the "Great Moderation," Greenspan and then Bernanke became the world's leading architects of the new approach to economics, with their successive appointments as Governor of the Fed (1987–2006 and 2006–14). They confidently designed a conservative monetary policy as the stabilizing backbone of the new epoch. Nothing could go wrong and a handful of well-chosen indicators were sufficient to monitor and regulate the economy. In case of financial mishap, a gentle loosening of the monetary tap could right any imbalance. No other state intervention was needed, certainly not fiscal policy. Both Governors felt comfortable weighing in on the virtues of balanced budgets and even of spending priorities.

As no alternative was imagined, the neoliberal consensus solidified. In 2007, mere months before the crisis boiled over, Christina Romer, who would soon become the leading advocate of stimulus policy as Chair of the Council of Economic Advisers in the Obama administration, chastened earlier Keynesian views on the benefits of stimulus, stating "we have seen the triumph of sensible ideas and reaped the rewards in terms of macroeconomic performance. The costly wrong turn in ideas and macropolicy of the 1960s/70s has been righted, and the future of stabilization looks bright."[3]

In the same sense and even the year after the crash, the chief economist of the IMF, Olivier Blanchard, could aver that "the state of macro is good," with a "broad convergence of vision." The dream of Milton Friedman had been realized.[4]

Yet such convergence has been more imagined than real. Friedman blamed the wrong monetary policy for the Great Depression and Hayek bluntly explained it as a government failure and not a market failure.[5] But Bernanke knew better: as historian of that history, he could understand both the mistakes by the institutions and the economic contradictions of that epoch.[6]

The "Great Moderation" implied that the business cycle was tamed and financial-market volatility had diminished. Soon it would be understood that this apparent change led to increasing risks.[7] In fact, it is hard to avoid metaphors of teeming underbellies and dangerous currents beneath calm surfaces. The 2007–8 financial crisis, precipitated by the bursting housing bubble and the collapse of the subprime mortgage market and its derivatives, and the deep long recession that followed shattered optimistic views. The domino effect of the Lehman Brothers collapse demonstrated how this interconnected market could repeat the "extraordinary popular delusions and the madness of crowds." Lehman Brothers' short-term notes

[2] *Wall Street Journal*, February 13, 2009; Freeland (2014), p. 196. [3] C. D. Romer (2007).
[4] Blanchard (2008). [5] Cassidy (2009), p. 73.
[6] Bernanke (2000). [7] Eichengreen (2015), p. 5.

were largely held by money market funds, on whom rattled fundholders promptly initiated a run. The fundholders then turned to the parent investment banks, and the entire securitization markets collapsed.

The surprise was embarrassing. Channeling Claude Rains in *Casablanca*, Alan Greenspan, the powerful Governor of the US Federal Reserve for almost two decades, reported to a committee of the US House of Representatives Committee on October 23, 2008, "I am shocked."

The next sections discuss some of the reasons for this shock and the resulting "madness of crowds" with their "popular delusions."

"DADDY, WHY IS EVERYONE SO SURPRISED?"

The crisis and the recession were not widely foreseen by a public that had been repeatedly calmed and reassured by scholarly prognostications of stability and growth. A very well known example is that of Queen Elizabeth II. At a ceremony at the London School of Economics, the Queen—who had just lost £25 million, or one quarter of her portfolio—asked her assembled sages, "Why did nobody foresee it?"[8]

The British economists felt obliged to prepare some notes on what had happened and why they had failed to anticipate such a problem. The final report of this endeavor, by July 2009, argued, deferring to the Queen, that "in summary, Your Majesty, the failure to foresee the timing, extent and severity of the crisis and to head it off, while it had many causes, was principally a failure of the collective imagination of many bright people, both in this country and internationally, to understand the risks to the system as a whole."[9] A "failure of the collective imagination of many bright people," sounds like explaining having been hijacked by a UFO from the highroad and brought back when the crisis was over.

Instead, Jamie Dimon, a giant of US finance, chair of J.P. Morgan, and, in the annals of the crisis, "the last man standing,"[10] had not had such a "failure of imagination" and preferred to tell a personal anecdote to the US Financial Crisis Inquiry Commission, when he was questioned on January 13, 2010: "My daughter called me up from school and said 'Daddy, what's a financial crisis?' And without trying to be funny, I said, 'It's something that happens every five to seven years'. And she says, 'So why is everyone so surprised?'."[11]

As his little daughter thoughtfully observed, Dimon too had failed to anticipate a regular twice-a-decade crisis. He had not "understood the risks" but in any case he responded swiftly and, when the opportunity presented at the vertex of the crisis, he bought a bank for nothing. Indeed.[12]

[8] A. Pierce (2008). [9] Stewart (2009). [10] D. McDonald (2009). [11] Dimon (2010), p. 78.

[12] Jamie Dimon was the CEO of J.P. Morgan, but also had a seat on the board of Federal Reserve Bank of New York. Under the guidance of the New York Fed, he brokered the deal of the sale of Bear Stearns to his own bank. He could not anticipate the business cycle, but is certainly notorious for his ability at business.

The "popular delusions" were not so plebeian after all. The scholars consulted by the Queen and a distinguished financier consulted by his own daughter struck the same chord. They knew that the end would come, but please not today.

Let's look at the theoretical reasons for ignoring the signs of the crisis.

FROM HAYEK TO FRIEDMAN: THE MONT PELERIN SOCIETY

In August 1938, the Colloque Walter Lippmann in Paris convened twenty-six academics, journalists, and businessmen. The previous year the well-known polemicist Walter Lippmann had published a successful book, *Inquiry into the Principles of the Good Society*, presented as "a defense of classical liberalism and gradual reform against totalitarian movements," and its French translation served as pretext for the gathering. The participants included, besides Lippmann himself and the organizer, Louis Rougier, well-known European and US conservatives and liberals, such as Raymond Aron, Hayek, Ludwig von Mises, Michael Polanyi, Wilhelm Ropke, and Jacques Rueff.

Lippmann was a famous journalist, and his column was syndicated in some of the most influential US newspapers. He was an unlikely supporter of liberalism: he maintained a close friendship with Keynes, before and after the publication of the book. He was in this case influenced by reading Hayek, the leading rival of Keynes in the London–Cambridge controversies on economics, philosophy, and politics. Lippmann, writing for a popular audience, scorned nineteenth-century *laissez-faire*, or classical economic liberalism, and developed the argument under the influence of the views of Hayek, who enthusiastically endorsed the book, on the post-1917 world.[13]

Rougier, the convener, was a cryptic character. An enthusiast of Lippmann's argument, he became enmeshed in the wreckage of the Second World War. A supporter of the collaborationist Vichy regime, Rougier was sent as a representative of Pétain to London for secret negotiations with Churchill. (Although the British later denied it, the evidence is sound.) After the War Rougier was dismissed from his university post and moved to the US and Canada. Upon his return he developed a close relationship to right-wing forces in France. Rougier was barred from entering the Mont Pelerin Society until the late 1950s.[14]

As the book was published and was highly successful, Hayek, Ropke (the German representative of the Ordoliberals, whose influence on the definition of the future European Union is discussed in other chapters), and Lippmann corresponded and a process of collaboration was defined, leading to the neoliberal expedition to Paris. This seminar was the first of many, as the participants accepted the move to create a new society to promote their views.[15] After the end of the War, this movement led to a new conference, at the invitation of Hayek, which met in April 1947 at a hotel at Mont Pèlerin, in Switzerland.

[13] The US philosopher John Dewey criticized the book as "encouragement and practical support to reactionaries" Burgin (2012), pp. 58, 61.

[14] Burgin (2012), p. 77.

[15] Ibid., p. 85. Yet, after the Colloquium, Lippmann preferred not to engage directly any more in the activities of the group.

Hayek was by then the prime mover of what became the Mont Pelerin Society (the alternative name "Acton-Tocqueville Society" was rejected, as both were European and religiously inclined personalities, a choice that could alienate possible participants). Established in London since 1931, Hayek was by then 48 years old and a well-known ideologue of the European neoliberals. A couple of years earlier, his 1944 book *The Road to Serfdom* had been summarized in a popular edition by *Reader's Digest* in the US, establishing his public image. It was a tremendous success, as large firms ordered in some cases thousands of copies of the pamphlet to distribute among their workers, but this had a price: the summary contributed to creating a reputation for Hayek as a "reactionary agitator," which he would fully deserve through his career, as noted in this chapter, but at that time it dismayed him, as he then favored some state intervention, for instance limiting working hours, and toyed with the idea of "planning for competition," instead of a simple Cold War narrative.[16] Hayek presided over the conference as an aristocrat leading his guests to a fancy party. He consequently was nominated President of the Society.

In the 1940s, the Society was a narrow movement and yet very contradictory. It represented just a small group of scholars. Most of them were in the initial phase of their careers and some of the elders were not convinced. Some were enthusiastic: for Friedman, then 35 years old, this was the first trip abroad. In contrast, Karl Popper, whom Friedman met for the first time and felt to be a "kindred spirit," was already an influential philosopher, but he did not feel at home, fearing the narrowness of the cult.[17] Others, including Polanyi, Allais, Jouvenel, and Aron, abandoned ship as soon as the conference ended.[18]

As a consequence, the Society was "far less doctrinaire than the conventional narrative would indicate,"[19] and it was divided among different social and philosophical views: it rejected "conservatism," associated with the status quo, but no alternative was clearly addressed; it glorified capitalism but not its cultural traits; it praised individualism but suspected democracy.

At the time of its foundation, the Society represented ideas and prophets that were quite marginal. Only the LSE with Robbins, some scholars at the University of Chicago, and the Geneva Institute for International Studies could count as bastions for the doctrine. But even Chicago was not exactly Hayekian: in the wake of the Great Depression, as the neoliberals quite unpopularly argued for "quietism," the Chicago professors, Frank Knight, Jacob Viner, and Henry Simons took a more moderate position and tried to dissociate from the radical views since, as Henry Simons put it, they are "often fanatically extreme" (he even defended nationalization against monopolies); and Oskar Lange, a Marxist, and Paul Douglas, a social democrat, were also there. Indeed, "the Chicago economists in this period did not perceive themselves to be part of a coherent group that agreed on any particular agenda."[20]

[16] Burgin (2012), pp. 88–9.

[17] Popper wrote to Hayek criticizing the danger of a ideologically closed organization, which would not match his own views of open science, discussion, and eventual refutation. Mises argued the other way round, that the Society's admission policy was not rigid enough, ibid., p. 95.

[18] Ibid., pp. 107, 116. [19] Ibid., p. 9.

[20] Viner repeatedly opposed Hayek's suggestion to create movements and institutions for the defense of the free market ideas, ibid., pp. 15, 33, 43, 54.

It would not have helped to have some of the founders of the Society engaged in strict Cold War parlance: Lionel Robbins, for instance, argued that the western societies should treat the Russians as "though they are not human beings."[21] The fact is that the 1950s were a difficult and unpromising period for the Society. Its divisions were aggravated by internal conflicts on management and financial issues. On its tenth anniversary, Hayek suggested winding up the Society. Although outright disbandment was not considered, by early 1960 Friedman and the other Chicagoans, such as Stigler and Machlup, threatened to resign if the director was not dismissed. Ludwig Erhard, then vice chancellor of Federal Republic of Germany, who commanded special respect within the Society, arbitrated the conflict.[22] The resolution gave more power to the Friedman faction and by the end of the 1960s Friedman had consolidated power within the Society. A page had turned.

The Mont Pelerin Society remained a small group.[23] It was not a major player in academic life. Only in rare cases did it obtain some social influence (with the exception of the German Ordoliberals, in no other country did the MPS count in political terms). Friedman himself had been the expression of that isolation but he was then on the verge of a political turn. Friedman became the main advisor for the Goldwater campaign in 1964. Lyndon Johnson delivered a crushing defeat, although later events proved that some roots of new liberal ideas had implanted in Republican quarters.

Capitalism and Freedom had been published a couple of years before and it was a propaganda hit. The book became a manifesto for reborn neoliberal ideas, and it presented them in the crude form of a radical statement: at the time Friedman had abandoned his previous sympathy for the programs of aid to the poor, and battled for the elimination of agricultural price supports, the minimum wage, the system of military draft, national parks, public housing, and even public social security or other forms of public regulation. Friedman advocated for open borders to all immigrants, although they would get no social welfare, and he was strongly opposed to the civil rights legislation.[24] It was a reactionary point of view, not only a conservative notion, but it was combined with total confidence in markets (at that time this was not shared by Hayek), and the power of attraction of his ideas and preaching emerged from that marriage.

Combating socialism and diffusing monetarism and neoliberalism became the purpose of Friedman's life, whose success is discussed in other sections of the book, in which we follow the Friedmanites in their endeavors in Latin American, the Ordoliberals in Europe, and neoliberal ideas in central banks everywhere.

[21] Ibid., p. 105. One possible interpretation is that the Cold War context provided cement to the Society and the political agenda saved it from its divisions. Furthermore, at the time of its foundation the Society was quite isolated in academia, not to mention that its members were not in the best of moods: Frank Knight was depressed; Robbins proclaimed that lay understanding of economics was doomed. Robbins even moved to a semi-Keynesian position, as is obvious from some of his seminars during the same year of 1947, claiming that his argument with Keynes had been "the greatest mistake of my professional career"; and Ropke conceded that the case for liberalism and capitalism was condemned. Confidence did not abound.

[22] Burgin (2012), pp. 124, 134.

[23] By 1947 it had thirty-nine members, by 1961 it was up to 258, ibid., p. 127.

[24] Ibid., pp. 182, 202.

Friedman himself would sometimes indulge in doubt but never abandon his crusade: "After World War II, opinion was socialist while practice was free market; currently, opinion is free market while practice is heavily socialist. We have largely won the battle of ideas (though no such battle is ever won permanently); we have succeeded in stalling the progress of socialism, but we have not succeeded in reversing its course. We are still far from bringing practice into conformity with opinion."[25] Still far, but, with a Nobel Prize, close to Reagan and Bush, with friends in governments and institutions, Friedman could claim to have created an "era" under his own name.

LIBERALIZERS...

Milton Friedman (1912–2006), the economist who so proudly explained the virtue of greed was for the *New York Times* the "most consequential public intellectual of the twentieth century"[26] and that century's final decades could be reasonably declared the *Age of Friedman*.[27]

The father of the modern Chicago School, Friedman is a curious exception in the history of US economic orthodoxy. Despite the hagiography affixed to both him and Hayek,[28] the foundational figures of neoliberalism, Friedman was far more successful in training cohorts of disciples and in shaping the intellectual mood of his time. He dedicated his life to that undertaking. As an outsider to the dominant scientific approaches of the 1960s and 1970s, he rejected Keynesianism and redistribution of wealth, as well as the gloominess of the later mathematical formulation of models. He thought differently, and his economics was historical, empirical, and mostly ideological: he led a crusade.

Friedman's pithy observations are revered by his followers, as when he criticized the notion of "social responsibility of the firms" as the "dumbest idea." Any business executives who pursued a goal other than making money were, according to Friedman, "unwitting puppets of the intellectual forces that have been undermining the basis of a free society these past decades." He savaged "the doctrine of 'social responsibility' " for its "acceptance of the socialist view that political mechanisms, not market mechanisms, are the appropriate way to determine the allocation of scarce resources to alternative uses."[29]

In this matter as well as in others, Friedman's task was public indoctrination. Beginning in 1966 he published a successful column in the *Wall Street Journal* and in 1980 aired a ten-part TV series, "Free to Choose" on the public television network. Perhaps because of their shared interest in Latin American economic policy, Citibank recruited Friedman for a time as an expert.[30] (More on Friedman's Latin American adventures in Chapter 7.) He initiated the fight for liberalization, for free markets ruling the world, greed moving people to the satisfaction of their inner nature.

[25] *Wall Street Journal*, December 9, 2004. [26] Denning (2013). [27] Shleifer (2009).

[28] Friedrich Hayek (1899–1992), was born in Vienna and taught at the London School of Economics and then Chicago. He was awarded the Nobel Prize in economics in 1974 and distinguished himself as an opponent of Keynes.

[29] M. Friedman (1970). [30] Dezalay and Garth (2002), p. 89.

The political turn of the 1980s proved that the time was ripe for him. Friedman was the right man at the right time and, when Thatcher, Reagan, and Deng Xiaoping came to power, his intellectual movement was moving, the faculty was onboard, and his students ascended to influential decision making posts. The dogma was established and it was named "consensus."

... AND THEIR CLUBS

The victory of the views of Milton Friedman surprised those who observed his long academic marginalization prior to the 1970s. Yet as we discussed earlier, the ascendancy was prepared by a powerful ideological machine, which organized the cavalry of the persistent neoclassical attack against the dominant Keynesian views: the Mont Pelerin Society.

The Society matched together Chicago neoclassicals, Hayekian Austrians, and German ordoliberals,[31] who, in spite of their differences, shared a vision on how to transform economics and politics. From Germany, it attracted Walter Eucken, Wilhelm Ropke, and Ludwig Erhard; from France, Maurice Allais, Jacques Rueff, and Bertrand de Jouvenel; from the US, Friedman, Gottfried Haberler, George Stigler, and Frank Knight; from Austria, Ludwig von Mises and Fritz Machlup besides Hayek and Popper; from Britain, Lionel Robbins. They were the core of what came to be known, through their conjoint effort, as neoliberal economics and philosophy.

As the dominant characters of this movement are well known, we will not describe their endeavors. Only some notes are in order on the German Ordoliberals, who were highly successful, in their own way. Just after the Mont Pelerin meeting, they created the journal *Ordo*, in 1948, from which they got the name Ordoliberalism. Eucken and Franz Bohm, two Freiburg economists, pursued the work of Ropke and his contempt for old-time liberalism, identified as the weakness having led to the collapsing Weimar Republic. Instead, they opted for a strong state imposing organized rules on the market but pursuing an agenda of economic liberalization, germane to monetarism. Ordoliberalism, embedded in the most powerful institutions of Germany—Ludwig Erhard was a member, and the influence of the current on the Bundesbank was dominant—determined the constitutive treaties of the European Union and the Eurozone and has ever since been the most influential brand of neoliberalism in Europe.[32]

In Europe, the US, and elsewhere, the Society guided a strategic action for the creation of a web of educational institutions, influencing universities and

[31] Mirowski (2013), p. 42, provides the most detailed account of the emergence of the Mont Pelerin Society as an ideological empire in modern times.

[32] Mirowski (2013), pp. 43, 53; Other researchers investigated another club, the Group of Thirty, which emerged in the 1980s and 1990s. It is a think tank and advocacy group, including always thirty members, with a varied composition (at some point, it included Paul Volcker, Kenneth Rogoff, Raghuram Rajan, Jacques de la Rosière, who led the IMF, Jean Claude Trichet and Mario Draghi, ECB, Pedro Aspe and Ernesto Zedillo from Mexico, Domingos Cavallo from Argentina, and the three will be protagonists of another chapter, Mark Carney, now at the Bank of England, Martin Feldstein, NBER, Stanley Fischer, IMF, Timothy Geithner, but also Paul Krugman and Lawrence Summers). This G30 was responsible for a famous 1993 report recommending the protection of over-the-counter derivatives, Tsingou (2015).

think tanks promoting ideas for governance. Some of these influential foundations for education are the Volcker Fund, Relm Foundation, Lilly Endowment, Olin Foundation, Scaife Foundation, Bradley Foundation, and the Foundation for Economic Education. Bolstered by the new foundations, the promoters of the Mont Pelerin Society dominated economics at the London School of Economics, at Geneva's Institut Universitaire des Hautes Etudes Internationales, at St Andrews in Scotland, at Freiburg University in Germany, at George Mason University (where they developed the "Virginia School" of public-choice economics), and, above all, at the University of Chicago (where they held sway in the law school as well).

Several Nobel Prize winners in economics are part of this story of the Mont Pelerin Society: Gary Becker, Ronald Coase, James Buchanan, Vernon Smith, Douglass North, besides Friedman, Stigler, and Hayek, a total of eight.[33]

A number of think tanks completed this map: Institute for Economic Affairs in Britain, American Enterprise Institute, Heritage Foundation, Hoover Institution at Stanford in the United States, Schweizerisches Institut für Auslandforschung in Switzerland, and recently the Fraser Institute in Canada, Center for Dissemination of Economic Information in Venezuela, Free Market Center in Belgrade, Liberty Institute in Romania, and Unirule in Beijing. The Koch Foundation in the US, led by the Koch brothers whom we met in the previous chapter, are also part of the network, which also involves the Mercatus Center, the Heritage Foundation and the Manhattan Institute in the US, the Center for a New Europe in Belgium, and the Stiftung Marktwirtschaft in Germany.[34]

In Chapter 7, we will look at the indoctrination in action and register how these institutions created a network of economists, members of government, and central bankers that moved the world. We will then meet Arnold Harberger, a Chicago veteran and member of the Mont Pelerin Society, who excelled in this recruiting of future members of government and policymakers.

RADICAL MONEY FOR A RADICAL RIGHT WING

James Buchanan, like Friedman a recipient of the Nobel Prize in Economics (1986), was born in the US south and began his conservative activity at the University of Virginia at the height of the US civil rights movement. (Buchanan shares the name but otherwise bears no relation to the pro-Slavery President who preceded Lincoln and the US Civil War.) Like Friedman, Buchanan was drawn to the Presidential campaign of Republican Barry Goldwater in 1964. Despite Goldwater's overwhelming defeat by Lyndon Johnson, the campaign initiated much of the modern right, launched the public persona of Friedman, and provided some

[33] The Society also includes other personalities, including publicists, such as Niall Ferguson. In recent times, it has been involved in the management of the aftermath of the economic crisis, and curiously, at a New York conference of the Society in March 2009, the keynote address by Deepak Lal raised the revealing but annoying question: why was there a crisis when so many Mont Pelerin Society members rule the world? Mirowski (2013), 6–7. This is the Shakespearean tragedy of real power.

[34] Ibid., p. 44.

recognition for Buchanan as well. Buchanan held truly reactionary perspectives as far as civil rights were concerned and chose to pursue aggressive action against late 1960s policies advancing civil rights and the welfare state.

Closely aligned with his radical liberal economic advisers, Goldwater had argued for extreme economic positions: abolish social security, reject state intervention for civil rights and against discrimination, privatize everything public, and promote the market as the social organizer. Buchanan pursued this agenda from the university, creating think tanks and propaganda in order to organize systematic campaigns around key issues to advance an explicitly political agenda.

Buchanan completed his doctorate at Chicago with Frank Knight, a co-founder if skeptic of the Mont Pelerin Society. Buchanan also inherited a family tradition of populism from his grandfather, an activist in the sometimes radical, sometimes racist and xenophobic Populist Party.

Buchanan's hostility towards the East Coast elites, anti-government sentiment, and subscription to the principle of racial discrimination led him to concentrate his initial academic efforts in advocacy for privatized education. In particular, Buchanan recommended public funding of private schools through a system of vouchers as an alternative to increasingly integrated public schools.

Buchanan meanwhile developed his public choice approach to political economy, which identifies the actions of government officials as fundamentally self-serving—in the narrowest sense of pursuing personal self-interest in their public decisions. Legislators seek re-election; regulators seek power, possibly even bribes, or revolving-door opportunities from the regulated. The mode of analysis, tautologically true because all actions by every actor are understood as optimal for that actor, fit well with the anti-government sentiment of the Reagan movement as it approached and then assumed power.

The support of the Koch brothers, who orbited around similar positions in the Republican Party, proved to be decisive for his career and lavishly funded several research centers created by Buchanan. The Kochs preferred the Virginia professor to Friedman, whom they considered a "sell out to the system"[35] because his liberalization schemes were intended to improve government function. The Koch brothers and Buchanan represented a purer right-wing libertarian view, which admits the need for government only to provide minimalist security and never to rule social or economic activity. Buchanan, as a spokesman of this movement, declared his project "to create, support, and activate an effective counter-intelligentsia" to transform "the way people think about government."[36]

Buchanan was part of the Mont Pelerin Society and, like Friedman, also visited Chile under Pinochet in 1980 to support the authoritarian free-market experiment, with special interest in the radical experiment of complete privatization of the social security system. His five conferences with officers of the dictatorship indicate his enchantment with the Pinochet politics. Buchanan himself organized, the following year, the world meeting of the Society at the Chilean village of Viña del Mar. The radical neoliberals felt at home.[37]

[35] MacLean (2017), pp. 181–2. [36] MacLean (2017), p. 160.

[37] In spite of Buchanan's crucial role, his disciples ultimately abandoned Buchanan. In a strange turn of history, it was Wendy Gramm, wife of Senator Phil Gramm—both appear in Chapter 6—a

ETERNAL JOY

Robert Lucas, mentored by Friedman and later a distinguished professor and one of the many Nobel Prize winners at the University of Chicago,[38] was sure that the Great Moderation had become the permanent status of properly managed advanced economies. Early in the twenty-first century, as part of his Presidential address to the American Economics Association, Lucas argued: "My thesis in this lecture is that macroeconomics in this original sense has succeeded: its central problem of depression prevention has been solved, for all practical purposes, and has in fact been solved for many decades,"[39] or, the perennial tribulation of the economic cycles is over as liberalization made the world flat.

Some decades before, in the early 1970s, the consensus was rather the opposite. Macroeconomic regulation was enforced by a Democratic Congress and accepted by Nixon, who proclaimed "we are all Keynesians now."[40] After this juncture the different theories parted ways and Friedman mounted his rebuttal of traditional remedies to recessions, arguing instead that deregulation was the key issue. The "social responsibility" of managers and entrepreneurs is to earn their keep, to liberate the market, and to praise free competition, not to care for employment or wellbeing. Lucas followed Friedman, confidently announcing that the "central problem of depression prevention has been solved ... for many decades."

In his self-congratulatory speeches, Lucas was not otherwise certain that the theory would be adequate in all its domains, and in the main he feared that central banks might fail to foresee major perturbations,[41] but nevertheless he argued that the overall picture could not be missed: the problem has been solved for many decades.

Only four years later, the veteran economist was shocked by the evidence that inadequate (de)regulation had fueled a major systemic failure. "I'm changing my views on bank regulation every week," Lucas confessed. "It was an area I saw as under control. Now I don't believe that," he added.[42] Lucas's surprise is no surprise. Lucas's models were highly stylized and without institutional detail and they modeled a virtual capitalism without real capitalists. Nothing could go really wrong in these models and nothing ever did, but reality is another thing.

In spite of his awakening, Lucas rapidly regressed to his previous confidence on the virtues of deregulation. Changing his views "every week" on the failure of

board member of Buchanan's center at George Mason University, who provoked his departure from his eponymous center. Gramm wrote a pamphlet on the purpose of the center that he felt to be at odds with his own conception and much too partisan.

[38] The Faculty of Economics of Chicago have received roughly one third of the Nobel Memorial Prizes in Economics awarded by the Swedish central bank since 1969.

[39] Lucas (2003b). [40] D. Harvey (2005), pp. 12–13.

[41] Lucas added shortly thereafter, "There's a residue of things they [the central banks' DSGE models] don't let us think about. They don't let us think about the US experience in the 1930s or about financial crises and their real consequences in Asia and Latin America; they don't let us think very well about Japan in the 1990s," Lucas (2004). This is a blunt confession: whenever something goes wrong, the model is irrelevant. It does not allow us to think about the problem whenever the problem arises.

[42] Lippert (2008).

regulation when the market is in turmoil is one thing, to challenge the virtues of the market itself is another thing.[43]

This is why, in 2013, Lucas could praise the essential changes in regulation, although lip servicing the advantages of the previous Glass-Steagall system. In his "Requiem for Glass Steagall" Lucas ascertained that "a system that differentiates between investment banks and commercial, deposit-taking banks is no longer possible. The 1999 repeal of the Glass-Steagall-Acts suggests that this belief is widely shared." It was the rigidity of the rules that "scattered demand deposits out into the world of 'shadow banking' and largely ended the constraints imposed by Glass-Steagall. The Act's actual repeal in 1999 was just a formality."[44] Everything came to be what it should be.

Even macroeconomists who did not share Lucas's optimistic views on the Great Moderation had limited their models to a world without crisis. In his vivid indictment of the state of "modern macro," Nobel Prize winner Robert Solow rejected the Chicagoan assumption of rational behavior of the agents and markets given that, moreover, his use of stylized facts was instrumental in removing his model from the messy world and from typical Walrasian assumptions. He "deliberately avoided recourse to the optimizing representative agent and instead used as building blocks only aggregative relationships that are in principle observable." Yet Solow acknowledged that his own alternative theory "restricted the applicability of the model to tranquil trajectories without stormy intervals" and he warned the reader of "the possibility of aggregative imbalances that would not fit into the model."[45]

Solow distances himself from Lucas's lineage. "I feel guilty about some things, but not about 'modern macro,'" he remarks.[46] But even rejecting assumptions about the wisdom of omniscient agents, his theory could not explain the "stormy intervals" such as the long immoderation after 2008.

FAMA AND THE NEW CRUSADE FROM CHICAGO

Lucas and Solow are giants of modern economics, with strong disagreements. In both cases, they devoted their energy to theory and abstract models of

[43] This was only a minor turn in Lucas's views through life. He was enamored with Marxism in his first steps in science: "I read [Karl Marx's *Communist Manifesto*] as an undergraduate student and I liked [his] sense that economic theory could give us a unified way about thinking about all known societies. I thought that ambition was a noble one, and an accurate one, and I bought into it. Economics is an extremely powerful way of looking at the forces that shape any society. In that sense, all of us economists are Marxists," I. P. King (2008). Then Lucas was impressed by the revelation of Friedman, his mentor at Chicago. "For many of us, the shock wave of Friedman's libertarian-conservative ideas forced a rethinking of our whole social philosophy," he insisted in his Nobel autobiography, Lucas (1995). Then he was a "kind of Austrian" to rapidly abandon such reference, after reading a book on the subject, Snowdon and Vane (1998), p. 121; Jenkins (2011), In politics, he voted mostly Republican, even if disgusted with the Keynesian leanings of Reagan, with the exception of a 2008 vote for Obama under the influence of his sister.

[44] Lucas (2013), pp. 43, 46; Posner (2010). Other academics questioned this view. Federal judge and legal scholar, Richard Posner, a lecturer at Chicago noted for the integration of law and economics, published a book asking for a new Glass-Steagall in order to address the "crisis of capitalist democracy."

[45] Solow (2008). [46] Ibid.

macroeconomics. At least equally influential in financial economics is Eugene Fama, who shared the 2013 Nobel Prize with Robert Shiller of Yale (and Lars Peter Hansen, from Chicago, another Friedmanite). Fama, with Fisher Black, Robert Merton, Myron Scholes, William Sharpe, Merton Miller, and Harry Markowitz, formed a powerful intellectual movement for establishing a brave new world for finance. Their success was immense, and Fama may be singled out as the foremost builder of that change: the University of Chicago proudly presents him as the "father of modern finance."

The Nobel Committee of the Central Bank of Sweden presented this feat in the following terms: "For many of us, the rise and fall of stock prices symbolizes economic development. In the 1960s, Eugene Fama demonstrated that stock price movements are impossible to predict in the short-term and that new information affects prices almost immediately, which means that the market is efficient."[47] Efficiency is all that matters, and all standard financial movements are efficient.

An outspoken prophet of the efficient-markets hypothesis, with the essential corollary that financial markets function best if undisturbed by regulators, Fama was interviewed for the *New Yorker* by John Cassidy after getting his 2013 Nobel—more than five years into the Great Recession. Cassidy asked Fama to assess how the efficient-markets hypothesis had held up during and after the crash. Fama responded: "I think it did quite well in this episode. Prices started to decline in advance of when people recognized that it was a recession and then continued to decline. There was nothing unusual about that. That was exactly what you would expect if markets were efficient." Cassidy probed further, noting that the credit bubble in the mortgage market could not be efficient. Fama replied: "I don't even know what that means. People who get credit have to get it from somewhere. Does a credit bubble mean that people save too much during that period? I don't know what a credit bubble means. I don't even know what a bubble means. These words have become popular. I don't think they have any meaning."[48] This turns out to be a confession of ignorance as the natural state of science: the events have no meaning if they do not conform with theory. Gary Becker, another Chicago man and another Nobel Prize winner—and another Mont Pelerin Society member, for that matter—was more prudent: "There are a lot of things that people got wrong, and I got wrong, and Chicago got wrong," since he figured that his colleagues did not understand derivatives.[49]

Dimon's daughter would be appalled: after all, the crash arrived on schedule because of the housing bubble. But Fama, the leading financial economist of the era, insists that bubble has no meaning: "I don't even know what that means." And the Nobel Prize winner insisted: "We don't know what causes recessions. I'm not a macroeconomist so I don't feel bad about that! We've never known. Debates go on to this day about what caused the Great Depression. Economics is not very good at explaining swings in economic activity...If I could have predicted the crisis, I would have. I didn't see it. I'd love to know more what causes business cycles." Cassidy persisted: "Are the markets efficient?" Fama replied "Yes. And if it isn't, then it's going to be impossible to tell."[50]

[47] Sveriges Riksbank (2013). [48] Cassidy (2010).
[49] Frank (2012), 36, quoted by John Cassidy, "After the Blow Up," *New Yorker*, January 11.
[50] Cassidy (2010).

How Fama came to this conclusion is a strange, under-appreciated story. In fact, at the beginning of his career, Fama stood for the opposite view. His first paper, published in early 1963 in the *Journal of Business* summarized his doctoral dissertation and discussed the work of a Polish-born and later Franco-American mathematician, Benoit Mandelbrot, who had just spent some time at Chicago, Fama's home faculty. The paper developed Mandelbrot's work on the identification of the dominant features of speculative markets, and he was not shy about the implications of his theories. Fama stated: "We shall see later that if Mandelbrot's hypothesis is up-held, it will radically revise our thinking concerning both the nature of speculative markets and the proper statistical tools to be used when dealing with speculative prices." He continued, "Mandelbrot feels that these departures from normality are sufficient to warrant a radically new approach to the theory of random walks in speculative prices."[51] Radical, indeed.

Fama stressed the importance of Mandelbrot's challenge: "the hypothesis implies that there are a larger number of abrupt changes in the economic variables that determine equilibrium prices in speculative markets than would be the case under a Gaussian hypothesis." This confirmed Fama's own research, because "[t]he conclusion of the dissertation is that for the important case of stock prices the stable Paretian hypothesis is more consistent with the data than the Gaussian hypothesis."[52]

Fama's argument is radical because it implies what statisticians call "fat tails" in financial returns. While large, wild movements in price are vanishingly rare in the tame Gaussian random walk widely assumed in the mainstream literature, they are shockingly frequent in Mandelbrot's alternative.[53] Young Fama would have known well "what a bubble means," unlike his own later self. The wild ride of Mandelbrot and the younger Fama might have lighted the way to a wiser approach to the dynamics—and regulation—of commodities and financial markets.

But Fama soon forgot his wild youth. Shortly after the heterodox paper, Fama published his iconic January 1965 piece in the *Journal of Business*, "The Behavior of Stock Market Prices," adopting a different point of view and building the efficient-market hypothesis based on the notion of the stock market following a random walk.

This theory was developed throughout his career. In 1970, Fama refined the notion, distinguishing three degrees of potential market efficiency: the weak form (the past does not predict the future); the semi-strong form (prices adjust rapidly to available information); and the strong form (market prices are always right, and no one has relevant information to predict future prices). Fama's empirical studies provided evidence for the semi-strong and strong forms. All of the forms imply that deregulation optimizes outcomes: securities and their derivatives should be traded with minimal interference or oversight so that new information can be integrated into prices without delay.

[51] Eugene F Fama (1963), p. 420. [52] Ibid., p. 429.

[53] Taleb (2007), Nassim Nicholas Taleb has thoroughly pursued this Black Swan hypothesis, drawing heavily from Mandelbrot, arguing that an important and unpredicted event may change the game.

In this context, Fama brings to finance the Chicago School doctrine of Milton Friedman, who influenced his work: liberate the market, suspect the government.[54] Indeed, the government matters for the anti-government proselytizers. Its mathematical elegance and straightforward implications have made Fama's work highly esteemed in the economics profession, following Bachelier (the mathematical expectation of the speculator is zero) and Samuelson (describing the returns of the speculative market as being generated by a random walk). But it has another implication with greater long-term importance: the efficient-markets hypothesis guided political choices and inspired the decades-long effort to change the laws, practices, and structure governing financial markets.

As might be feared, its adherents have taken the doctrine to extreme positions. *Bloomberg News* reports that John Cochrane, another Chicago professor (and Fama's son-in-law), led the late September 2008 revolt against Secretary of Treasury Paulson's initial attempt to buy securitized mortgages as the subprime crisis crested. Many Chicago faculty signed Cochrane's petition, and Cochrane congratulated the US House of Representatives for rejecting Paulson's plan. (A second, larger plan was approved days later, to the regret of the petitioners.)

Echoing Mellon's infamous "Liquidate labor, liquidate stocks, liquidate farmers, liquidate real estate...,"[55] Cochrane is quoted to have said, "We should have a recession. People who spend their lives pounding nails in Nevada need something else to do."[56] Recession, which is supposed to never happen, is nevertheless hailed as the purgative for the maladjustments of society. By early 2010, Cochrane added in the same spirit, "the economy can recover very quickly from a credit crunch if left on its own."[57]

Cochrane echoed the inspiration of Fama, who dared that "[t]he experiment we never ran is, suppose the government stepped aside and let these institutions fail? How long would it have taken to unscramble everything and figure everything out? My guess is we are talking a week or two."[58] Full deregulation, a purgative crisis, and one week or two would put things right.[59]

Furthermore, as Fama concluded in a 1992 revisionist paper, the historical patterns of stock returns prove mysterious since, if the dividend yields are low, they tend to misbehave for the next years, an impossibility if adjustment were complete and instantaneous.[60] Fama felt nevertheless comfortable to trust the market and

[54] Young, Henriksen, and Seabrooke (2016). Kevin Young and his co-authors demonstrate an irony in this suspicion of government among the great liberalizers, Friedman, Stigler, Sargent, Lucas, Wallace, Kydland, Prescott, Plosser, Long, and other Mont Pelerin people. Their first-generation disciples rose disproportionately to the top ranks of Economics, but the next generation, the "grandsons," failed to achieve top academic status. Young et al. note that the first generation was "markedly close to power" and "their ascendance had support from government agencies."

[55] See for instance Paul Krugman's column on the Mellon doctrine, Krugman (2011b).

[56] Fendrich (2009), Quoted by John Lippert in *Bloomberg*; Lippert (2008); although semi-repudiated by, Cochrane (2011), himself.

[57] J. Brown (2010). [58] Cassidy (2010).

[59] US Department of the Treasury (2014). In 2010, Ramin Toloui, then working at PIMCO, proved that the global output of the economy is a better guide to the value of government bonds than the sophisticated computations of their market value based on these theories. In fact, he showed that the government bond indices weighted by GDP outperform those weighted by value for the previous twenty years and with less volatility. By 2014 Toloui was nominated US Treasury's Assistant Secretary for International Finance, thus representing the Treasury in international monetary negotiations.

[60] Eugene F. Fame and French (1992); Dang, Gorton, and Holmstrom (2009). A refinement of Fama's theory went a step further, asking "how can the mispricing of tail risk exist in a world with fully rational

his own view of its perfection, since he joined in the meantime a firm managing index funds, the Dimensional Funds Advisors.[61]

The builder of this edifice, Fama was subject to three bodies of critique, two within the discipline and one among practitioners. The first argued that the slightest approximation to reality would doom the perfect model of efficiency in financial markets. In a 1990 article, Lawrence Summers with other distinguished scholars demonstrated that modest noise in market values could attract trend-chasing speculators whose trades create a significant and long-lived divergence between speculative prices and the ideal price implied by "fundamentals"—a divergence precluded by the religion of efficient markets.[62] Fischer Black, another of the "fathers of modern finance," had given intuition for the same result a couple of years earlier.[63]

The second wave of criticism came from professional investors and financiers. Charlie Munger, a partner of Warren Buffett in Berkshire Hathaway, argued in 2003: "Berkshire's whole record has been achieved without paying one ounce of attention to the efficient market theory in its hard form," and added that the ideas of efficient market doctrine in corporate finance "became even sillier than they were in the economics."[64]

Finally, Robert Shiller, who was awarded the Nobel Prize and shared the Oslo ceremony with Fama, was as outspoken and challenged the contradiction between Fama's discourse of the model and his perception of reality. Shiller's empirically oriented investigations demonstrated imperfections and inefficiency of the market. Furthermore, he considered that this was at odds with Chicago's point of view on the perfection of deregulation: "It must affect your thinking somehow that they (the Chicago school) really believe in markets. I think that maybe [Fama] has a cognitive dissonance. His research shows that markets are not efficient. So what do you do if you are living in the University of Chicago? It's like being a Catholic priest and then discovering that God doesn't exist or something, you can't deal with that, you've got to somehow rationalize it."[65]

The backstage of the Nobel gala dinner must have been as entertaining as that of the joint Nobel Prize to Hayek and Gunnar Myrdal in 1974, with award recipients who opposed each other in every economic concept.

DEREGULATION AND THE PINTO CASE

Liberalization, as described through this chapter, was not a product of some brilliant or devious minds, not less a conspiracy. It was the result of a precise social context and conflict, in which the forces of capital accumulation contributed

actors?" and providing the answer: namely, that debt contracts are optimal precisely because they generate opacity. The rationale is that opacity minimizes the incentives to get new information and that, in the dark, everybody tends to have the same perception of the market. The likelihood of bad shocks, however, increases the incentive of some speculators to collect information and can exacerbate adverse selection. The incorporation of this information in market prices amplifies negative effects. So, free markets do not necessarily mean transparency; on the contrary, free markets may mean equally distributed opacity and ignorance.

[61] Cassidy (2009), p. 91. [62] DeLong et al. (1990). [63] Black (1986).
[64] T. G. Ash (2016); Munger (2003). [65] Allen (2013).

to change the institutions, the legislation, the forms of power, and the popular perceptions. In banking and industry, protection of consumers, or the access to public goods, this liberalization process fought successive battles, winning some and losing others.

In any case, deregulation was a trench in that war. One telling example is that of Ford's Pinto, a car that was sold from 1971 to 1980. As it became known afterwards, the company detected defective gas tanks in the car. Its own tests identified danger of rupture in the gas tank, and yet the firm managed to delay for eight years the regulation on safety that would imply a change in its production process.

The rationale for that resistance was cost-benefit analysis: according to the computations of Ford, a safe gas tank would every year have prevented some 180 people from burning to death, another 180 people from experiencing serious injury, and 2,100 cars from bursting into flames. The computation was even more precise: pricing the value of death at 200,000 dollars, and extending other computations to the other losses, the total social value of the accidents would be US $49.5 million, whereas the cost of repairing and changing the production process would approximate US $137 million, or 11 dollars per car for 11 million cars and 1.5 million trucks. For this reason, Ford resisted regulation and prevented it for eight years. Finally it was obvious that the computation was not only socially dangerous but also wrong as far as costs were concerned: the price of fixing the problem was one dollar per tank.[66]

ENTER TRUMP

The surprising victory of Donald Trump was first taken as a threat by the financial markets and then as a relief: after all, the dream of deregulation is again on the table. Personal comparisons between Trump and Reagan, both being radical Republicans but outsiders, emerged as their political agendas were also paired, as both promised tax cuts and new approaches to the economic problems, believing in Friedmanite solutions. The liberalizers are back, the leaders of finance understood as a parade of Wall Street moguls was organized in the Trump Tower in order to pick the Treasury Secretary.

The final choice, after not much deliberation, was Steven Mnuchin, an ex-Goldman Sachs turned banker on his own and his friends' money as well as a Hollywood producer (who also played a minor role in Warren Beatty's 2016 prophetically titled "Rules Don't Apply" and he was the executive producer of "Wonder Woman"). As part of a government of radical billionaires, Mnuchin was saluted as a guarantee for further waves of liberalization, beginning with new tax cuts for the wealthy and for business. In the same vein, the rage against Obamacare, a timid program for health care that did not match, and by far, the proposals President Nixon had once presented and which were rejected by a Democratic Congress for being too pro-capital, emphasized the social credentials of Trump's White House.

[66] See, for instance, Clawson, Neustadtl, and Weller (1998), p. 191f, describing the computations of Ford in order to avoid repairing the gas tank.

In spite of this surprising victory and the enthusiasm it generated among the eventual beneficiaries of such fiscal and financial generosity, Trump's agenda may not be followed to the line. The impact of the proposed tax cuts could amount to 4 percent of GDP (the four-year impact of Reagan's tax cut was 3 percent),[67] and combined with the plan for public infrastructure investment this means huge deficits and higher interest rates on the national debt. In fact, government bond yields rose from the day of the election, anticipating such deficits.

The risks may be even greater than in the Reagan era. An influx of capital attracted by rising interest rates may overvalue the dollar, which would aggravate the already substantial US trade deficit and augment the service burden for countries and private debtors who have borrowed in dollars. Protectionist measures undertaken to offset these imbalances could trigger exchange rate wars, with China foremost although the European countries would not be sheltered from it.

In any case, this agenda promotes inequality and not only financial recklessness. In other words, instability.

CONCLUSION

Friedman, Lucas, Buchanan, and Fama have been the pillars of the new doctrines of deregulation. They shared a social motivation, propelled by the vision of liberated markets maximizing prosperity, and a political determination to resist alternatives because "the right to choose" meant choosing the efficiency of markets against social needs. Yet their victory was not engraved in marble, since they were ignored economists, radical if not extravagant thinkers, and defeated politicians for most of their careers. If these ideas won the day, it was because they were part of the neoliberal trend, if not consequences or voices of the social movement prevailing during the long phase of restructuring of the mode of production since the international crisis and recession of 1974–5. That movement imposed a setback on the social mobilization of the popular classes, a degradation of their capacity to keep the social contract of the previous decades in the developed economies, an offensive against social welfare. The preparation of cadres, central bankers, decision makers, and politicians under the spell of the ideal of deregulated markets—a theme we will pursue in the next chapters—was instrumental in this turn.

The Mont Pelerin Society, for long a minority if not a marginal movement among neoliberals, was instrumental in defining the power of Friedman. In any case, he was challenged by even more extremist points of view, such as that of Buchanan.

The victory of this movement generated major changes in rules, laws, conventions, and traditions, as the forces of finance were unleashed for a pyramid of new products, new accounts, and new tools. The previous forms of regulation were distorted or annihilated. The new ideas won the day.

As the Trump administration takes office, these ideas gain momentum as a project to dump the Dodd-Frank core regulations and to reestablish the deregulation creed as in the heyday of Reagan.

The next chapter presents the role of the central bankers in the making of this new order.

[67] Nunns et al. (2015).

6

Deeds and Doctrines of the Central Bankers

Our triptych of decision makers includes big business, liberalizers, and, in this chapter, the central bankers who were essential players in the process of deregulation, globalization, and financialization. Central bankers, operating under the doctrine and legislation of independence, assuring their power over the elected institutions and the pressure of public opinion, imposed their views on governments. The results are dangerous.

NOT SO MODERATE

The "modern theory of finance," an outgrowth of the application of standard economic theory bolstered by sophisticated mathematics and excited ideology, eventually became consensus among influential policymakers and public and private decision makers. But as recently as the mid-1970s, Friedman was preaching a gospel of *laissez-faire* that seemed grossly out of touch in the popular imagination and Fama's and Lucas's careers were just getting underway. Nevertheless, in a matter of two decades, they became dominant throughout academia and central banks. This process is the theme for the current chapter.

Central banking claimed two great triumphs in this era. One was institutional, as their independence was established, ratified by their success in moderating inflation, which had been a chronic feature of the postwar developed economies and then accelerated in the 1970s. Independence favored a large scope of action outside public scrutiny and democratic decision making in the name of expertise but also of independence itself, i.e., removal from politics. Central banks were able to impose major game changes in different countries. One telling example is that of the US Federal Reserve Chair Paul Volcker, appointed by Democratic President Jimmy Carter, applying high interest rates to tame inflation—and the organized working class.[1] Concurrent with its vigorous application on Wall Street and Main Street, independent central banking received the luster of academic respectability using innovations in macroeconomic and game theory.

[1] Carter's main advisor during the electoral campaign was Lawrence Klein, a Keynesian economist who had been persecuted by McCarthyism. But his appointed Chair of the Federal Reserve was Volcker, who pursued a hard line policy increasing the interest rates. Arthur Okun, another economist who had been the Chair of the Council of Economic Advisers for the President, famously exclaimed that "the gnomes of Zurich got their way," as austerity was being imposed, J. Stein (2010), p. 225.

Then came the "Great Moderation" and the notion that an economy managed by an independent central bank—mostly with rules but with occasional discretion—could avoid major turbulence and overcome the occasional hiccup. In terms of hiccups and discretion, the absence of fallout from the 1987 stock-market crash, in which a financial crisis did not infect the real economy, seemed to prove the point. Greenspan's Fed could even experiment with the limits of the unemployment-inflation tradeoff in the 1990s, as the US unemployment rate edged below 4.0 percent. Financial markets rested easy because the Fed's independence assured that the least hint of wage growth or inflation would spur immediate action by the central bank in order to increase the interest rate and cool off the economy and, with it, working-class wage demands.

In 2004 Ben Bernanke, at that point still a member of Greenspan's compliant board, popularized the concept of "Great Moderation." He attributed the twenty-year run of an apparently tamed business cycle to the independence of central banks, to strict monetary rules, and to sound economics,[2] in short, a well-managed economy. It was a beautiful but short-lived dream.

Before we describe the crisis of regulation and the breakdown of the subprime crash, we will survey the agents of change who propagated the dream and led the practical tasks of liberating the market. Most powerful among them were the central bankers.

SHOCKED AS I AM

To bring the new world to birth, heroes of change were deregulating regulators, allied to governments eager to deliver on the fruits of modern finance. Although they were acquainted with the theoreticians of Chicago, the real game changers were the practitioners. Alan Greenspan stands out as the central figure.

Greenspan had led a long career in business before finishing his PhD in 1977 at New York University, at the age of 51.[3] He had been founder and director of Townsend-Greenspan, a New York consulting firm, then chair of the Council of Economic Advisers under Gerald Ford in 1977,[4] and later adviser to President Reagan. But prior to his appointment as Fed Chair by Ronald Reagan in 1987, most of Greenspan's time was dedicated to serving on boards of private firms, both financial and industrial, including the Aluminum Corporation of America, Automatic Data Processing, General Foods, J.P. Morgan, Morgan Guaranty Trust Company of New York, and Mobil.[5] After his appointment to the Fed, he served as Chair for nineteen years under several presidents and gained unparalleled power.

[2] Bernanke (2004); The notion of "Great Moderation" was already discussed in previous chapters. An early source for this argument is the paper by Stock and Watson presented at the Federal Reserve Bank of Kansas City symposium, "Monetary Policy and Uncertainty," at Jackson Hole, Wyoming, August 28–30, 2003, under the title "Has the Business Cycle Changed? Evidence and Explanations," Stock and Watson (2003).

[3] His academic research is not well known because Greenspan forced New York University to withdraw his 1977 thesis from public eyes when he took office at the Fed. It is rumored to include warnings about speculation and housing bubbles.

[4] Mirowski (2013), p. 164. [5] Lebaron (2000), p. 224.

He managed the Fed through significant crashes, the Savings and Loan scandal, the 1987 stock market crash, the 1997–8 crashes in Russia, Asia, and Mexico, and the 2000 burst of the dot-com bubble. After stepping down in late 2005, Greenspan took a job as consultant at PIMCO, the largest player in the world bond market.[6] A consistent type, he fought for deregulation for his entire career.

Robert Shiller recounts a discussion with Greenspan in 1996. The topic was the danger of a new financial bubble. Shiller "stood before Alan Greenspan and the entire Federal Reserve Board in December 1996 and testified that the stock market was being blown into what seemed to be an irrational bubble." Apparently moved, Greenspan made his famous remarks on "irrational exuberance" three days later. But if Greenspan had been temporarily chastened by the conversation with the Yale economist and future Nobelist, Greenspan soon dropped his warnings of a brewing bubble in stock prices.[7] In contrast to William McChesney Martin, also a nineteen-year Fed chair in a different era, 1951–70, who described the role of the Fed Chair as being to "take away the punch bowl just as the party gets going," Greenspan saw himself as a booster, not a bear or a scold.[8]

Delivered in Greenspan's opaque, oblique style, the irrational exuberance speech at least recognized the possibility of bubbles. A true defense attorney for market efficiency, such as Fama, would never consider the charge. Not only did Greenspan entertain the possibility of bubbles, he accepted their inevitability. Greenspan added the extraordinary proposition that the Fed should not anticipate or squelch bubbles but only provide remedy afterward: "We as central bankers need not be concerned if a collapsing financial asset bubble does not threaten to impair the real economy, its production, jobs, and price stability."[9]

The bubbles that subjected the real economy of the nineteenth and twentieth centuries to doldrums often lasting as much as a decade became little more than a temporary nuisance in the hands of the "maestro" (as the journalist Bob Woodward's admiring biography dubbed Greenspan).

Armed with supreme confidence that the central bank could manage the occasional hiccup, Greenspan saw no need to hobble financial innovation with prosaic mid-twentieth-century regulation. Again and again, Greenspan delivered the same anti-regulation, techno-optimistic message: regulation is "inherently conservative," a new revolution is coming, and the new technology and financial products are its riders.

In a 1997 lecture to the annual conference of the Association of Private Enterprise Education, Greenspan presented his views on why regulators should stand down and allow the financial sector to watch itself:

> Regulation is inherently conservative. It endeavors to maintain the status quo and the special interests who benefit therefrom [...]. With technological change clearly accelerating, existing regulatory structures are being bypassed, freeing market forces

[6] Johnson (2009).

[7] This was not the first conflict generated by a statement by Shiller, since Geithner had removed him from the Fed Advisory Board after a presentation on the danger of bubbles. Suskind (2011), pp. 56–7; Although right on the prediction of the bubble, Shiller did not distance himself from the traditional remedies of neoclassical economics to the financial peccadilloes, and his recent proposals involve "baroque" securitization. Mirowski (2013), p. 260.

[8] Akerlof and Shiller (2009). [9] Greenspan (1996a).

> to enhance wealth creation and economic growth. In finance, regulatory restraints against interstate banking and combinations of investment and commercial banking are being swept away under the pressure of technological change [...]. As we move into a new century, the market-stabilizing private regulatory forces should gradually displace many cumbersome, increasingly ineffective government structures. This is a likely outcome since governments, by their nature, cannot adjust sufficiently quickly to a changing environment, which too often veers in unforeseen directions.[10]

The new century was coming and the cumbersome state would cede to technological change "freeing market forces to enhance wealth creation and economic growth." What a wonderful world.

Discussing over-the-counter derivatives, which are complex, customized, and unregulated financial transactions between major players, Greenspan reassured the Senate Banking Committee in 2003: "The vast increase in the size of the over-the-counter derivatives markets is the result of the market finding them a very useful vehicle. And the question is, should these be regulated? Well, indeed, for the United States, they are obviously regulated to the extent that banks, being the crucial creators of these derivatives, are regulated by the banking agencies, but not beyond that. And the reason why we think it would be a mistake to go beyond that degree of regulation is that these derivative transactions are transactions amongst professionals."[11]

"Amongst professionals" is the key phrase. US financial regulations use, without irony, the term "sophisticated investors" to describe agents who, by dint of income and net worth, are presumed competent to engage in complex, higher-risk transactions. Greenspan's modest proposal is the height of governance—norms and practice by participating, interested parties—supplanting government—regulation and enforcement by an elected, empowered, and disinterested public authority.

Regulation by counterparty became the doctrine of the Fed in the Greenspan era. In an essay "The Quiet Coup," former IMF Director of Research Simon Johnson quotes Bernanke arguing that: "The management of market risk and credit risk has become increasingly sophisticated [...]. Banking organizations of all sizes have made substantial strides over the past two decades in their ability to measure and manage risk."[12] Amongst professionals, indeed.

The doctrine of regulation by counterparty was repeated over and over again, as an article of faith. The market is the regulator, claimed Greenspan: "In the essence, prudential regulation is supplied by the market through counterparty evaluation and monitoring rather than by authorities [...] Private regulation generally has proved far better at constraining excessive risk taking than has government regulation."[13]

As unfolding events highlighted the dangers of deregulation, Greenspan, who departed the Fed two years before the subprime crash, acknowledged the disaster. Of course, that was a "once in a century tsunami," he alleged, but nevertheless the country and the regulators were unprepared. At the congressional session of hearings on the financial crisis, in the House of Representative's Government Oversight Committee, Greenspan accepted that mistakes were made. "I am shocked," he noted.

[10] Greenspan (1997b); Johnson and Kwak (2011), pp. 100–1.
[11] Edsall (2009). [12] Johnson (2009). [13] Greenspan (2005).

The Telegraph reports: "Mr. Waxman [chair of the committee] went further, however, and asked the former Fed chief whether he was wrong about the benefits of deregulation, to which Mr. Greenspan responded, 'partially'. He proceeded to admit that the 'flaw' in the assumptions he used over the past 40 years were [sic] that banks and other financial institutions were best able to protect the interest of their shareholders."[14] This "flaw"—the simplistic belief that "amongst professionals" private interest would protect general interest against lucrative and destabilizing looting—bears substantial responsibility for the tsunami.

In 2007, Greenspan's coterie, including Bernanke (Greenspan's successor as chair), as well as Vice Chair Kohn, and Governors Kroszner and Mishkin, voiced alarm and warned the general public about growing financial instability. But to no avail, even within their own institution, in principle the center of US financial regulation. Even at that late date, it was hard to visualize the threat because the institutional culture had promulgated the view that sophisticated professionals and the discipline of a self-regulating market would work things out.

Greenspan, who had returned to his entrepreneurial life shortly before the crash, continued his crusade for market freedom. In early 2008, as the defaulting loans and failing banks began to pile up and the crash approached its culmination an undaunted Greenspan argued in the *Financial Times*, "We will never be able to anticipate all discontinuities in financial markets. Discontinuities are, of necessity, a surprise. Anticipated events are arbitraged away. [...] Thus it is important, indeed crucial, that any reforms in, and adjustments to, the structure of markets and regulation not inhibit our most reliable and effective safeguards against cumulative economic failure: market flexibility and open competition."[15] With catastrophe in sight, the response to the piece was ferocious. The most distinguished practitioner of the doctrine of deregulation and former head of the central bank of the most powerful economy in the world was doubling down his bets with the dealer showing an ace.

The next year, a chastened Greenspan was more prudent and eventually retracted his own enthusiastic belief in the intelligence of the market and marketeers. At one point, he went so far as to propose splitting up the big banks: "If they are too big to fail, they're too big. [...] So, I mean, radical things, as you—you know, break them up, you know. In 1911, we broke Standard Oil.

[14] As reported in *The Telegraph*, October 23, 2008. In the inquiry the same day at the House Committee on Oversight and Government Reform, Chair Henry Waxman asked Greenspan: "Were you wrong?." Greenspan candidly replied: "Partially. I made a mistake in presuming that self-interests of organizations, specifically banks and others, were such that they were best capable of protecting their own shareholders and their equity in the firms ... The problem here is something which looked to be a very solid edifice, and, indeed, a critical pillar to market competition and free markets, did break down. And I think that, as I said, shocked me. I still do not fully understand why it happened and obviously, to the extent that I figure out what happened and why, I will change my views." House of Representatives, Committee on Oversight and Government Reform (2008), p. 34; Greenspan (2008a).

[15] Greenspan (2008b), The argument was that regulation was inherently dangerous, since "if, as I strongly suspect, periods of euphoria are very difficult to suppress as they build, they will not collapse until the speculative fever breaks on its own. Paradoxically, to the extent risk management succeeds in identifying such episodes, it can prolong and enlarge the period of euphoria. But risk management can never reach perfection. It will eventually fail and a disturbing reality will be laid bare, prompting an unexpected and sharp discontinuous response." The article was published in the *Financial Times*, under the title of "We will never have a perfect model of risk."

So what happened? The individual parts became more valuable than the whole. Maybe that's what we need."[16] Although his temporary zeal may constitute an excessive reaction on awaking from his torpor as regulator, and was indeed not followed by any serious advocacy for regulation on his part, at least he finally stated the problem. Deregulation and emergence of giant banks had, for the moment, run their course.

Bernanke followed Greenspan's lead closely. In testimony to the Congress, in 2006 Bernanke stated, "the best way to achieve good oversight of hedge funds is through market discipline [...]. I think the market discipline has shown its capability of keeping hedge funds well disciplined."[17] In March 2007 congressional testimony, Fed Chair Bernanke again declared that the subprime danger was contained.[18]

Taking to new heights Paul Samuelson's dictum that facts can only dent a theorist's hide, Bernanke accepted the facts but continued to express confidence in his theory. In 2010, as the recession was still raging in the world, he declared at Princeton, "I would argue that the recent financial crisis was more a failure of economic engineering and economic management than of what I have called economic science [...] I don't think the crisis by any means requires us to rethink economics and finance from the ground up."[19]

Timothy Geithner, a former Treasury Secretary under Obama, previously a longstanding officer of the New York branch of the Federal Reserve and then the head of the Financial Stability Oversight Council, played the same tune as Greenspan and Bernanke in 2011, giving that regulation "depends too much on the state of the world at the time. In the future, we may have to do exceptional things again if we face a shock that large [...]. You won't be able to make a judgment about what's systemic and what's not until you know the nature of the shock."[20] Wait and see.

These top regulators had drawn the lesson that no further financial regulation had been required and, after the crash, that no further regulation would be welcome if it led to excessive limits on the market. *Pace* the declarations on breaking the banks or on the malignancies of the financial shocks.

A LONG ROAD TO DEREGULATE

Deregulation had traveled a long road and not every waypoint is marked. Indeed, lobbying to deregulate financial markets began mere moments after the regulation of the stock market and creation of the Securities and Exchange Commission in the 1930s, in the wake of the Great Crash of 1929; the creation of oversight-free hedge funds—justified by the sophistication of participants—was the deregulation lobby's

[16] Greenspan (2009b). [17] Bernanke (2006b).

[18] Mirowski (2013), p. 187. In his memoir, Bernanke accepts that errors were made, namely that the failure to cut the Federal Funds Rate as monetary stimulus after the collapse of Lehman Brothers was a "mistake," Bernanke (2015a). But Bernanke still insists that there was no alternative to letting Lehman fall.

[19] Bernanke (2010). [20] *Financial Times* (2011).

first success.[21] While the roots of the deregulation movement preceded Greenspan, he became its prime mover.

As early as 1974, the US Commodities Futures Trading Commission Act accepted self-regulation in the derivatives market, where speculative contracts bet on future prices of assets, commodities, stock, and bonds. That was a pivotal change for flourishing new financial products, "innovations" in the language of advocates, which gave birth to modern shadow finance.[22] Financial deregulation accompanied industrial deregulation in a drive to restore profitability to the US and other developed economies and to contain the prices paid by consumers in an inflationary era. In addition to banking, traditionally regulated sectors such as trucking, rail, telecommunications, airlines, and postal services were key targets for deregulation, privatization, and introduction of competition. Furthermore, deregulation made for strange bedfellows. For instance, Ralph Nader represented consumer interests against the monopolistic practices and regulatory capture by the industries while cowboy capitalists and free-market economists challenged incumbent companies for their hold on lucrative sectors, and they converged in anti-regulation counsels. In the same sense, Democratic US President Jimmy Carter (1977–81) signed acts deregulating airlines and trucking with the support of both liberal (in the US sense of left-of-center) Senator Edward Kennedy and certified arch-conservative Milton Friedman.[23]

With the airline industry shaken up, the following president, Republican Ronald Reagan, responded to a strike of the publicly employed air traffic controllers by firing them. The broken strike imposed a major setback on the trade-union movement and was followed by an increase in harsh anti-union campaigns and a rapid deunionization in the US.[24]

Greenspan, Reagan's nominee for the Fed, was a major player in the deregulation movement, as we noted in the previous section. He favored deregulation and financial innovation, a crucial part of that change. Both socially and ideologically, his mandate was a turning point for the imposition of a new concept of the scope of the markets, as Friedman's "right to choose" was embodied in the neoliberal policies pursued with zeal.

Yet not every deregulatory effort turned out well. The deregulated banking sector embroiled itself in the Savings and Loan Crisis, as liberalization of borrowing and lending rates and deregulation of investment choices created opportunities for both honest follies and outright looting. In 1987, Greenspan responded to a stock market crash—an indirect consequence of the Savings and Loan Crisis—with a massive liquidity infusion. Although the US economy experienced a recession three years later, it avoided immediate turmoil and the financial crisis of 1987 did not change Greenspan's views on the regulation and rescue of financial markets. Another wake-up call would soon present itself.

In 1994, Orange County, California, then the epitome of wealthy, conservative Southern Californian suburbia and home to the Nixon Presidential Library,

[21] Taub (2014). [22] Pistor (2013). [23] On this conflict, see Avent-Holt (2012).

[24] During Carter's mandate, the emerging consensus favored liberalization. By 1978, the Federal Reserve Board of Governors accepted the authorization for banks to place short-term debt, including commercial paper, raising money for corporate clients, and this was considered not to be a violation of Glass-Steagall, Johnson and Kwak (2011), p. 83.

suffered massive losses to its public treasury when the enormous derivative-market bets of its financial manager, Robert Citron, a presumably "sophisticated investor," went belly up. A subsequent Congressional investigation of the financial industry uncovered systematic practices of misinforming clients in derivative markets. The fleecing of clients on inflated service fees for complex products has a venerable history in financial markets.[25]

Unfazed by market turmoil or Congressional findings, Greenspan defended the industry in 1997, a year marked by multiple significant crashes in international markets: the "need for US government regulation of derivatives instruments and markets should be carefully re-examined. The application of the Commodity Exchange Act to off-exchange transactions between institutions seems wholly unnecessary—private market regulation appears to be achieving public policy objectives quite effectively and efficiently."[26] The "unnecessary" intervention of which the Fed Chair warned was an emergent challenge by a determined regulator, Brooksley Born, an attorney then heading the Commodities Futures Trading Commission (CFTC).

A FIGHT FOR REGULATION

By the 1970s the Chicago Board of Trade for farm commodity futures was 130 years old; nominally introduced to provide market-based price insurance for farmers, who could sell their output at an assured price, the futures market was in fact long home to riotous speculation and profiteering. Coupled with volatility in world food, energy, and credit markets, the farm crisis of the 1970s generated widespread resentment against speculative commodity markets. Thus, the original charge when the CFTC was created in 1974 was to protect farmers from excessive risk in futures markets; so the agency had its roots in market skepticism. But, as the world had changed since the 1970s, a host of new financial products—derivatives—had joined farm futures in lucrative speculative trading. A Clinton appointee, Born became head of the CFTC in 1996 and took on the task of dealing with that futures business.

Born perceived not only the misuse of clients, including supposedly sophisticated investors, but also the potential for systemic risk from derivative markets. Derivative markets trade notional values many times larger than the capitalization of many of the largest stock markets. Although under most circumstances notional values do not actually change hands, volatile financial markets are capable of generating extreme circumstances that put notional values into play. Born insisted that a new approach to regulation of derivatives was required. To move in that direction, Born, familiar with resistance to increasing supervision among the regulatory community in Washington, felt obliged to confront the establishment.

And she was rightly understood: Greenspan—enamored of financial innovation in derivatives markets, cognizant of their profitability for the major players,

[25] M. M. Lewis (1989), describes the practice in the early years of the mortgage-backed security market.

[26] Greenspan (1997a).

confident in their capacity for self-regulation, and also aware of their increasing importance in global financial activity—mustered an army of academics and de-regulators to fight the CFTC and to crusade for regulation-free contracts.

By the peak of the crisis ten years later, the sheer size of the derivative market was so immense that one must wonder how a case against regulation could ever have been advanced. Yet over-the-counter derivatives were a giant and profitable industry, and its power helped the industry to avoid regulation and to spread the risk of mortgages through the whole financial system. By the time of the crash, the notional value of derivatives, namely what it would cost to resolve every contract, had grown to US $20 trillion. The resistance to regulation was powerful, and it prevailed under Greenspan's guidance.

In May 1998, Born issued a "concept paper" on derivative-market regulation, organized around a list a questions and leading to a proposal for regulation of derivatives. This generated a duel with the other regulators, through public confrontation of ideas and policies as well as through palace coups.

Journalist Rick Schmitt, who interviewed the protagonists of this debate for the Stanford University alumni magazine, describes a conversation between Born and Greenspan at a private lunch. In Born's account Greenspan told her, "Well, Brooksley, I guess you and I will never agree about fraud." To which she replied, "What is there not to agree on?" She recalls Greenspan elaborating, "Well, you probably will always believe there should be laws against fraud, and I don't think there is any need for a law against fraud," as he suggested that clients would learn to avoid cheating brokers through their own experience.

Greenspan himself rejects Born's account of the conversation. "This alleged conversation is wholly at variance with my decades-long held view," he said in an email to the journalist. Yet some of Born's collaborators confirm her account,[27] and the senior staff of the CFTC gave further insights on the political pressures against regulation of derivatives. Michael Greenberger, a University of Maryland law professor then serving as Born's director of the Division of Trading and Markets, remembers the fateful call from Larry Summers, who said, "I have 13 bankers in my office, and they say if you go forward with this you will cause the worst financial crisis since World War II."[28]

As Born developed her proposal, she sought to include credit default swaps under the regulatory jurisdiction of the CFTC. Among her concerns was that firms trading in swaps faced no capital requirements: a firm could promise to insure a bond in default, potentially requiring the outlay of billions of dollars without any money in the vault to back up the promise.

Born's jurisdictional proposal was emphatically rejected by other regulatory agencies.[29] The chief SEC regulator, Richard R. Lindsey, explained that his own agency, not the CFTC, should continue its light supervision: regulation, not speculation, was the greater danger.[30]

[27] Schmitt (2009). [28] Roig-Franzia (2009). [29] Cassidy (2009), p. 231.

[30] Lindsey (1998). "Uncertainty created by the CFTC's concept release and concerns about the imposition of new regulatory costs also may stifle innovation and push transactions offshore," Options Clearing Corporation (2017). After leaving his permissive SEC, Lindsey took a position at Bear Stearns and then as chief investment advisory for Janus Liquid Alternatives.

When the "concept paper" listing Born's proposals was published,[31] Greenspan, Rubin, and SEC head Arthur Levitt responded within hours with their own publication: a joint statement expressing "grave concern about this action and its possible consequences."[32] They asked for no less than Congressional legislation, not merely an administrative decision, to prevent the CFTC from regulating derivatives.

Greenspan defended the swaps market against the norms proposed by Born:

> The major element of control of leverage and capital in the international financial system is the structure of counterparty interrelationships. Ultimately, you have a system in which individuals who lend money to others have a very important interest in getting that money back ... The question is, do you have a level of failure which very seriously undermines the system? And the answer to that at this particular stage is very clearly no, and that as far as I can judge, the degree of supervision of regulation of the over-the-counter derivatives market is quite adequate to maintain a degree of stability in the system. And it is by no means clear to me that the expansion of regulation to that particular area of the economy serves the overall financial system of the United States. There is some regulation which is helpful and there is some which is negative, and I would not like to see regulation which inhibits the effective functioning of our financial system.[33]

But as if to demonstrate Born's prescience, Long-Term Capital Management (LTCM), a trading firm guided by two Nobel Prize winners, whose profit model rested on highly leveraged positions in derivative markets, sank because of its excessive exposure to unforeseen events. LTCM, with its enormous, leveraged bets in many markets, posed a systemic risk. Greenspan rode to the rescue again, organizing the purchase of LTCM and providing liquidity to forestall a more general crisis, which was, in fact, a serious possibility.

Unfazed by the LTCM debacle, Greenspan and Summers advanced their position. In October, one month after the LTCM rescue, a finance-beholden Congress approved a six-month moratorium that prevented the CFTC from regulating custom derivatives.

They collaborated with an abundance of Congressional allies and Washington insiders. One of these allies, in a House captured by Republicans since 1994, was Senator Phil Gramm of Texas, who played a key role in developing the Gramm-Leach-Bliley Act in 1999, which repealed Glass-Steagall. He was one of five co-sponsors of the Commodity Futures Modernization Act of 2000 that kept Born and regulation out of the derivative markets.[34] Senator Gramm's wife, Wendy Gramm, who served under President Ronald Reagan first as head of the Office of Information and Regulatory Affairs at the Office of Management and Budget and as head of the Commodity Futures Trading Commission, eventually left government service in 1993 to take a position on the Board of Directors and Audit Committee of

[31] Commodity Futures Trading Commission (1998).

[32] Frontline (2009). Levitt subsequently changed his view of the need for a regulation of derivatives. Born quotes him as saying, "You know, if she just would have gotten to know us,...maybe it would have gone a different way," and acknowledging that he was wrong and Born was right.

[33] See US House of Representatives, Committee on Banking and Financial Services (1998), in particular Born's comments on the dangers of the swap culture at page 142 ff; also see the PBS documentary *The Warning*, Kirk, Gilmore, and Wiser (2009).

[34] Brooksley Born recounts the story in an extensive interview, Frontline (2009).

Enron Corporation (a giant energy trading firm that went spectacularly bankrupt in a sea of fraudulent accounting in 2001). Gramm and Gramm, both PhDs in Economics, were an important advocacy team for financial deregulation.

In 1999, the President's Working Group on Financial Markets, including Greenspan, Summers, and chairs of the regulatory agencies, recommended that the exemption for derivatives from federal regulation be included in legislation, and so given the full force of law (rather than as simply an administrative matter subject to relatively easy revision). Clinton complied and included the exemption in the Commodity Futures Modernization Act, which Congress passed and the President signed in December 2000, one of his last acts in office. Born, defeated but defiant, had left the CFTC in June 1999. Her successor rapidly corrected the deviation from de-regulatory orthodoxy, assuring the financial world that there would be no Born legacy.[35]

The financial market liberation movement was at the time unstoppable. In January 1998, the Board of Governors of the Fed affirmed the prevailing practice "to not conduct consumer compliance examinations of, nor to investigate complaints regarding, nonbank subsidiaries of bank holding companies."[36] The system of special investment vehicles was safe from the regulatory threat. Shadow finance was shielded from any regulation whatsoever.

In 1999 the Gramm-Leach-Bliley Act, or the Financial Modernization Act, passed Congress and was signed by Clinton. The bipartisan consensus of the Washington establishment was clear and continued into the Bush era.[37] The Rooseveltian era of the Glass-Steagall insulation of commercial banks from speculative adventures came to an end. Greenspan and Wall Street were victorious in a seventy-year war.

For his whole career, Greenspan stood by the certainty that "markets get it right." Even in retirement and faced with a world-threatening financial crisis, Greenspan expressed shock at the existence of fraud and at the prospect that self-regulation could amplify danger, since the market could not get it wrong, or at least could not be fooled for long.

A SMALL CHANGE TO KEEP ON GOING

Until 2004 US investment banks were completely unregulated, as the Depression era compromise was that commercial banking, with its dependence on many individual depositors, would be both insured and regulated, whereas investment banks were invited to occupy the wild side of the street. And the two were to be kept safely apart. Investment banks occasionally submitted to some US regulator

[35] William Rainer, chair of the CFTC for 1999–2000, took the controversial stand to recommend lifting a ban on single-stock futures. That was accepted and, in 2001, he became the CEO of OneChicago, a trader of single-stock futures. Johnson and Kwak (2011), p. 95.

[36] Kregel (2014), pp. 12–13.

[37] When in October 2004 George Bush signed the Financial Services Regulatory Relief Act, allowing banks to have smaller reserves, the legislation was unanimous at the Senate and was passed by 417 to 15 at the House.

to satisfy an EU formality that banks identify a domestic regulator, which the bank itself could select—this was regulation in the spirit of a teenager convincing a young uncle to buy beer. Most investment banks selected the SEC for this *pro forma* regulation, for two sound, profitable reasons: the SEC lacked authority to impose capital requirements, which are anathema to banks' quest for leverage; and the SEC had only twenty-four people in charge of supervising the five largest banks.

After the end of the Greenspan era, business at the Fed proceeded apace. Bernanke proved a convenient and compliant successor. In June 2006, five months after his appointment, Bernanke repeated the party line: "banking organizations of all sizes have made substantial strides over the past two decades in their ability to measure and manage risks."[38] The Fed pursued its vision of finance as a market to be liberated from public interference. As a high officer of the Fed told the Financial Crisis Inquiry Commission (FCIC), the state of mind was there should be no regulation.[39]

And then came the crash of 2007–8. Of the five largest investment banks, one went bankrupt with the crash, two were rescued with drastic measures and restructuring, and the remaining two, Goldman Sachs and Morgan Stanley, modified their shadow activities to get access to the lifeline of public funding.[40]

The initial public outcry yielded an inquiry and some regulatory measures. The Congressionally appointed commission, inquiring into the failure of the supervision and the reasons for the crash, blamed Mr. Greenspan for advocating deregulation and cited the "pivotal failure to stem the flow of toxic mortgages" under Greenspan's leadership as a "prime example" of negligence. Greenspan's strategy, the report averred, favored greed. The report decried the decision to shield derivatives from regulation as "a key turning point in the march toward the financial crisis."[41] Events had proved Born right, but the damage was done.[42]

Yet even in the face of overwhelming public sentiment—and some Congressional mobilization—for regulating finance, the voices for deregulation quickly re-emerged. Camden Fine, head of the Independent Community Bankers of America that represents some 6,500 small banks, argued while the fallout was still warm, "the current regulatory regime has gone too far."[43] In other countries as well the deregulatory crusade did not demobilize fully or for long.

THE VIRTUE OF IGNORANCE

The inability of the central banks to promote or to defend financial stability was a consequence of the prevailing vision of the self-regulating markets and their capacity to tame volatility. This, in turn, was the consequence of the ideology, of

[38] Bernanke (2006a).

[39] Scott Alvarez testimony to US Financial Crisis Inquiry Commission (2011), p. 96; and see Wolf (2014), p. 172.

[40] Taub (2014), p. 452.

[41] Final conclusions of the US Financial Crisis Inquiry Commission (2011); and also see Chan (2011).

[42] US Financial Crisis Inquiry Commission (2011), p. 96; and also see Wolf (2014), p. 172.

[43] Carrick-Hagenbarth and Epstein (2012).

economic thinking, and of the behavior of the deregulating regulators. It was also a consequence of the tools they used and perhaps the most telling example is that of the verification of the health of banks.

After the crash, stress tests were redesigned to anticipate the reaction of each bank to extreme events, including once-in-a-lifetime tsunamis that Greenspan identified in the 2007–8 subprime crisis. But before the crash, stress tests were part of the business-as-usual, normal-tailed apparatus and failed to identify enormous mounting problems.

Take the case of HBOS, a giant retail bank resulting from the fusion of the Bank of Scotland with Halifax, whose operations were centered on risky lending. A stress test conducted in 2005 led to the impressive conclusion that the possibility of the bank having three consecutive years of negative results would happen once in five thousand years. HBOS required rescue in 2008.[44]

Stress tests constituted a peculiar form of organized misperception or ignorance. In Iceland, where the four largest banks owned assets representing 900 percent of the national GDP, the stress test conducted in 2008 by the IMF claimed to find resilience and confidence: yet their collapse followed immediately. This was not the exception but rather the norm: the previous year, 2007, on the verge of the subprime crisis, the IMF recommended the results of stress tests on banks that were highly exposed to the mortgage bubble, writing in a very enthusiastic vein "Stress tests conducted by investment banks show that, even under scenarios of nationwide house price declines that are historically unprecedented, most investors with exposure to subprime mortgages through securitized structures will not face losses." A bold conclusion of a bold test that was conducted by none other than a notorious bank, Lehman Brothers: both the tester and the tested would soon suffer the dramatic and costly effects of their misperception.[45]

In Europe, the same process demonstrated the inadequacy of banking oversight, and the European stress tests proved equally incapable of detecting stress. In August 2008, a full year after the beginning of the crash, the Committee of European Banking Supervision investigated twenty-two major banks, and all were approved. In 2009, it broadened the scope of the tests to ninety-one banks, and only seven failed. In 2011, the new European Banking Authority approved all the banks of Cyprus and Bankia, in Spain. This is a standard: the US authorities had failed to detect any major risk in Fannie Mae and Freddie Mac. In all cases, bankruptcies proved the inadequacy of the stress tests—and the supervisors did not learn lessons. Indeed they could not and they would not because the supervisors were firm believers in the new faith: finance should be outside the scope of public authorities that could be influenced by political or electoral choices.

THE VIRTUE OF INDEPENDENCE

The "Great Moderation," the claim that there was a period of macroeconomic stability and limited, or at least contained, financial crises across the developed

[44] Bank of England (2015).
[45] Reported in the 2007 Report according to World Economic and Financial Surveys (2009), p. 7.

world, appeared to vindicate the success of the movement for independence of central banking. Indeed, the very notion of "Great Moderation" commemorates a major modification of modern economies, that of the power of central banks: the ascendance of liberalized finance was anticipated by careful changes in the statutory definitions of the national central banks.

Central banks embody the sovereign power of printing money and the regulatory function of the financial system. The regulatory function includes the insurance guarantee on deposits and supervision of banks' use of deposits for safe, productive pursuits. The failsafe of the guarantee and supervisory system is the central banks' role as lenders of last resort, a source of liquidity in the event of crisis. All of these functions demonstrate that central banks are a crucial part of the power of the state.

Through modern history until the 1970s, in most developed economies the executive and legislative branches of government directed the activity of the central bank. The governors of most central banks, and other top management have been appointed by executives, with some countries requiring parliamentary consent. Central bank activity and outcomes were closely scrutinized by public authorities and the general public. In fact, the governments dictated the policy.

Take the case of the US and Homeric battles in order to establish a central bank as an expression of public management of money and the financial system. In the first years of the republic, Secretary of the Treasury Alexander Hamilton created the First Bank of the United States in 1791, headquartered in Philadelphia, as a publicly chartered private bank to issue money (although without an exclusive monopoly) and manage public debt. This charter, for twenty years, emerged from the first of many conflicts on the nature of central banking, as the United States has always had an agonistic relationship with its central bank. The epic battles on the role of the central bank began with the face-off between Secretary Hamilton and Thomas Jefferson, then Secretary of State.[46] Jefferson tried to convince President Washington to veto the law creating the bank, arguing that the power of issuing money was constitutionally reserved to the states and not the Federal government.[47] Hamilton won the skirmish and the bank was chartered for twenty years,[48] but the first partisan conflicts in the United States revolved around the opposition on the issue of the central bank between Jefferson's Democratic-Republican Party and Hamilton's Federalist Party.

The balance of power shifted under Jefferson's Presidency (1801–9) and in 1811 Congress decided—by a single vote—not to extend the charter. The practical consequences of running a country without a bank manifested themselves, and a Second Bank of the US was chartered in 1816. Ex-President Jefferson reaffirmed his position against banks and borrowing, in a letter to a correspondent: "I sincerely believe, with you, that banking establishments are more dangerous than standing armies; and that the principle of spending money to be paid by posterity, under the name of funding, is but swindling futurity on a large scale."[49]

[46] Johnson and Kwak (2011), 20fn. [47] Jack N. Rakove (2010), p. 236.

[48] The next year the US economy suffered its first financial crash. Hamilton bought federal bonds for a higher price, pouring money to lenders in trouble, and augmented the credit for banks—creating the central bank proved to be the right decision, Cowen, Sylla, and Wright (2006).

[49] Letter to John Taylor, May 28, 1816, in Jefferson (1907), p. 23.

President Andrew Jackson shared Jefferson's hatred against central banking (and also hated Nicholas Biddle, President of the Second Bank of the US). There were multiple strains at work in the contest between Jackson and the Bank—a conflict of states' rights against Federal authority, the attachment of elite northeastern banking interests to hard money, and a populist taste for soft money for infrastructure development and land speculation on the western frontier. Charter renewal for the Second Bank was denied in 1836 and Jackson's victory marked the beginning of the Free Banking Era (1836–65). The Free Banking Era was marked by generally softer money, gold as the final standard, rapid westward expansion, and alternating booms and busts.

Everything changed with the US Civil War, which transformed the conditions of monetary circulation (as well as the relationship between the states and Federal government, the role of slavery, and almost every other aspect of American life). To finance the war, the legislators passed a National Banking Act in 1863, establishing circulating notes, or Greenbacks, backed by US government securities. Greenbacks simultaneously softened the Federal stance from the gold standard but also represented the assertion of Federal authority over the states.

Fights over the hardness of the money dominated the political scene of the late nineteenth-century United States as soft-money populists advocated bimetallism (gold and silver standards) and made it a central (but ultimately unsuccessful) plank of both the insurgent Populist Party and, eventually, the Democratic Party. The US operated without a central bank in those years, and large private banks provided the financial and monetary infrastructure. Regional concerns—especially the reliance of farmers on credit—underpinned the conflict, with enormous popular resentment against the Eastern banking establishment. It was the golden age of the House of Morgan.

The panic of 1907, which private (and profitable) action coordinated by J.P. Morgan prevented from turning into a broader economic collapse,[50] moved the balance back towards central banking. The Federal Reserve was created by the US Congress in 1913, as a network of twelve decentralized private banks with public oversight, including the Presidential appointment of the Governors. The Fed's current structure remains a subsidiary of that past. Regulation of investment activities had already imposed some restrictions: since 1908, the national banks were limited to commercial banking activities, although state chartered banks could engage in securities markets with no restrictions. This would change with the 1927 Pepper-McFadden Act, as national banks were limited to commercial banking activities,[51] a decision reinforced and broadened by Glass-Steagall after the 1929 Crash.

That Crash blew open the doors to wholesale regulation. So deep was the damage to the country, so crooked the workings of finance, and so thorough the investigation and the assignment of blame that finance felt little choice but to comply. The alphabet soup of legislation enabling new regulators, including the Securities and Exchange Commission, the Federal Deposit Insurance Corporation, and the Federal Home Loan Bank Board, limited the scope of investment and

[50] In 1907, J. Pierpont Morgan was instrumental in bailing out the troubled banks. In one famous episode, he locked the bankers in his library until they reached a settlement.

[51] Kregel (2014), p. 6.

speculation, informed investors, installed deposit insurance, and provided for greater oversight of transactions and accounts. It would take nearly seventy years to dismantle this system of control and regulations.

INDEPENDENCE EVERYWHERE

The history of the most powerful central banks confirms the parallel between liberalization, deregulation, and depriving democratic institutions of their power of leading the central banks. Many of the central banks were born as private entities but always with public oversight because they were chartered to manage public debt and to issue banknotes. The first central bank appears to be the Sveriges Riksbank, a Swedish bank created in 1668. Shortly afterwards, the Bank of England, created in 1694 as the debt manager, has since 1844 enjoyed the monopoly of printing currency. As a response to the South Sea Bubble (see Chapter 8), the Bank of England was empowered as the lender of last resort, a concept explored by Walter Bagehot in *Lombard Street*. Always scrutinized by governments, the Bank was effectively nationalized during the Second World War and formally nationalized in 1946, although it had been for all effective purposes a public agency for much longer. The Bank of England, outside the European System, is independent since it was legally redefined in 1997 to lead monetary policy, setting the interest rates.

The Bank of France was created shortly after the first bank of Hamilton, in 1800. It was founded by Napoleon, who chartered it as the only issuer of notes in Paris. Later this prerogative was extended to other cities, and by 1848 the Bank enjoyed a monopoly in large parts of the country. It was nationalized in 1936, as a response to the turmoil caused by the depression. Its independence was enshrined in legislation in 1993.

The German Bundesbank was created in 1957, succeeding the Bank Deutscher Länder of 1948, founded after the end of the War to redevelop the devastated and occupied country. The Bundesbank was the keeper of currency reserves and issuer of currency and a staunch inflation fighter during West Germany's bountiful years. Then, along with the other central banks of the Eurozone, it became part of the European System, headquartered in Frankfurt and with a system designed in the image of the German bank. Of course, the Bundesbank was first among equals, serving as template for its Europe-wide offspring, the European Central Bank, as we will explore in what follows.

The German banking system is an interesting case of change, not least because of its influence on European policymaking. The credit system in the country corresponds to a bank-based financial system, with a small shadow system. Furthermore, state-owned savings banks play a large role (by 2012, they represented 29.4 percent of the total assets, the private banks 38 percent of assets, and the cooperative banks 22.8 percent). Although these were conceptually and legally universal banks, in fact foreign banks mostly developed investment banking.

This is partly due to historical constraints. After the Second World War the three major banks were nationalized and then divided into ten regional banks, and only in 1957 were the Deutsche Bank and Dresdner Bank reunified, and the Commerzbank was privatized in 1958. This banking system was a decisive player in the reconstitution of German capitalism, through credit and direct ownership and guidance of firms: by 1964, the banks had 50.5 percent of voting rights in non-financial firms.[52] Then they were instrumental for mergers and acquisitions that shaped the modern German economy,[53] and closely monitored by a powerful central bank and governments.

In any case, the time came for abolishing the controls of capital and for liberalization and deregulation (since 1981), although the public and cooperative part of the banking industry remained very large (the third largest bank is public, KfW Bankegrouppe). With the world financial crash of 2007–8, Hypo Real Estate was nationalized, the Commerzbank partly nationalized, and the regional governments intervened in the Landesbanken. Then Commerzbank took over Dresden in 2009 and Unicredit, an Italian group, grew to be the third-ranking private bank.[54]

In other parts of the world, independence of the central banks proceeded apace. Take the case of the Bank of Mexico, created in 1925 with a monopoly on issuing currency, under strict government control. Before 1910, Mexico had twenty-four issuing banks, including the Bank of London. It was the triumph of the Mexican Revolution that paved the way to the new and single central bank. Independence was granted to this bank in 1993, after the liberalization movement and the conclusion of the privatization of commercial banks the previous year, a major shock that will be discussed in another chapter.

THE SOCIAL LOGIC OF CENTRAL BANK INDEPENDENCE

In a small set of cases, largely in developing economies and in situations already charged by political and social crises, governments with direct control over the central bank implemented deficit financing via direct printing of money, using the "*maquina*" in Latin American parlance, with hyper-inflationary results. But in most developed countries, between the Second World War and the 1970s the central bank operated with state supervision to meet multiple mandates of economic growth, moderated inflation, and financial sector stability.

The late 1960s and early 1970s were marked by working-class militancy, significant wage gains, and relatively high inflation across the developed countries. Academic economists, particularly the camp around Milton Friedman, including the Mont Pelerin Society that we presented in the last chapter, converged with business-class organizations, e.g., the Business Roundtable in the United States, to

[52] Detzer et al. (2013), p. 39.

[53] This eventually led to contradictions and conflicts of interest: in the takeover of Hoesch by Krupp, in 1991, Krupp was supported by its bank, WestLB, which had a share of 12% in Hoesch. In the merger of Krupp with Thyssen in 1998, the Deutsche Bank advised Krupp in the unfriendly takeover bid, although the bank had a seat on the supervisory board of Thyssen. The Deutsche Bank also had a seat on the supervisory board of Mannesmann, which was a part of the 1999–2000 Vodafone-Mannesmann deal, rejected by the government, the trade unions, and the CEO of Mannesmann (this firm was advised by Morgan Stanley, Merrill Lynch, and J.P. Morgan, whereas Vodafone was advised by Goldman Sachs; ibid., p. 216.

[54] Ibid., pp. 73–4.

confront these challenges to profitability.[55] For reasons of political palatability, they focused on "inflation," rather than class conflict or wage gains, as the most effective way for the business class to discuss and respond to a crisis of profitability.

The Friedmanites and the business advocacy organizations, and the bank lobby itself, came to trumpet the doctrine of central bank independence as a key way to confront inflation. The wisdom of independence of the central banks is thus recent (although it was not exactly the concept of Friedman himself. [56] How right he was.)

With respect to monetary policy, printing money and setting policy interest rates, independence represents the victory of anti-inflationary dogma: central banks should contain the cycle during expansions and advocate politically against the Keynesian counter-cyclical fiscal policy in recessions.

Declaring the futility of monetary policy, the Friedmanites alerted the public to danger: unscrupulous politicians might, at the behest of uninformed labor unions, use the central bank to deliver an artificial, short-lived stimulus. Although ultimately of no avail and generative only of inflation, such a stimulus might prove irresistible to politicians facing an electoral challenge in a slumping economy. Only an independent central bank could provide a credible commitment to not tweaking the economy for short-term political gain, they argued.

To its advocates, independence implied a manifold process of neutralization: the disqualification of the legitimacy of politics in macroeconomic policy debates, with politics to be replaced by independent expertise, and the downplaying of discretion. The intellectual basis for the argument was twofold. First, Friedman's successors firmed up his arguments for the "neutrality" of money. Their position was that monetary policy could only change prices, i.e., stimulate inflation; the real side of the economy—hours worked, unemployment, the production of goods and services—was the true world of good-for-good exchange merely masked by the veil of money. Debate might continue about whether the separation applied instantaneously, in the short run, or in longer runs, but expansionary monetary policy was deemed at best futile and quite possibly destructive.[57] An additional neutralization was embedded in the academic case for independence: a muting of discussion of economic and social interests in macroeconomic policy. Labor unions and progressive politicians were held to be simply mistaken in their requests for interventionist monetary policy because it scientifically could not work.

This neutralization favored the deregulation process because, the argument goes, if the central bank and its policy embody the common beliefs of the economic agents and produce social equilibrium, then the construction of the institutions

[55] The Roundtable is a lobbying organization, formed in 1972 in order to influence labor legislation and tax policy and open only to CEOs. Its connection to the neoliberal milieus was instrumental in developing campaigns in favor of deregulation. In any case, it is noticeable that large firms tend to support or be part of different associations following the tides: in 1942 and the next years, large conglomerates, such as Goldman Sachs, J.P. Morgan, Ford, Lehman Brothers, Kodak, or Shell adhered to the Keynesian-oriented Committee for Economic Development (Clawson et al., 1998, pp. 96, 149; Kotz, 2015, pp. 69 ff, 53 ff).

[56] Friedman acknowledged that the independence of the central bank could establish excessive power on the part of the bankers: "an independent central bank will almost inevitably give undue emphasis to the point of view of bankers," Friedman (1962), p. 227.

[57] Lebaron (2000), p. 210.

should avoid any temptation for political or electoral interference. An independent central bank is the ideal counterpart to a deregulated financial system.

In any case, the neutralization campaign had positive feedback effects for itself. The part of the economics profession advocating for autonomous financial markets and a self-equilibrating market garnered increasing support in influential policy circles. This support translated into policy action that aided the rise of finance, which in turn raised the prestige and influence of the academic programs supplying ideas and graduates to these activities. Therefore, independence of the central banks protected the power of deregulators at the top of the most important regulatory public agency.

QUARRELS AT THE HEADQUARTERS

The dogma of the central bankers does not rest on its particular success in forecasting or moderating the macroeconomy. In this section another dimension of the action of central banks is investigated, namely the sorry state of their ideological or preferred theoretical approach.

The models and the technical approach of the central banks relied overwhelmingly on the assumption of equilibrating processes, and economic rationality is the term applied post hoc to whatever has occurred. But the equilibrating doctrine is in a shambles after the subprime crash because it cannot explain the gathering of fuels, the spark of ignition, or the spread of the fire. Charles Goodhart, a member of the Bank of England Monetary Committee from 1997 to 2000, did not mince words when he wrote: "The ruling workhorse models used by the central banks prior to the financial crisis that began in 2008 essentially ignored the financial system."[58] This is the strange case of the central bank, the chief financial officer for the economy, seeking to model and guide the economy while wholly ignoring its actual lever, the financial system.

Cornel Ban, a professor at Boston University, observes that, in the period after the financial crisis initiated in 2007 and 2008, an Atlantic-sized wedge grew between the regulatory institutions. In a paper under the provocative title of "Orthodox Washington versus Social Europe," Ban turned on its head the longstanding conception that US institutions are fundamentally more neoliberal than their counterparts in Europe, which are redeemed by their embeddedness in social states. It is true that Greenspan led the way for liberalizing central banks and liberated finance. But Ban argues that Europe trailed close behind and indeed became a font of aggressive political and economic strategies.

The individual central banks, their governing bodies, and research departments subscribed wholeheartedly to the doctrine of deregulation. Fiscal policy, once at the heart of democratic and parliamentary representation, was "largely removed from the space of democratic deliberation" in Europe, through the established

[58] Goodhart et al. (2013), p. 112, introduces a model of macroprudential regulation that would combine capital and liquidity regulations, margin requirements, and dynamic provisioning to moderate credit booms. The model considers commercial and shadow banking.

notions of fiscal consolidation, deficit management, and austerity.[59] The European Central Bank (ECB) and Euro system, infatuated with fiscal discipline, distilled and refined the neoliberal potion with distinguished zeal.

The European social state model had already been weakened by successive waves of privatization and, as a consequence of its demise, banished from the minds of the European central bankers, who focused on market solutions for the provision of public goods, including banking safety. Contrary to the established view, that consensus on the social state has given way to conflict over liberalization of finance, the struggle against the social functions of the state had already been waged and won in the halls of the research departments of the European Central Bank and its member central banks.

The crisis of 2008 and its deepening after 2010 created a new opening for debate. Ban notes: "some of the lead actors involved in the management of the crisis have radicalized pre-crisis orthodoxy by upholding the expansionary austerity thesis (the European Central Bank, ECB) while others have chosen to revise orthodox scripts using select Keynesian ideas (the IMF)."[60] Ban examines the web of citations in the papers of the research departments of the different institutions and contrasts the IMF (standing in for Washington) and the ECB, finding substantial divergence in their academic and intellectual milieus. "Revisionist" policy guidelines, new openings to expansionary fiscal policy, and capital controls and financial regulation, have found more fertile turf in orthodox Washington than in social Europe.

A case in point is the offensive by the European Central Bank against the fiscal stimulus package adopted by the EU in 2008: as early as January 2009, with the memory of utter financial collapse and the extraordinary extra-constitutional measures required to stem the bleeding still fresh and with the US and European economies hemorrhaging jobs, the ECB's Governing Council asked for the reversal of the stimulus decision, gloomily announcing that "if not reversed in due time, this will negatively affect in particular the younger and the future generations."[61] It's good to see that not every atheist in a foxhole will profess belief.

The IMF administration, too, maintained the faith. But the research department of the IMF acknowledged the crisis as more than a momentary error and undertook a fundamental epistemological self-examination. IMF researchers questioned the core tenets of central bank doctrine, the New Consensus dominant in the 1990s and early 2000s. These homegrown critiques challenged the program of "expansive austerity,"[62] which the ECB accepted, and the IMF research department joined early dissenters, such as Krugman, in condemning Depression Economics.

The critiques include core theorists and practitioners of the liberalization program.[63] Erstwhile *laissez-faire* economists argued for fiscal stimulus, currency

[59] Ilene Grabel of the University of Denver confirms the rise of this period of what she terms "productive incoherence," in which many practitioners embedded in orthodox institutions tested the limits of orthodoxy, Grabel (2011). Current explanations for the consistent and successful attacks on the role of fiscal policy include the power of corporations (Crouch (2011); Jabko (2013)); or that of a transnational superclass (Streeck (2014); Apeldoorn (2014)); or take this as a feature of liberalism (Blyth (2013)).

[60] Ban (2015), p. 3. [61] European Central Bank (2009).

[62] Alesina and Ardagna (2010); Alesina, Barbiero et al. (2015).

[63] That would be the case of neoliberal minded scholars such as Brad DeLong, Eichenbaum, Christiano, and Rebelo.

devaluations, unemployment insurance, and investment incentives.[64] Perhaps the most noteworthy change, the IMF issued arguments and guidelines for capital controls, a break with an article of faith, to be discussed in Chapter 10.

The changes were accelerated by the financial crisis but, as is often the case with doctrinal change, there were active nuclei of dissent at work beforehand.[65]

Before 2008 some departments of the IMF already operated with "selective Keynesian insights," recalibrating previous views.[66] Ban identifies the centers of orthodoxy and dissent: the crucial suppliers of orthodox arguments are the Cent*re* for Economic Policy Research (Europe, not to be confused with the center-left US think tank Cent*er* for Economic Policy Research), Bocconi University (a prestigious private school of economics and management in Milan), the University of Chicago (birthplace of Friedmanism), the Bank of Chile, the IMF Fiscal Affairs Department, and the ECB. The "revisionist" camp, favoring interventionist Keynesian policies, includes Northwestern University, Berkeley, the Soros-funded Institute for New Economic Thinking, the Paris School of Economics, and several central banks (including departments at the Fed and the Bank of England). The IMF Research Department and the National Bureau of Economic Research can be placed more reliably in the revisionist category, although both contribute to the orthodox camp as well.[67]

The revisionist emergence refers to ideas and models developed in universities and research sections and may not yet be reflected in practical decision making in central banks and parliaments. But the interplay between ideas, politics, and policy is strong. The intellectual debate on appropriate policy for financial and economic crisis is robust. With luck, economic science will advance faster than one funeral at a time.

Others voices have been more critical still. Joseph Stiglitz, Nobel Prize winner in economics, has openly criticized the independence doctrine, and has pointed out the responsibility of the international institutions such as the IMF for creating crisis conditions and exacerbating crises.[68]

[64] Auerbach and Gorodnichenko (2012); Woodford (2011).

[65] Less than 40% of the IMF staff is recruited from developing countries, Lebaron (2000), and it is not obvious that the new openings were not in any case deepened by the emergence of the general recession in developed countries.

[66] Ban (2015). [67] Ibid.

[68] 'The IMF reports to the ministers of finance and the governors of the central banks, and one of the important items on its agenda is to make these central banks more independent—and less democratically accountable [...] it always puts more weight on inflation than on jobs. The problem of having the rules of the game dictated by the IMF—and then by the financial community—is not just a question of values (though that is important) but also a question of ideology. The financial community's view of the world predominates—even when there is little evidence in its support," Stiglitz (2002). In addition to challenging policy, Stiglitz criticized contemporary theory and the discipline's resistance to engaging diverse views. One statement is the appeal published May 1992 by the *American Economic Review*, arguing that "economists today enforce a monopoly of method or core assumptions, often defended on no better ground than it constitutes the 'mainstream'. Economists will advocate free competition, but will not practice it in the marketplace of ideas. Consequently, we call for a new spirit of pluralism in economics," and signed by five Nobel Prize winners (Paul Samuelson, Clive Granger, Franco Modigliani, Herbert Simon, and Jan Tinbergen), together with other prominent economists (Hyman Minsky, Robert Axelrod, Charles Kindleberger, Christopher Freeman, and others).

MULTIPLIERS AND DIVIDERS

Greenspan's doctrine was followed to the letter in Europe, where radical central bankers imposed austerity policies and far outreached their monetary and exchange prerogative.

Through the long recession in Europe following the financial crash of 2007–8, the European Central Bank was both one of the most powerful institutions in the World and one of the most inefficient and misguided. In 2010, the ECB declared recovery to be underway and withdrew its emergency responses to the crisis. It still appears outrageous in hindsight that in 2011 the Bank twice raised interest rates,[69] having determined that inflation, rather than recession, was the greatest threat to European economic and social stability. The ECB and other European institutions together with the IMF mercilessly imposed austerity on the indebted countries of southern Europe, forcing further contractionary measures in their domestic fiscal politics.

The theory of expansionary austerity, one of the great oxymorons of our times, came from Alberto Alesina, an economics professor at Harvard. Alesina argued that public austerity, by boosting private profitability and confidence, might induce investment and thereby produce an expansionary effect. He recommended cutting the public budget and reducing wages and pensions of working people. Alesina denied a multiplier for public sector activity, and instead he perceived everywhere the potential for government borrowing and output crowding out private initiatives.[70]

In a subsequent paper reassessing "Austerity in 2009–13," Alesina and his coauthors argued that spending cuts were less costly than tax increases as far as output losses were concerned, comparing two types of austerity measures. Yet they added, in tortured prose, that "our results, however, are mute on the question whether the countries we study did the right thing implementing fiscal austerity at the time they did, that is 2009–13."[71] The results are "mute," meaning that the authors did not consider alternatives, such as increased public investment, yet they forcefully advocated austerity measures that impoverished the Southern European societies.

It may appear bizarre to have so many of the political choices depending on technical argument over a single figure, the Keynesian multiplier (the multiplier measures for instance the addition to total economic output of one additional dollar of government spending). Yet competing estimates were crucial for the argument because the New Consensus ruling economics from the 1980s onwards presented itself as based in fact and evidence against the superstitions of the Old Keynesians.

The New Consensus in fact contained a range of views from New Keynesian models that merely tempered Keynesian views on price rigidity with some accounting for expectations to full-fledged adherents of rational expectations, perfect capital markets, and Ricardian equivalence (assuming that government stimulus through increasing demand will have a null impact given the foresight of consumers, who anticipate future increases of taxes). But both substantially

[69] Eichengreen (2015), p. 8. [70] Alesina, Barbiero et al. (2015); Eichengreen (2015), p. 10.
[71] Alesina, Barbiero et al. (2015), p. 424.

downplayed the role of aggregate demand as the fundamental driver of money-based modern economies and both significantly subscribed to Say's Law, that supply would determine output in some reasonably short run.

The consensus of the Consensus was that the multiplier was less than their Depression-scarred predecessors believed. For some of the New Consensus economists, the multiplier might be less than one, meaning that an attempted fiscal expansion would be close to inconsequential, while for stricter adherents, such as Alesina, Robert Lucas, or John Taylor, the multiplier might be less than zero,[72] meaning that an attempted expansion of demand might actually depress the economy. Indeed, austerity might actually prove corrective, they argued.

Christina Romer, a Berkeley professor and the first chair of the Council of Economic Advisors for President Obama, computed the fiscal multipliers for government spending in the US at 1.6, larger than the preferred figure of the New Consensus. Uproar ensued, with Romer under heavy fire for politicizing economic science and with Robert Lucas and Paul Krugman wrangling over the figures on television and in the newspapers.[73]

A curiosity that divides the most ideological economics departments from the practical world of the central bank is that the models then used at the central banks employed substantially higher values for the multiplier, perhaps as high as three.[74] These models permitted even larger figures if many people in the economy are starved for current cash flow.

The argument is not esoteric. If one dollar of investment or spending in consumption leads to an increase of economic activity somewhere between 1.6 and 3 dollars, then the sound policy under a recession is for the government to borrow, spend, and invest.

But attached to the New Consensus doctrine of expansionary austerity, the ECB and other institutions responded to the long recession after 2007–8 by imposing austerity, insisting on balanced public budgets, with a particular emphasis on lowering spending rather than raising taxes. This formula, which Old Keynesians warned would constitute a drastic reduction of aggregate demand, was imposed on the countries with sizable foreign exchange deficits and large public debt. If the New Consensus gamble were correct, the economic impact would be minor and the recession would be at worst slightly deepened but the countries would emerge with smaller deficits and public debt and additional private-sector investment.

The failure of the policy and the prognostication in Europe, where austerity became standard policy, was impressive. The US followed a different, more (though still inadequate) expansionary course with some success. For that purpose, Chief Economist of the IMF Olivier Blanchard demonstrated that forecasts based on the New Consensus assumptions were simply wrong. These forecasts had served as the basis for policy, both imposed and chosen, in the weaker Eurozone economies. To the shock of the IMF staff, multipliers proved to be much larger than expected, meaning that austerity had a worse effect than forecasters predicted.

[72] Cogan et al. (2010), p. 18.

[73] Romer and Bernstein (2009a). Romer's report on the job impact of the investment plans was published; Lucas (2009), trashed it; Krugman (2015b), and Paul Krugman summarized the discussion in his *New York Times* blog.

[74] Christiano, Eichenbaum, and Rebelo (2011).

To forecast the effect of its austerity recommendations on the European economies, the IMF had applied an estimated multiplier of 0.5 (one euro of additional government spending would create only 50 cents of new economic activity). In the same vein, a cut of one percentage point of GDP from the public budget would imply a reduction of only 0.5 percent in GDP, a relatively cheap road to budget balance. But the actual and verified values substantially exceeded a multiplier of one early in the crisis, meaning that austerity reduced the productive and employment capacity of each country by more than the Consensus economists predicted.[75]

Blanchard did not shy away from offering an explanation: because fiscal multipliers were higher than expected, the fiscal consolidation through austerity lowered growth more sharply than predicted. Closer inspection demonstrated that public debt, far from declining with the effort to cut spending, had actually increased. In other words, the destructive implications of the strategy imposed on weak economies—such as Greece, Portugal, and Spain, but also Italy and France—proved both that the ECB was wrong and that an alternative was viable and available.

The consequences of austerity were devastating. The ECB-imposed spending cuts aggravated the recession and reduced Eurozone growth (by two percentage points in 2011 and three percentage points in 2012). The policy destroyed employment and led not towards budget sustainability but in the opposite direction. The leading economic institutions of Europe had endangered the European population.

Despite the evidence, the ECB (with the complicity of the IMF) and their partner institutions insisted and persisted: the process of structural reforms in Europe led to extensive austerity cuts and new adjustment through demand. The computation was wrong, the consequences were immense, and the policy was pursued against all evidence.

CONCLUSION

Before and through the financial crisis, the central bankers committed two mistakes, both intended consequences of intended actions and choices.

First, they favored deregulation and the delusionary view of self-regulating markets and, as we have shown in this chapter, their rare moments of repentance were rapidly submerged by new waves of doctrine and reassuring repetition of the neoliberal creed.

Second, independence of the central banks immunized them from public pressure and thus not only favored recessionary policies, but also led these banks to the political role of imposing vigilante fiscal restrictions. Through this transformation, the central banks became exactly the opposite of what they were conceived to insure and protect.

Central banks became the political and legislative conduits for the development of shadow finance and the central bankers became the certifiers and promoters

[75] Blanchard and Leigh (2013), p. 19; Eichengreen (2015), p. 301.

of its virtue. No obstacle remained, at the institutional level, for the growth of securitization, as the cycle of indebtedness and credit skyrocketed. The result was a monster and it was perceived by not a few of its agents.

John Mack, the ex-CEO of Morgan Stanley, is quoted as saying that banks could not be trusted (in a previous incarnation, in 2006 he had gone through the experience of being accused of insider trading; the accusation was dropped). Having led the investment bank from 2005 to 2009, through the turbulence of the crash, he warned his colleagues at a 2009 conference, by the end of his tenure, "We cannot control ourselves." Therefore, addressing the public authorities, he indulged in blasphemy: "You have to step in and control the [Wall] Street."[76] In the same desperate vein, Sandy Weill, chairman of Citigroup, asked for the breaking up of the banks.[77] At the same time, Greenspan said the same thing using other words. "I am shocked" for not having anticipated the "once in a century tsunami," and for not having noticed that regulators—himself—were unprepared.

Although this whole story is a stinging indictment of deregulation and of shadow finance and its dangers, the regulators, just after the crash, returned to their traditional views and ways. There was nobody to step in, not even at the request of Mack or Weill, some of the sharks in the tank (although they only thought this would be necessary *post festum*).

The independence of central banks thus became a trap: as pointed out by a former IMF staff member and currently an executive at PIMCO—the financial firm so keen to recruit ex-central bankers and regulators—as the "only game in town" has been reliance on central banks for macroeconomic stimulus, easy money favored financial risks,[78] while deregulation was being promoted by the guardians of the economy. The central banks proved to be part of the danger the world economy has been facing. As they failed, the tsunami went through to the shores.

[76] Pressler (2012); Yet Mack did not fully betray the solidarity due his colleagues. In 2014, Mack stepped in to defend Lloyd Blankfein from Goldman Sachs and Jamie Dimon from J.P. Morgan Chase, who were under scrutiny for their high fees. In an interview with Bloomberg he claimed he would prefer "to see people stop beating up on Lloyd and Jamie," Bloomberg (2014).

[77] "Wall Street Legend Sandy Weill: Break up Big Banks," *CNBC*, July 25, 2012.

[78] El-Erian (2016).

APPENDIX B

Skeptics and Critics vs. True Believers

After considering the deregulators and liberalizers—the academics, policymakers, and central bankers who created, implemented, and ruled the neoliberal dream—we turn in this Appendix to consider some of the critics of this course of thought and action. We find empirical skepticism and theoretical critiques. The skeptics and critics build from practical arguments based on recent and historical experience as well as from suspicion of the very concept of the self that dwells in the neoliberal vision. Finally we encounter growing critiques of the policies that have been conducted through the globalization and financialization era; we identify nine key policy errors of neoliberalism that represent the bulwark of its approach.

Readers interested in the debates of economic science will find familiar material in this Appendix; for those who find these discussions too parochial or abstract, we can only recommend looking at them if considered useful, otherwise go to the chapters on plutocracy and the management of consensus through education and indoctrination or the revolving door, which form Part III of the book.

True Believers

The revolution in academic economics marked by the Efficient Markets Hypothesis, Rational Expectations, and Friedman's market utopianism turned back the clock to a happier time for capitalism, before the Great Depression drove *laissez-faire* and unbridled finance into global disrepute. Let's review some of the key points of the argument that we traced in Chapters 5 and 6.

Capitalists need to be able to buy, sell, borrow, and lend capital. Budding entrepreneurs borrow for investment. Successful entrepreneurs cash out, converting the value from a single firm into a pool of liquid capital for diversification and further accumulation. Speculators place lucrative bets with leverage as borrowed funds amplify the outcomes of their bets. The aim is always, of course, to make capitalists richer. In all these cases, and if the market devotees' claim that capitalism allocates capital to its efficient, i.e., best, use is to be taken seriously, capitalists need to know what capital is worth—constantly and accurately. This need is fundamental for decision making because the alignment or misalignment between what capital costs and what capital is worth determines whether capitalists should buy more capital or sell off what they have.

But capital is fiendishly hard to value. Unlike simple commodities, say, copper or wheat, capital is heterogeneous. Physical capital can range from brand new robots in an auto plant to decades-old sewing machines in a sweatshop. Financial capital comprises anything from Treasury bills lent overnight between banks, to individual thirty-year mortgages, to securitized bundles of student-loan debt, to bets on the solvency of sovereign bonds. Heterogeneous capital gives only fleeting glimpses of its fundamental value, maybe, for example, in the price of brand new physical capital at the moment of purchase.

Furthermore, unlike the flow of spending on food or clothing or even cars, the stock of capital delivers its value only slowly and uncertainly, over time and with no guarantees. The value of the contemporary capital stock is supposed to be the value of the expected future stream of net profit flows from the stock. Given this reasoning, Joan Robinson attributes to Michal Kalecki an elegant expression of the difficulty: "I have found out what economics is; it is the science of confusing stocks with flows."[1] For capitalists, it is a needed science and a necessary confusion. Heterogeneity among forms of capital, the problem of comparing stocks and flows, and the challenge of predicting the future might appear to pose insurmountable difficulties for the valuation and allocation of capital.

To the rescue come financial markets, in which financial capital, and the physical capital it represents, has a constantly listed and updated price. Value is manifest in liquidity; if an asset can be sold at a price then that price is what the asset is worth. These principles are not so hard to profess. As narrator Nick Carraway explains at the beginning of F. Scott Fitzgerald's *Great Gatsby*, "I decided to go East and learn the bond business. Everybody I knew was in the bond business, so I supposed it could support one more single man."

While liquidity and continuous posting improve matters for the capitalist, liquidity is not the same as accuracy. Here the incentive-oriented mindset of economics makes its contribution. It is in the material interest of investors to make accurate estimates of the true value of capital. To do otherwise would be to forgo profits. Therefore, investors must make accurate, even if imprecise, estimates of the true value of capital. It is supposed that the human mind can solve messily, provisionally, but on average correctly, the computational problems of guessing what the future holds and converting between future flows and present-day stocks. The interplay of many investors in a liquid market, each investor with an incentive to value accurately, provides "efficient price discovery." That is, market participants, whose incentives direct them, on average, to guess correctly, thus bid, ask, and transact towards the true value. Liberal financial markets are the original crowd-sourced solution. The incentive to be right combined with the law of large numbers cannot be wrong.

Or so says the Efficient Markets Hypothesis, which has been mobilized at every step to stave off criticisms, let alone outright regulation, of financial markets. For any interference in the process of market participants engaging in efficient price discovery would disrupt its accuracy and immediacy. A more concrete offspring of the Efficient Markets Hypothesis, the Capital Assets Pricing Model (CAPM) provides a neat and applicable law of finance, tracing a straightforward tradeoff between expected risk and returns. Armed with these models, the financiers have tailored products for customers and fended off regulators.

The interplay between research and regulatory policy on finance has been an effective and tightly linked public-private intellectual partnership. Contemporary confidence in the Efficient Markets Hypothesis has historical antecedents. Active financial markets flourished from the nineteenth century onward, apparently solving the problems of valuing capital and maintaining its liquidity with the cult of the stabilizing speculator and a host of exotic instruments that are surprisingly current today. By the 1930s, John Maynard Keynes could speak meaningfully of "orthodox finance," already a century-old game.

There is a shortfall in the basic logic: wanting to be accurate or finding it profitable to be accurate does not mean that investors will, in fact, be accurate. And the tattered record of financial markets, of repeated cycles of boom and bust illustrate the systematic forces that point away from accuracy. The true value of capital most likely does not exist. It is, at best, fleeting and unknowable, because fundamental uncertainty dooms the enterprise. The frequent occurrence of once-in-a-lifetime events and multiple outcomes that are more correlated with each other and more dominated by macroeconomic context than microeconomic logic or past performance can predict in advance means that the innocent as well as the guilty will go down with a sinking ship.

That shortfall in logic (wanting it so does not make it so) and the implication of out-of-control financial markets in the most serious economic and political crises of the advanced economies in the eighteenth, nineteenth, twentieth, and twenty-first centuries has attracted critics within and outside Economics. In this chapter we focus on the skeptics and critics within Economics.

[1] Robinson (1982).

A basic dichotomy in disciplinary skepticism about financial markets is a difference in views on whether there are some blemishes on the skin of an otherwise wholesome fruit or whether the entire apple is rotten to the core. The former perspective has roots in research on anomalies in security prices. (Indeed, the name of the regular column by University of Chicago Professor Richard Thaler in the *Journal of Economic Perspectives* is "Anomalies"). Financial market anomalies are "surprising" violations of the Efficient Markets Hypothesis and its offspring such as the CAPM. The January Effect (stocks outperform expectations in January), Small Cap Premium Anomaly (there are bargains, even acknowledging risk, in the stock price of smaller firms), and a host of other anomalies demonstrate scratches in the shiny armor of the Efficient Markets Hypothesis. Even one of the true believers, Burton Malkiel, author of *A Random Walk Down Wall Street*,[2] which hybridizes a popular investment guide and a review of the academic literature exploring the Efficient Markets Hypothesis, has included anomalies in the closing chapters of recent editions. Bounded skepticism based on anomalies research has taken robust shape in the field of Behavioral Finance.

And their Beliefs: The Errors of Neoliberalism

What all three flavors of skeptics have failed to do is to bring down the house of the true believers. Indeed, not only in finance but in the framework of economic and financial management, bad economics has continued to drive out good. Part of the puzzle of the success of neoliberalism as guidance for leadership is that the neoliberals' economic explanations and prescriptions have not performed well. The neoliberals are wrong about everything, wrong with little consequence for their reputations or theories, and wrong with grave consequences for the rest of the world.

In the Introduction we examined some of the underlying reasons for the neoliberal errors—the attention to greed as singular motive and policy guide. John Cassidy's *How Markets Fail* has a thorough survey of the microeconomics of economic disaster. In this section, we look at nine concrete errors in analysis and prescription that neoliberalism has brought. These nine errors of neoliberalism, and the continued strict adherence of policymakers to these ideas with limited or waning empirical support offer plenty of food for thought of skeptics and critics.

Low Inflation

One of the key tenets of neoliberal macroeconomic policy has been the importance of maintaining price stability, i.e., low inflation. This goal has been pursued with the macroeconomic policy of inflation targeting in which macroeconomic authorities, typically the monetary authority, declare a desired rate of inflation and adjust monetary policy, via the policy interest rate, to meet the declared target.

As we shall see, the European Union has become in almost every dimension the realization of the neoliberal ideal in macroeconomic and financial management. The focus on price stability is a central case. Unlike the US Federal Reserve which has a twin mandate of price stability and full employment, the European Central Bank has, as its official mandate, only price stability. The ECB has assiduously followed its mandate, setting an inflation target of 2 percent and raising rates when inflation exceeds this target, even in the depths of the Great Recession.

Both the inclusion and the exclusion warrant reflection. The exclusion of full employment as a goal of the ECB emerged in large part from the success of the rational expectations turn in economics in the 1970s and the conclusion of significant portions of the Economics

[2] Malkiel (2011).

discipline that monetary policy cannot affect output and employment. In contrast, the twin mandate of the US Federal Reserve to include full employment was set in 1946 and reflected economic thinking at the height of the Keynesian era and concerns about secular stagnation and the return of the Great Depression. By the 1970s the thinking of Milton Friedman, Robert Lucas, and Thomas Sargent and the experience of stagflation—simultaneously high inflation and high unemployment, had eroded confidence in the ability of national governments to manage the macroeconomy. According to the Friedman-Lucas-Sargent critiques, what had appeared to be a substantive tradeoff between unemployment and inflation was in fact somewhere between a short-term tradeoff and altogether illusory. In any case, the economy would gravitate to a Natural Rate of Unemployment, in Friedman's terminology, for wholly real reasons, and monetary policy would merely determine the inflation rate and price level. There was no point in trying to adjust the unemployment rate with interest rates or monetary policy because it simply could not be done.

The inclusion of price stability as the goal of the ECB reflects a strongly anti-inflationary mindset, which was a core tenet of the ECB's predecessor, the Bundesbank. Every tightening of the European money supply is accompanied by the bromide that German bankers remember the Weimar inflation. The tightening is needed to avoid the inevitable inflationary spirals that occur when inflation exceeds 2 percent (or unemployment falls below 7 percent). We are piously informed that so painful is the ninety-year-old memory of the German inflation and its political consequences for democratic Weimar that responsible German bankers could never let it happen again. The sage German banker knows that without constant vigilance the road to ruin is certain: 3 percent inflation this year, 75,000 percent next year, and then the inevitable march of fascism. Of course it's only a tale half-told—the 1923 inflation was quelled and democratic Germany enjoyed six years of relative stability until the international Great Depression tore it apart—nor, as we shall see, are bankers' memories all that good. The tight money of the ECB and the Bundesbank thus represents the sometimes stern discipline that is nonetheless always for the greater good of social stability and democracy.

A populist gloss often accompanies anti-inflation rhetoric. In his 1982 economic report, Ronald Reagan described inflation as "tragic." Reagan bragged that he and Fed Chair Paul Volcker ensured that inflation, " 'the cruelest tax,' was taking less away from individual savings and taking less out of every working American's paycheck."[3]

Retirees on fixed incomes or workers on multi-year contracts appear to be at grave risk from inflation, which reduces the real value of their nominally fixed income. But inflation is, in fact, more of a problem for bankers than for workers or retirees. The problems that people on fixed incomes face from inflation can be trivially managed with automatic indexation, as has been the case for Social Security pension payments in the United States since the early 1970s. Indexation can also protect wages and salaries and, as has been the case in the United States since 1986, insulate a progressive tax structure from inflation. Inflation is not the cruelest tax for working people or people on fixed incomes. The real truth about inflation is that it is a problem for Fixed Income Departments of investment banks—bond traders and bondholders, not pensioners. Moderate inflation transfers wealth from creditors to debtors, who include working people and many productive enterprises.

In fact, moving up to the macroeconomic level for the economy as a whole, there is essentially no evidence that moderate inflation is bad for economic growth. Some key evidence on the unimportance of inflation comes from the heart of neoliberal economics: Michael Bruno, now deceased, who served both as Governor of the Central Bank of Israel and as Chief Economist of the World Bank, and William Easterly, Professor of Economics at New York University, analyzed more than six hundred episodes of—by the standards of the

[3] Reagan (1982).

neoliberal era—high inflation, annual inflation in excess of 20 percent per year. The majority of these cases had inflation between 20 and 40 percent, and in no case did inflation accelerate nor was economic growth diminished.[4] A more detailed econometric analysis confirms the finding.[5]

The Bruno and Easterly work points up the importance of simply examining the data to assess strong universal claims about macroeconomic policy. There are certainly cases in which inflation can damage economies, and no one doubts the significant damage that hyperinflation (annual price inflation in excess of 50 percent) can do—although most cases of hyperinflation occur in political situations of extreme stress.

What is remarkable is that the goal of very low inflation became universal dogma with essentially no evidence that it provides benefits. The Federal Reserve of the United States now targets roughly 2 percent inflation, the ECB targets something below 2 percent with true price stability, i.e., 0 percent inflation, as an implicit goal. Even many African countries, in which the price level is dominated by food and fuel, i.e., imported goods with highly volatile prices, have attempted inflation targeting.

So with essentially no evidence in its favor, the maintenance of low inflation became the law of the land.

"Developed," or Highly Liquid, Financial Markets

Another tenet of the neoliberal macro-regulatory regime is that "developed" financial markets contribute significantly to economic growth. What "developed" means in this context are active, or liquid, financial markets in which paper ownership of productive assets and other paper claims on output can change hands smoothly.

Gerald Epstein of University of Massachusetts Amherst identifies six functions of finance: (1) Channel finance to productive investment; (2) Provide mechanisms for households to save for retirement; (3) Reduce risk; (4) Provide stable and flexible liquidity; (5) Provide an efficient payments mechanism; and (6) Create useful financial innovations.[6] The argument for a liquid stock market is that active financial markets provide productive firms with access to capital and direct capital to efficient uses. Yet there is little evidence that liquid stock markets effectively meet any of Epstein's functions.

There was for a time a cottage industry in demonstrating the connection between developed financial markets and economic growth. In a series of empirical papers Ross Levine, then a Principal Economist at the World Bank, emphasized the importance of financial development for economic growth. The most influential, published in the *American Economic Review*, concludes that a liquid stock market makes a potentially very large contribution to economic growth.[7] Levine and Zervos report that between the mid-1970s and the early 1990s, the GDPs of countries that had highly liquid stock markets grew almost 1.5 percentage points per year faster than countries without liquid stock markets.

But this widely cited result turned out to depend critically on two peculiar cases, Korea and Taiwan.[8] Even by the most optimistic reading, those who heed the call of liquid financial markets will not find the road to riches.

It is not clear what benefits are provided by active stock markets. What Levine and Zervos call liquidity is really the amount of churn, the exchange of existing shares. The value of this churn exceeds many times over the amount of new productive investment, that is, actual creation of new plant and equipment.

International Capital Mobility

If there is one area in which the neoliberal consensus has yielded and the neoliberal institutions have backed down in terms of the practical enforcement of the rules governing

[4] Bruno and Easterly (1996, 1998). [5] Pollin and Zhu (2006). [6] Epstein (2016).
[7] Levine and Zervos (1998). [8] Zhu, M. Ash, and Pollin (2004).

country behavior, it is in International Capital Mobility. International capital mobility was a generation-long fetish for the international financial institutions. No interference of any sort or of any duration with the passage of capital outward or inward could be tolerated. We treat the emergent revision of neoliberal orthodoxy in the International Monetary Fund in Chapter 10.

As with "developed financial markets," liberalization of international financial markets was the object of much study by advocates. Opinions varied on how to measure liberalization, with some papers preferring policy—with several scoring systems coding the restrictions in the IMF's Annual Report on Exchange Arrangements and Exchange Restrictions, the OECD's Code of Liberalization Capital Movements, and various derived measures and others identifying actual activity, typically the sum of gross capital flows (sum of absolute values of inflows and outflows) divided by GDP or "accumulated" capital flows divided by GDP.

In any case, regardless of the measure, cross-country growth equations give no evidence in favor of international capital mobility as a lever of development. Figure B.1 reprints a key finding on how growth responded (or failed to respond) to increased capital account openness. At every level of increased capital account openness (on the horizontal axis), there was a wide range of subsequent observed growth with no evident relationship between more openness and more growth.

"Capital Account Liberalization: Theory, Evidence, and Speculation" attempts to demonstrate powerful beneficial effects of capital account liberalization[9] in the face of mounting evidence to the contrary. The theoretical basis for the rescue is that under the standard growth model in mainstream economics, a higher savings rate, i.e., faster capital accumulation, provides only a one-time boost to output per capita as the old capital-to-labor ratio converges to the new, higher ratio. This position taken to its fullest means accepting that essentially no interventions in the economy can raise the growth rate permanently.

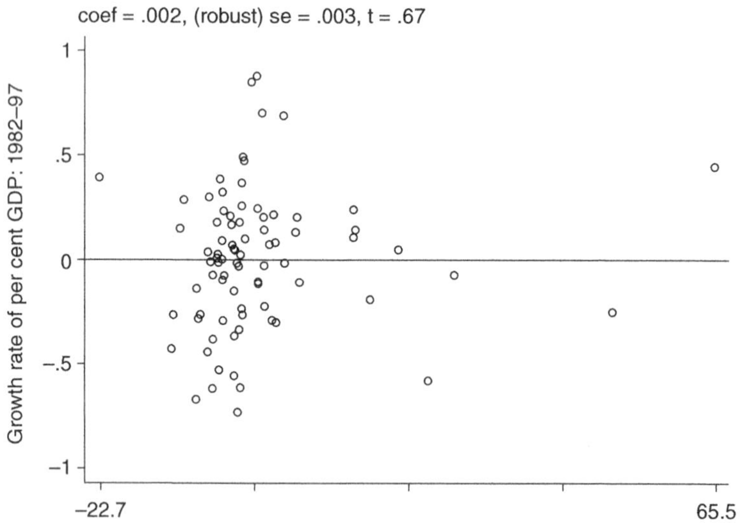

Figure B.1. Capital account liberalization and economic growth
Source: E. Prasad et al. (2003).

[9] Henry (2007).

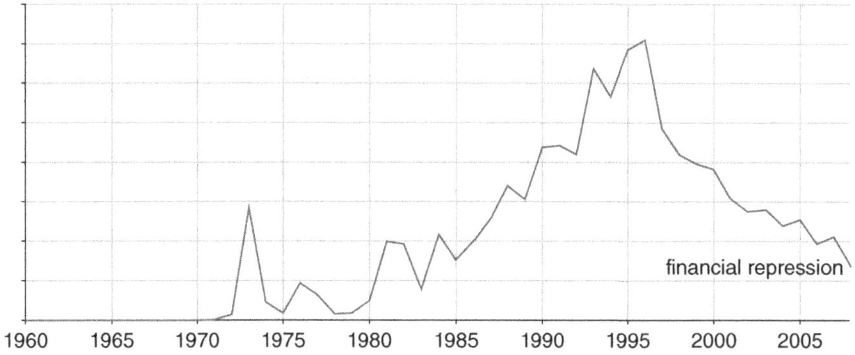

Figure B.2. The arc of financial repression

Notes: The figure shows the Google *n*-gram time series for the appearance of the term "financial repression" in the English-language corpus, 1960–present.

Source: Authors' analysis using Michel et al. (2011).

Applied to the question of capital account liberalization, the argument is both a strategic retreat and a good offense. As a retreat, the fall back on the standard growth model is revising the promise: "we never said that it would increase growth rates, only that there would be a nice one-time increase in per capita income." Of course the public usually hears stronger promises in the run up to market openings. Furthermore, with any lags or medium-run effects, the increased growth rate should show up in the data—the one-time increase occurring over some time horizon. Henry's event studies show an increase in investment, measured as investment in relation to the capital stock, following liberalization. However, over any window greater than three years there is no effect on investment or on growth.

Capital account liberalization has been the most important site of a break in orthodoxy, with cracks appearing as early as the Asian financial crisis in the late 1990s and widening sharply during the Great Crash of 2007–8. We explore the depth and longevity of the break in more detail in Chapter 10. The break is less remarkable than the preceding orthodoxy, and the vehemence of the conviction that capital controls were anathema to growth, even in the face of substantial evidence that capital controls could support growth, as in many of the high-growth Asian economies, and that the absence of capital controls could court financial and macroeconomic ruin.

The use of the term "financial repression" to describe controls on international movement of capital is a remarkable innovation in marketing policy. Figure B.2 shows the relative frequency of the term "financial repression." It is apparently unused (in the corpus of scanned texts in Google's collection) before 1970. It makes a brief appearance in the early 1970s and then rises to prominence beginning just before 1980 with peak application in 1995 at the height of the Washington Consensus.

As we discuss in more detail in Chapter 6, no area of the Washington Consensus has seen a more complete breakdown among policy elites than the case for perfect international capital mobility. The promulgating institutions, in particular the International Monetary Fund, have been in significant internal turmoil over the question, a civil war that some label "productive incoherence."

Distrust of Social Insurance

In his 2005 Presidential Address to the American Economics Association, Martin Feldstein summarized a career's worth of research against social insurance and the welfare state. Feldstein, Chair of President Ronald Reagan's Council of Economic Advisers, has waged war on social insurance since the early 1970s. The fundamental criticism stems from the greed-guided concepts of incentive and moral hazard.

In his attacks on unemployment insurance, Feldstein estimated replacement ratios, the percentage of a worker's salary that would be replaced in the event of unemployment. With replacement rates as high as 50 percent of employed earnings—and further advantaged by their untaxed status—the incentives to become or remain unemployed were large. The attack on unemployment insurance spilled over into views of unemployment itself. Even during the Great Recession, University of Chicago economists Casey Mulligan and John Cochrane pointed to the extension of the duration of unemployment benefits as the cause of the high unemployment rate. The American Liberal disease has now spread to European social democracies and question labor-market flexibility and entitlement reform.

A detailed analysis across most of the developed economies examines which came first, the unemployment insurance or the unemployment, and find that more generous unemployment benefits essentially never lead to higher unemployment.[10] In many countries, unemployment benefits have been, humanely, increased in response to periods of higher unemployment, and this increase has been effected without aggravating unemployment.[11]

So unemployment insurance had been widely accepted as progress, providing insurance against the vicissitudes of life in a capitalist economy. It provides automatic stabilization of the economy by buffering household spending against temporary economic downturns. And high quality evidence shows that this security can be delivered with no meaningful effect on the incentives to seek work. Yet the neoliberal dogma has converted unemployment insurance into something alien and perverse.

Feldstein sought to launch for public pensions the same attack that he initiated for unemployment benefits. In the case of pensions, national savings might be endangered by the moral hazard of a secure retirement. Who would save for retirement or incapacitation when a pay-as-you-go public retirement system would provide support for the elderly or disabled? Coupled with a neoclassical savings constrained model of investment, the macroeconomic and welfare effects could be considerable. By viewing the promised public pension as "wealth," the household would fail to provide savings for investment on the productive side of the economy.

Feldstein's econometric study using US data for the postwar period estimated rather substantial responses of private savings to perceived social security wealth.[12] Replication of the research found that a programming error accounted for the exciting result, which the author blamed on his graduate research assistant.[13]

Beyond the violation of the laws of arithmetic, Feldstein's argument fails to hold water on two levels: first, in its assumption that investment is savings constrained; and second, in its finding that perceived social security wealth meaningfully alters household incentives for savings for productive ends. Personal responsibility suggests prudence rather than the cruder "You're On Your Own."

Old-age and survivor insurance, health insurance, and unemployment insurance were great inventions of the late nineteenth and early twentieth centuries in response to restructured societies with enormous dislocations in the ability of communities and families to provide care. For most of the twentieth century and especially after the Second World War, the Western democracies broadened and deepened the reach of these programs, partially shielding the working classes from the heartlessness of the labor market. Sometimes workers organized insurance through the workplace and sometimes the state intervened directly to provide the social protection itself, the insurance, or access to fair, regulated markets for the insurance.

[10] D. R. Howell et al. (2007). [11] Boone et al. (2016). [12] Feldstein (1974).
[13] Feldstein (1982).

But through an extraordinary focus of intellectual power, the neoliberals turned virtue into vice.

Flexible Labor Markets

The provision of social insurance is one aspect of labor market structure, or "rigidity" as it is pejoratively known. In addition to social insurance, labor market structure refers in the broadest sense to the rules of the game for establishing the conditions of employment and work. Important aspects of labor market structure include laws, regulations, or norms concerning the terms under which employees may be disciplined or dismissed; the existence of laws concerning minimum wages, overtime or maximum hours, safety regulations, and other standards for the treatment of labor in the workplace; whether wages, wage-setting rules, and working conditions can be established by collective bargaining; whether collective bargaining agreements are extended from unionized firms or sectors to non-unionized firms or sectors; and the role of apprenticeships and qualifications in hiring and promotion.

The neoliberals have blamed poor macroeconomic results and high unemployment rates, especially in the social democracies of Western Europe, on rigid labor markets. The assault on labor market structures that favor workers has been conducted at every level, from macroeconomic claims that firms are inhibited from hiring by the prospect of workers who cannot be rapidly sanctioned to microeconomic arguments supporting irregular work and sub-minimum wages in the name of freedom to contract. The use of language in the terms rigid and flexible has been deft, and even workers have been mobilized to express a taste for flexible hours.

Labor market rigidity is not responsible for high unemployment rates. Indeed, the more structured labor markets of Europe, such as Austria, Finland, and Germany, have delivered better employment performance. Nor has increased labor market flexibility in the countries that have attempted to liberalize their labor markets likely produced a single new job.

Labor market flexibility implicitly contrasts with rigidity or sclerosis. If the markets are rusty, lubricate them with some layoffs.

Deposit Insurance

The neoliberals never met insurance that they liked. Deposit insurance, a Federal policy of the New Deal, which replaced a host of inadequate and variable local provisions, in response to the devastating effect of banks failures on the savings of the middle class during the Great Crash and Depression, provides that small depositors will not experience losses in case of bank failure. Banks in the US pay mandatory premiums to participate in the Federal Deposit Insurance Corporation.[14]

In the US Savings and Loan debacle, the simultaneous deregulation both of borrowing interest rates, lending interest rates, and investment choices for a numerous class of previously local banks, so-called Savings and Loans, led to extraordinary risk taking, outright looting, and massive losses. Conservative accounts of the disaster point to the combination of deregulated investment with insured deposits as the combustible mixture—as if astute individual depositors could have disciplined Savings and Loans from their outrageous bets on commercial developments in Texas suburbs. The individual depositor is perhaps the least qualified agent of so-called counterparty monitoring in the financial system.

Without doubt, deposit insurance works best in a well-regulated financial regime. But deposit insurance remains among the chimera of the deregulatory right.

[14] Federal Deposit Insurance Corporation (1998).

"Free" Trade

Few economics principles elicit more knee-jerk loyalty from academic economists than Free Trade. Going back to David Ricardo and Adam Smith the theories of comparative advantage and voluntary exchange provide positive and counterintuitive findings. Regardless of endowments or differential productivity, both parties to a transaction can be made better off. No parties will see their skills or effort rendered redundant. The effects of trade are more ambiguous when it involves multiple classes and countries (labor in the home country, labor in the foreign country, capital in the home country, capital in the foreign country), unemployment, and accumulated advantages in learning and technological change.

And the implementation of trade via policy always and everywhere deviates from the textbook characterization. Even the true history of David Ricardo's account of England specializing in textiles and Portugal specializing in wine, literally the textbook case, does not conform to the freetrade model. Dean Baker points out that the goods and services exposed to new competition under trade policy are rarely those in which the rich benefit from the exclusion; for example, trade policy does not generally seek to expose doctors, lawyers, filmmakers, or bankers to additional competition, but steelworkers, meatpackers, and fruit pickers are routinely additionally exposed to new competition.[15]

Furthermore, trade policy advocated by neoliberals as free trade typically excludes distinctions based on "Process and Production Methods" (PPM) from trade regulation. As part of its trade policy, this exclusion ignores legitimate collective decisions to regulate products based on ethical or environmental concerns about their production.

In the larger scheme, Ha-Joon Chang of Cambridge University demonstrates with historical case studies that none of today's developed countries arrived at development with free trade policies for themselves.[16]

A substantial literature, largely conducted or sponsored by the World Bank, which addressed the question "Do countries with lower barriers to international trade experience faster economic progress?" largely finds in favor of the virtues of liberal trade policy. Francisco Rodriguez and Dani Rodrik review and replicate (or fail to replicate) the original results.[17] They find the literature rife with misspecifications. They especially note the use of poor proxies for trade policy. Their revisitation of this literature leaves substantial doubt about the association between reduction of trade barriers and improved growth.

Balanced Budgets, Austerity, and Debt Reduction

The psychological hold of the balanced budget, a key component of what Keynes referred to as "The Treasury View" is enormously strong. In the depths of the Great Depression Franklin Delano Roosevelt campaigned for President of the United States against Herbert Hoover with the promise of a balanced budget and stopping Hoover's profligacy. In 2009, as the economies of the United States and Europe plunged into recession, newly inaugurated President Barack Obama made his first remarks to his senior staff with the guidance, "During this period of economic emergency, families are tightening their belts, and so should Washington," and he would repeat the obligation of belt tightening through 2013.[18] Expansionary austerity can join the Newspeak lexicon.

A pile of academic literature on the dangers of public debt emerged in tandem with the broadening of the financial crisis to Europe in 2010. Reinhart and Rogoff, Checherita-Westphal and Rother, Cecchetti, Mohanty, and Zampolli, and Kumar and Wu made

[15] D. Baker (2006). [16] Chang (2002, 2007). [17] Rodriguez and Rodrik (2001).

[18] See, for Obama administration examples, Obama (2009, 2010, 2013); Lew (2010); US Senate Committee on the Budget (2011). But for the Republican opposition, who were equally attracted to the belt-tightening metaphor, the constriction did not suffice, Ryan (2009); Ros-Lehtinen (2012); Rodgers (2015).

appearances, largely in a gray, or not-peer-reviewed, academic literature at this time. All four of these analyses, associated with Harvard, the Bank of International Settlements, and the International Monetary Fund, found that high public debt stymies growth.

Indeed, all four papers found a cliff in the relationship between economic growth and public debt at the point where public debt exceeded 90 percent of GDP. The papers used different datasets and different methods, both superficial indicators of robustness in economic findings.

The findings—that public debt inhibits growth and that the negative effect of public debt on growth is severe above public debt in excess of 90 percent of GDP—appeared at the height of public debate on recession, debt, and austerity in Europe. There is little question that the academic contribution influenced or at least emboldened public decision makers. The idea of austerity may not have originated in Reinhart and Rogoff, but with the most respected analysis from the most elite universities and institutions making the case, it was easier for politicians to insist on the anti-Keynesian austerity response.

Mistakes in these papers were exposed, beginning with the work of graduate Thomas Herndon at the University of Massachusetts Amherst, who demonstrated that the Reinhart and Rogoff result depended critically on a selected sample and indefensible methods of aggregation.[19] The spreadsheet that included the selected sample and the indefensible aggregation method also had other errors: five countries from the twenty-country sample were omitted and numbers were incorrectly transcribed.

Properly accounted, there is a modest association between public debt and growth, and much of the relationship comes not from public debt reducing growth but from recessions increasing public debt. A fundamental problem with the analysis is that the pathway from public debt to reduced economic performance is not specified. It is a faith in the unseen. At best, it is a foolish fallacy of composition from the household to the nation state because what is true for the household, that debt places a damper on future consumption, is not true for nations where most of the debt is held by nationals and will be paid back through taxes paid by nationals.

While the overturning of the Reinhart and Rogoff result received the most attention, all of the papers on the negative consequences of public debt are marked by significant methodological flaws that significantly reduce their relevance in the current political and economic conjuncture.

As the recession wore on, especially in the parts of Europe that had most assiduously implemented austerity, the second generation of analysis rediscovered the effectiveness of expansionary policy. Blanchard and Leigh demonstrated a strong relationship between deficit spending and growth, with a nearly perfect correlation between the austerity program and the depth of the recession. Additional analysis showed how ideological blinders at the international institutions systematically led to forecasting errors about the effect of austerity.[20] The conviction that austerity would not be contractionary made the forecasts far too optimistic for the countries that most aggressively implemented austerity plans.

Privatization

A final dimension of the neoliberal package is the belief that public agency is inept and corrupt and that private parties can better provide any good or service, including those that have been historically or universally provided by the public sector.

Several claims recur in the privatization campaigns. First, the privatization case rests on the proposition that the private sector can provide the same service at lower cost because the public sector lacks incentives to provide the service at the lowest possible cost and therefore wastes resources. Second, privatization is often couched in the language of choice, which

[19] Herndon, M. Ash, and Pollin (2014). [20] Blanchard and Leigh (2013).

collapses the public provision of fundamentals that depend on social solidarity, such as health, education, pensions, and insurance, into an individual consumer-choice model.

There are several fundamental problems with privatization.

The break with universalism is often a moral outrage but it is more than that. The state cannot in fact discharge its obligations by contracting them out. Privatizers pick and choose the most profitable pieces, whether it be picking and choosing state-owned industries for acquisition or selecting patients or students that are profitable to treat or to educate. Cream-skimming and cherry-picking are colorful terms for grabbing winners, and lemon-dropping means similarly avoiding expensive or difficult to manage cases. The state, which is the provider of ultimate responsibility and last resort, is left to provide for the most difficult or expensive case after having yielded capacity and revenue—a potential source of cross-subsidization to manage difficult cases—to privatizers.

Cost savings are often overestimated. It's often the case in privatizations that the public entity guarantees the costs or even the profitability of the private agent. For example, toll roads in Portugal have been privatized with a guarantee of a minimum traffic load and hence revenue and the public sector has been obligated to make whole a disappointed privatizer. In the US, companies operating private prisons have been promised numbers of occupied beds, with ensuing moral hazard for the administration of public justice.

The source of cost savings is often not efficiencies, but exploitation and speed-up. Privatization to evade unionized public labor may generate budgetary savings but the loss of well-paid jobs means that the savings are largely a transfer from workers to better-off taxpayers rather than a true gain in productivity.

States are likely to sell assets when they are fiscally strapped, in particular during downturns. Unfortunately, the price is often depressed and states excel at selling low on behalf of citizens. During downturns the state should not shed capacity but instead build its capacity, taking advantage of low interest rates and depressed private sector options.

A Taxonomy of Skeptics and Critics

The errors of neoliberal policy are buttressed with careful use of language. The language of neoliberalism is a worthy companion to Newspeak. The case against budget deficits is billed as Expansionary Austerity. Any proposed interference with the international movement of capital is attacked as Financial Repression. Interventions by fiscal and banking authorities are characterized as precise and therapeutic: shock therapy and inflation targeting. Free Trade is the grandparent of positive spin. Few words have more positive and fewer negative connotations than "Free." Financial Market Development associates liberal, liquid financial markets with economic and human development.

Against this half century neoliberal and deregulatory assault on these social protections and its Orwellian warping of language, we review some of the skeptics and critics of neoliberalism and deregulation. We begin with skepticism from within the contemporary mainstream of the profession and then turn to the more critical outsiders, such as Adam Smith.

Reluctant Skepticism from the Belly of the Beast

Caught in the middle of a tug-of-war between professional respectability and professional responsibility, some of the mainstream critics cannot decide which camp they occupy. Dante comments on the inability to take sides: "that wicked band / of angels who were neither rebels / nor faithful to God."[21] They are here called the "reluctant skeptics."

[21] Inf. III. 37–9.

Larry Summers

Before his ascendance to the US Treasury, as we discuss in more detail in Chapter 6 for his engagement in the Born affair and in Chapter 12 as a practitioner of the revolving door, Professor Larry Summers of Harvard University rose to academic prominence on a set of studies in the Keynesian tradition, some on unemployment and many on dysfunctions in financial markets.

In joint work, Summers identified noise traders, financial speculators who respond with alacrity to trends, rather than to the evaluation of fundamentals, as a potential barrier to financial markets arriving at the right price. Unlike the mainstream model, where savvy fundamentals traders can profit from the valuation mistake and thereby drive the speculative offenders from the market, noise traders can create enough of their own noise that the pricing deviation is potentially long-lived. Lest Summers' attention to the static generated by noise traders be considered merely more of the anomalies variant, Summers also developed the analysis of rational bubbles, long-term deviation of asset prices from fundamentals with no available recourse for a would-be stabilizing speculator. Summers also demonstrated the weakness of supposed empirical tests of market efficiency, observing that, while they fail to reject the hypothesis of efficient markets, the tests suffer from low power, i.e., cannot distinguish between the alternatives. Even a market price that deviates really substantially from fundamentals for a very long period, a clear violation of the Efficient Markets Hypothesis, will not necessarily trip the statistical wires that would reject the hypothesis once and for all.

One of his best known works asks, "Does the Stock Market Rationally Reflect Fundamental Values?" Summers begins by observing: "The proposition that securities markets are efficient forms the basis for most research in financial economics." After reviewing decades of empirical analysis, he closes, recommending "caution in treating stock prices or their changes as rational reflections of fundamental values" and notes the "very weak available evidence that market valuations are always rational."[22] With such a damning indictment of the Efficient Markets Hypothesis, Summers might be supposed to be soundly in the Keynesian, regulatory camp.

But the findings of Summers the professor seem to have taken only half root with Summers the policy insider. First the good news. As Deputy Secretary of the Treasury in the Clinton administration, Summers, along with Chair of the Fed Alan Greenspan and Secretary of the Treasury (and former Goldman Sachs Chair) Robert Rubin, helped to mitigate the effects of back-to-back economic meltdowns in Russia and Asia in 1997–8, for which they were hailed on the cover of *Time* as the Committee to Save the World.[23] The world-saving involved substantial extensions of liquidity to financial institutions in crisis and occasional writedowns of bad debt. The response might be less charitably described as orthodox crisis finance, in the tradition of Walter Bagehot, the nineteenth-century financial journalist (and founder of that field) who advocated unlimited lending at penalty rates to solvent institutions undergoing liquidity crises.

Then the bad news. Despite his illustrious academic career demonstrating the needless volatility of financial markets and his first-hand experience with the damage in Russia and Asia, Summers nonetheless advocated vigorously at every opportunity for the continued deregulation of US financial markets. Sophisticated investors and financial innovation were the watchwords of his campaigns. His practical hand in these matters was telling. Summers advocated for the repeal of the Glass-Steagall Act of 1933, a New Deal-era financial regulation that enforced separation of commercial banking (with its access to Federally insured customer deposits) and investment banking (with its practices of proprietary trading and other forms of taking risky bets. With Summers at the helm as Secretary of

[22] Summers (1986). [23] Ramo (1999).

the Treasury—he was promoted after Rubin retired—and with a stock-market bubble in Internet stocks (the "dot-com bubble") in full swing, Glass-Steagall was repealed in 1999. On the day of the Glass-Steagall repeal, Secretary Summers remarked: "Today Congress voted to update the rules that have governed financial services since the Great Depression and replace them with a system for the 21st century ...This historic legislation will better enable American companies to compete in the new economy."[24]

His advocacy and praise for other parts of the financial deregulation package was equally fulsome. Summers played a key role as a White House insider in preventing more aggressive regulation of derivative markets. Summers maneuvered and parried to prevent Commodity Futures Trading Commission (CFTC) Chair Brooksley Born from bringing derivatives under the jurisdiction of the Commission. Encouraged by Summers, Congress passed legislation in 1999 prohibiting the CFTC from regulating this form of financial asset, as we discussed in Chapter 6.

Thus, Summers, despite his outstanding intellectual achievements in the area of financial market unreliability and despite his close-up view of the Russian and Asian financial debacles, played a more aggressive and public role than even, say, Eugene Fama, whose contribution we reviewed in Chapter 5, in protecting financial markets from regulation.

Reinhart and Rogoff

In *This Time Is Different*, two orthodox insiders with strong policy credentials, Carmen Reinhart and Kenneth Rogoff, trace more than 200 years of bubbles and crashes[25] and provide a significant warning about the dangers of unbridled finance. The book indisputably starts as a clear warning of the danger of speculative private financial markets and early on makes the case for better regulation of finance. The title refers to the inevitable rationale that boosters give for why on the way up each particular boom can be simultaneously as enticing as it appears and still consistent with the laws of conventional finance. The phases of growth appear to mirror those of Minsky. Thus, on first encounter, *This Time Is Different* would appear to be a long-awaited antidote for belief in efficient markets at all times.

But the careful reader perceives a curious elision in progress over the course of the book. The cautionary tales of the dangers of private debt has quietly transformed by the end of the book into a warning against the dangers of public debt.

The distinction is very important. First, public debt is typically more transparent and scrutinized—and hence less prone to run up bubbles and less dangerous—than private debt. To be sure, there are exceptions, and some private financial firms have worked with national governments to mask the extent of public borrowing, as Goldman Sachs did with Greece in the early 2000s. But runaway bubbles in private debt are far more common. Second, the shift in focus avoids coming to grips with the problem of endogenous crisis in private financial markets. Followed to its logical conclusion, the indictment of private debt in *This Time Is Different* would point towards a much more regulated financial system. But by handing off the problem from private to public finance by the end of the tome, Reinhart and Rogoff avoid coming to terms with a difficult-to-swallow message for orthodox finance and economics.

Robert Shiller

Robert Shiller is Professor of Economics at Yale University and a winner of the Nobel Prize in Economics. Shiller has provided a technical exposition of Keynes's nth degree guessing game in his excellent June 1981 paper. The current price of a share of stock is supposed to be the discounted stream of its expected future dividends.[26] So for the stock price to move a lot, as it often does, there must be substantial movement in expectations about its future dividends.

[24] Labaton (1999). [25] Reinhart and Rogoff (2009). [26] Shiller (1981).

It would be reasonable for speculators to be surprised by true shocks, that is, for the actual unfolding of economic events to be more volatile than one's prior guess. Who could have foreseen, say, the 1970s oil shocks or the economic effects associated with the geopolitical shifts at the end of the Cold War. But it is absurd to be surprised, again and again, by how stable everything turns out to be.

In Figure B.3 reprinted from Shiller's classic work, the solid line (p) shows stock price, the best guesses about how the future will be. These guesses about the future move a lot (they are very noisy, in economics parlance), suggesting that views about the future change quickly. The dashed line (p*) shows the actual course of dividends (which, after the fact, would have been the best prediction). The solid line is more than five times more volatile than the dashed line. There also isn't much of a relationship between predictions about the future, represented by the price line, and how things actually turned out, represented by the actual dividends line. The lack of association between the guesses and the truth and the great volatility of the guesses suggests that speculators could have significantly improved their forecasts by ignoring rumors, hunches, and herding. But of course that wouldn't be nearly as entertaining for traders—and it would not generate fees for active management of investment portfolios.

At the same time that speculators see things that aren't there—indicated by the big unjustified movements in stock prices—they also fail to see things that are there. The housing bubble represents an enormous "Who could have known?" moment. Shiller was, along with Dean Baker of the Center for Economic Policy Research, among the first to identify a bubble in the US real estate market. Shiller's time series of housing prices is indeed an iconic representation of the bubble growing, peaking, and bursting. The graphic is a testament to the reality of enormous, devastating bubbles. The US housing bubble was accompanied by a bubble in complex derivatives. The bubble before that was the Spanish real estate bubble, which was preceded by the dot-com bubble in tech stocks, which was

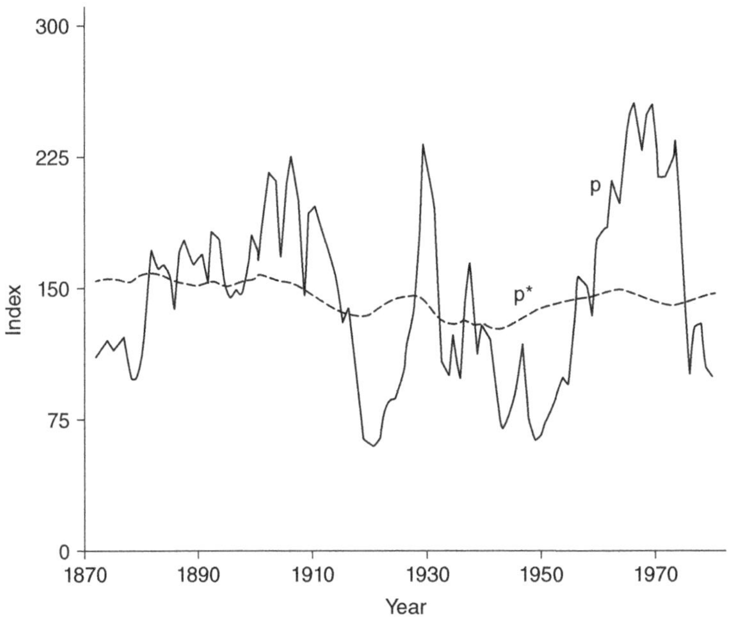

Figure B.3. Expected prices are more volatile than the real thing

Source: Shiller (1981).

preceded by the Japanese real estate bubble, and so on, with a long chain reaching back to the birth of modern finance in the seventeenth century. Charles Kindleberger, another brilliant but quiet skeptic, traces the sad path in *Manias, Panics, and Crashes*.[27]

Yet Shiller, the leading mainstream scholar of irrational markets, cannot fully shake his own confidence in financial markets. Each of his deviations from orthodoxy requires a hedge of its own,

> Don't get us wrong: [we] are certainly free-market advocates. In fact, I have argued for years that we need more such markets, like futures markets for single-family home prices or occupational incomes, or markets that would enable us to trade claims on gross domestic product. I've written about these things in this column.[28]

Shiller has proposed to tame volatile real estate markets by establishing futures markets where homeowners and speculators can trade risk. The scheme works as follows. For many working or middle-class households, the owned house is their greatest asset. The risk of neighborhood decline, say, because of deindustrialization or crime, sharply reducing the value of the family house poses an enormous threat to this single lumpy store of wealth. Shiller proposes that homeowners be enabled to insure against neighborhood decline by selling an interest in the house to speculators willing to take on additional risk.

Like ideas from the Fama camp, the proposal from Shiller the skeptic sounds fine in principle—if valuations are on-average accurate and reasonably stable, if the risk sales do not themselves affect the quality of the neighborhood, if housing prices do not launch on bubble paths that double prices in a matter of years, if spreading rumors, racialized panics, block-busting, rules of thumb, trampling herds, and other real-world factors do not distort the expected path of the value of housing over the years to come.

Nevertheless, the hedging proposal shows an inability to escape the financialized mindset. How does he imagine that the derived market in neighborhood risk will function smoothly and efficiently when the underlying market is warped by irrational bubbles and busts?

Many of Shiller's policy proposals, show-cased in his *New York Times* column, recommend advice and education especially for mortgage borrowers and small investors as the cures for financial errors, as if—in Shiller's words—a "clearer crystal ball" is all that is needed. It may be too little and too late.

Critical Views

Some critical points of view will be presented in the following, from Adam Smith to John Maynard Keynes to Hyman Minsky and James Crotty, proving that the debates on the neoliberal views were always present in the history of economics.

Adam Smith

The founder of classical liberalism was also its first critic. Smith was fascinated with both normal agents and rogues and the dangerous anomalies each could bring to life. Smith was the first not only to detect and point out those dangers but also to propose daring solutions.

A philosopher and keen observer of his society, Smith worried about the development of human sentiments and social relations. He was inclined to an empirical approach to the meaning of profit, capital, competition, and production. This led him to suspect the deviations that would prove injurious to the common good: "People of the same trade seldom meet together, even for merriment and diversion, but the conversation ends in a conspiracy against the public, or in some diversion to raise prices."[29]

[27] Kindleberger and Aliber (2005). [28] Shiller (2015). [29] Smith (1999), p. 232.

This sort of conspiracy eventually transforms the economy and endangers social life and cohesion. That was why Smith, contrary to today's deregulation movements, promoted rules to be strictly obeyed in order to prevent credit busts, and other risks. He did not flinch from the notion that this would imply contouring the pure claims of free markets, in order to impose social cohesion and protection against banking and financial collapses:

> These regulations may, no doubt, be considered in some respects a violation of natural liberty. But these exertions of the natural liberty of a few individuals, which might endanger the security of the whole society, are, and ought to be, restrained by the laws of all governments, of the most free, as well as the most despotic. The obligation of building party walls, in order to prevent the communication of fire, is a violation of natural liberty, exactly of the same kind with the regulations of the banking trade which are here proposed.[30]

This passage of Smith receives less attention than other more exuberant portions.

John Maynard Keynes

Keynes pursued the debate on what is normal and abnormal behavior in economic life, essentially in finance. In contrast to the anomaly perspective is the train wrecks view of financial markets, which has often proven a lonely corner of the profession. For those who see the train wreck, markets organized as casinos (or casinos disguised as markets) require constant totemic guesswork about what will come next:

> Thus the professional investor is forced to concern himself with the anticipation of impending changes, in the news or in the atmosphere, of the kind by which experience shows that the mass psychology of the market is most influenced ... This battle of wits to anticipate the basis of conventional valuation a few months hence, rather than the prospective yield of an investment over a long term of years, does not even require gulls amongst the public to feed the maws of the professional;—it can be played by professionals amongst themselves. Nor is it necessary that anyone should keep his simple faith in the conventional basis of valuation having any genuine long-term validity.

Markets organized as casinos also cultivate the profusion of dopey pundits and post-hoc explanations and validations. "The stock market went up—or down, it does not matter—today because ..." Meaningless and idiotic anthropomorphic metaphors for the institutions, such as "Markets liked the Election," "Markets were troubled by the Fed's latest move," "Markets reacted to the unemployment rate news," etc. abound in the popular media. The fundamental metaphor is Keynes's beauty contest:

> Professional investment may be likened to those newspaper competitions in which the competitors have to pick out the six prettiest faces from a hundred photographs, the prize being awarded to the competitor whose choice most nearly corresponds to the average preferences of the competitors as a whole; so that each competitor has to pick, not those faces which he himself finds prettiest, but those which he thinks likeliest to catch the fancy of the other competitors, all of whom are looking at the problem from the same point of view. It is not a case of choosing those which, to the best of one's judgment, are really the prettiest, nor even those which average opinion genuinely thinks the prettiest. We have reached the third degree where we devote our intelligences to anticipating what average opinion expects the average opinion to be. And there are some, I believe, who practice the fourth, fifth and higher degrees.[31]

The Keynesian critique reaches to the core of financial markets because the capitalists' twin ideals of financial markets are tightly integrated: liquidity and price discovery. The train wreck view ultimately finds the entire enterprise rotten to the core. To quote Keynes again:

[30] Ibid., pp. 423–4. [31] Keynes (2007), chapter 12.

> Of the maxims of orthodox finance none, surely, is more anti-social than the fetish of liquidity, the doctrine that it is a positive virtue on the part of investment institutions to concentrate their resources upon the holding of "liquid" securities. It forgets that there is no such thing as liquidity of investment for the community as a whole. The social object of skilled investment should be to defeat the dark forces of time and ignorance which envelop our future.[32]

Keynes observes a key problem that bears on the spillover damage from financial markets to real markets. Liquidity is more than a state of financial markets that can get casino-goers in trouble when it gives out—as it does in financial crises. The liquidity crunch is certainly a very serious problem when the music stops. But the problem goes deeper. The fetish of liquidity alters the relationship between capitalists and real investment and, hence, between capitalists and workers. Best performance for a capitalist is not running a company well; rather, best performance is cashing out when the opportunity to cash out is good. Liquidity is the virtue that protects the opportunity to cash out. Making sure that plentiful liquidity accompanies high prices has become a science for managers who manipulate buybacks and buyouts to maximize profits.

The skeptics, starting with Keynes, call out fraud in the Efficient Markets Hypothesis, the Capital Asset Pricing Model, and the fetish of liquidity. If the Great Crashes are not a sufficient demonstration, the skepticism needs refinement, an explanation of how the daily functioning of financial markets contributes to inefficiency and instability. While the EMH advocates point to a unitary abstract incentive, the most persuasive critics have drawn on historical experience and structured consistent and coherent observation of actual practice.

Joan Robinson

A contemporary and collaborator of Keynes at Cambridge University, Joan Robinson was present at the birth of Keynesianism. Puzzled like so many by the ferocity and tenaciousness of the Great Depression, Robinson was initially attached to imperfect competition and monopolization as the source of instability in capitalist economies and developed one of the first economy-wide theories of imperfect competition. Robinson and others hoped that monopolistic deviation from perfect competition could explain the catastrophic failure of the self-regulating market. However, imperfect competition, although both profitable for the monopolists and distortionary for the market, could not explain the periodic crises that culminated with the Great Depression. It took the Keynesian insight on aggregate demand, which Robinson helped to develop and then propound, to break the impasse in economics and in policy.

After the war, Robinson became one of the intellectual guarantors of untamed Keynesianism, which shared with domesticated Keynesianism a commitment to aggregate demand management, but also maintained Keynes's attention to the unreliability of capital markets. Robinson and her Cambridge, UK, collaborators explored the implications of the mismeasure of capital for understanding, or failing to understand, the short-term and long-term trajectories of capitalist economies. It is often dismissed as quaint,[33] but the Cambridge Capital Controversy, a debate between Cambridge University (UK) and Cambridge, Massachusetts, USA, home of Harvard University and MIT, disputed issues that lie at the center of the valuation of capital, the role of financial markets, and the distribution of output.

Hyman Minsky

At first pass an unlikely figure to become the intellectual champion of skepticism about financial markets, Hyman Minsky went through then conventional undergraduate and

[32] Keynes (2007), chapter 12. [33] Piketty (2014), p. 232.

graduate education in Economics. After undergraduate training at University of Chicago (before the Friedman-Fama revolution), Minsky graduated with his PhD in Economics from Harvard University in the mid-1940s and spent his career at Brown University, University of California, Washington University in St. Louis, and eventually the Levy Institute of Bard College.

Despite his academic origins in the center of orthodoxy, Minsky's methods and thought were anything but orthodox. Based on actual observation of banks, on conversation with bankers, and on close reading of Keynes, Minsky developed the Financial Instability Hypothesis, that financial systems tend, from their own logic and endogenous trajectory, towards out-of-control booms followed by severe financial and economic crises. Eschewing the type of technical detail that was becoming essential to be taken seriously in the Economics discipline during this period, Minsky's discursive style—in *Stabilizing an Unstable Economy*,[34] during his Keynes biography,[35] and in *Can "It" Happen Again?*[36] is based on historical and institutional analysis as well as deep familiarity with the financial markets.

In their insightful gloss on Minsky's contribution to economic thought, Dymski and Pollin dub Minsky a "hedgehog" for his single central vision of the Wall Street paradigm.[37] (According to the philosopher Isaiah Berlin, hedgehogs have single central vision in contradistinction to foxes who "know many things" but "related by no moral or aesthetic principle.") Two key ideas dominate the Wall Street paradigm: radical uncertainty about the future; and endogenous evolution towards instability.

After conventional retirement Minsky held an affiliation with the heterodox Levy Institute of Bard College through to his death. Long a popular figure in heterodox economics, Minsky was "discovered" by the mainstream after the crisis of 2007–8, in which the lock-up of the world financial system was dubbed a "Minsky moment" although Minsky might find objectionable the reduction of the full course of finance to the moment of crisis.[38] The whole point is that the crash is only the culmination of a continuum of moments in which finance destabilizes the economy.

Minsky emphasized and elaborated endogenous instability in the financial system. Traditional economic theories of finance of course understood that external shocks, such as revolutions, natural disasters, wars, oil crises, or mistakes by government regulators, could upset markets. But endogenous means that rather than external shocks triggering financial crises, these crises occur because the financial system has in itself an inherent tendency to move from stability towards instability and crisis—by the aggregated action of its individual actors making expected responses.

First, it is crucial to note the enormous contrast between Minsky's views and the equilibrium-seeking perspective of the mainstreamers. In the mainstream perspective the system is constantly moving towards ever more correct and stable prices, with speculators' bids and asks for assets guided towards each other, and towards truth, by the invisible hand. Only outside triggers—unforeseen news of war, crop failure, oil shortage, onerous regulations, insufficient or overabundant money printing—can disrupt the reliable path to equilibrium. In contrast, for Minsky, endogenous instability means that the financial system evolves consistently and predictably from stability towards instability.

Minsky identifies three phases in the evolution towards instability and crisis. In the first phase, which he designates "hedge finance," firms are able to cover both operating expenses, i.e., paying workers and suppliers, and capital costs, i.e., repaying bondholders, from their current revenue. This success in and of itself creates demand for liquidity (successful entrepreneurs cash out of their firms to diversify), for growth (successful enterprises reinvest), and for leverage (speculators keep betting on winners).

[34] Minsky (1986). [35] Minsky (1976). [36] Minsky (2015).
[37] Dymski and Pollin (1992). [38] Flanders (2015).

At this point in Minsky's progression, euphoria begins to grow. The psychological and social structures of interpretation and judgment about risks may change. As optimism takes over, not only do the risks grow but the very apparatus for evaluating risks becomes more tolerant of these risks. This phase is called speculative finance. In the speculative phase, firms avail themselves of the additional funds, i.e., borrowing and lending, which increases both liabilities and assets. The borrowers become dependent on ongoing rollover of their debts to maintain their capital stock. Current revenue can cover operating costs and interest payments, but the enlarged stock of debt requires constant refinancing. Often this financing involves new maturity structures (with terms typically shortening) and even new financing forms (with, for example, market finance supplanting bank finance).

Minsky entitles the final phase Ponzi finance. (Charles Ponzi will be a protagonist of Chapter 9.) The application of this term, usually reserved for illegal pyramid schemes, to (presumably) legal financial activity infuriates market true believers. In the Ponzi phase, firms take on additional liabilities that can be serviced only with ongoing expansion and growing capital gains, a manic treadmill that necessarily ends in disaster. Minsky's detailed description of actual behavior in financial markets, his systematic elaboration of the evolution of instability, and the ultimate accuracy of his prediction that this time is never different make his vision a clear and up-to-date indictment of financial markets.

Minsky identified the risks of the financial system, such as a deposit drain (affecting the holding reserves), non-performing loans (affecting the capital buffers), a liquidity crisis (demanding support by the central bank), and systemic insolvency (leading to resolution or nationalization). Consequently he noticed that the new forms of liquidity creation under the shadow banking system aggravated the dangers. He considered the primary function of banks to be the creation of liquidity for investment, not, per the neoclassical model, intermediation between savers and business. As a policy response, Minsky would propose new stability rules to change the functioning of the credit and financial system.

For that, Minsky favored the control of capital assets to be obtained via the issue of liabilities of two types, one collateralized by public debt and the other by private debts of business, and defining a stability rule such as income from financed assets should be enough to cover liabilities held by lenders. His work was followed by Crotty and other scholars.

James Crotty and Other Critics

James Crotty is one of the most important interpreters and deepeners of Keynes's and Minsky's thought. Crotty has integrated their insights about unstable financial markets with Marxist analysis of inter-capitalist competition and class exploitation. Crotty, by his own description a "working class kid from the Bronx," completed his PhD at Carnegie-Mellon University (Pittsburgh) in 1973 and has spent much of his career at the University of Massachusetts Amherst, where he joined the Economics faculty in the mid-1970s. Crotty's interests varied widely over the years, with insights gleaned from intensive study of the Korean economy and its chaebol conglomerates informing Crotty's perspectives on global competition.

While Minsky avoided political economy in the conventional sense, Crotty, who largely subscribes to the Minskyian model of the structure and evolution of financial markets, additionally pinpoints capitalists' drive towards excess capacity in real markets and their demand for leverage for expansion of physical capital. This excess capacity generated by competition is then followed by capitalist efforts to consolidate with even more leveraged efforts to establish monopoly control of overbuilt industries. Crotty uses examples from telecommunications, pharmaceuticals, airlines, and other industries to demonstrate the principles.

Crotty's work also includes a blistering critique of Friedman's positivist revolution in economics. The positivist turn advocated by Friedman posited that theories should be judged not by the realism of their assumptions but by the accuracy of their predictions.

In addition to observing that theories built on grossly unrealistic assumptions are unlikely to perform well, Crotty notes that the formulation permitted the presentation and rapid promulgation of theories that were highly advantageous to the financial services industry (and to the capitalist class as a whole)—with scrutiny deferred to a later date and then carried out using highly technical and often inconclusive methods. The failure of these theories to square with frequent outright disasters in financial markets, in Mexico and elsewhere in Latin America in the 1980s, in Russia, East Asia, and, again, Mexico in the 1990s, and the United States and Western Europe in the 2000s, should have given pause to economists. Instead typical analysis excludes these once-in-a-lifetime crashes that occur roughly every decade. In only a few cases have economists reexamined and revised their positions.

Another line of inquiry among the radical critics focuses on the subversion of academic and regulatory activity in the interest of the financial industry. The popular film *Inside Job* (2010) identified several high profile cases of academic economists who failed to disclose significant personal interest in policy decisions on which they offered expert commentary to public media. Gerald Epstein and Jessica Carrick-Hagenbarth examined the proposition of *Inside Job* through a scientific lens.[39]

Epstein and Carrick-Hagenbarth gathered data on the disclosure of conflict of interest by academic economists in academic publications or in media appearances on a set of policy-related debates in finance. Even though many of the academics had consulting engagement or direct employment with financial institutions whose interests were at stake in these matters of public policy, virtually none of the academic economists disclosed their conflicts of interest. Other disciplines, such as medicine, have codes of ethics and much stricter disclosure requirements, although even then questions remain.[40]

Jennifer Taub is professor of law at the Vermont College of Law with expertise in financial markets and regulation. Taub has studied the struggle of financial firms to free themselves from regulation. For example, she observed that financial firms sought wiggle room in Glass-Steagall as soon as the ink had dried, creating hedge fund exemptions to rules concerning oversight. More recently Taub has documented the systematic undermining of regulatory authority in financial markets, an effort by speculators that has paid off handsomely for themselves. Financial firms shop rigorously for regulatory venues that will keep the regulations light, badger regulators whom they perceive as overzealous, and outright corrupt public decision makers. One instance of investigations on eventual corruption was the Keating Five, the case of five US Senators, four Democrats and one Republican (John McCain), who were convinced by banker Charles Keating to go easy on the regulation and investigation of the accounts of his Lincoln Savings and Loans, which finally went bankrupt at a cost of three billion dollars.[41]

Conclusion

As we noted in the Introduction, the period after 1980 was termed by some "The Age of Milton Friedman." The appellation is fitting. The *Age of Friedman* consisted in large part of building and consolidating the neoliberal agenda that Friedman and his cohort had planned over the previous generation.

[39] Carrick-Hagenbarth and Epstein (2012). Epstein is on the Faculty of Economics at the University of Massachusetts Amherst where he co-directs the Political Economy Research Institute (PERI). Carrick-Hagenbarth was then a PhD student at University of Massachusetts Amherst and has joined the faculty of the State University of New York.

[40] See, for example, Angell (2009). The author is an MD and former editor of the prestigious *New England Journal of Medicine*.

[41] Taub (2014), pp. 102.

Even as Friedman ascended with his program carried forth by central bankers, Treasury ministers, and international financial institutions, a robust underworld of skeptics and critics was at work in the margins, documenting the inconsistencies, demonstrating the ways in which the emperors of the age wore no clothes, and warning of the short- and long-run consequences of the neoliberal program. The *Age of Friedman* did not bring exceptional growth but it did bring exceptional inequality and upward redistribution as the skeptic and critic Robert Pollin, professor of economics at the University of Massachusetts Amherst, documents in *Contours of Descent*.[42] The age ended—or perhaps more accurately the end of the age began—with a bang rather than a whimper, and we enter now the Trump Era, when everything becomes possible, including the combination of extreme liberalization as the apex of business and authoritarianism in unprecedented forms, at least since the middle of the twentieth century.

As we move into the next era, still traumatized from the Crash of 2008 and the Great Recession, the war of ideas will remain at the center. For now, the last word goes to Keynes: "Practical men who believe themselves to be quite exempt from any intellectual influence, are usually the slaves of some defunct economist. Madmen in authority, who hear voices in the air, are distilling their frenzy from some academic scribbler of a few years back."[43]

[42] Pollin (2005). [43] Keynes (2007), pp. 393–4.

Part III

Plutocracy and Oligarchy

7

Consensus by Schooling and Power: The Indoctrination of the Elites

The dominance of finance in the modern world, including that of shadow finance, has been discussed in the previous chapters from the point of view of its economic power and the ability to rule, to regulate, and to deregulate, to direct and to impose limits on the legal institutions. The growing interconnection between the world of business and politics, as well as trust in US capitalism as the leading force through the twentieth century were the pillars of the emergence of neoliberal economics. Its expansion and homogenization, based on precise tools for self-reproduction, institutional coherence, and ideological energy led to a precise pattern of professionalization of economics on a world scale.

We will discuss in this chapter how this process of homogenization proceeded, after looking at the agents of liberalization, academics, policymakers and central bankers, and their institutions, who constitute social networks that were scrutinized in previous parts of the book. Part III deals therefore with another dimension of the power of the shadows: the creation of a belief system generating widespread consensus on the prevalence of the financial markets and movements.[1]

This belief system has been prepared and nurtured through ideas and schooling. The two pillars of this consensus building have therefore been social learning (namely the process of mimetic convergence towards global patterns in social behavior, which in any case may have some national peculiarities, as we shall see) and the selective functioning of education and certification institutions (namely universities, research centers, the selection of grants, international connections in academia, and think tanks).[2]

The globalization and standardization of the profession of economist went hand in hand with the hegemony of neoliberal ideas, as the training was homogenized

[1] Simon Johnson, a professor at MIT who was chief economist at IMF for 2007–8 and was already quoted in earlier chapters, suggested the expression: "the American financial industry gained political power by amassing a kind of cultural capital—a belief system," Johnson (2009). In the same sense, Sarah Babb discussed the "national systems of expert knowledge shaped by its constituencies—organizations and social groups that provide professionals with resources" require a general belief and acceptance, Babb (2001), p. 209.

[2] The use of the concepts of "social learning" and "consensus" does not imply presuming uniformity or absence of conflict, instead it refers only to the dominant views in the society. As Dezalay and Bryant argue for the case of Latin America, discussed in the core of this chapter, "social learning in Latin America may be based on a consensus that excludes a significant portion of the population—a state of affairs that would not bode well for the region's political future," Dezalay and Garth (2002), p. 219.

across countries, creating a specialized group of people able to favor, to advance, and to interpret the transnationalization of political regulations and controls, including jurisdictions, treaties, and international bodies.[3] Furthermore, there is a universalistic rhetoric and technical dictionary that is subsidiary to the dominant views in economics, "good economics" as a bold Chicago professor, whom we will encounter in the following, once put it. This corresponds to a form of power: the specific language and coherent jurisdictional monopoly of globalized economic ideas are assured by liberalization, led by US and US-trained academics and policymakers.

The convergence to this pattern of ideas and institutions was imposed and fought for, but it would never have succeeded if it had only been attempted by either brute force or sophisticated coercion. Persuasion played a major role in this. As we will see in the examples illustrating this chapter, changes in universities, special programs for attracting foreign students to the US, hiring policies for essential institutions (central bank, government) creating invisible colleges, plus adaptation to membership of international fora (the World Bank, IMF, CEPAL, private banks) and to external legitimation (by the OECD, IMF, World Bank, and other institutions), were crucial for the legitimation of changes in economic thinking and policymaking in different countries. In this case, following the investigations of Fourcade and Babb, we also discuss expert isomorphism, or mimetism to the role models that propelled the neoliberal agenda in the cases of Mexico, Chile, Argentina, Brazil, France, Britain, and Germany or, in another part of the book, China.[4] The mentoring process, through recruiting and networking for the creation of discipline and disciples, will be discussed in this chapter.

Indoctrination is a social process, constituting powerful centripetal forces and certification processes. It is a means for the reproduction of social structures and relations. We present some cases to demonstrate how indoctrination, mentoring, and mimetization proceed in different frameworks. One illustration is the constitution of political "camarillas" in Mexico and the change of direction of the PRI, the political party that governed Mexico for most of the twentieth century. We will examine in some detail how the political wooing of the PRI and the constitution of the cabinet of President Salinas led to a major change in that country.[5]

In some countries, shocks and social and political defeats, such as the Chilean hyperinflation and the balance of payments crisis in 1973, but also the British sterling crisis in 1976; then the radical program of Margaret Thatcher and the defeat of the miners' strike, marking a new relationship of forces in social life; then the victory of Reagan and in particular his ability to fire the air traffic controllers and to crush their union; the Mexican debt collapse in 1982; the failure of the French

[3] Marion Fourcade, in particular, investigated the connection between the local ecologies of professions and the globalization process, namely that of economics and of economic ideas, Fourcade (2009), pp. 148, 156.

[4] Babb (2001), p. 189. Babb investigates how these isomorphisms were constructed through time and in different national cases.

[5] R. A. Camp (1990, 2002); Fourcade (2009). Fourcade-Gourinchas and Babb (2002) are the main sources for this chapter. Other views are relevant for this research on social reproduction: Domhoff (1983) for instance, discusses the relation between the ruling class and institutions, while from the opposite point of view Alesina and Drazen (1991), map the "pro and anti-(liberal)reform groups." We take a more empirically oriented and historically descriptive point of view in this chapter.

government expansionary policy in 1981; the crisis of the sovereign debts and the banking systems in Portugal and Spain (among other countries) opened windows on the allegiance to the new consensus around neoliberal alternatives. The road could be ideological (as in Britain under the pressure of the IMF, and Chile, under the pressure of a dictatorship) or pragmatic (as in Mexico and France). The change could be imposed through a financial crisis (as in Mexico and Argentina) or through largely domestic transformation of the state apparatus (France, Brazil, and China) or the emergence of a governing elite subordinated to financial interests (Portugal and Spain). But regardless of the pathways, the remarkable feature of this period was the coalescence on a single direction of change towards establishment of a new liberalism.[6]

US DOMINANCE

US dominance in the formation of the hegemonic ideas in economics and governance is an unsurprising feature of its world leadership through the twentieth century and thereafter. Consider the Nobel Prize in Economics, established since 1969 (a later addition to the Nobel awards and independently administered by the Central Bank of Sweden): until 2015 seventy-two of the seventy-seven prizes were awarded to US-based economists (sixty-three nationals and nine others)—an impressive preponderance (and all but one awarded to men). Although there is some diversity among the themes, the sub-disciplines, and the orientation of the winners, this essentially means the formation and consecration of orthodoxy, economics being presented as the science of the markets.

This dominance and the consequential "jurisdictional expansion" of the US universities formatting economic thought, leading to increased control and standardization of economics, we describe as the *Americanization* of economics, as other authors did. The full monty consisted, as Fourcade noted, in a coherent monopoly managing the globalization of economics, including a typical universalistic rhetoric, a technology of bureaucratic power, and transnational linkages dominated by the US universities and, specifically, by neoclassical economics.[7]

This represents a major turn as compared to the foundation of economics in the US. In the early days, the American Economic Association (AEA) was formed under the influence of progressive Christians, such a Richard T. Ely and John Bates Clark, and the ideas of free markets and liberalization were something of a curiosity, since the association was formed by "economists who repudiated *laissez-faire* as a scientific doctrine." They instead carved social reform as the purpose of the constitution of the association: "We regard the state as an agency whose progressive assistance is one of the indispensable conditions of human progress. [. . .] We hold that the conflict of labor and capital has brought into prominence a vast number of social problems whose solution requires the united effort, each in its own sphere, of the church, of the state, and of science."[8]

[6] Fourcade-Gourinchas and Babb (2002), p. 569.

[7] Fourcade (2009), p. 156.

[8] Ely (1910), p. 55n. In Ely's first draft of the AEA statement of principles he even declared that the "doctrine of *laissez faire* is unsafe in politics and unsound in morals."

Richard Ely, eventually the major mover of the association, its first Secretary and later President, was a fascinating character. A social militant, he was part of the Christian Social Union, fought child labor, argued for changes in the property of land, and defended unionization and labor rights. He was eventually threatened and even prosecuted for favoring strikes in Wisconsin.[9] As a very peculiar institutional economist, he marked the first years of the national association as a tool for social reform and fair distribution.

Although Ely described this constitution as a "general indication of the views and the purposes of those who founded the AEA but it is not regarded as binding upon individual members," the text soon became uncomfortable for most and was purged within two years, in 1887.[10] The turn of mood in US economics and the influx of neoclassical economists changed the Association, but it would take a long time for the new approach to prevail.

Ely represented the prolongation of the German Historical School, under which many of the young American economists were educated at the time, some of them rejecting liberal ideas and arguing for public intervention in order to correct social inequality. Their interest in institutions was a crucial part of their scientific research, and their intellectual movement was christened "institutionalist economics." John Commons, who was supervised by Ely in his PhD at Johns Hopkins University, and Wesley Clair Mitchell, from Columbia University and the founder of the National Bureau of Economic Research, became the main references for institutionalism. In the first decades of the twentieth century, the current grew in influence both in economic research and even in policymaking.

Mitchell was one of the most respected economists in the country. In 1933, he received the most votes in the first election for Fellow of the Econometric Society.[11] He took a job in the Hoover administration as chair of the Research Committee on Social Trends, and was nominated by Roosevelt as head of the National Planning Board, on which he served from 1933 to 1935, in the first New Deal administration.[12] In fact, these administrations included some institutionalists in relevant positions, but their numbers and influence increased mostly during the second New Deal period (at the Planning Board, the National Recovery Administration, and the National Labor Relations Board), although the state bureaucracy avoided the more interventionist economists. Other institutions were populated by economists more or less influenced by Keynesianism (at the Fed, and Department of Commerce) but also neoclassical economists (at the Treasury and State Department), although most mainstream economists were so alienated from policymaking that they played no role in the first Roosevelt administration.[13]

In any case, as late as the 1930s US economics remained an open science with rival schools. Moreover, the neoclassicals fell into disfavor because they could offer neither explanation nor remedy for the Great Depression. The institutionalists looked at monopoly power and imperfect competition as important causes of the Great Depression. Instead, this view attracted adherents in the US and the United Kingdom, including some who would go on to be foundational figures in Keynesianism. Congressional investigations of monopoly power,

[9] Fourcade (2009), p. 79. [10] Ely (1910), pp. 49–50; Fourcade (2009), pp. 78–80.
[11] Louçã (2007), p. 31. [12] Fourcade (2009), pp. 82, 84, 101.
[13] Babb (2001), pp. 51–2; Barber (1981); Stryker (1990).

e.g., at General Motors, were one response, as the more corporatist elements of the New Deal sought to get the institutions and the level of competition right.[14] But the institutionalists were ultimately unable to establish a convincing framework for understanding and responding to the Great Depression. As the views of the institutionalists failed to gain traction and the Depression deepened, Keynesian economics emerged as a radical alternative to standard equilibrium and neoclassical economics.

After the Second World War, the tide changed and the political and ideological references combined to make economics a more closed and mathematical or abstract discipline. The emergence of econometrics and its program of structural estimation rendered the empirical quantification approach of the institutionalists obsolete. Subsequently, Paul Samuelson's codification of the more conventional elements of Keynesian thought in a synthesis with neoclassical economics gave birth to modern macroeconomics. The huge resources of military research by RAND Corporation and its interpenetration of academic economics contributed to the dominance of formalized models in economics. In the meantime, the Cold War and McCarthyism, or the processes of repression against the left, alienated or exiled critically minded economists. All of these movements changed the map of economics.[15]

In previous chapters, while dealing with liberalizers and deregulators, we met many of the champions of this transformation in their glory, such as the Milton Friedman TV show from 1977 onwards, the nomination of Greenspan to the Fed, the incorporation of financiers and Goldman Sachs men at the top of government, and other instances of the same movement at different historical junctures. In the remainder of this chapter, we will meet some of the institutions that contributed to this apologetics of the market, such as the universities and global network of neoliberal think tanks (e.g., the Cato Institute, the Institute of Economic Affairs, the Institute of Public Affairs, the Heritage Foundation, the Hoover Institute, the Center for the Study of American Business, and the American Enterprise Institute).

The reconfiguration of the economics discipline paved the way for pretense and demagoguery. A famous case is that of the Laffer curve. *Wall Street Journal* editor Jude Wanniski promoted the argument of libertarian economist Arthur Laffer that US tax rates were so high that their chilling effect on business activity actually reduced net tax collection.[16] As a corollary tax cuts were presented as a beneficial

[14] Backhouse (1998), p. 87.

[15] McCarthyism sent Lawrence Klein and others into exile, Fourcade (2009), p. 84; Babb (2001), pp. 51–2. The postwar American turn towards mathematical economics was also related to McCarthyism, since this provided for a refuge in abstract reasoning, but it was mostly a result of the requirements of technification for government hiring during the War, of the orientation of research institutions such as the Cowles Commission, and the availability of new techniques for computation and simulation, Fourcade (2009), p. 140. But this homogenization movement was not without contradictions. For example, Kenneth Arrow worked on a collective utility function for the USSR while at RAND, Fourcade (2009), p. 157. Some of the juiciest episodes of this saga were recounted by Mirowski (2002, 2013). But it was the growing connection to resurgent business and the confidence of US capitalism as a dominant force through the twentieth century that finally promoted neoliberal economics to power. The expansion and homogeneity it has exhibited ever since, based on self-reproduction, institutional coherence, and ideological energy, have led to the professionalization of economics on a world scale.

[16] Wanniski was at the time the associate editor of the *Wall Street Journal*. A conservative economist, Wanniski abandoned journalism after he was found distributing leaflets for a Republican candidate to

program for public management and fiscal rectitude. Financed by conservative think tanks, such as the American Enterprise Institute, the Smith Richardson Foundation, the Scaife Foundation, and the Olin Foundation, and through the staunch support of US Representative Jack Kemp and Presidential candidate Ronald Reagan, the supply-side doctrine was incorporated in the mainstream thought of the Republican Party, although such thinking generated resistance among economists who were suspicious of its offer of an apparently free lunch. Of high profile academics only Robert Mundell, later a Nobel Prize winner, gave his benediction to the supply-side creed.[17] But President Reagan followed the line, and, as the popular perception of the promise of lower taxes changed the political mood, in particular after the assassination attempt he suffered, he received surprising bipartisan support: when large tax cuts were proposed in 1981, the Congress, under a Democratic majority, easily passed the bill.[18]

The deregulation movement became a near crusade for Washington, crossing political lines. Freeing business from cumbersome environmental protection as well as the campaigns against financial and transportation regulation were the vanguard of the movement. Even before the Reagan revolution, Ford and Carter had already fired the first rounds. Ford issued an executive order subjecting new regulations to a preliminary computation of their effects on inflation. Carter shuttered the Civil Aeronautics Board.[19] Cost-benefit requirements for new regulation and paperwork reduction were coordinated by the Office of Information and Regulatory Affairs (OIRA) of the Office of Management and Budget, the executive agency responsible for implementing Presidential positions in the Federal budget and regulations. Along with the Treasury and the Council of Economic Advisers, OIRA became one of three main beachheads for the invasion of economic orthodoxy in Federal administration, which had been previously rooted in institutions and constituencies.

But life comes with many surprises, and one is the pendular movement in political moods. Over the next decade, the Republican President George H. W. Bush, in conjunction with a Democratic Congress, oversaw a substantial expansion of regulation, including the environmentally focused Clean Air Act Amendments of 1990, and the Americans with Disability Act, which established comprehensive guidelines for accommodating disabilities in workplaces and schools. In contrast, and again confirming the pendulum in politics, President William J. Clinton significantly reduced the reach of the welfare state (with the support of Reaganite Arthur Laffer)[20] and terminated the Rooseveltian protection against unregulated speculative banking.

the Senate. In a later phase of his career, he supported the Nation of Islam and its controversial leader, Louis Farrakhan.

[17] Himmelstein (1992), p. 112; Prasad (2006), p. 54.

[18] In spite of this majority, Reagan approved this change of fiscal policy with the support of forty-eight Democrats who voted yes, whereas only twelve Republicans rejected the bill. At the Senate the majority was impressive: eighty-nine in favor, M. Prasad (2006), p. 57.

[19] Ralph Nader, advocating for consumers, had proposed such a move, arguing that it inflated airfares. In debate with the then-Governor Ronald Reagan, among others, Nader was invited to provide a list of official bodies to be scrapped, and he gladly did, to the praise of Reagan, M. Prasad (2006), pp. 62, 67; Shanahan, Humphrey, and American Enterprise Institute for Public Policy Research and Hoover Institution on War, Revolution, and Peace (1976).

[20] Prasad (2006), p. 97.

Triumphant in Washington and dominant in the Economics departments of elite universities, neoliberalism spread around the world as a powerful intellectual movement. Neoliberalism represents policy advocacy and action primarily in the interest of financial capital, with some benefits for selected extractive, industrial, and commercial agents. Unlike their nineteenth-century predecessors, neoclassical economics and neoliberal policies are indifferent and sometimes hostile to democratic issues raised by classical liberalism.[21]

This will be discussed through the remainder of this chapter. We will examine Latin American and some European cases, in which elites mobilized extreme authoritarianism or major political turns to launch neoliberal economics. As we will notice, Americanization proceeded through different channels, namely the institutions and the ecology of peers and the education and the ecology of mates.

THE US INTERNAL POLITICAL CONVERGENCE OF OLIGARCHIC PARTIES

Americanization in this context refers to a specific and historically situated diffusion and extension across the world of words, concepts, processes, institutions, forms of power, social connections, and rules. US capital and leadership became hegemonic, and neoliberalism was established as dogma in social and economic decision making.

A political scientist, E.E. Schattschneider, proposed as early as 1960 a concept of "the semi-sovereign people," indicating how democracy was being undermined by the coalitions of economic interests governing the major parties.[22] The investment theory of political parties takes this notion further and presents the dominant political parties in the US "as blocs of major investors who coalesce to advance candidates representing their interests," or as oligarchic parties, thus converging in policies and ideas in a "money-driven political system."[23]

The intricate connections between politics and business are the theme for the next chapter, but it is relevant to indicate now the plethora of studies on the selection of candidates for office in the US and the links between fortunes, firms, and covert interests organizing these "blocs of investors" leading the parties and governments.[24] In *Dollars and Votes*, Clawson and his coauthors establish how elections and reelections became more expensive, how gerrymandering makes

[21] One such case is that of the immediate decisions taken by the occupation authorities in Iraq, a case study for the combination of liberalization and authoritarianism: on September 19, 2003, Paul Bremer, the US-nominated head of the Coalition Provisional Authority, issued orders decreeing the full privatization of all public enterprises of the country, assuring the full ownership rights by foreign firms of Iraqi businesses, the unconditional and full repatriation of profits by foreign firms, the opening of Iraqi banks to foreign control, and the elimination of nearly all trade barriers, only exempting oil, which was under the control of the occupation army. Strikes were forbidden in several sectors and unionization was restricted, D. Harvey (2005), pp. 6–7. Chua (2003), made the case that exporting free market ideology and institutions has bred global instability.

[22] Schattschneider (1960). [23] Ferguson (1995), p. 27.

[24] E.g., Schattschneider (1960); Ferguson (1995); Clawson et al. (1998); Hacker and Pierson (2006); Cowie (2010); Frank (2012).

most seats safe for one party but the decisive disputes more dependent on big firms and dark money, how financing moved to promote conservative think tanks or specific purposes, such as changing the tax laws in order to favor the "haves," and how the agenda was transformed in order to emphasize privatization or market transformation of the two most important social programs of the past: FDR's Social Security and LBJ's Medicare.[25]

The "Reagan revolution" which has promoted this radical agenda since the 1980s was not the result of inspiration or of charisma and leadership. It was the expression of a major change in social relations. Since the decade after the Second World War, and until late in the 1970s, more than a third of North-American workers belonged to a union; indeed, this rate of unionization was greater than that of Canada at the time. In 1970, the country underwent the largest labor strike movement since 1946, involving some 2.4 million workers in large-scale work stoppages.[26] It was not until Reagan that a defeat with long-term effects was imposed on labor militancy, although it was already weakened by Carter's harsh austerity policy. As a consequence, by 2004 unionization in the US was reduced to 13.8 percent and by 2016 to 11 percent (whereas in Canada it was still at 27 percent).[27]

The 1970s were a decisive period for such transformations. It was when an organized labor force began suffering the pressure of high unemployment and declining wages, when the most important financial players grew in power, influence, and resolve. The turn towards finance was noted by astute journalists, economists, and political scientists—and experienced by many in the form of plant closures and erosion of working conditions.[28]

In Europe, the drive towards liberalization and austerity led to a result parallel to that of the US. The largest insurgencies of the late 1960s and the first half of the 1970s, combining revolt by workers and youth and, in some countries, democratic movements replacing the old dictatorships (Portugal, Spain, Greece) were first affected by the general recession and then by the imposition of neoliberal agendas. The impact was quite different in each country, as, for instance, unionization varies widely according to the history of social formations and class conflicts. It currently stands at 74 percent of the active labor force in Finland, 70 percent in Sweden, and 67 percent in Denmark, but only 8 percent in France and Lithuania, 19 percent in Portugal and Spain, and 12 percent in Hungary and Poland (the European Union average is 23 percent). In Germany that rate is 18 percent, although the largest union confederation, the DGB, has lost almost half of its membership since 1991, given huge losses in the former East Germany. In the UK unions suffered major setbacks since the 1980s under Thatcher, and union density declined to 25.6 percent.[29]

The neoliberal turn since the 1980s has had an immense impact. This electoral turn and the new governments and administrations to which it gave power, express an earlier change in class relations but also provided the tools for radicalizing the liberal agenda. So, as Thatcher, Reagan, and Deng Xiao Ping imposed new economic visions, the dominant political parties, the electoral systems, and the

[25] Clawson et al. (1998). [26] Cowie (2010), p. 2. [27] Bureau of Labor Statistics (2017).
[28] Cowie (2010); Frank (2012). [29] European Trade Union Institute (2017).

mass media were transformed. Finance became the victor of those changes and Americanization was its tool.

AMERICANIZATION THROUGH THE ECOLOGY OF THE IMF

Jeffrey Chwieroth, an LSE professor, studied eighty-one non-concessional loans by the IMF to twenty-two developing countries, for the period 1983–98. He found that "weak professional ties between the staff and borrowing-country officials lead to the application of more stringent conditionality,"[30] and otherwise stronger professional connections would lead to better deals. In other words, the IMF looks for friends and suspects the unfaithful.

The same author had already perused the connections among 300 IMF staff members and 1,173 officials, including chiefs of government, ministers of finance, and heads of central banks, from 1969 to 1998, of forty-four developing countries. He then checked in detail 143 loans to twenty-nine developing countries for the period 1975–98, to conclude that better loans went to governments with officials sharing their professional training with IMF staff: "The results provide evidence that the staff provide favorable treatment to government officials with similar professional characteristics," namely education in US and UK economic faculties, and of course "countries where there is significant exposure to US commercial banks receive more generous loans"[31]

Another inquiry into 486 loans by the IMF during the period from 1980 to 2000 proved that, when the local policymakers are neoliberal, the IMF adjustment program is less onerous, more generous, and requires lighter enforcement—this is again evidence of "playing favorites."[32]

This is strictly acknowledged by the IMF, at least if we take the word of its official historian, James Boughton. Boughton writes about a "silent revolution" since the 1980s, spreading through many countries, since, as officials close to the IMF's views and with similar professional training came to decision making positions, this "revolution" helped impose the IMF views.[33] Professional ties and shared views formatted the ecology of the IMF thinkers and practitioners.

AMERICANIZATION THROUGH EDUCATION AND POLITICAL CONVERGENCE

Neoliberal indoctrination has been interlinked with Americanization of institutions, in particular education and politics, in much of the world. Yet, this was not a homogeneous process. Neoliberalization without Americanization, as was the case in France, is a possible although rare configuration. In fact, the Americanization of the local elites was common and proceeded through different institutions,

[30] Chwieroth (2015), p. 22.
[31] Chwieroth (2013), pp. 286–8.
[32] Nelson (2014), p. 486.
[33] Boughton (2001).

strategies, and channels, with varying results. In this section and the next, we explore the first two of these channels, homogenization through education and, in particular, through education of international graduate students in the US, and the adoption of neoliberal ideas and curricula at educational institutions in different countries.

A survey in the 1990s investigated the origins of central bankers and found that fully one third had been educated in the US.[34] Therefore, it does not come as a surprise to verify that central banks were decisive in the Americanization of economics in Latin America. In Brazil, during the period 1965–95, more than half of central bank officials with graduate degrees had earned them in the US.[35] The pattern was not merely a reflection of large numbers of foreign students seeking higher education in the US but the result of a conscious political choice.[36] Indeed, some US universities developed specific programs for foreign students, with support from federal programs. Such was the case of the program created by the University of Chicago, for Latin Americans, predominantly from Argentina, Mexico, and—with significant consequences for the region and the world—Chile.

In the case of Chile, the result was impressive: for the initial period of 1957 to 1970, the conservative Universidad Católica sent around one hundred Chilean students to Chicago for specialized economics postgraduate courses. Chile had no more than 120 economists in the early 1960s, a number that grew to 700 during the following decade, many of them beneficiaries of US training. They would become the backbone of the political and economic turn in the early 1970s under the Pinochet dictatorship. After 1971, graduates of the Instituto Tecnológico Autónomo de México (ITAM), an important institution whose role we will discuss, also gravitated primarily to the University of Chicago, followed by MIT.[37]

Elites in developing countries rapidly changed their educational preference from law and Europe to economics and the US. US-trained economists played a prominent role in neoliberal changes in (at least) Chile, Colombia, Indonesia, Korea, Mexico, Turkey, Brazil, and Peru. More recently, Vietnam, Costa Rica, Pakistan, and China have sent ambitious youth to the US to learn the way of neoliberal economics and finance.[38] In many cases the training and the graduates were closely associated with particular universities. For example, the Department of Economics at the University of California trained what came to be known as the "Berkeley Mafia," which worked under President Suharto after his bloody military coup in Indonesia.[39] But Chicago was both the origin and the apotheosis of the practice.

[34] Lebaron (2000), p. 106. [35] M. Loureiro (1997), p. 49; Lebaron (2000), p. 173.

[36] In the US, the share of foreign students was one third from the 1960s to 1990s. But in economics, the proportion of foreign students (considering those requiring a visa) went up to 54% in 2000. In England, the proportion of foreign students was 47% as early as 1991. By the end of that decade, only 10% of PhD students in the top British faculties of economics were indigenous, Lebaron (2000), p. 172.

[37] Babb (2001), p. 133. [38] Haggard and Williamson (1994); Babb (2001), p. 19.

[39] After the eviction of the Dutch professors from Indonesian faculties, the Ford Foundation was approached to propose a new program for teaching economics. The students sent to Berkeley constituted the future backbone of liberal policy making, after the Suharto coup in 1966. Some generals who shared a more nationalistic view in any case opposed them. On this topic, see N. Klein (2007).

THE CHICAGO CONNECTION

Born in 1924, Arnold Harberger has remained influential well beyond his heyday at Chicago, elected President of the American Economic Association in 1988, serving between 2006 and 2010 as chief economic advisor of USAID, and continuing on the faculty of UCLA. In a 1994 interview, Harberger claimed that his courses trained more than 300 Latin American economists, among them twenty-five ministers and central bank governors. At that time, his students simultaneously headed the central banks in Israel, Chile, and Argentina and had recently left leadership in Argentina, Chile, and Costa Rica.[40] Some years later, the count would include the former presidents of Panama and El Salvador, more than forty-five cabinet ministers, and more than fifteen heads of central banks.[41] Harberger, as many others we will find throughout this chapter, is an eminent member of the Mont Pelerin Society.[42] Latin America was Harberger's battlefield.

Harberger is the pivotal figure of the Americanization of Latin American economics—"Good Economics Comes to Latin America," he modestly entitles a 1996 reminiscence (which does not contain the words "Pinochet" or "Allende").[43] Harberger's influence and keen eye for identifying promising policymakers also extended to the home country: he was the PhD advisor for Robert Lucas, the distinguished neoliberal economist. In 1955, he traveled to Chile to establish a protocol with the Catholic University at Santiago, accompanying Theodor W. Schultz (later on a Nobel Prize winner). Harberger, then in his early thirties, was picked for the expedition because he could speak Spanish and was therefore invited to spend a couple of months to put the project in motion.[44] In his account, Harberger was appalled that the Catholic University employed not a single full professor of economics. The Chicago team was persuasive: the local university accepted the terms of the proposed cooperation and committed itself to appoint four Chicago alumni.[45] It delivered much more than that.

On this first visit Harberger met and established a long-lasting friendship with Sergio de Castro, who would play an important role[46] as the pivotal economic manager of the Pinochet regime shortly after the *coup d'état*. Others he trained himself.

The program with Chicago lasted until 1964, and more would come. At the time, Chilean students traveling abroad preferred Cambridge (Massachusetts) rather than Chicago, but a well-financed program, supported by the Ford Foundation and

[40] See the interview in Levy (1999); and also Fourcade (2009), pp. 180–1.

[41] See the birthday interview by Harms (2014).

[42] The story of the Society was told in Chapter 5. Hayek, Friedman, and Popper founded this group of academics in the 1940s to provide a new vision for neoliberal policies through its focus on educational strategy and the occupation of institutional space.

[43] Harberger (1997). [44] Mansell-Carstens (2003), p. 343.

[45] Harberger (1997), p. 301. The Chilean project, from 1955 to 1964, finally engaged thirteen full-time professors at the end. See Harberger's interview in Harms (2014).

[46] Harberger was proud to announce that the program was a success since the beginning: "In the case of the first Chilean 'reformation,' if you want to call it that, I would say about eighty percent of the key players were Chicago alumni," and the same for the upper levels of the administration, Mansell-Carstens (2003), p. 343.

the US government changed their tastes. Chicago became the reference for young Chilean economists seeking further education and career advancement.

SKIRMISHES FROM WASHINGTON TO CHICAGO

Before pursuing our narrative on the success of the Americanization of economics in the south of Latin America, we shall look at some contradictions at home in the US.

Indeed, the American project of exporting the technology of "good economics" to the governing institutions of Latin America emerged from a variety of institutions. All of these operated in the ideological space of the Cold War and broadly aimed to secure allegiance to the US and to the laws of the market, but they nonetheless varied substantively in their orientation towards developmental states and towards the "military solution" that took shape in the Southern Cone with General Castelo Branco in Brazil (1964) and General Pinochet in Chile (1973), Bordaberry and the military Junta in Uruguay (1973), and General Videla and Admiral Massera in Argentina (1976).

Joining the University of Chicago, the northeastern elite universities, and the University of California, USAID and other public agencies, private funds and non-governmental organizations, such as the Ford Foundation and its beneficiaries, and the international institutions such as the World Bank and OECD, completed the picture. US Cold War foreign policy dominated but different views coexisted and competed.

The long-term educational project created a cadre ready to introduce neoliberal public management when the occasion presented. The involvement of the US institutions was a prolonged and heterogeneous investment. The Ford Foundation and USAID contributed to the professionalization of economics but peddled the "soft option": Ford's support for the Institute of Economics of the University of Chile, which generally favored structuralist over neoliberal approaches, was double Ford's support for Catholic University.[47]

The Chicago project otherwise focused on the formation of a body of elite economists with a strong free-market commitment prepared to take positions in government and the central bank. Within Latin America, Chicago operated on the *foquista* model: after establishing a beachhead at Catholic University in 1955, the project exported educational programs to other countries of the continent,[48] and as the Catholic University provided the core of the economic management of the dictatorship, Chile became, during and after the military regime, a home for the Chicago boys as the Latin American representatives of the Washington rules.

Nevertheless, after the defeat in Vietnam, social and public opinion brought pressure for a change in authoritarian-friendly foreign policies of the US. The emerging view was simultaneously neoliberal but tempered by a degree of respect

[47] Dezalay and Garth (2002), p. 113.

[48] Valdés (1989), pp. 278–9. For the recent trends in internationalization of economic ideas and management, see Dargent (2014). Here, *foquista* refers to the Latin American word for the guerrilla strategy concentrating military power in one single zone.

for formal democracy and liberal rights (against torture, coercion, and suppression of media). There certainly were exceptions to the latter proviso—in Nicaragua, Honduras, El Salvador, and Venezuela—but never to the former. What was eventually termed the Washington Consensus combined neoliberal economics and the human rights movement. As one economist announced, this is "the common core of wisdom embraced by all serious economists, whose implementation provides the minimum conditions that will give a developing country the chance to start down the road to the sort of prosperity enjoyed by the industrialized countries,"[49] meaning trade liberalization, privatization, and flexible markets.

This consensus was the result of intense investment, namely from the Council on Foreign Relations, a key consensus-building institution for US elites. Founded in 1921 by New York lawyers and financiers, such as J.P. Morgan and John Rockefeller, the Council on Foreign Relations rose to prominence in the early 1950s, when the Cold War was mounting, and it was instrumental in creating the International Commission of Jurists, in Geneva, offering the human rights movement as an alternative to peace movements supported by the USSR.[50]

Beginning in 1966, the powerful Ford Foundation developed anti-poverty programs in Latin America and also defended intellectuals from the dictatorships. For example, ignoring resistance from the US government and Ford Foundation headquarters, the Ford representatives in Brazil protected Fernando Henrique Cardoso after his university expulsion by the Brazilian military government.

Other institutions took a stance in these conflicts, providing a large scope for the Americanization process, including some critical views. That was the case of the Inter-American Dialogue, created by Washington insiders and financed by the Ford Foundation, which was designed to counter President Reagan and his Ambassador to the UN Jeane Kirkpatrick's hawkish foreign policy. It created an education program, promoting neoliberal economics combined with a view of evolution and economic dynamics, based on the notion of path dependence.

But the World Bank is the most interesting example. It first promoted the "religion of development," under President Kennedy and continuing with McNamara at the head of the World Bank and Hollis Chenery, a prestigious development economist, with previous service at USAID, as vice president of the Bank for development policy from 1972 to 1982.[51] With Reagan, the neoliberal discipline was instead imposed. Anne Krueger, a Mont Pelerin Society member, replaced Chenery as chief economist and served 1982–1986.[52] In 1987, Reagan appointed Republican politician Barber Conable President of the Bank. Conable brought an increased US financial contribution and increased control; as the stakeholders

[49] Williamson (1994), p. 18.

[50] The Irish politician Seán MacBride presided over the Commission from 1963 until 1971 and saved it when, in 1967, it emerged it was being financed if not actually controlled by the CIA. MacBride restructured the Commission and obtained new funding from the Ford Foundation, although one may consider that its best days were over. MacBride had been the director of intelligence of the IRA in Ireland, later abandoned the organization, and became the Irish foreign affairs minister and, as such, was a founder of the Council of Europe. He was also Assistant General Secretary and President of the General Assembly of the United Nations, and founder and chairman of Amnesty International from 1961 to 1975, and thus a recipient of the Nobel Prize awarded to the organization.

[51] Dezalay and Garth (2002), pp. 90, 104f, 180.

[52] She later became the first deputy managing director for the IMF, from 2001 to 2006.

rejected the previously proposed budget, he was able to move in, to take control, and to purge the personnel holding different views.[53]

This openly partisan interlude fueled the crisis in the institution and, in the 1990s, the World Bank responded to pressure brought by activists over inequality, degradation of environment and health, and underdevelopment, by adopting a more participatory and heterodox approach.[54] The new approach at the World Bank was stated, for instance, in the 1991 report on "the challenge of development," focusing on an institutional approach. It was repeated in the 1996 report and again in 1998 under the revealing title of *Beyond the Washington Consensus: Institutions Matter*. Meanwhile, the IMF, which had changed its postwar focus on developed economies to managing crises in the emerging economies, maintained strong neoliberal views. The IMF imposed these views repeatedly, exercising political management and enforcing elite-friendly resolution of domestic budgetary and labor conflict as a condition for financial support during emergencies.[55] IMF decisions intervened in the core of political struggle in Latin America.

THE BATTLEFIELD OF LATIN AMERICA

In spite of his tenacious efforts, Harberger lamented the failure of the Chicago strategy to spread throughout Latin America, bemoaning the shortage of faculties to enlist in the struggle for "good economics." According to him, the Chicago package only dominated in nine institutions: the two Chilean universities; in Brazil, the *Universidade de São Paulo* and the *Fundação Getúlio Vargas*; the Universities of Cordoba and Tucuman and CEMA in Argentina, and in Mexico, the ITAM and *Colegio de Mexico*. As he put it, "these institutions might be called the core group that dedicated itself to the modern science of economics from quite early on."[56]

This brave dedication to the modern science of economics is too modest a conclusion that understates the deep impact of indoctrination of the Latin American elites (not to mention the CIA and other US agencies' efforts). The US-trained economists, alumni from Chicago and other major schools, played a crucial role in elite disenchantment with developmentalist policies and their selection of the neoliberal option: this elite, which some call the "technopols,"[57] took dominant positions in the state, the central bank, political parties, universities, and think tanks in spreading the word. This change was instrumental in the economic turns pursued through military coups and, importantly, they were continued after the reestablishment of democratic rule during the 1980s and later.

Apart from the hard core of neoliberal economists in Chile, the "technopols" included intellectuals who were disillusioned with the left and became enamored of neoliberal policies, e.g., Alejandro Foxley in Chile, Fernando Henrique Cardoso in Brazil, and the writer Mario Vargas Llosa in Peru. Other standard bearers included young stars in economics and politics from the Chicago harvest or

[53] Dezalay and Garth (2002), p. 172. [54] Ibid., p. 187.

[55] See Easterly (2006), on the burden of the IMF impositions; and Teichman (2001), on IMF dealings with Chile, Argentina, and Mexico.

[56] Harberger (1997), pp. 307–8. [57] Domínguez (1997a).

other US elite institutions, including Pedro Aspe in Mexico, Hernando de Soto in Peru, Guillermo Perry in Colombia, and Domingo Cavallo in Argentina. In the following, we will look essentially to the revealing cases of these economists in Chile, Argentina, and Mexico, to then compare their dealings with the histories of Brazil and other countries in other continents.

The Case of Chile

A shock was crucial in Chile for the change of regime: the conflict between Salvador Allende's democratic left-wing policies and Chilean elites took the shape of a capital strike and spilled into hyperinflation and a balance of payments crisis in 1973, culminating with Pinochet's coup.[58] The episode illustrates the divergence between liberal political economy and neoliberal economics. The military dictatorship provided the major breakthrough for neoliberal policies in the economy that were obviously not matched by the anti-military and secularist turn in society which marked previous liberal ascendancies. The paradox did not prevent the neoliberal economists from availing themselves of the first photo opportunity to praise the new regime led by Pinochet.

Milton Friedman, then at the height of his career and mere months from receipt of the Nobel Prize, visited Chile in March 1975. For six days, he met with General Pinochet and lectured, accompanied by the inevitable Arnold Harberger, the primary mentor of the Chicago boys.[59] Friedman and the Chicagoans recognized former students among the ministers and staff, and the ambiance was enthusiastic.

In November 1977, Friedrich Hayek, himself a recent winner of the Nobel Prize, toured what the neoliberals increasingly recognized as the Chilean experiment.[60] He visited again in April 1981. After both visits he complained publicly about the prejudicial treatment of Pinochet in the Western media. He also advocated Pinochet's methods in a private letter to Margaret Thatcher; although his letter is not available, Thatcher's tantalizing reply includes the following: "However, I am sure you will agree that, in Britain with our democratic institutions and the need for a high degree of consent, some of the measures adopted in Chile are quite unacceptable. Our reform must be in line with our traditions and our Constitution. At times the process may seem painfully slow. But I am certain we shall achieve our reforms in our own way and in our own time. Then they will endure."[61] "Some of the measures adopted in Chile" disturbed Thatcher but apparently not so much Hayek.

Hayek, a very political scholar, pontificated in interviews for the official Chilean press—under censorship—about the power of the combination of a neoliberal economy and muscular government power to deliver a virtuous society, echoing a position he had long argued for.[62] Shortly after his last visit, the Mont Pelerin

[58] Fourcade-Gourinchas and Babb (2002), p. 569. [59] Cassidy (2009), p. 82.

[60] Caldwell and Montes (2015); Borzutzky (2005), p. 650. [61] DeLong (2011).

[62] "Liberalism and democracy, although compatible, are not the same [...], it is at least possible in principle that a democratic government may be totalitarian and that an authoritarian government may act on liberal principles," he stated in 1967, Hayek (1967), p. 161; Friedman agreed: "You can have a

Society, the strategic think tank of the neoliberal counter-revolution, which he had founded almost three decades before, chose Chile for its November 1981 meeting.

As everyone could have anticipated, this pro-dictatorship approach was not highly popular. So, forced by the facts, Harberger, the parent of the indoctrination program, felt it necessary to express discomfort with the more heavy-handed procedures of the Pinochet government, at least in his pronunciations outside Chile. He took pains to explain that he only accepted the invitation to act as a consultant to the dictatorship under exceptional circumstances: "I made a point to refuse requests to be a consultant to the Chilean government for something like five years after the coup. During this period I checked regularly with the American Ambassador and with the officials in the embassy who kept tabs on disappearances and other human rights violations. I only relaxed my 'boycott' after, sometime around 1978, the embassy reported zero disappearances." In the same vein, his students and friends, the Chicago boys, "took pains to keep a good distance between themselves and the military dictatorship," he reported with satisfaction.[63]

The local boys may have enjoyed—and needed—fewer updates from the Embassy on the improved "zero disappearance" policy of the military regime or on "other human rights violations." What is certain is that the Chicago economists became the masters of the liberalization program beginning in the third year of the dictatorship, and no "good distance" was maintained after they became part of the dictatorial government.

The first two years of the new regime were governed in compromise with General Gustavo Leigh, a man of developmentalist inclination and General Pinochet's main rival for power. But by 1975 the neoliberals came to power when Sergio de Castro, the first local friend of Harberger, was appointed economy minister (1974–76) and then finance minister (1977–82). A brisk negotiation with the IMF settled the major plans for liberalization.[64] The Planning Ministry was headed by Alvaro Donoso, another Harberger student, and the Chicago economist presented the successive waves of liberalization as the "triumph of good economics," an incantation of what they had learned from their gurus.

Harberger, many years after the disgrace of Pinochet, made the point that many essential staff of the military regime were not educated at Chicago, namely Hernan Buchi, the dominant personality in government after Sergio de Castro, and Jorge Cauas (both educated at Columbia University), and José Piñera (from Harvard University). In something of a cosmetic overstatement, Harberger added that some Chicago boys were even jailed for some months after the 1982–3 debt crisis.[65]

high degree of social freedom and a high degree of economic freedom without any political freedom," as quoted in Crouch (2011), p. 122.

[63] In a previous interview, Harberger pointed out that even when the dictatorship named Jorge Cauas, not a Chicago boy, but a "good friend," as the economic "super minister," he still "absolutely refused to be a 'consultant' to the Chilean government," Harberger (2010); Of course, he still did not have the assurance from the US Embassy that there had been "zero disappearances" (not even of US citizens, not to mention Chileans), Levy (1999).

[64] Fourcade-Gourinchas and Babb (2002), p. 545.

[65] Those would be the cases involving Rolf Luders and Ricardo Marin, Harberger (2010). This is certainly an overstatement: Luders was imprisoned for financial dealings leading to the bankruptcy of a major bank not for a democratic epiphany.

As a response to this crisis, the IMF opposed the expansionary policy led by finance minister Luis Cerda in 1983–4, and contacted Hernan Buchi, who had by then the responsibility of leading the financial system as "superintendent of Chile's banks." Buchi conducted informal discussions with the IMF from 1982 to late 1984, and, when he became finance minister in 1985, an agreement with the IMF was rapidly effected.[66] Buchi was not Harberger's man; he was simply the man of the IMF.

As Chile became the first Latin American country to apply a full package of free market measures shortly after the 1973 military coup, it became the center of attention for the continent and a laboratory for the neoliberal practices. Among the experiments, one with far-reaching consequences was the privatization of the social security, the public pension system. In the 1970s, Chilean social security covered 70 percent of the population, but it was outdated and a labyrinth of rules and exceptions, maintained since 1924 as four distinctive components (private sector, public sector, military, and police systems of retirement) and involving 160 different funds.[67]

In 1979, the dictatorship abolished the principle of maintaining parity within occupations and changed from counting years of work to age. In 1980, two more decisive steps followed: the elimination of the employer's contribution to the system; and the establishment of individual accounts, under management by specialized—and highly profitable—corporations.[68] Finally, in 1981, Minister Piñera, a neoliberal ally although not himself a Chicago alumnus, led outright privatization.

Over the following twenty years, coverage fell and the deficit of the pension system grew immensely.[69] Matters turned out better for the privatizers: José Piñera and Jorge Cauas, with three other former ministers, served as executives of the largest economic group in Chile, the Cruzat-Larraín conglomerate, which acquired Provida, the largest pension fund management corporation.[70] As public managers and private entrepreneurs, they did well by staying true to neoliberal economics, and liberalizing authoritarianism. Even after the failure of the project in Chile, as some years afterwards the social security system was nationalized given its high levels of debt, the same pattern has been proposed in many other countries, not only in Latin America.

In any case, continuity of economic management still prevailed many years after the fall of the Pinochet dictatorship: when Ricardo Lagos, supported by the Socialist Party, took the presidency of Chile after the rule of Christian Democrats, he nominated a finance minister who is a former IMF director, Nicolás Eyzaguirre.[71]

[66] Chwieroth (2013), p. 273.

[67] Fourcade-Gourinchas and Babb (2002), p. 545; Borzutzky (2005), pp. 656–7.

[68] The individual capitalization system was optional but there was substantial pressure favoring it (75% of the population was integrated in the new system, and the three largest corporations managed 69% of its volume).

[69] By 2003, only 52.5% of the population was under capitalization funds (plus 2.7% still in one of the old systems). The deficit generated by the pension system grew from 3.8% in 1981 to 6.1% of GDP in 2000.

[70] Borzutzky (2005), p. 661. [71] Babb (2001), p. 219.

The case of Argentina

The process of Americanization enjoyed a steady march to success in Chile but proved more challenging in Argentina. Harberger, as he triumphed in Chile, tried his charms in Argentina as well and helped negotiate Project Cuyo in the 1960s, consisting in sending Chilean Chicago-trained economists to set up a new course of study at the *Universidad de Cuyo*, Cordoba. But they were met with resistance and not even the validation for the course credit was granted for long. Harberger took a personal interest and taught there, but to no effect. It was only in Chile that the result was immediate, as "Chile has played an outsized, even legendary role in the diffusion of professional models in and beyond the region."[72]

Apart from Chicago, other institutions had a role in this process of change in Latin American economics. Harberger recounts that the Econometric Society made efforts to enlarge its Latin American membership in 1978 and 1979, culminating in a first regional meeting held in 1980 in Buenos Aires, then home to a ferocious dictatorship.[73] It is not recorded whether the participants at the scientific gathering noticed what was happening around them.

As in Chile, in Argentina it was the imposition of a military dictatorship that provided the first watershed between economic nationalism and neoliberal policies. In 1976, the military overthrew the presidency of Isabel Peron, the widow of the populist general who had ruled Argentina during the periods 1946–55 and 1973–74. The developmental state and close relationships with domestic capital and with the labor aristocracy had been central to the Peronist model.

After the fall of Isabel Peron and during the dictatorship, the leaders of the military Junta were divided on the choice of personnel and the political economic tenor of the new course. General Jorge Videla, the head of the Junta, supported the appointment of neoliberal economists for the strategic posts of the new administration. But Admiral Emilio Massera and the Air Force generals, supported by the powerful newspaper *Clarin*, opposed the turn to liberalization because they were more nationalist and developmentalist than their Army colleagues.[74]

In the end, José Alfredo Martinez de Hoz, the neoliberal Minister of the Economy for 1976–81, followed a strict monetarist policy and reduced import and export tariffs; he also, in an extraordinary and decidedly illiberal economic measure, froze wages, demonstrating the possibility of peaceful coexistence between neoliberal and authoritarian policies. The whole package delighted the IMF, which supported and financed this government scarcely days after it came into power. In 1977, a banking reform law opened the banks to foreign capital, and de Hoz

[72] Montecinos and Markoff (2009), p. xiii.

[73] The Conference met under the Argentinian military dictatorship in its darkest hours, but there is no record, as far as we are aware, of qualms about the venue. In contrast, when a European conference of the Econometric Society was scheduled for Barcelona in 1971, under Franco's dictatorship, some of the founders of the Society not only protested but also declined to participate, Louçã (2007), p. 302. The Argentine Dirty War apparently raised no concerns for the organizers of the 1980 meeting. One can only hypothesize how the emergence of mathematics as the symbolic language for universalization and of econometrics as the language of economics facilitates the integration of different students, in the current case under the auspices of an ideologically minded education in the neoliberal creed.

[74] Trowbridge (2001), p. 80; Biglaiser (2009), pp. 80, 89.

pursued his agenda to dismantle the barriers and protections that had long supported the import substitution strategy.

After the initial hesitation, the Junta, which ruled from 1976 until 1983, arrived at solid support for market-oriented reforms. This rupture with structuralist orientation and nationally focused economic action faced significant resistance, including from within the ruling military elite, but the neoliberal bloc slowly solidified its position.

The same change of mood occurred in academia. The rise of neoliberalism in the faculties of economics in Argentina benefited from the flight of many professors critical of military rule. The dictatorship was ruthless and its Dirty War ultimately claimed more victims than the notorious General Pinochet in neighboring Chile. The education system was fragmented, and only some survivors were tolerated by the generals in power.[75]

Argentina deviates to some extent from the Chilean and Mexican models in that the success of the neoliberal consensus was more home-grown and less dependent on US imports. In fact, in Argentina the think tanks and educational institutions completed their struggle for the neoliberal turn and standardized pedagogy in economics before the intervention of US programs and funding.

The epicenter of this educational strategy was the Instituto Di Tella, a private research center created in 1958 and later transformed into a university by 1991. Torcuato di Tella was an Italian immigrant who made a fortune producing automobiles and refrigerators and understood the importance of ideas in order to consolidate social changes and economic power. Despite the eventual bankruptcy of the firm, his family has remained an influential player in Argentina, and Tella's son Guido became minister of foreign affairs in 1991.

The Centro de Estudios Macroeconomicos de Argentina (CEMA), one of Harberger's favorites, was created in 1978, during the period of the military Junta; it became a university by 1995, under the leadership of four Chicago PhDs. Another player was the Centro de Estudios de Estado y Sociedad.

But the most important think tanks were those of the Domingo Cavallo's constellation: his Fundación Mediterranea, based in Cordoba, his home base, and its Instituto de Estudios Economicos sobre la Realidad Argentina, IEERAL. Forty years after his first Latin American excursion, Harberger helped Cavallo to create the *Instituto Superior de Economistas de Gobierno* in 1994, which offered postgraduate courses for the preparation of state officials, in cooperation with a selected group of neoliberal faculties, the *Instituto Di Tella, CEMA*, and others and recruits its teachers from the Universidad Catolica of Chile.[76]

Cavallo, with twin PhDs in economics from Cordoba and Harvard, was the most influential economist who pursued his career before and after the military dictatorship and led the economic policy of the new regime. He was the president of the central bank in 1982, under the military regime, and returned to power as minister

[75] Until the late 1970s, Chicago had little influence, and not until the 1990s was there a significant influx of neoliberal economists in government. During the Peronist regime and the dictatorship, the degradation of the universities was evident, as from the 1940s to the 1970s frequent interventions by government in universities, in contrast to Chile, undermined the education system. This got worse in the last years of the Peronist regime and under the military dictatorship.

[76] Biglaiser (2009), pp. 79, 84.

of foreign affairs for the controversial Carlos Menem presidency (1989–99). He was then appointed in 1991 the minister of the economy and took most of his IEERAL collaborators to the ministry. In the most powerful post in government and for a long period (1991–96), he excelled in trade liberalization, lowering labor costs and imposing the controversial dollarization of the Argentinian economy.[77]

The strength of these think tanks and the indoctrination and social networks they represent explain how, after the end in disgrace of the military Junta, the neoliberal politics it had pursued could regain momentum in a new government, that of the Peronist Menem. Cavallo, who proudly presents himself as "the most important minister of Menem's administration during seven years,"[78] was the strategist of that continuity.

Under Cavallo, liberalization enjoyed impressive victories with the privatization of over 400 public firms, including the oil company YPF (to Repsol), the telecom company Emtel (to France Telecom, Telecom Italia, and Spanish Telefonica), Aerolineas Argentinas (to Iberia), but also health facilities, railways, state gas, and the Buenos Aires electrical network. In 1991, the Mercosur, an agreement for a free trade zone with Brazil, Uruguay, and Paraguay, was signed.[79]

Cavallo, who had resigned in 1996, returned again to the ministry of the economy under President De la Rua in 2001, until the rapid collapse of the regime, when the President was forced by riots to resign and to flee the Presidential palace by helicopter. Cavallo was then one of the most criticized if not hated ministers, given the "corralito," or the freezing of the bank accounts, and the austerity measures affecting most of the population and leading to an unending recession.

The most distinguished neoliberal yet authoritarian economist and politician was ousted from government and for the following years persecuted by successive accusations, such as contraband of arms and different financial malfeasances, including corruption.

The Case of Mexico

Throughout most of the twentieth century, Mexico's political system combined formal democratic rules and an effectively single party system with weak democratic institutions and strong corporatism. One of the many consequences of this disposition was the ability to insulate the technocrats from political pressures from below and from requirements of transparency and accountability.[80]

In fact, the Mexican Revolution, from 1910 to 1920, had eliminated the power of the traditional oligarchy led by Porfirio Diaz and gave rise to a new state bureaucracy, firmly ruling the government through the official party, the Party

[77] Trowbridge (2001), p. 9.

[78] Cavallo (2004), p. 23. Cavallo's views on Chile are revealing of this attitude of prioritizing the neoliberal agenda: praising the "neoliberal revolution led by Augusto Pinochet," he still laments the fact that "economic liberal reforms had been decided and implemented by a repressive regime [which] had added more passion to an already heated debate" but defends the idea that authority was nevertheless crucial since "Chile's success should be explained due to the ability of the State not only to establish new rules of the game, but also what is more important to sustain them," Cavallo (2004), pp. 10–11.

[79] Ronchi (2007).

[80] Fourcade-Gourinchas and Babb (2002), p. 561.

of the Institutionalized Revolution (PRI), an extraordinary oxymoron. After this game change, the Bank of Mexico and the ministry of finance concentrated the economic intelligentsia, and a new university, the National Autonomous University of Mexico (UNAM), was created as a major project for the education of state officials, namely for those two institutions.

The new power was stable enough to use the new opportunities and to modernize the economic structures under a populist regime distributing social benefits. After the 1929 crisis, which led to the abandonment of *laissez-faire* in Latin America, the creation of the UN Commission for Latin America (CEPAL), in 1948, provided the leadership for the developmentalist conceptions that dominated the continent. In 1942, the government signed a favorable agreement of debt restructuring with the US and, in the following decades (1940–70), the "Mexican miracle" was registered as producing high growth rates. The dominant ideology of this period was "developmentalism," or "structuralism," a heterogeneous combination of the contributions of W. Arthur Lewis, Walt Rostow, and Ragnar Nurske, oscillating between neoclassical and Keynesian economics in order to analyze the terms of unequal change between the core economies and their peripheries.

Raul Prebisch, who presided at CEPAL, established in Santiago do Chile in 1948, guided this current and gave it enough institutional power to determine political choices in different countries, such as Brazil and Argentina.[81] Later, from the 1950s, dependency theory challenged the CEPAL, under the influence of Marxism and other critiques of capitalism and imperialism.

The equilibrium among the three forces (Keynesian-developmentalist in the lead, with neoclassical and Marxist critical on the right and left margins) broke down with the debt crises, which culminated in 1982. The market orientation rapidly became dominant in the 1980s and 1990s.

The turn in the dominant economic conceptions and in the orientation of public action depended on a major change of personnel, and that was carefully prepared through time. The Bank of Mexico was instrumental for that change: it "was the single organization most responsible for the internationalization of the Mexican economics profession in the postwar period,"[82] developing a specific program for scholarship favoring a major reconceptualization of economics, favoring new options in the management of the Mexican economy.

Babb, who wrote one of the most complete appraisals of these changes, concludes: "From a historical perspective, the Banco was the government organization most responsible for the Americanization of Mexican economics. The central bank was responsible for Mexico's first foreign scholarship program for economists, and played a role in the founding of economics at the ITM (later ITAM) and the Colegio of Mexico and the renovation of economics at the University of Nuevo Léon. Furthermore, Bank of Mexico officials were instrumental in the remaking of ITAM economics into a much more Americanized program oriented toward sending students to postgraduate studies in the United States."[83] As with the Bank of Mexico, the central banks of Colombia and Argentina constituted the anchor institution for the neoliberal turn in their countries.[84]

[81] Namely influencing President Kubitschek in Brazil (1956–61) and President Frondizi in Argentina (1958–62).

[82] Babb (2001), p. 90.

[83] Ibid., pp. 126, 189.

[84] Urrutia (1994); Dagnino Pastore (1989).

For such a result, the Bank of Mexico and its allies mobilized several tools. The first was a new teaching of economics, through the creation of ITAM as early as 1946, as the center for neoliberal economics. This was a strategic move and "a small group of central bankers remade a second rate night school into the world-famous bastion of neoclassical economics known as the ITAM."[85] This was combined with the selection process for the internationalization of students in economics: Harberger, the same Chicago professor previously quoted on the numbers of disciples who took the strategic ministries and governorships at the central banks, noted that CONACYT, the Mexican National Council for Science and Technology, constituted "a secret weapon without which Mexico's economic transformation would never have been accomplished."[86] The "secret weapon" of the Council was its careful selection of candidates for scholarships in economics at designated US universities under the mantle of scientific training.

The second tool involved an ideological and political battle when a crisis occurred as in August 1982 Mexico defaulted on its debt. At the same time, President Lopez Portillo nationalized the banking system, nationalizing and consolidating 764 banks into fewer than twenty, and imposing capital controls. This exceptional move towards a more regulated economy would prove short-lived.

Over the year preceding the default, a conflict had emerged between the developmentalists, some trained at Cambridge, UK, and the monetarists, many trained in the US. Isolated, the government accepted the terms of an agreement with the IMF, accepting an agenda of liberalization.[87] That was the triumph of the fiscal and monetary conservatives.[88] This victory of the latter was completed when the new President De la Madrid, the same year, nominated two Yale-trained economists to the finance ministry and the central bank and favored the beginning of a long adjustment process towards liberalization. Under De la Madrid, six years of austerity followed with immense social consequences.[89]

Carlos Salinas de Gortiari, the next President (1988–94), a graduate from UNAM and then Harvard University (PhD, 1978), came to power in Mexico after a long international career, namely as alternate director of the IMF for 1956–8. As expected, Salinas selected many US graduates for his administration. His finance minister was Pedro Aspe (PhD at the MIT, 1978), the minister of commerce was Jaime Serra Puche (PhD at Yale, 1979), the NAFTA's chief negotiator was Herminio Mendoza (PhD at Chicago, 1978), and the minister of budget was Ernesto Zedillo (PhD at Yale, 1981). The combination of international finance pressures through the debt crisis, and the rise of US and other foreign-trained technocrats in government delivered the neoliberal reforms.[90]

The Salinas privatization program included the telephone company, airlines, chemical and steel industries, national insurance companies and banks, television, radio, and the communications system. At the rural level Salinas destroyed the

[85] Babb (2001), p. 201. [86] Quoted in ibid., p. 190.

[87] This was the first agreement signed by the IMF imposing a full-scale plan of liberalization, as discussed in D. Harvey (2005).

[88] Babb (2001), 179.

[89] For the period 1983–8, per capita income fell 5% a year and the real value of workers' wages fell at least 40%, MacLeod (2004); Lomnitz (2003).

[90] Santiso (2004), p. 33; Babb (2001), pp. 83, 171f, 191.

rules of sharing community land, liberalizing land markets for sale or rental. In 1992, Salinas signed the NAFTA agreement with the US and Canada, assuring free movement of goods and capital. The result was a reconfiguration of the Mexican industry with the intensification of "maquiladoras," the border factories for intensive use of labor for finishing products. The concentrators of riches included Carlos Slim, the beneficiary of the privatization of communications whose wealth grew to be equivalent to 6 percent of Mexico's GDP (in the US, Rockefeller, in his best years, reached only 2 percent of GDP, and Bill Gates nowadays less than 0.5 percent).[91]

The Mexican crack was not without political and social struggle. The PRI, the completely dominant party for sixty years, lost a local election to an opposition party in 1989, and in 1988 the first contested Presidential race was held: Salinas won by a slim majority of only 50.4 percent against Cuauhtemóc Cardenas, a popular dissident of his own party and the son of a respected past President. (Salinas is said to have benefited from the strange breakdown of the computer system, an "apagón," or blackout, when the votes were being counted.)

Ernesto Zedillo Ponce de Leon replaced Salinas, after the term of his office. Zedillo was a Yale-trained economist who pursued the liberalization process which has been "dominated by economists trained at Harvard, Yale, MIT, and the University of Chicago, [as] three consecutive Presidential administrations transformed the Mexican economy with a series of neoliberal reforms."[92]

Only in 2000 would a different party win a Presidential election, ending the absolute dominance of the PRI. The victor was Vicente Fox, of the right-wing PAN, but to no surprise he appointed neoliberal economists from the previous government: Francisco Gil Diaz, his minister of finance, was the former deputy finance minister of Salinas and a Chicago boy.

This neoliberal evolution since the debt crisis of 1982 represented a major rupture with tradition and prevalent economic conceptions in Mexico, which had inspired the views of the Mexican state bureaucracy. With the debt crisis of the 1980s, the victor in Mexico came to be neoliberalism.

The Network of Good Economics

Domingos Cavallo, the pompous minister of finance of Argentina, was the protagonist of the previous section on his country, but his remarks on Chile were also registered. Now it is convenient to go back in time, to his education years, to uncover the virtues of Americanization and indoctrination of the Latin American elites.

For his education, Cavallo had come to Harvard, where he spent several years (1974–77, decisive years, with *coups d'ètat* in both Chile and Argentina). At that time, Latin Americans students from Harvard or MIT used to gather to discuss the events and their visions. The Boston circle included Cavallo, the narrator of the saga, José Piñera, future minister of mines and labor of Pinochet, his brother

[91] Freeland (2014), p. 260. On the careers of the Mexican mandarins, see R. A. Camp (2002).

[92] The road was not without some setbacks and scandals: Luis Colosio, the appointed candidate for replacing Salinas, was assassinated in 1994, and immediately replaced by Zedillo who was more trusted by the PRI bureaucracy, Babb (2001), p. 182.

Sebastian Piñera, future senator, and the visiting Alejandro Foxley. Cavallo was also a mate of Pedro Aspe (a 1978 PhD from MIT), the future finance minister of Salinas in Mexico (who was also at Harvard at the time—he got his PhD there in 1978). Aspe was then the head of ITAM, the most important neoliberal center in Mexico and the pillar of the Americanization of economics in the country.

In the concluding years of his stay in Harvard, Cavallo was recruited for a mission to Bolivia with Arnold Harberger (1976–77), the mentor of the Chicago boys.[93] Then Cavallo went back to Argentina to create his own think tank and shortly after to lead the central bank.

The links to Aspe and Harberger proved to be decisive. The Chicago connection helped Cavallo to prepare his think tanks and teams for government, and the Boston connection helped him to keep the best relations with other like-minded economists who were simultaneously changing the social map of their own and neighboring countries.

The Boston connection also worked in another sense, as all the protagonists followed the same strategy, or perfected it after the Boston student experience or the Chicago illumination by "good economics": Foxley had already created his own think tank in 1970, Cavallo created the IEERAL, and Aspe was leading the ITAM when they met.[94] All would have key positions in government for the neoliberal turn.

The Chilean Alejandro Foxley was by then a visiting professor at MIT. A Democratic-Christian politician and the founder of the *Corporación de Estudios para Latinoamérica* (CIEPLAN), Foxley headed a think tank that generated the argument for the opposition against the Allende government and contributed to the imposition of the Pinochet dictatorship and its government.[95]

Like Cavallo and Aspe, Foxley pursued a career in government, in his case and unlike his friends, after the end of the dictatorship. He was the finance minister of the Aylwin government from 1990 to 1994, a Democratic-Christian government following a neoliberal agenda, and simultaneously governor at the World Bank, and then, as a man for all seasons, he returned to power as minister of foreign affairs for a socialist government (2006–9).

In Chile and Argentina in the 1970s and under the military dictatorships, economic liberalization was promoted as part of a program for societal change. In the case of Argentina, the dictatorship created the conditions for the turn, as it imposed monetarist policies and the drastic compression of labor costs, but it was after its fall, with Menem and Cavallo, that the privatization program was developed to its heights. In the case of Mexico, it was the pressure from the debt crisis and the internal changes in the leading party that provided for the neoliberal turn under Salinas and then Zedillo, during the 1980s. In Mexico, Chile, and Argentina, the economists and politicians who pursued privatization and liberalization had been formed by the Americanization of economics, and they became the chief advocates for developing financial markets.

[93] Cavallo (2004), pp. 12, 15. [94] Centeno (2010), pp. 34–5.

[95] Santiso (2003), pp. 114–17. Foxley was later finance minister (1990–4) and minister of foreign affairs (2006–9), after the Pinochet era.

The Case of Brazil

In Argentina, the imposition of a military dictatorship did not necessarily imply the Chilean curse, the combination of neoliberal measures under socially authoritarian rules, because disagreement within government circles prevented or postponed measures favoring the financial markets. In Brazil, too, the ideas of the nationalist and developmentalist economists, under the guidance of Raul Prebisch's CEPAL and Celso Furtado, who followed the same orientation towards the creation of a national accumulation process, permeated the military apparatus. After the 1964 military coup, the government was divided between the neoliberals and those preferring to maintain a focus on national industries and companies, albeit imposing a severe corporatist compression of working and democratic rights. In 1964, developmentalism was still going strong; it was too early for the acceptance of the gems of neoliberalism.

The Brazilian Armed Forces benefited from its close relationship with Washington, formed through the training of the Brazilian Expeditionary Force during the Second World War. General Castelo Branco, the eventual coordinator of the 1964 military coup, was prominent in the US relationship. After the war, a Joint Brazil-US Commission for Economic Development was formed, with World Bank involvement, leading to the creation of BNDES (National Bank for Economic Development) under the presidency of João Goulart.[96] The program represented the strategy to create a protected national economy.

Roberto Campos, a conservative economist who was for some time part of the team that created BNDES, was a protagonist of that turn since, after his alienation from the Vargas government, he was named Ambassador to Washington where he built influence. He was the first neoliberal to occupy a strategic post for the military regime, as he was nominated minister for planning by Castelo Branco. Campos, a devotee of Hayek, had studied at Columbia (he had an unfinished PhD) and claimed to be a monetarist.

In Brazil, the equivalent of the ITAM in Mexico and the Institute Di Tella in Argentina is the Fundação Getúlio Vargas. The Fundação was created in 1946 in Rio de Janeiro and, with the Faculdade Nacional de Ciências Economicas (FNCE) created the previous year in São Paulo, became the center for the Americanization of Brazilian economics providing the link to the US universities.[97]

The connections of the Foundation to the military regime precipitated the separation of a group of professors who moved to the Catholic University of Rio de Janeiro (PUC-RJ), under the influence of Pedro Malan and a group of economists, graduates from Berkeley. The PUC benefited from strong support from the Ford Foundation to send students to the US. Malan would then take a post at the UN and as executive director of the World Bank, and later would be the minister of finance under President Fernando Henrique Cardoso.

Fernando Henrique Cardoso was a distinguished sociologist who gained international acclaim as a proponent of the dependency theory. A disciple of Florestan Fernandes, a Brazilian Marxist, he wrote his PhD dissertation as a critique of the

[96] Dezalay and Garth (2002), p. 97.

[97] Valdés (1989), p. 102; Dezalay and Garth (2002), pp. 98, 100.

traditional views of slavery as proposed by Gilberto Freire, and from then he held top positions in Brazilian academia, until the dictatorship drove him into exile. When he returned with democracy, he was elected Senator and then President, but changed his previous views and endorsed strict neoliberal solutions. Cardoso changed the Constitution in order to be able to be reelected, an objective he attained. Lula da Silva, who followed him as President, was a metal worker in São Paulo and was the founder and leader of the Workers Party. Although promoting active social policies against extreme poverty, he did not challenge the neoliberal approach then dominant at the top level of the regime.

A corruption investigation on a major construction firm, Odebrecht, and the public oil company, Petrobrás, led to a political crisis from 2015 to 2016 and was instrumental in the impeachment of President Dilma Rousseff, who lost the support of most of her allies, in particular of the vice president Michel Temer, who was then empowered by Congress (in spite of the fact that he was then accused of corruption, unlike the toppled President). As the new government took office, a new program for ultra-liberal reforms was presented.

EUROPE AND THE FINANCIAL LOBBIES

We now briefly discuss five European cases, Britain, France, Germany, Spain, and Portugal, for comparison with the Latin American processes of indoctrination of the elites and find different patterns of allegiance to neoliberal policies. Yet in all of them the consecration of ideas through schooling and the emergence of dominant academic centers and think tanks, the composition of social interests and representations in governments leading privatizations and deregulation and the disciplinary power of international connections match the patterns we have found in the countries studied so far.

These different national processes differ in method and protagonists: whereas in France it was not academic conversion to the new ideas but a strategic choice of the state apparatus that led to liberalization, in Germany the path was defined by the connection between a doctrine, ordoliberalism, accepted both in faculties and by the central bank, and the convergence of the main parties around free market ideas, and in Britain the City and the Treasury were the decisive factors for the alignment of the country under the leadership of global shadow finance. Finally, in Spain and Portugal neoliberalism transformed the socialist or social-democratic parties, and privatization and austerity policies became embedded in most governments.

Lobbies and their ability to create social networks were in any case instrumental for this travel. In that sense, a book, *Europe, Inc.*, suggests that think tanks and lobby groups have succeeded in influencing important choices of the EU, namely the European Roundtable of Industrialists, the Transatlantic Business Dialogue, the International Chamber of Commerce, and the Association for Monetary Union of Europe. They were eventually decisive in decisions on transports, biotechnology, and climate change policies, as well as key economic projects such as the negotiation on the Transatlantic Economic Partnership,[98] which came under attack by Trump.

[98] Balanyá et al. (2000).

THE CASE OF BRITAIN AND THE POWER OF THE CITY

The process of Americanization of British universities took a long time, because there was a well-established alternative school of thought, based on Cambridge and the Keynesian tradition. This tradition has roots in the influence of Alfred Marshall, who presided over the spread of economic ideas from the turn of the century until the early years of the twentieth century: by 1888, half of the Economics chairs in England were populated by students of Marshall, and they shared a peculiar vision of social motivation and ethical principles, unlike the positive claims of the emerging neoclassical economists from the European continent. Even Arthur Cecil Pigou, the disciple of Marshall whom young Keynes would take as the epitome of standard economics to be challenged if not ridiculed, nonetheless claimed that economic science was inspired by that "social enthusiasm which revolts from the sordidness of mean streets and the joylessness of withered lives" and defended progressive taxation and other social measures that would be seen as radical not many years afterwards (even if he was quite conservative, for long opposing government regulation and supporting the Gold Standard).[99] In any case, with the 1929 recession, Keynesian views opened an avenue to dominate British economics and had an impact in different latitudes as well.

Although the London School of Economics, hosting Hayek, became a center for neoliberal economics, the intellectual landscape remained contradictory if not hostile to neoclassical economics for a long period and the Cambridge group not only resisted but also prevailed in the major controversies. Therefore, as the faculties would side with Keynesian politics in most cases, it was outside academia that the neoliberal tents were set up. It was not through economics but through political choices and the coagulation of social interests that Britain was converted to the neoliberal alternative.

Despite social tensions and the alternating electoral success of the two parties, from the 1950s forward institutional continuity rather than social transformation dominated British politics. The two essential moments defining British politics, the landslide victories of Labour in 1945 and that of Thatcher in 1979, suggest otherwise. But Labour's Keynesian politics retreated after 1947, and an austerity budget was imposed;[100] as a consequence of the disarray, the conservatives under Churchill regained power in 1951. Consistency and continuity became the pillars of British politics, as power was managed through the triptych of the City of London, the Bank of England, and the Treasury.[101]

[99] Fourcade (2009), pp. 136–7, 143, 155.

[100] Kerr (2001), p. 95.

[101] Kerr (2001), p. 64; According to Kerr, "The problem for policy-makers has been the historically close association between all three of Britain's central institutions: the Treasury, the Bank of England, and the City of London. The links between these have their origins in the pre-industrial era and 'were based upon the Bank's management of the state's debts by means of loans raised in the City, the interest on which the Treasury levied through the protectionist customs duties and tariffs' (Ingham, 1984, p. 128). Ironically the strengthening of this relationship in the nineteenth century sprung from an attempt by the state to provide the Treasury with greater independence from the city, by allowing the Treasury to pursue a 'general strategy of rigorous parsimony and balanced budgets' (ibid., p. 130). However, through time as the City expanded its overseas interests and laid the foundations for the international gold-sterling standard, the Treasury's fiscal prudence became an important cornerstone for guaranteeing the stability of the sterling area [...] Thus, by the late nineteenth century the relationship between the Treasury, the City and the Bank had been built around an 'integrated system of interdependencies' (ibid.) The foundation of this system was a general antipathy towards increases

Policy orthodoxy was to avoid endangering the financial system, and governments conceded to austerity when the time came. It was a Labour government that asked for the IMF intervention in 1975–6, and as a consequence a monetarist and deflationary plan was adopted: the recession doomed Labor, which had in fact initiated the Tory program. The government was forced by the IMF to sell parts of British Petroleum, in an unprecedented inauguration of privatizations.[102]

Economists played a role in this continuity, although not so much from academia but from the pinnacles of the Treasury and the Bank of England, as an official clergy managing the connections between the dominant public institutions.[103] Journalists at the *Observer*, *The Times*, the *Independent*, and, especially, Samuel Brittan at the *Financial Times* digested the orthodox view for popular consumption. Its further reproduction on TV made the wisdom of financial markets into common sense.[104] On the other hand, the monetarist discourse was well established before Thatcher, namely as part of the political apparatus of the Conservative Party and its connections to industry. This was established through the Institute of Economic Affairs, created in 1955 under the leadership of Keith Joseph, who would become a crucial adviser to Thatcher, and then the Center for Policy Studies and the Adam Smith Institute, created respectively in 1974 and 1976.[105] As in the other cases we have addressed earlier in this chapter, the neoliberal think tanks educated many of the key players for future governments.

But it was the City, the huge and powerful private banks, which encouraged the allegiance of a large number of economists and political officials to neoliberal ideas, as the expression of the predominance of finance. Under its influence, the Conservative Party adopted a free market platform in 1970 and Labour agreed in its 1976 platform to weaken the emphasis on fiscal policy and to abandon the objective of full employment.[106]

The stage was set for a right-wing turn and the opportunity would present itself when Margaret Thatcher was chosen by the Conservatives to replace Ted Heath.[107] Although Thatcher, when she was minister of education, favored an increase of the budget for her own sake, she then led, as prime minister, a highly successful liberalization plan: at the end of her term, half of the public assets in industry had been sold, including some important public utilities that were traditionally protected, since they represented natural monopolies. The sale of British Telecom was the largest stock-based privatization, but even it accounted for only one

in state expenditure and a consensus on the need to secure sterling's world role." And further: ' "The influence of the Treasury on the state has been based only partly on structural features. It has also been based to a considerable extent on the willingness of politicians to submit to the workings of these structures' (Cronin, 1991). Through a combination of these factors, Britain has developed over the years a state and party system which is inherently conservative and generally hostile to *dirigiste* measures," Kerr (2001), 149, and see also pp. 138, 140–3.

[102] Kerr (2001), p. 160; M. Prasad (2006), p. 135.

[103] As Fourcade notes, referring to the public officials, "In the British 'model,' the identity of economists has been historically shaped by their embeddedness in the high-status, well educated clerisy whose knowledge ought to be put to the general service of the society," Fourcade (2009), p. 183.

[104] Ibid., p. 181. [105] D. Harvey (2005), p. 22.

[106] Fourcade-Gourinchas and Babb (2002), p. 552.

[107] M. Prasad (2006), pp. 258, 122, 126, 133; Keegan (1984), p. 42.

seventh the value and a small fraction of the social impact of the sale of roughly 1 million council houses to their tenants.[108]

The ideological argument was that "denationalization" was required: the state should establish markets to coordinate social life and then retreat to the minimal function of protecting persons and property. Thatcher shared Hayek's intuition that neoliberalism could succeed only if it changed the popular conceptions of economy, society, and even personhood: people should identify as earners, taxpayers, and consumers, not as workers, social actors, or decision makers.

THE CASES OF FRANCE AND GERMANY

In contrast to Britain where the triumvirate of the City, the Bank of England, and the Treasury structured the political space, the political and economic core in France and Germany formed around state technocracy.

Fourcade investigated the three routes for economics in France: first, the *laissez-faire* approach of the physiocrats as the first liberals; second, the sociological tradition; and third, the marginalist tradition, mostly developed by trained mathematicians "turned public engineers,"[109] but who lived outside the academic community of French economists. This third track to nineteenth-century economics was taken by Antoine Cournot, a mathematician, by Jules Dupuit, an engineer, as well by Léon Walras, who failed to secure a position in his home country and emigrated to Switzerland.

Instead of the "public minded elitism" prevailing in Britain, in France a nobility of public officers was composed of high-level civil servants and engineers,[110] frequently favoring a strategic role of the state and indicative planning combined with strong support for national industries and firms. Jacques Rueff and Maurice Allais, two of the most distinguished neoliberal economists, accepted or favored state intervention, and Allais even came to admit the "potential efficiency of centrally managed public utilities,"[111] in spite of his paradoxical ideological excursions and invective against some of his colleagues who could not share his faith in free markets.[112]

Unlike what happened in US academia, in France modern economics was not the result of the incorporation of mathematics and econometrics in equilibrium and neoclassical teachings, but of ideological choices in different faculties, which have always been dominantly conservative, and then of pragmatism in government and official institutions. Neoliberalism became the dominant economic school in France, beginning in the 1970s at the Ecole Nationale d'Administration, where

[108] Campbell (2011), 235–6. This was quite exceptional in Europe: the privatization process in France took twenty years to achieve what Britain under Thatcher did in three, M. Prasad (2006), p. 12.

[109] Fourcade, Ollion, and Algan (2015), p. 200.

[110] Ibid., pp. 10, 231.

[111] Ibid., p. 204.

[112] That was the case of an epic confrontation with Ragnar Frisch, the founder of econometrics, at a Vatican seminar in 1963, Louçã (2007), pp. 295–7.

future high-ranking public officers were educated, then at the Institut d'Etudes Politiques, under Jacques Rueff.[113]

Politically, France went through two liberalization periods: in 1976–8 with right-wing President Giscard D'Estaing and Prime Minister Raymond Barre, and in 1986–8 during the cohabitation of socialist President Mitterrand and conservative Prime Minister Jacques Chirac. Immediately following his election in 1981, Mitterrand had conducted a policy of nationalization of all the financial systems and major industrial groups, but he was vanquished both by internal and external pressures—a foreign exchange crisis and a domestic capital strike—leading to the collapse of the government and a rapid reversal of course. Since 1983, the dismantling of price controls and of restrictions on capital markets, privatizations and free market reforms set a new course; this ended Mitterand's experiment of "Keynesianism in one country" and began France's neoliberal epoch.

In Germany, Helmut Kohl was elected in 1982, shortly after Mitterrand in France, and only three years after Thatcher. Following thirteen years of social democratic government and capitalizing on European doldrums, Kohl proposed the first successful neoliberal program in Germany aided by several influential institutions which favored that orientation. The Bundesbank and the Council of Economic Experts had turned to neoliberalism earlier. Nevertheless, Kohl did not pursue a vast privatization program as in Britain: the German state held no large industrial stakes. While he did deregulate telecommunications and broadcasting, he did not go further.

Resistance against a more Thatcherite program came from inside the ruling Christian Democratic Union. Kohl himself presented Thatcher critically as an example of "unrestrained and dangerous capitalism."[114] A complex of political reasons and personal convictions related to his project of unifying Germany and to managing pressures posed by the eastern frontier, Kohl favored a conciliatory approach. Hand-in-hand with Mitterrand, Kohl joined the duo that led the European Union for some years.

Furthermore, the dominant German intellectual tradition at the universities and major institutions was not that of contemporary standard economics, much less of traditional neoliberal economics, it was that of Law faculties and of ordoliberalism, a peculiar brand proposing economic liberalization measures under the auspices of strong state control, which inspired the European treaties and solutions with a distinctive interventionist flavor. Ordoliberalism played a dominant role in the configuration of the European Union treaties and workings despite Euroskepticism among some of the most ardent ordoliberals.[115]

[113] For instance, by 1957 most French members of the Econometric Society were engineers or mathematicians and not economists, Fourcade (2009), pp. 188, 192; Fourcade-Gourinchas and Babb (2002), p. 567; M. Prasad (2006), pp. 260–1.

[114] Geppert (2003), p. 9; M. Prasad (2006), p. 162.

[115] Hans Werner Sinn, one of the most influential of the Ordoliberals, became a critic of the euro as he suspected it could not deliver the same discipline the German mark required, Sinn (2014). In the event of the continuation of the recession and its aggravation in the periphery of Europe, Sinn defended restructuring the public debt of the southern countries, although under the condition of strong controls. Some authors of the Eucken Institute defended the mutualization of public debt in Europe: "We conclude that Germany may have followed ordoliberal thinking rather too little than too much.

The ordoliberal economists and politicians can nevertheless claim that the essential choices of the European Union, such as its constitutive and ruling treaties, from the Rome Treaty to the current dispositions, follow their recommendations, as the core of the European edifice is freeing the movements of capital and imposing strict social order. Angela Merkel, the German Chancellor, led the way for this program and has imposed it through the legal arrangements and political choices in Europe for more than a decade; she will have served for the longest term in German government. Anxious to play a central role in the creation of the euro, successive French governments overcame reservations and accepted the structure of free movement of capital with strictly national fiscal accounts. This structure created sharp regional asymmetries and degraded prospects for European convergence.[116]

SPAIN, A CASE OF EMBEDDED NEOLIBERALISM

The recent history of Spain's allegiance to austerity programs is a case of "embedded neoliberalism": in particular since the election of a government of the socialist party, the PSOE, in 1982, which represents a neoliberal turn towards privatization, deregulation, and pro-business policies, economic orthodoxy was pursued but simultaneously public services, progressive taxation, and a public investment strategy were established, or "a neoliberalism ensconced with measures that compensate citizens for the dislocating effects of the market."[117] The Gonzalez government accepted a typical IMF package, including a liberalization of the labor market with the introduction of temporary contracts, but simultaneously tried to address the hopes of a population that had recently lived through the dictatorship of Franco. This took place in a difficult international context: as Mitterrand had been elected in 1981 and his attempt at nationalization and public control of some economic tools had collapsed, the Spanish government was also under pressure not to follow the same path.

The adaptation to the neoliberal agenda proceeded similarly to other cases discussed in this chapter. The central bank provided the brains and the brawn for the job. Its economists first embraced neoliberal ideas. In the 1970s the Research Service of the Bank of Spain became the first national research institution.[118] Veterans of the Bank then moved to government positions to apply the recipe. The connections among central bank bureaucrats, Economics faculties, and ministers tell the story of these decades of liberal modernization, as "beginning in the 1970s, a group of Spanish economists who regularly switched hats between their roles as central bankers, academic mandarins, and government bureaucrats acted as the translators of neoliberal theories about fiscal, monetary, and labor market policy."[119]

It would have been more prudent to trade a partial (legacy) debt mutualization against the preservation of independence of the ECB and national debt brakes," Feld, Köhler, and Nientiedt (2015).

[116] A critique of ordoliberalism, arguing that its policy increased the asymmetry and costs of the crisis, is to be found for instance in Munchau, *Financial Times*, November 16, 2014.

[117] Ban (2016), pp. 5, 33. [118] Ban (2016), pp. 22, 39–40. [119] Ibid., p. 245.

Yet, the roots of these ideas go deeper in history. In 1944, a German dissident, Heinrich von Stackelberg, came to Spain and took a position at the Complutense University in Madrid. He had been a Nazi: a member of the party from 1931, sergeant in the SS from 1933, and then professor at the Berlin and Bonn universities. But he became estranged from Nazism, grew close to the Freiburg Circle, a dissident version of ordoliberalism, and decided to move to Spain. Francisco Franco had recently won the civil war and established a dictatorship, and von Stackelberg could be accepted without too many questions. Although he lived there for only two years, until his death in 1946, von Stackelberg influenced the teaching of economics, introducing game theory, regional and industrial economics, and models of duopoly and imperfect competition.

This move to internationalization opened up new avenues for economics in Spain, but it obviously could not be classified as a liberal view of the future of the country. Neither do the other promoters of right-wing policies within the framework of the new regime emerging after the end of the civil war, but most of these founders of economic neoliberalism plus authoritarian politics obtained their credentials from the London School of Economics. There, in the 1930s, Lucas Beltrán, who came to be the main figure for the introduction of neoliberalism in Spain, studied under the guidance of the Austrian School with Hayek and Lionel Robbins, the two challengers of John Maynard Keynes, then the towering patriarch of economics in Britain. Beltrán developed his Austrian leanings and introduced these views in his home country, inviting Hayek for a visit in 1951 (in a previous section we discussed the effect of this traveling strategy of Hayek, much later, in Chile), as he did with other scholars of the same orientation. Beltrán, who belonged to the Mont Pelerin Society, also developed close links to the German Ordoliberals, such as Ropke, whom he also brought to Spain.

Benefiting from a strategic grant policy, two other economists, Luis Rojo and Pedro Schwartz, also came to the LSE, to study with Popper and Robbins. Both became members of the Mont Pelerin Society. Schwartz, whose first publication was a translation of a political essay by Popper, had been mostly a teacher, although for a period he took a job at the research department of the Bank of Spain. He developed a network of connections in the neoliberal universe, through the Cato Institute and the Thatcherite Institute of Economic Affairs and went briefly into politics, as the small Liberal Party elected him to Parliament in 1982. But his political influence was marginal, as was that of his student Jesus Huerta de Soto, who became a vice president of the Mont Pelerin Society and was also part of a politically marginal movement.[120]

In contrast, Rojo had a distinguished career at the national bank. He became its director of investigation and then governor (1992–2000), through the decisive period of the preparation for the euro, and then moved to the private sector at Santander.[121]

[120] Instead, Jose Toribio, with a PhD from Chicago, obtained under Friedman and who is credited with having converted Schwartz to monetarism, has had a distinguished career in the bridge between university and business: he was the chairman of Caixabank Monaco and Inverban, as well as member of different boards (La Caixa, Nestlé, Abertis Telecom, La Caixa Corporate Finance, Yoigo, Amper, ITM Club), after being research director at different banks (Banco Urquijo and Banco Hispano Americano). He is invited, on a weekly basis, to elaborate his views for CNN.

[121] Ban (2016), pp. 105, 109, 134.

The Americanization of economics in Spain is part of the education of these "switching hats" professors and bankers, and the same pattern is to be found across the political divide. Carlos Solchaga, whose first professional assignment was established by Rojo in the central bank, spent one year at MIT and became the superminister of finance and economics for the PSOE government, over a long period during its first term in power (1982–93). In spite of his ministerial position, in 1991 he simultaneously accepted appointment to the internal review board of the IMF.[122]

After the governments of Felipe Gonzalez (1982–96) and Jose Maria Aznar (1996–2004), the socialists came to power again with Jose Luis Zapatero, whose government is a standard case of Americanization: his economic team, including key advisors and ministers, had PhDs from the University of Minnesota and various other US and British universities. Having presided over the adjustment measures in the wake of the financial crisis, Zapatero ended his career in government imposing a change in the Constitution in order to impose permanent structural surpluses by force of law,[123] a concession to the populist versions of neoliberalism that few governments dared to follow.

Finally, as the right-wing Popular Party regained the government with Mariano Rajoy in 2011, the choice for finance minister was Luis de Guindos, an ex-CEO of the infamous Lehman Brothers.[124]

THE CASE OF PORTUGAL AND THE STRATEGY OF AUSTERITY

Our final case study concerns the adoption of austerity policies in Portugal, in parallel to some other European countries following the financial crash and then the debt crisis, and concentrates on showing how, again, Americanization and neoliberal indoctrination paved the way for major shifts in social and economic policies.

In the spring of 2011, as the turbulent crisis of sovereign debt extended from one country to another on the periphery of the Eurozone, the Portuguese government was forced to accept a bailout led by the European Commission, the European Central Bank, and the International Monetary Fund. Greece and Ireland had already accepted the austerity measures that were the condition for funding, and the Portuguese authorities approved the same type of adjustment program.

The correspondent of the *Financial Times* in Lisbon was the only journalist to notice that something odd had happened as the representatives of these institutions, popularly called the *Troika*, began their procedures with the local authorities. Indeed, the Troika representatives went missing for several hours during the first day of negotiations, and the official schedule gave no hint of their whereabouts. As the newspaper discovered, they met with some professors of economics at the Nova Business School before driving to the Ministry of Finance. "The Easter

[122] Ban (2016), p. 135. [123] Ibid., pp. 6, 136, 194, 202. [124] Ibid., p. 205.

breakfast with the troika delegation, held in a former palace on the Nova campus, has only just come to light," he wrote.

Peter Wise, the journalist, talked to the economists invited to this preparatory meeting with the Troika officers and reported their happy description of the meeting: "'They (the Troika officers) were eager to hear our views,' says José Ferreira Machado, dean of the faculty. The meeting reflects the degree of influence that Portugal's top business and economics schools have always had on government policy and national debate. 'In a small country like ours, the leading economics faculties are in a sense co-leaders of the nation in a way that would not be possible in bigger countries,' says Prof Ferreira Machado."

As the dean explained, both Nova and the Catholic University are agenda setters: "we are a meeting point for the elites of today and tomorrow, and our obligation is to point out possible directions for the future leaders of the country." He added: "bigger faculties in bigger countries may have the money to recruit Nobel Prize-winning economists, but they don't have the same kind of impact on society as the leading schools in a small country."[125]

The Catholic University and Nova were created in 1972 and 1973, just before the fall of the old dictatorship that had ruled Portugal since 1926, and they were conceived as alternatives to the main universities that, already by that time and in particular over the following years, had, become centers of critical thought. Neoclassical economics was reestablished at Nova and Católica, which developed a powerful plan for academic Americanization and education of the elites, thus becoming what the dean would call the "co-leaders of the nation" as the tide of liberalization and privatization followed the turmoil of the fall of the dictatorship.

When the adjustment program ruled by the Troika was negotiated, the opportunity for a major game change was perceived by the liberalizers. The director of the school, Ferreira Machado, could then proudly claim that the Memorandum bears "the intellectual mark of our school."[126]

Even before the discussions of the wording of the Memorandum defining the austerity measures were concluded, Nova published a collection of papers on its main topics, anticipating the conclusions they knew beforehand.[127] In the preface, Machado vigorously endorses the strategy, stating: "if carried out with enthusiasm and rigor, these reforms will change Portugal for the better" and that "the crisis has forced cooperation and silenced the reservations."[128]

Ferreira Machado is himself a product of the Americanization process. Holding a PhD from the University of Illinois, Machado led a faculty for which the key academic criterion is holding a doctorate from a US university. The other participants at the meeting, the self-proclaimed "co-leaders of the nation," follow the same pattern. Pedro Portugal, who inspired the labor law reforms, has a PhD from the University of South Carolina and made a career both at Nova and the Bank of Portugal, a stronghold of neoliberal positions. Francesco Franco, who proposed the reduction of labor costs through cuts in the pension deductions paid by employees, received his PhD from MIT, under the supervision of Olivier Blanchard.

[125] Wise (2011).
[126] Ibid. See the Wise article.
[127] Lains (2013).
[128] Machado (2011), p. 2.

Blanchard was indeed one of the intellectual movers of this approach, both as an influential MIT professor and as the IMF chief economist for the crucial period between 2008 and 2015. In the case of Portugal, he sketched this program even before the crash and the debt crisis: in a 2007 paper, he suggested that the Portuguese economy was doomed by a competitive deficit generated by the mismatch between wages and productivity, and suggested ways to actually reduce the wages as a solution.

In this influential paper, Blanchard considered several alternatives. One would be to restrain the nominal wage growth, but this would meet resistance given the trade union tradition and organization. But, as the impact of inflation was by that time very small, given that the euro imposed a strict monetary policy biased against price changes, this would take a long time and therefore he indicated his preference for another solution, a composite package for reductions in nominal wages. The remaining alternative would be to use industrial policies to stimulate exports, but European rules precluded that option and Blanchard himself did not believe the country had the comparative advantage for that, since it should preferably specialize in tourism and attracting rich pensioners.[129]

Blanchard concentrated therefore on ways to reduce wages. "If successful, a devaluation [. . .] decreases the real consumption wage," he proclaimed. And, "a decrease in nominal wages sounds exotic, but it is the same in essence as a successful devaluation," or a "competitive disinflation." For this, a "period of sustained high unemployment" is required, as "more total unemployment is needed to achieve a given improvement in competitiveness." Consequently, "the adjustment is likely to be long and painful" as "many years of high unemployment may be needed to convince workers of the need for adjustment."[130]

As did his followers, Blanchard enumerates the real and nominal wage rigidities that should be addressed: the unions, the wage bargaining process, the labor laws, the "psychological" and other "legal" obstacles as, in particular, "the labor law forbids 'unjustified wage decreases' and in practice rules out decreases in nominal wages for economic reasons."[131] The Memorandum agreement signed by the local authorities carefully addresses these obstacles and describes the legal changes required by the Troika.

The proceedings of a 2006 conference that reunited Blanchard and his disciples explain why real wages should be reduced even if inflation cannot achieve the reduction.[132] Internal devaluation, reduction of redundancy payments, reducing unemployment benefits, reducing extra-time compensation, changing the rules for wage bargaining, and a number of other changes became effective during the Troika years and were successful, as they imposed an important transfer of income from labor to capital.

As the austerity program followed the script, the "co-leaders" fulfilled the positions of power: all the leading officials during the Troika period were recruited from US banks and institutions or had a US university pedigree. Vítor Gaspar, with a PhD from Nova, was the minister of finance (he then left to take a job as director of research at the IMF). Moreira Rato, who led the agency managing the public

[129] Blanchard (2007), pp. 12–13, 15, 7. [130] Ibid., pp. 7, 13, 15, 29. [131] Ibid., 8.
[132] Franco (2008), p. 84; Portugal (2008); and in the same vein Portugal (2011).

debt, was a Nova graduate with a Chicago PhD and a career beginning at Goldman Sachs and then moving to executive director at Lehman Brothers and Morgan Stanley. António Borges, professor at Nova, had a Stanford PhD and a career as executive vice chairman of Goldman Sachs for 2000–8 (but simultaneously he took administrative jobs at Citibank, BNP Paribas, Santander, and at the two dominant firms in distribution in Portugal, Sonae and Jerónimo Martins), then moved to Santander. He was subsequently the director of the European Department of the IMF and finally took charge of the privatization program defined by the Memorandum agreement.

This austerity program achieved social success as far as the legal changes it defined and the privatization plan it established, but the economic result was nevertheless a failure. The recession was deeper and the adjustment was too destructive, so that Blanchard himself, and later the IMF as such, were forced to recognize that the model did not work. In his *New York Times* blog, Krugman was the first to note that Blanchard acknowledged that extreme austerity proved to be self-defeating.[133] But the die was cast.

CONCLUSION

Through several distinctive cases from Latin America and Europe, we have discussed in this chapter the essential forms of education and specifically of neoliberal indoctrination of the elites. The management of academic programs and special programs for students to travel to reference universities; the selection process for hiring for institutions such as the central bank and public office; social learning through the evolution of political parties, think tanks, associations, media, and public opinion; the participation at international fora, such as the World Bank, the IMF, the CEPAL, the OECD; and the conditioning rules, e.g., treaties, and forms of external legitimation, have been investigated as part of the construction of hegemony in each country.

History highlights the distinctions and the parallels among these cases. For the more dependent economies, with a recent university system, Americanization was the dominant means for the education of the elite and for the creation of a neoliberal consensus among the major players and institutions. The University of Chicago programs for attracting students from Chile or Mexico, the Boston connection involving some of the future finance ministers in Argentina, Mexico, and Chile, and the Berkeley connection in Indonesia are examples of the results of these plans. In Europe, on the other hand, think tanks and media played a major role, but academic circles could oppose neoliberalism, such as in Britain, or could propose a very specific approach to state intervention, such as in Germany.

Ruling class hegemony requires cohesion, control of policy, reproduction of ideas, and the exclusion of alternative ideas or projects emerging from competing social movements. A hegemonic ruling class establishes control of education, knowledge, and action by mobilizing institutions, such as faculties and think tanks, that certify valid knowledge and exclude alternatives. Willem Buiter, an economist

[133] Krugman (2011a).

who was on the staff of the Bank of England and was then chief economist of Citigroup after 2010, called this process the "cognitive capture" of economics and economists, specifically referring to regulators.[134]

We have shown why and how the neoliberal agenda, namely that of the Mont Pelerin Society, was so intent on this long-term strategy to channel students to Chicago, to help found neoliberal think tanks in different countries, and to establish the patterns for political choices, independently of the democratic allegiance of different governments. The coups creating the Chilean and Argentinian dictatorships were the turning points for the ascension of neoliberalism in those countries, in spite of the specificities between them, Chile being the successful story of the first military regime (until its collapse) and Argentina being the portrait of unresolved contradictions that postponed the neoliberal impetus (after the collapse of the dictatorship).

The neoliberal path was therefore imposed in Chile through political outsiders, the military, whereas in Britain it came from organic intellectuals of the Conservative Party in a hegemonic position that would then extend to the Blairite *Third Way*, and in the US it was imposed through the configuration of the political system according to a general convergence around the interests of finance and big firms, whereas in Mexico and France it would be the result of insiders pursuing a career in public office. The elites of Chile and Britain were therefore ideologically equipped for a monetarist revolution, whereas those in Mexico and France justified their choices as forced adaptation to the global economy.[135] In Brazil and Germany national traditions and economic schools, plus a different configuration of the social forces, distorted and adjourned participation in this movement. In Portugal and Spain, in contrast, neoliberal ideas became the mantra for the ruling parties, both conservative and social-democratic.

In any case, globalization, essentially a force of financialization for the last decades, has reinforced this process as it absorbed large parts of the world economy.

For the Latin American cases discussed here, the turn was precipitated by a crisis in the balance of payments, leading to very short-term changes and liberalization measures, in every instance under dictatorships or authoritarian regimes. For the European cases, the institution of the rule of free movement of capital destroyed the viability of exchange rate policies and limited that of monetary policies, as the development of the European Union represented the culmination of the process of financialization and liberalization.

Another form of power will be discussed in the next chapter, investigating the linkages between members of government and central banks and finance, as their professional careers and particular interests evolved both before and after official positions, or the revolving door between politics and business.

[134] Buiter (2013).

[135] Fourcade-Gourinchas and Babb (2002), pp. 556, 533. Prasad presents an alternative interpretation. According to her thesis, neoliberalism triumphed in the US and Britain not because the Left was weak but rather because it was strong, and "the socioeconomic transformations of the postwar period had moved most voters to the other side of the adversarial divide," anchoring the neoliberal alternative in a general dissatisfaction with the status quo. Instead, given the nonadversarial political traditions in Germany and France, under a more centralized and stable power, there was less room for status quo change, according to her analysis, M. Prasad (2006), p. 3, 40.

8

The Revolving Door

The wide consensus leading the new society under the spell of finance has been established by indoctrination and the Americanization of universities and other institutions such as central banks, media and think tanks, and by schooling. But its victory depended on the organization of power and social differentiation, including the construction of networks that captured the elites and imposed the selection of governments and institutions, and the transformation of the economic and financial forces leading economies and politics, as discussed in the two previous chapters.

The explanations for the success of financialization that have been offered in the literature vary from the power of corporations,[1] to that of a transnational "superclass,"[2] or simply present it as a feature of neoliberalism.[3] Taking these views into consideration, in this book we concentrate on the discussion of the mechanisms of power and the social and institutional conflicts leading to their transformation. This chapter presents some evidence on that process of capture through the revolving door between politics and business. Other mechanisms and social contradictions will be discussed in the remaining chapters.

The revolving door has been studied and discussed, mostly in recent years, after it became apparent that states are, even in well-established democratic societies, a sort of "public-private partnership," leading to the widespread use of public resources for satisfying private interests.

In some cases, the revolving door is justified on the basis that it selects the best for office with neither regret nor shame among those promoting the revolving door. In some sophisticated cases, the business connections are even presented as a rational form of career planning for government officials. The Bloomberg agency made such an argument in a provoking article, "Why the Revolving Door Might Be a Good Thing," stating that the door provides an opportunity for maximizing future benefits:

> The argument could be made that government jobs would attract an entirely different caliber of person if they didn't hold out the possibility of a coveted private-sector gig and cushy paycheck at the end of them. But because this track exists, ambitious people with fancy degrees from good schools who would otherwise pursue other options might choose to earn less money working for the federal government, at least for a time. Of course there's potential for corrosion inherent in the relationship, but there are benefits to this private-sector subsidy, too.[4]

[1] Crouch (2011); Jabko (2013). [2] Streeck (2014); Apeldoorn (2014). [3] Blyth (2013).
[4] Kolhatkar (2013).

Although not everyone would be ready to adopt this extremely cynical view, the examples discussed in this chapter show that the "cushy paycheck" of the revolving door is a crucial part of modern societies. This was not always accepted. By 1933 Louis Brandeis, a distinguished judge at the US Supreme Court, famously challenged the interlocking between bank and industry as "the root of many evils." This chapter investigates the mechanisms for the change of perceptions, from such "evils" to the revolving door presented by business as a "good thing."

DOORS EVERYWHERE

Many cases of revolving doors have been investigated in different contexts and some examples will be examined in this section.

A sample of forty-two countries was examined for firms whose controlling shareholders and top managers are members of national parliaments or governments.[5] The company is defined by the author, Faccio, as politically connected if at least one of the its large shareholders (anybody directly or indirectly controlling at least 10 percent of votes) or top directors (the CEO, president, vice president, or secretary) is a member of the parliament, a minister (including the prime minister), or the head of state (dictator, president, monarch), or is "closely-related" to a top politician. The data sources allowed identification of 17,033 politicians for the forty-two countries, who were in office during the first half of 2001. The variables used to measure the spread of political connections at the country level were, first, the "% of politically connected listed firms," the ratio of connected firms over the total number of firms listed in a particular country, and, second, "connected firms as % of market capitalization," or the ratio of the market capitalization of connected firms over the overall capitalization of each country.

The findings were, first, that connections are widespread (out of a sample of forty-two countries, 532 firms have top directors or large shareholders who sit in the national parliament or government). These firms represent 2.68 percent of listed corporations but 7.76 percent of the world's market capitalization—they are quite large. Furthermore, connections provide significant benefits to firms in terms of easier access to debt financing, lower income taxation, and market power, although connected firms exhibit significantly lower performance than their non-connected counterparts. Rent-seeking by politicians, who are appointed as directors and managers of firms, cannot alone explain the poorer returns by these connected firms. The underperformance of connected firms also suggests distortions that connections introduce in the allocation of capital, investment decisions, and therefore the long-term growth of these corporations. It may be bad business.

Taking some national cases, let's consider very different economies. Evidence from Indonesia demonstrates that firms connected to President Suharto suffered a larger impact than others when rumors of his illness were spread in the mid-1990s, as the fall of their stocks was 23 percent greater as compared to other traded firms.[6] Evidence of special protection of private interests is also relevant, and another

[5] Faccio (2006). [6] Fisman (2001).

investigation established how the two businessmen closest to President Suharto used their position to enrich themselves.[7] A similar case emerged in Malaysia in the 1990s, when firms connected to the circles around Prime Minister Mahathir fell by 20 percent more than others when he left power. A comparable case was also demonstrated for Pakistan.[8] For the US there is a large literature on the connections between the lobbies and the Congressional staff and high-ranking policymakers.[9]

A 2006–7 study of Germany investigated publicly available information on connections between 605 publicly traded and influential companies and the non-parliamentary activity of 611 Bundestag members.[10] This study found that twenty-eight companies, representing the largest, most globalized firms were politically connected through the actual employment of a member of Parliament. Political links were more evident for financial institutions, insurance, stock exchange, energy, and automobile manufacturers. Some MPs had connections with firms related to their official roles. For example, members of the Bundestag Finance Committee work for Allianz, Deutsche Bank, Deutsche Börse, and Commerzbank, and members of the Committee on Educational, Research, and Technology Assessment work for firms in the energy or pharmaceutical sectors. Parties in power were more connected: 76 percent of all connected members of Parliament belonged to the governing parties. A political preference was found: the conservative CDU/CSU and the liberal FDP on the right wing of Parliament were more connected to corporations than were the center or center-left parties.

In Germany, politically connected firms had higher market capitalization, higher sales, and higher total assets than the others. The standard deviations for stock market return were quite different for politically connected firms and politically unconnected firms, with that for the former being almost half the value of that of the unconnected ones. This indicates that German politicians undertake work at large, wealthy, low-risk companies. In terms of performance, the politically connected German firms exhibit better results and excess returns. Political connections and firm performance are positively correlated although it is not possible to establish a causal relation. MPs may help firm performance, or successful firms and politicians may seek each other out.

A similar investigation on France traced the networks between political leaders and CEOs of some publicly traded companies in France, between 1989 and 2002.[11] The investigators focused on whether CEOs of publicly traded companies who enjoy educational and professional relations with the political elite bestow "economic favors" on politicians to help them get re-elected. Well-connected companies realize lower returns but create more jobs near election time. But these are pieces of evidence for political connections rather than for social mobility.[12]

[7] Harvey (2005), p. 34. [8] Johnson and Mitton (2003); Khwaja and Mian (2005).

[9] The *New York Times* conducted research on these links, pointing out some examples, such as that of a top environmental advisor in the Obama administration who is a consultant to the nuclear power industry, or the leader of the health program at the Brookings Institution who is on the board of Johnson & Johnson Lipton, Confessore, and Williams (2016).

[10] Niessen and Ruenzi (2010). [11] Bertrand et at. (2005).

[12] Many other investigations discussed other countries or economic processes, reaching the same conclusions. For instance, Agrawal and Knoeber (2001), evaluated the importance of outside directors with a background in politics on the boards of US firms and proved that politically-connected directors are more frequent in firms with larger sales to government. Cull and Xu (2005), showed that politically-connected firms have preferential access to debt financing. Khwaja and Mian (2005); Dinç (2005).

We turn now to harder evidence on the social and systemic mechanisms of revolving doors.

The influence of business on politics has attracted renewed interest because of growing inequality and public awareness plus the politicization of inequality and economic control as highlighted by concepts such as that of "the 1 percent" and "the 99 percent," in particular after the works of Atkinson, Piketty, Stiglitz, and others. Political connections, *lato sensu*, concern the relationship between political power (in the form of its representatives or agents) and industry (once again in the form of its representatives or agents). In some cases, agents of business may influence agents of political power, e.g., in lobbying for legislation, regulation, implementation, or non-enforcement. In other cases agents who act on the behalf of one another may perhaps just be interchanging positions over time, a process referred to as the revolving door.

New tools have also emerged for the rigorous analysis of political connectedness and the revolving door. Network analysis makes it possible to trace the pathways of power. Advances in coding text enable us to assess many relationships at a time, increasing the scale and pace beyond what was previously possible only through detailed case studies. We have recourse to both in the following.

The next sections present the result of three studies of political connectedness and interconnections. The first study gathers key biographical information about the careers of professionals in the governments and central banks of twelve developed countries on three continents: Brazil, Chile, Mexico, the US, Canada, the UK, France, Spain, Belgium, Germany, Portugal, and Greece in the years 1975 and 2015. We track the academic training of these bureaucrats and their careers before and after their period of public service. The next study presents data on the careers of center or center-left governments for different countries spanning the entire period which are examined in order to detect evidence for the revolving door. Finally the specific cases of Portugal and Spain are studied: in the case of Portugal we do not take a sample but examine the entire population of members of all governments through that long period, and in the case of Spain we consider some examples.

Three Hypotheses: Internationalization, Economization, and Financialization

In the following, we examine three main hypotheses concerning the change trajectories, i.e., in the education and career of elite bureaucrats: internationalization, economization, and financialization. Internationalization means that elite

To investigate political connections in newly privatized firms, Boubakri, Cosset, and Saffar (2008), used a sample of 245 privatized firms from forty-one countries (twenty-seven developing and fourteen developed countries) between 1980 and 2002. They found eighty-seven of these firms to be politically connected as they have a politician or ex-politician on their boards. Stijn Claessens, Feijen, and Laeven (2008), show that Brazilian corporations which contribute significantly to political campaigns exhibit an increase in bank leverage. This was also found by Hongbin Li et al. (2008), concerning China, where the authors demonstrate that affiliation with the ruling Communist Party of China helps in obtaining loans from banks and other institutions. Szwarcberg (2012), provides a network analysis of clientelism in the context of Argentina. Mendieta et al. (1997), investigated Mexico governmental officers' network with firms. R. Camp (2007); Sinclair (2007, 2011).

bureaucrats in the neoliberal era are more likely to have international experience prior to assuming their key offices than did their predecessors. International experience might come in the form of education, in particular, graduate and postgraduate education.[13] It might also come in the form of participation in international institutions, e.g., the European Union bureaucracy or international institutions such as the World Bank or IMF, in the form of participation of other countries' institutions, or in the form of participation in international rather than national business or financial activity. In this sense, internationalization aids the exchange of ideas and the international norming of the bureaucratic elite. It has reduced dependence, both economic and intellectual, on domestic political and economic processes and increased dependence on international fora.[14]

In a major study on the ecology of the managements of the top world firms, this hypothesis of internationalization was discussed. The authors took the directorates of the 176 largest corporations in the world (135 corporations and 42 banks), for 1976, 1999, 2006, and 2013, and detected the formation of communities: the business elite is more densely connected, as this process of transnationalization has accelerated since 1996, in particular being regionally centered in the North Atlantic.[15]

The second hypothesis, economization, means that the rise of economics and economistic thinking has come to play a more central role in the formation of the elite bureaucratic type. We hypothesize that law has been to some degree displaced by economics or management as the preferred or modal training ground of public officials.

This change, which we expect to see at least in part in the formal education of bureaucrats, also signals a larger epistemological change in the governance mentality, the rise of economistic thinking as the basis of public decision making. Within the US government, the "Economics 101" mindset—named for the introductory course in economics at many universities[16]—was once the exclusive province of the Council of Economic Advisers (CEA) and the Office of Management and Budget (OMB), government agencies that would seek to impose economic logic on public decision making. The economistic government agencies would seek to discipline the other agencies, such as the Department of Labor, Department of Agriculture, or Environmental Protection Agency. But the economistic approach is now widespread: since the victory of the neoliberal turn in the 1980s, the ideas of the free market replaced those of public management and regulation. CEA and OMB, once the lonely outposts of the standard approach emphasizing market equilibrium, marginal analysis, and cost-benefit analysis, now find allies

[13] Bourdieu (1998). In a groundbreaking work, Bourdieu proved the relevance of elite shared backgrounds and educational ties forming networks of influence and social reproduction.

[14] In more restricted research on governments and central banks of the UK, Germany, France, Spain, Belgium, Greece, and Brazil, the target universe for the analysis was the five top decision makers or economists at central banks from each of these countries in 1975 and 2015 and five or more cabinet-level public officials from the same countries for the same years, based on a variety of sources. The research found evidence for a rapid growth of internationalization and education abroad, mostly for the central bankers, Dias et al. (2015). Other investigations will be discussed in the following.

[15] Heemskerk, Fennema, and Carroll (2016).

[16] See Kwak and Johnson (2017), for a scathing discussion of the impact of economism on public discourse and decision making.

everywhere.[17] The larger bureaucratic agencies that formerly had close ties to constituencies, such as Agriculture, Labor, or Commerce, now find themselves sharing in the economic mindset. As a concrete hypothesis, we expect to see an increase in the formal study of economics in the training of bureaucratic elites with displacement both of law, as the generic training ground of bureaucratic elites, and of specific sector expertise, as in the case of agriculture, labor, or industry.

This change in the pattern of education of public officials is obvious from data. In Mexico, the long tradition of lawyer or engineer presidents was displaced when President Salinas, educated in public management at the Harvard Kennedy School, took office. In the United States, President George W. Bush was the first president to hold an MBA (also from Harvard). The notion that the economistic mindset is essential for governance has some historical roots in the businessperson president, although formal neoclassical economics education is actually quite different from the business mindset.

Our third hypothesis concerning bureaucratic elites, financialization, means that participation in financial institutions, i.e., private or central banks or international financial institutions, has become a key part of the development of the bureaucrat. Previous generations may have come through other powerful economic institutions, e.g., through industrial firms, as Robert S. McNamara, the powerful US Secretary of Defense in the Johnson administration, came through Ford Motor Company,[18] but also through law firms, through local elective bodies, e.g., through mayoralties, regional legislatures, or even through labor unions.

Obviously, the connections to the world of finance can occur outside the bounds of employment. Peer Steinbrück, the social-democratic candidate for chancellor in the 2013 German elections, experienced the embarrassing revelation that he had earned €1.25 million by giving eighty-nine speeches between 2009 and 2012 at companies and banks including Deutsche Bank, J.P. Morgan Chase, BNP Paribas, Sal. Oppenheim, Union Investment, Ernst & Young, Freshfields Bruckhaus Deringer, and Baker & McKenzie. At the same time, he said the chancellor's salary, at about €250,000 annually, is too low because regional savings bank directors are paid more.[19]

This damaged his campaign and, indeed, Steinbrück canceled a speech at Bank Sarasin & Cie after a German newspaper reported that the Swiss private bank was being investigated by German prosecutors for tax evasion.[20]

Financialization of the nomenclature closely accompanies internationalization as potential key pathways for the disconnection of the bureaucratic elite from the domestic real economy, since the growth of finance plays out differently for the national economic elite and the working class. The former have the option of financializing, joining the pool of global liquidity. Some individual members of the domestic economic elite, owners of small and medium businesses, may be left behind but, as a class, the domestic economic elite financializes or dies. But

[17] DeLong (1996).

[18] "The Fog of War: Eleven Lessons from the Life of Robert S. McNamara," a 2003 documentary by Errol Morris, presented the life and deeds of McNamara. The film won the Academy Award for best documentary.

[19] Deutsche Welle (2012). [20] Weck (2013).

for the working class, the real economy is, along with the state of class struggle, a prime determinant of wellbeing. In any case, considering the elite bureaucrats, financialization provides both a new fraternity and a new outlook.

In terms of outlook, the financialized type is an individual agent operating in a financialized economy, including agency in or with financialized firms.[21] Key elements in the financialized type include engagement in outright speculative activity with special attachment to leverage, transactions of risk, and interest in commodification via the establishment of property rights and terms of alienation for new or complex forms of property. These new commodities pertain to risky or contingent property, intellectual property, transformed (in the sense of privatized) commons or common pool property, and transformed (in the sense of privatized) public or state-owned property.

In terms of fraternity, financialization of the bureaucratic elite is closely related to the revolving-door proposition. Finance grew as a share of the economy, became dominant as a social force, and became more sensitive to the regulatory apparatus. The revolving door between finance and regulators therefore became increasingly important in maintaining the operating space and profitability of finance, the new leading industry. The growth of finance has established its enormous appeal among ambitious young people. In 2006, on the eve of the financial crisis, Princeton University, an elite institution with an engineering school and a long tradition of liberal arts education and without a business school sent 46 percent of its new graduates into financial services.[22]

Although Princeton led the elite pack as a feeder for Wall Street, Harvard and Yale were not far behind with between one quarter and one third of graduates typically heading into finance. The near monoculture of graduates has a strong cyclical component: the share going into financial services rises during manias and ebbs during crises and their aftermath. But the flow has been strong for the past four decades. So it has simply become more likely that an elite bureaucrat has been through finance at some point in her or his career.

Thus, in the data we expect to see more elite government bureaucrats with some period of activity in banks or other areas of finance. For example, Hillary Rodham Clinton, elitely educated (Wellesley College and Yale University), trained as a lawyer, and attracted early to public service, nonetheless also had a period as a successful financial speculator in real estate and commodities before her full-time entry into the political arena as First Lady (of Governor and later President William J. Clinton), as US Senator, as Secretary of State, and as Presidential candidate. In the administration of President George W. Bush, which began in 2000, the fact that Bush's first Secretary of the Treasury Paul O'Neill had come from Alcoa, a large aluminum producer, was considered noteworthy because of O'Neill's non-financial roots. His successors, more typical of the Age of Finance, came from a large holding company (Snow, of CSX) and then from Goldman Sachs (Paulson). We hypothesize that for politically ambitious actors of one generation earlier, a finance phase is less common.

These networks affect the nature and quality of regulation, as shown in previous chapters. Different case studies on advocacy and lobbying, on the role of former

[21] Epstein (2005a); Crotty (2008). [22] Rampell (2011).

US congressional staff, or on politicians recruited for administrations of banks, lead to the same conclusion: closeness and inclusion matter.[23]

The revolving door hypothesis is consistent with more and less venal mechanisms, although there is a distinction between financial acculturation and outright corruption. Ideological capture may be more important than vulgar self-interest in terms of high-paid jobs in the finance sector awaiting former regulators who were willing to "play ball." A host of transitions back and forth between the private financial institutions and the alphabet soup of regulatory agencies have been documented.[24]

Data

For the first investigation, we hypothesize that 1975 and 2015 are appropriate for specifying a time before and a time after (or during) the neoliberal transformation. Our aim is to identify patterns, in particular, to establish systematic changes over time. One key feature of the neoliberal era is the rapid adoption and rise to dominance of the neoliberal tenets, as discussed in Chapter 5. In the current chapter, we instead investigate the role of individuals and career pathways in this process, including the social class background, the universities attended, including the option between domestic versus international study, and the subject and type of degree, which are potential sites of the change between the elite bureaucrats on the before and after sides of the neoliberal revolution.

There are several alternative, not mutually exclusive, hypotheses. Bureaucrats today may be from substantially different family or class, education, and career backgrounds than were bureaucrats in the mid-1970s. An alternative is that bureaucrats come from similar family and class origins but that their education and experience have changed substantially.

Our questions also concern the career paths of politicians and central bank directors before and after their mandates. Both past activity and future prospects may affect public performance professional careers. We also examine patterns in their academic and professional background.

For this research on center-left and center parties in governments, we rely heavily on Wikipedia for biographical data on the large number of administrators and bureaucrats whom we examine, and complement Wikipedia with other sources.[25]

[23] Young, Marple, and Heilman (2017), For instance, studies on a sample of twenty firms for 1999–2014 showed that close ties to the SEC expanded advocacy, Blanes i Vidal, Draca, and Fons-Rosen (2012). The role of former congressional staffers was highlighted, Braun and Raddatz (2010), And the number of former politicians on bank boards in different countries is related to the weaker quality of regulation.

[24] For instance, Taub (2010b).

[25] An analysis published in the journal *Nature* that examined articles on the natural sciences concluded: "Wikipedia comes close to Britannica in terms of the accuracy of its science entries" (Giles (2005)). However, political biography is not the same as the natural sciences, and Wikipedia's own article "Reliability of Wikipedia" warns about "false biographical information," and "political interests and advocacy" citing, inter alia, a peer-reviewed study that finds that in crowd-sourced political information negative biographic information is more likely to be deleted than positive information, Kalla and Aronow (2015). In some cases Wikipedia is more accurate than professional biographies. For example, Wendy Gramm's professional biography at the Mercatus Center at George Mason University, where she headed the Regulatory Studies Program, did not mention her term of service on the Enron board of directors while her Wikipedia entry does discuss the Enron affiliation.

We keep in mind that politically charged affiliations, e.g., with Goldman Sachs, are more likely to be reported in error, with either false negatives or false positives, than are less charged affiliations, e.g., whether, where, and in what field someone completed a doctorate.

The twelve countries represented in the study are Belgium, Brazil, Canada, Chile, France, Germany, Greece, Mexico, Portugal, Spain, the UK, and the US. We sampled 1975 and 2015, accepting that there might be different governments in the two years. For example, France had a center-right government (UDF under Giscard d'Estaing, a party that has effectively become the Republican Party of France) in 1975 and a center-left government (François Hollande, Socialist) in 2015, while the UK had a center-left government (Labour under Harold Wilson in 1975) and a center-right government (Conservative under David Cameron) in 2015. For each government we attempted to collect biographical data on the entire upper administration (head of state or government and cabinet ministers).

We used the same sample of countries and years for a sample of upper-level central bank management.

We attempted to extract a total of 512 biographies or curricula vitae from the web. We made 474 total successful extractions; of these thirty-three came from organizational websites and 441 came from Wikipedia. We then analyzed the 474 biographies using searches for "regular expressions" that would provide information on the education and career trajectory of the people in the sample.

The Center and Center-left Governments

In *The Death of the Liberal Class*, political commentator Chris Hedges laments that the professional class and elements of the elite in the United States have abandoned the center-left principles and policies that emerged from Franklin Roosevelt's New Deal. In this section we examine the material and ideological basis for this claim.

In the US as in other countries, the elites of different sectors have relationships to the political parties that are both historically determined and determined by contemporary economic interests. One way to track these affiliations is via the political campaign contributions by industry.[26]

For example, the legal profession in the US has been on the whole and as a sector oriented towards the Democratic Party. The manufacturing sector and extractive industries have been overwhelmingly towards the Republican. Wall Street, unlike finance in other countries, is evenly split, with contributions to Democrats not falling below 40 percent of total sectoral contributions (until the most recent election cycles, in any case exhibiting how the two-party system represented a convergence between them). There is a certain element of historical accident that New York is home both to the financial industry and to one of the most highly unionized workforces in the US.

In the US, the close relationship between finance and the centrist Democratic Party has historically contingent roots. But this is clearly not the case in other countries where the rentier class has been firmly associated with the parties of the

[26] Lorica (2011). Access to the public data is provided by public-interest organizations such as Center for Responsive Politics (2017a).

right, e.g., the City of London was strictly Tory for more than a century before the Blair era, electing Conservative MPs with typically a large majority.

Portugal is an exception because of the historical realignment after the fall of the dictatorship in 1974. In France, finance has been close to the parties of the right with the specter of nationalization looming (and even attempted by Mitterrand in the early 1980s, effectively spurring a capital strike).

So how did financial capital and austerity get inside the minds and spirits of the center and center-left parties? This was partly a reaction to the electoral sweeps of the parties of the right in the age of Reagan, Thatcher, and Kohl. In all of these countries the center-left and center parties were under enormous pressure to reinvent themselves. "Reinvent" meant in practice developing greater connections to finance, establishing distance from the labor movement, reducing labor involvement in internal party politics, and adopting austerity balanced-budget politics with reduced aspirations for a welfare state.

In the United States, Senator Gary Hart, a political predecessor of Bill Clinton, gave the traditional New Deal candidate Walter Mondale a close run for the Democratic Presidential nomination in 1984 with the vague campaign theme of "new ideas." His campaign dismissed unions, one of the core constituencies of the Democratic Party from the New Deal through the early 1980s, as "political action committees," a pejorative term for self-interested special interests.[27] Reviewing Hart's campaign literature decades later,[28] it is clear that the new way was still in progress. It would take eight more years, including another disastrous Presidential election with a candidate more closely tied to the New Deal, before Clinton solidified the Democratic Party transformation, but the turn was already in progress.

Center or center-left parties resurged in the 1990s and 2000s, first with Clinton in the United States (1992), followed by Chrétien and the Liberals in Canada (1993), Prodi and the Olive Tree coalition in Italy (1996), Blair's Labour in the UK (1997), Jospin and the Parti Socialiste in France (1997), Schroeder and the SPD in Germany (1998), Zapatero in Spain (2004), and similar center or center-left electoral success in smaller countries, Purple Coalitions in the Netherlands (1994), Gyurcsany in Hungary (2004), and Sócrates in Portugal (2005). In most of these cases, the center or center-left party initiated a period of continued electoral success. But in every case, these were transformed center and center-left parties that were at ease or in bed with finance, distant from labor, and practically and ideologically attached to neoliberal models for microeconomic and macroeconomic policy and management.

The case of Blair and New Labour is illustrative if extreme. Blair's New Labour positively fled from the association with the labor movement and the trade unions, which had been quite powerful within the Labour Party until the 1980s. The memoir of the Labour Party expert on focus groups reports that appearing "tough on the unions" was one of three key factors in constructing New Labour.[29] The Secretary General of the Trades Union Congress (TUC) commented during Blair's first term that for New Labour, the unions' "primary role is to be used to define what New Labour isn't."[30] In more concrete terms, the Blairites altered the very

[27] Krieger (1986), p. 155. [28] 4President.org (2017). [29] C. Howell (2005), p. 175.
[30] Ibid.

structure of the Labour Party to keep labor away from decision making. Until the 1990s, membership in the Labour Party was defined by membership or activism in trade unions. Unions financed the party, held 90 percent of the votes at the Labour Party conferences, and had substantial and automatic representation on the National Executive Committee.[31] The situation changed rapidly with the rise of New Labour under Blair. Their government task forces studiously avoided representation from trade unionists, with 2 percent of membership from unions and 36 percent from private business or industry groups.[32] Within weeks of winning the 1997 election, Blair and Chancellor of the Exchequer Gordon Brown established the formal independence of the central bank. Independence for the central bank. Independence from labor.

Unlike Labour in Britain, the US Democratic Party was less explicitly tied to the labor movement of its country. So the Democrats' turn to the Third Way required less by way of a formal divorce. Since the 1930s, the Democratic Party had been allied with the labor movement and trade unions and had relied heavily on the unions for funds and voter mobilization. But the integration of the party and the movement was limited, with the Democratic Party representing a complex alliance of regional and economic interests.[33] With the Democrats stung by the portentous if not overwhelming 1980 loss followed by the landslide 1984 loss to Republican Ronald Reagan, conservative members of the party founded the Democratic Leadership Council (DLC), asserted longstanding corporate interests, and advocated reduction of the welfare state, fiscal probity, and reduced association with "special interests" (code for labor unions and the social movements for ethnic minorities and women). The break with organized labor was an explicit rallying point for the DLC and its eventually triumphant—both in the Democratic Party and in national elections—candidate Bill Clinton.[34]

Even in the most riven case of Brazil, the ascendant PT (Workers' Party), a left-wing party from its origin, could still adhere to the neoliberal macroeconomic framework while expanding some aspects of the welfare state under the banner of "fiscally sound social inclusion." A recent book remarks (approvingly): "Lula drastically reduced uncertainty by providing credible evidence that his administration would not abandon fiscal and monetary orthodoxy."[35] The model is currently in crisis because "fiscally sound" has turned out to mean to the extent that extraordinary profits on petroleum permit. Social inclusion that comes from truly redistributive politics is not yet feasible in Brazil. Indeed, as the petroleum-financed polity runs into trouble, social inclusion is very much in jeopardy.

Our goal is to document some of the effects of the transformation of the center and center-left parties. We look at the party leaders themselves and assess whether their backgrounds changed, e.g., from children of unionists to children of professionals, their educations changed, e.g., more university graduates or even graduates with advanced degrees, from law to economics, from domestic education to international education, their career paths change, e.g., from civil service to private activity, particularly in finance or from domestic activity to work in the international sector. As the United States was the first to undergo the

[31] Cronin, Ross, and Shoch (2011), p. 124. [32] C. Howell (2005), p. 178. [33] Baer (2000).
[34] Pierce (2016). [35] Alston et al. (2016).

Table 8.1. Experience *before* service, government minister sample, 1975 and 2015

	1975	2015
IFIs	2.3	9.9
Banking	8.0	12.3
Big banks	1.7	1.5
Industrial	12.0	30.0
Post-baccalaureate education		
None	83.9	74.4
Domestic Econ PhD	1.1	3.0
Inter'l Econ PhD	0.0	4.9
Law	11.5	12.3
Humanities	2.3	0.5
Domestic Sci/Med	0.6	3.4
Inter'l Sci/Med	0.6	1.5
Wikipedia *N*/Target *N*	174/185	203/208

Notes: Authors' analysis of sample of cabinet-level personnel for twelve countries for 1975 and 2015. The table reports the share of the samples who had service in the listed fields or who had graduate education, by discipline.

transformation and was also the source of its intellectual inspiration, we look for indications of Americanization in the trajectory of the center-liberal leaders in the other countries.

For the center and center-left party analysis, we sought to analyze the universe, i.e., the complete list, of center or center-left party leaders from the sample of twelve countries (Belgium, Brazil, Canada, Chile, France, Germany, Greece, Mexico, Portugal, Spain, UK, and US) for the period 1975–2012. For countries under military rule during the first portion of this period, the analysis begins with the re-establishment of party politics. For Mexico, which continued its decades of one-party government for a substantial portion of this period, we analyze the one party (the PRI), rather than trying to disentangle its left and right wings. Babb provides an excellent intellectual history of the transformation of PRI from economic nationalism (Keynesianism, import substitution industrialization, public ownership) to neoliberalism.[36]

Table 8.2 indicates, not surprisingly, that previous experience in banking was and remains an important criterion for enlistment in the highest levels of management. Around 30 percent of the sample had previous banking experience. In the case of government ministers, banking has risen in significance as an important early career stage for high-level administrators. Prior to assuming office in 1975, 8 percent of these officials had experience in private banking, a share which increased to 12 percent in the 2015 sample. If banking is broadly defined to include the international financial institutions and big banks, prior experience in banking increased from 12 percent to around 24 percent between 1975 to 2015. Curiously, prior affiliation with the big banks did not increase in prevalence for either the government sample (stable at 1.5 percent) or the central bank sample (stable at just over 4 percent) between 1975 and 2015. But considering the central banks

[36] Babb (2001).

Table 8.2. Experience *before* service, central bank sample, 1975 and 2015

	1975	2015
IFIs	12.5	38.9
Banking	31.3	29.2
Big banks	4.2	4.2
Industrial	6.3	20.8
Post-baccalaureate education		
None	77.1	29.2
Domestic Econ PhD	14.6	33.3
Inter'l Econ PhD	8.3	31.9
Law	0.0	5.6
Wikipedia (+ Website) *N*/Target *N*	26/48	(38 + 9)/63

Notes: Authors' analysis of sample of cabinet-level personnel for twelve countries for 1975 and 2015. The table reports the share of the samples who had service in the listed fields or who had graduate education, by discipline.

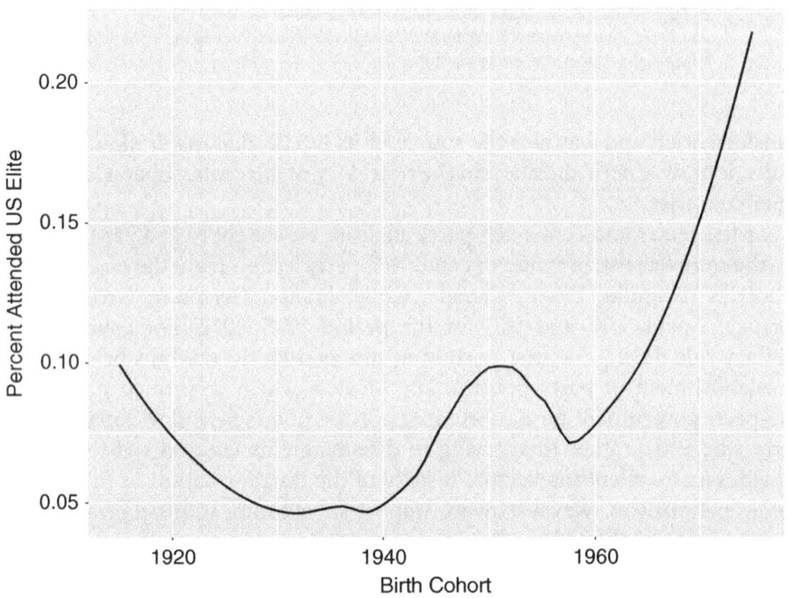

Figure 8.1. Education at elite US institutions

Note: Authors' analysis of sample of center and center-left party leadership for twelve countries, 1975–2016. The time series reports the percentage, by birth cohort, who received baccalaureate or graduate education at elite US institutions of higher education (Ivy League universities or equivalent—the target list is available from the authors).

sample, total prior affiliation to international financial agencies and different banks increased from 47 percent to an outstanding figure of 72.3 percent.

There is some evidence for the rise of economics in the education of high-level administrators. In the early, 1975, sample a substantial number of administrators did not have a university degree, very few had PhDs, and most degrees among degree holders were in law. In the later, 2015, sample almost all of the

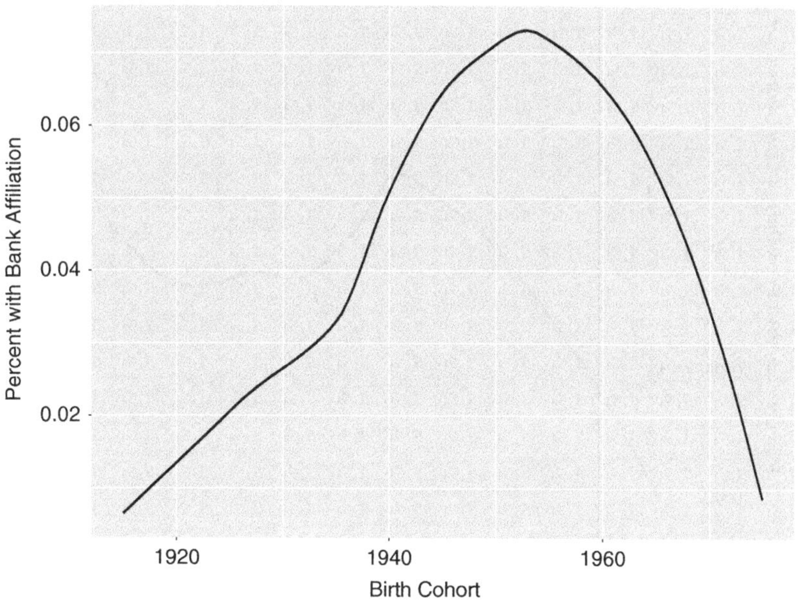

Figure 8.2. Bank affiliation

Note: Authors' analysis of sample of center and center-left party leadership for twelve countries, 1975–2016. The time series reports the percentage, by birth cohort, who worked for a major bank. (The target list is available from the authors.)

administrators held college degrees, and many held PhDs. Although law remains well represented, the share of those administrators holding doctorates in law, political science, or public administration remained stable at 12 percent of the high-level public administrators, while economics at both the undergraduate and graduate level has increased substantially in importance. Economics PhDs in the upper levels of administration increased from 1 percent in 1975 to more than 7 percent in 2015. At the graduate level, if both PhDs and MBAs are considered, economic education now challenges law as the dominant educational preparation for high-level administration. (Interestingly, doctorates in science, medicine, and technology among these high-level administrators have also increased, from 1 percent to just under 5 percent, while humanities PhDs have decreased from 2 percent to less than 0.5 percent.)

There is some evidence for the rise of international experience in both the education and career trajectories of high-level administrators. In particular, education in the United States has become relatively common with elite US institutions, e.g., Harvard, MIT, and Yale among the key destinations. International education in other leading sites, e.g., the elite British institutions, the Catholic Universities of both Leuven and Louvain-la-Neuve in Belgium, and some leading French universities appear in the educational trajectory of many in the sample. The important national schools in France, e.g., the Ecole Nationale d'Administration (ENA) and the Ecole Normale Supérieure (ENS), remain uniquely French in their reach.

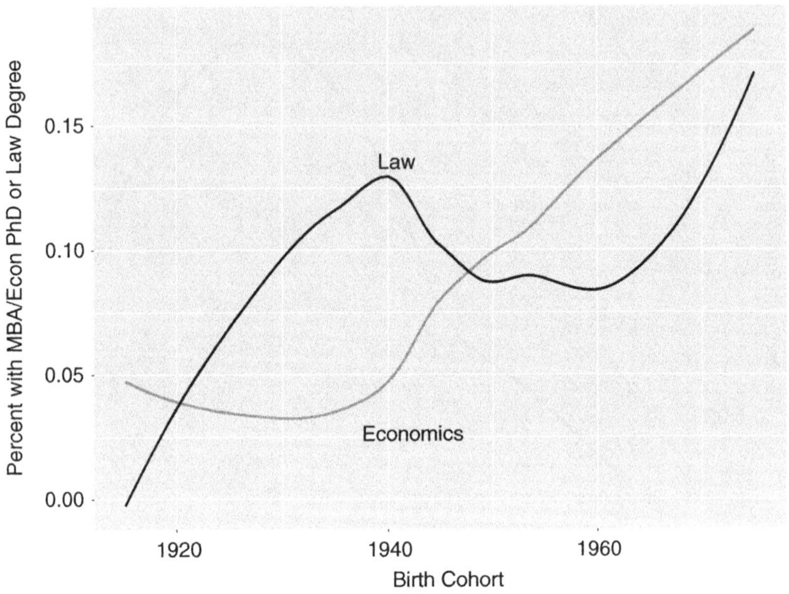

Figure 8.3. Education in economics or law

Note: Authors' analysis of sample of center and center-left party leadership for twelve countries, 1975–2016. The time series reports the percentage by birth cohort whose education was in law or graduate study of economics.

In the analysis of this sample we find more evidence for economization and internationalization than evidence that direct involvement with the big banks was or has become an important component of the career trajectory of high-level public officials. By the end of the sample, only 6 percent of the high-level functionaries of the center or center-left parties had their own banking experience. Therefore, the signs of intellectual capture may dominate, as the educational and career trajectories of public officials have taken them through institutions. A significant portion of the government sample shows experience with international financial institutions or international governance institutions.

The Revolving Door—the Portuguese Case

A previous investigation on the revolving door between government and business in Portugal provides another example, in this case of a recent democracy (Portugal lived under a dictatorship until April 1974). The fact that the society recently underwent a substantial alteration in the social order offers insight into the role of the revolving door in creating a new ruling bureaucracy.

The study followed the professional career of all members of all governments in Portugal, beginning with the first constitutional government in 1976 through 2013. The universe includes the 776 ministers and junior ministers who occupied 1,281

Table 8.3. Type of connections among Portuguese politicians and managers

Members of government	Number of cabinet members (%)	Number of posts they occupied in government (%)
In large economic groups	170 (22.9%)	311 (24.3%)
In the PSI20 firms[a]	140 (18.0%)	
In the firms related to PPP	107 (13.8%)	196 (15.3%)
In the financial sector	230 (29.6%)	382 (29.8%)
In industry	193 (24.9%)	187 (14.6%)
In real estate and building firms	94 (12.1%)	173 (13.5%)
In communications firms	95 (12.2%)	159 (12.4%)

[a] PSI20 is the index for the 20 largest firms in the stock market. Some types of connection may overlap.
Source: Louçã, Lopes, and Costa (2014).

posts in government during that period.[37] The connections to business (defined as being a partner, a high-level manager, or a member of the board) were examined in detail. These 776 cabinet members represent the recent political and social groups emerging after the fall of the dictatorship, and therefore the Portuguese case may present some differences as compared to more stabilized democracies.

Some of these politicians occupied several responsibilities: 148 of them were in government two or more times, 32 three or more, 17 five or more. Although there are some differences according to the political origin of the members of government, there is in general a high rate of connections to business, with 64 percent of those from the right-wing party PSD (295 ministers and junior ministers) being connected, and 47 percent from for the center-left party PS (296), and 63 percent for the minor right-wing party CDS (54 members of government).

Tables 8.3 and 8.4 summarize the results. Table 8.3 describes the prevalence of each type of connection in terms of persons and posts. Table 8.4 examines the evolution of the connections and indicates the relative importance of promotions, politicians whose first business connection followed government service, and veterans, those who had previous attachments to business and returned to business after government service. With respect to promotions, Table 8.4 shows that one in four of the members of government had no prior business connection but made one upon leaving office.

A high level of connections was found, as shown by the table. Approximately one in three members of government either came from or went to the administration of a financial firm, one in five did so to the largest stock market firms, one in four to the larger economic groups, and one in seven came from or went to firms benefiting from public-private partnerships, which result from contracts established by crucial decisions by governments.

For one quarter of the universe, the presence in government ensured a promotion to the board of different firms. One fifth were already veterans of corporate leadership and were selected for government on the basis of their previous experience in business.

[37] Louçã, Lopes, and Costa (2014), presents the full dataset in an online appendix.

Table 8.4. Evolution of connections among Portuguese politicians

	Number of members of government (%)	Number of posts they occupied while in government (%)
Promotion effect (were not previously but became connected)	187 (24.1%)	337 (26.3%)
Veterans (were connected and returned to business after govt)	143 (18.4%)	354 (27.6%)

Source: Louçã, Lopes, and Costa (2014)

The Spanish Case

Recent prime ministers of Spain are examples of successful careers via the revolving door. Felipe Gonzalez, a socialist, took a consultancy job at Gas Natural Fenosa and with Carlos Slim, the Mexican ultra-billionaire. José Maria Aznar, from the Popular Party, took a job at Endesa. Energy firms have recruited extensively from ex-members of government, and their board membership is publicly available.

But other distinguished personalities of both the governing parties stand out as well in the revolving door department. Further examples of socialist ex-ministers of the economy would be: Elena Salgado (Endesa), Pedro Solbes (Evel), Miguel Boyer (Red Eléctrica España), as well as Jordi Sevilla, ex-minister of public administrations, who went to Pricewaterhouse, and Virgilio Zapatero, who took a job at Bankia.

On the right wing of the political spectrum, the most distinguished example is that of Rodrigo Rato, who was the vice president of the Aznar government and then director of the IMF, and led Bankia from 2010 to 2012 (the bank collapsed and Rato was arrested for suspected tax misconduct).[38]

CRONYISM

After presenting evidence on the revolving door for some countries, we will verify in the second part of this chapter its concrete development as cronyism and namely the effect on the capture of regulation.

Simon Johnson, the MIT professor who was previously a chief economist at the IMF for 2007–8, argues that this process of capture goes both ways. It involves the capture of regulation and the protection of specific business interests, but also the selection of officials and offering jobs to ex-members of government and regulatory agencies. This is what he calls "crony capitalism." It is based upon a system of socially unequal favors, since "at the outset of the crisis, the oligarchs are usually among the first to get extra help from the government,"[39] a certainty comfortably established by doctrine and common practice of different governments. Indeed, the elite of business, namely the financiers, know from experience that the

[38] Vélez (2011). On energy in the revolving door in Spain, see Jiménez (2014), and *El Pais*, September 2, 2012.

[39] Johnson (2009).

doctrine of the "too large to fail" is an assurance for generous bailouts, even when they are responsible for the creation of the crash. But the right people must be at the right place at the right time in order to operate these connections.

Capture of Regulation

George Stigler, a Chicago Nobel laureate of the neoclassical school (and a member of the Mont Pelerin Society), first proposed the notion of a revolving door in a 1971 paper on "The Theory of Economic Regulation." He stated: "as a rule, regulation is acquired by the industry and designed and operated primarily for its benefit."[40] That was almost half a century ago, before Greenspan chaired the Federal Reserve, before one could imagine Ronald Reagan as President, before the tsunami of deregulation. But Stigler was right. The specific interests of the firms and markets to be regulated tend to capture regulation and that went together with globalization, becoming an indistinguishable feature of modern economies and nowhere has this been more evident than in finance.

Yet the capture of regulators has been a difficult and long process, since it had to remove a number of legal and institutional rules and limitations, along with habits, beliefs, and conventions. For one, the creation of the new common sense of unregulated markets contradicted the whole previous history of economic management and public action since the early twentieth century. The challenge was revolutionary, but it required a long process of dismantling the previous mainstream views and deeds (in a previous chapter we discussed the example of Keynes's views on the need to control flows of capital and the battles over it).

The road to deregulation was thus difficult. But it was traveled with the utmost enthusiasm of both academics (Fama) and regulators (Greenspan), developing the Friedmanite ideology of the liberty of the markets and acting accordingly. For Greenspan, as noted before, this ideology was protected by the justification of technological and product innovation and this became the *motum* for institutional action of the deregulating regulators.

The US Securities and Exchange Commission, for instance, argued that, given the power of the mathematical tools for assessing risk, self-regulation should become the standard, as it proposed changes in the law: "These amendments are introduced to reduce regulatory costs for broker-dealers by allowing very highly capitalized firms that have developed robust internal risk management practices to use those risk management practices, such as mathematical risk measurement models, for regulatory purposes."[41] In that case, the most powerful financial firms should be allowed to escape the costs and forms of regulation, even if they were to become the more dangerous to the market, given precisely their power.

The deregulation machine has been at work and it has delivered in successive waves, as the examples presented in previous chapters attest. Another case was the campaign just preceding the subprime crash, against new financial regulations,

[40] Stigler (1971). There is also a left/institutionalist tradition of criticizing regulation in the interest of the regulated. The railroads dominated the Interstate Commerce Commission and the airlines the Federal Aviation Administration.

[41] The rule became effective August 20, 2004, Securities and Exchange Commission (2004).

which was launched in a report by McKinsey Global Consulting. Published in 2006, it argued that New York would lose its role as financial capital if derivatives were to be regulated. Michael Bloomberg, the millionaire who was then the Mayor of the city, joined forces with Senator Charles Schumer and made a battering ram of the report. John Thain, then the executive director of the New York Stock Exchange, wrote a supportive letter to the editor of *Wall Street Journal*.[42] Yet, as the director of Merrill Lynch, two years later, he would be responsible for selling the firm to the Bank of America in despair, the victim of his own deeds and inadequate regulation. Henry Paulson, the Secretary of Treasury, added to the choir that "optimal balances" were expected to be attained by self-regulation.[43] Lawrence Summers, who had been chief economist at the World Bank and would be the Treasury Secretary for the following President (and the scholar who, in a previous incarnation, presented a model opposed to that of Fama), also kept the flame, intensely opposing regulation of derivatives and becoming the protagonist of a major fight against a regulation agency, as recounted in a previous chapter.[44]

They all agreed, they were all "amongst professionals," to recall Greenspan's words.

Yet, the New York Federal Reserve, worried about the vulnerability of the "professionals," proceeded to examine a large sample of banking regulators and to study the revolving door. Taking the careers of 35,604 regulators of all US agencies from the 1980s until 2013, the researchers found higher inflows and outflows from the agencies to firms in periods of more intense regulatory activity: after the recession of 2008, when shadow finance was under scrutiny and new rules were being discussed, the study registers the doubling of flows from public agencies to firms.[45] The revolving door opens wide when it is required.

Crony Capitalism: Goldman Sachs and Carlyle

The professionals of finance, the promoters of innovation and stabilization that Greenspan and other decision makers considered a sufficient standard for an efficient market, were at the center of the deregulation revolution. They ensured, through their fidelity to the cause, that no harm would befall the institutions and their new norms, that the markets would be protected from intrusion, and that a carapace of legislation would be built around the fortress.[46] So, looking

[42] *Wall Street Journal*, November 11, and 25, 2006. [43] Freeland (2014), p. 283.

[44] Johnson and Kwak (2011), p. 99. Geithner recalls in his memoir that, in a meeting with John Thain, Merrill Lynch's chief, he was surprised to gather that Thain did not know the name of his chief officer of risk assessment sitting next to him, Geithner (2014); Komlos (2014), p. 97. One may reckon that Thain was indeed uninterested in regulation.

[45] Lucca, Seru, and Trebbi (2014), p. 43.

[46] We do not suggest that payment was always the major motivation for entering the revolving door. Ideological commitment and professional identification may have frequently played a major role. In fact, in some cases the gain was occasional: Glenn Hubbard, chairman of Bush's Council of Economic Advisors, was paid a handsome US $100,000 by the defense to testify for two Bear Stearns executives, Carrick-Hagenbarth and Epstein (2012), p. 44.

at it the other way round, the revolving door also paved the way for members of government to secure important jobs in finance, following the suggestion by Bloomberg, the firm that we met in the introduction to this chapter. The founder Michael Bloomberg made a fortune in the business of business information and was the engine of a public campaign for deregulation.

Both Thain and Paulson shared his radical views on regulation, but they had in common another feature: they were both *alumni* of Goldman Sachs, albeit in different capacities. Thain had been the head of the mortgage securities division between 1985 and 1990, long enough to understand about bubbles, Paulson was placed even higher since, prior to his government appointment by Bush (1999–2006), he had been the powerful CEO of Goldman Sachs. Steve Mnuchin, the Secretary of the Treasury under the Trump administration, is another Goldman Sachs man. In a previous chapter, we discussed the role of Goldman Sachs. Given its notoriety and dimension, as well as its political implications, it stands as one of the more telling examples of the revolving door.

"What's good for General Motors is good for the country, and vice versa,' former General Motors CEO Charlie Wilson responded when asked about the potential for conflict of interest during his 1957 Senate hearings to become Secretary of Defense under President Eisenhower. It is somewhat odd, given the context, that the remark has come to represent the high-water mark of monopoly capitalism, in which the interests of the great industries and the interests of the nation were presumed indistinguishable, more than a glaring instance of the revolving door. Wilson's answer was in some sense so open and ingenuous that it actually allayed concern that he would take advantage of his position to benefit General Motors at the expense of other industrial concerns or the populace. The alignment of interests in a high-wage military-industrial partnership was obvious.

Fewer people are comfortable with the proposition that what is good for Goldman Sachs is good for the country. Suspicion of connections has often been the case with speculative and financial activity in relation to the public trust. In the early years of the United States, speculation in the debt of the predecessor regime brought accusations that an insider, Secretary of the Treasury Alexander Hamilton, had leaked word that the outstanding obligations would pay off at their full value. (Hamilton adamantly denied the leak, confessing to a highly embarrassing and politically damaging sex scandal rather than face prosecution for financial impropriety.) Since then the competing interests of Wall Street and Main Street have been a standard of American politics, with the competition forgotten only on the upswing of ultimately ruinous financial booms as Main Street has fallen for the promise that we're all going to get rich.

The policy implementation of the Friedman-Fama synthesis by Phil Gramm, Alan Greenspan, Robert Rubin, Lawrence Summers, and Bill Clinton promised that financial modernization would bring a host of benefits: easy-to-use financial products; and access to low-cost capital for home mortgages and firm investment. But because insider information is so valuable and because the busts have been so destructive, public uptake of "what's good for the banks is good for the country" has always been limited.

So the revolving door in finance has depended less on mutualism with the public than on mutualism with ambitious individuals.

There is no question that Goldman Sachs holds sway at the commanding heights. *The Independent* identified a few "masters of the eurozone" whose careers passed through or near Goldman Sachs.[47]

Four held positions of direct employment prior to public service and at least three of these were positions with significant managerial power. Three held the somewhat nebulous position of adviser or international adviser likely invited for existing influence. Another was, as head of the Greek Central Bank, in close relations with Goldman Sachs, hired to manage the accounting of the national debt:

- Peter Sutherland, former Attorney General of Ireland, founding director-general of the World Trade Organization, and European Commissioner for competition, who became the non-executive chairman of Goldman Sachs International for ten years;
- Mario Draghi, former managing director of Goldman Sachs International;
- Mario Monti, European Commissioner (1995–2004) and Italian prime minister (2011–13), and former international adviser to Goldman Sachs;
- Antonio Borges, former head of the IMF's European Department, and former vice chairman of Goldman Sachs International (and then the leader of the Portuguese government team responsible for an ambitious program of privatizations);
- Petros Christodoulou, head of Greek debt management agency and former employee of Goldman Sachs;
- Lucas Papademos, former Greek prime minister (2011–12), head of the central bank when it hired Goldman Sachs for controversial derivatives involving Greek debt;
- Karel van Miert, former EU Competition Commissioner, ex-international adviser to Goldman Sachs; and
- Otmar Issing, former board member of the Bundesbank and the ECB, adviser to Goldman Sachs.

A more international list, not only for the Eurozone, would also include: Romano Prodi, President of the European Commission (1999–2004) and Italian prime minister (2006–8); Malcolm Turnball, prime minister of Australia (2015–present); Carlos Moedas, European Commissioner (2014–present); Robert Zoellick, who went from the leadership of Goldman Sachs' international affairs to being head of the World Bank and then back to chairman of the advisory board of Sachs; and finally José Manuel Barroso, President of the European Commission for ten years, who replaced Sutherland as the chairman of Goldman Sachs. These are some of the distinguished men of Goldman Sachs at the top of governments and institutions or recruited by the bank after their political mandates.

The US-based website OpenSecrets.org provides a revolving door database of US political lobbying, joining a private database of lobbyists with data on federal employment or uncompensated appointments (for example to boards or

[47] Foley (2011).

working groups).[48] This database identifies forty people as having Goldman Sachs affiliations.[49]

But when we examined the sample of cabinet ministers and central bank administrators, Goldman Sachs did not have a high incidence in the career trajectories. In the entire sample of cabinet ministers and central bank administrators, only two Britons (Ben Broadbent and Mark Carney, the latter also Canadian), one Greek (Gikas Hardouvelis), one German (Hans Friderichs), and one American (Ashton Carter) register as having direct employment by Goldman Sachs. All five of these were in the more recent 2015 sample, but the connections are nonetheless rather limited. Indeed a search for direct affiliations with some of the large investment banks, namely, Goldman Sachs, Bank of America, Chase, J.P. Morgan, and Citibank, finds few connections, only 1.5 percent of the 1975 sample, tripling to roughly 5 percent of the 2015 sample.

The Goldman Sachs ring includes the aforementioned Henry Paulson, and also the Treasury undersecretaries Robert Stell (who served under Bush and then became CEO of the doomed Wachovia mortgage company) and Gary Gensler (who served under Bill Clinton), Joshua Bolten, chief of staff of President Bush, Senator Jon Corzine (who co-chaired Goldman Sachs with Paulson and later became CEO of MF Global, which went bankrupt in 2011), Stephen Friedman, chair of New York Fed and then its president. William Dudley, who replaced Geithner at the head of the New York Fed,[50] is also a former employee of Goldman Sachs. So are Rahm Emanuel, Mayor of Chicago, and many others.

But, if the Goldman Sachs ring is certainly one of the larger if not the most extensive and included a bipartisan connection (in a previous chapter this ring was disclosed in some detail), other stars shine in this constellation, such as the private equity Carlyle Group, which recruited many distinguished members of government all over the world. Once led by Frank Carlucci, an ex-head of the CIA, Carlyle's payroll included George H.W. Bush, a former President of the US, as well as James Baker III, a Secretary of the Treasury under Reagan and then Bush's Secretary of State, and John Major, former prime minister of the UK, and other former members of different governments.

Indeed, there is a long tradition of financial giants being represented in Washington. Nicholas Brady, after a thirty-four-year career at Dillon Read, an investment bank, then moved to government as Secretary of the Treasury. When he left, he took the job of chairman of Darby Overseas Investment, established 1994.[51] That was also the case of Frank Newman, chief financial officer of the Bank of America, who joined the Treasury as under secretary for domestic finance in 1993; of Roger Altman, from Lehman Brothers, deputy Treasury Secretary;

[48] Center for Responsive Politics (2017b).

[49] Of the forty people identified as one-time Goldman Sachs employees in the opensecrets.org Revolving Door database, twenty-four have Wikipedia entries. Twenty of the twenty-four Wikipedia entries identify the Goldman Sachs connection and all but one cites a source other than the Revolving Door database. Others that appear in the Revolving Door database did not have Wikipedia entries, but at least one was identified by *The Hill*, a trade journal about government, as among the fifty most beautiful Washington, D.C., people of 2009.

[50] The close ties of Goldman Sachs and the New York Federal Reserve Bank came frequently under attention and were often presented as evidence of coziness (*New York Times*, November 19, 2014).

[51] Centeno (2010), p. 49.

of Lee Sachs, from Bear Stearns, assistant secretary for financial markets, also under the Clinton administration; of Richard Clarida, from Columbia University and then assistant Treasury Secretary under George Bush, to become then the executive vice president of PIMCO—among many others.

It was also the case of John Snow, Treasury Secretary under George W. Bush, who went to Cerberus Capital Management, a private equity firm that also recruited the ex-vice president Dan Quayle. The list goes on and on: Pete Peterson, US Treasury Secretary, formed with Steve Schwarzman a new firm, Blackstone, now a financial giant; Michael Froman, chief of staff at Treasury with Rubin, who became an executive of Citigroup, as Rubin did; Gerald Corrigan, President of New York Federal Reserve from 1985 to 1993, then moved to Goldman Sachs as partner and senior executive; David Mullins, assistant Secretary at Treasury, then vice chair of the Federal Reserve Board of Governors, from which he resigned to go to the infamous LTCM.[52] Other examples include David Petraeus, the four-star general and head of the CIA, who joined KKR, a private equity firm specialized in buyouts, and Alan Greenspan, who, after leaving the Federal Reserve, accepted a job as a consultant to PIMCO the biggest agency in bond markets, but also to Deutsche Bank and to the hedge fund Paulson & Co.[53] So did Bernanke, his successor at the FED, and Jean-Claude Trichet, former head of the European Central Bank, and Gordon Brown, former UK prime minister, all at PIMCO. This practice is standard, and our examples are telling: Condoleezza Rice, former Secretary of State with Bush, had a career at Chevron and, after leaving government, combined a faculty appointment with consultancy and a strategic partnership with RWC, an investment house.[54]

Central Banks and the Selection of Senior Staff

As we have shown, the central banks are an essential part of the plot of liberalization. Given their independence from governments and parliaments and their effective influence, they have been prime movers of deregulation and financialization. In any case, the explanation for the coherence of central banks, notwithstanding the tumultuous events and the Great Recession after the financial crash of 2007–8, in spite of the collapse of systemic banks and the turmoil of massive bailouts, is beyond the purview of economics as such and requires an examination of political history. They form a regime, acid-tested through the recession, and yet prevailing after all it endured, and they cannot be understood except as part of a power system—and a very closed one, since central bankers are mostly recruited in-house,[55] with some exceptions that merit special attention, some of which are exemplified in what follows.

The coherence is constructed by a close connection between governments, big business and the financial industry, and central banks, expressed not only in the convergence of visions on regulation and other matters, but also in professional ties. In this section the web of decision makers or the revolving door between the

[52] Johnson and Kwak (2011), p. 95. [53] Ibid. [54] *Financial Times*, February 13, 2017.

[55] Lebaron studied the professional careers of ninety-four governors of central banks (1999–2000) and detected that they predominantly ascended in the bank itself, Lebaron (2000), pp. 211, 215.

central banks and governments is demonstrated through examples from various countries.

We begin with the example of the European Central Bank (ECB). Wim Duisenberg, former leader of the Social Democrats in the Netherlands, and former minister of finance (1973–7), was the first president of the ECB, for the period 1998–2003, the founding years.[56] Other ex-ministers followed him, although he was the most high-profile politician to hold the job. Different examples prove the same point, namely how European social democrats became part of the financial ruling elite: Djisselbloem, Dutch finance minister and president of the Eurogroup (the conference of finance ministers of the Eurozone, in charge of following the budgets and applying punitive measures) until the end of 2017, himself a Social Democrat, became the closest ally of Merkel in the context of the debt crisis which engulfed Greece and the southern European countries debt crisis.

Other political agents took jobs at the central banks. For example, Ernst Welteke from Germany: he was a member of parliament in Hesse, then minister of economy in the region (1991–4), then federal finance minister (1995), president of the central bank of Hesse, then the successor of Hans Tietmeyer at the Bundesbank (1999). His was a long career culminating at the central bank. Birgir Gunnarson, from Iceland, and Urban Baskstrom, from Sweden, followed the same path from parliament and government to the central bank.

Moving in the other direction, several central bankers became president or prime minister: Guntis Ulmanus (Latvia, President 1993–9), Mugur Isarescu (Romania, prime minister 1999–2000), Josef Tosovsky (Czech Republic, prime minister 1997–8), Viktor Yushchenko (Ukraine, prime minister 1999–2001), Siim Kallas (Estonia, prime minister 2002–3), and Einars Repse (Latvia, prime minister 2002–4), among others.

Yet, the most common path is from the central bank to private finance. A former governor of the German Bundesbank, Axel Weber, became the chairman of a major Swiss bank, UBS, and Philipp Hildebrand, of the Swiss National Bank, took on the position of vice chairman of BlackRock.

Other types of connection are as visible under the form of lobbying. The Nippon Kaigi, or Japan Conference, is an old grouping of selected politicians and influential people, and distinguished itself with a long history of supporting the war effort, in which Japan was defeated. Still, it may number some 38,000 members, including one third of parliament and over half of the ministers, including the prime minister, who is designated a "special advisor," for the lobby.[57] Japan has a special term for the revolving door: *amakudari*, or "descended from heaven."

CHANGING TIDES

The third and last part of this chapter is dedicated to some brief case studies of different protagonists of the revolving door between official positions and shadow or traditional finance. A book by Charles Ferguson calls this the *Predator Nation*,

[56] Adolph (2013), p. 146. [57] Mizohata (2016), p. 2.

and presents portraits of Summers, Feldstein, and others to prove the point that the revolving door is a dangerous threat to democratic life.[58]

Even association with failure or scandal carries little consequence. Take the case of the Harvard professor Martin Feldstein, who spent twenty-two years on the board of AIG, having resigned in June 2009, well after the global financial crash and specifically that of AIG. He was the chair of the finance and risk committee of the firm, which had been investigated for fraud since 2005 and was finally bailed out in 2008 in order to avoid bankruptcy—it was the largest bailout in the history of the US. In spite of this, Feldstein was appointed by Obama to the Presidential Economic Recovery Advisory Board in the same year.[59] As we will show through the examples which follow, success in the careers of the "revolving door people" is not exactly reassuring for the common good.

A Case Study on Cronyism: Lawrence Summers

A young Harvard professor, Lawrence Summers, then thirty-two, was not convinced about the glorification of financial markets, and published a paper challenging Fama, the creator of the efficient markets hypothesis.[60] His argument was not that the efficiency hypothesis was wrong but simply that it could not be proved with the available data and, furthermore, he demonstrated that the statistical power of the tests then used is very low and cannot reject alternative explanations. Considering monthly data of stock returns, Summers dared to prove that, in order to reject the null of efficiency of speculative markets, the researcher would be required to have access to data for over 5,000 years, even noticing that market prices frequently deviate from the rational expectation of the present value of the flow of future cash by over 30 percent, indicating large persistent errors that remain unexplained by the theory. Therefore, Fama's conclusions are suspect, since asset prices cannot be assumed to be rationally related to the fundamentals of the economy. Alternative explanations would be excessive volatility from speculation, and error caused by irrational decision making, or by money illusion.[61] Keynes's "animal spirits" and Tversky's and Kahneman's experiments on individual behavior came to mind and were quoted by Summers.

At that time, Summers advocated Tobin taxes on various financial transactions.[62] Another bold move by a somewhat radical economist.

Now meet the second Lawrence Summers, who left Harvard for the World Bank (chief economist, 1991–3), then moved to the Treasury, where he was soon appointed Deputy Secretary (1999) and finally replaced his patron Robert Rubin as Secretary (1999–2001) under Clinton. With Obama, Summers returned to the White House as the director of the National Economic Council (2009–10). After a career in public service, he returned to Harvard as its President for a short period, but also entered the financial market, becoming the director of the hedge fund

[58] Ferguson (2013). [59] Mirowski (2013), p. 208. [60] Summers (1986).

[61] Shiller (1981); Modigliani and Cohn (1979); Arrow (1982).

[62] Mirowski (2013), p. 221; Cassidy (2009). The late Nobel Prize winner James Tobin (1918–2002) proposed a small tax on currency transactions to fund development and to discourage excessive speculation. His proposal was rejected by international or national institutions.

D.E. Shaw and taking a position on the board of Taconic Capital Advisors, a Goldman alumni hedge fund. In relation to his financial activity, Summers was paid more than US $20 million during the period from 2001 to 2008.[63]

This second Summers held controversial but effective views on how to deregulate the financial industry. He was a decisive player in the repeal of the last provisions of the Glass-Steagall Act, with the approval of the Commodity Futures Modernization Act in 1999. For ending an epoch and burying the Rooseveltian heritage, his argument was forceful:

> First, by breaking down outdated barriers between banks and other financial service companies, the 1999 Financial Modernization Act opened the door to greater innovation and competition. We have equipped the financial industry to take advantage of the rapid technological changes that are taking place, while providing consumers with greater choice and lower costs... And third, we have made significant progress towards the enactment of legislation that would reform the legal and regulatory framework affecting the OTC derivatives market. Taken together, these changes would provide legal certainty, contribute to the reduction of systemic risk, protect retail customers, stimulate the competitiveness of America's financial markets, and thereby help to create jobs and lower costs for American consumers and businesses. We have achieved an extraordinary bipartisan consensus this year on these very complex issues. Let me take this opportunity to urge Congress to enact these reforms as soon as possible.[64]

The Congress heard his plea, as we discussed in a previous chapter. The financial market, efficient or not, rational or not, was vindicated. Curiously enough, Martin Wolf, a renowned *Financial Times* analyst, interviewed Summers and was treated to a raft of quotations from Bagehot and Kindleberger, both critics of financial misadventures.[65] Summers also quoted Keynes, the outspoken critic of free market ideas, and Minsky, the prophet of financial doom, not Fama, the founder of the creed of efficient markets. But the gulf between what he believed and what he actually did was huge for one of the most influential policymakers in the era of deregulation.

Summers, flagrantly changing his earlier views, opposed derivative regulation even more than Rubin, and was the champion of the deregulating campaign against Brooksley Born, the head of the public agency who dared to propose checking the market for derivatives, as we described in a previous chapter. Rubin took pleasure in censuring the extremist views of his former collaborator and then successor in his own 2004 autobiography: "Larry characterized my concern about derivatives as a preference for playing tennis with wooden racquets—as opposed to the more powerful graphite and titanium ones used today."[66] In any case, the economist assured politicians and regulators that the powerful racket of deregulation would liven up the game, which set the stage for disaster.

Case Studies on Networking: Geithner and Rubin

By November 2008, Timothy Geithner, then head of the powerful Federal Reserve Bank of New York, was announced by the President-elect Obama as the nominee

[63] Carrick-Hagenbarth and Epstein (2012), p. 44. [64] Summers (2000). [65] Wolf (2014).
[66] Rubin and Weisberg (2004), pp. 197–8.

for Secretary of the Treasury. This ended some controversy and speculation on alternative candidates, including personalities who had a previous career at the White House, the Treasury, or the Fed, such as Summers or Volcker.

Geithner had a consistent record in public management, with an initial career in the diplomatic service and then in Treasury. He had been Under Secretary of International Affairs at the Treasury, with both Rubin and Summers and, from 2001 to 2003, a director at the IMF, while at the same time he took a position at the Council on Foreign Relations. From 2003 to 2009 he presided the New York Federal Reserve Bank.

Consequently, the partners and administrators of the financial institutions welcomed his nomination. There was no surprise and Geithner appeared as the favorite for the betting houses. He was well known and respected, he had contacts, and he was part of the game.[67]

What was nevertheless noticeable was the reaction of the market itself: an important and selected group of firms registered an abnormal return of 6 percent the day of the announcement, and ten days later they had achieved a 12 percent increase. Acemoglu and his co-authors identified and investigated this sudden change and argued that these firms were Geithner-connected and that the mood of the market was caused by the "perceived impact of relying on the advice of a small network of financial executives during a time of acute crisis and heightened political discretion."[68] The authors attribute the increase not to crude corruption or direct interest but to the anticipation of the resolution of uncertainty provoked by the enormous financial crisis of fall 2008.

Nevertheless, this emergence of confidence and business did not happen in the past, it was a specific event created by the nomination of Geithner. In previous cases, rather the opposite had happened. When Henry Paulson, a Goldman Sachs president, took office as Secretary of the Treasury for Bush, the stock of his own firm fell by 5.2 percent the same day and was still 3.3 percent down ten days later, while the S&P 500 index declined less (1.6 percent and 3.3 percent). When Paul O'Neill, the Alcoa CEO, was nominated, the stock fell by 6.1 percent the first day and 1.1 percent at the end of ten days, in both cases more than the general index S&P. For John Snow, the head of a railroad company, CSX, the stock fell 1.5 percent and recovered by the same amount after ten days. With the nomination of Jack Lew, from Citigroup, the numbers went up, 1.9 percent the same day and 2 percent after ten days, but the S&P grew 0.8 percent and 2.9 percent.[69] In the case of Dick Cheney, the head of Blackwater (which would be one of the major contractors for the Iraq war) who became a powerful vice president under Bush, the value of his connections was estimated at zero.[70] So, what happened to Geithner?

Acemoglu and his co-authors used three measures of connections: the list of the executives of financial firms meeting with Geithner as the President of the Federal Reserve Bank of New York, the list of personal connections as established through common participation in organizations, such as nonprofit boards and groups, and,

[67] Geithner is perhaps another example of a regulator intellectually captured by the dominant views on the financial market. One instance is that, defining himself as a "technocrat," Geithner compared the financial crisis to an "inferno," a "fire," an exogenous and surprising event he could neither predict nor avoid, *New York Times*, May 15, 2014 and Komlos (2014).

[68] Acemoglu et al. (2016). [69] Ibid. [70] Fisman et al. (2012).

finally, the location of the firms. For each and every one of these criteria, they compared the "connected firms" to the control group constituted by all the others, in a universe of 603 financial firms and concluded that the "Geithner-connected firms" benefited from an exceptional return following his nomination. This was further confirmed by an equally exceptional, although momentary, setback when his nomination was questioned in relation to an accusation of non-payment of taxes while he was at the IMF. The same pattern was detected in the credit default swaps, the insurance against risks of those firms, and both measures were interpreted by the investigators as the impact of the "perceived benefit to creditors."

Acemoglu and his colleagues reject any explanation from corruption or the anticipation of material compensation for the firms with connections to Geithner. He was considered to be a standard banker and public servant and the revolving door between politics and business did not appear to be the reason for the stock market effect. Acemoglu et al. did not pursue the possibility of intellectual or cultural capture, which suggests that the financial sector recognizes and rewards consonant policy preferences. The previous cases of irrelevant or negative impact of the nomination of executives of Goldman Sachs or other financial firms seem to lessen the eventual impact of this effect in these cases. Instead, they propose another interpretation: that this effect was generated by the perception of the crash and that "social connections meet the crisis." This enthusiasm of the stock market would be a crisis-specific attitude: after all, during that same period Citigroup and AIG (from February 27 to March 3, 2009) were bailed out and the perception of the dangers associated with the ongoing financial meltdown was very acute.

Therefore, the market acted following herd-like behavior and the firms connected to Geithner, albeit indirectly, were considered to be the safer bet. Geithner's case is not anomalous: firms connected to the politically influential are more likely to get bailed-out in both developed and emerging economies.[71]

This explanation emphasizes the relevance of the networks implicitly identified by the nomination and then mobilized by the consequent selection of the cabinet. Yet, this effect requires a socially visible network.

As Geithner was active in different social and professional circles that assembled influential people in the financial and business world, the map of such connections is relevant for this inquiry. These organizations were, in 2009, the Council on Foreign Relations, the RAND Corporation, the Federal Reserve Bank of New York, the Partnership for New York, the Economic Club of New York, and the Group of Thirty. Out of the fifty-two personal relations identified by Acemoglu and his colleagues, through the common participation on boards of different organizations, the Council on Foreign Relations accounts for eighteen of those.[72]

[71] Fisman (2001); Faccio, Masulis, and McConnell (2006), for Indonesia; Johnson and Mitton (2003), for Malaysia; and Khwaja and Mian (2005), for Pakistan.

[72] They are: Patricia Mitchell, director, Bank of America; J. Tomilson Hill, vice chairman of the Blackstone Group; Richard Salomon, board chair, Blackstone Group; Patrick Gross, director, Capital One; C. Armstrong, Judith Rodin, and Kenneth Derr, directors, Citigroup; Michael Froman, managing director, Citigroup; Pamela Flaherty, director, Citigroup; Richard Haas, director, Fortress Investment Group; James Johnson, Ruth Simmons, and Stephen Friedman, directors, Goldman Sachs; Ellen Futter, director, J.P. Morgan Chase; William Daley, chairman for the Midwest, J.P. Morgan Chase; Robert Wilmers, chairman, M&T Bank; Frederick Whittemore, partner and managing director, Morgan Stanley; Shirley Jackson, director, NYSE.

The network of perceived and prominent social connections was established through these organizations, and not only by strictly professional contacts.

Geithner's cabinet defined the second network. Geithner's team included his chief of staff Mark Patterson (a former Goldman Sachs lobbyist), Lee Sachs (senior advisor, previously at Bear Stearns and Mariner Investment Group), Matt Kabaker (from Blackstone, an equity firm), for a short period, Meg McConnell (from the New York Fed), Gene Sperling (formerly Goldman Sachs and Clinton administration),[73] Lew Alexander (from Citigroup), David Miller (formerly Goldman Sachs), Herb Allison, in charge of running the rescue program (he was previously an executive at Merrill Lynch), and Neal Wolin (from an insurance company). This was a dream team of financiers and lobbyists.

Acemoglu and his co-authors argue that these two rings of connections provided market signals and that this explains the enthusiasm of finance when Geithner was appointed, given the exceptional stress after the subprime crash.

The role of Timothy Geithner is enlightening from this point of view. Confessing in his 2014 book, *Stress Tests: Reflections on Financial Crises*, to be a "technocrat," neither "a banker, an economist, a politician, or even a Democrat," Geithner presided over the New York Federal Reserve Bank, the gravity center of the Fed, through the years preceding the crisis, and then the Treasury itself in its aftermath. During his mandate, he would never indulge the idea of following the solution both Rubin and he himself had previously recommended: the takeover of banks for good.[74] Greenspan himself, in a moment of weakness, even accepted that "it may be necessary to temporarily nationalize the banks in order to facilitate a swift and orderly restructuring,"[75] but not Geithner. The financial system of the US was spared such boldness. Geithner proved to be a trustworthy banker and politician.

The revolving door was quite successful in all the previous stories we have presented and, as it revolves in both directions, also in that of Geithner. After leaving the Treasury, by March 2014 Geithner had become the President of Warburg Pincus, a private equity firm. This was his first job in a financial firm, in spite of the legends surrounding his past. Geithner was frequently presented as an alumnus of Goldman Sachs. Michael Bloomberg, the *Washington Post*, the CBS, and even a congressman at a congressional hearing referred to Geithner's alleged Goldman Sachs connection. The *New York Times* found some humor in this ongoing urban legend.[76] For the record, Geithner never worked at Goldman. His career began at Kissinger Associates, a firm run by Henry Kissinger, but he then moved to the public service in banking.

The Council of Foreign Relations, where Geithner found so many of his institutional relations, was co-chaired at that time by Robert Rubin, frequently presented as Geithner's and Summers' mentor, and simultaneously director of Citigroup. Rubin's history is also representative of the revolving door scenario. He had been a specialist in risk arbitrage and co-headed its fixed income-trading department, then became the co-chair of Goldman Sachs, then director of the National

[73] Carrick-Hagenbarth and Epstein (2012). [74] Johnson and Kwak (2011), pp. 168f, 177.

[75] Interview with *Financial Times*, February 17; also quoted in *Wall Street Journal*, February 21, 2009.

[76] DealBook (2010) and Calmes (2010); and other sources clarified the facts, including Kiely (2012). Of course this was in more innocent times before the rise of "fake news."

Economic Council for Bill Clinton and then his second Secretary of Treasury, and then he left for business and became the chairman of the executive committee of Citigroup in 1999 (after the repeal of Glass-Steagall Act that allowed the creation of Citigroup).[77] He was handsomely paid (1999 to 2008, US $166 million),[78] but resigned in January 2009.

Cronyism at its Apex: Trump

One financial newspaper described Trump and his ascension to power in the following terms:

> Although he styles himself as a chief executive who can turn the country around, Donald Trump is an outsider in the world of American business. His commercial operation is tiny by the standards of the country's mega-firms and few of their bosses have ever viewed the President-elect as an equal or ally. He has "no friends" among the business elite, sniffed a private equity baron a few weeks ago, who will now doubtless join the queue of executives waiting at Trump Tower to curry favour and to assess the new man's priorities before he takes office.[79]

In fact, Trump's empire is small by American standards; the 833rd largest firm in the US or the 1925th by sales. Ross Perot, Mitt Romney, and Michael Bloomberg, just to mention some recent political contenders, managed larger fortunes and firms. Furthermore, his hotels in Panama, Mumbai, Toronto, and Manila scarcely count as an international operation, as his assets are concentrated in the US for 93 percent, 66 percent of which in New York.

In spite of this outsider status and the dimension of his exploits, since he opened his avenue to the White House Trump has been able to attract business moguls and billionaires, distributing the strategic jobs to Wall Street and to some captains of industry. As he proceeded, Trump formed the richest and the most business-representative administration ever, as we noted in the Introduction.

The comparison that comes to mind is with the Warren Harding administration in the 1920s, which was dubbed the "Ohio gang" (not fair to Ohio, since people from other states were also included). Andrew Mellon, one of the richest men in the country, only behind Rockefeller and Ford, was Secretary of the Treasury; as the founder of Alcoa, Union Steel, and Gulf Oil, he represented money through his long tenure (1921–32), imposing his liberal and pro-finance politics. His crucial plan was to reduce the top income tax rate from 77 to 24 percent, expecting large fortunes to invest. After the beginning of the Great Depression, Roosevelt reversed this policy.

The extreme case of cronyism in the Harding administration led to the 1921–2 Teapot Dome scandal, as the Secretary of the Interior, Albert Fall, leased two petroleum land reserves of the Navy to Mammoth Oil Company and Pan American Petroleum Company without competitive bids, pocketing a large bribe. There is nothing new under the sun, as far as cronyism goes.

[77] Eichengreen (2015), pp. 69, 290.
[78] Millet and Toussaint (2009), pp. 58–9; Johnson and Kwak (2011), p. 94.
[79] *The Economist*, November 12, 2016.

Cases Studies on Promotion: John Major and Tony Blair

John Major, a former UK prime minister (1990–7), early in his retirement accepted membership of Carlyle's European Advisory Board (since 1998). He was later the chairman of Carlyle Europe, from 2001 to 2004.

A retired politician, he became a prolix dinner speaker, comfortably paid. In a remarkable turn of phrase, *The Independent* stated that he speaks on "insights and his own opinions on the expanding European Union, the future of the world in the 21st century, and also about Britain."[80]

Tony Blair, the prime minister of the UK following Major from 1997 to 2007, presides over his empire from Grosvenor Square, in the heart of London. Several firms and at least one hundred people are installed in the five-storey building, generating cumulated revenue of £30 to £60 million a year in trading. His managers include the ex-director of Barclays Capital, David Lyons, who now leads Firefish Ventures, the financial branch of "Tony Blair Inc," as well as an ex-executive of Lehman Brothers and another from J.P. Morgan.

Blair himself presides the international advisory council of J.P. Morgan,[81] apart from conducting his own business, plus some foundations.[82] But he did not completely abandon politics, either in the UK or at the international level (he was the envoy of the Quartet for the Middle East, including the UN, US, Russia, and the EU, despite his own business interests with Saudi Arabia).[83]

A witness and participant at the social events during the Davos conference notes the effect of Blair's appearance at the J.P. Morgan cocktail, as he is, "a highly desirable anchor who draws other influential guests."[84] The same author comments that Blair created an immense list of clients: Abu Dhabi's sovereign wealth fund, the controversial Kazakhstan President Nursultan Nazarbayev, and Paul Kagame, the President of Rwanda, plus different arrangements with China, Kuwait, Azerbaijan, Mongolia, Sierra Leone, Liberia, Mozambique, and East Timor, in a highly profitable manner.[85]

This evolution is not exceptional in Britain or, for that matter, in any other developed economy. A well-known case is that of an ex-member of parliament and minister of Blair, Stephen Byers, who was interviewed in 2010 by a TV journalist posing as a potential employer and admitted "I'm a bit like a sort of cab for hire," suggesting his willingness to arrange appointments with the prime minister and other officials. Other politicians took the same stance,[86] and one US senator is

[80] Andrew Buncombe, *The Independent*, February 24, 2007.

[81] *Financial Times*, "Fine Dining for Dimon at the Palace," November 23–24, 2014.

[82] The list is exhibited on Tony Blair's website, http://institute.global/.

[83] Stevens (2014). [84] Navidi (2017), p. 40.

[85] "As chairman of the JPMorgan Advisory Council, he has made himself available for corporate events and high-level client meetings, rendering advice on international matters for a reported $3 million a year. He was also on retainer for Petro Saudi, an oil company related to the Saudi royal family, for $66,000 a month plus an additional 2% of any deal resulting from his efforts, as well as to Zürich Insurance for $750,000 a year. [...] For a three-hour engagement, facilitating the $66 billion merger negotiations between Glencore, Xstrata, and the Qatari ruling family, he received $1 million. He is also a highly sought-after speaker and on average charges $200,000 per speaking engagement. As one paper put it, he logs enough frequent flyer miles in one year to make it to the moon" (Navidi, ibid., p. 204).

[86] Channel 4 (2015). For the Byers interview and follow-up, see *The Telegraph* (2010).

famous for proposing in the same mood, "my vote can't bought but it can be rented."[87]

A report by Transparency International, an agency promoting anti-corruption measures, presents some other disturbing examples of the effects of the revolving door:

> Former Health Minister Alan Milburn has been criticised for taking several jobs with private health companies since leaving office, as well as working for private equity firm Bridgepoint Capital, which obtained several NHS contacts. Again, allegations of impropriety arise partly because of the details of particular contracts. The NHS concluded a contract with Bridgepoint Capital's daughter company, Alliance Medical, six months after Milburn joined the parent company. Under the contract, Alliance Medical agreed to supply 130,000 MRI scans, of which fewer than half were eventually used. The government was nevertheless compelled to pay the full £16m contract price. Milburn's case is also interesting because he undertook extensive paid work in the private sector while he was an MP, following his tenure as a Minister.
>
> Patricia Hewitt MP, who had been Secretary of State for Health from May 2005 until June 2007 (and previously Secretary of State for Trade and Industry), accepted a consultancy worth £45,000 with retail and pharmacy company Alliance Boots just seven months after standing down as a Minister, in January 2008. She also took a £55,000 job with Cinven, an investment company which in 2007 bought 25 private hospitals from Bupa.
>
> Another former health Minister, Norman Warner, became non-executive chairman of UK Health Gateway less than two years after resigning as a Minister. UK Health Gateway "help[s] pharmaceutical, equipment & device manufacturers to enter the UK market successfully." He also became adviser to technology firm Xansa and anti-microbial company Byotrol, both of which sell services and products to the NHS."[88]

Many pieces can come together in determining capture or its opposite.

Although modest class origins are no guarantee of alternative politics, fewer and fewer party power brokers have origins like that of Robin Cook, a Labour MP who resigned from his high party posts in protest against the 2003 invasion of Iraq. Cook's father was a chemistry teacher and his grandfather was a miner before being blacklisted for striking.[89] His relationship to Old and New Labour was nuanced[90] with the relationship to both Blair and the EU (then EEC) evolving towards centrist positions but consistently couched in the language of equality and social solidarity. Instead, the former Labour prime minister Gordon Brown, as previously indicated, accepted a job at PIMCO, the world largest bond fund, just as George Osborne, the Chancellor for the Exchequer for the Conservative government of David Cameron, took a job at BlackRock, the world's largest fund.[91]

The revolving door is a way of life.

A Case Study on Bridging from Institutions to Business: Dominique Strauss-Kahn

Dominique Strauss-Kahn, minister of economy and finance of France (1991–3) and then director of the IMF (2007–11), was ousted in disgrace after being

[87] The remarkable admission came from Senator John Breaux. See Edsall (2011); and Chait (2005).

[88] David-Barrett (2011). See also the OECD report, Miller and Dinan (2009).

[89] Cameron (2005). [90] Castle (1997). [91] *Financial Times*, February 13, 2017.

involved in a sexual harassment accusation. He would soon reconstruct his career in the private sector, becoming in 2013 the President of the Anatevka Group, re-baptized Leyne, Strauss-Kahn and Partners, Compagnie Financière (LSK), an investment bank present in six countries (Luxembourg, Belgium, Monaco, Israel, Switzerland, and Romania). Furthermore, the specialized press writes that he acted as a consultant for different governments, such as Serbia and South Sudan, the Russian bank of Regional Development, the Russian Direct Investment Fund, the National Credit Bank, and a consortium of banks from Morocco.

Business seemed promising and the partners prepared together a DSK Global Fund, a hedge fund to speculate on currency, commodities, and interest rates, trying to raise US $2 billion from different investors, in particular from China.[92]

But LSK met unexpected difficulties when Thierry Leyne, one of the partners, committed suicide in Tel Aviv on October 23, 2014. Strauss-Kahn declared "no knowledge" of money laundering, and blamed the decision for "excessive borrowing" on his partner.[93]

Two weeks before the death of the partner, a court in Luxembourg condemned the company, one of its branches, and Thierry Leyne to pay €2 million to another firm, Bâloise-Vie Luxembourg, which asked for repayment of titles. By November 2014, LSK had filed for bankruptcy in a Luxembourg court.[94]

A Case Study on Promotion and Interests: the Barroso Commission

One in three of the commissioners under the presidency of José Barroso took a job in the private sector as soon as they left office.[95] This was immediately noticed, but the description of the jobs is even more relevant than the career strategies of the highest ranking officers of the European Union.

Indeed, Barroso himself accepted the honorary presidency of the European Business Summit and to be part of the Bilderberg Conference board, two valuable lobbies, and of a number of firms. Then Barroso, as soon as he retired as President of the Commission, accepted a chairmanship at Goldman, igniting a ferocious debate on the revolving door and the European norms. Others followed his lead.

For instance, Viviane Reding, the ex-commissioner for justice, went to Agfa and to Bertelsmann; Kaerl de Gucht to Merit Capital; and Jane Potocnik to Syngenta. Neelie Kroes is a special case: she went to the Bank of America Merrill Lynch after leaving the post of commissioner, but then it was revealed that she was the director of two firms registered in the Bahamas, including during her tenure at the Commission.[96]

CONCLUSION

In this chapter we reviewed evidence on the capture of elites through the working of the revolving door between politics and business, and eventually between central banks and politics or business.

[92] *Financial Times*, "Strauss-Kahn to launch fund," March 21, 2014. [93] Les Echos (2014).
[94] Le Monde (2014). [95] *Brussels Times*, December 15, 2015.
[96] *The Guardian*, September 21, 2016.

The first section was argued with evidence from an investigation conducted on the careers of members of government for a large sample of countries for two years (1975 and 2015). Next we examined the makeup of the central banks themselves. Finally we tracked the leadership of the center and center-left parties in several countries for the entire 1975–2015 period, both from the perspective of when they were in government and also across all members of government in one country (Portugal). We checked for the transitions proving our three hypotheses: internationalization, economization, and financialization.

In the second installment, cases of the revolving door were listed, namely those generated around Goldman Sachs and Carlyle, giants in the shadows of finance. It is apparent that there is a political agenda in their recruitment efforts in different countries and conditions.

Finally, we considered some case studies, from the US, Britain, and France. Although they only indicate tendencies, they provide the examples to confirm the practical working of the revolving door and to explain its success.

The revolving door proves a powerful instrument for constructing a dominant social network. Connections between governments and business create opportunities for social mobility and also for the constitution of a cohesive group leading political parties and powerful firms. Changing places in smart career moves, reassuring the protagonists of their support via back doors, and providing opportunities for social elevation is just business as usual in modern societies.

Part IV

The Web of Power

9

The Wild Side of the Street

Although it may have not been obvious at the time, a wave of change was unleashed during the summer of 2007. That surprising development was the topic for one of the previous chapters, but as we have argued, the groundwork was prepared by years of deregulation and globalization led by a corps of liberalizers, central bankers, and powerful private and public economic managers. As we noted, the danger signs were hidden from most because business looked good at the time. For instance, net revenues of one of the largest investment banks, Goldman Sachs, exceeded the GDP of at least 100 countries. Never before had finance concentrated so much power at the global scale. But one of its pillars, the mortgage industry, was on the verge of a series of bankruptcies that would eventually precipitate a domino effect of panic and a major recession. The world suddenly discovered the cost of financial chicanery.

As the preceding chapters concentrated on the role of academics, ideologues, and central bankers, we have dealt until now only with the misadventures of respected gentlemen (and occasionally gentlewomen) and with the schooling and acculturation that brought them together. This chapter describes instead the larger spectrum of decision makers on the wild side of the street, the practical operatives. We examine the incentives, institutions, choices, and other people that contributed to hide the danger and led to the meltdown. And although many examples of illegal activities will be listed, we will concentrate principally on legal rather than illegal procedures, namely those protected by law, tradition, or simply power. The shadow economy is protected, as this book demonstrates, by a forest of well-behaved and conservative tycoons. This chapter points out some of their strategies.

AGAIN AND AGAIN

Robbery and fraud are as old as wealth itself, with accounts of crime and sometimes punishment pervading ancient and modern texts. The deceptions have became more sophisticated and encompassing because the tools for the circulation of capital and resources are wider, and greed's reach is ever longer.

The historical record shows that one of the first modern speculative bubbles was the Dutch Tulipmania after 1624. As an appreciating commodity, with some truly rare and precious specimens, tulips became a traded asset in Holland. When the prices spiked for some months, speculators invested massively in these flowers.

The appreciation, beginning in 1636, attracted those expecting huge rewards. From a price of approximately ten guilders on November 12, 1636, the price for an average bulb soared through the fall and winter of 1636–7, attaining an apex of 200 guilders—more than one year's wage for a skilled laborer—by February 3, 1637. Auctions for rare bulbs captured the popular imagination: in one extraordinary affair, forty rare bulbs garnered a price of one hundred thousand guilders. Then the bubble burst when a buyer failed to pay for the bulbs purchased at auction. Mistrust rapidly replaced enthusiasm, and prices fell catastrophically, generating a wave of bankruptcies and losses.

If the Tulipmania was generated in the street market and the auction houses, other bubbles and frauds were initiated at high levels of intermingled government and private finance. The case of the South Sea Bubble in the eighteenth century provides an early example of how those controlling information can, at least for a time, manage expectations and induce speculation for profit.[1] The South Sea Company was founded as a joint stock company in 1711, designed to consolidate and finance public debt and to hold a monopoly on British trade, which included the slave trade, with South America. (Legend has it that Daniel Defoe, the author of *Robinson Crusoe*, proposed the scheme, but the claim cannot be documented.) The function of the South Sea Company was to absorb the unsecured debt held by creditors, offering stock in exchange for debt. As a consequence, the public debt was transferred to the company, and the government was relieved of the obligation of paying the principal of that debt.[2]

The problem was that this vaunted trade monopoly was not actually worth very much because the region was dominated by Spain. Few benefits were recorded from its business. But hopes ran high, especially when the popular imagination was captured by the rumor that Francis Drake had uncovered a paradise awaiting exploitation in the South Seas. In any case, the shareholders were promised annual interest of 4–5 percent plus a share of the eventual profits from trade. Thanks to a combination of bribes to members of parliament and insider trading on forthcoming debt, the South Sea Company flourished for some years and its stock rose. The company financed current dividends by borrowing and by increasing the number of shares. That is, this government-promoted private company operated a classic pyramid, or Ponzi, scheme. (Ponzi himself will be the protagonist of some of the following pages.)

Even when Spain seized the vital properties of the South Sea Company in South America in 1718, enthusiasm persisted and prices increased tenfold from 1719 to 1720. The company went bankrupt only when confidence vanished.[3] Among the victims of the fraud, Isaac Newton lost £20,000, a fortune. Indeed, in 1720 Newton sold his shares for a 100 percent profit, but moved by the general enthusiasm, bought again at a higher price (and lost the equivalent of US $3 or 4 million today). George Handel, the musician, made a fortune because he was wise enough to sell at the appropriate time.[4]

[1] *The Economist*, March 1, 2014. [2] Mirowski (2013), p. 229.

[3] After the crash of the South Sea Bubble, a first wave of regulation was imposed on finance: "In reaction to the South Sea Bubble and the ensuing decade of depression, institutional constraints were imposed on the capitalist firm and finance, which did act to reduce instability in the economy," ibid., p. 278.

[4] Soll (2014), pp. 16–18.

New worlds to conquer have provided fuel for bubbles. At approximately the same time as the South Sea Bubble, the Scottish banker John Law was nominated Controller General of the Finances of France by the Duke of Orléans, regent for the young Louis XV. Law created the Banque Générale of France, a private enterprise issuing paper money under public authorization, and then founded the Mississippi Company for exploring and trading with New France. The stock initially soared, fueled by Law's optimistic claims. When the project collapsed Law fled the country.

One century later, Gregor MacGregor, self-professed descendant of the heroic Rob Roy MacGregor, achieved notoriety as one of history's more inventive con men. After buying a commission and serving a tour in the British Army in the 1809–10 peninsular campaign in Portugal, MacGregor crossed the Atlantic and the Equator, joining Simon Bolivar. MacGregor was appointed Major-General in the Bolivaran forces and returned to England by 1821 as self-proclaimed "cazique" of Poyais, an invented country roughly in the location of modern-day Honduras. He also presented himself as the "Inca" of New Granada. He styled the marvelous nation of Poyais as the dream destination for those seeking to abandon Europe, which was still suffering from the Napoleonic Wars and inflation, and to settle in a rich new land. As government bonds and private alternatives were paying very low interest after the wars, MacGregor's opportunity attracted an audience. Two ships and 250 settlers were sent, under the illusion of high returns, and more ships were prepared to follow. Ultimately, the settlement was a disaster, finding unfriendly Indians, high fevers, inclement weather, and unforgiving forests. The "cazique" had taken, at today's prices, 3.6 billion pounds (Two centuries later Bernard Madoff would get twenty times more, but the key method was already in place).[5] As news of the collapse of the project spread, MacGregor moved to France. He would later travel to Venezuela where he was received as a hero of the independence struggle.

In 1899, at the turn of the century, a new society had already emerged. New industries, new cities, new banks, and new hopes populated the new world. A Brooklyn bookkeeper, William Miller, found a promising path to fortune: he promised 10 percent interest a week to the eventual depositors, and he attracted so many people to his home and office that the tale states that his staircase was crushed. He was nicknamed Mr. "520 percent" and, of course, the scheme collapsed. Miller, who defrauded his clients of one million dollars (25 million would be the modern equivalent), was sentenced to ten years in prison. After his release he opened a grocery store and no more was heard of William Miller.[6]

Charles Ponzi, unlike the "cazique," could not claim descent from a prestigious clan and, unlike Miller, did not give up. A poor immigrant from Parma, Italy, to the US in the 1910s, Ponzi invented an ingenious pyramid scheme using the emerging market of foreign exchange. In fact, he benefited from a new product, international postal reply coupons, created in 1906 to enable transfer of funds from one country to another. As the First World War ravaged Europe, governments turned to the printing press to pay for armies, and many currencies depreciated against the dollar. International postal reply coupons, bought cheap in the devalued currency, would allow the owner to buy more than the initial cost in stamps in the US. Ponzi grasped the arbitrage opportunity and created a flamboyant Securities Exchange

[5] *The Economist*, December 22, 2012. [6] *Time*, March 7, 2012.

Company in 1920, promising to double every investment in three months. The company attracted much investment but, as one might expect, soon went bankrupt. Ponzi was convicted and sentenced to three and a half years in jail. In prison he was prosecuted for additional frauds, but he eventually got out.

Free from prison, Ponzi created a second chance for himself. Moving to Florida, Ponzi noticed the escalating real-estate boom, now the source of many jokes about "selling swamp land in Florida." In 1925, Ponzi created Charpon Land Corporation, more daring than his earlier ride in the financial market. Ponzi promised to *triple* the investment every two months. When the scheme collapsed Ponzi was again sentenced to prison. He escaped briefly but was caught while in disguise and returned to prison. Deported to Italy in 1934, Ponzi then moved to Brazil, where he finished his life, accompanied by tales of smuggling. Arbitrage, new financial products, and confidence in human cupidity doomed the ingenious Charles Ponzi.[7]

Continuing into the new century, new products and sophisticated methods of accounting and reporting preceded great collapses, such as that of Enron in 2001, or WorldCom in 2002. Enron, an energy trading company, had been heralded the most innovative firm for six years in a row by *Fortune Magazine*, only to be exposed in a scandal of false accounting and corruption. WorldCom, which was for a time the second largest provider of long distance telephone calls in the US, admitted a bookkeeping fraud of almost four billion dollars.[8] Its CEO, Bernard Ebbers, was sentenced to twenty-five years in prison.

Despite these impressive cases, the 2008 exposure of the scheme of Bernard Madoff revealed fraud of still larger proportions. Madoff had a long career managing one of the top Wall Street firms, specializing in over-the-counter brokerage, i.e., dealing in specialized and customized financial products, with a large, ostensibly sophisticated clientele who were promised huge returns. In fact, Madoff's empire was a simple Ponzi scheme—old investors paid off with the deposits of new investors—that went undetected by US regulators including the Securities and Exchange Commission. Several individual analysts, such as the Bank of Ireland, with which Madoff had dealings, tried to blow the whistle, but the regulators were not listening, thanks to a combination of anti-regulatory ideology and disbelief that such a large, successful enterprise could be no more than a house of cards.

Madoff himself expressed surprise that he had not been caught by a 2003 SEC investigation. Instead he happily pursued his business. In the end, clients' losses amounted to some US $65 billion with at least US $18 billion lost outright.

The Madoff scandal emerged at the intersection of incompetent and indifferent regulation with a culture of greed. In these cases, fraud and failure were the consequence of deviant practices. In other cases, financial crashes emerge from normalized patterns of behavior generated by business itself. Nick Leeson, who destroyed the venerable Barings Bank in 1995, argued that the loss of £862 million and the consequent bankruptcy resulted from his understandable attempt to cover losses of a mere £20,000 by a junior colleague.[9]

[7] Eichengreen (2015), pp. 17–19. [8] *New York Times*, July 22, 2002.

[9] Walne (2012). As Leeson himself relates to *The Telegraph*.

Ezubao, the largest peer-to-peer credit firm in China, was created in 2014 by Ding Ning, a manufacturer, with huge success. Soon he attracted one million investors and a government institution presented it as a "model enterprise." In 2016 it was revealed to be a Ponzi scheme.[10]

In the approach to the abyss of 2007–8 and in its aftermath, fraud has ceased to be a form of misbehavior; fraud is the name of the game.

THE DANGER LIES AT HOME, NOT ELSEWHERE

The same Michael Lewis, whose true-life first-person account of working in the bond trade in the 1980s accidentally inspired many young Americans to choose finance, would later uncover market manipulation in high frequency trading and conclude that, indeed, Wall Street resisted quite well, since apparently nothing "could sink the system" and instead the late scandals fortified it.[11]

In the next sections, we discuss some of the reasons why Lewis and others were beaten by the system of beliefs generated in and by the economies, in spite of the damaging evidence of successive banking and financial crashes. In particular, three explanations for this failure will be explored throughout this book: excessive confidence in the rating agencies' signals about the health of the market products; confidence in the regulatory agencies; and confidence in the self-preservation virtue of the big players in the financial world (which led to Greenspan's "I am shocked"). Confidence was the pillar of the most innovative, risky, and daring industries in modern times. And confidence led to a major systemic failure, if not on the scale of Lewis's prediction.

IF YOU AIN'T CHEATING, YOU AIN'T TRYING

The culture of Wall Street and the City of London—or for that matter of Frankfurt, Tokyo, or Shanghai—represents a mixture of greed, ingenuity, and power that drives our contemporary world. Power is its primary mover.

This is how an investigator describes one important event in the market for public debt:

> At 10.28 a.m. on Monday 2 August 2004, four traders at Citigroup's European government bond trading desk activated a proprietary software program they called 'Dr.Evil' (after a character in the spy spoof movie *Austin Powers*) to sell a large number of bonds very quickly. Twenty seconds later, unsure whether the trades had succeeded, they submitted another sell order. By 10.29 a.m. Citigroup had sold 13 billion euros worth of 119 different European government bonds across 11 platforms of the Rome-based

[10] *Financial Times* (2016).

[11] Lewis (2014). Yet permanent instability is a feature of the financial market and in particular of global banks: when in 2015 the rumor was that lots of toxic waste was still in the balance sheets of the banks, J.P. Morgan Chase felt obliged to inform investors it would not be broken up, Eavis (2015); and Deutsche Bank was forced to sell off assets, Thomas, Jr. (2016).

> Mercato dei Titoli di Stato (public bonds market). This was roughly the same amount of bonds as the entire market would typically trade over one day, and it happened in one minute. After reconfiguring their program, the traders bought back four billion euros in bonds, realizing a profit of 15 million euros by 11.25 a.m. Although Citigroup was not charged with market abuse, which is illegal, the operation was highly controversial. At the time, it provoked (the other) "bankers' wrath"[12]

The UK's Financial Services Authority ruled on the transaction in June 2005, imposing a fine of £14 million on this "bond coup."

Other events prove that this form of ruse is a market standard. On March 8, 2011, at precisely 15:34:40 and lasting for only 11 seconds, Goldman Sachs launched an intense robot war at the New York Stock Exchange, bombarding the market with orders and vertiginously buying and selling stocks at different prices. The authorities deemed the practice strange and threatening but not technically illegal. The real motivation seemed to be testing the algorithms of its competitors, in order to get information on how fast Goldman Sachs could or should proceed, and how it should tune its software in order to get marginal benefits from this advantage.

These cases are not exceptional. Computational power, control of information, high speed trading, these are some of the advantages of the giants in finance. In *Flash Boys*: Lewis investigated a scheme by some of the major players in the financial market to get their information 13 milliseconds before the competition—quicker than blinking. High frequency trading became the mode of operation of the stock market. Technical capacity defines the victor.

A headstart faster than the blink of an eye may prove a very important advantage because, in these markets, financial power is instead based upon the secrecy of the decision process. Take the example of the long-lived "Cartel." By May 20, 2015, the supervisors reached a non-prosecution agreement with six banks, the Bank of America, UBS, Barclays, Citigroup, J.P. Morgan Chase, and Royal Bank of Scotland for the payment of a €5.6 billion fine.[13]

These banks had already paid US $4.25 billion six months earlier and then pleaded guilty and accepted the fines for collusion in the currency market.[14] The text of the indictment registered a coded communication system through an online chat room, involving some traders modestly calling themselves "The Cartel," for manipulating the foreign exchange market and, in particular, for fixing the exchange rate between dollar and euro from 2007 until 2013. For Citigroup, this was the single most important fine for violation of the Sherman Act, the US antitrust legislation. UBS had already paid a previous fine of US $1.5 billion for a scandal we will discuss later, the manipulation of the Libor rate (more on the Libor scandal later in this chapter).

The public complaint records the emailed remark of a Barclays' vice president in New York: "if you ain't cheating, you ain't trying."[15] An expression worthy of Gordon Gekko.

[12] Gomes (2012); *The Daily Telegraph*, August 11, 2004.

[13] *Financial Times* (2015a).

[14] Corkery and Protess (2015).

[15] Although most of the directors and staff involved were already out of the banks, the New York financial regulator, Benjamin Lawsky, forced Barclays to dismiss another eight employees.

SWINDLES AS A WAY OF BUSINESS

In some cases, the thin line between market dealings and swindling is overstepped—or the line can move according to convenience. Sometimes the supervisors act willingly or are forced. The long list of fines and accusations proves how the financial shadows menace the transparency of the markets.

Sometimes penalties have been applied for narrowly defined criminal activity or dealings with foreign powers under national or international sanction. In 2005 the US authorities hit the Banco Delta Asia, of Macau, China, for dealings with North Korea. Other banks were also punished for violating international sanctions or rules: the HSBC in 2012 (condemned to pay US $1.9 billion to the US authorities for violating sanctions against Libya and Sudan and for dealings with Mexican drug cartels), then the Standard Chartered Bank on negotiations with Iran (a US $340 million fine), BNP Paribas (US $2,200 million for dealings with Iran and Sudan), the Bank of Tokyo-Mitsubishi (US $565 million for violating sanctions on Iran), Commerzbank (US $610 million fine on Iran), HSBC and Citigroup (money laundering of Mexican criminal associations), and Deutsche Bank (US $827 million for laundering and other offences in 2017).[16]

In 2016, a scandal in Malaysia revealed some of the complex tentacles of the political-financial connections. Investigations on allegations of personal misappropriation of billions of dollars in the 1MDB scandal, a state investment fund formed in cooperation with companies from Saudi Arabia to Abu Dhabi, have shaken Malaysia: US $680 million were found in the account of the prime minister, Najib Razak, allegedly paid by the Saudi royal family (the prime minister acknowledged this was a gift by Prince Turki bin Abdullah, who one year afterwards would be arrested in his own country for alleged corruption), and other funds were detected in the personal accounts of Malaysian and United Arab Emirates officials. Goldman Sachs, a giant in finance that we shall encounter again later in this chapter, was one of the agents raising capital for the fund, which was supposed to promote investment. The US Department of Justice computes US $3,500 million allegedly misappropriated. To make things even worse, French justice investigates bribery in a submarine sale, involving the same people, and the Swiss criminal authorities have investigated firms connected to the fund. To add to the political tempest, the Malaysian government suspended publication of critical newspapers, opposition members of parliament were prevented from traveling, and the central bank announced a criminal investigation, which was quickly shut down by the attorney general. Finally, one opposition politician, Rafizi Ramli, who denounced the affair, was sentenced to prison.[17]

Indeed, bribery has been a frequent reason for penalties imposed on major financial and industrial firms:[18] since 2008, Siemens has spent US $3 billion on fines and internal investigations or lawyers on accusations for bribes in emerging markets; Walmart was fined US $800 million for bribes in Mexico, and spent more than US $1 billion in lawyers' fees; in 2014, US regulators imposed a fine of US $772 million on Alstom, a major French industrial group, for alleged US $75 million

[16] *The Economist*, March 7, 2015, November 4, 2017.

[17] *Financial Times*, February 16, 2016; *The Economist*, November 19, 2016.

[18] *The Economist*, May 9, 2015.

bribes in Egypt and Indonesia; Petrobrás, the public monopoly of oil extraction in Brazil, has been involved in a deep scandal on party corruption; and China attacked GSK, a British pharmaceutical, company and Avon (fines of US $350 million), accused of bribery.

For what it's worth, much of the elite managerial class sees bribery as a reasonable and acceptable cost of business.[19]

As with legitimate business expenses, there is a marginal cost (the amount of the bribe itself, the risk of discovery, and the magnitude of punishment) and a marginal benefit (the likelihood of the success of the project) from bribes. Economic doctrine may even suggest that a wise manager will optimize by investing in bribes until the cost outweighs the benefits, although this is not frequently confessed.[20]

Additional crackdowns on the giants of industry and finance have been for doctoring accounts or for tax evasion. Fallout from the Enron case—the giant energy trading firm that manipulated the electricity market in California—included the collapse of Arthur Andersen, one of the world's largest consulting and accounting firms, that was found guilty of obstruction of justice in 2002. In 1996, Dick Cheney, then CEO of Halliburton and soon to become vice president of the United States under George W. Bush, made an endorsement video for Arthur Andersen in which he attests that the accounting firm gave advice "over and above" what would normally be expected from auditors. Cheney praises Andersen, saying, "I get good advice, if you will, from their people, based upon how we are doing business and how we are operating, over and above the normal, by-the-books auditing arrangement."[21]

A dozen years after the Enron episode, in May 2014, Crédit Suisse pleaded guilty to criminal charges for helping clients to evade US taxes, and agreed to pay an impressive US $2,800 million fine. Five years earlier, another Swiss bank, UBS, had already paid a fine of US $780 million for the same offence. Yet, the US government failed to demand the identities of Crédit Suisse's tax-evading clients as part of the agreement. The bank's shares actually rose the day the plea agreement was announced.[22] In contrast, the German parliament bluntly rejected a deal to recover the lost tax revenue because it would have allowed the banks to keep the names under wraps.[23]

Not all the Swiss banks escaped with impunity. The 2012 indictment of Wegelin in New York on charges of money laundering put it out of business. Under the pressure from US tax authorities, 285 of the roughly 300 Swiss banks agreed to

[19] Karabell (2015). Although the reliable data on bribery are reduced to those on criminal prosecutions, and this may represent only a small sample of the procedure, the group of cases involving CEOs is relevant. As *Forbes* summarized, "The World Bank estimates that globally more than $1 trillion is handed over annually to corrupt government officials, while the OECD's 2014 Foreign Bribery Report shows a substantial increase in the number of bribery cases brought annually around the world since the OECD began monitoring these activities seriously in 1999. Of 427 cases identified last year, 53% involved corporate management or CEOs; 80 individuals received jail terms of up to 13 years; and another 38 were given suspended sentences. The largest individual fine was $149 million".

[20] An outspoken exception, but not the only one, is "In Defense of Bribery," Lemieux (2005).

[21] BBC (2002).

[22] *The Economist*, May 24, 2014. The trial of Raoul Weil, the head of UBS private banking, who was arrested in Italy and then extradited to the US, was a major blow for the authorities: he was acquitted after one hour of jury deliberations.

[23] *The Economist*, September 7, 2013.

provide information on their American clients in order to avoid prosecution, and to pay penalties of between 20 and 50 percent of the clients' account balances. Despite years of investigation, the first agreement did not include the fourteen largest banks.[24]

HSBC was the epicenter of a tax-dodging scandal, when a list of more than one hundred thousand clients of the Geneva branch of HSBC were implicated in undertaking a gigantic tax evasion scheme from 2005 to 2007. Hervé Falciani, a systems engineer for the bank, leaked the files to judicial authorities and the IMF, where a subset was named the "Lagarde list." It came out that Falciani's boss, Stuart Gulliver, received his pay in a Swiss account owned by a Panama-based shell corporation, and that many of these clients were indeed avoiding their tax responsibilities. HSBC, which had already paid US $1,900 million in the US for laundering drug money for drug cartels in its Mexican branch, was forced to publish a one-page apology in the newspapers, acknowledging that the case was a "source of shame."[25] Nor was it the bank's first brush with laundering: in 2008, HSBC Cayman had been used by organized crime.

Another form of crime is mass murder. BNP accepted in 2014 a $9 billion fine for having helped Sudan's government in 2006 to finance the militias responsible for the massacre in Darfur (other charges included breaking the embargo to Cuba and Iran). Other accusations made against the bank because of payments that may have favored the Rwanda 1994 massacre (800,000 people dead) resurfaced, following the findings of a report presented to the Security Council of the United Nations in 1998.

After the financial crash ignited by the subprime meltdown and the subsequent explosion of public outrage, institutional tolerance towards sketchy financial products narrowed significantly. The big banks faced consequences of their earlier victories against regulation: central bankers and regulatory agencies could not afford the suspicion of being manipulated by finance and became more willing to punish especially visible or controversial excesses.

Conventional crime such as money laundering drug revenues, tax evasion, and financial manipulation appear repeatedly in the same banks at the commanding heights of finance. In other cases, banks make their own trouble trying to beat the market or fleece the credulous.[26]

Insider trading is certainly one of the most dangerous games in the world of finance and sometimes those responsible get caught. The three largest penalties for trading in privileged information were imposed on Ivan Boesky in 1989 (fined US $600 million, an exposé that also lead to the conviction of Michael Milken, the king of junk bonds), Raj Rajaratnam in 2009 (fined US $157 million in a 2011 investigation that also brought down Rajat Gupta, CEO of McKinsey), and finally in 2012 SAC Capital, a medium-sized capital management firm with US $15 billion

[24] Ibid. [25] *The Economist*, February 14, 2015; February 28, 2015; May 3, 2014.

[26] Johnson and Kwak (2011), p. 230. Other cases are dealt with through settlements in order to avoid criminal prosecution and bad press. For instance, in July 2010, Goldman Sachs agreed to a fine of US $550 million, imposed by the SEC, as a settlement for marketing CDOs that "contained incomplete information," a euphemism for collaborating with speculators to produce and sell bundled assets with a high probability of failure. Criminal charges were discussed as this appeared to be a case of a large investment bank intentionally fleecing its clients. But the settlement closed that possibility.

under management, headed by Steven Cohen, a star in the shadow banking system, which paid a fine of US $8 billion to the Securities and Exchange Commission (SEC). The SEC established that the firm obtained insider information on the upcoming financial results of hardware manufacturers Dell and NVidia, and to top it off, gathered advance details on the performance of a new medicine from a professor of neurology, Sidney Gilman, whom Cohen's firm had carefully cultivated for several years as a source.[27] But it should be noticed that at least three successful businessmen condemned for fraud, in spite of that setback, remained on the *Forbes* list of billionaires: that is the case of the aforementioned Michael Milken, sentenced to twenty-two months in jail for securities fraud, and Steve Cohen, the head of SAC Capital Advisors, who pleaded guilty for insider trading, and of Wong Kwong Yu, from China, condemned to fourteen years in jail for bribery and insider trading.

As the United States moved ahead with heavily contested financial reform legislation, the Dodd-Frank Act of 2010, this type of penalty was aggravated. As the Act, somewhat weakened by lobbying, went into effect and was guided by new regulations and the spirit of financial reform, the intensity of scrutiny increased. As a consequence, some large fines were imposed on Bank of America (US $11.8 billion in February 2012, for misbehavior in home mortgage foreclosures); Wells Fargo (US $5.3 billion in February 2012 for misbehavior in home mortgage foreclosures with an additional payment of US $125 million to compensate borrowers and US $50 million more as a fine for an information program that eventually overcharged 30,000 people, then again under pressure for the revelation of having imposed unnecessary insurance to car loans customers and of having opened a large number of unauthorized retail deposit accounts in 2017[28]); J.P. Morgan (US $5.3 billion, February 2012, for violating foreign policy sanctions): Bank of America (US $11.6 billion, January 2013, for errors in mortgage repurchases, and US $2.9 billion, for misbehavior in home mortgage foreclosures); again J.P. Morgan Chase (the record sum of US $13 billion, October 2013, for unscrupulous dealings with mortgage based securities), and yet again J.P. Morgan (US $5.1 billion, October 2013, for dubious mortgage securities repurchases); again the Bank of America (US $9.3 billion, March 2014, also for activity in the MBS market); Crédit Suisse (US $2.6 billion, May 2014, for tax evasion); and BNP Paribas (US $8.9 billion, June 2014, for violation of foreign policy sanctions).[29]

Since 2009, in the aftermath of the crash, the settlements by financial firms in the US amounted to US $219 billion in 188 cases, with 278 still pending at the end of 2016. The Bank of America alone paid US $7.7 billion, or half of its net worth.[30]

These regulatory procedures only scratch the surface of the hidden economy and finance. In India, a journalist with a hidden camera and a plausible story recently asked managers of several banks if they would launder money. All happily agreed.[31] In London, the property boom in the 2010s largely depends on anonymous offshore companies, many supposedly connected to money laundering,[32] and the Bank of England calculates that no less than half of United Kingdom banknotes

[27] *New Yorker*, October 13, 2014. [28] *Forbes*, August 31, 2017.

[29] Eichengreen (2015), and *The Economist*, July 5, 2014. In 2014 the fines paid by major banks was up to US $87 billion (*The Economist*, August 8, 2015).

[30] *The Economist*, August 13, 2016. [31] *The Economist*, March 23, 2013.

[32] *Independent*, March 4, 2015.

are used for the shadow economy and crime.[33] In any case, shameful accusations spread everywhere: in Spain, the Banco Madrid filed for bankruptcy by March 2015, as the US Treasury accused its Andorran parent firm of money laundering. As a consequence, the Banca Privada d'Andorra was nationalized.[34]

If you ain't cheating, you ain't trying—and you will not prevail.

THE LIBOR CONNECTION

Although great banks are not above occasional profitable sorties into crime, serious people also engage in greed and deception within the boundaries of the law. In this and the next sections we explore some of these shadows, beginning with Libor.

Libor is the acronym for London Interbank Offered Rate (and *Euribor* for Euro Interbank Offered Rate). Every night, some banks need to borrow to meet "reserve requirements" and other banks with excess reserves have the opportunity to lend to these banks in need. Libor summarizes the overnight interest rates that the large banks charge each other, or the bids by banks on the basis of the expectation of what other banks would do (on the London market). Overnight lending between large banks is generally considered a safe lending practice, and the Libor usually represents the opportunity cost of low-risk short-term access to money. As such, it is an important benchmark rate on which other transactions are based. But sharp increases in the Libor may indicate severe trouble brewing in financial markets as banks become unwilling to lend to other banks even for very short periods. Libor thus plays important roles in the official banking system and in the shadow banking system as well as a barometer of systemic risk.

Libor is supposed to summarize the actual rates paid by borrower banks to lender banks in a myriad of private lending agreements. Each morning, at 11 o'clock, a small committee gathers in London to get the estimates from a panel of sixteen of the largest banks on the costs of borrowing money in several currencies over different time periods. The British Bankers' Association manages the process and Reuters computes an index rate reflecting the average of rates excluding extreme values among the estimates. The conclusion is published daily at noon.[35]

These rates have a direct influence on the world of non-financial businesses and households. Banks follow the Libor to set the interest rates on mortgages, credit cards, other household credit, and even corporate loans. Fluctuations of the Libor (and Euribor) decide the payments and ultimately the debt of households, which can represent a significant share of disposable income for indebted populations.

Libor has another use and not a trivial one: it is central in pricing US $300 trillion of derivatives. With so much at stake, even small changes of the Libor can transfer significant amounts of debt and wealth among contracting parties. Successful manipulation, leveraged and multiplied a trillion-fold, would be very lucrative indeed.

[33] Fish and Whymark (2015). [34] *The Economist*, February 27, 2016.

[35] Stenfors (2014). The *Euribor* is slightly different, the index is computed only on the basis of estimates of what the rate between two banks would be.

The Federal Reserve Bank of New York learned as early as 2007 that the participating banks were colluding and manipulating the morning report of the Libor. Yet the Fed took no action. Only by 2012 were nine of the world's largest banks investigated for participation in the Libor scandal: the Bank of America, Bank of Tokyo Mitsubishi, Crédit Suisse, Lloyds, Rabobank, Royal Bank of Canada, Société Générale, Norinchukin Bank, and WestLB.[36] But when in 2013 the media found out about the manipulation, the revelations provoked public outcry and further investigations. The Swiss UBS and RBS, and the British bank Barclays paid fines (and a prominent candidate for the position of Governor of the Bank of England, Paul Tucker, was sidelined given his connections to Bob Diamond, the CEO of Barclays, after being questioned by a parliamentary committee). Although a New York court ruled in March 2013 that the manipulation did not violate the law, banks nonetheless agreed to settle the question with a sizable payment.[37] The regulatory authority for the State of New York, the Department of Financial Services, agreed with Deutsche Bank a fine for manipulation of Libor.[38]

By 2015, more banks agreed to pay approximately €2 billion in fines: HSBC, Barclays, Citigroup, BNP Paribas, Goldman Sachs, Royal Bank of Scotland, and Union de Banques Suisses.[39] In August 2015, Tom Hayes, a senior officer in Citigroup and the central figure in the Libor fixing scheme, was sentenced to 14 years in prison (this was reduced to 11 years by a British appeal court).[40]

The same applies to the manipulation of Euribor. In this case, the European authorities settled the case with the Royal Bank of Scotland, Barclays, Deutsche Bank, and Société Générale in 2015 for a fine of €820 million. In 2016, three other banks, HSBC, J.P. Morgan, and Crédit Agricole, that had not accepted the settlement, were fined €468 million.[41]

The giants of the banking industry were involved in this case, a cartel for manipulating the information to their benefit.

OFFSHORING CAPITAL

During his first Presidential campaign in 2008, candidate Barack Obama enlightened a crowd of supporters about the financial haven in the Cayman Islands. Obama stunned his audience, innocent of the ways of high finance, with the news that a single building in the Caymans registered 40,000 firms. Obama was right, and that was just a single example.

Distance from traditional financial centers and small size do not limit opportunities. Vanuatu, a small archipelago in the Pacific Ocean, has its share of misadventures: as the President traveled abroad, his temporary replacement, the speaker of parliament, pardoned himself and thirteen MPs already convicted for bribery. Pardons were revoked upon return of the President, but the fragility of the system

[36] *Wall Street Journal*, October 26, 2012. [37] *The Economist*, April 6, 2013.

[38] DFS has acted as supervisor since 2011, given that, as the banks have a subsidiary in New York, it has the power to investigate their dealings although not to prosecute (*The Economist*, March 28, 2015).

[39] *Le Monde*, August 14, 2015. [40] *New York Times*, December 22, 2015.

[41] *The Guardian*, December 7, 2016.

became obvious. Not so for finance: Vanuatu houses some thousands of shell companies, apparently with no threatening interference from local politics.

An International Consortium of Investigative Journalists, a worldwide network of reporters, published in 2013 what was called the Offshore Leaks, pointing out 100,000 entities sheltered in different offshore locations for tax avoidance, including in tax havens in the most developed economies—not Vanuatu. The same Consortium published in 2016 evidence on 214,000 firms, mostly created by a law firm in Panama, Mossack Fonseca, in different havens from Nevada to Hong Kong. The *Panama Papers* constituted the most detailed investigation to date on hiding money.

In late 2016, an additional product of this investigation emerged: a list of banks and firms using the Bahamas offshore to evade their fiscal responsibilities. One in ten among the firms installed in the Bahamas since 1990 were created by Crédit Suisse and UBS, 25,000 each, although the champion was Mossack Fonseca.[42]

But it would be a mistake to imagine that offshore companies are only harbored in the distant tropics. Instead offshores are at the heart of major financial systems. US Representative Devin Nunes, then chair of a Congressional working group on taxation, declared his goal that America become "the largest tax haven in human history." In the European Union, the official list of non-cooperative tax jurisdictions includes Andorra, Guernsey, Liechtenstein, and Monaco and other respected Member States shelter offshore operations promoting illegal activity.[43] Devin Nunes, as Trump was elected, took a job in his transition team, generating some expectation that he might be able to fight for his "largest tax haven in human history."

Luxembourg, in particular, has been accused of tax malpractices, as the Consortium uncovered in 2014 what came to be called *Luxleaks*: it was shown that the state had created, under the guidance of PricewaterhouseCoopers since 2002, a scheme for benefiting tax avoidance by multinational companies. Jean Claude Juncker, the prime minister (1995–2013, and also minister of finance until 2009) was the prime mover of the tax avoidance scheme, which damaged the tax systems of many countries in Europe and beyond. He was then nominated the president of the European Commission.[44]

The Netherlands is another case. The state accepts at least 10,000 "letterbox firms," located for tax reduction, as does Ireland. This duo gives its name to a favored technique of multinationals seeking to decrease their tax liabilities: "the Double Irish with Dutch sandwich." The firm pays itself royalties at an Irish subsidiary, then moves through a Dutch entity, and finally to a second Irish subsidiary registered in a tax haven. These strategies and others may amount to large sums of tax losses. Tax Research, a UK analyst, computes Italian tax evasion at €180 billion, that of Germany at €159, France at €120, Britain at €74, Spain at €73, respectively around 27, 16, 15, 14, and 22 percent of their total tax income.[45] And this is only the illegal portion.

Sheer greed and volume can spur the recourse to tax havens. In 2013, Google (in spite of its fun-loving corporate motto, "Don't be evil") avoided paying some

[42] Swissinfo (2016).
[43] *The Economist*, November 7, 2015; August 22, 2015; February 20, 2016.
[44] Galizia, et al. (2014).
[45] *The Economist*, October 10, 2015.

€2 billion in taxes by transferring almost €10 billion to Bermuda, where the corporate tax rate is only 5 percent, through a company in the Netherlands that specializes in routing income to advantageous destinations.[46] The result for Google was an effective tax rate of 2.4 percent.

An investigation by Gabriel Zucman, a professor at the University of California, Berkeley, concluded that offshore havens harbor some 8 percent of global private financial wealth, of which some three-quarters is unrecorded. Moreover, according to his computation, two-thirds of the decline of the effective tax rate on US corporations for the last fifteen years, from 30 to 20 percent, is due to operations in tax havens.[47] The IMF concurs and presents a similar computation: 8 trillion of the world total US $123 trillion of private financial wealth sit in offshore havens, and most of this is due to tax evasion. If we come to financial flows, for instance in the case of foreign direct investment, over 30 percent of the total is booked through offshore financial centers.

From the smaller jurisdictions such as Vanuatu, to the huge business centers of the Channel Islands or even the State of Delaware (which charges no tax on sales or personal income and welcomes 945,000 registered companies to enjoy reduced corporate taxation), the tax havens protect shadow business, with significant tolerance for money laundering and other non-legal action. A well-researched case is that of Augusto Pinochet, the dictator of Chile from 1973 to 1981, who hid his money in different bank accounts at Citigroup, Bank of America, Espírito Santo, and others. A 2004 investigation by the US Senate uncovered this secretive network.[48] Cases of criminals using offshore accounts surface frequently.

The liberalization of capital movement has ushered in a golden age for offshore (and onshore) havens. This has created a culture, and three researchers, Findley, Nielson, and Sharman, found compelling evidence for the deep change going on, as they conducted an experiment posing as financiers trying to hide money through untraceable companies and asking for advice on how to proceed: they found much more openness from bankers in OECD countries than in offshores, given the pressure for disclosure to which these are submitted.[49] As Devin Nunes, the US congressman, put it, the competition is to create the largest inshore tax haven.

THE SWISS PARADISE

The forerunners of this new attitude towards capital movements were a handful of countries specialized in assisting tax evasion, often at substantial cost to their neighbors. The most famous and successful of these tax havens has been Switzerland.

Switzerland has long protected discreet capital movements enabling its banking industry to become one of the most powerful in Europe. The twentieth-century convulsions threatening Europe further enhanced the financial system of the enclave to service the diversified funds that knocked at its door. The proprietors

[46] *Financial Times* (2013). [47] Zucman (2015). [48] US Senate (2004).
[49] Findley, Nielson, and Sharman (2014).

of those fortunes required discretion, and discretion they got, as Switzerland has been the fatherland of banking secrecy. The force of the law with the threat of prison discouraged bankers and bureaucrats from revealing the identity of depositors.

The principle of banking secrecy was a long-held tradition of Swiss banks, but it was reinforced following a scandal in France in the 1930s. After the Global Crash of 1929 and the ensuing Depression, banks were in trouble and in need of capital and state budgets were threatened and in need of tax revenue. Seeking evidence of tax evasion, the French authorities raided the Paris headquarters of the Banque Commerciale de Bâle (Basel, Switzerland) on October 27, 1932. They found more than they expected, as they opened the files on several personages whose income had been hidden in the Swiss vaults. Depositors included two bishops, three senators, some ex-ministers, ten generals, the Peugeot brothers, and François Coty. (Coty, owner of a perfume enterprise, proprietor of the often anti-Semitic *Figaro*, and admirer of Mussolini, was elected senator for Corsica but lost his position after accusations of bribery.) A good portion of the French elite was implicated in this scandal with the accounts in the Banque de Bâle. Each time the French police inspected another bank, the same picture emerged. The scandal was immense: in Parliament, tax evasion was denounced amidst calls for action.

But change proved difficult. The French government asked to check the books of the bank in Basel itself, but the local authorities rejected the petition. France even imprisoned the director and vice director of the Paris branch of the Bank of Bâle, but to no avail; the books were not revealed.

Meanwhile, the Swiss authorities were in the process of preparation of a new law enhancing banking secrecy. Although the convenient legend was that this was motivated by the Nazi persecution of Jews (the first version of the Swiss law was drafted eighteen days after Hitler came to power), the real turning point was the French crackdown on tax evasion. It was finally approved in 1934.[50]

This was not the end of the story. When the US entered the Second World War in 1941, US authorities blocked the deposits of Swiss banks because they correctly suspected the Swiss authorities of excessive cooperation with the Axis interests. After the war, US authorities imposed two conditions for the release of those deposits: a thorough identification of Nazi assets in Switzerland; and the disclosure of the origin of the deposits in the US. It took more seventy years to extract some of the banking secrets of Switzerland.

In spite of this tenacious effort, exposing irregularities of financial powers can be dangerous, and whistleblowers in the fight against tax evasion have been prosecuted: Heinrich Kieber, who sold data from Liechtenstein banks to Germany in 2008, is listed as one of Interpol's most wanted criminals for violating Liechtenstein's cryptic banking laws; Brad Birkenfeld, who received a whistleblowing reward of US $104 million from US authorities for data on North American UBS clients, was nevertheless sentenced to three years in jail; and Rudolf Elmer, who worked in the Cayman office of a Zurich bank and accused it of tax evasion, was himself arrested.

[50] Guex (1999).

IF YOU'RE SMART, WHY AIN'T YOU RICH?

Finance, shadow or bright, cannot be understood without its oligarchs, a specific brand of people managing the financial movements, organizing social and institutional relations, brokering the deals, and getting out of trouble whenever required. Let's consider some revealing cases.

Stanley O'Neal, CEO of Merrill Lynch during 2005 and 2006, pushed mortgage-backed securities. By October 2007, after the subprime crash, he accepted that "The bottom line is, we—I—got it wrong by being overexposed to subprime, and we suffered as a result of impaired liquidity in that market. No one is more disappointed than I am in that result."[51] Disappointed as he was, he enjoyed a US $14 million bonus in 2006 and indicated his shame by negotiating a US $162 million severance package in 2007. When the Bank of America bought Merrill Lynch, on January 1 of the following year, the new CEO would discover that US $4 billion of bonus payments had been paid in advance the previous month, just before the new management came in. The oligarchs are part of the game and never give up.

The bonuses are generous even in hard times: in 2008, as the financial crisis was cresting, 1,626 employees of J.P. Morgan Chase received bonuses exceeding US $1 million; at Goldman Sachs 953 employees were that lucky with 212 receiving more than US $3 million. In all, in 2008, while the government disbursed US $243 billion in emergency assistance in order to rescue the banks, US $18 billion were diverted to be paid as bonuses. By September 2009, Goldman Sachs' sum was reduced to a paltry half a million per employee.[52]

In keeping with the best tournament-like compensation practices worked out by some economists,[53] the rewards must grow at the top. The year before the crash, the CEOs were awarded nice payments: James Cayne, of Bear Sterns, US $34 million, Richard Fuld, of Lehman Brothers, US $41 million, Lloyd Blankfein, of Goldman Sachs, US $55 million, Stanley O'Neal, of Merrill Lynch, US $48 million, John Mack, of Morgan Stanley, US $41 million, Charles Prince, of Citigroup, US $26 million, and Kenneth Lewis, of the Bank of America, US $28 million. Not bad.

Generous compensation during an expanding bubble is expected. But even during the year of the crash, 2007, Lloyd Blankfein of Goldman Sachs received US $54 million. John Thain of Merrill Lynch got US $84 million, and next year, the firm was sold to the Bank of America as the only solution to avoid the collapse. Richard Fuld, of Lehman Brothers, received US $21 million in 2007, the year of all perils; Kenneth Lewis, of the Bank of America, US $20 million; Charles Price, of Citigroup, in spite of the government rescue, got US $20 million and then US $38 million.[54] Angelo Mozillo, of Countrywide Financial, accepted a US $68 million fine for insider trading, which was paid in part by the Bank of America that bought the firm. Yet Mozillo had received US $522 million in bonuses and other executive payments from 2000 to 2008. Impressive pay for impressive performance.

[51] Johnson (2009). [52] Johnson and Kwak (2011), pp. 12, 116.

[53] Among them the New Institutional economists, Lazear and Rosen (1981); Milgrom and J. Roberts (1992).

[54] Wolf (2014), p. 150.

The oligarchs became more prudent for a while: Dimon, of J.P. Morgan, graciously volunteered to forgo a bonus in 2008, but still received US $19.7 million in stock awards.[55] Still, John Mack of Morgan Stanley got US $41 million.[56]

These bankers are smart and rich, as are so many others who got their comfortable rewards, in spite of their responsibility in major bankruptcies during and after the crash. Only one senior banker was convicted in the US after the subprime crash.

But they were unrepentant. Blankfein, the head of Goldman Sachs and a top bonus recipient, rejected any notion of abuse in these practices: "If you examine our practices on compensation, you will see a complete correlation throughout our history of having remuneration match performance over the long term."[57]

The bonuses paid during the years of 2007 and 2008 indicate the meaning of that "complete correlation," of course considering a savior "long term."

THE THREE SISTERS

Weren't they watched? You know the answer. The oversight committees indeed committed oversights. Greenspan, the supreme head of the supreme supervising agency, was "shocked" to discover what had been going on. Other supervisors said the same. But they should not have been alone in the forest of finance. Other powerful institutions should have been setting market rules, but instead they were part of the market and playing the game. They are the rating agencies.

Three decades of financial innovation produced a cornucopia of sophisticated products. One of the authors of this book recalls a conversation with the President of his country, a distinguished attorney innocent of the shifting world of finance, who recalled asking a leading banker for some details on short selling and other financial operations, only to receive the answer that the banker himself could not understand the transactions he was promoting. From each crisis new products emerged, with assets transformed into derivatives, or derivatives insured by additional derivatives, a growing chain of diversity and complexity.

The path of innovation was chosen to avoid regulation, to limit the required capital, to increase leverage, and, ultimately, to maximize profits. Indeed, the banking system used to be the most regulated province of finance. The special purpose vehicle was mobilized specifically to clear debt from the balance sheets and relax the requirement to use capital as a funding cushion for that debt. Mortgage loans and other assets could be stripped out of the balance sheets, transformed into securities, and sold. These securities were collateral debt obligations and they were packaged in successively different forms with the "synthetic CDO" as the most distilled form and with payments backed by portfolios of insurance contracts on credits (or credit default swaps), instruments well removed from actual monthly mortgage payments on housing debt. As an historian puts it, "they were backed

[55] Johnson and Kwak (2011), pp. 58–9; Freeland (2014), p. 167.
[56] *New York Times*, April 5, 2008. [57] *Sunday Times*, November 8, 2009.

by nothing more than the promise of the issuer to pay in the event that the default in question occurred."[58]

Someone was supposed to be minding the store. Even in the case of complicated assets transacted between sophisticated parties, "trust me" requires something more than a handshake.[59] The rating agencies are supposed to be the pillars of trust.

Rating agencies investigate and proclaim the quality and risk of debt. The three largest agencies, Standard & Poor's, Moody's, and Fitch, each use similar rating systems to describe the probability of default for a particular type of debt. All three rank Prime bonds with very low risk at AAA, and the scales vary slightly. For example, Moody's describes investment-grade corporate bonds as BAA, while Fitch and Standard & Poor's use a BBB designation. Once the rating is issued, the seller and potential buyers of the bond should be in significant agreement about the default risk of the bond and pricing, in terms of the interest rate to be paid, and can proceed accordingly. For historical reasons and very significantly as we shall see, the issuer pays for the rating agency's investigative effort.

Standard & Poor's and Moody's each represent around 40 percent of the world rating market (by the end of 2013 S&P rated 1.1 million and Moody's 0.9 million issues), and Fitch, the smaller sister, around 14 percent. All together, this is around 95 percent of the market, a dominant position that is virtually unparalleled in any other market, as heavy regulation makes it difficult to create new agencies.

All three agencies choose the recipe and the ingredients and collect handsome fees: the payments vary from 1.2 to 1.5 percent of the value of the rated financial paper. These agencies also advise lenders on how to structure Collateralized Debt Obligations (CDOs), advise buyers on what to buy, advise the markets on the perspectives for profit. The introduction of new products and any growth in uncertainty increases profits for these firms. Shares of Moody's have gone up sixfold since 2009, and the three agencies have raised their prices by 4 percent per year since 2010, proving again that a crisis can lead to good business.

Their advice not only establishes the conditions for issuing debt; the rating agencies are themselves an investment opportunity. Fitch, the smallest of the three sisters, is part of the French group Fimalac, S&P is owned by McGraw-Hill, and Moody's, until 2000 a subsidiary of Dun and Bradstreet, now boasts Warren Buffett as its largest shareholder.[60] But interest is broad: Vanguard holds 5.02 percent of Moody's and 6.9 percent of S&P, T. Rowe Price has 2.61 percent and 4.81 percent, Alliance Bernstein 3.94 percent and 1.63 percent, Capital World Investments 12.6 percent and 9.99 percent respectively. As a result, four of the largest shareholders are common to both firms, owning 24.17 percent in Moody's (with Buffett holding another 10 percent) and 23.33 percent in S&P. The sisters augur for the world and a small group of shareholders simultaneously hold two of the three.

There are no neutrals here: the investors get their money from firms advising and rating investments, their own and the competitors'. To make matters worse, it is the issuer of the bond who chooses among the three rating agencies and pays

[58] Eichengreen (2015), pp. 75–6.

[59] As Fons (2008), noted in his testimony before the House Committee on Government Oversight and Reform.

[60] Cassidy (2009), p. 263.

for the service of rating. Anxious to maintain market share, the rating agencies are under constant pressure to provide favorable ratings or to watch their business go elsewhere. Jerome Fons, an economist at the Fed who spent several years at Moody's, testifying in the US House of Representative, put it bluntly: "a large part of the blame can be placed on the inherent conflicts of interest found in the issuer-pays business model and rating shopping by issuers of structured securities. [...] Originators of structured securities typically chose the agency with the lowest standards, engendering a race to the bottom in terms of rating quality."[61]

One could still imagine problems if, say, the bond buyers paid, but the issuer-pays model greatly decreases the scrutiny in what should be an adversarial investigative process. The race to the bottom, with its adventurous and imaginative innovations, could not even exist if the markets, in their infinite wisdom, were not led to trust. But, if trust can be proclaimed, the new products will flourish, as they did.

If the potential conflict of interests would not be enough, the public indications by these firms delivered poorly, mostly during crises, precisely when their information was most crucial. In fact, their negative record is impressive. In 2001, just four days before the bankruptcy of Enron, all three rating agencies still recommended buying shares of the energy giant. During the Great Crash, the highest rating of triple-A was awarded to AIG and to Bear Stearns shortly before both were nationalized to avoid going out of business. Lehman Brothers got the same positive rating by all three agencies until minutes before bankruptcy was declared. Freddie Mac was proudly awarded A1, until Warren Buffett trumpeted his reservations, and Moody's felt forced to downgrade it by five degrees; it was immediately nationalized.

Lloyd Blankfein, head of Goldman Sachs, noted that on the eve of the crash only twelve firms globally were rated triple-A while 64,000 structured financial instruments garnered the triple-A designation.[62] Furthermore, as the criteria of the rating agencies are that the damaging notation is BB+ or below, considered to be junk, and "investment grade" is BBB- or higher, evidence shows that the agencies are so frequently wrong that they are not to be trusted. Historical evidence from S&P notations proves that, for BBB American corporate bonds, 1.1 percent default three years later; for BB, 4.8 percent default, but for B-rated issues, the figure is 14.7 percent, or increasing noted risk implies decreasing default rates.[63] Therefore, the evidence is that notations are artificial if not misleading.

After all these failures, the rating agencies were criticized for excessive proximity with some firms and conflicts of interest. In 2013, the US Department of Justice filed a civil suit for US $5,000 million against S&P for inflating the ratings of CDOs and mortgage-backed securities, presenting internal mails as proof that the managers of some accounts intentionally misinformed their clients. A curious note of that process is evidence that, in response to a damaging *Fortune* article, the company preferred to hire someone to improve the public relations and press service instead of revising its procedures.[64] Some official action followed, although it was inconsequential. Business went on as usual.

[61] Fons (2008). [62] Blankfein (2009). [63] *The Economist*, April 23, 2015.
[64] US Department of Justice quoted in Eichengreen (2015), pp. 78–9.

In other cases, charges were presented against the three sisters for wrongdoings in disservice to transparency and information for the market. In the US, the SEC was mandated to create an Office of Credit Ratings in order to supervise the rating agencies, under the Dodd-Frank Act.[65] Yet, it required that regulations imposing ratings be subject to further deliberation and consultation and nothing happened.

In the European Union, the alarm rang earlier but to no purpose.

In December 2010, a bill for the regulation of the rating agencies was approved and then amended the following May. The law increased the frequency of rating updates from annual to semi-annual, forbade dominant shareholders from owning more than 5 percent in any of the sisters, and defined rules for more public information. But the EU rejected the proposal of a publicly funded rating agency. The rating agencies understood the message: they would have no competition.

Despite the catastrophic failure of the rating agencies to distinguish the best possible investment from garbage, the financial markets would not have another source of rating risk on titles and debt. The markets should renew their trust in the producers of the most toxic systemic mistakes.

GOLDMAN SACHS, SO CLOSE TO GOD

One may wonder why nobody at the major institutions noticed the crisis coming, from regulators to rating agencies and other institutions. Why were so many people so surprised, as Jamie Dimon's daughter and the Queen of England naively asked, when the financial crisis spread from Lehman Brothers to other banks and institutions?

Alerts had come both from official bodies and from astute academic observers. Economists Robert Shiller and Dean Baker and journalist John Cassidy pointed out the housing bubble—on the basis of deviation of rents from prices.[66] Nouriel Roubini, who made it his trade, predicted the crash.[67]

Others expressed suspicion of the major players in the financial market. Mark Carney, an alumnus of Goldman Sachs who headed the Bank of Canada for thirteen years saw signs. After the crash, he moved to the Bank of England and directed the Financial Stability Board set by the G20 to investigate wrongdoing in financial speculation. When Carney confronted Blankfein over regulation in 2011, they quarreled in public. Carney personified the worried central banker who hopes never to see another month like September 2008.[68]

Lloyd Blankfein, CEO of Goldman Sachs, the most powerful of all investment banks, assiduously cultivates his own legend. His tone is controversial and defiant, defending the record of his company and of the financial system during and after the Great Crash of 2007. As early as November 2009, he was interviewed by the London *Times*, which asked him to justify the monumental compensation of managers and analysts whose work led to the crisis and to huge losses for their clients. The *Wall Street Journal* eagerly reprinted the interview:

[65] Eichengreen (2015), pp. 78–9.
[66] D. Baker (2002); Case and Shiller (2003); Cassidy (2004).
[67] Roubini (2006). [68] Freeland (2014), p. 332.

> Is it possible to make too much money? "Is it possible to have too much ambition? Is it possible to be too successful?" Blankfein shoots back. "I don't want people in this firm to think that they have accomplished as much for themselves as they can and go on vacation. As the guardian of the interests of the shareholders and, by the way, for the purposes of society, I'd like them to continue to do what they are doing. I don't want to put a cap on their ambition. It's hard for me to argue for a cap on their compensation."
>
> So, it's business as usual, then, regardless of whether it makes most people howl at the moon with rage? Goldman Sachs, this pillar of the free market, breeder of super-citizens, object of envy and awe will go on raking it in, getting richer than God? An impish grin spreads across Blankfein's face. Call him a fat cat who mocks the public. Call him wicked. Call him what you will. He is, he says, just a banker "doing God's work".[69]

And so "doing God's work," became the *motum* for Blankfein's legend. Yet, in spite of the glamour of such work, the reality is somber.

Goldman Sachs developed multiple lines of operation across the world. After the crash problems compounded. Goldman Sachs was accused of helping past Greek governments to doctor national accounts and hide deficits. With some of the European statistical authorities looking the other way, Goldman advised Greece to register as "currency trades" cash advances obtained in exchange for future income on airport landing fees and the national lottery.[70] Goldman also explained how to hide costs of acquisition of material for the armed forces, an important expense for Greece. These practices damaged the ability of the Greek authorities to manage their budget and external commitments and ultimately damaged Greece's reputation. The stories end sadly for Greece but not for Mario Draghi, who headed the European branch of Goldman Sachs at the time of these exploits and went on to become governor of the ECB in charge of punishing Greece for, among other things, its failure to present clean accounts. God's position is that of power, not of accountability.

In the US, Goldman Sachs earned fees by creating and distributing mortgage-backed securities, earning fees for that while the bank was betting its own money against its products.[71] The justification for the procedure was that the investors should be sophisticated enough to understand what they were about, in spite of the fact that they were paying Goldman Sachs precisely to get advice on how to deal with uncertainty and risk. The Department of Justice investigated the matter but found not enough evidence to sue, but the Securities and Exchange Commission still obtained from the firm a settlement for US $550 million. A US Senate subcommittee concluded in 2011 that Goldman Sachs had misled investors in this matter. Some years later Goldman Sachs agreed to pay another fine, of five billion, for fraud with mortgage-backed securities.[72]

Goldman Sachs vice president Tourre was in deeper trouble because an email surfaced showing that in January 2007 he anticipated the crash, even if he did put himself in the place of God, a surviving but slightly ignorant God: "The whole building is about to collapse anytime now [...]. Only potential survivor, the fabulous Fab[rice] [...] standing in the middle of all these complex, highly leveraged, exotic trades he created without necessarily understanding all implications

[69] Phillips (2009). [70] Eichengreen (2015), p. 94; Clark, Stewart, and Moya (2010).
[71] Eichengreen (2015), p. 168. [72] Ibid., 436–437, and *The Economist*, January 23, 2016.

of those monstrosities."[73] The fabulous Fabrice, in the fabric of God, discovered the "exotic trades he created without necessarily understanding all implications of those monstrosities." No one could put it better.

Nevertheless, by its very nature, this God's work was not supervised or even verified in most cases (and it could father these "monstrosities"). But that seems to be the deep meaning of Blankfein's claim about his firm's own role in the global economy.

But this God of business still worked in another direction, that of political connections: four out of seven of the last Treasury Secretaries of the US came from Goldman Sachs,[74] as well as many other high-ranking officers in different administrations, a topic we discussed in Chapter 8 on the revolving door between finance and politics.

CONCLUSION

After the ideologues, the academics and opinion makers, the indoctrinators and the managers, and the central bankers, we turned in this chapter to the financiers and their dealings. Offshores, imaginative frauds, legal schemes, daring maneuvers, coziness with governments and other authorities, we found substantial evidence for that confession by a banker according to whom, "if you ain't cheating, you ain't trying."

The portrait of these shadow movements is crony capitalism, with high rewards to failed bankers, farcical regulations, dense connections between powerful firms and central banks and the executive power, and a wonderful sense of opportunity by the major players. "At the outset of the crisis, the oligarchs are usually among the first to get extra help from the government," wrote an ex-chief economist at the IMF.[75] In some cases, even the disgraced bankers try to get something out of their misadventures: the former CEO of AIG, Hank Greenberg, sued the US government for illegal bailout and requested 25 billion in damages.[76] One is reminded of the patricide who begs the mercy of the court as an orphan.

They are always trying and sometimes cheating, and they get away with it most of the time.

[73] Quoted in the complaint *US Securities and Exchange Commission v. Goldman Sachs & Co.* and Fabrice Tourre (2010).

[74] Freeland (2014), p. 357.

[75] Johnson (2009).

[76] Walsh (2014). Nine years later Greenberg settled and eventually agreed to pay a fine but denied any wrongdoing (*New York Times*, February 10, 2017).

10

Capital Controls: The Emergency Brakes

Joseph Stiglitz, a Nobel Prize winner who has devoted much of his intellectual powers over the past decade to advocating a social reorganization that would tame finance, put it bluntly: "capital account liberalization was the single most important factor leading to the crisis."[1] No less. As Chair of the Council of Economic Advisers of the Clinton White House and senior vice president of the World Bank, Stiglitz witnessed firsthand how major economies tremble under the impact of financial perturbations. To understand the crises we need, like Stiglitz, to follow the trail of capital account liberalization.

This has been the argument of this book so far, as we have unveiled a shadow world in which indoctrination, the revolving door, and other efficient mechanisms of social consolidation and power increased the risks of global financial crises with toxic products and unbounded greed. In this chapter we will discuss a possible back door: the mechanisms of capital control. As we shall see, that door has been known and recognized for many years, but liberalization creates further obstacles in the way of recourse to the required measures to protect economies and societies.

THE TRADITION OF CAPITAL CONTROLS

The question of capital movement and its regulation has a distinguished lineage in economic theory. For most of the modern epoch, the key actors—nations, banks, and international institutions—accepted that flows of capital should be monitored and managed by governments with significant support even for active direction. John Maynard Keynes advocated that "control of capital movements, both inward and outward, should be a permanent feature of the postwar system," a basis for a rational and safe international monetary exchange system.[2] At the Bretton Woods conference, both Keynes, for the British delegation, and Harry Dexter White, leading the North American delegation,[3] proposed a double check

[1] Stiglitz (2003), p. 99. [2] US Department of State (1948).

[3] Dexter White, the chief international economist at the US Treasury in 1942–4, led the US delegation to Bretton Woods. It is now well established that, for ideological reasons, he regularly passed information to the Soviet government. The IMF denied this for some time, then accepted the fact but reduced the evidence to some "meetings" and finally recognized the dual role of White: "there is enough reliable evidence from Soviet archives to suggest that White clandestinely gave information to Soviet intelligence, although it is impossible to know how much," as reported in Rauchway (2013). See also Boughton (1998). See also the thorough investigation by Steil (2013).

on capital movements, at "both ends" of the capital flows, tracking and managing the flow of capital from origin to destination.

For that purpose, Article VI of the 1944 founding Agreement of the IMF dealt with capital transfers, affirming that "Members may exercise such controls as are necessary to regulate international capital movements, but no member may exercise these controls in a manner which will restrict payments for current transactions or which will unduly delay transfers of funds in settlement of commitments." In summary, short of reneging on payments immediately due, nation states could control capital flow across their borders.[4] National control of capital flows went hand-in-hand with the coordination of exchange rates under the Bretton Woods system.[5]

The question was debated because *laissez-faire* advocates have long rejected the notion of public management of capital flows. Harrod, the most distinguished disciple of Keynes, rejected his mentor's views on this point. Yet Keynes was adamant and, in a 1942 letter to Harrod, he argued:

> I disagree most strongly with your view that the control of capital movements may very possibly be unnecessary . . . I see no reason to feel confidence that the more stable conditions [of the post-war era] will remove the more dangerous movements [of capital]. These are likely to be caused by political issues. Surely in the post-war years there is hardly a country in which we ought not to expect keen political discussions affecting the position of the wealthier classes and the treatment of private property. If so, there will be a number of people constantly taking fright because they think the degree of leftism in one country looks for the time being likely to be greater than somewhere else.
>
> [Moreover,] you overlook the most fundamental long-run theoretical reason. Freedom of capital movements is an essential part of the old *laissez-faire* system and assumes that it is right and desirable to have an equalisation of interest rates in all parts of the world [. . .]. In my view the whole management of the domestic economy depends upon being free to have the appropriate rate of interest without reference to the rates prevailing elsewhere in the world. Capital control is a corollary to this.[6]

Keynes continued by noting "advisable domestic policies might be easier to compass if the phenomenon known as the 'flight of capital' could be ruled out."

It is a different world from our own in which capital control was presumed as a corollary to domestic management of the economy. Indeed, for four fine decades in the middle of the twentieth century, sovereign states were presumed to have the right and duty to manage interest rates with the aim of full employment. Although international interest rate differentials might create temptations for the "wealthier classes" to relocate assets to more tempting shores, international cooperation should prevent them from doing so.

[4] Nevertheless, it should be noted that "legally speaking, they (the IMF countries) enjoy full freedom to regulate capital movements. This does not apply to countries that have given up this freedom, in part or in total, by their membership of the OECD, of the euro area, or that they have signed bilateral investment agreements or free trade agreements with the United States," Paulo Nogueira Batista (2012), p. 98.

[5] Fourcade and Babb argue that this postwar consensus was convenient since capital controls were used in order to avoid upsetting pegged exchange rates, so that governments could concentrate on domestic policies, Fourcade-Gourinchas and Babb (2002), p. 537.

[6] Keynes (1980), pp. 148–9.

In fact, international coordination via the Bretton Woods system gave nation states the power to control the movement of capital across their borders. Indeed, they used this capacity.[7] In 1947, Britain itself, for more than a century preceding the Second World War the guarantor and chief advocate of the free movement of capital, imposed the Exchange Control Act which forced all external flows of capital to be denominated in pounds, a rule that prevailed until 1979. The Companies Acts of 1948 and 1967, the Prevention of Frauds Act of 1958, and the Protection of Depositors Act of 1963 strengthened these controls. Like Britain, the other developed economies protected against destabilizing the flow of capital.

Keynes carried the day—which helped to launch the Golden Age, or the *Trente Glorieuses*, the long period of intensive growth in the most developed economies following the Second World War. But much would change three decades later with the collapse of the Bretton Woods system.

THE CASE FOR FREE CIRCULATION OF CAPITAL

The Bretton Woods system persisted until its breakdown in the early 1970s, which opened the opportunity for a major change. Stretched by domestic political and social demands and imperial war abroad (and the defeat in Vietnam) the United States government exploited the dollar's position as international currency. The overvalued dollar was among several significant imbalances that developed in the Bretton Woods system. The system was not shredded but holes had opened up, and *laissez-faire* policy entrepreneurs stepped artfully into the gap, as a response to the social tensions and political dangers. As a result, the neoliberal era was inaugurated by Reagan and Thatcher at the same time that controls on the international movement of capital were dismantled. At the time, the new pieces were perceived as fragmented, provisional, and experimental. In retrospect, armed with the concept of neoliberalism, we can see the emergence of a whole cloth revisioning of domestic and international relations.

Even in the heyday of the Bretton Woods regime, the powers of the shadow economy were gathering force. In the decades following the end of the Second World War, the IMF and other international institutions fought for reconsideration of the previous restrictive views encapsulated in the original agreement. Another prime mover for change was the argument developed by academics: working independently yet simultaneously in academia, Milton Friedman, Paul Samuelson, and Robert Mundell built a forceful intellectual case for capital mobility. The case rested on three propositions.

First, Friedman argued that speculators are never destabilizing. Indeed, speculators will drive the market quickly towards equilibrium, and a speculator who bets the wrong way, i.e., in the destabilizing direction against the "natural" equilibrium, punishes no one but himself. While the proposition is obviously false to survivors (and victims) of Great Crashes, the simplicity of the indisputable theoretical construction, the fading from collective memory of the speculative excesses of the

[7] Ferguson (2014), p. 68fn.

1920s, and the lure of profit in financial markets brought this perspective (back) into fashion.

Second, physical capital should move to places where its marginal productivity is higher. Respected theoretical work as well as the actual rapid growth of emerging economies in the postwar world created an argument that unimpeded movement of capital would favor development.[8] With rising standards of living for workers in the industrialized countries temporarily muting zero-sum considerations, additional capital movement towards areas of efficient use would appear to benefit both the users of capital in the less-developed world and the owners of capital. Knowledge transfer associated with the migration of capital would be an additional benefit. Such movement might even undermine the monopolistic power of entrenched local elites, even giving the proposition some currency on the US liberal left let alone among the standard bearers for *laissez-faire*.

Third comes the idea that exchange rate adjustments in currency markets can permit smooth adjustment of international imbalances. The Mundell-Fleming model both illustrated the limits of policy for small open economies and also provided a vision of a future free of the tyranny of the Gold Standard, which had aggravated the Great Depression.[9] According to this view, with floating exchange rates set in foreign-exchange markets, international imbalances could be relatively painlessly resolved by market-driven exchange-rate adjustments. The currency of a country with a surplus in the trade balance would experience appreciation pressure, and the appreciation would resolve the surplus—consumers in the country with the appreciating currency would happily buy more stuff. Similarly the currency of a country in deficit would tend to depreciate and, if permitted to do so in open foreign exchange markets, to resolve the deficit. Delay in adjustment, created by ultimately futile government policy, would create hard landings. In particular, these theories even demonstrated the opportunity for macroeconomic recovery from regional recessions if only local currencies could adjust.

The last two arguments in particular are noteworthy for their view of the beneficence of markets. It would be a mistake to overlook the rhetoric of fairness that appears in the arguments. Indeed variants of these arguments had some purchase on the left. Access to capital for development received solid support from the New Deal coalition still dominant in the United States through the late 1960s, both for humanitarian reasons and with an eye to developing new markets for US products. With respect to foreign exchange, Abba Lerner, parent of functional finance,[10] developed an analog to Mundell's optimal-currency areas. There was a significant left critique—shared as well by nationalists such as de Gaulle—of the hegemonic dollar standard that replaced the Gold Standard and permitted the United States

[8] The intellectual building blocks of that approach were the contributions by Heckscher and Ohlin and by Stolper and Samuelson.

[9] Robert Mundell (1932–) and Marcus Fleming (1911–76) extended the IS-LM model, a neoclassical representation of the Keynesian model, in order to apply it to an open economy, considering not only the interest rate and output but also the exchange rate and trade balance. Their research led to the conclusion that an economy cannot maintain simultaneously autonomous monetary policy, free circulation of capital, and a fixed exchange rate.

[10] Abba Lerner (1903–82) studied under the supervision of Hayek, but moved in another intellectual direction, namely formulating the idea of functional finance, defined by the achievement of goals such as full employment.

to spend "beyond its means" with effectively international seigniorage privilege. More recently, some critical voices on the left have adopted essentially a Mundell-Fleming type of critique of the euro, arguing for its inevitable unsustainability without a capacity for inter-regional adjustment in exchange rates.

Thus, it is important to realize that we cannot and should not "go home again" to a Golden Age that was rife with contradictions and power imbalances. Yet in both its intellectual and practical aspects, capital mobility in the neoliberal system offered a one-word solution at every turn—liberalize—with disastrous consequences.

With respect to the second case for the liberalization of capital movement, i.e., to encourage the efficient flow of capital to places with high marginal productivity as a tool for development, the evidence was weak at best. There is a highly contested literature on how capital-account liberalization affected the cost of capital, investment, and economic growth in less-developed countries.[11] In any case, the evidence for growth enhancement under business-as-usual conditions is not clear-cut. There was a growing body of evidence that fast-moving capital contributes to the frequency and intensity of crises in emerging markets and this was driven home when, some decades after Reagan-Thatcher gave form to modern *laissez-faire*, the "flat globe" of capital movements was shocked by such huge financial perturbations.

STORMS INSIDE THE IMF

So grave was the financial shock ignited by the subprime crash in 2007 and 2008 that the liberal canon was questioned from within. No less a veteran of the IMF than Kenneth Rogoff argued, in a book with his co-author Carmen Reinhart, that periods of liberalization of capital flows have been more prone to crashes and banking crises.[12] Indeed, such crashes and crises were current in the years preceding their book.

Emergency response opened the door for the reemergence of capital controls. As a matter of fact, having held the line for capital mobility during the Asian crisis of 1997–8, the IMF was more open to experimentation on recourse to capital control measures after the subprime crash. Perhaps the facts had done more than dent the theorist's hide. In any case, the IMF itself nurtured the breakdown of the previous dogmatic consensus.[13]

The actual emergence of the new capital controls was similar in character to a Kuhn-type scientific revolution—experimentation at the margins. Latvia and Iceland, both small countries engulfed at the center of the major global crisis beginning in 2007–8, imposed capital controls, even on outflows. In both cases the controls were imposed before the agreement with the IMF, in the breach and in the spirit of experimentation, but the international institution did not challenge them, accepting the fait accompli of "stringent capital controls," even on outflows.[14]

[11] Levine (1997); Arestis and Demetriades (1997); Henry (2007).

[12] Reinhart and Rogoff (2009), pp. 92–4, 205, 403.

[13] Grabel (2011), pp. 807, 816.

[14] Ibid., p. 819–20.

Shortly after those experiences, a joint IMF-WB report (2009) listed six other countries—substantially larger economies—imposing capital controls during the crisis: China, Colombia, Ecuador, Indonesia, Russia, and Ukraine. (South Korea could be added to the list.) The joint report presented the argument verbatim: "nonetheless, capital controls might need to be imposed as a last resort to help mitigate a financial crisis or stabilize macroeconomic developments."[15] If you are living through a crisis, nontraditional remedies may be acceptable, or, in other words, the door had opened.

In February 2010, the IMF published a staff report acknowledging that, for the previous fifteen years, capital account regulations had been fairly effective. By March 2011, the executive board of the IMF discussed a "possible framework" for provisional measures of capital control and published guidelines for using capital controls. For that, a new and elegant acronym was proposed: CFMs, capital flow management measures, including macroprudential measures and capital controls. Management sounds more technical and less conspicuous, avoiding the stigma of the notion of control. For the IMF, these would be last resort measures, to be taken only temporarily and after the accumulation of sufficient reserves and adjusting interest rates; furthermore, the controls should be price-based and avoid "discrimination" against foreign agents.

Thus, it did not come as a complete surprise when, in 2012, the IMF, a stronghold of traditional views in finance and economic policy, issued a report accepting that "under certain circumstances" capital controls would be acceptable.[16] Shortly after that report, Cyprus provided a new case for the argument.[17]

Yet the opposite view maintains a firm hold. Liberalization has been the standard for decades, firmly entrenched since the Reagan-Thatcher ideological revolution in the early 1980s. Most changes in capital control regimes over this period operated in the direction of liberalization. An examination of 664 cases of changes in capital control regimes in emerging countries during the 2000s found that fully 274 changes constituted an easing on restriction of outflows, by far the largest case in the sample, with other forms of liberalization constituting much of the remainder. That was the dogma and that was what happened under the watch of the IMF.[18]

The recourse to capital controls was instead challenged by the deregulators: even as cracks and fissures appeared, defenders of the faith argue that, outside the case of Malaysia, there is little evidence for the usefulness of capital controls.[19] Given the debate, the new proposals of the IMF 2012 report were not unnoticed. But, as we have just pointed out, it was not a surprise move. The previous year, the board of the IMF was mandated to prepare "further work on a comprehensive, flexible, and balanced approach for the management of capital flows." The result was the list of recommendations, approved by Olivier Blanchard, an MIT professor who was then the head of the Research Department of the IMF, and others. Although the language is elliptical, the report acknowledges that liberalization is "less risky"

[15] World Bank and International Monetary Fund (2009), p. 65.

[16] *The Economist*, December 13, 2014.

[17] As we recounted earlier, Ban (2015), describes the development of the contrarian case within the IMF.

[18] Aizenman and Pasricha (2013).

[19] Magud, Reinhart, and Rogoff (2011); Kaplan and Rodrik (2001).

if "countries have reached a "certain level or thresholds of financial and institutional development," with the tacit implication that it is risky otherwise. Thus, the CFMs, the capital flow management measures, could eventually be recommended only in order to limit capital inflows and to impose prudential measures "under certain circumstances, if capital flows pose risks to macroeconomic or financial system stability." The report certainly suggests that the reimposition of CFMs, a tool widely used in the past by pre-liberalized economies, should be "targeted, transparent and generally temporary."[20]

That may not be the case, since the IMF has a long record of biased action. Professor Jeffrey, a researcher at LSE, London, studied the effect of this change of heart at the IMF and noted that, after the Asian crisis, there was an attempt even to amend the statutes of the institution in order to include the forced commitment of governments to remove all forms of capital control and requiring the IMF to approve any momentary reintroduction of such action. Although the proposal failed, it indicated a movement. Afterwards, in particular as a response to long-term contestation, the IMF accepted "endorsing controls more strongly but refraining from fundamentally assaulting the long-run desirability of freedom of capital movements."[21]

Other economists saw a broader opening and have taken a more radical view, pointing out the severe dangers of free capital flows with little evidence for compensation by growth-enhancing effects. Indeed, free capital flows increase the volatile exchange rates, increase risk of both emergency and endemic capital flight, and reduce the capacity of independent monetary policy. The radicals will consider permanent quantity-based capital controls as effective measures for counter-cyclical policy. They are furthermore willing to distinguish agents by residence (to "discriminate against foreigners") to protect the national economies from external pressures.[22]

Paulo Nogueira Batista, the executive director of IMF for Brazil and other Latin American countries, voiced a critical view of his own institution, given the "hesitant nature of the IMF's recent shift toward the acceptance of capital account regulations" and conceding that "one of the worst things that can happen to a country is to fall into the good graces of international capital markets," with the emerging countries getting an uncontrolled inflow of capital.[23] Noting the error of the standard approach for large capital inflows, leading to a currency appreciation and relaxing capital outflows restrictions, Nogueira Baptista challenged this orientation and claimed it led to failure. Furthermore, after the 2007–8 crash, "as time goes by, we will probably come to realize that capital account management policies may be necessary not only in emerging markets but also in advanced economies."[24]

In spite of the novelty and relevance of the new approach discussed at the IMF, two other distinguished scholars noted that this was not the dominant view and challenged the rationale of the traditional approach. For this purpose, Eichengreen and Rose discussed the two dominant justifications for capital controls in the IMF-led literature: (1) large inflows, caused by a decline in world interest rates, should

[20] Blanchard, Hagan, et al. (2012), pp. 35–6. Other authors suggest the acceptance by the IMF of capital controls, Gabor (2015); Gallagher (2015).

[21] Chwieroth (2014), p. 4.

[22] Gallagher, Griffith-Jones, and Ocampo (2012), p. 3.

[23] Paulo Nogueira Batista (2012), pp. 94–5.

[24] Ibid.

be prevented in order to avoid wage increases, and (2) large outflows should be prevented in order to avoid financial instability, the latter being the topic of the IMF preoccupation. In both cases, measures of capital control are presented as the second best alternatives to traditional monetary and financial policies. But this does not match with reality, according to Eichengreen and Rose. Following their research, governments have rarely imposed capital control as a response to short-term fluctuations in output, terms of trade, or financial conditions.

But that certainly happened in Iceland, 2008, as the government was confronted with a massive outflow of capital, and similar intervention was approved by the Eurozone authorities for Cyprus in, 2013, as the banking system collapsed. Nevertheless, these are the exception rather than the rule, they write: capital control regimes are not responses to emergencies but rather strategies to change the internal conditions of a stressed economy and, when they are imposed, controls are persistent and not temporary, since "the capital control regime is slow moving, almost glacial."[25] Their explanation for such an evolution is that the new regimes imply redistributional effects, and therefore require the establishment of coalitions that would prevent changes of these regimes afterwards.

The contestants know what is at stake. The evidence confirms that a capital control regime, once established, is persistent. For the fifty-one examples they investigate of re-imposition of controls after a period of liberalization, persistence is the dominant case. From this evidence, they conclude that "capital controls are not strongly correlated with exchange rate regimes, financial crisis, or fluctuations in other macroeconomic and financial variables," they are rather connected to the quality of regulatory institutions, all moving slowly.[26]

Liberalization was not the only possible answer to international financial imbalances in the 1970s but it was the answer that fit with the political agenda of the new dominant political configurations, led by neoliberal policies, and it was the answer that took hold and pushed out all alternatives. It was also the name of the game: in order to prevent major challenges to the prevailing economic order, neoliberal solutions radicalized the protection of capital accumulation and circulation, including tax fraud and evasion. So, in the framework of the international debates on the opacity of capital flows, the hardliners continue to reject any intervention in capital mobility. But the IMF has allowed heterodoxy—heresy?—to get its foot in the door.

The IMF apostates fall into several camps, all opposed to the liberalized orthodoxy. Beginning with the most cautious break with orthodoxy, some would control inflows as a prudential matter but would stand out of the way on outflows. Bolder interventions might add temporary outflow restrictions as a reasonable response to emergency. Bolder still would include control on both inflow and outflow as appropriate tools for guiding long-term development.

In any case, the apostates are catching up with actual practice. Historically, governments have to establish limits to capital outflows not as a short-term response to financial threats, although that happened in rather exceptional cases, but as a tool to repair long-term economic damage and imbalances. Capital control is not only a counter-cyclical emergency kit to be used after a crash or a disturbance, it can be a tool for structural repair.

[25] Eichengreen and Rose (2014), p. 2. [26] Ibid., p. 9.

PROTECTION EVERYWHERE

Protection against uncontrolled capital flows appears therefore to be common, as several cases indicate.

In the early 1990s, in response to a financial and banking crisis, North European governments established strict measures of capital control, including a comprehensive nationalization of banks.[27] The Finnish government merged more than forty banks into one public savings bank and the Swedish government took control of the two largest banks and created a bad bank for toxic assets.

For the whole period 1991–2001, Chile ruled that a proportion of earnings of foreign companies should be kept in Chilean deposit accounts paying no interest.[28] Uruguay imposed capital controls in 1998, after the Asian crisis, although this was a short-lived decision reversed the following year. Indonesia, South Korea, and Thailand followed with temporary capital controls.[29] In the last case, the country never entirely dismantled several capital controls as the central bank issued guidelines to monitor credit to non-residents and directed the financial institutions to refrain from buying and selling certain debt instruments to non-residents. In 2006 at the high-water mark of liberalization, Thailand established a forceful reserve requirement, similar to Chile's, on inward foreign investment.[30]

Brazil has a long record of capital control. For example, since 1962 Brazil has required registration of transfers of capital with the central bank; many of these measures were lifted during the last decade, under the governments of Lula da Silva and Dilma Rousseff. Some economists dispute the effectiveness of the measures, but a new wave of capital controls was introduced in 2009. At least one intervention, a 2011 tax targeting offshore equity derivatives, generated a desired depreciation of the Brazilian currency, the real, by as much as 10 percent.[31] Chamon and Garcia, writing for an IMF conference, conclude that these measures obtained a major positive result. The measures were effective in isolating Brazilian finance from the contagious crisis in global financial markets and "controls may have helped Brazil to avoid a bubble and perhaps worse." As they investigate the cocktail of measures that both loosened and tightened capital controls between 2009 and 2011, they conclude that Brazil largely avoided bubbles over this period. The same authors point out the controls of inflows, such as those in Chile (1991–8) and Colombia (1993–8 and 2007–8) had less impact, except for "tilting the composition of flows towards longer maturities," a nevertheless crucial anti-speculative feature.[32]

Closer inspection of these measures reveals the ingenuity and diversity of the protections. In October 2009, Brazil imposed a tax on portfolio investment, which provoked a mild reaction from the world institutions. Strauss-Kahn, then director of the IMF, said "I have no ideology on this" and accepted that capital controls are "not something that come from hell."[33] The following year, in October 2010, this control was strengthened, and in March 2011 new controls on the purchase

[27] Cassidy (2009), p. 321.

[28] *The Economist*, October 12, 2013. In Thailand, the measures for capital control were reversed in some days, as the result of a coup (December 2006).

[29] Grabel (2011), p. 12. [30] Eichengreen and Rose (2014), pp. 5, 10.

[31] Chamon and Garcia (2016). [32] Ibid., pp. 2, 24. [33] Grabel (2012), p. 62.

of farmland by foreigners were approved, aimed at managing the pressure of Chinese investment. Brazil additionally approved a 6 percent tax on repatriated funds raised through international bond sales and loans with maturity up to two years. In August 2011, a tax on bets against the US dollar in futures markets was added to the menu. That same month in its review of Brazil, the IMF deemed these measures "appropriate."[34] In October 2010, the director of the IMF argued, unsuccessfully, for the use of capital controls in Colombia to address the rapid and unwelcome appreciation of its currency.[35] Although the Colombian tax was ultimately rejected, signs of IMF heterodoxy or pragmatism in this case demonstrated that a changing conception of currency instability can lead to more sensitive policies.

As many now recognize, countries deploying capital controls were better protected from the global financial crisis and able to manage volatile capital flows, including Brazil, Taiwan, and South Korea.[36]

Other countries use different tools, the most common being taxes on short-term borrowing or defining a minimum required duration for foreign direct investment. But emergency measures have also been applied when banking crises threatened national economies. That was the case of Iceland, where the IMF accepted or encouraged the control of outflow capital.[37] The Stand-by Arrangement with the IMF, signed by Iceland in October 2008, included provisions for stringent capital controls, accepting the reality that they were already in place. The same type of agreement signed in December 2008 by Latvia accepted that country's imposition of a deposit freeze at the largest national bank. In Cyprus, the IMF and the European Council also accepted such controls, which could not be avoided.[38] The meaning is clear: in case of emergency, recourse to forbidden measures is effective and acceptable.

Some emerging economies used similar legislation. India imposed capital controls in 2013. Peru and Taiwan controlled inflows of capital (2008 and 2009), Indonesia managed short-term investment (2010), Argentina and Venezuela restricted outflows (2010). China of course never abandoned its power; compulsory joint ventures for foreign investment have been the norm, and national regulators closely investigate foreign companies.[39]

Other protectionist practices are rather common even if sophisticatedly disguised under arcane rules. The government bailout of national firms, most recently of banks and insurance companies on a massive scale, was an implicit intervention in international capital flows. The subtle world of trade promotion policies, including wage subsidies, export-tax and VAT rebates, lines of credits for exports, directed credit from public banks, requirements of investment in R&D, programs for financing and promoting special fields of research, such as biotech, are accepted

[34] This was a "tax on foreign purchases of Brazilian securities and later a reserve requirement and taxes for firms going short on the nation's currency and holding some derivative positions in foreign currency," Gallagher, Griffith-Jones, and Ocampo (2012), p. 1.

[35] Grabel (2012), p. 64.

[36] Gallagher, Griffith-Jones, and Ocampo (2012), p. 1; Magud, Reinhart, and Rogoff (2011).

[37] Epstein (2012), p. 48.

[38] World Economic and Financial Surveys (2009), and *The Economist*, April 6, 2013.

[39] *The Economist*, October 12, 2013.

and justified, both in continental Europe and in the heartlands of liberalization, Britain, Australia, and the US, and they all constitute forms of protectionism.

CONCLUSION

After the financial crisis of the late 2000s, the doctrine of *laissez-faire* economics trembled. The most powerful and neoliberal governments and international institutions, both molded by Friedman's doctrines on the free circulation of capital, resorted to intensely activist policies, nationalized banks, bailed out financial firms, inundated the shadow system with liquidity, controlled the international flows of capital, and prayed to strange gods.

After a short digestion period, which one investigator calls "productive incoherence,"[40] the IMF, first among the constitutive bodies of the international economic order, proceeded through initially discrete and then increasingly outspoken revision of its pillars of action and discourse. Capital controls were first presented as emergency brakes for the system with growing recognition that they could be a permanent solution for some economies.

Another expression of this incoherence was some afterthought on austerity programs in Europe. By June 2016, the journal published by the IMF, *Finance and Development*, included a surprising piece stating that "instead of delivering growth, some neoliberal policies have increased inequality, in turn jeopardizing durable expansion," under the provocative title of "Neoliberalism: Oversold?" Maurice Obstfeld, the chief economist of the institution, was called in to prevent the turmoil generated by this view and, in an interview quickly published in the same journal, watered down the excitation,[41] reassuring readers and lecturing on the virtues of liberalization.

Notwithstanding such implicit recognition of previous errors in crisis management, the IMF still favored pro-cyclical programs, such as those applied in southern Europe to discipline their sovereign debt, despite the collapse of the banking systems and deep recession. Even if its application can be circumstantially overcome by necessary and pragmatic action, the doctrine prevails.

The question of capital controls is closely intertwined with that of sovereign debt restructuring. The IMF announced that it favored a solution for the Greek case that would include a sovereign debt restructuring mechanism.[42]

In the same vein, the General Assembly of the United Nations in New York adopted a resolution in 2015 entitled *Basic Principles on Sovereign Debt Restructuring Processes*. The consensus is substantial, with 136 member states voting for, but six powerful countries, including Germany, the UK, and the US, voted against, and forty-one countries, including most of Europe, abstained.[43] In the following years, no change happened. In any case, as in the past, when different economists or governments challenged the prevailing rules, the status quo was maintained. Much water will pass under the bridges before a useful conclusion is reached.

[40] Grabel (2011). [41] Ostry, Loungani, and Furceri (2016); Obstfeld (2016).
[42] Xafa (2014); Pelagidis (2016). [43] United Nations General Assembly (2015).

APPENDIX C

Can the Institutions Be Trusted?

In previous chapters we navigated through the debris of frauds enabled by opaque financial practices and weak financial regulation and we examined the deregulators, academic ideologues, rating agencies, and central bankers who made it possible. Now we turn to the history of rule changes to understand how financial institutions and decision makers pursued a patient campaign to diminish public control and free the movement of capital and to impose their aims.

In a world of global finance, financial and banking deregulation proceeded through three main channels: the dismantlement in the US of the New Deal reforms; downsizing the state in Europe; and the growth of international agreements to outflank national institutions.

The first part of this appendix will briefly examine the age of regulation, and the second part will discuss the channels of deregulation. The third part will summarize the new wave of regulation that followed the 2007–8 financial crash: the Dodd-Frank Act of 2010, Britain's Bank Reform Bill of 2012; the EU new Capital Requirement Directive of 2013, and the Basel Accord for 2010–19.

What is Regulation About?

From the origins of the modern monetary and banking system, prudential regulation concentrated on achieving the full redemption of bank notes, which were circulated by state-chartered banks dominating the issue of means of payment or by private banks. In the case of the US and in the early twentieth century, following more than a quarter century of crashes, a reserve system was constituted in order to "pool private bank reserves." After the Great Crash of 1929, the Glass-Steagall Act imposed a separation between commercial banking and investment banking to "ensure public deposits in terms of Federal Reserve notes," constituting a major civilizational watershed.[1]

Although in European countries the banking and monetary system is older, the development of supervision and regulatory authority had followed roughly the same pattern. Because sovereignty depends on the right to issue the national currency, regulation was defined on the basis of the needs of the state to protect its notes and their value and circulation.

Twentieth-century regulation was organized around financial institutions, namely commercial banks, investment banks, and insurance companies. Financial institution and financial functions were closely mapped: commercial banks made loans to households and to businesses, investment banks underwrote the issuance of securities and sometimes speculated themselves, and insurance companies sold insurance for a variety of types of unexpected loss. State sovereignty both enabled and required a set of functions, including the maintenance of reserves and provision of convertibility.

By the late twentieth century, the concept of regulation had changed dramatically. First, products and agents—brokers, dealers, and underwriters—replaced functional institutions as the object of regulation, and markets replaced the state as the main source of reserves, liquidity, and convertibility. Second, from the early days of liberalization of financial flows in the 1980s, commercial banks expanded their reach, developing a foothold in securities

[1] Kregel (2014), p. 3.

markets. The measurement and management of risk, previously a world of acquaintance and handshakes, became fictitious, because in most cases the identity of the counterparty responsible for risk became unknown.

Although popular legend assigns them the roles of unexpected insurgents into politics as usual, Thatcher and Reagan in fact joined a deregulatory revolution already in progress. In the US, the deregulatory drive had manifold origins, ranging from Ralph Nader and Edward Kennedy, who were stalwart advocates of transportation deregulation to benefit consumers and the little guy, to Friedman and Hayek. Reagan and Thatcher gave the process an overarching political context, but one deep root lies in the emergence of new financial powers.

Throughout the same period the function and profit model of the banking system changed: banking depends far less on profits generated by the interest-rate spread between borrowing and lending, but rather on profits from fees, commissions, and the rapid sale of loans into markets (securitization). The new model has increased risk exposure. The banking system has itself become a part of the shadow system, in which the investor takes the risks and the provider takes the fees.

Special purpose entities moved risk off inspectable balance sheets and out of regulatory sight. Off-balance financial ghosts first received widespread attention when Enron, one of the largest distributors of energy in the world, collapsed in 2001. Enron's mysteriously named special purpose entities dragged their parent into bankruptcy. In the cleanup, new accounting rules were defined, but by October 2003 an exemption was approved for new special purpose entities used for securitization. Then a permanent exemption was established from July 2004.[2] Special purpose entities grew in importance as concerns developed about the quality of complex loans to support home mortgage and other types of lending.

The three main operating arenas for those changes were the US and the European economies and the international regulations defined by the Basel accords.

US and the Case of AIG

We explored the US liberalization process in earlier chapters, in particular how the 1999 Gramm-Leach-Bliley Act eliminated the Roosevelt-era rules preventing speculation by commercial banks. Here we recapitulate some of its institutional features, most prominently the birth of the incentive structure in the mortgage market and the related spread of new products generated by the snowball effect of securitization and diversification of risk.

Because state rather than Federal authorities license mortgage brokers, the agents who match homebuyers with banks or other lenders, their supervision was local and soft. Furthermore, economic incentives worked smoothly in favor of making the deal: local economies benefited from an expansion of credit, local governments reaped public fees associated with home sales and property taxes based on inflated prices, and the agents and brokers benefited from large commissions for mortgages to be sold down the line in securitized packages. Everybody was happy, the indebted homeowners holding a sure-thing speculative asset, the overpaid intermediaries, the credit institutions, the construction companies, and the local authorities. The more daring the deal, the happier the happiness, as the subprime loans generated 15 percent margins, instead of the typical 1–2 percent on other loans.[3]

In fact, a world of inventive financial products was emerging, of which subprime lending represented only a small portion. New markets grew rapidly as lenders hired the rating

[2] Thiemann (2014), p. 1216.

[3] It was not until 2009 that the Federal Reserve Board forbade payments to mortgage brokers based on interest rate charged, Eichengreen (2015), pp. 78, 80.

agencies, first to advise them on how to manage complex products and to structure titles on debt and then to rate these very products for professional market information and assessment. Investment banks were paid fees to hide public and private debt under inventive accounting tricks, and the show went on. Regulators were regularly misled, regulations were forum-shopped or, at best, avoided outright.

The case of AIG is an exuberant example: as European rules required financial institutions operating in Europe to be subject to some supervision agency and, therefore, when the authorities accurately identified AIG as a bank, the insurance giant sought to comply in the least burdensome manner possible and it purchased American General Bank which, as a savings and loan, qualified for supervision by the small and weak Office of Thrift Supervision.[4]

Facing minimal regulation, AIG continued with business as usual, specializing in insuring supposedly safe bonds, until its September 2008 collapse required an infusion of US $85 billion by the Fed, a bailout that acquired 80 percent of AIG ownership for the public. As old habits die hard, even after the bailout AIG paid US $6.4 million to seventy-three employees as retention bonuses, and US $165 million in bonuses to the staff of the department responsible for the fall. Most significantly, despite its bankruptcy and its dependence on public money, AIG paid its debt obligations to Goldman Sachs at 100 cents on the dollar (the Fed instructed AIG not to disclose to the Securities and Exchange Commission the memoranda on the payments).[5]

In spite of the public outcry, the agencies and consultants that helped firms to play this game have been insulated from any impacts of their miscalculations, obfuscations, and gross errors. For instance, in a revealing move and at the apex of the crisis, the US Secretary of Treasury Geithner engaged the consultancy Oliver Wyman for stress testing the banks. Wyman had already won notoriety for its 2007 report presenting Anglo Irish as the best bank in the world, shortly before Anglo Irish's dealings required a public rescue worth €30 billion.[6]

Europe Before and During the Crash

European liberalization followed a different course from the US. Unlike the US, where the separation of commercial from investment banking was a central and long-lasting tenet of the New Deal, universal banking remained legal and common in much of Europe. Like commercial banks in the US, European banks hold the deposits of households with public insurance protecting depositors, and like investment banks in the US, they engage in proprietary trading. In the US that mix was seen as the toxic brew that enabled the Great Crash of 1929, but in Europe universal banking was seen as integral to financing investment and growth. The association between universal banking and productive investment was strong enough to give a name, "bank capitalism," to the particular variety of capitalism that

[4] Eichengreen (2015), p. 205. For that, AIG purchased the American General Bank, a savings and loan institution, to avoid the pressure of the European supervisors, who considered it an insurance company and not a bank. The US supervision system is based on four main agencies: the Federal Reserve is responsible for the big bank holding companies (Morgan, Citigroup); the Office of Comptroller of the Currency, an independent division of the Treasury, for the nationally chartered banks (Citibank, Wells Fargo); the Federal Deposit Insurance Corporation (FDIC) supervises the banks that are not part of the Federal Reserve System and acts in case of bankruptcies, insuring depositors and restructuring bank management and assets; and the Office of Thrift Supervision regulates the savings and loans institutions (such as Washington Mutual or Countrywide), Cassidy (2009), p. 265. As these agencies get a handsome income from fees levied on regulated entities, they fight for the regulation market, although, in this case, demand creates its own supply.

[5] Johnson and Kwak (2011), p. 3; Andrews and P. Baker (2009).

[6] Eichengreen (2015), p. 363.

prevailed in Europe, especially Germany. Although this system of universal banking may have been functional for many years, it clearly shares responsibility for many collapses after 2007 (e.g., Northern Rock, Fortis, Dexia, Bankia, and Espírito Santo).

A second difference is that the European banks were governed by distinct, strict, sometimes arcane, national regulations. These regulations limited international competition and granted substantial monopoly power to national banks, which could charge depositors high transaction fees and operate with little pressure for customer service. The European Union played a key role in dismantling these national structures and replacing them with international competition and European banking and bank regulation.[7]

It has been a long process. Europe began to liberalize the circulation of capital in 1960,[8] but liberalization accelerated in the late 1980s under the combination of the political spell of Thatcherism and the European movement towards monetary union.

The First Banking Directive in 1977 paved the way for deregulation, but it was the Second Directive in 1989 that established total freedom of movement for capital and financial products by July 1, 1990. (The deadline was extended for Greece, Ireland, Spain, and Portugal until January 1, 1994 when the second phase of European Monetary Union began.) The Second Directive established a crucial element of deregulation: the obligation of mutual recognition, or that a bank established in one EU country is necessarily permitted to operate in any other. Coupled with home country control, meaning that decisions by home country authorities cannot be challenged by other countries, the Second Directive provided a potent structure for deregulation. Furthermore, this Directive favored universal banking: all forms of transaction were allowed, including dealing with securities and other products, and banks were allowed to own insurance companies.[9] Unlike the US, which severely restricted branch banking until 1999, the Second Banking Directive spearheaded a fast and deep deregulation process, enabling branch banking across the entire EU beginning in 1993.[10]

The 1986 Single European Act, inaugurating the road to the euro, was also a major step in the direction of banking liberalization. It imposed a single objective for monetary management: price stability. Consequently, it established rules for the participating nations: a maximum rate of inflation, maximum fiscal and debt positions, similar interest rates, and a sustainable current account in the balance of payments. To support current-account balance, the Single European Act provided for unregulated international financial movements. Indeed, free finance was a building block of that process. For that, "the enduring regulatory dispute between strict application of prudential rules versus discretionary interpretation of financial regulations by national supervisors was won by the latter."[11]

The super-national mandate for free capital movement coupled with national responsibility for regulation had consequences. Regulatory havens nurtured the rapid growth of finance, whence finance could nimbly reach outwards to new speculative opportunities. Over the longer run, countries followed a race to the bottom in regulation to remain attractive to footloose finance.

Deregulation favored more short-term lending and cross-national profit-seeking. In several countries, asset prices, especially in real estate, rose chased by both domestic and

[7] Of course, liberalization is a rewarding game for those with decision power and the ideology of free movements of capital may be slightly overrated. In many cases, the national authorities of powerful economies and states used their discretionary action to impose restrictions, even at the margin of the law: for instance, when Unicredit, an Italian firm, bought HVBB, the German's second largest, the Berlin authorities restricted the amount of cash it could transfer to the headquarters (*The Economist*, October 12, 2013).

[8] Benink and Benston (2005), p. 291.

[9] Some limits were imposed: all the different banks' holdings cannot exceed 60% of a credit institution's equity, and each one can have no more than 15%, although this does not apply to insurance.

[10] Benink and Benston (2005), p. 289.

[11] Kregel, Kattel, and Tonveronachi (2015).

imported capital. But this first financial boom ended abruptly: with a recession in the early 1990s asset prices fell, eroding the value of the collateral, much of it in real estate, that had previously supported credit chains. Restrictive monetary policy, which had recently become the law of the land to combat inflation, aggravated the crisis. Banking crises emerged in Sweden, Norway, and Finland,[12] and soon extended to banking giants Crédit Lyonnais and Banco di Napoli. Then came the 1991 collapse of BCCI, once the seventh largest bank in the world and the secret owner of the bank First American, in a scandal in which the line between finance as usual and criminality could not be meaningfully resolved (it was accused of money laundering for the Medellin Cartel and other criminal enterprises, and it also included some secret accounts of the CIA). The venerable Barings Banks followed in 1995.

This first shock failed to rouse the European authorities, who in fact reinforced and accelerated the liberalization process. In 1997 Tony Blair, entirely the heir of Thatcher in the matter of liberated finance, stripped the Bank of England of some of its supervisory authority, transferring it to a separate office, the Financial Services Authority. The transfer neglected a fundamental principle of supervision, coherent oversight of the supervised.

Throughout Europe, forum shopping drove a race to the bottom in regulations, which converged in the same low standards. The results are appalling: the capital-assets ratio for the ten largest European economies suffered a historical decline, from 30 percent in 1850 to a rapid decline by the end of the twentieth century, reaching 5 to 6 percent around 2000 (whereas the non-financial companies necessarily have a much larger capital-assets ratio).[13] In spite of its ups and downs, leverage has been mounting over a long period.

European Deregulation

The overall trend to international convergence has been imposed over distinct national regulatory approaches. The cases of France, Germany, Italy, and Spain, which we will briefly examine, show how diverse historical and institutional frameworks shaped regulatory convergence.[14]

Postwar France had strict limitations on so-called universal banking with a separation of functions that paralleled Glass-Steagall in the United States. As of 1980, finance was largely in private hands, and a partial liberalization had already been staged with the Debré Law in 1966. But the French state still administered a public system of credit and exercised substantial administrative control on capital and trade. This would change in 1981, when President François Mitterrand, leading France's first postwar Socialist government, promptly nationalized all the major banks and insurance companies. Then, under economic and political pressure from domestic capital and international institutions, Mitterrand backed down and accepted re-privatization. The process of deregulation followed in 1984 with a Banking Act that introduced universal banks.

Yet France retained its capacity to impose temporary restrictions on the free movement of capital until the EU imposed the decisive turn, as the 1988 EU Directive opened cross-border activities. In 1989 the Directive on capital requirements opened the path for liberalization reinforced in 1993 by the inclusion of investment services, in 1994 by legislation on deposit guarantees, and finally in 2001 by the introduction of crisis management schemes. Even so, France retained a real if narrow scope for national regulations, and it adopted stricter rules for control of capital movement in 1999 (but then reversed them in 2004). Overall, the European framework was imposed as the decisive boundary of local choice.

Germany has a long legacy of universal banking and an economy dominated by very large banks with structures that predate even the crisis of the 1930s and the Second World War.

[12] The costs of public support for banks in Norway, Sweden, and Finland by 1992 were 2.8%, 3.1%, and 7.2% of their respective GNP.

[13] Eichengreen (2015), pp. 182, 295.

[14] Kregel, Kattel, and Tonveronachi (2015).

It is the only EU country with a "continuous history of universal banking and more market directed credit allocation" and this system delivered "an enviable record of stability with the same financial structure in the post-war period."[15] Although private banking dominates the high ground, an important system of cooperative and local saving banks is controlled by regional governments.

The 1990s witnessed disagreements between the European Commission at the time, when it generally favored more prudential regulation, and French and German authorities, which opposed the European Commission's regulatory impulses. The Commission considered limitations on universal banking, an expedited process of resolution in case large banks failed, and prohibition on proprietary trading by banks and bank holding companies, but the banks reacted quickly and their influence carried the day.

Italy has a segmented system of public regional savings banks with substantial responsibility for credit allocation within their regions. The Bank of Italy bears national responsibility for regulation and supervision. With the Amato Act of 1990, these public savings banks were allowed to operate as universal banks, relieved of regulatory constraints between short- and long-term operations, and ultimately opened to privatization. Although exposure to public debt was huge, Italy was spared the worst effects of liberalization and privatization because relatively modest private debt limited vulnerability. In particular, Italian regulators prevented banks from participating in the market for securitized mortgages, the market that triggered the global meltdown in 2007–8.[16]

In Spain, the 1976 financial crisis was ignited by an excessive credit expansion, which led to early adoption of solvency standards and other rules that foreshadowed EU directives on macro-prudential rules, counter-cyclical, dynamic and statistical provisioning, and establishment of loan-loss provisions. Despite this promising prudential start, Spain experienced a large late-century housing bubble that generated large imbalances in the banking industry. With the impact of the 2007 crash, one of the Spain's largest banks, Bankia, was saved only by nationalization, and a massive bailout with borrowed money from the ECB and the Commission rescued the Spanish banks. Later, in 2017, Banco Popular was delivered to Santander, which acquired the bank for just one euro and promised a €7 billion infusion of capital to save Banco Popular, once one of the most powerful banks in Spain and closely connected with the religious sect Opus Dei.

The different yet convergent European cases in the run-up to the 2007 crash demonstrate that international rules favored deregulation and liberalization of the financial markets. And indeed little has changed since the crash. The shadow system depends on consistent rejection of structural regulation instead of reliance on a market-based risk-hedging approach.

A paradox of banking is that its minimal capital requirements, which would represent outright bankruptcy in any other sector of the economy, receive steady public subsidies, including regulatory forbearance, implicit and explicit guarantees, and—ultimately—bailouts. The paradox intensifies after financial crashes that simultaneously demonstrate the fragility of the system yet mobilize its resources in financially profitable bailouts.

The First Basel Concerts

In an ideal world, dangerous deregulatory innovation would punish only the innovating state. But financial deregulatory innovation leads other countries in a race to the bottom in the quality of regulation, both through competitive pressures and through institutions of international harmonization. Under pressure from domestic banking interests, which

[15] Jeffers and Plihon (2014), p. 13.

[16] Ibid., pp. 16, 30. By 2014, France and Germany were blamed by other governments for undermining efforts to raise capital requirements, protecting the level of leverage (*The Economist*, January 18, 2014).

face international competitive pressure, national jurisdictions are forced to adapt national laws and practices in the direction of liberalization. These changes were coordinated by the Basel Committee on Banking Supervision, an initiative of the G20 headquartered in Basel, Switzerland, which brokers negotiation for international financial rules.

In 1988, the Basel I Accord, going beyond its initial mandate to regulate only banks operating internationally, imposed an increase in the value of the risk-weighted capital requirement from 5.6 percent to 8 percent for all banks. But while the number went up, the quality went down, as Basel I broadened the scope of eligible capital assets. Under the new rule, all public debt was defined as risk-free eligible for finance with zero capital requirements, but increasingly risky classes of assets, starting from triple-A mortgage credit and ranging to riskier financial products, required maintenance of additional capital in the vault. As 8 percent was at that time the average retained capital, the requirements were not notably burdensome and did not immediately alter the value of the implicit and explicit guarantees of the system.

The Basel I achievement appeared to reach a coherent conclusion, that each bank would face the same rules, which limited damaging competition, and the system in its parts and as a whole would be protected against risk. Yet beneath this apparently benign and smooth surface, the opposite occurred, and Basel I initiated a stealthy but massive shift towards greater risk.

Because many securitized assets carried—indiscriminately as we later learned—Triple A ratings, Basel I encouraged inventive techniques for avoiding transparency and accountability and for maintaining the highest level of leverage. These accelerated the trend towards securitization, as banks sought to circumvent banking regulation and to minimize the impact of core capital requirements on lending.[17] As balance sheets were to be scrutinized, the banks transferred assets off their balance sheets to special purpose entities, "essentially robot firms that have no employees, make no substantive economic decisions, have no physical location, and cannot go bankrupt."[18] They exist only to cleanse the books of their parent banks and thereby enlarge the shadow system to unchartered territories.

In an impressive instance of regulatory responsiveness, the banks restructured their liquidity support to securitization into special entities each time one day before the delay imposed by Basel I rules.[19] These off-balance sheet vehicles fed the shadow system and its risky habit of funding long-term assets with short-term debt, initiating a spiral of debt that was only revealed by the crash. The growth of the shadow banking system was instrumental for banks to evade core capital requirements.

Already by 1999 astute observers had noted some of these dangers and, as securitization was identified as problematic or as increasing tail risk, a new round of negotiations sought to avert the danger. The discussion of the new rules took from 1999 until 2004, although implementation was only established for 2008, a very long delay that would allow most institutions to adapt if not to explore different loopholes.

The Basel II rules were certainly too late, but they were also too little. Basel II asked the banks to use their own models and conduct their own measurement of the value at risk, or VaR.[20] The regulation continued to require that banks hold capital equal in value to 8 percent of assets on a risk-weighted basis—but risk was to be measured by the risk-taking entity.

17 Thiemann (2014), p. 1213. 18 Gorton and Souleles (2007), p. 550.

19 Thiemann (2014), pp. 1209, 1205.

20 Kregel, Kattel, and Tonveronachi (2015). The market-risk exposure measured in terms of VaR understates the risk, namely that of market covariance (Benink and Benston, 2005, p. 307), or the risk of an avalanche in a financial system. The Basel Committee tried to address and overcome the shortcomings of this model by multiplying the VaR predictions by a factor of three, even if this is recognition that the methodology it is championing is a failure.

In a well-meaning attempt to articulate a counter-cyclical strategy that would increase capital requirements to cool off booms or potential bubbles, a capital buffer of 2.5 percent was added to the basic 8 percent capital requirement. A much larger variable buffer would have helped: Switzerland had discussed a 19 percent total capital requirement and an independent commission in the UK recommended 17–20 percent, with some experts at the Bank of England advocating for capital reserves ranging from 20 percent up to 45 percent in some cases.[21] The reliance on self-valuation of risk was widely recognized as the Achilles heel of the approach, and the Basel Committee tried to overcome this shortcoming by multiplying VaR predictions by a factor of three. Even tripling the risk estimate would prove grossly inadequate.

In the same sense, Basel II initiated stress tests which, following in the spirit of the expensive medical monitoring available to the middle-aged men who run banks, ostensibly subjected banks to simulations of performance in case of catastrophe. Basel II also introduced required intermediation chambers for operating over-the-counter derivatives.[22] But some key topics were outside Basel regulation and proved to be crucial for the development of shadow banking: the structured investment "vehicles," the special purpose "entities," and the streams of liquidity granted by banks to their own securitization "special entities." In particular, it became obvious that exemption of securitization activities from global regulation, as allowed by Basel II, would precipitate the multiplication of new forms of avoiding regulation. A major event, the subprime crash, proved how dangerous these choices were even before Basel II came into effect: under the sway of such a crisis, structured vehicles with US $400 billion and asset-based commercial paper with US $550 billion vanished.[23]

Even the mild requirements of Basel received a cold welcome from most central bankers and supervisors. But Greenspan himself, in a rare moment of regulatory advocacy, attacked the Basel rules as insufficient.[24] Throughout his career he had found solace in the certainty that because no perfect prediction was possible, no regulation could be justified, and Greenspan missed no opportunity to advocate for markets free of regulation. His late repentance proved brief, and Greenspan returned rapidly to his long-held anti-regulatory views. Others simply understood that these weak rules would be circumvented and evidence proved that the successive Basel Accords encouraged the shadow system in each iteration and that, while these loopholes remain, the shadows will dominate finance.

After the Crash, a New Wave of Regulations

After the crash, different national and international authorities initiated the first major increase in regulation since the US Savings and Loan scandal of the late 1980s. Parliaments, central banks, and international agencies piously promised a new approach to stricter regulation. The Federal Deposit Insurance Corporation (FDIC), one of the US bank supervisors, closed over three hundred small and medium banks since the onset of the 2007–8 crisis. But, as Reinhart and Rogoff quipped in the caustic title of their book, the general discourse was that *This Time is Different*—and if not this time, then maybe next time.[25] But in a few short years the mood of contrition and temperance was diluted by carefully phrased, relentlessly lobbied, and ultimately inconsequential laws—or forgotten outright.

[21] Miles, Yang, and Marcheggiano (2013). [22] Kregel, Kattel, and Tonveronachi (2015).

[23] Thiemann (2014), p. 1207.

[24] "The Basel Committee on Banking Supervision, representing regulatory authorities from the world's major financial systems, promulgated a set of capital rules that failed to foresee the need that arose in August 2007 for large capital buffers," (Greenspan, in a speech at the Economic Club of New York, February 17, 2009).

[25] Reinhart and Rogoff (2009).

Some true believers could even find signs of over-regulation in the run-up to the crash, and have cautioned against what they considered to be an overwrought regulatory over-response. That has been the case of the best-selling economic historian Niall Ferguson, who blamed regulation for the subprime crash. He is right on only one point: insured banks and not only their uninsured hedge funds were at the center of the crash. The banks understood the incentive created by Basel II and used their own estimation of risk as the norm for fixing capital requirements, thus promoting a cornucopia of "special entities." The US Congress did favor cheap credit for lower-income families. Ferguson, who ultimately concedes only that derivatives require some regulation, otherwise presents the financial markets as a Darwinian economy, as befits a faithful promoter of the Mont Pelerin Society (see Chapter 5 for details).[26] However, even Ferguson's modest concession refers to wrong regulations or to deregulatory extremes, and not to the need for rules establishing the basic requirement of market transparency and with the capacity to unwind in case of crisis.

In any case, in the US and in Europe, the years immediately following the subprime crash were dominated by a wave of new regulations. The G20 imposed limits on some shadow financial contracts, adding the requirement that some contracts be registered with a central office and, beginning in February 2014, that the two parties cannot proceed to a contract without recourse to a swap execution facility.[27] But then came a wave of lobbying, interpretation, and reinterpretation, which re-arranged the new legislation in order to comply with the advantages of shadow finance.

After the crash and under its impact, the third round of negotiations at Basel was finalized, and a new package of regulations was approved in the US in the form of the Dodd-Frank Act. In the European Union, the discussion pitted the British Vickers commission proposal for partial separation of commercial and investment banks through separate capitalization and the Liikanen proposal to delimit trading from retail outright. We will briefly examine each one in the following sections of this chapter.

Changes in the US Regulation: Dodd-Frank and Volcker Rules

The complete title of the law commonly known as the Dodd-Frank Act of 2010 is a declaration by itself: "An act to promote the financial stability of the United States by improving accountability and transparency in the financial system, to end 'too big to fail,' to protect the American taxpayer by ending bailouts, to protect consumers from abusive financial services practices, and for other purposes."[28]

Approved by a highly partisan vote in 2010, Dodd-Frank provided a brisk and substantive response to the 2007–8 crash and the financial instability and innovation the crash exposed.[29] The law was championed by an unlikely team. Barney Frank, then chair of the House Financial Services Committees, registered the securities industry as his top donor. Christopher Dodd, then chair of the Senate Banking Committee, received some US $2.9 million of donations from the securities industry in the very years of the meltdown, more than any other senator (other than the Presidential candidates Senator Barack Obama and Senator John McCain).[30]

[26] Ferguson (2014), p. 70. [27] *The Economist*, May 10, 2014.

[28] For some challenging critiques, see Konczal (2010); Lee (2010); Pollin and Heintz (2013).

[29] By June 2009 the Financial Accounting Standards Board amended the existing rules for consolidation of securitization operations; by September the same year, the US banking regulators defined that depository institutions should hold regulatory capital against consolidated securitization operations, considering the risk-weighted assets and increasing the capital requirements, Adrian and Ashcraft (2012), p. 26.

[30] *New York Times*, December 13, 2008, "A Champion of Wall Street Reaps Benefits."

The clarity and thirty-seven-page brevity of Roosevelt's core New Deal financial legislation, the Glass-Steagall Act, mocks the jungle of laws, rules, reports, papers, and agencies created by the legislation adopted after the subprime crash. Dodd-Frank, as approved in 2010, spans 884 pages and demands 243 complementary regulations, sixty-seven research papers, and twenty-two periodical reports.

By the end of 2015 the regulatory page count had reached 8,843 pages and some experts predicted it might approach 30,000, given that some rules were still delayed or even suspended because several regulatory agencies failed to provide needed cost and benefit computations. Five years after its approval, Dodd-Frank remained incomplete with only half of the 400 mandated regulations actually in place and many not even proposed. For the European directives and regulations, the comparable count had reached over 2,000 pages by the end of 2015 on its way to an ultimate 60,000 pages.[31]

The larger banks enrolled armies of lawyers and other specialists to cope with and avoid the new rules. J.P. Morgan Chase mobilized 950 employees for Dodd-Frank, with an additional 400 dedicated to dealing with the hundreds of rules on the liquidity of assets and 300 more for complying only with the Volcker Rule, that is, working directly on compliance; Morgan Chase had 24,000 people in 2011 before Dodd-Frank and 43,000 in 2015.[32] This is not a typo: General Electric employs 900 technicians for its tax division.

The Volcker Rule (named for its most prominent champion, Paul Volcker, chair of the Fed 1979–87), a seventy-one-page piece of the Dodd-Frank Act,[33] developed by the agencies into almost one thousand pages of regulation, banning banks from proprietary trading and restricting their connections to hedge and private equity funds. Banning banks from trading on their own account was as close as Dodd-Frank came to reestablishing Rooseveltian rules, and unfortunately the terms were badly defined and remained mired in controversy and murk. Five different agencies participated in the 891-page report, and the Volcker Rule did not come into effect until July 21, 2015. As with previous legislation, the array of agencies and arcane rules did more to encourage the pathways to shadow banking than to regulate financial firms into responsible behavior.[34]

Volcker himself expressed discontent with Dodd-Frank's "chaotic and overlapping" regulation system. He proposed several alternatives. First he suggested giving more power to the Fed not only to decide on monetary policy but to draft regulations. Second he proposed to merge the SEC and the Commodity Futures Trading Commission to establish the Financial Stability Oversight Council, a new agency responsible for monitoring financial stability that would join the new Consumer Financial Protection Bureau.

Other supervisors expressed distrust of current routines. The SEC even called for personal stress tests on managers to anticipate how they would deal with a crisis, a sorry statement on the difficulty of predicting and correcting the behavior of the market and its players in times of trial.[35] In a more constructive vein and in the face of some dissent, SEC advanced new restrictions on reliance on bond ratings, to limit risk and maturity transformation and proposed the creation of further capital and liquidity buffers.

[31] Haldane and Madouros (2012); Ferguson (2014), p. 76; Kregel, Kattel, and Tonveronachi (2015).

[32] *The Economist*, April 18, 2015, May 6, 2017.

[33] Volcker was appointed Chair of the Fed by US President James Carter in October 1979. He sharply raised the policy interest rate to fight inflation. Federal Reserve History (2013), provides a detailed official history.

[34] The Volcker Rule also included some 900 pages of exclusions from the rule: exemptions for transactions such as securities lending, liquidity management, derivatives clearing, covering short sales, direct and reverse repurchase agreements, plus proprietary trading by foreign banks not controlled by US entities, Kregel (2014), p. 26.

[35] *The Economist*, April 18, and 25, 2015.

After Dodd-Frank, the US Imbroglio

Despite public outcry at the height of the crisis against "too big to fail" and "too interconnected to fail," the regulations imposed, at most, modest limits on size and interconnectedness. The surviving banks, having weathered both the crisis and the regulatory onslaught, understood the new terms as a green light for a renewal of securitization and new adventures of debt creating debt.[36] The Volcker Rule forced banks to limit their involvement in hedge funds, but the shadow system was largely untouched.

The political stalemate in regulation forced the regulatory agencies to adopt novel rules as stopgaps for the major holes of the new regulatory system and each major regulator developed its own framework and measures. The newly created labyrinth added to the complexity of already outdated financial regulation.

For instance, the Office of Credit Ratings declared it would fine firms that relied too uncritically on rating agencies or that failed to use third parties appropriately or failed to disclose mandated information. OCR additionally sought to close, or at least slow, the revolving door between government and firms, by requiring firms to report hiring of former agency personnel within five years of leaving government service.

The Fed mandated "living wills," first from banks with over US $250 billion and later extended to include US $100-billion banks. These "wills," designed to clarify obligations in case of crisis and to prevent the formation of insolvent zombie banks, require resolution plans in case of insolvency and exposure reports, including a "description of ownership, assets, liabilities, contractual obligations" of the financial firms at risk.[37]

With respect to prudential regulation, the Fed required banks to hold a thirty-day buffer of very liquid assets, initiated liquidity stress tests, and defined new risk management standards. To discipline high frequency trading, which was rightly held up as the epitome of rent-seeking financial behavior with no conceivable social benefit yet significant risk of generating stampedes, a fifteen-second delay was imposed on brokers and dealers in executing customers' trades.[38]

Critics abounded on the left and the right. While some legislators remained attached to the liberalized model, others complained about excessive support for the financial system, arguing that regulation favored or enabled malpractice. In mid-2015, unlikely allies in the US Senate, Democrat Elizabeth Warren and Republican David Vitter, presented a bill to restrict the Fed's capacity to lend during a financial panic.[39] They argued that the US $13 trillion mobilized over 2007–9 to support the financial firms under stress rewarded bad behavior. Furthermore, they critiqued the Fed for failing to issue the regulations mandated by Dodd-Frank in 2010. As they rightly intuited, after the crash, business returned to its usual state of affairs, namely present and imminent danger.

With the victory of Donald Trump, a new wave of deregulation was promised. In spite of the ambiguous claims (for every new regulation, two will be eliminated) and the inconsistency (the Volcker Rule should be dismissed and Dodd-Frank rewritten, but the principles of Glass-Steagall should be implemented, said Trump), the new administration empowers a hedge fund mogul, Mnuchin, and appears to favor new forms of financial products. As for the regulatory agencies, the executive power of the President is very large: he has the right to nominate the vice president of the Federal Reserve who is in charge of

[36] A maximum leverage of 15:1 was imposed for identified firms supposed to threaten stability and to have more than US $50 billion in assets, Kregel (2014), p. 49. But again this is crucially dependent on the classification of assets.

[37] The FDIC rejected in 2015 the "living wills" of the US subsidiaries of three of world's largest banks (BNP, HSBC, and RBS). The previous year all the "wills" of the eleven banks larger than US $250 billion were rejected (*The Economist*, March 28, 2015).

[38] Kregel (2014), p. 36. [39] *The Economist*, April 25, 2015.

regulation, the board members of the Financial Stability Oversight Council, and the director of the Consumer Financial Protection Bureau, two institutions created by Dodd-Frank.

Europe after the Crash

The usually more neoliberal US outpaced Europe in financial reform, but both economies share a comparable fragility, since the EU matched the US in fragmentation among the regulatory agencies. In any case, the European institutions reacted coldly to the regulatory spirit emanating from the US. The European integration process had for decades adopted the German model of universal banks. Indeed there was a longstanding literature proselytizing on the benefits of universal banking to the real economy. Strong arguments combined with the lobbying power of modern finance assured that the reintroduction of any rule delimiting commercial and investment banks was soundly rejected,[40] and, as the American-style Volcker Rule banning of proprietary trading by banks was off the table, European authorities sought alternative approaches, but there was no consensus on the best direction.

Two main alternatives to the Volcker Rule's ban on proprietary trading and bank engagement in hedge and equity funds were considered. The Vickers Report of the UK Independent Commission on Banking[41] proposed, in lieu of separating commercial and investment banks, separating capitalization of bank activities. Retail banking would be "ring fenced" from trading and universal banking.

Erkki Liikanen, governor of the Bank of Finland and member of the ECB board, offered an even less strict separation in a 2012 report for the European authorities. The Liikanen report proposed that proprietary trading above a threshold would be undertaken by a different bank, which could belong to the same holding company. The rule would isolate high-risk trading in one institution—but not in the financial group—and also offered some stricter risk-management rules and bail-in mechanisms, meaning that in case of resolution the cost would be imputed to equity and to the creditors of the bank.

A discrete change was nevertheless imposed by the Markets in Financial Instruments Directive, called MiFID II, in force since January 3, 2018. Whereas the previous directive (MiFID I) only included shares, the second installment promises to alter the norms of trading of stocks, bonds, and derivatives, limiting the amount of dark trades and defining some other restrictions, including the use of electronic trading platforms, distinct from the banks, and contributing to some price transparency. In spite of these words and actions, most derivatives and bonds are traded over-the-counter and are not regulated.[42]

Basel III and the Future of Regulation

Basel III, negotiated from 2010 to 2013 and to be implemented from 2013 through 2019, constitutes an international response to the subprime crash and ensuing financial disruption. Basel III strengthens the prudential requirements of capital, but the provisions are likely insufficient and unlikely to deliver stability because of their short-term bias and their dependence on national regulations, in particular on the measure of capital.[43]

The fundamental shortcoming of the re-regulation effort is that using unsupervised, off-balance sheet vehicles to acquire long-term assets with short-term debt is the source both

[40] Kregel (2014), pp. 61, 63.

[41] Vickers (2011). Named for its chair John Vickers, former chief economist of the Bank of England.

[42] *The Economist*, September 30, 2017.

[43] Basel III rules have been criticized for being prejudiced against long-term loans, for example, those required for infrastructure projects (*The Economist* computes that approximately US $60 trillion is required for maintaining world roads, power plants, and pipelines for the period 2014–2030, and one trillion a year is missing; *The Economist*, March 22, 2014), Benink and Benston (2005), pp. 299–300.

of profitable leverage for banks and of risk and instability that threaten the global economy. Without challenging that fundamental problem, and fueled by fiscal competition and the self-interest of banks in maintaining their shadow system, international action is promoting a race to the bottom in national supervision systems.

Furthermore, the Basel guidelines accept that national regulations will govern bank competition, and Basel III did not specify how a firm or a "vehicle" would qualify as subsidiary, because responsibility for establishing the boundaries of financial institutions was relegated to national jurisdiction. Most national (or regional, in the case of the EU) legislatures, as expected, opted to protect adventurous special purpose "entities" from the regulatory net. In the same sense, in France the stricter rules passed in 1999 were actually reversed in 2004 as the legislature sought to restore international competitiveness in finance with lax regulation.

The several rounds of Basel negotiations and decisions did not seriously address the shadow system and missed the most important connections between bank and shadow finance. Basel III ignored the role of offshoring special investment vehicles, the use of special purpose entities that are in fact subsidiaries of banks, all the way to the liquidity lines granted by banks to their own securitization entities. The regulatory loopholes persisted and Basel even allowed exemption of securitization activities from global regulation. When the revision of Basel III was concluded by the end of 2017, to take full effect not before 2027, these loopholes remained untouched and the European banks entered the last years of the 2010 decade with large shortfalls of capital and exposed to new and old systemic risks.

One further contradiction is that the conditions for competition of banks depend on international regulations, but the application of Basel depends on national laws. Because it is up to national laws to define the perimeter of consolidation, Basel does not specify which companies are in fact subsidiaries. It is advantageous to banks to have the definition of supervision exclude special purpose entities and so it happened. The shadow system has been the main beneficiary of this legislative flux.

In the case of the Eurozone, the European Central Bank strictly favored securitization: since the banks have been reluctant to raise capital, they were simply authorized to increase their leverage, in hopes of generating new credit.[44]

The fragmentation of regulations, "competition in laxity," and "principled minimalism"[45] are results of these global mechanisms undermining the regulatory capacity which is required to address the major dangers in the financial markets. As one researcher asks, "what if global governance mechanisms themselves undermine the capacity of national banking regulators to deal with the regulatory capital arbitrage activities of their banks?"[46] The answer signals the danger.

As it has evolved in modern capitalist economies, the financial system is a public-private partnership, with the "government ceding the right to produce means of payment with the related permission on leveraged lending services, against the acceptance of rules designed to ensure stability for both individual institutions and the financial system."[47] But in this partnership the public monopoly on control of the money system and of speculation is compromised. Credit is a key element of the money supply, and the shadow system, flying below the regulatory radar, makes the economy more unstable and unpredictable.

All of the forces at work on regulators point in the same direction. Cognitive capture, the revolving door, the sophistication of financial rent-seekers, structural and legislative constraints imposed on national regulators, and even mere uncoordinated action make regulation a weak match for finance.[48] The cult of "counterparty regulation," the hope that

[44] *The Economist*, January 11, 2014.

[45] Murphy (2004); Rodrik and Subramanian (2009); Pistor (2010).

[46] Thiemann (2014), p. 1205; Murphy (2004), See also Rodrik and Subramanian (2009); Pistor (2010).

[47] Kregel, Kattel, and Tonveronachi (2015).

[48] Thiemann (2014), pp. 1212–13.

the skepticism of the other party would alone discipline markets and speculators resulted in catastrophe.

There are alternatives to this decay of regulation but each has its challenges. Rules-based regulation is prone to regulatory evasion, namely by financial innovation, an ongoing cat-and-mouse between regulators and regulated. This is why some authors suggest forms of regulation based on function—providing liquidity—may be more comprehensive and efficient, penetrating the black boxes of the shadows. That was the proposal of Minsky and of James Tobin, among others, as previously discussed.

The critical fragility of the financial system—which threatens entire economies—lies in the shadow banking system. The verification of cross-border capital movements (to be discussed in the next chapter), the robustness of deposit guarantee schemes, and the sharpness of recovery and resolution procedures, plus rules on liquidity, competition, incentives, and taxes, should be part of a consistent regulation tool kit.

In any case, even before the full application of Basel III in 2019, some of its rules became the ground for a contentious dispute between US and European authorities. The US side proposes a higher evaluation of risk-weighted assets, generating larger requirements of capital cushions. For the US banks, this is not a problem, since they sell most of their mortgages to the public agencies, Fannie Mae and Freddie Mac, and do not keep them on their books, unlike the European banks. Furthermore, the US firms get most of their capital in the market and not from credit, again unlike the European firms. Consequently, the European banks would require much larger injections of capital and their operations would impact more on the firms; Morgan Stanley anticipated that the necessary extra capital could come close to €400 billion. If the sum is so large, the debate on the rules is certainly part of the growth of uncertainty.

Auditors and the Virtue of Silence

The behavior of regulators and supervisors can certainly be explained by the theory of cognitive capture: they could just believe the interests of finance were essential to develop a sound economy and that regulation by itself, or excessive regulation, would damage market forces and unleash dismal consequences.[49] In Chapter 7 we explored convincing evidence for this capture. But this appears to be insufficient to explain the magnitude of the overzealous lack of regulation or deregulation. Other authors suggest that the structural constraints of national regulators also played a role, if not essential at least substantial, not only and not mainly their cognitive assimilation of the doctrine of free markets.[50]

In two different ways, supervisors protected the supervised and avoided using their own powers, or even misused them. First, the supervisors resisted coordinated action, providing for important opportunities in regulatory arbitrage. In the US, the alphabet soup of financial regulatory agencies provided a forum for every possibility. In Europe, national regulations chased each other to the bottom.[51] Second, the supervisors rested on global mechanisms undermining their effective regulatory capacity and providing for easy justifications of errors.

Lack of coordination can even compete with ideological capture as an explanation. Uncoordinated national efforts make the national capacity for supervision fragile. Can the institutions be trusted? Our reply is that they cannot. The constitutive rules and modes of

[49] Baker (2006); Turner (2012); Buiter (2009). [50] Thiemann (2014), pp. 1212–13.

[51] Recent episodes belie the notion that the era of national control is over. When Unicredit, an Italian financial firm, bought HVBB, German's second larger lender, the local authorities restricted the amount of cash Unicredit could transfer to the headquarters. If the state is powerful enough, it can bend the liberalization rules.

action are designed to favor shadow finance, and personnel are selected for their allegiance to deregulation.

The institutions not only fail to anticipate market failures but also reject evidence of failure in progress. Take the case of the whistleblowers on the financial monstrosities pervading some of the big firms. Alayne Fleischmann, associate at J.P. Morgan, working at the department establishing standards for credit, understood that mortgage-based securities were not sound and, by the end of 2006 and early 2007 presented the case to management. That was before the subprime crash. After the crash, in February 2008, as experience proved her right, Fleischmann was fired. She testified before the SEC and the Justice Department; her deposition in March 2013 allowed for a case to be settled for US $13 billion. She was never admitted back in the banking business. Richard Bowen III, senior executive at Citigroup, detected wrongdoings with mortgage securities and discussed his concerns with the top levels of management, including Rubin—Bowen was fired. Michael Winston, managing director at Countrywide Financial, uncovered excessive lending and bad mortgages—he was dismissed.[52]

If these appear to be isolated cases or misunderstandings by managers used to business as usual, consider the giant accounting firms whose high pay, reputation, and legal foundations depend on their capacity to audit and detect problems in the accounts and to confirm their findings.

There are four global-scale accounting firms: Deloitte, PricewaterhouseCoopers, EY (formerly Ernst and Young), and KPMG—the last is the smallest but larger than the next four combined. They dominate the market: the four auditing giants check the accounts of 99 percent of the firms in the S&P500 and FTSE indexes, and typically for a long period. Their exploits provide a chronicle of systemic malfunction. Price was determined negligent in the case of the enormous retailer Tesco. Tesco overstated the rebate income expected from suppliers and produced cosmetic changes in the accounts. Other scandals emerged with the accounts of Olympus, the Japanese optical device maker, Hewlett-Packard, and Bankia. KPMG was accused of inaccurately reporting full-capacity utilization of the industrial units of China Integrated Energy. Deloitte settled the largest fine in Brazilian history in 2016 for wrongdoings and false audits on behalf of an airline.[53] In 2016, PWC settled a $5.5 billion lawsuit following its previous approval of the Colonial Bank accounts, although the bank collapsed in 2009—it was proved that the bank made loans based on nonexistent assets.[54]

Previous histories of Enron and WorldCom, the great collapses of 2001–2 implying losses of some US $200 billions for investors, suggest a pattern. EY was the auditor of Lehman Brothers. Price and EY were both the auditors of BCCI, the giant bank that collapsed in 1991.

Institutions are vulnerable to their own agenda.

Conclusion

If the two great financial crashes and two reform attempts are compared, the difference between the 1930s and the 2010s is striking. Under Glass-Steagall, the principle of supervision was based on the identity between the function of finance, the creation of liquidity, and its institutions. In unwinding the crash of 2007–8, insufficient attention has been paid to liquidity creation and how the shadow system became the mirror image of the financial system. The reform is unlikely to take root, precisely because, unlike what happened in the 1930s, the shadow system was the victor of the crash of which it was also the culprit.

[52] *New York Times*, February 16, 2016.
[53] *The Economist*, December 13, 2014; *Reuters*, December 5, 2016.
[54] *Independent*, August 15, 2016.

As deregulation or liberalizing regulation led to the gigantic financial shadow system, after the crash the new regulation framework maintained or aggravated the asymmetry between the proclaimed intentions and the effective regulatory action. In other words, the national states, once the guardians of financial and monetary stability, pursued the race to the degradation of their regulatory powers under the pretense that competition leads finance.

In this universe, no government has an incentive to regulate stringently for fear of disadvantaging domestic banks and driving financial business elsewhere. Furthermore, the Basel Accords on banking regulation left substantial incentives for individual countries to exempt domestic financial schemes from bank regulation, namely those with the sole purpose of holding risk off the books of banks. As a consequence, almost a decade after the financial crash of 2007–8 the world is endangered by another meltdown.

As the primary function of banks moved from the creation of liquidity for investment to the intermediation between savers and business, as they shadowed their activities, the financial networks became simply the recognizable part of the shadow system. This is the critical point of the contemporary economic system.

Can these institutions be trusted? Experience speaks for itself. If they can be trusted, since their action is consistent, then the crises are simply either an effect of lacunae in previous regulations or of fraud, and therefore the solution would be public injection of liquidity by any means necessary when necessary, resolution of large banks if required, and safety commissions everywhere. If this trust is unwarranted, then the shadow system is a problem.

There is a consequence for the first approach: let's complete the markets, let's have a unified capital market under no restrictions, let's make true the dream of *laissez-faire*. There is also a consequence for the alternative view: let's take care.

Is financial liberalization an advantage for modern societies? A possible answer, as a conclusion to this chapter, is to evoke the testimony of Sanford Weill. He was the co-chair of Citicorp, a firm that began merging with the Travelers Insurance Group in 1998, and then formed Citigroup in 1999. This merger would be impossible under the conditions of the Glass-Steagall Act and the firm lobbied for its repeal. This battle was quite simple, as we indicated, since the emerging consensus had already settled the fate of the old rules inherited from Roosevelt. By 2012, a repentant Weill, already out of business, recognized that the decision had been an error: "What we should probably do is go and split up investment banking from banking, have banks be deposit takers, have banks make commercial loans and real estate loans, have banks do something that's not going to risk the taxpayer dollars, that's not too big to fail."[55] But the too-big-to-fail system has already failed, and now it has won the political battles that will enable it to fail again and perhaps worse.

[55] *Wall Street Journal*, July, 26 2012.

Part V

The World We Live In

11

A Long Stagnation, or Capitalism without Growth

The crisis ignited by the subprime crash exposed the sorry illusion of orthodox economics on the virtues of equilibrium and perpetual growth without perturbations. The cavalier and brazen impudence of the authorities promoting the emergence of shadow finance and protecting it through deregulation paved the way not only for the crisis and recession but also for new waves of measures deepening the recession. Indoctrination and the close connection between politicians and business interests, through golden revolving doors, favored the hegemony of the ideas and the institutions that imposed the survival of the choices that led to the meltdown.

As a consequence, the first big crisis of the twenty-first century has had an impact that contrasts with that of 1929, the deepest crisis of the previous century. By 1936, ten years after the Great Crash, both government responses (albeit provisionally) and new academic thinking favored counter-cyclical measures and had rejected hard money views. The current crisis, in contrast, was met with more neoliberal policies. Lucas's and Cochrane's suggestion, ludicrous on its face, that the market, free of any public intervention, would reboot in a matter of weeks after a recession, and the most unabashed justifications for the continuation of neoliberalism have largely prevailed, even if there were gigantic public interventions nationalizing private losses and bailing out the financial firms that had promoted the speculative misadventures. At the time of the largest state intervention ever, neoliberalism pursued its quest for *laissez-faire*, as if such ideas were living on another planet.

The facts, notwithstanding, remain: the economic leadership was a disaster. The figures are telling, since between 1933 and 1937 real GDP recovered at the annual rate of 8 percent in the US, but in 2010–13 it only grew at 2 percent.[1] In the Eurozone, only in 2016 was the level of the pre-crash GDP per capita attained. Furthermore, almost a decade after the crash, recovery is anemic. That is why some economists looked back to the past and found, in conditions they paralleled to the present, the somber anticipation of a "secular stagnation." That is the theme for the current chapter.

[1] Eichengreen (2015), p. 7.

THE DOOMSAYERS

The mood could not have been upbeat as the US economists gathered in Detroit, on December 28, 1938. The country continued to suffer from the effects of the Great Recession. Europe was plunged into hatred, war scares, and *fait accompli*: in March, Germany had effectuated the *Anschluss* of Austria and in September the western governments forced Czechoslovakia to cede its Sudeten territory to Hitler. Japan had been ravaging China for most of the decade. A sense of doom hung over the world.

The newly elected President of the American Economic Association was Alvin Hansen, fifty-one years old and recently appointed at Harvard after successful terms at Brown and Minnesota Universities. Hansen was advising President Roosevelt, a task he would continue with Truman. He combined his background in the American institutional economics tradition with appreciation for the new discoveries of Keynes. He was already a specialist in the theory of economic cycles, and he rapidly became the most illustrious importer of Keynesian doctrine to the US, where his prestigious pedigree eased concerns about deviations from orthodoxy. Hansen combined the tools, motivation, and standing to move the profession and policymakers who would listen to confront the Depression, the collapse of international cooperation, and the march towards war.

Preparing his AEA Presidential address,[2] Hansen consulted a recent lecture by Keynes on the danger that demographic slowdown posed for ongoing depression, which may have surprised the audience at the Eugenics Society in London.[3] Hansen himself had anticipated the problem as early as 1934.[4] In a nutshell, the demographic menace was that slow population growth would leave a chronic shortage of demand, undermining incentives for investment. In this sense, "secular stagnation," the term he proposed specifically for this demographically induced slowdown, would lead to a "hard and seemingly immovable core of unemployment" with, at most, a jobless recovery, or "depressions feeding on themselves."[5]

The proposition came as a shock to most economists, and Hansen was aware of the impact of his words. His colleagues were surely used to the idea of a recession; almost a decade of frightening difficulties had passed since Black Tuesday, October 29, 1929. But some recovery was evident, at least in the US. Malthusian leanings die hard and the notion that slower demographic growth would leave more to go around resonated with the same common sense that falling prices would equilibrate markets.

But Hansen stood his ground against received wisdom and expressed himself bluntly: "Not until the problem of full employment of our productive resources from the long-run, secular standpoint was upon us, were we compelled to give serious consideration to those factors and forces in our economy which tend to

[2] Hansen (1939).

[3] The lecture appears in Keynes (1937). In a 1912 lecture, Keynes expressed his early eugenic view which echoed Malthus's approach to population. But in the 1920s Keynes changed his opinion, and after the 1929 crisis, Keynes emphasized instead the threat of population decline, discussing the other Malthusian devil, that of underemployed resources. The Galton Lecture of 1937, delivered at the Eugenics Society, presented those "economic consequences of a declining population."

[4] Hansen (1934). [5] Ibid., p. 11.

make business recoveries weak and anemic and which tend to prolong and deepen the course of depressions. This is the essence of secular stagnation—sick recoveries which die in their infancy and depressions which feed on themselves."[6]

The historical impact of population growth on capital formation was difficult to measure, not least because National Accounts were in their infancy. In any case, Hansen estimated that population growth accounted for 40 percent of the capital formation in Western Europe and 60 percent of that in the US during the second half of the nineteenth century.[7] He predicted that faltering population growth could push capital formation into decline and the world into an abyss of permanent recession.

But Hansen also offered a redemptive vision: fostering inventiveness, raising the rate of profit of prospective investments or, if necessary, even increasing public spending, could provide crucial incentives to maintain both production and demand. "We are thus rapidly entering a world in which we must fall back upon a more rapid advance of technology than in the past if we are to find private investment opportunities adequate to maintain full employment," he argued.[8]

Hansen presented "economic progress" itself as the crux of the matter, with a clear role for social scientists: "The great transition, incident to a rapid decline in population growth and its impact upon capital formation and the workability of a system of free enterprise, calls for high scientific adventure along all the fronts represented by the social science disciplines."[9]

Was Hansen right or wrong? He is sometimes quoted today to gainsay predictions of doom. After all, "economic progress" accelerated in following decades while population surged, leaving the next generation to worry about the "population bomb." At the time, the Second World War and its aftermath generated a gigantic upsurge in aggregate demand, and a baby boom rapidly compensated for the war's short-term deadly effects. By 1944, US real GDP was double the 1939 level. The upsurge was caused by war, but the experience had demonstrated the possibility of coordinated action to maintain aggregate demand.

The civilization that emerged from the war promised prosperity and indeed delivered nearly full employment in the most developed economies and impressive rates of growth in much of the world.

THE UNDERCONSUMPTIONISTS

Even in the postwar boom, the spectre of the Great Depression and its consequences lurked in the background. In the mainstream, Paul Samuelson, the leading bourgeois economist of the day, promised to finetune the economy with

[6] Ibid., p. 4. [7] Ibid., p. 8.

[8] Hansen shows his admiration for Knut Wicksell (1851–1926), a prestigious Swedish scholar who influenced the first theories of money and interest, and took from him the idea that lack of investment was explained by the low prospective rate of profit—Keynes would say "marginal efficiency of capital" to respect the "classical," i.e., neoclassical tradition—the interest rate being rather a passive variable. Hansen concluded that innovation was a key element to change that impasse (Hansen, 1934, p. 10).

[9] Ibid., p. 15.

aggregate-demand management, a blend of fiscal and monetary policy. Radical economists Paul Baran and Paul Sweezy painted a bleaker vision of *Monopoly Capital*.[10] They argued that the highly capital-intensive, highly productive corporations that completed their consolidation in the US postwar order endogenously generate systemic risks. These corporations create and reap an enormous surplus, but because profits in capitalism are concentrated, the production fails to generate mass demand for its own products. They labeled this systematic failure to complete the circuit of circular flow the underconsumptionist tendency in monopoly capitalism.

In their analysis, Baran and Sweezy explain the dodges that contemporary capitalism was employing to stave off an underconsumption crisis. Monopoly capitalism requires a societal infrastructure that is capable of absorbing the surplus, often in wasteful ways. The choice of output, including the production of luxury goods and explicit design of mass-market goods for obsolescence and repeat purchase, organizes product markets to absorb some of the surplus. Advertising serves two purposes: the sales effort itself employs designers, account executives, broadcasters, and large staffs, and the advertising stimulates consumers to keep buying. Government spending, a demonstrated success in consuming and spurring consumption during the recovery from the Great Depression, can absorb surplus and complement consumption of private output, for example, through the construction of highways. But government activity must be strictly controlled to avoid altering the underlying shares of class wealth and power. Military spending offers another way to burn rapidly and repeatedly through the output of the productive capacity.

Interestingly finance receives only passing mention in *Monopoly Capital*, where Baran and Sweezy remark that finance, insurance, and real estate are similar in scale and importance to the sales effort in the attempt to generate new surplus-absorbing sectors to consume the vast output of industrial society.[11] They focus on the quantity rather than the distinctive quality of finance in their analysis, an indication of how the reign of monopoly capitalism had not yet given way to the rise of finance capitalism. The focus at that time was the underconsumption problem of monopoly capitalism. Their argument gave analytic depth and historical continuity to the threat of secular stagnation in advanced capitalism. Sweezy and fellow *Monthly Review* colleague Harry Magdoff would soon perceive and elaborate the critical role of finance in bolstering capitalism's flagging fortunes in the 1970s.

DOOM AGAIN?

By the turn of the century, however, the mood had reverted throughout the developed countries: declining populations, slower economic growth, and chronically high unemployment.

The crisis that began in 2008 with its precursors in the Japanese slump after 1989 and the rise in depression thinking renewed interest in Hansen's concept of "secular stagnation." Krugman, who had early understood the significance of the

[10] Baran and Sweezy (1966). [11] Ibid., pp. 139–140.

Japanese slump with the corollary "it could happen here," continued to warn of "bubbles, regulation, and secular stagnation," Krugman in fact offers asset deflation induced by demographic slowdown in Japan as one facet in his model of that country's decades-long slump.[12]

Summers, whose adventures as academic and public official were previously discussed, took up the campaign in November 2013 proposing to the IMF Forum that a new crisis could be ignited by the unreformed financial system and that the ongoing stagnation plaguing Europe and the US was the consequence of the current direction of policy.[13] In February 2014, Summers presented "US economic prospects: secular stagnation, hysteresis, and the zero lower bound" to the National Association for Business Economics. He argued that the mandate of macroeconomics had changed (or had better change) from "manage cycles," to "avoid secular stagnation." In other words, action is needed to save the world from permanent depression.

In some circles Summers and Krugman were derided, like Hansen, as doomsayers. But their direct observations that a decade-long slump and anemic recovery indicated to many that something was deeply wrong in the economic structure of the developed countries—and in the theories that cannot explain the slowdown.

It is easy to mock doomsday predictions, and not every economist subscribes to the secular stagnation hypothesis. Dani Rodrik, himself a frequent critic of the mainstream, is more confident than the doomsayers. Rodrik notes that the richest and poorest parts of the world, beginning with an income gap of 2:1 on the eve of the Industrial Revolution, underwent a "great divergence" that has expanded the gap to 80:1. This historical divergence process moved a powerful cycle of growth and the development of human and technical capabilities and institutions. High productivity industries attracted labor. The result has been increased global inequality but the optimist in Rodrik nonetheless holds out hope, observing that global median income consistently grew in the late twentieth century and at the turn of the century—at least until the subprime crash and recession.[14]

Bernanke turns the argument on its head: increased global risk and slow growth have generated a savings glut as the capital generated in the less-developed economies seeks safe investments in the developed world. The glut has lowered interest rates in the long term—at least in the most developed economies, since the excess of savings leads to abundance of capital but no accumulation or investment.[15]

Other economists show more skepticism about secular stagnation, arguing that debt is the monster consuming the economies. Kenneth Rogoff points to a "debt super-cycle, not secular stagnation," as the underlying source of imbalances.[16] Still others offer that the burst of the subprime bubble created a "balance sheet recession"; the liabilities of affected firms remain on their books, and these analysts fear that firms will need to pay back their debts in a depressed market.[17]

[12] Krugman (1998, 2013b). [13] Summers (2013).

[14] According to Rodrik and Subramanian (2009), pp. 9–10, the 1988 world median income was US $846 (2005 purchasing power parity-adjusted dollar) and increased by 43% to $1,209 by 2005. But Rodrik notes that within-country inequality increased, for instance, in the US and China.

[15] For instance, the argument by Bernanke (2015b). [16] Rogoff (2015). [17] Koo (2014).

FROM GREAT MODERATION TO GREAT DANGER

Ben Bernanke, the head of the US Federal Reserve who inherited the system on the eve of the subprime crash and managed it through the crisis, once promulgated the concept of the Great Moderation, discussed in previous chapters.[18] He knows history, which is rare in the profession. In his pre-Fed and academic incarnation, Bernanke was an expert on business cycles and the Great Depression. So perhaps greater caution was in order when he, eerily echoing Irving Fisher's optimistic 1928 pronouncement, declared a permanent plateau of good business, with the era of output volatility and inflation happily left behind.

Bernanke was not alone. Robert Lucas boldly declared that the problem of depression prevention had been solved for many decades.[19] Stanley Fischer, Bernanke's PhD adviser and a prominent advocate of central bank independence, instead attributed the success to the stricter rules adopted by the central banks. For Bernanke himself, as he was already a member of the Board of Governors of the Fed and would become Chair on the eve of the crash, his proclamation of the "Great Moderation" in his 2004 speech appears self-indulgent in retrospect.

These are not merely innocent bystanders. The central banks were deeply enmeshed in the plot, and the financial crash induced a highly volatile impact not only on the major economies but everywhere. For the first time since the end of the Second World War, the planet's GDP contracted. Bernanke and the "great moderators" were wrong about everything: wrong about predictions because the cycle exploded when it was supposed to have vanished and wrong about policies, which led the world over the brink of economic disaster. Anyway, all signs of moderation disappeared as the crisis unleashed the forces of financial bankruptcy. As the crisis turned into recession and the recession refused to end, secular stagnation returned to vogue.[20]

As with all grand predictions, there is a danger in words. Some of the protagonists of secular stagnation are recent migrants from the land of "great moderation." Perhaps the dictum of US baseball great Yogi Berra, known for his wise-fool aphorisms, is most appropriate, "It's tough to make predictions, especially about the future." An alternative interpretation of the current sluggishness that some see as deeply embedded secular stagnation is that the malaise is systemic but interpretable and even reversible. As a consequence, there is an orthodox response to the crash, the combination of austerity policy and the blowback of decades of inflation fighting, that is responsible for the prolonged crisis.

The orthodox argument goes as follows. Under the post-crash conditions, a negative real interest rate is needed to equate savings and investment at full employment.[21] But negative real interest rates cannot be realized because there is a zero lower bound on policy interest rates. So we are condemned to a jobless recovery and a mediocre recovery at most. Simply put, there will be not enough investment. Furthermore, the slump accentuates the risk of deflation, which can

[18] Bernanke (2004). [19] Lucas (2003b), p. 1703.

[20] The debate is summarized in Teulings and Baldwin (2014), which includes pieces from the major contenders.

[21] This is the so-called Wicksellian rate, from the work of Swedish economist Knut Wicksell (1851–1926).

reinforce depression tendencies. And staying at the zero lower bound brings risks of its own: Ponzi schemes are likely because the supply of safe assets has been drastically reduced and, armed with low interest rates, the incentive to play risky games is elevated.[22]

Economists bemoan the inadequacy of two policy tools, monetary and fiscal policy, to address three necessary targets, full employment and output growth, fiscal probity, and price stability. Lawrence Summers writes in the same text that "it may be impossible for an economy to achieve full employment, satisfactory growth, and financial stability simultaneously simply through the operation of conventional monetary policy."[23] If the interest rate cannot be low enough to promote full employment and if, furthermore, flexible wages and prices only exacerbate the problem through deflation, Summers concludes that the economic structure itself may condemn the world to lasting depression.

Summers identifies multiple headwinds, factors accounting for deficient demand and long-term low interest rates, leading to slower population growth; to innovation slowdown (although Robert J. Gordon of Northwestern University has been a more forceful advocate for the technology dry-well hypothesis); given the reduced capital intensity of the available new technologies, to low impact on employment; and to high inequality concentrating wealth among people with the lowest propensity to spend. These forces reduce the demand for capital goods and reduce aggregate demand altogether. Extended stagnation can even permanently reduce potential growth: lower aggregate output today lowers potential output in the future, a process called hysteresis, in which recessions are not merely unpleasant deviations from a steady growth trend but have the potential for degrading growth tomorrow.[24]

The other side of the coin of scarcity of investment is an excess of savings, funds not used to purchase goods and services from labor and physical capital but instead diverted to the financial markets searching for the nut under the shell. These funds fuel the world of the shadows we are investigating in this book. In some cases, such as in Europe, that trajectory was reinforced by direct, elite decisions imposing austerity on fragile economies. For fifteen years prior to the onset of the crisis the European authorities, in particular those of the Eurozone, had carved in stone the obligation for its governments to curb demand. Even when the crisis came, the mandate for fiscal rectitude dictated policies to reduce the total output and to increase unemployment in order to correct the effects of recession, which exacerbated the crisis.[25]

Excess of savings without opportunities for productive investment poses a problem. It leads to bubbles. For some time the "US housing bubble absorbed China's excess saving,"[26] but the solution is unsustainable and dangerous.

[22] Teulings and Baldwin (2014), p. 10. The global safe asset stock was reduced from 37% of world GDP in 2007 to 18% in 2011 according the Barclays Equity Gilt Study of 2012 as quoted by Caballero and Farhi (2014), pp. 112–13, due in particular to the reclassification of public debt from European countries as unsafe. On the history of Charles Ponzi and his schemes, see Chapter 8.

[23] Summers (2014a). [24] Ibid., p. 29.

[25] The rules of austerity in Europe require a permanent reduction of deficit and debt, or a very strong contraction of the public spending, which aggravates the excess of savings, Teulings and Baldwin (2014), p. 20.

[26] Ibid., p. 14.

Although some authors charitably argue about the usefulness of "rational bubbles" to absorb excess savings, reality is harsh.[27]

Collapsing confidence in speculative markets creates a domino effect without boundaries.

The financial bubble has become a permanent feature of contemporary economies. Without substantive structural changes to tame financial speculation, there is no alternative to future events of collapse and recessions. Investment remains low in spite of capital being cheaper. Policy interest rates throughout the developed economies have been close to zero for years. As Summers has noted, today's leading investment opportunities require modest amounts of physical capital. WhatsApp has greater market value than Sony; Google's valuation far exceeds that of General Motors. Today's success stories make clear that capital is available, capital is cheap, and capital is spending most of its time chasing financial assets.

INNOVATION TO SOLVE THE CONUNDRUM

Hansen's answer is to foster innovation. But even innovation can prove a double-edged sword depending on the ability to substitute labor for capital.

The contenders in the technological stalemate debate are among the most respected scholars in the US. Eichengreen of Berkeley and Mokyr of Northwestern University argue that innovation continues to play as central a role as in previous periods of the history of capitalism.[28] But Robert Gordon, also at Northwestern, anticipated this debate, pointing out "faltering innovation," and highlights major new trends violating the classical pattern of growth. Gordon argues that the innovation slowdown is not required to reduce growth over the long run. A no-growth horizon could emerge from any of the following: stagnant population growth, a completed education revolution with little possibility of a repeat performance, gross inequality reducing aggregate demand, and substantial public debt justifying public austerity. Taking the long perspective, Gordon estimates that the four headwinds could reduce the average annual performance of the 1891–2007 high-growth period by 2 full percentage points. A growth fall-off that powerful would impact potential output even if technological progress follows the historical norm.[29] It would be stagnation at best, a disaster at worst.

In Europe, although the discussion does not follow the US pattern, it is possible to find EU staff repeating the warnings of the secular-stagnationists: the slowdown of the growth rate of the working age population, the increase in the "non-accelerating inflation rate of unemployment," reduced "total factor productivity" growth, i.e., the pace of innovation, and low rates of capital formation are responsible for "chronic demand shortage" and no recovery of investment, the argument goes. The prospects are dark, given aging, rising income inequality, and

[27] Gross (2009). See, for example, the pop book *Pop!*.

[28] This is the perspective of Eichengreen (2014); Mokyr (2014); and E. Glaeser (2014).

[29] By 2012 Gordon had developed this notion of a reduction in the long-term growth rate of the US economy (2012 and 2014, p. 52), with more complete development in Gordon (2016).

the reduction in investment and consumption. "The euro area is mostly facing a secular decline in productivity growth and aging, which started before the great recession and continues today," one economist working for the European Commission concludes.[30] Although the European Commission acts otherwise, this analysis confirms the danger.

The fear of stagnation is indeed based on facts. As we write this book, the recession or stagnation lingers in the most powerful economies and the recovery is limited and unbalanced across countries and classes. The case for stagnation seems particularly strong because different theories, from the innovation slowdown (Gordon) to inequality (Stiglitz), to all of the above combined with a global capital glut and a reduction in the capital needs of production (Summers). There are indeed more snakes than ladders.

FINANCIAL BUBBLES, DEBT, AND...

This disagreement on secular stagnation is more than an academic kerfuffle. Although carried out in polite circles, the debate concerns imminent danger. "The global economy is in serious danger," claims Summers, considering the risk to be as great as in the moments following the Lehman Brothers debacle.[31] Inequality, slow productivity growth, and uncertainty have increased the propensity to save.

The savings are channeled to risky assets, and Summers offers the unconventional wisdom, "Western bond markets are sending a strong signal that there is too little, rather than too much, outstanding government debt." Summers continues to advocate unorthodox measures including deficit spending and the expansion of central bank balance sheets because "it is an irony of today's secular stagnation that what is conventionally regarded as imprudent offers the only prudent way forward." Krugman strikes the same chord, provocatively claiming, "Debt is good."[32]

They have several good points. First, loose monetary policy, or the central banks pouring liquidity into financial markets failed to deliver growth, investment, or employment. The old adage "you can't push on a string" applied. The systematic downgrading of IMF forecasts documents the progress of pessimism.[33] One report calculates that the twenty-three richest countries cumulatively lost 8.4 percent of their potential output between the onset of the recession and 2015, as if "the entire German economy had evaporated."[34]

Pits without ladders reawakened interest in hysteresis, the absence of self-correcting forces, and the prospect that economies once down would stay down.

[30] Roeger (2014), pp. 23, 29; Pichelmann (2015). In another research note, an economist from the EU Directorate for Economic and Financial Affairs rejects the stagnation hypothesis but admits that "enduring lack of demand and persistent periods of weak growth cannot be ruled out."

[31] Summers (2015), in the *Washington Post*.

[32] Summers (2015); Krugman (2015a).

[33] Relative to its own previsions by 2012, the IMF anticipated in 2015 a US GDP for 2020 smaller by 6%, in Europe by 3%, in China by 14%, and in the World by 6%. The World Bank concurred.

[34] Ball (2014), computed the long-term damage imposed by the recession on twenty-three OECD economies. The comparison of magnitude to Germany is from *The Economist* (June 14, 2014).

Economic policy, as conducted by the dominant states and their central banks under the sway of economic orthodoxy, failed to respond to the long recession.

Second, orthodox policy is based on poor historical perspective. Summers observes that if Europe imposed on itself a limit of 60 percent for the ratio of public debt to GDP when the costs of borrowing were around 5 percent, then the contemporary situation, with interest rates close to 0 percent, would support a much larger public debt (all the more so, given the two decades of austere living). The Maastricht Treaty limit of the ratio of public debt to GDP proved to be not a rule based on the likely cost of debt service but a fetish based on numerology and superstition—indeed, the rules imposed in the Treaty were invented as pure political cosmetics.[35]

Above all, debt was accumulating in the wrong places: for the more fragile economies of Europe, public debt and current account deficits generated a vicious cycle. The larger economies, which could have easily afforded additional public debt, declined to issue the stimulus.

Too much debt, or too little, is that the question? The question must include its composition between public and private: with public debt between large countries with sovereign currency and smaller countries constrained by trade balance and currency unions; and with private debt among the financial sector, non-financial firms, and households. But certainly debt is increasing in the global economy. *The Economist*, a venerable voice of neoliberalism, is intimidated by this imminent danger: "spotting future disaster," it denounces the "debt surge, [and the] ill-understood interconnections and uncertainty about safety nets."[36]

According to the reports by McKinsey, debt has grown mostly as bond issues by governments and by non-financial firms, which then in some cases turned into lenders.[37] Conventional economic theory is mute on the matter of debt, with the greatest theoretical result on corporate finance suggesting an indifference to the amount of debt. More Keynesian perspectives suggest that the growth of debt could be good news if firms and governments transform the borrowed funds into spending on investment and employment generation. But if we are trapped in a status quo of low investment and high propensity to save, the money is likely to find its way into financial markets.

As a consequence, the Hansen nightmare could happen again (not only during the Great Recession) and it can happen everywhere (not only in Japan). Declining population growth, public and private purchasing power choked by austerity, and stalling "technological progress" suggest limited effective demand for investment. We may face long-term "secular stagnation."

It's always easy to look silly as a pessimist. The technological stall could relent autonomously. Perhaps a 3-D printer in every home can do for the global north what backyard steel furnaces failed to do for China during its attempted Great Leap Forward of the late 1950s. The effect on productivity of the spread of personal computers remains controversial more than thirty-five years after the introduction

[35] The numbers for the Maastricht Treaty were picked out of the hat of a French official, Guy Abeille, for political convenience, with no technical support (*Le Parisien*, September 28, 2012). See also Pasinetti (1998).

[36] *The Economist*, September 7, 2013.

[37] Dobbs, Lund, et al. (2015).

of the PC. But as we write, strong political forces are brewing in Europe and the United States and the disputes over the immediate future are tainted by uncertainty.

... ITS PERILS

The IMF has been a key hinge for the global policy debate. Its actions, especially in the most vulnerable and depressed economies, undoubtedly aggravated the crisis of 2007–8 into the lengthy recession of 2009–13. Yet the IMF has also adopted a new openness to extravagant measures to meet the demands of extreme times, including forms of capital control. The IMF has defended, against its more orthodox partners, the need for public investment and economic growth to reduce the weight of the public debt, taking advantage of a cost of borrowing very close to zero.[38] The IMF has also appreciated the failure of monetary activism to spur investment and concluded that governments may invest directly. The IMF now apparently accepts that a debt-financed expansion can turn the tide against long-term stagnation. This could be the opening for a remarkable change of mood by a major international institution, perhaps not seen since the demise of the Treasury View on austerity and gold in the 1930s, if fiscal restrictions were not simultaneously imposed together with those restrictions. If contradictory orientations are suggested at the same time, the new ideas are reduced to mockery and the traditional institutional view dominates.

Nevertheless, inside the IMF—and the tension between two views inside the institution was already discussed in previous chapters—some voices indicate that the prevailing anti-expansionary policy leads to inequality, and therefore undermines the eventual and desired recovery. By 2010, two researchers had already made the point that inequality and debt precede and may also explain recessions,[39] and by 2016 a new team from the IMF targeted the neoliberal creed and argued that the traditional cocktail of austerity measures leads at least to further social differentiation and thus reduced growth potential, not to mention scarce benefits in terms of actual growth.[40] The impact of this challenge led the IMF to publish a hurried interview with its chief economist, Maurice Obstfeld, claiming that the argument of his colleagues had been "widely misinterpreted—it does not signify a major change in the Fund's approach."[41] He added that the authors were suggesting a tranquil evolution and not revolution in ideas.

Considering the stalemate of prevailing budgetary austerity, another path was also proposed and put into action during the long crisis. As governments remained wary of expansionary responses to recession, central banks turned to unconventional monetary activism. The central banks injected large amounts of money directly into firms and financial institutions, on a scale unprecedented in the era of independent central banking and with a scope of instruments that had previously been limited to after-dinner musing by post-Keynesian economists. This turn to quantitative easing, or the injection of liquidity into the market,

[38] International Monetary Fund (2014a).
[39] Kumhof and Rancière (2010).
[40] Ostry, Loungani, and Furceri (2016).
[41] Obstfeld (2016).

was a shocking repudiation of decades of monetary rectitude, with inflation as an intended, desired, and stated consequence. The money infusion directly provided the means to invest and indirectly encouraged currency depreciation to promote exports and a more favorable external balance. Such was the choice of the US and lately of the Eurozone monetary authorities. The US pioneered the strategy, with apparently effective results. In 2015, ECB President Mario Draghi proposed a Eurozone program of quantitative easing with planned purchases of more than €1 trillion of assets beginning that year, but perhaps too late as austerity and deflation hobbled aggregate demand beyond redemption.

Yet a specter haunts this expansionary monetary policy, the specter of financial speculation. Financial speculation raises the likelihood of bubbles but also bears on class politics: the inflation of prices of financial assets raises the wealth of the wealthy, who disproportionately hold those riches.

Criticisms of quantitative easing created curious bedfellows. Richard Fisher, a conservative economist and President of the Federal Reserve Bank of Dallas, opposed Bernanke's quantitative easing operation. Invoking a metaphor from military history, Fisher argued that the money would circumvent that "Maginot Line" of presumed fair use. Like a sweep through a previously impassable forest the new funds would find their way into unproductive but profitable uses, unfairly enriching the financial institutions that had been entrusted with their use in the broad public interest.[42]

Fisher, in a provocative argument for a conservative banker, suggests that the outflanking was inevitable or even intended. In a literary flourish that included quotes from Shakespeare and articulate former Fed chair Paul Volcker, Fisher notes the insidiousness of money when it fails to follow "proper circulation," quoting a 1735 poem by Jonathan Swift:

> Money, the life-blood of the nation,
> Corrupts and stagnates in the veins,
> Unless a proper circulation
> Its motion and its heat maintains.

While we concur regarding the corrupting role of money, we favor a broader explanation that encompasses the larger picture of strong and deliberate choices and decisions made in the breach but also in the business-as-usual governance of national and international monetary systems.

This global process at work at times responds to the interests and motivations of particular institutions but also tilts the playing field towards the economic and social advantages of groups and institutions. Never have policy interest rates been so low for so long. Cheap money abounds but investment and the growth it could lead remain absent in Europe. The means were available. If even before quantitative

[42] R. W. Fisher (2014), argues that "this liquidity can be used by financial intermediaries to lend to businesses to invest in job-creating capital expansion or by investors to finance the repairing of balance sheets at cheaper cost or on better terms, or for myriad other uses, including feeding speculative flows into financial markets. [...] But with low interest rates and abundant availability of credit in the non-depository market, the bond markets and other trading markets have spawned an abundance of speculative activity. There is no greater gift to a financial market operator—or anyone, for that matter—than free and abundant money. It reduces the cost of taking risk. But it also burns a hole in the proverbial pocket. It enhances the appeal of things that might not otherwise look so comely."

easing, the larger multinationals could borrow money more cheaply than European governments, with the advent of the new monetary policy funds were close to free. And yet no recovery was detected. Animal spirits, the domain of expectations about future profitability, prevented investment. In other words, no matter how cheap the money, the markets and the capitalists believed in secular stagnation.

Nevertheless, quantitative easing could not ease the long and deep slump suffered by the Eurozone because neither aggregate demand nor favorable expectations supported investment. Nonetheless liquidity poured forth liberally by the central banks provided a valuable option to private banks, to take refuge in financial assets that prop up equity values. This increases the potential for new bubbles, from rising prices in housing, especially in London, to real estate in China, or to stock and bond prices throughout the developed economies.

Worse still, the institutional adaptations to favor the recovery of the financial markets, promoting securitization again, accepting the return to the malpractices of the shadow system, incentivizing speculative applications, tend to aggravate the dangers. The push towards banking union in Europe and the unification of capital markets to re-invigorate securitization contain the seeds of the next crisis.

CHANGING A CHANGING WORLD, OR CAPITALISM WITHOUT GROWTH?

In the previous chapters of this book, we have argued that, despite their responsibility for the subprime crash, the most powerful financial institutions have actually increasingly gained in power since. We followed the money and found how, following the initial shock waves of devaluation of capital during the recession, regulation and policy have reset the terms to the advantage of the financial institutions, rather like pushing the snooze bar on a demanding alarm clock.

A McKinsey report gives a sense of the magnitude of the reallocation in favor of the financial institutions. Transnational corporations, themselves sites of enormously concentrated economic power, are predicted to see their profit decrease from 9.8 percent of the world GDP in 2013 to 7.9 percent in 2025.[43] Meanwhile, financial profits approach a postwar high,[44] and five banks control half of the world's equity trading.[45] Power is finance, and finance generates an extractive economy.

The result is stagnation, be it secular or for a long period. The explanation in the dominant academic debate turns around the Hansen factor (a demographic winter and its consequences on demand), Gordon's headwinds, the Summers synthesis of explanations for the lack of investment, and Stiglitz's and Piketty's focus on rising inequality.

[43] Dobbs, Koller, et al. (2015), As 80% of world trade requires the intervention of a transnational firm, and 36% of the trade is internal to these firms, that prospective change may have large implications on investment and trade.

[44] Admati and Hellwig (2014).

[45] The five are Goldman Sachs, Morgan Stanley, Credit Suisse, J.P. Morgan, and Bank of America.

Although we acknowledge these interpretations and subscribe to parts of them, our explanation is fundamentally different because our attention is concentrated on the course of the profit rate and the process of accumulation as the main driving force for the world economy.[46]

Rather than simply registering the deficit of investment, we look at the mismatch between profit and accumulation, reinforced by policies leading to the reduction of aggregate demand both caused by and subsequently reinforcing growing inequality. This is the Kalecki problem.

Michal Kalecki (1899–1970) was a fascinating Polish economist, who anticipated Keynes's views on effective demand (but never contested Keynes's primacy).[47] As continental Europe descended towards the abyss during the 1930s, Kalecki took refuge at the London School of Economics and later at Cambridge and Oxford, before returning to Warsaw after the war. One of his most famous papers discusses how the logic of power among capitalists may prevent a rational solution for the economy as a whole. Capitalists resist wage increases to augment their profits, but thereby tolerate lower aggregate demand and, hence, higher unemployment than efficiency would dictate. In recessions, capitalists consistently advocate austerity in lieu of counter-cyclical stimulus because crises offer opportunities to break trade unions, to otherwise curtail the power of labor, and to impose social discipline. Even as profits mount, accumulation, as measured by physical investment, may lag, both from low expectations and from deliberate social action of capitalists favoring downward wage pressure created by mass unemployment, or a regime-building strategy.

An analysis by, of all sources, Goldman Sachs supports the Kaleckian prediction. The return on physical capital—with profit measured as net operating surplus—in the ten largest world economies, representing 75 percent of the world GDP, has increased steadily since 1982.[48]

Even excluding the capital gains for holding and selling investments, the net yields of capital have grown comfortably. The profit rate peaked by the end of the century, in 1997, but remains robust. Even after the subprime crash and recession, the profit rate stayed positive. Yet, investment is failing.

The reasons for this result are straightforward and revealing. First, the fundamental source of profit is the extraction of value from labor, and the terms of extraction have been very convenient for capital.[49] Second, the emerging economies are a new driving force of the world economy, leading to an increase in the global labor supply, which raises the return on physical capital. Hansen's demographic winter really applies only in Europe and Japan (with hints of it in the United States) but the effective world labor force continues to grow, as emerging economies are integrated in the world market, with especially rapid contributions from the ex-Soviet Union,

[46] See Kotz and Basu (2015).

[47] Joan Robinson, who certainly admired Keynes, nonetheless insisted that Kalecki formulated the main threads of the theory of effective demand before Keynes.

[48] Daly and Broadbent (2009). Other alternative measures may be more sensitive to the distinction between the production of value and financial intermediation. See for instance M. Roberts (2012b).

[49] For the US, the Bureau of Labor Statistics indicates that, from 2000 to 2011, real output per person rose 2.5% a year, whereas real pay rose only 1%.

China, and also India. From 1980 to 2000, the global work force expanded by one to one-and-a-half billion people and then rapidly doubled to three billion.[50]

Never before has modern capitalism benefited from such a rapid extension of the market and such an increase of the labor force. So much for Hansen's demographic drama.

The impact of this changing world is also obvious in another dimension, that of an enlarged market in goods, services, and capital. The emergence of China and the transformation of the old USSR bloc are equivalent to the discovery of a new continent full of desirous consumers. More than any other factor, the incorporation of China in the global market prevented the subprime recession from deepening into a long depression. Together with other emerging markets, it also created new opportunities for finance.[51]

This evidence of growth in the rate of profit on physical capital provides a critique of the Bernanke's savings glut story. Money flows to speculative markets because it is especially profitable, not because other alternatives are lacking.

The Goldman Sachs analysts go even further. They argue that normal risk-averse behavior reversed itself. As risk-free government bonds offered vanishingly small returns, the equity risk premia increased, and speculation was the option.[52]

This finance-led economic regime makes this sort of extraction of value the backbone of hegemony. The social struggle Kalecki described enabled high unemployment and suppressed scarce demand. Globalized markets provided a short-term offsetting stimulus. Servicing large public debts consumes public budgets, which builds the case for austerity measures and leads, in turn, to more unemployment.

The vicious circle of the new economy of the twenty-first century is based on stagnation but it is a chosen stagnation rather than an inevitable outcome of unknown cosmic forces. In this sense, Hansen's vision of "depressions feeding on themselves," as he put it in the dark days of 1939, is applicable to our time.

MELTDOWN?

The mechanics of this financialized economic regime are overwhelming. Some of its extraction tools have already been presented: through financial intermediation it absorbs profits from those sectors of the economy producing goods and services, through the creation of debt it generates fees and interest payments, and through austerity it disciplines wages under huge permanent unemployment.

[50] Dobbs, Madgavkar, et al. (2012).

[51] The annual returns of the average mutual funds investment in emerging markets debt is 10.4% since 1998, and even these markets' stock funds get 8.2% a year. As a comparison, the big American stocks get 4.3% and the long-dated treasuries an average of 7.8% a year, for the past fifteen years (*The Economist*, April 20, 2013).

[52] The same Goldman Sachs analysts argue that there was no generalized asset bubble before the crash, yet one cannot but recognize that the mortgage market was inflated and ignited a contamination effect on a fragile and highly interdependent financial system.

Another tool, typically imposed by agreement of national authorities with international institutions such as the IMF, has been privatization. The first large wave of privatization of public assets began in the mid-1980s and grew to a peak around 2000. A second wave of privatization, with the new form of public-private partnerships, began on the eve of the crash in the mid-2000s.

Then, the crash forced a temporary reversal, as governments and central banks came to the rescue of finance. The bailout for banks, which sometimes took the form of outright nationalization, changed the landscape briefly.

Shortly after this exercise in emergency nationalization, both the banks and other public property returned to the auction block. There are plenty of state assets available for transfer. The combined value of the different state-owned entities in the OECD (excluding the US, for which there are no data) amounts to US $2.2 trillion, comparable to the value of all hedge funds combined. Adding the US $2 trillion value of the minority public stakes in firms and a host of non-financial assets (land, subsoil, buildings) for more than US $35 trillion, the public assets of the developed economies approximately equal world GDP, according to *The Economist* computation.[53] A host of profitable privatizations awaits the daring, although it may only reinforce the power of the financiers, and that is a gloomy prospect.

The schedule of profit is a crucial variable in the evolution of the economies, since it leads investment, employment, and social distribution, and represents by itself a social relationship describing the structure of the mode of production. Its long-term process was discussed by one of the authors, recapitulating the insights of Marx, Kondratiev, and Schumpeter, in a book with Chris Freeman, *As Time Goes By*.[54] The role of the industrial and technological revolutions was discussed in that work, emphasizing how financialization changed the form of modern capitalism and its accumulation conflicts.

AND THEN ENTERS TRUMP

Citigroup's changes of mood over *Trumponomics* are one of the revealing details of the surprising result of the Presidential race in the US: by November 4, 2016, just four days before the election, the bank's experts anticipated a drop of the S&P500 index by 5 percent; eight days after the election, they claimed that the announced cut of the corporate tax to 20 percent (Trump seemed to prefer 15 percent) could boost the earnings per share for the S&P500 firms by 9 percent, even offsetting the damaging effect of a stronger dollar and higher interest rates. In the four months following the election, the S&P index of banks soared by 34 percent.[55] After the tempest, the bonanza, although the plan was exactly the same.

The economic plan proposed by Trump, written by the then appointed Secretary of Commerce, the billionaire Wilbur Ross, proposed a tax cut for the wealthier and

[53] The US government owns one fifth of the land and, according to this *Economist* computation, this "saleable" property is worth US $9 trillion (*The Economist*, January 11, 2014).

[54] Freeman and Louçã (2001).

[55] *CNBC*, November 4, *CNBC*, November 16, 2016 and *The Economist*, May 6, 2017.

the corporations amounting to a loss of revenue of US $7 trillion over one decade. That would raise the debt ratio at least 26 percent. Adding the proposed investment in infrastructure (one billion more) and the increase of spending in defence—this is the most militarily staffed administration ever—implies large deficits and, as a consequence, higher debt, higher interest rates, and a stronger dollar, damaging exports and favoring imports. But Trump does not accept this consequence and intends to compensate for it with trade wars and protectionist threats.

Dan DiMicco, former CEO of the steelmaker Nucor and Trump's trade advisor during the campaign, appreciatively quotes Reagan's 45 percent tariff on Japanese motorcycles in the 1980s as an example. Yet, this example is not relevant, as more than thirty years ago the economies were not so globalized, US hegemony was stronger, and the US firms were less engaged in global production. DiMicco is called "the most protectionist guy in Washington," pressing for the end of different trade agreements, but apparently ignores the fact that 44 percent of the sales of the S&P500 firms are abroad or that, for instance, General Motors sells more cars in China than in the US. As a consequence, Trump's plan may fail: it is difficult to deliver on jobs with trade wars when so much of US consumption is based on imports, its public debt is partially owned by China, and its production is global.

On the campaign trail, Trump promised jobs for citizens and the expulsion of 11 million people to create job openings. The selection of Jeff Sessions, who as Senator aggressively advocated deportation, as Attorney General showed that Trump was serious. In the early years of the Trump administration deportations have increased in quantity and in ostentatious cruelty. But it remains to be seen if Trump's bourgeois voters will offer wages and working conditions sufficient to attract Trump's working class voters into the jobs of the expelled.

In summary, Trump threatens to create new deficits, changes in tax policy favoring inequality, exchange stress, and higher interest rates with huge consequences on world finance. In short, more instability.

CONCLUSION

The risks of a large-scale meltdown, in particular for the euro area, are significant. The crisis of 2007 revealed significant flaws, the huge scale of shadow finance, and the imbalances encouraged by deregulation, and how both are magnified by the interconnectedness of the financial system. Globalization, one of few forces offsetting Hansen factors, simultaneously becomes the phantom threatening the global markets.

In fact, the interdependencies have grown to an unprecedented scale: the financial market in Britain reaches five times its GDP, in Switzerland ten times, in the US eight times[56] and some financial firms have single-handedly reached the scale of US GDP or that of France or Germany. Global banking assets went up from 50 percent of world GDP in the 1960s to 200 percent by the late 2000s. Even for the large and somewhat isolated US, about 40 percent of profits and one third of

[56] In 1980 it was four times, but the weight doubled in thirty years.

the revenue of large publicly traded firms currently come from abroad. The same applies to the debt of firms: for instance, borrowing in dollars by non-financial Asian firms tripled from 2008 to 2014. Offshore companies pump out everywhere, Ponzi schemes resurface, debt skyrockets: the world of global finance is as unstable as it was in summer 2007.

Throughout the neoliberal era, deregulating rules, indoctrination, and selection of state and non-state actors delivered an outstanding result of social hegemony for finance. This is why stagnation is the hegemonic policy of our epoch.

12

China, A New Global Player

When, in June 2015, Jack Ma, one of the richest men in China and in the world, took the floor at the Economic Club of New York, in the luxurious salons of the Waldorf Astoria Hotel, the surprise was not the circumstances but the speech itself. The hotel is now owned by a Chinese insurance company run by Deng Xiaoping's grandson-in-law, a turn of events that no alarmed and xenophobic advocate of an earlier decade could ever have imagined. But such an advocate would be even more surprised to hear what Ma had to say: that the 650 million internet users in China spend more than those in the entire US do,[1] and consequently that there is a market opportunity to be seized. That is the business of Ma's company, Alibaba, which proceeded to the most splendorous entrance in the international stock market—never had a firm obtained such a high value of capitalization in its first day. Ma was heard and essentially understood.

By any measure, this number as well as others describing the Chinese economy are impressive: between 2011 and 2013 China poured more concrete than the US throughout the whole of the twentieth century, and its surplus capacity in steelmaking is larger than the combined steel production of Japan, the US, and Germany. As a consequence, it nowadays imports more materials for the semiconductor industry than oil, and its savings approach half of the total of all the emerging economies.[2]

This chapter presents a brief overview of the recent development of China and in particular of the social problems lying ahead, in order to reassess the view of financialization and the danger of secular stagnation that was laid out in the previous chapter. Discussing whether the Chinese economy, grand as it is, has the conditions to prevent that stagnation and to generate a new wave of growth, we conclude that such prospects are dim.

CHINA, A FORERUNNER OF (STATE) NEOLIBERALISM

In almost any recounting of the history of neoliberalism, two elections, Margaret Thatcher's in Britain in May 1979 and Ronald Reagan's in the US in November 1980

[1] *The Economist*, October 3, 2015. Anbang, an insurer, bought the symbolic Waldorf Astoria, and also bought Fidea Assurances, in Belgium, and Woori, the second bank in South Korea; *The Economist*, February 7, 2015.

[2] Larry Summers, October 7, 2015, *Washington Post*; *The Economist*, February 27, 2016 and July 25, 2015.

mark the ascendancy. The elections brought neoliberal standard-bearers to power and, with them, the return of *laissez-faire* policies and politics. Yet the emergence of the neoliberals was immediately preceded by another triumph: the rise of an older statesman conducting a new campaign for reform in China. The time was December 1978, and the man was Deng Xiaoping (1904–97), an old Communist Party dignitary who had suffered imprisonment and internal exile during the tumultuous Cultural Revolution.

Deng capped his return to power in a fierce battle for control of the Party, vanquishing and annihilating the widow and other close allies of the deceased Chairman Mao Zedong, the "Gang of Four," who were purged in 1976. Although Deng never held the highest state, government, or party office he nonetheless led China as "paramount leader." In December 1978, his internal power struggle largely complete, he proclaimed a new epoch of modernization and introduced a strategic opening to international capital. From 1978 to 1992, a program of reforms was imposed, beginning with market-oriented experiments in Guangdong province near Hong Kong, and then extended to other parts of the country.

Deng, already known for his aphorisms, such as, "it doesn't matter whether the cat is black or white, as long as it catches mice," declared in 1992, "to get rich is glorious."[3] Glorious days would come for Deng and China at the end of the century. Yet Deng's opening did not extend to the social realm: he was responsible for the massacre of protesting students in Tiananmen Square in June 1989. (The objects of the protests were ambiguous and multifarious; students oriented towards concepts of politics predominant in the West and North joined forces with people resisting market reforms, including many dislocated by the new economy. Yet the brutality of the repression bore witness to the difficulties of the regime.) Strict control of the Party remained a pillar in the new economy. Economic liberalism does not necessarily match with civil liberties, as we noted in other cases.

China's continued growth with a model that includes economic liberalism and export orientation holds out hope for widespread resuscitation of the globalization model.

CHINA AS THE LARGEST WORLD ECONOMY

In this economic reform process, transnational firms were welcomed to obtain technology transfers and foreign reserves. Their success was conditioned by political choices, by fast learning, and, when needed, by economic retaliation.[4] Benefiting from that investment and from the mobilization of its resources, China

[3] Hong Li (1977), p. 107.

[4] Many multinationals made large profits from their Chinese operation, which became a crucial part of their enterprise. That is the case of Apple, of Adidas, and of Samsonite; one of the first to get established Yum Brands, owns thousands of KFC restaurants. In other cases, the multinationals suffer from the conditions for competition: IBM and Cisco were under pressure in 2016 as they were sidelined in public procurement, to the advantage of Huawei and Lenovo, as the US authorities blacklisted Huawei from official contracts. GlaxoSmithKline, a major British drug-maker, was fined under the anti-corruption law, and other firms went through the same process (Bloomberg, September 30, 2016).

rapidly became the factory of the world. The country joined the World Trade Organization in 2001, and after 2005 virtually the entire territory was opened to foreign investment. In the ensuing years, massive trade surpluses made China a player in the international flows of capital. China holds the largest national stock of US sovereign debt, more than US $1.2 trillion of Treasury bills.

Such was the result that Romano Prodi, former Prime Minister of Italy and President of the European Commission, noted with sadness: "Italian industrial policy is now made in Beijing."[5] Indeed, China became the biggest foreign investor in Italy by 2014, and its European investments increased nine-fold from 2010 to 2014.[6] The Chinese National Chemical Corporation, CNCC, bought Pirelli, but it also bid against Monsanto for the Swiss giant Syngenta. The diversity of Chinese direct investment abroad includes a public company buying a stake at a French-built nuclear plant in the UK, the Ninebot robotics firm buying Segway in the US, the property and entertainment conglomerate and Dalian Wanda buying Legendary Entertainment (the studio for *Jurassic Park*) on the same day that Beijing Kunlun Tech bought Grindr, a social media network for gay men.[7] Other Chinese investors bought shares in Heathrow, Toulouse airport, and Club Med, as well as Kuka, the largest German builder of robots, and McCormick, the truck constructor. In France, Dongfeng bought a part of Peugeot; Weichai bought the investment fund Axa Private Equity; and China Investment Corporation bought part of GDF-Suez. Zhang Guohua bought the European leader in plywood, Plysorol, essentially to obtain its property of 600 thousand acres of forest in Gabon. The Chinese company Geely also owns Volvo in Sweden and other national firms own the major electricity supplier and its distributor in Portugal, as well as insurance and financial companies. Great Wall bid to buy Fiat-Chrysler or at least its subsidiary, Jeep. Weichai Power controls Kion, a major player in the production of transport for logistics.[8]

This investment is the result of an important surplus, obtained from impressive growth. In 1990 China manufacturing accounted for less than 3 percent of the world industrial production. By the mid-2010s, China produced 80 percent of the world's air conditioners, 70 percent of its mobile phones, and 60 percent of its shoes. China's share in global clothing exports exceeds 40 percent. One in four laptops are made in China, and the share is increasing.[9] At market exchange rates, the US represents a share of 23 percent of the world's roughly US $80 trillion GDP and China only 14 percent, but by measures that account for the purchasing power of the yuan, China is already the largest economy in the world, with 17 percent to the US 16 percent.[10] Considering trends in trade and foreign investment, China will eventually even move ahead and is expected to become the world's largest economy at market prices early in the next decade.[11]

[5] *The Economist*, March 28, 2015.
[6] From €2 billion to €18 billion, *Financial Times*, March 10, 2016.
[7] *The Economist*, September 12, 2015, October 24, 2015, January 16, 2016,
[8] *Frankfurter Allgemeine Zeitung*, August 22, 2017.
[9] *China Daily*, June 16, 2014. [10] World Bank (2017a).
[11] One of the consequences of growth was that between 1980 and 2000, 600 million people were lifted out of poverty. Wolf (2014), p. 30.

IS ASIA THE CENTER OF THE WORLD?

In spite of this extraordinary performance and perhaps contrary to conventional wisdom, Asia is not the economic center of the world. Not yet, at least. While Asian growth is one of the more impressive feats of contemporary times, the historical gap between Asia and other parts of the world is so large that differential growth will still take some years to bring Asia to the top.

Its rapid growth is narrowing the gap. Asia's 26.5 percent share of total manufacturing in 1990 almost doubled by 2013 to 46.5 percent. Asia's share in the global trade of intermediate inputs rose from 14 percent in 2000 to 50 percent in 2012.[12] But, while Asia already produces almost half of manufacturing (and 45 percent of carbon emissions), in some ways Asia remains isolated and distinct. Its firms represent only 27 percent of market capitalization and a little more than one quarter of world exports. Large Asian firms export more than the average of their economies, but not much: Asia's 100 largest corporations register only 32 percent of sales abroad compared to a 52 percent export share of output for Western corporations.

Because the region runs persistent trade surpluses, it already concentrates half of the world's currency reserves and boasts one quarter of the world's billionaires, facts with enormous consequences for the future. The region's economy is certainly preparing for that future: Asian firms and institutions invested 28 percent of world R&D spending and registered 41 percent of the patents by the mid-2010s. This is an exceptional level of activity in forward-looking investment,[13] and provides for a rapid change of the structure of the economy and society. Yet new social problems come with success.

THE STATE AND THE MARKET IN THE ECONOMY

One explanation for this rapid growth is the concentration of capacities and resources, made possible by the fact that most of these economies are typically controlled or managed by the state. This control takes different forms in different countries, from China, where the state has had a leading role in planning and manufacturing, to South Korea, where the public authorities played a significant role in the allocation of credit to designated private actors.

Europeans and North Americans who criticize these types of public involvement in economic development would do well to recall the building of empires and how capital accumulation proceeded in Europe through a bloody combination of piracy, invention, and royal charters; the advance of market control under the guns of flagships; and dramatic social transformation under both dispossession and industrial revolution. In any case, the world trembling under the threat of brute force was the condition for Western success for many years, and it is impossible to conceive a more state interventionist path to national wealth.

One consequence of this political control is that Asia remains relatively closed to foreign direct investment, of which the region receives only 17 percent of the

[12] World Bank (2017a). By 2014, the annual growth rate was 6.0% in India and 6.7% in China, but for Indonesia it is 3.7%, as compared to 0.1% for Japan and 1.6% for the USA.

[13] Intellectual Property Watch (2015).

world total. In China, foreign stockholders are forbidden in internet companies. In this epoch of globalization, the profit share of foreign-owned Chinese banks actually decreased and their share of the Chinese banking industry was reduced from 2.4 percent in 2012 to 1.7 percent in 2013.[14] Nevertheless, there is some wiggle room in these accounts: according to the Bank for International Settlements, international bank lending to China doubled in the same period as Chinese firms issued debt through foreign subsidiaries.

The peculiarity of contemporary Chinese development, as compared to other societies, is the extension of public property, as state-owned firms continue to dominate the landscape in China. Among the ninety-five Chinese companies in the 2014 *Fortune 500*, some four-fifths are publicly owned firms.[15] Still other firms technically listed as private adhere strictly to official control.

Take the case of Legend Holdings, which acquired IBM's PC division, renamed it Lenovo, and is now the world's largest producer of personal computers. It owes its origins to a 1984 loan by the Chinese Academy of Science, which still retains 36 percent of the operation. Under the guidance of Liu Chuanzhi, Legend Holdings has integrated a majority of private capital.[16] The public and the private in the partnership cannot be meaningfully disentangled.

The evolution of capital ownership is also slow and politically managed by the state in most Asian countries. As a consequence, only 28 percent of the region's stock market corresponds to firms with several owners, i.e., conventional joint stock companies. States own a towering 40 percent of stock with families holding an additional 27 percent, and only 5 percent are exclusively foreign property. Even compared to emerging economies, where the state may be a powerful economic player, Asia stands out for the degree of state involvement. The outstanding case is that of China, for obvious historical reasons: it has the most extensive and comprehensive public management of the economic and financial system. Chinese state-owned firms account for 60 percent of stock market capitalization,[17] while for Russia and Brazil the share of this type of firm is around 40 percent (counting both majority and minority stakes). Yet Chinese public firms represent only around one tenth of exports (down from two-thirds in 1995) and only one third of capital spending, whereas the private sector accounts for two-thirds of total output.

In spite of this level of control by the Chinese state,[18] the Chinese economy is already permeated by market forces, and the Chinese state accommodates market pressures.

ADVENTURES AND PERILOUS ESCAPES

Among the Asian economies, China stands out as an intriguing case of structural and institutional change, and in terms of conventional growth measures it is a success story.

[14] *The Economist*, June 20, 2015; June 28, 2014.
[15] Fortune (2017).
[16] Credit Suisse Asia Pacific/China Equity Research (2015).
[17] *The Economist*, May 31, 2014. By December 2013 Canada had allowed a Chinese public firm to buy a Canadian oil company, suggesting it would be the last (*Wall Street Journal*, June 22, 2015).
[18] *Financial Times*, November 9, 2012. According to China's company law, a Communist Party cell must exist in each firm of a certain size, and the government effectively manages the firms.

China's advantages include substantial and growing self-sufficiency: 65 percent of the inputs for goods produced in China are of domestic origin, up from 40 percent in the mid-1990s. The enormous national polity and market gives the additional advantage of concentrating power and resources, enabling a vast program of investment in public infrastructure and the potential for macroeconomic stabilization. As the global economy slowed during the Great Recession, and as the internal social pressures mounted, China adopted a new approach to the economy, replacing investment in export capacity with new investment for domestic consumption.

Yet even China faces the menace of slower growth and an increase in national debt, with a decline in construction being responsible for a significant reduction in GDP growth.[19] At the center of the difficulties is the financial system. China has a grafted financial system that relies simultaneously on: a high household savings rate in regulated banks and other vehicles; elements of shadow banking that mobilize large sums outside the regulated banking sector; and extensive state regulation with, for now, at least, public support in the case of malfunction. In this section, we examine how the shadow banking system developed in China as part of that success story, and how it now threatens the system.

The development of modern financial labyrinths in China is more homegrown than due to foreign transplants. In other sectors, foreign companies own substantial shares of China's exports. For example, in high-tech goods the foreign-owned share of exports is 82 percent, and a huge number of Chinese workers toil at assembly lines of electronic products mostly for foreign-owned firms.[20] But the most important financial innovation of the last decades, shadow finance, grew from the national banking and industrial systems under the vigilance of the state in China. Indeed, the main conflicts over economic policy in China concern financial liberalization and the fate of the state-owned enterprises.

Banking grew rapidly under Deng Xiaoping: from 1985 to 1993 alone, the number of branches of the state-owned banks increased from 61,000 to 144,000, and the number of employees doubled as well.[21] Furthermore, banking in China is subject to strict supervision and complex supports that are unparalleled in other economies navigating the waters of financial globalization, but strict supervision and complex support are not necessarily coherently integrated.

The trade press account of the optimistically named Credit Equals Gold No. 1 bond provides a telling story of supervision and intervention. The bond, issued in 2011 by the Industrial and Commercial Bank of China (ICBC), the largest bank in China, raised 3 billion yuan (US $490 million) with a promise of annual returns of 10 percent on the basis of the future dividends from a mining company. Payments

[19] Since 2007, growth in China is the consequence of internal demand, not external, and a large investment effort fueled by credit, that represents more than 50% of GDP. In spite of this effort, the diminishing marginal increase explains a GDP growth of 7% expected for 2015, the slowest in a quarter-century. Curiously, the budget still registers a 10.1% increase in the military budget, compared to 12.2% the previous year. The total debt in 2014 was more than 250% of GDP, growing 100% since 2008, although most of the debt is internal (*The Economist*, March 7, 2015; April 18, 2015, October 18, 2014). Studying the impact of changes in investment, UBS estimates that cutting 10% in construction investment, a typical response to this type of bubble, explains a GDP decrease of 3%.

[20] *The Economist*, May 31, 2014, October 4, 2014.

[21] See Harvey (2005), p. 103, and *Asian Times*, June 1, 2002.

lapsed, but days before default an unknown buyer acquired the assets of the mining company. The principal was repaid, although the investors did lose part of the interest.[22] The regulators chose to intervene—albeit silently and without public comment—in bailing out Credit Equals Gold No. 1.

A second bailout was not forthcoming: the equally moribund mining bond Credit Equals Gold No. 2 played the role of Lehman Brothers to Credit Equals Gold No. 1's Bear Stearns. In this second case, the coal-mining firm went bankrupt, and the clients lost both interest and principal.[23] The choice of response again went unexplained. In other countries publicly managed rescue operations are common, but silence is not typical. In China, the visible hand of the state became invisible. These shadow responses to crises in shadow finance reveal much about the financial connections in China and how the government promotes, directs, and disciplines the shadow finance system.

Can it keep such control? The tensions are evident. China is the third largest world bond market, after the US and Japan, but even so the capital market is small relative to the population and growing economy, as less than one fifth of household wealth is applied in shares. The dangers of capital flight, as in the last months of 2015, may thus disturb future economic policy choices.[24]

THE FINANCIAL AND BANKING SYSTEM

The four largest lenders in China are the Industrial and Commercial Bank of China,[25] the China Construction Bank, the Bank of China, and the Agricultural Bank of China. The first two are gigantic firms of over 400,000 employees each (the size of Volkswagen).[26] They operate as retail banks and institutions for private credit allocation but also as branches of the Treasury, implementing a particular form of *dirigiste* finance to fund state debt and their assets represent 40 percent of national GDP. This banking sector is the biggest in the world, while the Chinese stock market is second to that of the US and the bond market is the third in the world—but the fastest growing.

Besides the four giants, a host of asset management companies has emerged in the recent years, financed by complex securitization procedures. For example, in a typical scheme, a bank establishes a special purpose vehicle to buy a package of loans from an industrial trust. The special purpose vehicle sells the rights to the income to its own bank, which in turn sells the presumptive income stream to another bank. A chain of collaborating institutions without distinct boundaries of interests, with high promised payment streams, and with some expectations of bailout in case of crisis, creates opportunities for the development of bubbles.

[22] *Financial Times*, August 31, 2014. [23] *Forbes*, January 27, 2014.

[24] This happened in the last month of 2015, for instance, and that risk had already been pointed out (*The Guardian*, January 23, 2016). The level of capital flight by the end of 2015 would imply an annualized movement of US $1 trillion.

[25] China's ICBC is the largest shareholder in the Standard Bank, the largest in Africa. Brazil's BTG Pactual Bank is allied with VTB, Russia's second largest bank, and Citic Securities, a Chinese bank (*Financial Times*, June 12, 2012).

[26] *The Economist*, August 31, 2013.

These intermediary institutions have surged in the past five years, growing fivefold to manage 12.5 trillion yuan (US $2 trillion). Yet they represent only part of the shadow banking system, whose total assets currently represent more than 30 trillion yuan (around US $4.9 trillion), roughly half of Chinese GDP. The shadow banking system receives deposits and provides loans, using resources from different origins and often promising large interest payments, and accounted for one third of the rise of lending in 2013. In recent years, its growth has been over 50 percent a year.[27]

Chinese unlisted lenders now represent one third of the deposits in the banking sector, or some US $8 trillion in assets, the equivalent of the entire Japanese banking system or half of the US sector. Among the assets of unlisted banks, one third can be categorized as shadow assets (as presumed loan payments are recorded as investment).[28] Savings are increasingly channeled to these institutions and not only to commercial banks. And debts soar: at least one eighth of the 1,000 largest Chinese companies owed more in interest than they get in earnings before tax.

In its defense, shadow finance has provided the means for the transition from an export- and investment-led economy towards a consumption-led economy, a necessary realignment of the Chinese economy both for domestic reasons and for international balances, as it increased popular credit through the economy. However, for some industrial firms financial intermediation has become the core business, a process of financialization of the nonfinancial firm.[29] For instance, one of the largest shipyards in China, Yangzijiang Shipbuilding, receives two-thirds of its income from lending money.[30] The recycling of industrial profits as credit and other financial operations has thus become a dominant feature of capital accumulation in China.

Consequently, speculation in an increasingly overvalued stock market has reshaped the industrial map of the economy, with several notable accidents. China's energy industry teems with examples: Suntech, led by Shi Zhengrong, then the richest man in China, went bust in 2013; Chaori Solar followed in 2014, and it only survived with a bailout; Hanergy, led by Li Hejun, Zhengrong's successor as the richest man in China, rose rapidly and then collapsed in 2015 when regulators opened an investigation into the firm.[31] The previous year, a first run on a bank, the Sheyang Rural Commercial Bank, alarmed the authorities.[32]

No country has ever experienced such a credit boom without it leading to a crash, as Reinhart and Rogoff document in *This Time Is Different* (2009). In fact, the first tremors emerged with the stock-price crash of summer 2015, which then spilled into world financial markets. But the crisis demonstrated the determination and resilience of the Chinese government in managing the financial sector and the economy: the government pressed state-owned firms to buy stocks, forbade sales and speculation, changed the interest rate and exchange rate, inundated the market with liquidity and easy credit, and threatened non-complying managers. China mobilized huge resources that no other government would, or could, have at their disposal. Furthermore, this is a nationally controlled system (foreign banks only represent 1.5% of the banking sector in China).

[27] *Wall Street Journal*, October 30, 2015. [28] *The Economist*, July 4, 2015; April 18, 2015.
[29] Epstein (2005a); Crotty (2008). [30] *Financial Times*, September 6, 2011.
[31] *South China Morning Post*, December 28, 2015. [32] *Reuters*, March 26, 2014.

Yet the vigorous response also indicates signs of vulnerability as the stock market grows. The course of action was possible in summer 2015 only because the Chinese stock market remains small compared to the economy: the free float market capitalization is 40 percent of GDP, compared to more than 100 percent in other major economies.[33] Indeed, the financial turmoil, although staunched for the moment, revealed major threats. The combination of a housing bubble (house prices climbed 16 percent in 2015, but to twice or three times that in big cities, and this continued in 2016) and a large exposure of the banking system to bad loans and overvalued assets may yet ignite a new crash. This vulnerability is extended by the growth of indebtedness: total national debt (private and public) increased from 160 percent to 240 percent of GDP in the eight years ending in 2016.

As Clément Juglar, the statistician who first detected business cycles, once noted, it is prosperity that leads to crisis.

SUPPLY-SIDE ECONOMICS WITH CHINESE CHARACTERISTICS

The historical experience of capital accumulation should prompt the Chinese leadership to control the movements of capital and to manage the pressures of globalization. They apparently think otherwise.

As this book goes to press, the dominant doctrine in Chinese government is a curious recapitulation of supply-side economics, the theory put forward under President Ronald Reagan and igniting the neoliberal revolution in the US, more than three decades ago. The choice of words is certainly not innocent, as Xi Jinping, the Chinese President and General Secretary of the Communist Party, points out that the new course is supply-side economics, in order to break with credit-driven and state-controlled development.

A call by the Central Committee for a "decisive" role for market forces is published in the *People's Daily*, the official newspaper, in which the President calls this move "China Model 2.0 Edition."[34]

There are precedents to this supply-side orientation: the early visits of Milton Friedman to China in 1980 and 1988. But, as he describes his efforts to convert the officials he met to the market approach, Friedman shows how far away he was to convince his hosts to adopt monetarism.[35] China traveled at lightning speed to get back to the *laissez-faire* orientation of the past.

AN INTERNATIONAL PLAYER

As the world's largest holder of foreign exchange reserves, China is both a major player in exchange markets and a beneficiary of a stable financial and monetary

[33] The accumulation of large reserves of foreign currency kept the yuan down, which was a good strategy for development at the price of enormous external pressures from the US and other economies.

[34] *The Economist*, January 2, 2016, January 16, 2016.

[35] Friedman (1990).

international system.[36] China is, for now, reaping benefits from globalization and the neoliberal era, which has transformed its economy and society. The government has relaxed capital controls, accelerating the process.[37] The central bank anticipates full liberalization and in 2015 asked the IMF to recognize the yuan as a fully convertible currency the same year.

With these negotiations pending, China took the initiative of creating the Asian Infrastructure Investment Bank (AIIB),[38] aiming to provide US $8 trillion of infrastructure spending in Asia within one decade, with urbanization and other modernization investments central to the program, such as electricity generation, roads, and telecommunications. That would mean the world's largest market for public works.

The Obama administration in the US opposed the AIIB proposal, but its traditional ally Britain was the first non-Asian country to apply, and many others followed, including all the major European economies.

THE SOCIAL CONSEQUENCES

Deng's reform process and the engine of liberalization were an impressive success in launching China as an economic power. The Chinese economy has grown, but the recipe of export-led growth based on repressed consumption and wages, severe labor discipline, and public silence is dangerous.

Two major consequences of this process of capital accumulation stand out.

The first is massive structural change: in the cities, 250 million jobs have been created by the private sector since 1978 and almost 300 million people moved from villages to towns; this is, in one generation, the "biggest voluntary migration ever" in the history of mankind (with enormous consequences, as at least nine million children were left behind),[39] as well as the largest transformation of property ever registered in a modern economy. Urbanization, mass migration, and the rise of consumption are the main trends of this change. The consequences are immense: for the same period, 700 million Chinese left poverty, but inequality increased as well, as the Gini coefficient, measuring the social contrast of incomes, is double that of Germany and is larger than that of the US.

As the masses of peasants came to the towns and China's economy was rapidly growing, this generated "the biggest bubble in history," as Wang Jianlin, the richest man in the country and its largest real estate developer suggested.[40] The imbalance of land supply, in particular in big cities, tends to augment the bubble as, to meet demand, 800 million square meters would be required, the size of Singapore, every year until 2030. Prices will keep climbing.

In any case, with the expansion of production, consumption, and private ownership, expectations and social organization changed rapidly. While public control

[36] Wolf (2014), p. 129.

[37] The requirement of public authorization for foreign capital flows only applies to those over US $1 billion, whereas the previous limit was $100 million (*The Economist*, April 18, 2015), but personal transfers have been more strictly limited (*Wall Street Journal*, October 1, 2015).

[38] *Reuters*, January 17, 2016. [39] *China Daily*, November 10, 2016.

[40] *Business Insider*, September 28, 2016.

has remained important, the share of workers employed by the state has fallen from 99 percent in 1978 to only 18 percent in 2011 and it keeps diminishing. Urban life has changed the popular mood, and aspirations for a better standard of living have spread. Many people aim to acquire the same consumer goods they are producing for export. Furthermore, since 2001, the hourly manufacturing wage has risen by 12 percent a year; the average factory worker now receives 27.50 dollars a day compared to 6.70 dollars a day in Vietnam. Even so, the number of strikes doubled in 2014.[41] The minimum wage is only 270 dollars a month, or less than a quarter of that of the US, and aspirations for change appear to mount.

In the province of Guangdong, precisely where Deng Xiaoping initiated the vast social experiment in liberalization, the authorities have been forced to accept the right to collective bargaining to address labor unrest. Democratization of labor relations may change the social and political structure of China. This still does not fully extend to the right of travel within the country. But 2016 witnessed some limited changes in the *hukou* system, the rules for household registration that significantly restrict migration by rationing access to public services in cities.[42]

But other puzzles, threats, and imbalances remain. There may be massive layoffs in China if publicly owned firms are privatized or otherwise rapidly forced to meet hard budget constraints as industry is modernized.[43] New large flows of peasants to the towns will create social and ecological imbalances both in the countryside and in urban areas. Social pressures to increase wages and to set aside certain political and ideological controls, the dangers of unemployment, and an aging population are therefore some of the difficult prospects for the near future.

A second consequence of this process of capital accumulation is the tremendous economic and social change brought about by the formation of a new national bourgeoisie, topped by one million millionaires and many of the world's largest fortunes.[44] With it, we may see levels of corruption, cronyism, and clientelism that rival the West's and North's top 1 percent.

Take the example of Dalian Wanda, the largest property developer which registers annual revenues of US $40 billion. Its owner, Wang Jianlin, the son of a military hero of the Mao period and a deputy at the National Congress, now lives in another world: he has used his riches to buy one fifth of the shares of Atletico Madrid.[45] He is not a unique case: according to a report, the seventy richest members of China's National Assembly enjoy approximately US $90 billion in wealth[46]—they are richer than the richest members of the US House of Representatives. Anbang, the insurance company that bought Waldorf Astoria and bid for Marriott, is one example, as its Chairman is Wu Xiaohui, married to the grand-daughter of Deng

[41] *The Guardian*, April 22, 2014. [42] The Guardian, July 31, 2014.

[43] This also provides the opportunity for further changes in the labor force. While China is the world's biggest market for robots, buying 20% of world robot production, robotization, at thirty robots per ten thousand workers, remains well below that of Japan's 323 per ten thousand workers.

[44] The rapid emergence of wealth owners had a huge impact on the state itself, changing social references and procedures. One of the consequences is corruption: in 2013, 182,000 officials were punished for corruption (*The Telegraph*, March 7, 2016) and some of the processes had a large public audience and political significance.

[45] *The Economist*, February 14, 2015.

[46] *Bloomberg News*, February 27, 2012, quoting the Hurun Report.

Xiaoping, and the company includes in its leadership the son of Chen Yi, a military commander under Mao, and Levin Zhu, the son of a former prime minister.

Through families or arrangements, this concentration of wealth proceeds at a rapid pace. Beijing hosts more billionaires than New York and the top 1 percent in China own one third of the national assets.[47] No such concentration of wealth has ever been known in the history of the world.

CORRUPTION

As a consequence, examples of corruption emerge at different levels of the administration, including the most sacred niches of power. A chief of logistics of the People's Liberation Army, the huge Chinese armed forces, was arrested for economic crimes; among the extravagant goods in his mansion was found a statue of Mao in gold. When the former deputy chief of the nuclear arsenal and fourteen other generals were investigated for graft, ten trucks were needed to evacuate the ill-gotten gains of General Xu Caihou.[48]

Prevalence and perception have pushed corruption to the top of the public agenda. Opposing corruption is an effective stratagem in struggles within the ruling party and government. Throughout his rise, President Jinping Xi presented himself as the "cleaner."

Although some cases may refer to political dissidence or infighting (in summer 2015, Zhao Shaolin, the retired party boss of Jiangsu province, was taken away by the anti-corruption commission for criticizing the government), Ponzi frauds are frequent. The failure of the Ezubao, the largest peer-to-peer lender, led to losses of US $7.6 billion for over 900,000 investors, and, as its boss was arrested, the police had to use backhoes for some twenty hours to excavate the deeply buried account ledgers. Evidence of corruption emerges in unsuspected places: the chief of the national statistics bureau, Wang Bao'an, was investigated for the crime.[49]

Mismanagement of public funds has also become widespread. Song Lin, the former chairman of China Resources Group, was prosecuted; Su Shulin, the former chairman of Sinopec, a public oil company, and governor of Fujian province, is under investigation; Jiang Jiemin, the former head of Petrochina, was sentenced to sixteen years in jail; the European head of ICBC was arrested, under the accusation of illegal channeling of funds from Madrid to China, and similar accusations were made against the Bank of China for movements of capital from Italy; Sam Pa, a middleman for deals of public firms in Africa, was arrested; and Guo Guanchang, the boss of Fosun, a large private financial firm, was detained for a short period.[50]

Greed, again moving the world.

[47] *The Telegraph*, February 25, 2016. [48] CNN, March 15, 2015.

[49] Wang Bao'an was also accused of "superstitious activities" (*Fortune*, January 28, 2016).

[50] *The Economist*, December 5, 2015, October 24, 2015, December 19, 2015, February 27, 2016, February 6, 2016.

CONCLUSION

The architecture of the Chinese economy and society was presented in the recent pre-Deng past as unpropitious for capitalism. China's performance has provided a resounding rebuttal of the skeptics, as the country is today not only the largest economy in the world but also the fastest growing market by any standard.

The peculiarity of the contemporary Chinese economy is that production and labor are developed primarily by the private sector but under strong ongoing guidance of a single-party system.

The incorporation of China in the world economic system thus provided a counterweight to Hansen's predicted demographic winter. The centers of production and capital accumulation may change, and the consequences of such displacement are instability and possible conflict, but global secular stagnation has perhaps been postponed.

A vulnerability of Chinese development is finance. It is not the only vulnerability—grave ecological concerns, inequality, and massive population shifts from rural to urban areas also pose challenges for the Chinese model. China faces choices in the development of its financial system. The goose that laid the golden eggs was a hybrid system, combining the mobilization of household savings at very low interest rates for directed loans (an old-fashioned model of postal savings banks that had widespread subscription in both Asia and Europe), significant direction of state funds to preferred ventures, and new horizons in nontraditional finance, that is, shadow banking. The government has directed, overseen, and rescued finance, accepting financial imbalances, in particular, insolvent banks, over long periods, much longer than could persist in fully liberalized economies, where runs or bailouts would force a resolution.

Even with its enormous capacity for regulation and support, the Chinese model may soon come to the end with respect to maintaining the current regime, an accretion of practices from several eras that leaves substantial and risky gaps. Chinese finance is at a crossroads, and the current model is likely unsustainable. Which way forward is the central question.

As finance has emerged as a shadow system benefiting from the protection of the state and the publicly owned banks, it is prone to runs, to speculative bubbles, and to collapses. Nonetheless, there are strong pressures to liberalize finance. The case for liberalized finance builds on free-market ideology and economic models, but greed, plain and simple, plays a role as well. Some financiers will profit enormously from liberalized capital markets. They either expect to have cashed in their chips before the crash or suspect that liberalization's commitment to let the chips fall where they may will prove less than credible in the breach, i.e., bailouts will be provided as needed.

Yet China has other options in the oversight and management of its financial system. Its longstanding *dirigiste* institutions and practices will not wither rapidly. Zombie banks, i.e., banks that are insolvent on paper were mark-to-market accounting applied, can survive functionally and fruitfully in China in ways that they cannot in non-state-controlled economies. As long as the state provides clear instructions or direction for the continued provision of intermediation services, the banks do not have to turn around their balance sheets in short order. Chinese financial and regulatory institutions mean that, in the short run at least, China may not face the same threat of financial meltdown,[51] although it does risk other dangers.

Many China commentators perceive clearly the potential for disaster that rests in the full adoption of the liberalized model. For now, the state remains large relative to finance. The state was able to cushion a potentially catastrophic stock-market crash in summer 2015 as well as manage the many incidental busts of schemes to turn credit into gold. If liberalization permits finance to grow and in particular to grow without oversight, then future shocks may not be as easily managed.

[51] Roach (2015).

13

The Shadow Society and Its Fictitious Capital

The subprime crash was the result of rampant speculation provoking the explosion of the contradictions of shadow finance. It would be naive to interpret the contamination of the financial sector and its immense implications for social life as the consequence of the deviant behavior of one or two bad apples in an otherwise wholesome barrel. Our accumulated evidence demonstrates that the crash was, instead, the foreseeable outcome of financial system development through the epoch of deregulation and liberalization. Shadow finance encouraged the shadow economy and shadow politics. The interface between open and legitimated elite networks and the world of unregulated opportunism proved remarkably smooth and ultimately undifferentiated. The model dominated alternatives, for example, regulated capitalism or social democracy, as the desired outcome of strategic planning and social process.

Neoliberalism roared back in the last quarter of the twentieth century, regaining hegemony lost after the calamitous Great Depression. Its political success is evident in its capacities: to inform, mobilize, and constrain the decisions of legislators and regulators; to attract allies; and to indoctrinate experts, e.g., economists, and decision makers. It corresponds to a social force, and our thesis is that it is part of the emergence of finance and of financiers as the dominant *rentiers* in the world. That is the topic of our concluding chapter.

THE CONSTRUCTION OF INEQUALITY

Four years after the crash, Warren Buffett, an outspoken financier, wrote in the *New York Times* an indictment of the tax benefits he himself receives alongside his "super-rich friends." He marshaled compelling evidence that the US tax system is biased towards the top of society and establishes a marked class difference between poorest and richest:

> Our leaders have asked for "shared sacrifice". But when they did the asking, they spared me. I checked with my mega-rich friends to learn what pain they were expecting. They, too, were left untouched.
>
> While the poor and middle class fight for us in Afghanistan, and while most Americans struggle to make ends meet, we mega-rich continue to get our extraordinary tax breaks. Some of us are investment managers who earn billions from our daily labors but are allowed to classify our income as "carried interest," thereby getting a bargain 15 percent tax rate. Others own stock index futures for 10 minutes and have

> 60 percent of their gain taxed at 15 percent, as if they'd been long-term investors. These and other blessings are showered upon us by legislators in Washington who feel compelled to protect us, much as if we were spotted owls or some other endangered species. It's nice to have friends in high places.
>
> Last year my federal tax bill—the income tax I paid, as well as payroll taxes paid by me and on my behalf—was $6,938,744. That sounds like a lot of money. But what I paid was only 17.4 percent of my taxable income—and that's actually a lower percentage than was paid by any of the other twenty people in our office. Their tax burdens ranged from 33 percent to 41 percent and averaged 36 percent. If you make money with money, as some of my super-rich friends do, your percentage may be a bit lower than mine. But if you earn money from a job, your percentage will surely exceed mine—most likely by a lot.[1]

The provocative and wry remarks of Buffett, one of the richest people in the world, reminds us that inequality is an old script, an outcome of normal accumulation that is protected by law, by institutions. But crises favor it especially.

Emmanuel Saez, a professor at Berkeley whose research treats inequality, observes that during the 2009–12 recovery from recession in the US, the incomes of the top 1 percent of the social scale grew by 34.7 percent whereas that of the other 99 percent increased by 0.8 percent, a meager sum. Over the last twenty years of liberalization and deregulation, from 1993 to 2013 the incomes of the top 1 percent went up by 62.4 percent, whereas those of the remaining 99 percent grew by 7.3 percent.[2] So, not only did low taxes protect Buffett's super-rich friends, but the economy treated them rather well in the first place.

In previous chapters, we remarked on hefty compensation of both successful and disgraced CEOs of the firms involved in the hurricane of the crash. They were not isolated examples. In 1965, the CEOs of the 200 largest US corporations received 20 times the average full-time worker's pay; in 1980, 42 times. By 2000, the ratio had increased to 383:1. The vagaries of the Great Crash somewhat reduced CEO pay, but by 2015 the average had already recovered to a healthy 335:1.[3] The same applies to European firms. As Buffett noted, it is as if these managers were treated as "spotted owls or some other endangered species," and moreover "it's nice to have friends in high places."

The other face of this ostentation is poverty, exclusion, or simple exploitation feeding inequality. Indeed, inequality is not only a world feature, distinguishing among "developed" and "emerging" or "underdeveloped" countries, it is a mark of a social disease inside the very rich countries: in the UK, to take an example, official statistics highlight that boys born in Chelsea can expect to live nine years more than boys born in Blackpool.[4]

Still, the soaring heights of the very rich are just the most obvious characteristic of inequality. The glittering surface of the haves hides the sorrows of the have-nots. As rewards skyrocket and golden parachutes are guaranteed, wages are compressed. The recent course of wage income has fed finance.[5] This extraction

[1] Buffett (2011).

[2] Saez (2015). Milanovic, another researcher on global inequality, who argues for a different point of view, concedes that if, after industrialization, inequality across countries contributes most to world inequality, class-based inequality is nowadays growing, Milanovic (2016).

[3] AFL-CIO (2017), 2014 had been even better at 373:1, but the financial markets are prone to vagaries.

[4] Office of National Statistics, United Kingdom, November 4, 2015.

[5] Lapavitsas (2009). Costas Lapavitsas, a professor at SOAS, London University, calls this a process of "financial expropriation."

proceeds via four different paths. In the first instance, underpaid labor enables the vast rewards of the rich: labor creates value, and this value is expropriated by owners. Second, wage earners pay the taxes that finance the bailouts and subsidies for the largest and most connected firms. Third, high finance increasingly takes a slice of the pie to manage the accounts of the welfare state, with private pensions ensuring generous service fees for banks. Finally, the credit society reroutes a portion of wages to pay the interest on increasingly available instruments of consumer credit, mortgages, and credit cards.

In the face of declining wages, cheap credit established the illusion of sustained purchasing power. The credit society created a supplementary form of dependence and vulnerability, both for families who faced mounting obligations and for the society as aggregate demand came to depend on the health of the financial system. The expected stream of payments from the loans financing house and car purchases and credit cards were bundled into packages that became central assets of the financial system. These loan bundles were lucrative; they were also considered safe under the assumption that the debts of many diverse households were unlikely to default simultaneously.

But this garden of new financial products required frequent watering and intensive cultivation and protection from pests. The prospect of banking restrictions poses the threat of raising the cost of funding and requiring speculators to hold more capital in reserve rather than putting it into play.

The minimal capital requirements of banking would represent outright bankruptcy in any other sector of the economy. Yet, instead of being shuttered by regulators, banking receives massive public subsides, including regulatory forbearance, implicit and explicit guarantees, and—ultimately—bailouts. This paradox intensifies after financial crashes. Crashes demonstrate the fragility of the private financial system yet also mobilize the resources of the public in bailouts that add to the wealth and influence of the owners and high executives of the private financial system.

Past attempts to channel profits to social ends, to tame the advantages of managers and financiers, and to improve the distribution of income have constituted intense moments of social conflict in our time, and have rarely succeeded.[6] In fact, the triumph of neoliberalism established greed and inequality as threats to democracy. Finance maintains its hegemonic capacity: despite triggering a decade-long recession, finance thrives, while democracy is under threat. That threat is our first conclusion.

THE INTERCONNECTEDNESS OF THE SHADOWS

Inequality has been justified as the inevitable state of nature. Indeed many students in economics and management will expound on capitalism as "human nature."

[6] One generally forgotten example is that of Sweden in the 1960s, when the Rehn-Meidner plan was approved imposing a 20% tax on profits, to be used to buy shares in the firms by social funds. A Conservative government reversed course in 1991, and the preparation for joining the European Community through 1993–4 was the crucial step in stopping this redistributive policy.

A new division in social life pretends to distinguish between the beneficiaries of popular capitalism and those deprived of capital ambitions. That has been called "shareholding capitalism."[7]

Although the concept then fell into disgrace, shareholder capitalism provided for some time the illusion of novelty and redemption. Enron declared its mission to "create significant value for our shareholders," Lehman Brothers claimed its objective was "maximizing shareholder value," and MCI WorldCom was proud about its "proven record of shareholder value creation"—although these overly optimistic slogans were heralds of disaster, they were the motto of the era of finance. Yet, in spite of the setbacks, shareholder capitalism remained the social structure for the movements of capital and savings, as if the rollercoaster of the financial markets could be the ultimate judge and distributor of the claims on the gold mines.

Therefore, our second conclusion is that, in spite of the grave damage caused by the financial crisis both in reputation and liquidity in the financial system, when a decade has passed its vulnerability to new perturbations has still increased, even after several waves of cleansing and new regulation. This only highlights the fact that finance is the epitome of globalization and that it is a functional network, which augments the risks of contamination through dense interdependence and concentration.[8] This network is headquartered in dispersed centers, such as Chicago (for futures), New York (for the stock market), Frankfurt (for financial activity first around the deutschmark and now the euro), London (for financial enterprises), and Shanghai (for industrial production and emerging finance), and its susceptibility to havoc is amplified by their interconnectedness.

Costas Lapavitsas pointed out that three major changes are part of this network emerging from the rise of finance: non-financial firms become more involved in financial processes as part of their current operations; banks aim to profit from financial trading rather than the spread between borrowing and lending, which changes the scope of their business; and households rely more on the financial system for consumption. The first consequence of this transformation of conduct of non-financial firms, households, and banks is to create a social economy of debt, and debt is vulnerable to panics and runs.[9]

The second consequence is to accentuate the interconnectedness of the financial firms and not only institutions. Indeed, for some major players, globalization is their way of life: HSBC, the second bank in the world system, with J.P. Morgan, gets 60 percent of its profits from Asia,[10] and the examples abound. Therefore, when China trembles, Wall Street and the City panic and, as demonstrated by the subprime crash, even marginal disturbances, such as those occurring in a small part of the bond market but magnified by the securitization of subprime

[7] A critique may be found in Plihon (2010).

[8] The discourse on networks and globalization has prevailed for the last few decades, Castells (1996); but it has also been criticized, D. Harvey (1989); Arrighi (1994); Fine (2004); Duménil and Lévy (2005). Concentration is another consequence of these trends: the five largest banks' share in total assets rose from 25% in 2000 to 45% in 2016.

[9] Lapavitsas (2014), pp. 3–4, 38.

[10] By net revenue, the first would be ICBC, then Morgan Chase, then China Reconstruction Bank, Bank of America, Citigroup, Bank of China, HSBC, BNP Paribas, Deutsche Bank, and then Standard Chartered (*The Economist*, February 6, 2016). By assets, the four Chinese banks are at the top of the list.

mortgages, ricocheted as a bullet through the entire system and led to the brink of a world collapse.

Nevertheless, it would be naive to attribute the crisis to malfunction or to the purposeful action of socially deviant bankers and financiers. Indeed, throughout this book we have repeatedly shown otherwise. Instead, we found the resilient building blocks of a society transformed and managed by power and strategy, including freeing the gigantic capital movements that require and induce immense changes in the way of living and conducting business and political decision making in world affairs. Therefore, our third conclusion is that the adaptation of the states as public-private partnerships that constitute the pillars of financialization is a deeply rooted process that has shown extraordinary capacity to survive setbacks.

As a consequence and forced to choose between market-conforming and market-negating regulation, or between generic (including the function of the lender of last resort, which narrows the market processes) and systemic market negating regulation (capital controls), the developed economies were led always to choose the first and to pursue deregulatory regulation.[11]

The financial system and its political extensions, under stress and pressed to change course after the subprime episode, preferred to protect the shadows. This process is amplified by financial innovation, opening the door to successive forms of capturing savings and managing money, and to fierce competition and instability.[12] This has one obvious implication: the financial regime is in permanent trouble.

IRRATIONAL OR RATIONAL SPECULATION?

We are certainly not the first to note trouble as the middle name of finance. By the middle of the nineteenth century in response to the first "generalized crises," a brilliant and perceptive classical economist and polymath, John Stuart Mill, wrote that it would be unwise to expect milder oscillations and crises in the future, since the search for profit is the prime mover of the economy and it leads to violent

[11] Lapavitsas (2014), p. 306f. See also Jarsulic (2012), on the anatomy of the bubble, the failure of regulation, and the relation between investment banks and hedge funds. An ex-US Senate staffer, after his experience, argued that "the underlying assumption that regulators can effectively micromanage the market is flawed. Giving regulators more levers to pull and buttons to push with respect to the financial system only creates a false sense of security," Peirce et al. (2012).

[12] To date, the most influential examples of financial innovation are the money market mutual funds, asset- and mortgage-backed securities, and derivative trading. Crotty pointed out the "Volcker paradox": innovation leads to higher profits in finance. Crotty explains the paradox by noting increased demand for the new differentiated products (Crotty (2008), p. 170). Curious and recent examples of financial innovation are: automated wealth managers, or robot-advisors, that use algorithms to make real-time decisions with some US $20 billion in assets currently under management, a small but growing proportion of the total assets; or non-tradable "mini-bonds" issued by firms such as Chilango, a Mexican food chain in London, which pays 8% interest, Hotel Chocolate, a confectioner, whose 2010 bond issue pays its interest in chocolate, and King of Shaves which was paying 7% interest in 2009; and lending groups, which may grow to become a large market. The Goldman Sachs estimate is that new competitors could reduce profits of American banks by up to 7 percent (*The Economist*, August 16, 2014; May 9, 2015).

explosions: "Such vicissitudes, beginning with irrational speculation and ending with a commercial crisis, have not hitherto become less frequent or less violent with the growth of capital and the extension of industry. Rather they may be said to have become more so: in consequence, it is often said of increased competition; but, as I prefer to say, of a low rate of profit and interest, which makes the capitalists dissatisfied with the ordinary course of safe mercantile gains."[13] The growth of capital, indeed, provoked more and more such vicissitudes: they are in the nature of capitalism.

But how did capital grow? How is it that this accumulation developed with historically unprecedented success? The answer is, obviously, capitalism, the modern society generating the industrial revolution and the following two centuries of radical change. This section thus refers to discussions on the historical evolution of the rate of profit and the accumulation process.

For the last fifty years, the return on capital settled around 10 percent in the US, with only some sectors enjoying abnormal profit, the two most profitable industries being health care (one quarter of total abnormal profit in the US economy is retained by pharma) and information and communication technology. But finance can surpass the exceptional profitability of those sectors: according to the Boston Consulting Group, the profit rate of the asset management industry attained 39 percent in 2014, PIMCO being the largest firm, while profit was 20 percent for pharmaceuticals and a median 8 percent for consumer goods.[14] This dominance is new: in the 1973–85 period, financial sector profits were never more than 16 percent of total US domestic corporate profits; in 1986 they rose to 19 percent and, in the 2000s, they reached as much as 41 percent.

This process also changed over time. During the 1970s, the rate of profit was down to a trough, and then it recovered in the 1980s and 1990s, although the exact computation is a matter of dispute, given different statistical and conceptual approaches. Some researchers note a boom in the 1980s, since low interest raised the return on capital but also favored the gigantic consumer debt and bubbles, and there was a flow of profits from industry to finance.[15] Others note that the US rate of profit remained below the pre-1975 level even with the recovery from the mid-1980s, whereas still others point out that, even if profitability recovered, there has been no accumulation, or that there is no equivalent growth of investment.[16]

Therefore, the realm of finance, irrational as it appears in its eventual devastating consequences, is a rational form of power, concentrated in its aims, devoted to its methods, and meticulous in its proceedings as the market functions as an amplifier of the financial operations and innovations.[17] Our fourth conclusion is that financialization is not a consequence of errors in regulation or of the simple arbitrage of opportunities; it is a social regime.

[13] Mill (2008), pp. 81–2. [14] *The Economist*, March 26, 2016.
[15] Shaikh (2011); Stockhammer (2004). [16] Kliman (2011); Husson (2008).
[17] Orléan (1999). For this reason, the financial regime will protect its havens: one third of the total world foreign direct investment is managed through tax havens (the Virgin Islands are the world's fifth recipient of direct investment, practically doubling Britain).

THE ERA OF GLOBAL CAPITAL

In a curious book on the narrative of globalization and the cultures of financialization, Max Haiven, a professor of art history and cultural studies at Nova Scotia College of Art and Design, Canada, takes aim at the discourse, the metaphors, and even the idiomatic construction of the notions and procedures of financialization. His case studies extend from Walmart, the largest world employer and an example of aggressive commercial and labor practices, to Pokémon, the Nintendo children's game, and he applies the concept of "fictitious capital," a notion used although not invented by Karl Marx. Haiven mobilizes the concept including in the most literal sense: the financial regime creates fictions.[18]

The fictional discourse is certainly prevalent in modern times. Take the case of the famous aphorism by Schumpeter, the "creative destruction" identifying that drive of capitalism towards innovation. This concept is turned upside down and the adapted concept of "creative industries" populates a new vision of innovative economies as continuity and incremental progress, as opposed to radical innovations perturbing the business-as-usual mode of affairs.

But fictions are invented in a more material sense, and not only as new stories. Indeed, the meaning of the creation of new things has been a topic of discussion among sociologists and other social scientists for some time now. Scott Lash, a professor at the University of London, long pursued this line of investigation and he discussed globalization from the point of view of the differential reception, understanding, and cultural assimilation and use of global objects. His case studies were the Euro Football Cup of 1996, the films *Trainspotting* and *Toy Story*, the series *Wallace and Gromit*, and commodities from the brands Swatch and Nike. As culture produces not only symbols but things, as if to illustrate Marx's dictum that the "fetishism of money invaded all social grounds," the commodification of the communication and the construction of references became a world market process, even if the interpretation of these cultural artifacts is biased by national semantics.[19]

In this universe of fictions, there is a universal equivalent, money, the creator of the fetish and the religion of modernity. But, as we argue throughout this book, money is more than a measure of value, a medium of exchange, and a form of stored wealth; money is the social result of market society, an outcome of competition and economic power. Therefore, in the "era of money," as Keynes once put it, money, in the form of capital, is the socially recognized form of dominance. Then, why is this based on fictions?

In the third volume of his *Capital* an incomplete and sketchy book, Marx opens his remarks on fictitious capital quoting a Yorkshire banker who suggested that this capital is a form of circulation, a representation of a commercial value to be transferred between two entrepreneurs. Then he adds another dimension of the fiction: the speculation on the eventual appreciation of goods transported from far away to another market. But it is as part of the banking industry that the notion of fictitious capital enters as a major player in the theory.

[18] Haiven (2014).

[19] The expression is used by Marx, in *Capital*, volume 4, in the chapter "The Circuit of Money-Capital,"(Marx (1977)) as noted by Scott Lash and Celia Lury (2007).

For the banker, whose business is the expansion of credit and the enlargement of his claims on present and future capital, "the greater portion of the banking capital is, therefore, purely fictitious and consists of certificates of indebtedness (bills of exchange), government securities (which represent spent capital), and stocks (claims on future yields of production)."[20] These three forms of fictitious capital depend therefore on the development of a credit economy, first, since a future part of surplus and income is used to pay the various forms of debt, then, second, they depend on the ongoing extraction of taxes to pay for capital spent by public authorities, and third they depend on the changing value of stocks.[21]

Banking and central banks were formed as the basis of national credit systems and, originally, dedicated to the emission of money to finance public debt. By permitting claims on the future income of the state to be transacted as a financial asset, public debt was the original and central form of fictitious capital. The credit system emerged afterwards and then we got to the shores of the gigantic amplification of the markets for public debt and securitization of other types of debt.[22]

Marx noted the "antediluvian" origins of interest-bearing capital while also observing that the modern enlargement of the credit system has speeded the conversion of money-capital into interest-bearing capital through the growth of debt. The interplay of capital in function and capital as property implies that all forms of increasing value will appear as interest. Furthermore, the interest rate appears as the minimum profitability of capital and the expected income discounted by the market interest rate is the criterion for valuing capital, not that of traditional worth according to its capacity for generating surplus as it mobilizes labor and production.[23]

Marx, considering the system of credit developed as part of the expansion of the mode of production of commodities, describes new forms of financing being made available for the competing corporations. The dominant one is capitalization as the register of fictional, or the uncertain valuation of future flows of returns.[24] The present value is waged on the future through the current effect of manipulation of risk and beliefs.

Rudolf Hilferding developed the concept of finance capital from Marx and noticed that, with the generalization of the market, the exchange of commodities is split into different operations, leading to the intermediation and dominance of credit and finance.[25] Financialization is therefore more than the production

[20] Marx (1977), p. 435.

[21] Stocks are fictitious capital in the strictest sense of the word, since their value can be counted twice, both for the firm and for their owner, and for instance may generate two autonomous credit operations based on the very same value. Another kind of fictitious capital is that emerging from speculation.

[22] Gabor points out that securitized money markets benefited from the action of central banks, as sterilization operations promoted securitization in order to recycle the excess of liquidity from external creditors, Gabor (2010). They also benefited from financial innovation and the excessive confidence generated by the "great moderation" and deregulation period.

[23] Mello Belluzzo (2009), pp. 238, 241.

[24] Marx (1977), p. 371f., 432; Duménil and Lévy (2011), explores this concept of fictitious capital as the capitalized actual value of future revenues.

[25] Hilferding and Bottomore (1990). Marx distinguished between money capital, productive capital, and commodities capital, and Hilferding suggests that the generalization of credit generated finance capital.

of commodities by commodities supported by credit, it is the reign of abstract capital, and it is the regime that permits capital to establish property rights on future profits, or claims on future income. As the extension of credit became the basis for accumulation, this implies that financialization is the backbone of the expansion of capitalism.

This expansion is expressed through the obsessive search for liquidity, for convertibility of debt titles and assets into capital, and for short-term operations, although frequently valued at the uncertain price of the uncertain future.[26] Organized and financialized capitalism, or the era of money, is generated as a consequence of an unstable society.

Appreciation of financial assets is therefore a form of competition and, from this perspective, there is no surprise in securitization or other procedures of fictional increases in future claims on capital and profit, including the extraction rights of fictitious capital. Our fifth conclusion is that financialization is a mechanism of power; its power rests on the ability to project an image of capital as self-reproducing.[27]

RENTIERS AND CONCENTRATION

Since the crash, the largest and leading economy of the world, the US, has lived through a ten-trillion-dollar wave of mergers, promoting an increased concentration of market power in some firms. Considering the top four firms controlling between one third and two-thirds of the market in the very concentrated industries, they receive between 24 and 33 percent of the total revenues in the economy; considering the smaller number of firms that hold more than two-thirds of the market, in even more highly concentrated sectors (telecoms, pharmacies, credit cards), they still absorb one tenth of the revenues.

Although this is impressive, financial power is so concentrated that it can lead to shadow controls of firms through portfolios: as one magazine points out, "BlackRock, State Street and Capital Group, together they own 10–20 percent of most American companies," including firms competing among themselves.[28] Globalization, presented as the window of opportunity for the daring, turned out to be a rapid concentration process, at a scale unknown to date in the history of capitalism.

Furthermore, and this is our sixth conclusion, the contemporary structure of capital, public governance, and corporate control creates a prerogative for more

[26] Istvan Meszaros described this as the "regime of capital." The liquidity obsession is discussed by Aglietta (1995), and Madrick (2011).

[27] Hilferding rightly distinguishes between interest-bearing capital and fictitious capital, as the first finances accumulation and investment, and the second is unrelated to the direct production of surplus. Fictitious capital gets a part of profits not directly as a division of surplus, but instead as "differential profits," Hilferding and Bottomore (1990). Fictitious capital is not limited by the total of social surplus, although it may establish a right to a payment that can be traded; its exponential growth is the expression of fierce competition on the available surplus and therefore anticipates major losses for some of the players.

[28] *The Economist*, March 26, 2016.

rentier extraction, with both pressure and means to transform profits into dividends. In a global market, this process is mostly home based.[29] In spite of the stakes of ultra-billionaires, it depends on the managerial power behind financial expropriation; and the four largest types of financial institution—commercial banks, mutual funds, pension funds, also government sponsored agencies—together with regulators and political decision makers, are at the heart of this extraction process. They are the *rentiers* and owners of the shadows. The thirst for dividends is a major driving force for these trends. The head of research and two other researchers of the Bank of International Settlements proved this point as they published a paper computing the dividends paid by ninety Eurozone banks from 2007 to 2015, to obtain the total of €223 billion, retaining earnings of just €348 billion.[30]

Certainly, some of the changes imposed after the subprime crash have an effect. Trading in derivatives fell 90 percent immediately after the crisis, and the US bank's core capital doubled the pre-crisis level, but some dangers become evident. First, the mortgage system requires increases of capital, both in the US and in the Eurozone; in China, the housing bubble and debt inflation will impact on the banking system, and that is eventually why the longstanding governor of the central bank of China has warned about the danger of a "Minsky Moment" since the end of 2017. Second, and most of all, the Trumponomics drive for deregulation and its impact on the rise of interest rates will motivate flows of capital that may precipitate major difficulties for several economies, in particular in Europe. By the end of the second decade of the twenty-first century, the shadow economy again casts a mantle of uncertainty and danger over the world economy, which is more fragile than before the previous crisis.

KNOWN AND UNKNOWN, SHADOW AND LIGHT

In a famous soundbite at a NATO press conference in 2002, Donald Rumsfeld, then the US Secretary of Defense and one of the villains of the new wars in the Middle East (and of the revolving door between business and politics), presented the case for sending troops in the framework of radical uncertainty: "The message is that there are no 'knowns.' There are things we know that we know. There are known unknowns. That is to say there are things that we now know we don't know. But there are also unknown unknowns. There are things we don't know we don't know."[31]

Although we can only speculate on the effect of such words on an audience expecting the military chiefs to deliver enthusiasm and to cheer for the next moves on the battle front, this sort of declared and perplexed ignorance on the future—and present—is an example of how many choices are beyond the purview of recognized politics, simple economics, and even dark military arts. Yet, this quiz may constitute a useful guide.

[29] The home returns on equity are much larger for the US firms than those obtained abroad, by a difference of 40%. On the *rentier* regime, see Epstein and Jayadev (2005); Epstein (2005b,a).

[30] Acharya, Le, and Shin (2016). [31] Rumsfeld (2002).

We know that we know, and that may be, in our case, the sorry state of economics, attributing a scientific veneer and an unquestionable status to old ideas already proven dramatically wrong in the twenties and the early thirties of the twentieth century: *laissez-faire* led the world to the long depression by that time and again threatens a secular stagnation. As a response, an economist disillusioned with the mainstream called this Zombie Economics and argued for abandoning neoliberal ideas and not simply returning to Keynesianism, and not a few distinguished voices considered that the theory was doomed from the beginning.[32]

There are also known unknowns. Network finance and its dangers are some of them. As the shadow banking system was developed as a "subterranean credit system of vast proportions," network finance became more unstable since, contrary to old-fashioned market finance, and even investment banking, these are "dealer networks," furthermore powered by the dominant "minimalist view of finance as passive residual and comprising efficient markets." They are prone to instability but we cannot anticipate how it will manifest.[33] In fact, we know we don't know: network finance is a cartel, but how much does it represent, how deep does it go, how far-reaching is it? The full dimension and structure of shadow society is essentially ignored, since it has been developed in part through tax havens, occult operations, and subtle complicities. This is what we know that we don't know.

Finally, there are the darkest unknown unknowns, those dimensions in life we don't even know we don't know, according to Rumsfeld's perspicacity. The eventuality of a next collapse, the trigger and the forms of eventual contamination are unknowns. As "business as usual" is presented as discrete variations in the stock indexes, the claimed certainty that "this time is different," although echoing the announcement of "great moderation" and the taming of economic cycles, tends to promote resignation and nonchalance. We would do better preparing for difficult times, since mediocre recovery after the crash and recession, or even secular stagnation, are evidence of the exhaustion of the current remedies.

Pace Rumsfeld and his military language, the real unknown is quite obvious: it is the timing of the next crisis. Warnings about the present danger are as widespread as the euphoria in the markets. One is the statistics proving that the shadows are back: the weight of shadow banking creation of credit as part of the GDP is since 2014 above that of 2007 in twenty-seven jurisdictions reporting to the Financial Stability Board. The second comes from the shadow agencies themselves: Goldman Sachs analysts compare a measure of prices of dividends, stock, and debt to conclude that never since 1900 has it been so high, or that we live in a bubble.[34] A third alert is once again sounded by Robert Shiller, who was awarded the Nobel Prize in economics in 2013 for anticipating the subprime crash and the real estate bubble: if one takes the cyclically adjusted price-earnings ratio, or a measure of how expensive stocks are, for the last 136 years, only twice were the 2017 values surpassed, prior to the Great Crash and during the end-of-the-century

[32] For the critique of post-subprime economics, Kirman (2009); for Zombie economics, Quiggin (2012). Their plea may or may be not heard: as one study states with sorrow, there is even less pluralism in academic economics after the crash, F. S. Lee, Pham, and Gu (2013), not to mention the decision makers.

[33] Guttmann (2015). [34] Bloomberg, November 29, 2017.

dot.com bubble. Consequently, buying capital has become expensive, investment is reduced, and efforts to find adventurous ways are rewarded.[35] Furthermore, the very response of central banks to the recession, imposing large increases of easy money, of liquidity in the economy in order to keep the interest rates low, necessary as it was, provided an incentive for investment in riskier assets and delivered a wealth effect for those accumulating a patrimony in financial titles, thus feeding the bubble. All this is a recipe for disaster, since we know the result of a bubble: it bursts.

REMEDIES THAT DO NOT CURE

Perhaps the most ambitious and thoroughly unrealistic of the mainstream proposals is a return to narrow banking. Narrow banking, the imposition of a 100 percent reserve requirement on banks, appears to challenge the instability effect created by fractional reserve banking. Narrow banking was favored by Milton Friedman and at least some of the Chicago School, having been previously endorsed by Irving Fisher and Maurice Allais.[36] Laurence Kotlikoff made it a basis of his quixotic run for the 2016 Presidency of the United States, with an affirming nod from Gregory Mankiw.

The proposition is simply to impose 100 percent reserves on the banks, to be formed exclusively by public fiat money, meaning a total control of money supply by the state authorities. Banks would be forbidden from dabbling in the alchemy of speculative financial markets. Risky investment would be the prerogative of entrepreneurs and adventurers who would proceed with the absolute certainty that return and risk would be theirs alone.

No more leverage, no more moral hazard, no more financial crises.

If only it were that simple. This big step in state interventionism appears to be at odds with the neoliberal credentials of all the inventors and followers of the idea, and indeed it is. Narrow banking did not survive the narrow space of theoretical conceptualization. For banks ooze leverage. If leverage through legitimate channels is denied, even questioned, banks take to the shadows instead.

Hyman Minsky, a distinguished heterodox economist whose critique was mentioned in a previous chapter, once adhered to this proposal of narrow banking in the middle of the 1990s. But he soon abandoned it, considering the deflationary and recessive implications of this concept of the bank as a safe home for deposits and not as an institution creating credit and therefore demand. This banking system would eliminate banks rather than leverage, Minsky intuited.[37]

Other alternatives abound but did not impress either the decision makers or the regulators. Some researchers suggest, for instance, that finance is no more efficient than at the end of nineteenth century, considering the costs of intermediation, and therefore that gigantism is dangerous. Sensible proposals under debate include stronger capital requirements for banks, dampening opportunities

[35] Shiller (2017b). [36] Fisher (1935, 1936); Allais (1948); Friedman (1960).
[37] Kregel (2012).

for high-frequency trading, and linking executive bonuses not to share price but to long-term objectives.[38] These are all fine plans, but resistance to reform is fierce.

PROFESSIONALISM AND DEMOCRACY

Finance has five primary functions: (1) channel savings to productive investment, (2) provide mechanisms for households to save for retirement, (3) help businesses and households reduce risk, (4) provide stable and flexible liquidity, and (5) provide an efficient payments mechanism. A sixth function is to manage financial innovation to achieve the five primary functions.[39] Much of this book has argued that finance is failing, often grotesquely, in all six functions. The failure is systematic, political, and anti-egalitarian.

As we move towards conclusions, we recommend some immediate solutions to tame finance in the interest of the broad public in the developed and developing countries. The ability of managers and owners of capital to move capital across national borders at will has: created long destabilizing financial chains that are prone to crisis; shifted the domestic balance of political and economic power from workers to capitalists; and undermined the capacity of states to use fiscal, monetary, or industrial policy to manage their economies in the interest of the vast majority of their citizens.

Re-establishing controls on the international movement of capital is a key first step to better governance and more egalitarian outcomes. For example, containing international capital mobility would directly restore an important fiscal instrument that is historically important for less developed countries: duties on international trade and international finance. For both developed and developing countries, removing international outlets for capital flight and tax evasion would ease fiscal pressures. Restrictions on capital movement would also contain "whipsawing," the action or threat of setting workers in race-to-the-bottom bidding wars to attract capital. Cooling off hot flows of portfolio investment would limit crises and smooth growth. The majority of the world's nations are democracies, but international capital mobility locks them in an international structure in which domestic democracy cannot function effectively.

At this point, merely slowing and regulating the passage of capital across borders would be a good start, but a constructive program for international finance can do much better. A system of international reconciliation along the lines of the Bancor envisioned by Keynes at the end of the Second World War could enable stable growth in developing countries and prevent the development of international financial and trade imbalances. At its core, such a system would regulate financial flows, early and systematically tilt exchange rates in the direction of balance, and nudge both creditor and debtor countries back towards balance with fees on excess credit and depreciation assistance for debtors. While a Bancor-like system of international financial regulation would enable competent management, which would displace the current system of financial adventurism, we do not pretend that such

[38] Davis, Lukomnik, and Pitt-Watson (2016). [39] Epstein (2016).

an institution only offers competence in the management of international financial affairs. Bancor disciplines neo-mercantilists and tames speculators. It is a positive program in the interest of stability and balanced growth. Once implemented—and getting there will be an enormous political challenge—it would have strong homeostatic properties.

We also advocate stricter policing of shadow finance, a matter for the financial regulatory authorities of individual countries—as well as requiring coordination among countries to avoid regulatory arbitrage and races to the bottom. The modest progress in the United States with the Dodd-Frank Act indicates the potential for well-informed interventions yet also points up the strength of the opposition from the financial services industry. The Dodd-Frank Act has been contested at every phase, beginning with its initial passage through the Legislature. Since its passage, rulemaking by regulatory authorities has been the object of intense lobbying. The platform of the Republican Party and the Trump campaign explicitly called for overturning Dodd-Frank, and the Trump administration has introduced legislation to weaken regulation and widen loopholes.[40]

We also go beyond regulation and advocate the formal socialization of much of finance, insurance, and real estate to be managed in the public interest. This proposal, while jarring to neoliberal sensibilities, would greatly enhance efficiency by recognizing the great extent to which much of finance, insurance, and real estate is already publicly owned and publicly subsidized but not publicly controlled, with enormous benefit to narrow private interests.

Big banks have now enjoyed nearly a decade of oligopolistic profits on an interest-rate spread provided by the central banks. There is no force to compete away these profits and indeed we do not mourn the absence of wildcat competitors who have time and again proven to be dangerously destabilizing in finance. The big banks have an unimpressive record of delivering credit to productive activity. A more efficient solution would be to have central banks themselves operate as public allocators of credit.

The United States now operates a semi-public system of health insurance with residents under mandate to possess health insurance. Slightly more than half of non-elderly households use employment-based health insurance where employers contract with private providers and both employers and employees receive substantial public subsidies for the purchase of private health insurance. In the extension of health insurance developed by the administration of President Barack Obama, a significant share of the remaining non-elderly population is insured by private health insurance companies partly or fully subsidized by public spending.[41]

In the United States, the government-sponsored enterprises Fannie Mae and Freddie Mac hold, in the form of securitized mortgages, fully half of the ten trillion dollars in US mortgage debt. In 2016 alone, these public entities issued almost 1 trillion dollars in mortgage-backed securities. Previously stockholder

[40] See the Republican Party platform at Republican National Committee (2017). President Trump remarked on February 3, 2017, days after taking office, "We expect to be cutting a lot of Dodd-Frank, because frankly, I have so many people, friends of mine that had nice businesses, they can't borrow money" (Trump, 2017).

[41] US Census Bureau (2016).

corporations, both were effectively renationalized as part of the resolution of the 2007–8 financial crisis.[42] With mortgage debt representing more than one third of housing wealth in the United States,[43] Federal government is by far the biggest landlord in the United States. Public housing has arrived by an unlikely path and without full public benefit. Fannie Mae and Freddie Mac do not have retail windows. Loan originators and loan servicers take private cuts of the transaction.

In finance, insurance, and real estate, a tangled system of private provision, public subsidy, and socialized losses has contributed to inefficient and inequitable provision, monopolistic profits at public expense, and risk of crisis induced by moral hazard. The neoliberal solution of full privatization of responsibility simply cannot support the financial functions of a modern economy and is guaranteed to break down at the moment of crisis. The public role is already a substantial reality; it is time to embrace it, take responsibility for it, and reap and distribute the benefits from having these key financialized sectors operated for the public welfare.

In addition to the specific policies we sketch here we also propose guidance for governance to reform the shadow economy. Solutions must be guided by the principles of democracy and a socially oriented policy. The shadow economy has tilted an increasingly zero-sum game in favor of ruling elites. As we have shown, the shadow economy is undemocratic in its workings, in its day-to-day consequences, in its creation of crises, and in its resolution of crises. The core of any solution must come from a commitment to egalitarian democratic principles.

Yet, more democracy and socially consistent economic action is an abstract answer. What does more democracy look like? What options will a more democratic polity be able to imagine or to consider?

Some economists, for example, Alberto Alesina, worry that democratic egalitarian movements will demand so much redistribution that they upend productive behavior. In the early twenty-first century, the concern seems absurd. Far from reaching too far into markets and daily life, recent democratic surges, often arising from political frustration, have demanded remarkably little, and overall they have been deferential to the cults of balanced budgets and unregulated markets.

For example, the Pink Tide governments in Latin America effected modest redistribution of the rents from natural assets, especially oil and gas revenue, to poverty alleviation while for the most part accepting international capital mobility, balanced budgets, and the prerogative of the ruling class to manage the productive assets of their societies. Consider how much bitter resistance the Pink Tide faced from domestic elites and international capital. As rents from natural assets ebbed with falling commodity prices, elites organized violent and reactionary political responses, for example, in Brazil and Venezuela, fighting to limit the bounds of redistribution to the dwindling resource rents.

In the United States, the Occupy Wall Street movement of 2011 deeply touched hearts and captured popular imagination with its indictment of an economy built for the One Percent. But Occupy Wall Street was unable to translate itself into a transformative movement. Its failure can be narrowly attributed to geography,

[42] Solomon (2017); Board of Governors of the Federal Reserve System (2017b).

[43] Board of Governors of the Federal Reserve System (2017a),

spontaneity, and failure to articulate demands, but ultimately Occupy failed to connect with daily life and work.

As we reviewed at length in Chapter 8, social democratic parties throughout the developed and developing economies have abandoned their advocacy for substantially different ends and different means for their societies. On an even grimmer note, the electoral success of right-wing populist movements shows the sensitivity of the response of popular discontent to specific features of the organizational and informational context.

Democracy has come unmoored without mediating institutions, such as unions and mass membership political parties, and without confidence and capacity for economic management by dedicated public servants. The networks that constitute the shadow economy waged a largely successful war against both democratic capacity and democratic confidence.

An extreme instance of the war on confidence appears after the crash of 2008. Elites promulgated the message in corporate media and in lobbying that even the catastrophic errors of the managerial class were too complicated for simple democrats to comprehend. Indeed, they argued quite explicitly in the media and in public politics that the very elites who brought about the crisis were the only agents who could manage the clean-up. Perhaps swayed by these arguments, the governments of the crash countries were reluctant to expropriate and nationalize banks and other financial institutions at the very moment that these institutions had brought both themselves and their economies to the brink of ruin.

Democratic movements will need to reconstitute capacity and confidence if they are to transform their societies. But as we reviewed in our survey of the economics profession, much of the relevant expertise has been corrupted. Professional expertise has turned against the broader public interest.

We have seen the unfortunate consequences of expertise let loose in its own self-interest. Quants and Flashboys put math, physics, and computer science training to work. In Eastern Europe, the revolution-from-above was led by a business-oriented managerial class, who displaced a musty regime, violently bureaucratic but egalitarian in rights, with a hybrid of corporate and crony capitalism. The finest minds in the American academy have been dedicated to developing exquisitely-argued cases against public regulation. Carefully trained regulators have failed to regulate their charges, with regulatory capture reflecting in some cases the material rewards of the revolving door and in others intellectual capture.

Yet professional expertise is critical. Finance, climate, media, information, and privacy, education, and health care are indeed complex. They are not too complex for democracy, but they are overwhelming for democracy without reliable mediating institutions. The construction of those institutions is therefore the condition for professionals to break free from the service of the ruling financial interests.

CONCLUSION: WHAT CAN BE DONE?

If the choice of terms were innocent, no one would care if the earlier epoch of capital controls were to be called "financial repression." Instead, deregulation opened the door for forms of economic terrorism, a term just as controversial but proposed by the most unexpected head of state.[44] In any case, terminology apart, is it enough to travel back in time and to erect new waves of regulations, hoping they will deliver as they did before financialization? As we have gone through the facts and interpretations discussed in this book, our conclusion is negative.

Multiple forms of regulation may be welcome or they may just promote new strategies of shadow making, but what will be essential, at the end of the day, is to have public control of money and credit creation. Only a democratically-controlled system can tame speculation and reorient banking, money, and credit towards building an inclusive economy. Otherwise, speculation, rentism, and cronyism will reign. For this reason, the dependence of central banks on the requirements and leadership of democratic authorities will be a crucial part of the necessary transformation of money creation and policy management.

The immense expansion of the credit system, or of debt, the emergence of new forms of fictitious capital and other financial assets disputing claims on future income, the organization of a kleptocracy, and a *rentier* elite managing the economies: this will define our times if we fail to establish an alternative.

[44] The Holy Father Francis (2013). Pope Francis, of the Catholic Church, famously announced, "Finance kills".

Bibliography

4President.org (2017). *Gary Hart for President 1984 Campaign Brochure.* http://www.4President.org/brochures/garyhart1984brochure.htm.

Acemoglu, Daron et al. (2016). "The Value of Connections in Turbulent Times: Evidence from the United States," *Journal of Financial Economics*. National Bureau of Economic Research Working Paper 19701, December 2013.

Acharya, Viral V. and M. Richardson (2008). *Repairing a Failed System: An Introduction.* New York University Stern Papers. http://whitepapers.stern.nyu.edu/ summaries/intro.html.

Acharya, Viral V., Hanh Le, and Hyun Song Shin (2016). *Bank Capital and Dividend Externalities.* BIS Working Paper No 580. http://www.bis.org/publ/work580.htm.

Acharya, Viral V., Philipp Schnabl, and Gustavo Suarez (2013). "Securitization without Risk Transfer," *Journal of Financial Economics* 107(3) 515–36. http://pages.stern.nyu.edu/~pschnabl/public_html/AcharyaSchnablSuarez2013.pdf.

Admati, Anat and Martin Hellwig (2014). *The Bankers' New Clothes: What's Wrong with Banking and What to Do about It.* Princeton University Press.

Adolph, Christopher (2013). *Bankers, Bureaucrats, and Central Bank Politics: The Myth of Neutrality.* Cambridge University Press.

Adrian, Tobias and Adam B. Ashcraft (2012). *Shadow Banking: A Review of the Literature.* Federal Reserve Bank of New York Staff Report 580.

Adrian, Tobias, Brian Begalle, et al. (2013). "Repo and securities lending," in *Risk Topography: Systemic Risk and Macro Modeling.* Federal Reserve Bank of New York Staff Report 529. University of Chicago Press, pp. 131–48. http://www.newyorkfed.org/research/staff_reports/sr529.pdf.

Adrian, Tobias and Hyun Song Shin (2007). *Liquidity and Leverage.* Federal Reserve Bank of New York Staff Report 328. http://www.newyorkfed.org/research/staff_reports/sr328.pdf.

Adrian, Tobias and Hyun Song Shin (2008). "Liquidity, Monetary Policy, and Financial Cycles," *FRBNY Current Issues in Economics and Finance* 14(1) (January/February), 1–7. http://www.newyorkfed.org/research/current_issues/ci14-1.pdf.

Adrian, Tobias and Hyun Song Shin (2009). "Money, Liquidity, and Monetary Policy," in Federal Reserve Bank of New York Staff Report 360. http://www.newyorkfed. org/research/staff_reports/sr360.pdf.

Adrian, Tobias and Hyun Song Shin (2010). "The Changing Nature of Financial Intermediation and the Financial Crisis of 2007–2009," *Annual Review of Economics* 2(1) 603–18. https://www.newyorkfed.org/research/staff_reports/sr439.html.

AFL-CIO (2017). *Executive Paywatch.* https://aflcio.org/paywatch.

Aglietta, Michel (1995). *Macroéconomie Financière.* Paris: La Découverte.

Agrawal, A. and C. Knoeber (2001). "Do Some Outside Directors Play a Political Role?" *Journal of Law and Economics* 44(1) 179–98.

Aizenman, Joshua and Gurnain Kaur Pasricha (2013). *Why do Emerging Markets Liberalize Capital Outflow Controls? Fiscal versus net capital flow concerns.* NBER Working Paper.

Akerlof, George and Robert J. Shiller (2009). "Disputations: Our new theory of macroeconomics," *New Republic.* http://www.newrepublic. com/article/books-and-arts/disputations-our-new-theorymacroeconomics.

Alesina, Alberto and Silvia Ardagna (2010). "Large Changes in Fiscal Policy: Taxes versus spending," in *Tax Policy and the Economy, Vol 24.* Edited by Jeffrey Brown.

University of Chicago Press/National Bureau of Economic Research, pp. 35–68. http://www.nber.org/chapters/c11970.

Alesina, Alberto and Allan Drazen (1991). "Why Are Stabilizations Delayed?" *American Economic Review* 81(5) 1170–88.

Alesina, Alberto, Omar Barbiero, et al. (2015). "Austerity in 2009–13," *Economic Policy* 30(83) 383–437. http://scholar.harvard.edu/alesina/publications/austerity-2009-2013.

Alessandri, Piergiorgio and Andrew G. Haldane (2009). *Banking on the State*. London: Bank of England. http://www.bankofengland.co.uk/archive/ Documents/historicpubs/speeches/2009/speech409.pdf.

Allais, Maurice (1948). *Economie et Intérêt: Exposition Nouvelle des Problèmes Fondamentaux Relatifs au Rôle Economique du Taux d'Intérêt et de leurs Solutions*. Paris: Librairie des Publications Officielles.

Allen, Katie (2013). "Nobel Prize-Winning Economists Take Disagreement to Whole New Level," *The Guardian*. http://www.theguardian.com/business/2013/dec/10/nobel-prize-economists-robert-shillereugene-fama.

Almeida, Heitor V. and Daniel Wolfenzon (2006). "A Theory of Pyramidal Ownership and Family Business Groups," *Journal of Finance* 61(6) 2637–80. https://business.illinois.edu/halmeida/pyramids.pdf.

Alpert, Daniel (2013). *The Age of Oversupply: Overcoming the Greatest Challenge to the Global Economy*. Penguin.

Alston, Lee J., et al. (2016). *Brazil in Transition: Beliefs, Leadership, and Institutional Change*. Princeton University Press.

Alvaredo, Facundo, et al. (2016). *WID – The World Wealth and Income Database, 07/14/2016*. http://www.wid.world/.

Amromin, Gene and Anna L. Paulson (2010). *Default Rates on Prime and Subprime Mortgages: Differences and similarities*. Profitwise News and Views. Federal Reserve Bank of Chicago. https://www.chicagofed. org/~/media/publications/profitwise-news-and-views/2010/pnvaug2010-reed-final-web-pdf.pdf.

Anderson, Perry (2009). *The New Old World*. London: Verso.

Andrew, A. Piatt (1908a). "Hoarding in the Panic of 1907," *Quarterly Journal of Economics* 22(2) 290–9.

Andrew, A. Piatt (1908b). "Substitutes for Cash in the Panic of 1907," *Quarterly Journal of Economics* 22(4) 497–516.

Andrews, Edmund L. and Peter Baker (2009). "A.I.G. Planning Huge Bonuses After $170 Billion Bailout," *New York Times*, March 15. http://www.nytimes.com/2009/03/15/business/15AIG.html.

Angell, Marcia (2009). "Drug Companies and Doctors: A Story of Corruption," *New York Review of Books*. http://www.nybooks. com/articles/2009/01/15/drug-companies-doctorsa-story-ofcorruption/.

Apeldoorn, Bastiaan van (2014). "The European Capitalist Class and the Crisis of its Hegemonic Project," *Socialist Register* 50 189–206.

Arestis, Philip (2004). "Washington consensus and financial liberalization," *Journal of Post Keynesian Economics* 27(2) 251–71.

Arestis, Philip and Panicos Demetriades (1997). "Financial Development and Economic Growth: Assessing the evidence," *The Economic Journal* 107(442) 783–99.

Arestis, Philip, Georgios Chortareas, and Georgios Magkonis (2014). "The Financial Development and Growth Nexus: A meta-analysis," *Journal of Economic Surveys* 19(1). issn: 1467-6419. doi: 10.1111/joes.12086.

Ariely, Dan et al. (2009). "Large Stakes and Big Mistakes," *Review of Economic Studies* 76(2) 451–69.

Armenter, Roc (2012). "The Rise of Corporate Savings," *Federal Reserve Bank of Philadelphia, Philadelphia Business Review*, Q3, 1–8.

Arrighi, G. (1994). *The Long Twentieth Century: Money, Power and the Origins of Our Times*. New York: Verso.

Arrow, Kenneth J. (1982). "Risk Perception in Psychology and Economics," *Economic Inquiry* 20(1) 1–9.

Ash, Timothy Garton (2016). "When Economists Ignore the Human Factor, We All Pay the Price," *The Guardian*, February 5. https://www.theguardian.com/commentisfree/2016/feb/05/economics-global-crash-humanbehaviour.

Associated Press (2007). "BNP Paribas Freezes Security Funds," *Washington Post*, August 9. http://www.washingtonpost.com/wp-dyn/content/article/2007/08/09/AR2007080900450.html.

Atkinson, Anthony B. (2015). *Inequality*. Harvard University Press.

Auerbach, Alan J. and Yuriy Gorodnichenko (2012). "Measuring the Output Responses to Fiscal Policy," *American Economic Journal: Economic Policy* 4(2) 1–27.

Avent-Holt, Dustin (2012). "The Political Dynamics of Market Organization Cultural Framing, Neoliberalism, and the Case of Airline Deregulation," *Sociological Theory* 30(4) 283–302.

Axelrod, Robert (1980a). "Effective Choice in the Prisoner's Dilemma," *Journal of Conflict Resolution* 24(1) 3–25.

Axelrod, Robert (1980b). "More Effective Choice in the Prisoner's Dilemma," *Journal of Conflict Resolution* 24.3 379–403.

Axelrod, Robert M. (1984). *The Evolution of Cooperation*. Basic Books.

Azar, José, Sahil Raina, and Martin C. Schmalz (2016). "Ultimate Ownership and Bank Competition," Working Paper SSRN 2710252. http://papers.ssrn.com/sol3/papers.cfm?abstract_id=2710252.

Babb, Sarah L (2001). *Managing Mexico: Economists from Nationalism to Neoliberalism*. Princeton University Press.

Backhouse, Roger E (1998). "The Transformation of US Economics, 1920–1960, Viewed through a Survey of Journal Articles," *History of Political Economy* 30 (Supplement) 85.

Baer, Kenneth S. (2000). *Reinventing Democrats: The Politics of Liberalism from Reagan to Clinton*. University Press of Kansas.

Bagehot, Walter (1873). *Lombard Street: A Description of the Money Market*. King.

Baker, Dean (2002). "The Run-up in Home Prices: A bubble," *Challenge* 45(6) 93–119.

Baker, Dean (2006). *The Conservative Nanny State: How the Wealthy Use the Government to Stay Rich and Get Richer*. Center for Economic and Policy Research.

Baker, Dean, et al. (2004). "Labor Market Institutions and Unemployment: Assessment of the cross-country evidence," in *Fighting Unemployment: The Limits of Free Market Orthodoxy*. Edited by David R. Howell, pp. 72–118.

Balanyá, Belén, et al. (2000). *Europe Inc: Regional and Global Restructuring and the Rise of Corporate Power*. London: Pluto Press.

Ball, Laurence (2014). "Long-term Damage from the Great Recession in OECD Countries," *European Journal of Economics and Economic Policies: Intervention* 11(2) 149–60. http://www.nber.org/papers/w20185.

Ban, Cornel (2015). *"Orthodox" Washington versus "Social" Europe? The Politics of Fiscal Doctrine in the IMF and the ECB*. Boston University: Pardee School of Global Studies, pp. 1–22.

Ban, Cornel (2016). *Ruling Ideas: How Global Neoliberalism Goes Local*. Oxford University Press.

Bank of England (2015). *The Failure of HBOS Plc*. A Report by the Financial Conduct Authority (FCA) and the Prudential Regulation Authority (PRA). http://www.bankofengland.co.uk/pra/Documents/publications/reports/hbos.pdf.

BanksDaily (2017a). *The World's 10 Largest Banks (2007)*. http://banksdaily.com/topbanks/World/2007.html.

BanksDaily (2017b). *The World's 30 Largest Banks and Banking Groups (2012).* http://banksdaily.com/topbanks/World/2012.html.

Baran, Paul and Paul Sweezy (1966). *Monopoly Capital.* Monthly Review Press.

Barber, William J. (1981). "The United States: Economists in a pluralistic polity," *History of Political Economy* 13(3) 513–47.

Barca, Fabrizio and Marco Becht (2001). *The Control of Corporate Europe.* Oxford University Press.

Barone, Guglielmo and Sauro Mocetti (2016). "*Intergenerational Mobility in the Very Long Run: Florence 1427–2011,*" Banco d'Italia Eurosistema.

Barro, Robert (2007). *Macroeconomics: A Modern Approach.* Cengage Learning.

Barth, James R., Gerard Caprio, and Ross Levine (2004). "Bank Regulation and Supervision: What works best?" *Journal of Financial Intermediation* 13(2) 205–48.

BBC (2002). *Cheney Accused of Corporate Fraud.* Americas. http://news.bbc.co.uk/1/hi/world/americas/2119981.stm.

Beck, Thorsten, Asli Demirgüç-Kunt, and Ross Levine (2000). "A New Database on the Structure and Development of the Financial Sector," *The World Bank Economic Review* 14(3) 597–605.

Beck, Thorsten, Asli Demirgüç-Kunt, and Ross Levine (2010). *A New Database on Financial Development and Structure. June, 1999* (updated April 2010). http://documents.worldbank.org/curated/en/164081468779345058/A-new-database-on-financial-development-and-structure.

Bekaert, Geert, Campbell R. Harvey, and Christian Lundblad (2005). "Does Financial Liberalization Spur Growth?" *Journal of Financial Economics* 77(1) 3–55.

Belenzon, Sharon, Aaron K. Chatterji, and Brendan Daley (2017). "Eponymous Entrepreneurs," *American Economic Review* 107(6) 1638–55. doi: 10.1257/aer.20141524. http://www.aeaweb.org/articles? id=10.1257/aer.20141524.

Benink, Harald and George Benston (2005). "The Future of Banking Regulation in Developed Countries: Lessons from and for Europe," *Financial Markets, Institutions & Instruments* 14(5) 289–328.

Bernanke, Ben S. (2000). *Essays on the Great Depression.* Princeton University Press.

Bernanke, Ben S. (2004). "The Great Moderation," *Meetings of the Eastern Economic Association, Washington, DC.* http://www.federalreserve.gov/Boarddocs/Speeches/2004/20040220/default.htm.

Bernanke, Ben S. (2005). *The Global Saving Glut and the US Current Account Deficit.* Speech delivered for the Sandridge Lecture at the Virginia Association of Economists, Richmond.

Bernanke, Ben S. (2006a). *Modern Risk Management and Banking Supervision.* Speech at the Stonier Graduate School of Banking. https://www.federalreserve.gov/newsevents/speech/bernanke20060612a.htm.

Bernanke, Ben S. (2006b). *Monetary Policy and the State of the Economy.* Hearing before the Committee on Financial Services, US House of Representatives, One Hundred Ninth Congress, Second Session. https://www.gpo.gov/fdsys/pkg/CHRG-109hhrg31539/html/CHRG-109hhrg31539.htm.

Bernanke, Ben S. (2010). *Implications of the Financial Crisis for Economics.* Speech at the Conference Co-sponsored by the Center for Economic Policy Studies and the Bendheim Center for Finance, Princeton University, Princeton, New Jersey. http://www.federalreserve.gov/newsevents/speech/bernanke20100924a.htm.

Bernanke, Ben S. (2015a). *The Courage to Act: A Memoir of a Crisis and its Aftermath.* WW Norton.

Bernanke, Ben S. (2015b). *Why are Interest Rates so Low?* Brookings Institution Blog. https: // www.brookings.edu / blog/ben-bernanke/2015/03/30/whyare-interest-rates-so-low/.

Bertrand, Marianne et al. (2005). *Politically Connected CEOs and Corporate Outcomes: Evidence from France.* CREST Working Paper.

Beveridge, William Henry (1942). *Social Insurance and Allied Services*. Cmd. 6404, Parliamentary Papers 1942–43, vol. vi, pp. 119–417. http://news.bbc.co.uk/2/shared/bsp/hi/pdfs/19_07_05_beveridge.pdf.

Bhalla, Surjit S. (2012). *Devaluing to Prosperity: Misaligned Currencies and Their Growth Consequence*. Peterson Institute.

Bhattacharya, Sudipto, et al. (2015). "A Reconsideration of Minsky's Financial Instability Hypothesis," *Journal of Money, Credit and Banking* 47(5) 931–73.

Biglaiser, Glen (2009). "The Internationalization of Ideas in Argentina's Economics Profession," in *Economists in the Americas*. Edited by Verónica Montecinos and John Markoff. Northampton: Edward Elgar Publishing, pp. 63–99.

Black, Fischer (1986). "Noise," *Journal of Finance* 41(3) 528–43.

BlackRock (2017). *About Us*. https://www.blackrock.com/au/individual/about-blackrock.

Blanchard, Olivier J. (2007). "Adjustment within the Euro. The difficult case of Portugal," *Portuguese Economic Journal* 6(1) 1–21.

Blanchard, Olivier J. (2008). *The State of Macro*. National Bureau of Economic Research Working Paper 14259.

Blanchard, Olivier J. and Daniel Leigh (2013). "Growth forecast errors and fiscal multipliers," *American Economic Review* 103(3) 117–20.

Blanchard, Olivier J., Giovanni Dell'Ariccia, and Paolo Mauro (2010). *Rethinking Macroeconomic Policy*. Washington, DC: International Monetary Fund. http://www.imf.org/external/pubs/ft/spn/2010/spn1003.pdf.

Blanchard, Olivier J., Sean Hagan, et al., eds. (2012). *The Liberalization and Management of Capital Flows: An Institutional View*. International Monetary Fund, p. 48. http://www.imf.org/external/np/pp/eng/2012/111412.pdf.

Blanes i Vidal, Jordi, Mirko Draca, and Christian Fons-Rosen (2012). "Revolving Door Lobbyists," *American Economic Review* 102(7) 3731–48.

Blankfein, Lloyd (2009). *Remarks to the Council of Institutional Investors*.

Blankfein, Lloyd (2016). *Letter to Shareholders in Annual Report of Goldman Sachs*.

Blinder, Alan S. (2013). *After the Music Stopped: The Financial Crisis, the Response, and the Work Ahead*. Penguin Group USA.

Bloomberg (2014). *John Mack Says Wall Street Pay Debate Is "Healthy."* http://www.bloomberg.com / news / videos / b / e0a7652e-a4bf-42f2-99a0-6b3cc276968a (no longer available).

Blyth, Mark (2002). *Great Transformations: Economic Ideas and Institutional Change in the Twentieth Century*. Cambridge University Press.

Blyth, Mark (2013). *Austerity: The History of a Dangerous Idea*. Oxford University Press.

Board of Governors of the Federal Reserve System (2017a). *B.1 Derivation of Net Wealth*. Financial Accounts of the United States - Z.1. https://www.federalreserve.gov/releases/z1/current/html/b1.htm.

Board of Governors of the Federal Reserve System (2017b). *Mortgage Debt Outstanding*. Table 1.54. https://www. federalreserve.gov/data/mortoutstand/current.htm.

Board of Governors of the Federal Reserve System (US), Federal Reserve Bank of St. Louis (2017). *Various series*. https://fred.stlouisfed.org/.

Boone, Christopher, et al. (2016). *Unemployment Insurance Generosity and Aggregate Employment*. Unpublished manuscript.

Borzutzky, Silvia (2005). "From Chicago to Santiago: Neoliberalism and social security privatization in Chile," *Governance: An International Journal of Policy, Administration and Institutions* 18(4) 655–74.

Boubakri, N., J. C. Cosset, and W. Saffar (2008). "Political Connections of Newly Privatized Firms," *Journal of Corporate Finance* 14(5) 654–73.

Boughton, James M. (1998). "Harry Dexter White and the International Monetary Fund," *Finance and Development (IMF)* 35, 39. http://www.imf.org/external/pubs/ft/fandd/1998/09/boughton.htm.

Boughton, James M. (2001). *The Silent Revolution: The International Monetary Fund 1979–1989*. Washington, DC: International Monetary Fund.

Bourdieu, Pierre (1998). *The State Nobility: Elite Schools in the Field of Power*. Stanford University Press.

Boyce, James and Léonce Ndikumana (2011). *Africa's Odious Debts: How Foreign Loans and Capital Flight Bled a Continent*. Zed Books.

Boyd, John H. and Mark Gertler (1993). "US Commercial Banking: Trends, cycles, and policy," *NBER Macroeconomics Annual 1993, Vol 8*. MIT Press, pp. 319–77.

Boyd, Sebastian (2007). "BNP Paribas Freezes Funds as Loan Losses Roil Market," *Bloomberg News*. https://fcic-static.law.stanford.edu/cdn_media/fcic-docs/2007-08-09%20Bloomberg%20-%20BNP%20Paribas%20Freezes%20Funds%20as%20Loan%20Losses%20Roil%20Markets.pdf.

Bratton, Ethan and Jahanzaib Mehmood Chaudhary (2016). *Largest 100 Banks In The World*. S&P Global Market Intelligence. http://marketintelligence.spglobal.com/our-thinking/ideas/largest-100-banks-in-the-world.

Braun, Matías and Claudio Raddatz (2010). "Banking on Politics: When former high-ranking politicians become bank directors," *The World Bank Economic Review* 24(2) 234–79.

Brenner, Robert (2003). *The Boom and the Bubble: The US in the World Economy*. Verso.

Brown, Greg (2009). *Greenspan Suggests Bank Nationalization in Financial Times Interview*. NewsMax Finance. http://www.newsmax.com/Finance/StreetTalk/greenspan-nationalization/2009/02/18/id/328329/.

Brown, Jeffrey (2010). *One Year Later, Stimulus Appears to Yield Mixed Results*. PBS. http://www.pbs.org/newshour/bb/business-janjune10-stimulus%5C_02-17/ (no longer available).

Brua, Lynn (1975). "Top Bankers Compared," *The Banker* 125(592) 625–7.

Brunnermeier, Markus K. (2009). "Deciphering the Liquidity and Credit Crunch 2007–2008," *Journal of Economic Perspectives* 23(1) 77–100.

Bruno, Michael and William Easterly (1996). "Inflation and Growth: In search of a stable relationship," *Federal Reserve Bank of St. Louis Proceedings* 78, 139–46.

Bruno, Michael and William Easterly (1998). "Inflation Crises and Long-run Growth," *Journal of Monetary Economics* 41(1) 3–26.

Bryan, Dick and Michael Rafferty (2006). *Capitalism with Derivatives: A Political Economy of Financial Derivatives, Capital and Class*. New York: Palgrave Macmillan.

Buchanan, James M. (1965). *The Inconsistencies of the National Health Service: A Study in the Conflict between Individual Demand and Collective Supply*. Institute of Economic Affairs.

Buchanan, James M. (1991). *The Economics and the Ethics of Constitutional Order*. University of Michigan Press.

Buckley, Adrian (2011). *Financial Crisis: Causes, Context, and Consequences*. UK: Financial Times Prentice Hall.

Buffett, Warren E. (2011). "Stop Coddling the Super-Rich." *New York Times*. http://www.nytimes.com/2011/08/15/opinion/stopcoddling-the-super-rich.html.

Buiter, Willem H. (2009). "The Unfortunate Uselessness of Most 'State of the Art' Academic Monetary Economics," *VoxEU and Financial Times*, March 6.

Buiter, Willem H. (2013). "Interview of Buiter with the Federal Reserve Bank of Atlanta." https://www.frbatlanta.org/news/conferences-and-events/conferences/2013/0408-fmc/media/buiter.aspx.

Bureau of Labor Statistics (2017). *Union Member–2016*. Economic News Release. https://www.bls.gov/news.release/union2.nr0.htm.

Burgin, Angus (2012). *The Great Persuasion: Reinventing Free Markets since the Depression*. Harvard University Press.

Caballero, Ricardo and Emmanuel Farhi (2014). "On the Role of Safe Asset Shortages in Secular Stagnation," in *Secular Stagnation: Facts, Causes and Cures*. Edited by Coen Teulings and Richard Baldwin. Centre for Economic Policy Research. https://voxeu.org/article/role-safe-asset-shortages-secular-stagnation.

Caldwell, Bruce and Leonidas Montes (2015). "Friedrich Hayek and his Visits to Chile," *The Review of Austrian Economics* 28(3) 261–309. http://ssrn.com/abstract=2488106.

Callon, Michel (1998). *The Laws of the Markets*. Blackwell Publishers/Sociological Review.

Calmes, Jackie (2010). "At Treasury, Geithner Struggles to Escape a Past He Never Had," *The New York Times*, August 19.

Camerer, Colin, et al. (1997). "Labor Supply of New York City Cabdrivers: One day at a time," *Quarterly Journal of Economics*, 112(2) 407–41.

Cameron, Sue (2005). "Brilliant Orator and a Principled Politician," *Financial Times*. http://www.ft.com/cms/s/0/425b453e-074c-11da-a742-00000e2511c8.html.

Camp, Roderic A. (2007). *Politics in Mexico. The Democratic Consolidation*, 5th edn. Oxford University Press.

Camp, Roderic A. (1990). "Camarillas in Mexican Politics: The case of the Salinas cabinet," *Mexican Studies/Estudios Mexicanos* 6, 85–107.

Camp, Roderic A. (2002). *Mexico's Mandarins: Crafting a Power Elite for the Twenty-first Century*. Berkeley: University of California Press.

Camp, Roderic A. (2013). *Political Recruitment Across Two Centuries: Mexico, 1884–1991*. University of Texas Press.

Campbell, John (2011). *Margaret Thatcher Volume Two: The Iron Lady*. Random House.

Carrick-Hagenbarth, Jessica and Gerald A. Epstein (2012). "Dangerous Interconnectedness: Economists' conflicts of interest, ideology and financial crisis," *Cambridge Journal of Economics* 36(1) 43–63.

Carroll, William K. and Jean-Philippe Sapinski (2010). "The Global Corporate Elite and the Transnational Policy-Planning Network, 1996–2006: A Structural Analysis," *International Sociology* 25(4) 501–38.

Case, K. and Robert J. Shiller (2003). "Is There a Bubble in the Housing Market?" in *Brookings Papers on Economic Activity* 2. The Brookings Institution, pp. 299–342.

Cassidy, John (2004). "Blowing Bubbles," *The New Yorker*, July 12.

Cassidy, John (2009). *How Markets Fail: The Logic of Economic Calamities*. Macmillan.

Cassidy, John (2010). "Interview with Eugene Fama," *The New Yorker*, January 13. http://www.newyorker.com/news/john-cassidy/interview-with-eugenefama.

Castells, Manuel (1996). *The Network Society*. Oxford: Blackwell.

Castle, Stephen (1997). "Profile: Robin Cook: Left to Sort out the World. Just the World to Sort Out," *The Independent*, May 17. http://www.independent.co.uk/voices/profile-robin-cook-left-to-sort-out-the-worldjust-the-world-to-sort-out-1262251.html.

Catão, Luis A. V. and Gian Maria Milesi-Ferretti (2014). "External Liabilities and Crises," *Journal of International Economics* 94(1) 18–32.

Cavallo, Domingo (2004). *Latin America and the Washington Consensus*. Economics Department, Harvard University, spring term lectures.

CBInsight (2015). *SNL Financial ranks highest-paid US bank CEOs in 2014, Jamie Dimon on top*. CBInsight. https://www.snl.com/InteractiveX/Article.aspx?cdid=A-33115907-13868.

Centeno, Miguel Angel (2010). *Democracy within Reason: Technocratic Revolution in Mexico*. Penn State Press.

Center for Responsive Politics (2017a). *OpenSecrets.org Report on Influence & Lobbying, by Industry*. https://www.opensecrets.org/industries/indus.php?ind=F.

Center for Responsive Politics (2017b). *OpenSecrets.org Report on Influence & Lobbying, by Organization*. https://www.opensecrets.org/orgs/summary.php?id= d000000085.

Chait, Jonathan (2005). "John Breaux, Hero or Hack?" *Los Angeles* Times, January 14. http://articles.latimes.com/2005/jan/14/opinion/oechait14.

Chakravorty, Sanjoy, Devesh Kapur, and Nirvikar Singh (2016). *The Other One Percent: Indians in America*. Oxford University Press.

Chamon, Marcos and Marcio Garcia (2016). "Capital Controls in Brazil: Effective?" *Journal of International Money and Finance* 61, 163–87.

Chan, Sewell (2011). "Financial Crisis Was Avoidable, Inquiry Finds," *New York Times*, January 25. http://www.nytimes.com/2011/01/26/business/economy/26inquiry.html.

Chang, Ha-Joon (2002). *Kicking away the Ladder: Development strategy in historical perspective*. Anthem Press.

Chang, Ha-Joon (2007). *Bad Samaritans: The Myth of Free Trade and the Secret History of Capitalism*. Bloomsbury Publishing USA.

Channel 4 (2015). *Politicians for Hire*. http://www.channel4.com/info/press/news/politicians-for-hire.

Chibber, Vivek (2003). *Locked in Place: State-building and Late Industrialization in India*. Princeton University Press.

Chortareas, Georgios et al. (2015). "Financial Development and Economic Activity in Advanced and Developing Open Economies: Evidence from Panel Cointegration," *Review of Development Economics* 19(1) 163–77.

Christiano, Lawrence, Martin Eichenbaum, and Sergio Rebelo (2011). "When is the Government Spending Multiplier Large?" *Journal of Political Economy* 119(1) 78–121.

Chua, Amy (2003). *World on Fire: How the Exportation of Free Market Democracy Breeds Ethnic and Global Instability*. New York: Doubleday.

Chwieroth, Jeffrey M. (2010). *Capital Ideas: The IMF and the Rise of Financial Liberalization*. Princeton University Press.

Chwieroth, Jeffrey M. (2013). "'The Silent Revolution': How the staff exercise informal governance over IMF lending," *Review of International Organizations* 8 265–90.

Chwieroth, Jeffrey M. (2014). "Controlling Capital: The International Monetary Fund and transformative incremental change from within international organisations," *New Political Economy* 19(3) 445–69.

Chwieroth, Jeffrey M. (2015). "Professional Ties that Bind: How normative orientations shape IMF conditionality," *Review of International Political Economy* 22(4) 757–87.

Claessens, Stijn, Erik Feijen, and Luc Laeven (2008). "Political Connections and Preferential Access to Finance: The role of campaign contributions," *Journal of Financial Economics* 88(3). Technology Report 6045, C.E.P.R. Discussion Papers, 2007, pp. 554–80.

Claessens, Stijn, et al. (2012). *Shadow Banking: Economics and Policy*. IMF Staff Discussion Note SDN/12/12, pp. 1–36. http://www.imf.org/external/pubs/ft/sdn/2012/sdn1212.pdf.

Clark, Andrew, Heather Stewart, and Elena Moya (2010). "Goldman Sachs Faces Fed Inquiry Over Greek Crisis," *The Guardian*, February 26.

Clawson, Dan, Alan Neustadtl, and Mark Weller (1998). *Dollars and Votes: How Business Campaign Contributions Subvert Democracy*. Philadelphia: Temple University Press.

CNN (2017). *Presidential Results*. http://edition.cnn.com/election/results/President.

Coates, J. C. and R. Kraakman (2007). "CEO Tenure, Performance and Turnover in S&P 500 Companies," Harvard Law School, John M. Olin Center for Law, Economics, and Business Discussion Paper Series 595. http://papers.ssrn.com/sol3/papers.cfm?abstract_id=925532.

Coats, A.W. (1981). "Economists in Government," *History of Political Economy* 13(3) 341–64.

Cochrane, John H. (2011). "How Did Paul Krugman Get it so Wrong?" *Economic Affairs* 31(2) 36–40.

Cogan, John F., et al. (2010). "New Keynesian versus Old Keynesian Government Spending Multipliers," *Journal of Economic Dynamics and Control* 34(3) 281–95.

Collier, Paul (2008). *The Bottom Billion: Why the Poorest Countries are Failing and What Can be Done About it*. Oxford University Press.

Colpan, Asli M., Takashi Hikino, and James R. Lincoln (2010). *The Oxford Handbook of Business Groups*. Oxford University Press.

Commodity Futures Trading Commission (1998). *CFTC Issues Concept Release Concerning Over-the-Counter Derivatives Market*. Release #4142-98. http://www.cftc.gov/opa/press98/opa4142-98.htm.

Conti-Brown, Peter (2010). "A Proposed Fat-Tail Risk Metric: Disclosures, derivatives, and the measurement of financial risk," *Washington University Law Review* 87(6) 1461–74.

Copeland, Adam M., Antoine Martin, and Michael Walker (2010). "The Triparty Repo Market before the 2010 Reforms," *FRB of New York Staff Report* 477, 1–81. http://www.newyorkfed.org/research/staff_reports/sr477.pdf.

Corkery, Michael and Ben Protess (2015). "Rigging of Foreign Exchange Market Makes Felons of Top Banks," *New York Times*, May 20. https://www.nytimes.com/2015/05/21/business/dealbook/5-big-banksto-pay-billions-and-plead-guilty-in-currency-and-interestrate-cases.html.

Costa, Jorge, João Teixeira Lopes, and Francisco Louçã (2014). *Os donos angolanos de Portugal*. Bertrand.

Covitz, Daniel, Nellie Liang, and Gustavo A. Suarez (2009). "The Anatomy of a Financial Crisis: The evolution of panic-driven runs in the asset backed commercial paper market," Washington: Federal Reserve Board Finance and Economics Discussion Series Working Paper 36, pp. 1–46. http://www.federalreserve.gov/pubs/feds/2009/200936/200936pap.pdf.

Covitz, Daniel, Nellie Liang, and Gustavo A. Suarez (2013). "The Evolution of a Financial Crisis: Collapse of the asset-backed commercial paper market," *Journal of Finance* 68(3) 815–48.

Cowen, David, Richard Sylla, and Robert Wright (2006). "The US Panic of 1792: Financial crisis management and the lender of last resort," New York University Working Paper. http://www.helsinki.fi/iehc2006/papers1/Sylla.pdf.

Cowie, Jefferson (2010). *Stayin' Alive: The 1970s and the Last Days of the Working Class*. New York: The New Press.

Credit Suisse Asia Pacific/China Equity Research (2015). *Legend Holdings*. https://doc.research-and-analytics.csfb.com/docView? sourceid=em&document_id=x650959&serialid=Vfe6XzRDuj8FRKQnwWboVF8CgsdEBFSu0vjgP93SKS 5C%3d.

Credit Suisse Research (2014). *Global Wealth Report 2014*. https://publications.credit-suisse.com/tasks/render/file/?fileID=60931FDE-A2D2-F568-B041B58C5EA591A4.

Cronin, James E., George Ross, and James Shoch (2011). *What's Left of the Left*. Duke University Press Books.

Crotty, James R. (1983). "On Keynes and Capital Flight," *Journal of Economic Literature* 21(1) 59–65.

Crotty, James R. (2008). "If Financial Market Competition is so Intense, Why Are Financial Firm Profits so High? Reflections on the Current 'Golden Age' of Finance," *Competition & Change* 12(2) 167–83.

Crouch, Colin (2011). *The Strange Non-Death of Neo-liberalism*. Cambridge, UK: Polity Press.

Cuadros, Alex (2016). *Brazillionaires: The Godfathers of Modern Brazil*. New York: Spiegel and Grau.

Cull, Robert and Lixin Colin Xu (2005). "Institutions, Ownership, and Finance: The determinants of profit reinvestment among Chinese firms," *Journal of Financial Economics* 77(1) 117–46.

Dagnino Pastore, José Maria (1989). "Argentina," *The Role of the Economist in Government: An International Perspective*. Edited by Joseph A. Pechman. Harvester and Wheatsheaf.

Daly, Kevin and Ben Broadbent (2009). "The Savings Glut, the Return on Capital and the Rise in Risk Aversion," *Goldman Sachs Global Economics Paper* 195.

Dang, Tri Vi, Gary B. Gorton, and Bengt Holmstrom (2009). "Opacity and the optimality of debt for liquidity provision," *Manuscript Yale University*.

Darai, Donja and Silvia Grätz (2010). *Golden Balls: A Prisoner's Dilemma Experiment*. Working Paper 1006, Socioeconomic Institute, University of Zurich.

Dargent, Eduardo (2014). *Technocracy and Democracy in Latin America: The Experts Running Government*. Cambridge University Press.

D'Arista, J. and T. Schlesinger (1993a). "The Parallel Banking System," in *Transforming the US Financial System: Equity and Efficiency for the 21st Century*. Edited by Gary Dymski, Gerald A. Epstein, and Robert Pollin. ME Sharpe.

D'Arista, J. and T. Schlesinger (1993b). *The Parallel Banking System*. Washington: Economic Policy Institute Briefing Paper No 37, p. 45. http://s1.epi.org/files/page/-/old/briefingpapers/1993_bp_parallel.pdf.

Darling, Alistair (2011). *Back from the Brink: 1000 days at Number 11*. Atlantic Books Ltd.

Das, Satyajit (2006). *Traders, Guns & Money: Knowns and Unknowns in the Dazzling World of Derivatives*. Pearson Education.

David-Barrett, Liz (2011). "Cabs for Hire? Fixing the revolving door between Government and Business," *Transparency International*. http://sro.sussex.ac.uk/52110/.

Davies, James, Rodrigo Lluberas, and Anthony Shorrocks (2016). *Credit Suisse Global Wealth Databook 2016*. https://www.credit-suisse.com/microsites/next/en/financial-literacy-expertise/articles/the-global-wealth-report-2016.html.

Davis, John Bryan (2011). *The Elgar Companion to Recent Economic Methodology*. Edward Elgar Publishing.

Davis, Stephen, Jon Lukomnik, and David Pitt-Watson (2016). *What They Do with Your Money: How the Financial System Fails Us, and How to Fix It*. Yale University Press.

DealBook (2010). "Geithner Haunted by a Goldman Past He Never Had," *The New York Times*, August 19.

DeLong, J. Bradford (1996). "Keynesianism, Pennsylvania Avenue Style: Some Economic Consequences of the Employment Act of 1946," *Journal of Economic Perspectives* 10(3) 41–53.

DeLong, J. Bradford (2011). *Letter from Margaret Thatcher to Friedrich Hayek*. http://delong.typepad.com/sdj/2011/12/letter-frommargaret-thatcher-to-friedrich-hayek.html.

DeLong, J. Bradford, et al. (1990). "Noise Trader Risk in Financial Markets," *Journal of Political Economy* 98, 703–38.

Denning, Steve (2013). "The Origin Of 'The World's Dumbest Idea': Milton Friedman," *Forbes*, June 26. https://www.forbes.com/sites/stevedenning/2013/06/26/the-origin-of-the-worlds-dumbestidea-milton-friedman/#22716d94870e.

Detzer, Daniel, et al. (2013). *Studies in Financial Systems: No 3 The German Financial System*. Financialisation, Economy, Society & Sustainable Development (FESSUD) Project.

Deutsche Welle (2012). *Steinbrück Admits to over a Million Euros in Lecture Fees*. http://www.dw.com/en/steinbr%C3%BCck-admits-to-over-a-million-euros-in-lecture-fees/a-16341986.

Dezalay, Yves and Bryant G. Garth (2002). *The Internationalization of Palace Wars: Lawyers, Economists, and the Contest to Transform Latin American States*. University of Chicago Press.

Dias, A. C., et al. (2015). *The Revolving Door: Evidence from the United Kingdom, Germany, France, Spain, Belgium, Greece and Brazil*. University of Lisbon, ISEG–Departamento de Economia.

Dimon, Jamie (2010). *First Public Hearing of the Financial Crisis Inquiry Commission*. The Official Transcript. http://fcic-static.law. stanford.edu/cdn_media/fcic-testimony/2010-0113-Transcript. pdf.

Dimon, Jamie (2017). *Dear Fellow Shareholders*. 2016 CEO Letter to JPMorganChase Shareholders. https://www.jpmorganchase.com/corporate/investor-relations/document/ar2016-ceolettershareholders.pdf.

Dinç, I. Serdar (2005). "Politicians and Banks: Political influences on government owned banks in emerging markets," *Journal of Financial Economics* 77(2) 453–79.

Dobbs, Richard, Tim Koller, et al. (2015). "The New Global Competition for Corporate Profits," *McKinsey Global Institute Report*. http://www.mckinsey.com/business-functions/strategy-and-corporatefinance/our-insights/the-new-global-competition-for-corporateprofits.

Dobbs, Richard, Susan Lund, et al. (2015). "Debt and (not much) Deleveraging," *McKinsey Global Institute Report*. http://www.mckinsey. com/global-themes/employment-and-growth/debt-and-not-muchdeleveraging.

Dobbs, Richard, Anu Madgavkar, et al. (2012). *The World at Work: Jobs, Pay, and Skills for 3.5 Billion People*. McKinsey Global Institute. http://www.mckinsey.com/insights/employment_and_growth/the_world_at_work.

Dolan, K. A. and L. Kroll (2015). "Inside the 2015 Forbes Billionaires List: Facts and figures," *Forbes*, March 2. http://www.forbes.com/sites/kerryadolan/2015/03/02/inside-the-2015-forbes-billionaireslist-facts-and-figures/.

Domhoff, G. William (1983). *Who Rules America Now? A View for the '80s*. Englewood Cliffs, NJ: Prentice Hall.

Domínguez, Jorge I. (1997a). *Technopols: Freeing Politics and Markets in Latin America in the 1990s*. Penn State Press.

Domínguez, Jorge I. (1997b). "Technopols: Ideas and Leaders in Freeing Politics and Markets in Latin America in the 1990s," in *Technopols: Freeing Politics and Markets in Latin America in the 1990s*. Edited by Jorge I. Domínguez. Penn State Press.

Dowd, Kevin, et al. (2008). "How Unlucky Is 25-Sigma?" *Journal of Portfolio Management* 34(4) 76–80.

Dreyfuss, Robert (2001). "How the DLC Does It," *American Prospect*, April 23.

Drezner, D. W. (2014). "The System Worked: Global economic governance during the Great Recession," *World Politics* 66(1) 123–64.

Duarte, Pedro Garcia (2011). "16 Recent Developments in Macroeconomics: The DSGE approach to business cycles in perspective," in *The Elgar Companion to Recent Economic Methodology*. Edward Elgar Publishing, p. 375.

Dube, Arindrajit (2013). "Guest Post: Reinhart/Rogoff and Growth in a Time Before Debt," *Next New Deal: The Blog of the Roosevelt Institute*. http://rooseveltinstitute.org/guest-post-reinhartrogoff-andgrowth-time-debt/.

Ductor, Lorenzo and Daryna Grechyna (2015). "Financial Development, Real Sector, and Economic Growth," *International Review of Economics & Finance* 37(0) 393–405. issn: 1059-0560. doi: http://dx.doi.org/10.1016/j.iref.2015.01.001.

Duménil, Gérard and Dominique Lévy (2004). *Capital Resurgent: Roots of the Neoliberal Revolution*. Harvard University Press.

Duménil, Gérard and Dominique Lévy (2005). "Costs and Benefits of Neoliberalism: A class analysis," in *Financialization and the World Economy*. Edited by Gerald A. Epstein. Cheltenham, UK: Edward Elgar.

Duménil, Gérard and Dominique Lévy (2011). *The Crisis of Neoliberalism*. Harvard University Press.

Dymski, Gary and Robert Pollin (1992). "Hyman Minsky as Hedgehog: The power of the Wall Street paradigm," *Financial Conditions and Macroeconomic Performance: Essays in Honor of Hyman P. Minsky*. Edited by S. Fazzari and D. Papadimitriou. ME Sharpe, pp. 27–61.

Dymski, Gary, Gerald A. Epstein, and Robert Pollin (1993). *Transforming the US Financial System: Equity and Efficiency for the 21st Century*. ME Sharpe.

Easterly, William (2006). *The White Man's Burden: Why the West's Efforts to Aid the Rest Have Done so Much Ill and so Little Good*. New York: Penguin.

Eavis, Peter (2015). "The Break-Up Question Over JPMorgan Chase," *New York Times*. http://dealbook.nytimes.com/2015/01/14/thebreak-up-question-over-jpmorgan/.

The Economist (2014). *An On-Off Relationship: Counter-cyclical Capital Controls are Great in Theory but Less Useful in Practice.* http://www.economist.com/news/finance-and-economics/21636082-counter-cyclicalcapital-controls-are-great-theory-less-useful.

Edison, Hali J., et al. (2004). "Capital Account Liberalization and Economic Performance: Survey and synthesis," *IMF Staff Papers*, pp. 220–56.

Edlund, Lena and Evelyn Korn (2002). "A Theory of Prostitution," *Journal of Political Economy* 110(1) 181–214.

Edsall, Thomas B. (2009). "Alan Greenspan: The oracle or the master of disaster?" *Huffington Post*, February 20.

Edsall, Thomas B. (2011). "The Trouble With That Revolving Door," *New York Times*, December 17. http://campaignstops.blogs.nytimes.com/2011/12/18/the-trouble-with-that-revolving-door/.

Eggertsson, Gauti B. and Neil Mehrotra (2014). "A Model of Secular Stagnation," *Secular Stagnation: Facts, Causes and Cures*. Edited by Coen Teulings and Richard Baldwin. Centre for Economic Policy Research. https://voxeu.org/content/secular-stagnation-facts-causes-and-cures.

Eichengreen, Barry (2014). "Secular Stagnation: A Review of the Issues," *Secular Stagnation: Facts, Causes and Cures*. Edited by Coen Teulings and Richard Baldwin. Centre for Economic Policy Research, pp. 41–6. https://voxeu.org/content/secular-stagnation-facts-causes-and-cures.

Eichengreen, Barry (2015). *Hall of mirrors: The Great Depression, the Great Recession, and the uses—and misuses—of history*. New York: Oxford University Press.

Eichengreen, Barry and Kevin H. O'Rourke (2010). "A Tale of Two Depressions: What do the new data tell us?" *VoxEU.org*, March 23.

Eichengreen, Barry and Andrew Rose (2014). "Capital Controls in the 21st Century," *Journal of International Money and Finance* 48 1–16.

El-Erian, Mohamed A. (2016). *The Only Game in Town: Central Banks, Instability, and Avoiding the Next Collapse*. Yale University Press.

Ely, Richard T. (1910). "The American Economic Association 1885–1909," *American Economic Association Quarterly* 11(1) 47–111.

Engel, Kathleen C. and Patricia A. McCoy (2016). *The Subprime Virus: Reckless Credit, Regulatory Failure, and Next Steps*. Oxford University Press.

Epstein, Gerald A. (2005a). *Financialization and the World Economy*. Edward Elgar Publishing.

Epstein, Gerald A. (2005b). "Introduction: Financialization and the World Economy," *Financialization and the World Economy*. Edited by Gerald A. Epstein. Cheltenham, UK: Edward Elgar, p. 3.

Epstein, Gerald A. (2012). "Regulating Global Capital Flows for Long-Run Development," Edited by Kevin P. Gallagher, Stephany Griffith-Jones, and José Antonio Ocampo. Pardee Center, Boston University, Chap. "Capital Outflow Regulation: Economic Management, Development and Transformation," pp. 59–70.

Epstein, Gerald A. (2016). "From Boring Banking to Roaring Banking: How the financial sector grew out of control, and how we can change it," *Dollars & Sense*. http://www.dollarsandsense.org/archives/2015/0715epstein.html.

Epstein, Gerald A. and Arjun Jayadev (2005). "The Rise of Rentier Incomes in OECD Countries: Financialization, central bank policy and labor solidarity," *Financialization and the World Economy*. Edited by Gerald A. Epstein. Cheltenham, UK: Edward Elgar, pp. 46–74.

Equilar (2016). *Equilar/Associated Press S&P 500 CEO Pay Study 2016*. http://www.equilar.com/reports/37-associated-press-paystudy-2016.html.

Ernst and Young (2015). *Future Directions for Foreign Banks in China 2014*. http://www.ey.com/Publication/vwLUAssets/EY-foreignbank-china-report-2014/%24FILE/EY-foreign-bank-china-report-2014.pdf.

Errico, Luca, et al. (2014). *Mapping the Shadow Banking System Through a Global Flow of Funds Analysis*, IMF Working Paper.
European Central Bank (2009). *Introductory Statement with Q & A*. Press Conference, Jean-Claude Trichet, President of the ECB, and Lucas Papademos, Vice President of the ECB. https://www.ecb.europa.eu/press/pressconf/2009/html/is090115.en.html.
European Central Bank (2015). "The Fiscal Impact of Financial Sector Support During the Crisis," *Economic Bulletin* 6 74–87.
European Economic and Social Committee (EESC) (2012). *Green Paper–Shadow Banking*. INT/643. http://www.eesc.europa.eu/?i= portal.en.int-opinions.22753.
European Trade Union Institute (2017). *National Industrial Relations—Trade Unions*. Gateway to Information on Worker Participation Issues in Europe. https://www.worker-participation.eu/National-Industrial-Relations/Across-Europe/Trade-Unions2.
Faccio, Mara (2006). "Politically Connected Firms," *The American Economic Review* 96(1) 369–86.
Faccio, Mara and Larry H. P. Lang (2002). "The Ultimate Ownership of Western European Corporations," *Journal of Financial Economics* 65(3) 365–95.
Faccio, Mara, Ronald W. Masulis, and John McConnell (2006). "Political Connections and Corporate Bailouts," *Journal of Finance* 61(6) 2597–635.
Fama, Eugene F. (1963). "Mandelbrot and the Stable Paretian Hypothesis," *Journal of Business* 36(4) 420–9.
Fama, Eugene F. and Kenneth R. French (1992). "The Cross-section of Expected Stock Returns," *Journal of Finance* 47(2) 427–65.
Family Business Institute (2017). *Succession Planning*. http://www.familybusinessinstitute.com/index.php/Succession-Planning/.
Federal Deposit Insurance Corporation (1998). *A Brief History of Deposit Insurance in the United States*. Prepared for the International Conference on Deposit Insurance, Washington, DC. https://www.fdic.gov/bank/historical/brief/brhist.pdf.
Federal Reserve History (2013). *Volcker's Announcement of Anti-Inflation Measures*. http://www.federalreservehistory.org/Events/DetailView/41.
Feld, Lars P., Ekkehard A. Köhler, and Daniel Nientiedt (2015). "Ordoliberalism, Pragmatism and the Eurozone Crisis: How the German tradition shaped economic policy in Europe," CESifo Working Paper Series No 5368. http://papers.ssrn.com/sol3/papers.cfm?abstract_id=2613901.
Feldstein, Martin S. (1974). "Social Security, Induced Retirement, and Aggregate Capital Accumulation," *Journal of Political Economy* 82(5) 905–26.
Feldstein, Martin S. (1982). "Social Security and Private Saving: Reply," *Journal of Political Economy* 90(3) 630–42.
Fendrich, Laurie (2009). *Life Is Messy but True, Economics Is Clean but Wrong*. Chronicle of Higher Education Brainstorm Blog. http://www.chronicle.com/blogs/brainstorm/life-is-messy-but-trueeconomics-is-clean-but-wrong/7938.
Ferguson, Charles H. (2012). *Inside Job: The Financiers who Pulled off the Heist of the Century*. Oneworld Publications.
Ferguson, Charles H. (2013). *Predator Nation: Corporate Criminals, Political Corruption, and the Hijacking of America*. Crown Business.
Ferguson, Niall (2014). *The Great Degeneration: How Institutions Decay and Economies Die*. Penguin.
Ferguson, Thomas (1995). *Golden Rule: The Investment Theory of Party Competition and the Logic of Money-Driven Political Systems*. Chicago: University of Chicago Press.
Fernández, Andrés, Alessandro Rebucci, and Martín Uribe (2013). *Are Capital Controls Prudential? An Empirical Investigation*. National Bureau of Economic Research Working Paper 19671. doi: 10.3386/w19671. http://www.nber.org/papers/w19671.

Financial Stability Board (2011a). "Shadow Banking: Scoping the Issues—A Background Note of the Financial Stability Board," in *Basel: Financial Stability Board*, pp. 1–9. http://www.financialstabilityboard. org/wp-content/uploads/r_110412a.pdf.

Financial Stability Board (2011b). "Shadow Banking: Strengthening oversight and regulation," in *Basel: Financial Stability Board*, pp. 1–43. http://www.financialstabilityboard.org/wp-content/uploads/r_111027a.pdf.

Financial Stability Board (2014). "Global Shadow Banking Monitoring Report 2012," *Basel: Financial Stability Board*, pp. 1–55. http://www.fsb.org/2014/11/global-shadow-banking-monitoring-report-2014/.

Financial Times (2011). "Geithner Doubts Ability to Spot Vital Banks," January 14.

Financial Times (2013). "Dutch Sandwich" Grows as Google Shifts e8.8bn to Bermuda," October 10.

Financial Times (2015a). "Barclays Fined $2.4bn for Forex Rigging," May 20.

Financial Times (2015b). "Meet the Wallenbergs" June 5.

Financial Times (2016). "Arrests in China over $7.6bn Ponzi Scheme," January 31.

Findley, Michael G., Daniel L. Nielson, and Jason Campbell Sharman (2014). *Global Shell Games: Experiments in Transnational Relations, Crime, and Terrorism*. Vol. 128. Cambridge University Press.

Fine, Ben (2004). "Examining the Ideas of Globalisation and Development Critically: What Role for Political Economy?" *New Political Economy* 9(2) 213–31.

Fish, Tom and Roy Whymark (2015). "How has Cash Usage Evolved in Recent Decades? What Might Drive Demand in the Future?" *Bank of England Quarterly Bulletin* (Q3). http://www.bankofengland.co.uk/publications/Pages/quarterlybulletin/2015/q3prerelease_1.aspx.

Fisher, Irving (1935). *100 Percent Money*. George Allen & Unwin.

Fisher, Irving (1936). "100% Money and the Public Debt," *Economic Forum* Spring (April–June), 406–20. http://realmoneyecon.org/lev2/images/pdfs/100percent_money.pdf.

Fisher, Richard W. (2014). *Monetary Policy and the Maginot Line (with reference to Jonathan Swift, Neil Irwin, Shakespeare's Portia, Duck Hunting, the Virtues of Nuisance and Paul Volcker)*. Federal Reserve Bank of Dallas.

Fisman, David, et al. (2012). "Estimating the Value of Connections to Vice President Cheney," *The BE Journal of Economic Analysis & Policy* 12(3).

Fisman, Raymond J. (2001). "Estimating the Value of Political Connections," *American Economic Review* 91(4) 1095–102.

Flanders, M. June (2015). "It's not a Minsky Moment, it's a Minsky Era, or: Inevitable instability," *Econ Journal Watch* 12(1) 84.

Foley, Stephen (2011). "What Price the New Democracy? Goldman Sachs Conquers Europe," *The Independent*. http://www.independent. co.uk/news/business/analysis-and-features/what-price-thenew-democracy-goldman-sachs-conquers-europe-6264091.html.

Fons, Jerome S. (2008). *Testimony*. Committee on Government Oversight and Reform. https://democrats-oversight.house.gov/sites/democrats.oversight.house.gov/files/documents/20081022102726.pdf.

Forbes (2017). *The World's Billionaires*. Forbes. https://www.forbes.com/billionaires/list/.

Fortune (2017). *Rankings*. http://fortune.com/rankings/.

Fourcade, Marion (2009). *Economists and Societies: Discipline and Profession in the United States, Britain, and France, 1890s to 1990s*. Princeton University Press.

Fourcade, Marion, Etienne Ollion, and Yann Algan (2015). "The Superiority of Economists," *Journal of Economic Perspectives* 29(1) 89–114.

Fourcade-Gourinchas, Marion and Sarah L Babb (2002). "The Rebirth of the Liberal Creed: Paths to Neoliberalism in Four Countries," *American Journal of Sociology* 108(3) 533–79.

Fracchia, Eduardo, Luiz Mesquita, and Juan Quiroga (2010). "Business Groups in Argentina," *The Oxford Handbook of Business Groups*. Edited by Asli M. Colpan, Takashi Hikino, and James R. Lincoln. Oxford University Press.

Franco, Francesco (2008). *Challenges Ahead for the Portuguese Economy*. Lisbon: Instituto Ci encias Sociais.

Franco, Francesco (2011). *Macroeconomia. Memorandum of Economic and Financial Policies: 11 Perspectivas*. Nova School of Business and Economics. http://exed.novasbe.pt/difusao-conhecimento/applied-knowledge/261memorandum-of-economic-and-financial-policies-11-perspectivasv2.

Frank, Thomas (2012). *Pity the Billionaire: The Hard-Times Swindle and the Unlikely Comeback of the Right*. New York: Macmillan.

Franks, Julian and Colin Mayer (2001). "Ownership and Control of German Corporations," *Review of Financial Studies* 14(4) 943–77. doi: 10.1093/rfs/14.4.943. eprint: http://rfs.oxfordjournals.org/content/14/4/943.full.pdf+html.

Freeland, Chrystia (2014). *Plutocratas*. Lisbon: Temas e Debates.

Freeman, Christopher and Francisco Louçã (2001). *As Time Goes By: From the Industrial Revolutions to the Information Revolution*. Oxford University Press.

Freund, Caroline (2016). *Rich People Poor Countries: The Rise of Emerging Market Tycoons and their Mega Firms*. Peterson Institute for International Economics.

Freund, Caroline and Sarah Oliver (2016). "The Origins of the Superrich: The Billionaire Characteristics Database," Peterson Institute for International Economics Working Paper 16.1.

Friedman, Milton (1960). *A Program for Monetary Stability*. Vol. 541. New York: Fordham University Press.

Friedman, Milton (1962). "Should There Be an Independent Monetary Authority?" in *In Search of a Monetary Constitution*. Edited by Leland B. Yeager. Cambridge, MA: Harvard University Press.

Friedman, Milton (1970). "A Friedman Doctrine—The Social Responsibility of Business is to Increase its Profits," *New York Times*, September 13. http://www.nytimes. com/1970/09/13/archives/a-friedman-doctrine-the-socialresponsibility-of-business-is-to.html.

Friedman, Milton (1990). *Friedman in China*. Hong Kong Centre for Economic Research.

Friedman, Milton (2002). "Preface: Economic Freedom Behind the Scenes," *Economic Freedom of the World 2002 Annual Report*. Edited by James Gwartney and Robert Lawson. Vancouver: Fraser Institute, pp. xvii–xxi.

Friedman, Rose and Milton Friedman (1979). *Free to Choose: A Personal Statement*. Harcourt Brace Jovanovich. https://www.youtube.com/watch?v=RWsx1X8PV_A.

Frontline (2009). *Interview: Brooksley Born*. http://www.pbs.org/wgbh/pages/frontline/warning/interviews/born.html.

Gabor, Daniela (2010). "(De) Financialization and Crisis in Eastern Europe." in *Competition & Change* 14(3–4), 248–70.

Gabor, Daniela (2015). "The IMF's Rethink of Global Banks: Critical in theory, orthodox in practice," *Governance* 28(2) 199–218.

Gabor, Daniela (2016). "The (Impossible) Repo Trinity: The political economy of repo markets," *Review of International Political Economy*, 1–34.

Galbraith, James K. (2015). *The End of Normal: The Great Crisis and the Future of Growth*. New York: Simon and Schuster.

Galizia, Matthew Caruana, et al. (2014). *Explore the Documents: Luxembourg Leaks Database*. International Consortium of Investigative Journalists. http://www.icij.org/project/luxembourg-leaks/exploredocuments-luxembourg-leaks-database.

Gallagher, Kevin P. (2011). "Regaining Control? Capital controls and the global financial crisis," Political Economy Research Institute, University of Massachusetts Amherst, PERI Working Paper 250.

Gallagher, Kevin P. (2015). "Contesting the Governance of Capital Flows at the IMF," *Governance* 28(2) 185–98. issn: 1468-0491. doi: 10.1111/gove.12100. http://dx.doi.org/10.1111/gove.12100.

Gallagher, Kevin P., Stephany Griffith-Jones, and José Antonio Ocampo (2012). "Regulating Global Capital Flows for Long-run Development," in *Pardee Center Task Force Report*, pp. 13–22.

Gandhi, Aditi and Michael Walton (2012). "Where Do India's Billionaires Get Their Wealth?" in *Economic and Political Weekly* 47(40) 10–14. http://www.michaelwalton.info/wp-content/uploads/2012/10/Where-Do-Indias-Billionaires-Get-Th%20eir-Wealth-Aditi-Walton.pdf.

Geanakoplos, John (2010). "The Leverage Cycle," in *NBER Macroeconomics Annual 2009, Vol 24*. University of Chicago Press, pp. 1–65.

Geithner, Timothy (2014). *Stress Test: Reflections on Financial Crises*. Random House.

Gennaioli, Nicola, Andrei Shleifer, and Robert W. Vishny (2012). "Neglected Risks, Financial Innovation, and Financial Fragility," *Journal of Financial Economics* 104(3) 452–68.

Geppert, Dominik (2003). *Thatchers Konservative Revolution: Der Richtungswandel der Britischen Tories, 1975–1979*. Munich: Oldenbourg Verlag.

Giles, Jim (2005). "Internet Encyclopædias go Head to Head," *Nature* 438(7070) 900–1.

Glaeser, Edward (2014). "Secular Joblessness," in *Secular Stagnation: Facts, Causes and Cures*. Edited by Coen Teulings and Richard Baldwin. Centre for Economic Policy Research, pp. 69–80. https://voxeu.org/content/secular-stagnation-facts-causes-and-cures.

Glaeser, Edward L. (2013). "A Nation of Gamblers: Real Estate Speculation and American History," *American Economic Review* 103(3) 1–42.

Golden Balls (2008). *£100,000 Split Or Steal?* https://www.youtube.com/watch?v=p3Uos2fzIJ0.

Golden Balls (2012). *The Weirdest Split or Steal Ever*. https://www.youtube. com/watch?v=S0qjK3TWZE8.

Gomes, Rafael A. R. P. (2012). "Ethics in Finance, Robin Cosgrove Prize Global Edition 2012–2013," *Finance and the Common Good. Corporate Market Responsibility: Ethical Regulation for Orderly Financial Markets*. http://www.ethicsinfinance.org/.

Goodhart, Charles A. E. et al. (2013). "An Integrated Framework for Analyzing Multiple Financial Regulations," *International Journal of Central Banking* 9(1) 109–43.

Goolsbee, Austan (2007). "'Irresponsible' Mortgages Have Opened Doors to Many of the Excluded," *New York Times*, March 29. http://www.nytimes.com/2007/03/29/business/29scene.html.

Gordon, Robert J. (2012). *Is U.S. Economic Growth Over? Faltering Innovation Confronts the Six Headwinds*. National Bureau of Economic Research Working Paper 18315. doi: 10.3386/w18315. http://www.nber.org/papers/w18315.

Gordon, Robert J. (2014). "The Turtle's Progress: Secular Stagnation Meets the Headwinds," in *Secular Stagnation: Facts, Causes and Cures*. Edited by Coen Teulings and Richard Baldwin. Centre for Economic Policy Research, pp. 61–8. https://voxeu.org/content/secular-stagnation-facts-causes-and-cures.

Gordon, Robert J. (2016). *The Rise and Fall of American Growth: The US standard of living since the Civil War*. Princeton University Press.

Gorton, Gary B. (2008). "The Panic of 2007," Maintaining Stability in a Changing Financial System: Proceedings of the 2008 Jackson Hole Conference, Federal Reserve Bank of Kansas City. NBER Working Paper 14358, pp. 131–262.

Gorton, Gary B. (2009a). "Information, Liquidity, and the (Ongoing) Panic of 2007," *American Economic Review* 99(2) 567–72. http://papers.ssrn. com/sol3/papers.cfm?abstract_id=1324195.

Gorton, Gary B. (2009b). "Slapped in the Face by the Invisible Hand," Federal Reserve Bank of Atlanta Conference on Financial Markets: Financial Innovation and Crisis. https://www.frbatlanta.org/news/CONFEREN/09fmc/gorton.pdf, p. 52.

Gorton, Gary B. (2009c). "The Subprime Panic," *European Financial Management* 15(1) 10–46. http://ssrn.com/abstract=1276047.

Gorton, Gary B. (2010). *Slapped by the Invisible Hand: The Panic of 2007*. Oxford University Press.

Gorton, Gary B. and Andrew Metrick (2010). "Regulating the Shadow Banking System," *Brookings Papers on Economic Activity* 2010(2) 261–97. https://www.brookings.edu/wp-content/uploads/2010/09/2010b_bpea_gorton.pdf.

Gorton, Gary B. and Andrew Metrick (2012). "Securitized Banking and the Run on Repo," *Journal of Financial Economics* 104(3) 425–51. http://www. nber.org/papers/w15223. http://papers.ssrn. com/sol3/papers.cfm?abstract_id=1440752.

Gorton, Gary B. and Guillermo Ordoñez (2014). "Collateral Crises," *American Economic Review* 104(2) 343–78.

Gorton, Gary B. and Nicholas S. Souleles (2007). "Special Purpose Vehicles and Securitization," in *The Risks of Financial Institutions*. Edited by Mark Carey and René M. Stulz. University of Chicago Press, pp. 549–602.

Gorton, Gary B., Stefan Lewellen, and Andrew Metrick (2012). "The Safe-asset Share," *The American Economic Review* 102(3) 101–6.

Gowan, Peter (2009). "Crisis in the Heartland. Consequences of the New Wall Street System," *New Left Review* 55 01–02.

Grabel, Ilene (2011). "Not your grandfather's IMF: global crisis, 'productive incoherence' and developmental policy space," *Cambridge Journal of Economics* 35(5) 805–30.

Grabel, Ilene (2012). "Regulating Global Capital Flows for Long-Run Development," in Kevin P. Gallagher, Stephany Griffith-Jones, and José Antonio Ocampo. Pardee Center, Boston University. Chap. Dynamic Capital Regulations, IMF Irrelevance and the Crisis, pp. 59–70.

Graeber, David (2011). *Debt: The First 5,000 Years*. Brooklyn, NY: Melville House Publishing.

Granovetter, Mark and Patrick McGuire (1998). "The Making of an Industry: Electricity in the United States," *The Sociological Review* 46(S1) 147–73.

Greenfield, Jill (2010). "In the Echo of Gekko, a Rebuttal: Scaramucci explains why 'greed is bad,'" *Harvard Law Today*. https://today.law. harvard.edu/in-the-echo-of-gekko-a-rebuttal-scaramucciexplains-why-greed-is-bad-video/.

Greenspan, Alan (1996a). *Lecture at the American Enterprise Institute*. http://www. federalreserve.gov/boarddocs/speeches/1996/19961205.htm.

Greenspan, Alan (1996b). *Question: Is There a New Economy?* Remarks by Chairman Alan Greenspan At the Haas Annual Business Faculty Research Dialogue, University of California, Berkeley, California. https://www. federalreserve.gov/boarddocs/speeches/1998/19980904.htm.

Greenspan, Alan (1997a). Lecture at the Financial Markets Conference of the Federal Reserve Bank of Atlanta. http://online.wsj.com/public/resources/documents/EconClub.PDF.

Greenspan, Alan (1997b). *The Evolution of Banking in a Market Economy*. Remarks by Chairman Alan Greenspan At the Annual Conference of the Association of Private Enterprise Education, Arlington, Virginia. http://www.federalreserve.gov/boarddocs/speeches/1997/19970412.htm.

Greenspan, Alan (2002). *Testimony to the US Senate Banking Committee.* http://www.federalreserve.gov/boarddocs/hh/2002/july/testimony.htm.

Greenspan, Alan (2005). *Risk Transfer and Financial Stability.* Remarks by Chairman Alan Greenspan to the Federal Reserve Bank of Chicago's Forty-first Annual Conference on Bank Structure, Chicago, Illinois. http://www.federalreserve.gov/boarddocs/speeches/2005/20050505/default.htm.

Greenspan, Alan (2008a). *Testimony.* Committee on Government Oversight and Reform. https://democrats-oversight.house.gov/sites/democrats.oversight.house.gov/files/migrated/20081023100438.pdf.

Greenspan, Alan (2008b). "We Will Never Have a Perfect Model of Risk," *Financial Times,* March 17.

Greenspan, Alan (2009a). Speech at the Economic Club of New York. http://online.wsj.com/public/resources/documents/EconClub.PDF.

Greenspan, Alan (2009b). *The Global Financial Crisis: Causes and Consequences.* Council of Foreign Relations, C. Peter McColough Series on International Economics. https://www.cfr.org/event/c-peter-mccolough-seriesinternational-economics-global-financial-crisis-causes-and.

Greenwood, Robin, Samuel G. Hanson, and Jeremy C. Stein (2015). "A Comparative-Advantage Approach to Government Debt Maturity," *The Journal of Finance* 70(4) 1683–722.

Grice, Dylan (2013). ZeroHedge Blog. http://www.zerohedge.com/news/2013-03-11/dylan-grice-explains-how-crackpot-centralbankers-are-destroying-human-society.

Gross, Daniel (2009). *Pop! Why Bubbles are Great for the Economy.* Harper Collins.

Guex, Sébastien (1999). "Les origines du secret bancaire suisse et son rôle dans la politique de la Confédération au sortir de la Seconde Guerre mondiale," *Genèses* 34(1) 4–27.

Guttmann, Robert (2015). "The Transformation of Banking." Unpublished manuscript.

Guttmann, Robert (2016). *Finance-Led Capitalism: Shadow Banking, Re-Regulation, and the Future of Global Markets.* Springer.

Haas, Peter M. (1992). "Introduction: Epistemic Communities and International Policy Coordination," *International Organization* 46(1) 1–35. issn: 00208183, 15315088.

Hacker, Jacob S. and Paul Pierson (2006). *Off Center: The Republican Revolution and the Erosion of American Democracy.* New Haven: Yale University Press.

Haggard, Stephan and John Williamson (1994). "The Political Conditions for Economic Reform," *The Political Economy of Policy Reform.* Edited by J. Williamson. Washington DC: Institute for International Economics, pp. 527–96.

Haiven, Max (2014). *Cultures of Financialization: Fictitious Capital in Popular Culture and Everyday Life.* London: Springer.

Haldane, Andrew (2009). *Why Banks Failed the Stress Tests.* Speech given at the Marcus-Evans Conference on Stress-Testing. London: Bank of England. http://www.bankofengland.co.uk/archive/documents/historicpubs/speeches/2009/speech374.pdf.

Haldane, Andrew and Vasileios Madouros (2012). "The Dog and the Frisbee," Given at the Federal Reserve Bank of Kansas City's 36th economic policy symposium, The Changing Policy Landscape, Jackson Hole, Wyoming. London: Bank of England. http://www.bankofengland.co.uk/archive/Documents/historicpubs/speeches/2012/speech596.pdf.

Hale, David D. and Lyric Hughes Hale (2008). "Reconsidering Revaluation," *Foreign Affairs* 87(1) (January/February) 57.

Hansen, Alvin H. (1934). "Capital Goods and the Restoration of Purchasing Power," *Proceedings of the Academy of Political Science* 16(1) 11–19.

Hansen, Alvin H. (1939). "Economic Progress and Declining Population Growth," *American Economic Review* 29(1) 1–15.

Harberger, Arnold C. (1997). "Good Economics Comes to Latin America, 1955–95," *The Post 1945 Internationalization of Economics, Annual Supplement to History of Political Economy*. Edited by A. W. Coats. Vol. 28. MIT Press, pp. 301–11.

Harberger, Arnold C. (2010). *Arnold Harberger on the Chicago Boys*. Letter to the Editor. http://blog.independent.org/2010/12/04/arnold-harberger-onthe-chicago-boys/.

Hardoon, Deborah (2017). *An Economy for the 99%: It's time to build a human economy that benefits everyone, not just the privileged few*. https://www.oxfam.org/en/research/economy-99.

Hardoon, Deborah, Ricardo Fuentes-Nieva, and Sophia Ayele (2016). *An Economy for the 1%: How Privilege and Power in the Economy Drive Extreme Inequality and how This Can be Stopped*. https://www.oxfam. org/en/research/economy-1.

Harms, William (2014). *Professor to World's Economists: Harberger's 90th Birthday Marks Decades of Influence*. Division of the Social Sciences, University of Chicago. https://socialsciences.uchicago.edu/story/professor-worlds-economists-harbergers-90th-birthdaymarks-decades-influence.

Harvey, David (1989). *The Condition of Postmodernity*. Vol. 14. Oxford: Blackwell.

Harvey, David (2005). *Neoliberalism: A Brief History*. Oxford University Press.

Hayek, Friedrich A. von (1967). *Studies in Philosophy, Politics and Economics*. University of Chicago Press.

Hedges, C. (2010). *Death of the Liberal Class*. Nation Books. Heemskerk, Eelke, M., Meindert Fennema, and William K. Carroll (2016). "The Global Corporate Elite after the Financial Crisis: Evidence from the transnational network of interlocking directorates," *Global Networks* 16(1) 68–88.

Henrich, Joseph, et al. (2005). " 'Economic man' in Cross-cultural Perspective: Behavioral experiments in 15 small-scale societies," *Behavioral and Brain Sciences* 28(6) 795–815.

Henry, Peter Blair (2000). "Do Stock Market Liberalizations Cause Investment Booms?" in *Journal of Financial Economics* 58(1) 301–34.

Henry, Peter Blair (2003). "Capital-Account Liberalization, the Cost of Capital, and Economic Growth," *American Economic Review* 93(2) 91–6.

Henry, Peter Blair (2007). "Capital Account Liberalization: Theory, Evidence, and Speculation," *Journal of Economic Literature* 45(4) 887–935.

Herndon, Thomas, Michael Ash, and Robert Pollin (2014). "Does High Public Debt Consistently Stifle Economic Growth? A critique of Reinhart and Rogoff," *Cambridge Journal of Economics* 38(2) 257–79. doi: 10.1093/cje/bet075. eprint: http://cje.oxfordjournals.org/content/38/2/257.full.pdf+html.

Hilferding, Rudolf and Thomas Burton Bottomore (1990). *Finance Capital: A Study in the Latest Phase of Capitalist Development*. London: Routledge.

Himmelstein, Jerome L. (1992). *To the Right: The Transformation of American Conservatism*. University of California Press.

Hogfeldt, Peter (2005). "The History and Politics of Corporate Ownership in Sweden," in *A History of Corporate Governance around the World: Family Business Groups to Professional Managers*. Edited by Randall Morck. University of Chicago Press, pp. 517–80.

The Holy Father Francis (2013). *Apostolic Exhortation Evangelii Gaudium of the Holy Father Francis to the Bishops, Clergy, Consecrated Persons and the Lay Faithful on the Proclamation of the Gospel in Today's World*. http://w2.vatican.va/content/francesco/en/apost_exhortations/documents/papa-francesco_esortazioneap_20131124_evangelii-gaudium.html.

Hong Li (1977). *China's Political Situation and the Power Struggle in Peking*. University of Michigan, 2007: Lung Men Press.

Hördahl, Peter and Michael R. King (2008). "Developments in Repo Markets during the Financial Turmoil," *BIS Quarterly Review*, 37–53. http://www.bis.org/publ/qtrpdf/r_qt0812.pdf.

House of Representatives, Committee on Oversight and Government Reform (2008). *The Financial Crisis and the Role of Federal Regulators*. Preliminary Transcript. https://democrats-oversight.house.gov/sites/democrats.oversight.house.gov/files/migrated/20081024163819.pdf.

Howell, Chris (2005). *Trade Unions and the State: The Construction of Industrial Relations Institutions in Britain, 1890–2000*. Princeton University Press.

Howell, David R., et al. (2007). "Are Protective Labor Market Institutions at the Root of Unemployment? A critical review of the evidence," *Capitalism and Society* 2(1).

Hull, John (2009). *Options, Futures and Other Derivatives*. Chichester: John Wiley & Sons.

Husson, Michel (2008). *Un pur capitalisme*. Lausanne: Ed. Page Deux.

Husson, Michel (2015). "Les coordonnées de la crise qui vient," *A l'Encontre*. http://alencontre.org/laune/economie-les-coordonnees-de-lacrise-qui-vient.html#27052100.

Intellectual Property Watch (2015). *A Look At The Huge Upswing In China Patent Filings*. Inside Views. https://www.ip-watch.org/2015/04/22/a-look-at-the-huge-upswing-in-china-patent-filings/.

International Monetary Fund (2012). *Annual Report 2012: Working Together to Support Global Recovery*. Washington: International Monetary Fund. https://www.imf.org/external/pubs/ft/ar/2012/eng/.

International Monetary Fund (2014a). "Is It Time for an Infrastructure Push? The Macroeconomic Effects of Public Investment," *World Economic Outlook*. http://www.imf.org/external/pubs/ft/weo/2014/02/pdf/c3.pdf.

International Monetary Fund (2014b). *World Economic Outlook*. Washington: International Monetary Fund. http://www.imf.org/external/pubs/ft/weo/2014/02/.

International Monetary Fund Country Report 13/156 (2013). *Greece: Ex Post Evaluation of Exceptional Access under the 2010 Stand-By Arrangement*. International Monetary Fund.

International Monetary Fund Monetary and Capital Markets Department (2010). *Annual Report on Exchange Arrangements and Exchange Restrictions 2009*. USA. http://www.imf.org/external/pubs/cat/longres_gsause.aspx?sk=22924&gsa=true.

Jabko, Nicolas (2013). "The Political Appeal of Austerity," *Comparative European Politics* 11(6) 705–12.

Jameson, Fredric (2005). *Archaeologies of the Future: The Desire Called Utopia and Other Science Fictions*. London: Verso.

Jarsulic, Marc (2012). *Anatomy of a Financial Crisis: A Real Estate Bubble, Runaway Credit Markets, and Regulatory Failure*. New York: Palgrave Macmillan.

Jeffers, E. and Dominique Plihon (2014). "Universal Banking and Shadow Banking in Europe," *Economie Politique et Démocratie*. Association Française d'Economie Politique, p. 23.

Jenkins, Holman W. (2011). "The Weekend Interview with Robert Lucas: Chicago Economics on Trial," *Wall Street Journal*, September 24.

Jiménez, Francisco S. (2014). *Puertas giratorias: más de 50 políticos enchufados a la energía*. Diario Digital. https://dirigentesdigital.com/articulo/economia-y-empresas/12013/puertas-giratorias-masde-50-politicos-enchufados-a-la-energia.html.

Johnson, Simon (2009). "The Quiet Coup," *The Atlantic*, May. http://www.theatlantic.com/magazine/archive/2009/05/the-quietcoup/307364/.

Johnson, Simon and James Kwak (2011). *13 Bankers: The Wall Street Takeover and the Next Financial Meltdown*. Vintage Books USA.

Johnson, Simon and Todd Mitton (2003). "Cronyism and Capital Controls: Evidence from Malaysia," *Journal of Financial Economics* 67(2) 351–82.

Kahneman, Daniel (2011). *Thinking, Fast and Slow*. Macmillan.

Kalla, Joshua L. and Peter M. Aronow (2015). "Editorial Bias in Crowd Sourced Political Information," *PLOS ONE* 10(9) 1–8. doi: 10.1371/journal.pone.0136327.

Kaplan, Ethan and Dani Rodrik (2001). *Did the Malaysian Capital Controls Work?* National Bureau of Economic Research Working Paper 8142.

Kar, Dev and Joseph Spanjers (2015). *Illicit Financial Flows from Developing Countries: 2004–2013.* Global Financial Integrity Report 2014. http://www.gfintegrity.org/report/illicit-financial-flows-fromdeveloping-countries-2004-2013/.

Karabell, Shellie (2015). "Corruption 101: The Dark Side Of Leadership," *Forbes.* https://www.forbes.com/sites/shelliekarabell/2015/06/19/corruption-101-the-dark-side-of-leadership/.

Keegan, William (1984). *Mrs Thatcher's Economic Experiment.* London: Penguin Books.

Kennedy, David (2016). *A World of Struggle: How Power, Law, and Expertise Shape Global Political Economy.* Princeton University Press.

Kerr, Peter (2001). *From Conflict to Consensus: The Evolution of Post-War British Politics, 1945–1997.* London: Routledge.

Keynes, John Maynard (1933). "National Self-Sufficiency," *The Yale Review* 22(4) 755–69.

Keynes, John Maynard (1937). "Some Economic Consequences of a Declining Population (Galton lecture at the Eugenics Society)," *The Eugenics Review* 29(1) 13–17.

Keynes, John Maynard (1980). "Vol. 25, Activities 1940–1944: Shaping the Post-War World: The Clearing Union," in *The Collected Writings of John Maynard Keynes.* Edited by D. Moggridge. Macmillan/Cambridge University Press for the Royal Economic Society.

Keynes, John Maynard (2007). *General Theory of Employment, Interest and Money.* Atlantic Publishers & Dist.

Khwaja, Asim Ijaz and Atif Mian (2005). "Do Lenders Favor Politically Connected Firms? Rent Provision in an Emerging Financial Market," *Quarterly Journal of Economics* 120(4) 1371–411.

Kiely, Eugene (2012). *Obama White House "Full of Wall Street Executives"?* FactCheck.org. https://www.factcheck.org/2012/02/obama-white-house-full-of-wall-street-executives/.

Kindleberger, Charles P. and Robert Z. Aliber (2005). *Manias, Panics, and Crashes* Hoboken, NJ: John Wiley & Sons.

King, Ian P. (2008). "Interview: A Conversation with Robert E. Lucas, Jr., Nobel Laureate in Economics, 1995," *New Zealand Economic Papers* 42(1) 1–16. doi: 10.1080/00779950809544411.

Kirk, Michael, Jim Gilmore, and Mike Wiser (2009). *The Warning.* PBS. http://www.pbs.org/wgbh/pages/frontline/warning/view/.

Kirman, Alan (2009). "Economic Theory and the crisis," *VoxEU.org* 14. http://www.voxeu.org/index.php?q=node/4208.

Kiyosaki, Robert T. and Sharon L. Lechter (1997). *Rich Dad Poor Dad: What the Rich Teach Their Kids About Money That the Poor and the Middle Class Do Not!* New York: Warner Books.

Klebnikov, Paul (2002). "Theft of the Century: Privatization and the Looting of Russia," *The Multinational Monitor* 23(1 & 2) (January/February). http://multinationalmonitor.org/mm2002/02jan-feb/janfeb02interviewklebniko.html.

Klein, Michael W. (2003). *Capital Account Openness and the Varieties of Growth Experience.* Working Paper 9500. National Bureau of Economic Research. doi: 10.3386/w9500. http://www.nber.org/papers/w9500.

Klein, Michael W. (2005). *Capital Account Liberalization, Institutional Quality and Economic Growth: Theory and Evidence.* Working Paper 11112. National Bureau of Economic Research. doi: 10.3386/w11112. http://www.nber.org/papers/w11112.

Klein, Naomi (2007). *The Shock Doctrine: The Rise of Disaster Capitalism.* Macmillan.

Kliman, Andrew (2011). *The Failure of Capitalist Production: Underlying Causes of the Great Recession.* London: Pluto Press.

Kolhatkar, Sheelah (2013). "Timothy Geithner and Why the Revolving Door Might Be a Good Thing," *Bloomsberg Businessweek.* https://www.bloomberg.com/news/articles/2013-11-18/timothy-geithnerand-why-the-revolving-door-might-be-a-good-thing.

Komlos, John (2014). "The Banality of a Bureaucrat: Timothy Geithner and the Sinking of the US Economy," *Challenge* 57(5) 87–99.

Konczal, Michael, ed. (2010). *Will it Work? How Will we Know? The Future of Financial Reform*. New York: Roosevelt Institute.

Koo, Richard (2014). "Balance Sheet Recessions is the Reason for Secular Stagnation," *Secular Stagnation: Facts, Causes and Cures*. Edited by Coen Teulings and Richard Baldwin. Centre for Economic Policy Research, pp. 131–42. https://voxeu.org/content/secular-stagnation-facts-causes-and-cures.

Kose, M Ayhan et al. (2009). "Financial Globalization, A Reappraisal," *International Monetary Fund Staff Papers* 56(1).

Kotz, David M. (2009). "The Financial and Economic Crisis of 2008: A Systemic Crisis of Neoliberal Capitalism," *Review of Radical Political Economics* 41(3) 305–17.

Kotz, David M. (2013). "Social Structures of Accumulation, the Rate of Profit, and Economic Crises," in *Capitalism on Trial: Explorations in the Tradition of Thomas E. Weisskopf*. Edited by Jeannette Wicks-Lim and Robert Pollin. Edward Elgar Publishing. http://people.umass.edu/dmkotz/SSA_Profit_Rate_and_Crisis_V4_12_01.pdf.

Kotz, David M. (2015). *The Rise and Fall of Neoliberal Capitalism*. Harvard University Press.

Kotz, David M. and Deepankar Basu (2015). "Stagnation and Institutional Structures," University of Massachusetts Amherst Economics Working Paper. https://www.umass.edu/economics/sites/default/files/Kotz_Basu.pdf.

Kregel, Jan (2012). *Minsky and the Narrow Banking Proposal: No Solution for Financial Reform*, Levy Economics Institute of Bard College, Public Policy Brief No 125.

Kregel, Jan (2014). "Regulating the Financial System in a Minskian Perspective," in *Financial Stability and Growth: Perspectives on Financial Regulation and New Developmentalism*. Routledge, p. 127.

Kregel, Jan, Rainer Kattel, and Mario Tonveronachi (2015). *Financial Regulation in the European Union*. Vol. 7. Routledge.

Krieger, Joel (1986). *Reagan, Thatcher, and the Politics of Decline*. Oxford University Press.

Krishnamurthy, Arvind, Stefan Nagel, and Dmitry Orlov (2014). "Sizing Up Repo," *Journal of Finance* 69(6) 2381–417. https://ideas.repec.org/a/bla/jfinan/v69y2014i6p2381-2417.html.

Krugman, Paul (1998). "It's Baaack: Japan's slump and the return of the liquidity trap," *Brookings Papers on Economic Activity* 1998(2) 137–205.

Krugman, Paul (2011a). "Olivier Blanchard Isn't Very Serious," *The Conscience of a Liberal, The New York Times*, December 21. http://krugman.blogs.nytimes. com/2011/12/21/olivier-blanchard-isnt-very-serious/.

Krugman, Paul (2011b). "The Mellon Doctrine," *New York Times*, April 1. http://www.nytimes.com/2011/04/01/opinion/01krugman.html.

Krugman, Paul (2013a). "Bubbles, Regulation, and Secular Stagnation," *The Conscience of a Liberal, The New York Times*, September 25. http://krugman. blogs.nytimes.com/2013/09/25/bubbles-regulation-and-secularstagnation/.

Krugman, Paul (2013b). "Bubbles, Regulation, and Secular Stagnation," *New York Times*, September 25. http://krugman.blogs.nytimes.com/2013/09/25/bubbles-regulation-and-secular-stagnation/.

Krugman, Paul (2013c). "How the Case for Austerity has Crumbled," *The New York Review of Books* 6. http://www.nybooks.com/articles/archives/2013/jun/06/how-case-austerity-has-crumbled.

Krugman, Paul (2015a). "Debt Is Good," *New York Times*, August 21. http://www.nytimes.com/2015/08/21/opinion/paul-krugman-debt-is-good-for-theeconomy.html.

Krugman, Paul (2015b). "Multipliers and Reality," *New York Times*, June 3. https://krugman.blogs.nytimes.com/2015/06/03/multipliers-andreality/.

Kumhof, Michael and Romain G. Rancière (2010). "Inequality, Leverage and Crises," IMF Working Papers (Research Department) WP/10/268, pp. 1–37. https://www.imf.org/external/pubs/ft/wp/2010/wp10268.pdf.

Kwak, James and Simon Johnson (2017). *Economism: Bad Economics and the Rise of Inequality*. Pantheon Books. https://books.google.pt/books?id=NPaxDQAAQBAJ.

Labaton, Stephen (1999). "Congress Passes Wide-Ranging Bill Easing Banks Laws," *New York Times*, November 5. http://www.nytimes.com/1999/11/05/business/congress-passes-wide-ranging-bill-easing-banklaws.html.

Lains, Pedro (2013). *The Rise and Demise of the Troika Virtues*. Paper presented at: *Direitos e Desigualdades. Paradoxos e Alternativas*, Instituto de Cîencias Sociais, Universidade de Lisboa.

Lapavitsas, Costas (2009). "Financialised Capitalism: Crisis and financial expropriation," *Historical Materialism* 17(2) 114–48.

Lapavitsas, Costas (2014). *Profiting Without Producing: How Finance Exploits us All*. Verso.

Lapavitsas, Costas and Paulo L. Dos Santos (2008). "Globalization and Contemporary Banking: On the impact of new technology," *Contributions to Political Economy* 27(1) 31–56. http://econpapers.repec.org/article/oupcopoec/v_3a27_3ay_3a2008_3ai_3a1_3ap_3a31-56.htm.

Larsen, Peter Thal (2007). "Goldman Pays the Price of Being Big," *Financial Times*, August 13, p. 3.

Lash, Scott and Celia Lury (2007). *Global Culture Industry: The Mediation of Things*. John Wiley & Sons.

Lavoie, Marc and Engelbert Stockhammer (2013). *Wage-led Growth: An Equitable Strategy for Economic Recovery*. Springer.

Lazear, Edward P. and Sherwin Rosen (1981). "Rank-Order Tournaments as Optimum Labor Contracts," *Journal of Political Economy* 89(5) 841–64.

Le Monde (2014). "LSK, l'ancien fonds d'investissement de DSK, se déclare en cessation de paiements," *Argent & Placement*. http://www. lemonde.fr/argent/article/ 2014/11/05/lsk-l-ancienne-societefinanciere-de-dsk-se-declare-en-cessation-de-paiements_4518706_1657007.html.

Lebaron, Frédéric (2000). "The Space of Economic Neutrality: Types of legitimacy and trajectories of central bank managers," *International Journal of Contemporary Sociology* 37(2) 208–29.

Lebaron, Frédéric (2010). "European Central Bank Leaders in the Global Space of Central Bankers: A Geometric Data Analysis approach," *French Politics* 8(3) 294–320.

Lee, Frederic S., Xuan Pham, and Gyun Gu (2013). "The UK Research Assessment Exercise and the Narrowing of UK Economics," *Cambridge Journal of Economics* 37(4) 693–717.

Lee, Ruben (2010). *Running the World's Markets: The Governance of Financial Infrastructure*. Princeton University Press.

Lemieux, Pierre (2005). *In Defense of Bribery*. Auburn: Mises Institute. https://mises.org/library/defense-bribery.

Les Echos (2014). "Affaire LSK : DSK charge son associé," *LesEchos.fr*. http://www.lesechos.fr/finance-marches/gestion-actifs/0203900048430-dsk-jai-probablement-perdu-mon-investissementdans-lsk-1059132.php.

Levine, Ross (1997). "Financial Development and Economic Growth: Views and agenda," *Journal of Economic Literature* XXXV(2) 688–726.

Levine, Ross (2001). "International Financial Liberalization and Economic Growth," in *Review of International Economics* 9(4) 688–702.

Levine, Ross and Sara Zervos (1998). "Stock Markets, Banks, and Economic Growth," *American Economic Review* 88(3) 537–58.

Levitt, Steven D. and Stephen J. Dubner (2005). *Freakonomics: A Rogue Economist Explores the Hidden Side of Everything*. William Morrow.

Levy, David (1999). "Interview with Arnold Harberger," *Federal Reserve Bank of Minneapolis*. https://www.minneapolisfed.org/publications/the-region/interview-with-arnold-harberger.

Lew, Jack (2010). *Tightening Our Belts*. White House Blog Entry. https://obamawhitehouse.archives.gov/blog/2010/11/29/tighteningour-belts.

Lewis, Michael (2010). *The Big Short: Inside the Doomsday Machine*. WW Norton.

Lewis, Michael (2014). *Flash Boys: A Wall Street Revolt*. WW Norton.

Lewis, Michael (2015). "The End: How Wall Street Did Itself in," *Upstart Business Journal: From the Archives of Conde Nast Portfolio*.

Lewis, Michael and David Einhorn (2009). "The End of the Financial World as we Know It," *New York Times*, January 3.

Lewis, Michael (1989). *Liar's Poker: Rising Through the Wreckage on Wall Street*. WW Norton.

Li, H. (1977). *China's Political Situation and the Power Struggle in Peking*. Lung Men Press.

Li, Hongbin, et al. (2008). "Political Connections, Financing and Firm Performance: Evidence from Chinese private firms," *Journal of Development Economics* 87(2) 283–99.

Lindsey, Richard R. (1998). *Testimony before the House Committee on Banking and Financial Services Concerning Regulation of the Over-the-Counter Derivatives Market and Hybrid Instruments*. US Securities and Exchange Commission. https://www.sec.gov/news/testimony/testarchive/1998/tsty0898.htm.

Lippert, John (2008). *Friedman Would Be Roiled as Chicago Disciples Rue Repudiation*. Reprinted from Bloomberg. http://economistsview.typepad.com/economistsview/2008/12/friedman-would.html.

Lipscomb, Andrew A. and Albert Ellery Bergh, eds. (1907). *The Writings of Thomas Jefferson*. Vol. 15. Washington, DC: Thomas Jefferson Memorial Association of the United States.

Lipton, E., N. Confessore, and B. Williams (2016). "Think Tank Scholar or Corporate Consultant: It depends on the day," *The New York Times*, August 8. http://www.nytimes.com/2016/08/09/us/politics/thinktank-scholars-corporate-consultants.html.

Lo, Andrew W. (2017). *Adaptive Markets: Financial Evolution at the Speed of Thought*. Princeton University Press.

Lockwood, David (2012). *The Indian Bourgeoisie: A Political History of the Indian Capitalist Class in the Early Twentieth Century*. Vol. 5. IB Tauris.

Lomnitz, Claudio (2003). "The Depreciation of Life during Mexico City's Transition into the 'Crisis,'" in *Wounded Cities: Destruction and Reconstruction in a Globalized World*. Edited by J. Schneider and I. Susser. New York: Berg Publishers, pp. 47–69.

López-de-Silanes, Florencio and Rafael La Porta (1999). "The Benefits of Privatization: Evidence from Mexico," *Quarterly Journal of Economics* 114(4) 1193–242.

Lorica, Ben (2011). *Campaign Finance & Lobbying by the Numbers*. http://www.verisi.com/resources/campaign-finance.htm.

Louçã, Francisco (2007). *The Years of High Econometrics: A Short History of the Generation that Reinvented Economics*. London: Routledge.

Louçã, Francisco, João Teixeira Lopes, and Jorge Costa (2014). *Os Burgueses. Quem são, como vivem como mandam*. Lisboa: Bertrand Editora.

Loureiro, Maria Rita (1997). *Os economistas no governo: gestão econômica e democracia*. Fundação Getúlio Vargas Editora. http://osburgueses.net.

Lucas, Robert E., Jr. (1995). "Biographical," *Les Prix Nobel: The Nobel Prizes*. Edited by Tore Frangsmyr. Stockholm: Nobel Foundation. http://www.nobelprize.org/nobel_prizes/economic-sciences/laureates/1995/lucas-bio.html.

Lucas, Robert E., Jr. (2003a). "Colonialism and Growth," *Historically Speaking: The Bulletin of the Historical Society (Boston, Mass.)* 4(4) 29–31. doi: 10.1353/hsp.2003.0068.

Lucas, Robert E., Jr. (2003b). "Macroeconomic Priorities," *American Economic Review* 93(1) 1–14.

Lucas, Robert E., Jr. (2004). "Keynote Address to the 2003 HOPE Conference: My Keynesian Education," *History of Political Economy* 36(5) 12–24.

Lucas, Robert E., Jr. (2009). *Why a Second Look Matters*. Council on Foreign Relations. https://www.youtube.com/watch?v=CJaOuZ91pIw.

Lucas, Robert E., Jr. (2013). "Glass-Steagall: A requiem," *American Economic Review* 103(3) 43–7. http://web.ntpu.edu.tw/~guan/courses/Lucas13.pdf.

Lucca, David, Amit Seru, and Francesco Trebbi (2014). "The Revolving Door and Worker Flows in Banking Regulation," *Journal of Monetary Economics* 65, 17–32. https://www.newyorkfed.org/research/staff_reports/sr678.html.

Luckerson, Victor (2015). "This Guy Got $58 Million for 15 Months of Work," *Time*. http://time.com/66646/yahoo-executive-henriquede-castro-gets-58-million-severance/.

Machado, João (2011). *Introdução. Memorandum of Economic and Financial Policies: 11 Perspectivas*. Nova School of Business and Economics. http://exed.novasbe.pt/difusao-conhecimento/appliedknowledge/261-memorandum-of-economic-and-financial-policies-11-perspectivasv2.

MacKenzie, Donald, Fabian Muniesa, and Lucia Siu (2007). *Do Economists Make Markets? On the Performativity of Economics*. Princeton University Press.

MacLean, Nancy (2017). *Democracy in Chains: The Deep History of the Radical Right's Secret Plan for America*. Penguin.

MacLeod, Dag (2004). *Downsizing the State: Privatization and the Limits of Neoliberal Reform in Mexico*. Penn State Press.

Madrick, Jeff (2011). *Age of Greed*. New York: Alfred A. Knopf.

Magud, Nicolas E., Carmen M. Reinhart, and Kenneth S. Rogoff (2011). *Capital Controls: Myth and Reality—A Portfolio Balance Approach*. National Bureau of Economic Research Working Paper 16805. doi: 10.3386/w16805. http://www.nber.org/papers/w16805.

Malkiel, Burton (2011). *A Random Walk Down Wall Street*, 11thedn. WW Norton.

Mansell-Carstens, Catherine (2003). "Interview with Arnold C. Harberger," *Economía Mexicana. Nueva Epocá* 12(2) 337–66.

Markoff, John and Verónica Montecinos (1993). "The Ubiquitous Rise of Economists," *Journal of Public Policy* 13(01) 37–68.

Marlow, Ben (2014). "Who are Sweden's Powerful Wallenberg Family?" *The Telegraph*, June 21. http://www.telegraph.co.uk/finance/newsbysector/banksandfinance/10916991/Who-are-Swedens-powerful-Wallenbergfamily.html.

Marshall, Josh (2016). *Trump Rolls Out Anti-Semitic Closing Ad*. Talking Points Memo. http://talkingpointsmemo.com/edblog/trumprolls-out-anti-semitic-closing-ad.

Martin, Antoine, David Skeie, and Ernst-Ludwig Von Thadden (2014). "Repo Runs," *Review of Financial Studies* 27(4) 957–89. http://www.newyorkfed.org/research/staff_reports/sr444.pdf.

Marx, Karl (1977). *Le Capital, vol. III*. Paris: Editions Sociales.

Mason, Paul (2009). *Meltdown: The End of the Age of Greed*. Verso.

McCloskey, Donald N. (1978). "The Achievements of the Cliometric School," *Journal of Economic History* 38(01) 13–28.

McCulley, Paul A. (2007). "Teton Reflections," *PIMCO Global Central Bank Focus* 2 (August/September). http://www.pimco.com/EN/Insights/Pages/GCBF%20August-%20September%202007.aspx.

McCulley, Paul A. (2009). "The Shadow Banking System and Hyman Minsky's Economic Journey," *PIMCO Global Central Bank Focus* 2.2.

McCulley, Paul A. (2010). *Statement of Paul A. McCulley, Managing Director, PIMCO, Before the Financial Crisis Inquiry Commission*. Written Testimony at the Financial

Crisis Inquiry Commission Shadow Banking Hearing. http://fcic-static.law.stanford.edu/cdn_media/fcic-testimony/2010-0506-McCulley.pdf.

McDonald, Duff (2009). *Last Man Standing: The Ascent of Jamie Dimon and JPMorgan Chase*. Simon and Schuster.

McDonald, O. (2015). *Lehman Brothers: A Crisis of Value*. Bloomsbury Academic.

Mello Belluzzo, Luiz Gonzaga de (2009). *Os antecedentes da tormenta: origens da crise global*. UNESP.

Mendieta, Jorge Gil, et al. (1997). "A Dynamic Analysis of the Mexican Power Network," *Connections* 20(2) 34–55.

Meszaros, Istvan (2016). *Aspects of History and Class Consciousness*. Routledge.

Meyer, Thomas (2014). "The Galapagos Islands of Finance," in *Private Equity Unchained: Strategy Insights for the Institutional Investor*. London: Palgrave Macmillan, pp. 172–83. doi: 10.1057/9781137286826_16. http://dx.doi.org/10.1057/9781137286826_16.

Michel, Jean-Baptiste, et al. (2011). "Quantitative Analysis of Culture Using Millions of Digitized Books," *Science* 331(6014) 176–82.

Michell, Jo (2015). *The Monetary Circuit in the Shadows*. EEA Conference, New York, Special Session: Modern Advances in the Monetary Theory of Production (MTP): Contributions in Honour of Augusto Graziani.

Milanovic, Branko (2016). *Global Inequality: A New Approach for the Age of Globalization*. Harvard University Press.

Miles, David, Jing Yang, and Gilberto Marcheggiano (2013). "Optimal Bank Capital," *The Economic Journal* 123(567) 1–37. issn: 1468-0297. doi: 10.1111/j.1468-0297.2012.02521.x.

Milgrom, Paul and John Roberts (1992). *Economics, Organization and Management*. New Jersey: Prentice Hall.

Mill, John Stuart (2008). *Principles of Political Economy and Chapters on Socialism*. Oxford University Press.

Miller, David and William Dinan (2009). *Revolving Doors, Accountability and Transparency-Emerging Regulatory Concerns and Policy Solutions in the Financial Crisis*, OECD Report of the Expert Group on Conflict of Interest.

Millet, Damien and Eric Toussaint (2009). *La Crise, Quelles Crises?* Editions Aden.

Minsky, Hyman (1976). *John Maynard Keynes*. Springer.

Minsky, Hyman (1986). *Stabilizing an Unstable Economy*. Yale University Press.

Minsky, Hyman (2015). *Can "It" Happen Again? Essays on Instability and Finance*. Routledge.

Mirowski, Philip (2002). *Machine Dreams: Economics Becomes a Cyborg Science*. Cambridge University Press.

Mirowski, Philip (2013). *Never Let a Serious Crisis go to Waste: How Neoliberalism Survived the Financial Meltdown*. Verso.

Mizohata, Sachie (2016). "Nippon Kaigi: Empire, Contradiction, and Japan's Future," *The Asia-Pacific Journal: Japan Focus Volume* 14(21).

Mnuchin, Steven T. (2017). *A Financial System That Creates Economic Opportunities: Asset Management and Insurance*. US Department of the Treasury. https://www.treasury.gov/press-center/pressreleases/Documents/A-Financial-System-That-Creates-Economic-Opportunities-Asset_Management-Insurance.pdf.

Modigliani, Franco and Richard A. Cohn (1979). "Inflation, Rational Valuation and the Market," *Financial Analysts Journal* 35(2) 24–44.

Moghadam, R. (2009). "Review of Recent Crisis Programs," *International Monetary Fund Strategy, Policy, and Review Department* 14, 47. https://www.imf.org/external/np/pp/eng/2009/091409.pdf.

Mokyr, Joel (2014). "Secular Stagnation? Not in Your Life," *Secular Stagnation: Facts, Causes and Cures*. Edited by Coen Teulings and Richard Baldwin. Centre for Economic

Policy Research, pp. 83–90. https://voxeu.org/content/secular-stagnation-facts-causes-and-cures.

Montecinos, Verónica and John Markoff, eds. (2009). *Economists in the Americas*. Edward Elgar Publishing.

Morck, Randall and Masao Nakamura (1999). "Banks and Corporate Control in Japan," *Journal of Finance* 54(1) 319–39.

Morck, Randall and Bernard Yeung (2006). *Some Obstacles to Good Corporate Governance in Canada and How to Overcome Them*, Research Study Commissioned by the Task Force to Modernize Securities Legislation in Canada, p. 36.

Morck, Randall and Bernard Yeung (2014). "Enterprise Models: Freestanding Firms versus Family Pyramids," in *The Cambridge History of Capitalism: Volume 2, The Spread of Capitalism: From 1848 to the Present*. Edited by Larry Neal and Jeffrey G. Williamson. Vol. 2. Cambridge University Press, pp. 201–29.

Morck, Randall, K., David A. Stangeland, and Bernard Yeung (2000). "Inherited Wealth, Corporate Control, and Economic Growth," *Concentrated Corporate Ownership*. Edited by Randall Morck. University of Chicago Press.

Morgan, Mary S. and Malcolm Rutherford (1998). *From Interwar Pluralism to Postwar Neoclassicism*. Vol. 30. Durham, NC: Duke University Press.

Munger, Charles T. (2003). *Academic Economics: Strengths and Faults After Considering Interdisciplinary Needs*. Herb Kay Undergraduate Lecture, University of California, Santa Barbara, Economics Department. http://www.tilsonfunds.com/MungerUCSBspeech.pdf.

Murphy, Dale D (2004). *The Structure of Regulatory Competition: Corporations and Public Policies in a Global Economy*. Oxford University Press.

Murphy, E. V. (2013). *Shadow Banking: Background and Policy Issues*. Report prepared for members and committees of Congress, Congressional Research Service. https://www.fas.org/sgp/crs/misc/R43345.pdf.

Navidi, Sandra (2017). *Superhubs: How the Financial Elite and their Networks Rule Our World*. Boston: Nicholas Brealey. https://books.google.com/books?id=O3WfDAAAQBAJ.

Nelson, Stephen C. (2014). "Playing Favorites: How shared beliefs shape the IMF's lending decisions," *International Organization* 68(2) 297.

Niessen, Alexandra and Stefan Ruenzi (2010). "Political Connectedness and Firm Performance: Evidence from Germany," *German Economic Review* 11(4) 441–64.

Nogueira Batista, Paulo, Jr. (2012). "Regulating Global Capital Flows for Long-Run Development," edited by Kevin P. Gallagher, Stephany Griffith-Jones, and José Antonio Ocampo. Pardee Center, Boston University. Chap. "The IMF, Capital Account Regulation, and Emerging Market Economies," pp. 93–102.

Norfield, Tony (2012). "Derivatives and Capitalist Markets: The speculative heart of capital," *Historical Materialism* 20(1) 103–32.

Nunns, James R., et al. (2015). *Analysis of Donald Trump's Tax Plan*. Urban Institute & Brookings Institution Tax Policy Center. http://www.taxpolicycenter.org/publications/analysis-donald-trumps-taxplan/full.

Obama, Barack (2009). *Remarks to White House Senior Staff*. White House. https://www.gpo.gov/fdsys/pkg/PPP-2009-book1/pdf/PPP-2009-book1-Doc-pg4.pdf.

Obama, Barack (2010). *Remarks on Tax Relief*. White House. https://www.gpo. gov/fdsys/pkg/DCPD-200900260/pdf/DCPD-200900260.pdf.

Obama, Barack (2013). *Cutting Waste, Reducing the Deficit, and Asking All to Pay Their Fair Share*. White House. https://obamawhitehouse.archives. gov/sites/default/files/omb/budget/fy2013/assets/cutting. pdf.

Obstfeld, Maurice (2016). "Chief Economist Interview: Evolution Not Revolution: Rethinking Policy at the IMF," *IMF Survey*. http://www.imf.org/external/pubs/ft/survey/so/2016/POL060216A.htm.

OECD (2013). *Illicit Financial Flows from Developing Countries: Measuring OECD Responses*. http://www.gfintegrity.org/wp-content/uploads/2014/05/OECDIFF-Responses-2013.pdf. https://www.oecd.org/corruption/Illicit_Financial_Flows_from_Developing_Countries.pdf.

Options Clearing Corporation (2017). *Dr. Richard R. Lindsey, Managing Partner, Windham Capital Management Inc.* http://www. optionsclearing.com/about/corporate-information/board/bio_ lindsey.jsp.

Orléan, André (1999). *Le pouvoir de la finance*. Paris: Odile Jacob.

Oster, Shai, et al. (2012). *Heirs of Mao's Comrades Rise as New Capitalist Nobility*. Bloomberg News. http://www.bloomberg.com/news/2012-12-26/immortals-beget-china-capitalism-from-citic-togodfather-of-golf.html.

Ostry, Jonathan D., Prakash Loungani, and Davide Furceri (2016). "Neoliberalism: Oversold," *Finance & Development (IMF)* 53(2) 38–41. http://www.imf.org/external/pubs/ft/fandd/2016/06/ostry.htm.

Pasinetti, Luigi L. (1998). "The Myth (or Folly) of the 3% Deficit/GDP Maastricht 'Parameter,'" *Cambridge Journal of Economics* 22(1) 103–16.

Paulson, Henry (2013). *On the Brink: Inside the Race to Stop the Collapse of the Global Financial System—With Original New Material on the Five Year Anniversary of the Financial Crisis*. New York: Business Plus.

Paxton, Robert O. (2007). *The Anatomy of Fascism*. Vintage.

Peden, George C. (1991). *British Economic and Social Policy: Lloyd George to Margaret Thatcher*. Hemel Hempstead: Philip Allan.

Peirce, Hester, et al. (2012). *Dodd-Frank: What It Does and Why It's Flawed*. The Mercatus Center at George Mason University.

Pelagidis, Theodore (2016). *The IMF and the New Greek Restructuring Program*. Brookings. https://www.brookings.edu/blog/upfront/2016/02/25/the-imf-and-the-new-greek-restructuringprogram/.

Perkins, Susan, Randall Morck, and Bernard Yeung (2014). "Innocents Abroad: The hazards of international joint ventures with pyramidal group firms," *Global Strategy Journal* 4(4) and National Bureau of Economic Research Working Paper 13914, 2008, pp. 310–30.

Perrow, Charles (2011). *Normal Accidents: Living with High Risk Technologies*. Princeton University Press.

Phillips, Matt (2009). "Goldman Sachs' Blankfein on Banking: 'Doing God's Work,'" *Wall Street Journal*. https://blogs.wsj.com/marketbeat/2009/11/09/goldman-sachs-blankfein-on-banking-doing-gods-work/.

Phillips-Fein, Kim (2017). *Fear City—New York's Fiscal Crisis and the Rise of Austerity Politics*. New York: Metropolitan Books.

Pichelmann, Karl (2015). "When "Secular Stagnation" Meets Piketty's Capitalism in the 21st Century. Growth and Inequality Trends in Europe Reconsidered," in *Stagnation Versus Growth in Europe: Capitalism in the 21st Century*. Springer, pp. 19–39.

Pierce, Andrew (2008). "The Queen Asks why no one Saw the Credit Crunch Coming," *The Telegraph*, November 5. http://www.telegraph.co.uk/news/uknews/theroyalfamily/3386353/The-Queen-asks-why-no-one-sawthe-credit-crunch-coming.html.

Pierce, Michael (2016). "How Bill Clinton Remade the Democratic Party by Abandoning Unions: An Arkansas Story," *The Law and Working Class History Association*, November 26.

Piketty, Thomas (2014). *Capital in the 21st Century*. Harvard University Press.

Pistor, Katharina (2010). *Host's Dilemma: Rethinking EU Banking Regulation in Light of the Global Crisis*. European Corporate Governance Institute Working Paper No 286/2010. http://www.ecgi.org/wp/wp_id. php?id=447.

Pistor, Katharina (2013). "A Legal Theory of Finance," *Journal of Comparative Economics* 41(2) 315–30.

Plihon, Dominique (2010). *Le nouveau capitalisme*. Paris: La Découverte.

Pollin, Robert (2005). *Contours of Descent: US Economic Fractures and the Landscape of Global Austerity*. Verso.

Pollin, Robert (2010). "Austerity is Not a Solution: Why the deficit hawks are wrong," *Challenge* 53(6) 6–36.

Pollin, Robert and Heidi Garrett-Peltier (2009). "The US Employment Effects of Military and Domestic Spending Priorities," *International Journal of Health Services* 39(3) 443–60.

Pollin, Robert and James Heintz (2013). *Study of US Financial System*. Financialisation, Economy, Society & Sustainable Development (FESSUD) Project Working Paper No 10.

Pollin, Robert and Andong Zhu (2006). "Inflation and Economic Growth: A cross-country nonlinear analysis," *Journal of Post Keynesian Economics* 28(4) 593–614.

Porta, Rafael, Florencio López-de-Silanes, and Andrei Shleifer (1999). "Corporate Ownership around the World," *Journal of Finance* 54(2) 471–517.

Portugal, Pedro (2008). "Wage Setting in the Portuguese Labor Market: A Microeconomic Approach," in *Challenges Ahead for the Portuguese Economy*. Edied by Francesco Franco. Lisbon: Instituto de Cîencias Sociais.

Portugal, Pedro (2011). *Mercado de Trabalho. Memorandum of Economic and Financial Policies: 11 Perspectivas*. Nova School of Business and Economics. http://exed.novasbe.pt/difusao-conhecimento/appliedknowledge/261-memorandum-of-economic-and-financial-policies11-perspectivasv2.

Portugal, Pedro and H. Vilares (2013). "Labour Unions, Union Density and the Union Wage Premium," *Economic Bulletin and Financial Stability Report Articles*. Bank of Portugal.

Posner, Richard A. (2010). *The Crisis of Capitalist Democracy*. Harvard University Press.

Poundstone, William (1992). *Prisoner's Dilemma: John von Neuman, Game Theory, and the Puzzle of the Bomb*. Doubleday.

Pozsar, Zoltan (2013). "Institutional Cash Pools and the Triffin Dilemma of the US Banking System," *Financial Markets, Institutions & Instruments* 22(5) 283–318. http://www.imf.org/external/pubs/cat/longres.aspx?sk=25155.

Pozsar, Zoltan (2014). *Shadow Banking: The Money View*. Office of Financial Research, US Department of the Treasury Working Paper 14-04. http://financialresearch.gov/working-papers/files/OFRwp2014-04_Pozsar_ShadowBankingTheMoneyView.pdf.

Pozsar, Zoltan, et al. (2013). "Shadow Banking," *FRBNY Economic Policy Review* 19(2) 1–16. https://www.newyorkfed.org/research/epr/2013/0713adri.html.

Prasad, Eswar, et al. (2003). "Effects of Financial Globalisation on Developing Countries: Some empirical evidence," *Economic and Political Weekly* 4319–330.

Prasad, Monica (2006). *The Politics of Free Markets: The Rise of Neoliberal Economic Policies in Britain, France, Germany, and the United States*. Vol. 19. Cambridge University Press.

Pressler, Jessica (2012). "Look Who's Back: John Mack is no longer at the top of Morgan Stanley. So he's getting his fix elsewhere," *New York Magazine*, April 8. http://nymag.com/news/business/themoney/johnmack-2012-4/.

Quiggin, John (2012). *Zombie Economics: How Dead Ideas Still Walk Among Us*. Princeton University Press.

RadioLab (2014). *The Golden Rule*. Season 12, Episode 6. http://www.radiolab.org/story/golden-rule/.

Rajan, Raghuram G. (2005). *Has Financial Development Made the World Riskier?* Presented in the session, Financial Markets, Financial Fragility, and Central Banking, at "The Greenspan Era: Lessons for the Future" symposium, Proceedings of the 2005 Jackson Hole Economic Policy Symposium, Federal Reserve Bank of Kansas City at Jackson Hole, Wyoming. Also at http://www.nber.org/papers/w11728.pdf. http://www. kansascityfed.org/publicat/sympos/2005/pdf/rajan2005.pdf.

Rakove, Jack N. (1997/2010). *Original Meanings: Politics and Ideas in the Making of the Constitution*. Vintage. Knopf Doubleday Publishing Group. https://books.google.pt/books?id= zJlJkNZ897MC.

Ramo, Joshua Cooper (1999). "The Three Marketeers," *Time*, February 15.

Rampell, Catherine (2011). "Out of Harvard, and Into Finance," *New York Times*, December 21. http://economix.blogs.nytimes.com/2011/12/21/outof-harvard-and-into-finance.

Rauchway, Eric (2013). "Whitewashing History: Review of *The Battle of Bretton Woods* (Steil)," in *Finance and Development (IMF)*. http://www.imf.org/external/pubs/ft/fandd/2013/03/books.htm.

Reagan, Ronald (1982). *Message to the Congress Transmitting the Annual Economic Report of the President*. http://www.presidency.ucsb. edu/ws/?pid=42121.

Reinhart, Carmen M. and Kenneth S. Rogoff (2009). *This Time is Different: Eight Centuries of Financial Folly*. Princeton University Press.

Reinhart, Carmen M. and Kenneth S. Rogoff (2010a). "Growth in a Time of Debt," *American Economic Review: Papers & Proceedings* 100, 573–8.

Reinhart, Carmen M. and Kenneth S. Rogoff (2010b). *Growth in a Time of Debt*. National Bureau of Economic Research Working Paper 15639. http://www.nber.org/papers/w15639.

Republican National Committee (2017). *Freeing Financial Markets*. Republican Platform: Restoring the American Dream. https://gop.com/platform/restoring-the-american-dream/.

Roach, Stephen S. (2015). "Why the Stock Meltdown Doesn't Spell Doom for China," *Slate*, July 8. http://www.slate.com/articles/business/moneybox/2015/07/china_stock_meltdown_why_its_actual_economy_will_be_just_fine.html.

Roberts, Michael (2012a). *A World Rate of Profit*. The Next Recession Blog. http://thenextrecession.files.wordpress.com/2012/07/roberts_michael-a_world_rate_of_ profit.pdf.

Roberts, Michael (2012b). "A World Rate of Profit," Paper presented to the WAPE/AHE/IIPPE conference. https://thenextrecession. files.wordpress.com/2012/07/roberts_michael-a_world_rate_of_ profit.pdf.

Robinson, Joan (1982). "Shedding Darkness," *Cambridge Journal of Economics* 6(3) 295–96.

Rodgers, McMorris (2015). *America's New Congress: Ready to Change the Story*. Republican Leadership Press Conference. https://www.gop. gov/americas-new-congress-ready-to-change-the-story/.

Rodriguez, Francisco and Dani Rodrik (2001). "Trade Policy and Economic Growth: A skeptic's guide to the cross-national evidence," *NBER Macroeconomics Annual 2000, Vol 15*. Edited by Ben S. Bernanke and Kenneth S. Rogoff. MIT Press, pp. 261–338.

Rodrik, Dani (2014). "The Past, Present, and Future of Economic Growth," *Challenge* 57(3) 5–39.

Rodrik, Dani and Arvind Subramanian (2009). "Why Did Financial Globalization Disappoint?" in *IMF Staff Papers* 56(1) 112–38.

Roeger, Werner (2014). "Special Topics on the Euro Area Economy," *Quarterly Report on the Euro Area, European Commission* 13(4) 23–9. http://ec.europa.eu/economy_finance/publications/qr_ euro_area/2014/pdf/qrea4_section_2_en.pdf.

Rogoff, Kenneth S. (2015). "Debt Supercycle, not Secular Stagnation," in *Voxeu, CEPR's Policy Portal*. http://www.voxeu.org/article/debt-supercycle-not-secular-stagnation.

Roig-Franzia, Manuel (2009). "Brooksley Born, the Cassandra of the Derivatives Crisis," *The Washington Post*, May 25. http://www.washingtonpost. com/wp-dyn/content/article/2009/05/25/AR2009052502108.html.

Romer, Christina D. (2007). "Macroeconomic Policy in the 1960s: The causes and consequences of a mistaken revolution," Plenary Session, Economic History Association Annual Meeting, Lyndon B. Johnson Presidential Library.

Romer, Christina and Jared Bernstein (2009a). *The Job Impact of the American Recovery and Reinvestment Plan*. Council of Economic Advisers and Office of the Vice President. https://www.economy.com/mark-zandi/documents/The_Job_Impact_of_the_American_Recovery_and_Reinvestment_Plan.pdf.

Romer, Christina and Jared Bernstein (2009b). *The Job Impact of the American Recovery and Reinvestment Plan*. Office of the President-Elect. http://oversight.house.gov/wpcontent/uploads/2012/01/6-12-09-The-Job-Impact-of-the-American-Recovery-and-Reinvestment-Plan.pdf.

Ronchi, Veronica (2007). "The Neoliberal Myth in Latin America: The Cases of Mexico and Argentina in the '90s," *Fondazione Eni Enrico Mattei Nota di Lavoro 42.2007*.

Ros-Lehtinen, Ileana (2012). *Ros-Lehtinen Says President Obama Just Doesn't Get It*. https://ros-lehtinen.house.gov/press-release/roslehtinen-says-President-obama-just-doesn%5C%E2%5C%80%5C%99tget-it.

Roubini, Nouriel (2006). *International Monetary Fund Book Forums and International Seminars Lecture and Discussion with Nouriel Roubini*. Transcript of an IMF Seminar Nouriel Roubini on the U.S. and Global Outlook, Washington, DC. http://www.economonitor.com/nouriel/2010/09/02/economonitor-flashback-roubinis-imf-speech-september-72006/.

Rubin, Robert Edward and Jacob Weisberg (2004). *In an Uncertain World: Tough Choices from Wall Street to Washington*. Random House.

Rumsfeld, Donald (2002). Press Conference at NATO Headquarters, Brussels. http://www.nato.int/docu/speech/2002/s020606g.htm.

Ryan, Paul (2009). *President Obama's Half-Hearted Budget Cuts Dwarfed by Exploding Debt*. http://www.speaker.gov/general/presidentobama%5C%C3%5C%A2%5C%E2%5C%82%5C%AC%5C%E2%5C%84%5C%A2s-halfhearted-budget-cuts-dwarfed-exploding-debt (no longer available).

Saez, Emmanuel (2013). "Striking it Richer: The Evolution of Top Incomes in the United States (updated with 2012 preliminary estimates)," Berkeley: University of California, Department of Economics. http://elsa.berkeley.edu/~saez/saez-UStopincomes-2012.pdf.

Saez, Emmanuel (2015). "Striking it Richer: The Evolution of Top Incomes in the United States (updated with 2014 preliminary estimates)," University of California, Berkeley, Working Paper. https://eml.berkeley.edu/~saez/saez-UStopincomes-2014.pdf.

Saez, Emmanuel and Gabriel Zucman (2016). "Wealth Inequality in the United States since 1913: Evidence from Capitalized Income Tax Data," *Quarterly Journal of Economics* 131(2) 519–78. http://www.nber.org/papers/w20625.

Samargandi, Nahla, Jan Fidrmuc, and Sugata Ghosh (2015). "Is the Relationship Between Financial Development and Economic Growth Monotonic? Evidence from a Sample of Middle-Income Countries," *World Development* 68(0) 66–81. issn: 0305-750X. doi: http://dx.doi.org/10.1016/j.worlddev.2014.11.010.

Sanders, Bernard (2012). *Jamie Dimon is not Alone*. Office of the US Senator Bernard Sanders. http://www.sanders.senate.gov/imo/media/doc/061212DimonIsNotAlone.pdf.

Santiso, Javier (2003). *The Political Economy of Emerging Markets: Actors, Institutions and Financial Crises in Latin America*. Springer.

Santiso, Javier (2004). "Inside the Black Box: A journey towards Latin American emerging markets," *Documentos CIDOB. América Latina* 4.1.

Scaramucci, Anthony (2010). *Goodbye Gordon Gekko: How to Find Your Fortune without Losing Your Soul*. John Wiley & Sons.

Schattschneider, Elmer E. (1960). *The Semi-Sovereign People: A realist's view of democracy in America*. Holt, Rinehart and Winston.

Schmitt, Rick (2009). "Prophet and Loss." *Stanford Alumni* (March/April).

Securities and Exchange Commission (2004). *Final Rule: Alternative Net Capital Requirements for Broker-Dealers That Are Part of Consolidated Supervised Entities*. https://www.sec.gov/rules/final/34-49830.htm.

Shaikh, Anwar (2011). "The First Great Depression of the 21st Century," *Socialist Register* 47 (Fall) 44–63.

Shanahan, E., H. H. Humphrey, and American Enterprise Institute for Public Policy Research and Hoover Institution on War, Revolution, and Peace (1976). *Government Regulation: What Kind of Reform? A Round Table Held on 11 September 1975 and Sponsored by the American Enterprise Institute for Public Policy Research and the Hoover Institution on War, Revolution and Peace.* AEI Public Policy Forum. American Enterprise Institute for Public Policy Research. https://books.google.pt/books?id=AQguAAAAMAAJ.

Shiller, Robert J. (1981). "Do Stock Prices Move Too Much to be Justified by Subsequent Changes in Dividends?" *The American Economic Review* 71(3) 421–36.

Shiller, Robert J. (2005). *Irrational Exuberance* 2nd Edition. Princeton University Press.

Shiller, Robert J. (2007). "Understanding Recent Trends in House Prices and Homeownership," Proceedings—Economic Policy Symposium—Jackson Hole, pp. 89–123. https://ideas.repec.org/a/fip/fedkpr/y2007p89-123.html.

Shiller, Robert J. (2015). "Faith in an Unregulated Free Market? Don't Fall for It," *New York Times*, October 11. http://www.nytimes.com/2015/10/11/upshot/faith-in-an-unregulated-free-market-dont-fall-for-it.html.

Shiller, Robert J. (2017a). *Home Page of Robert J. Shiller.* http://www.econ.yale. edu/~shiller.

Shiller, Robert J. (2017b). "The Coming Bear Market?" in *Project Syndicate.* https://www.project-syndicate.org/commentary/us-stock-volatilitybear-market-by-robert-j-shiller-2017-09.

Shin, Hyun Song (2009). "Securitisation and Financial Stability," *The Economic Journal* 119(536) 309–32.

Shin, Hyun Song (2011). "Global Banking Glut and Loan risk Premium," *12th Jacques Polak Annual Research Conference.* International Monetary Fund. Washington, DC.

Shleifer, Andrei (2009). "The Age of Milton Friedman," *Journal of Economic Literature* 47(1) 123–35. http://scholar.harvard.edu/shleifer/publications/age-milton-friedman.

Shleifer, Andrei and Robert W. Vishny (2010). "Unstable Banking," *Journal of Financial Economics* 97(3) 306–18. http://www.nber.org/papers/w14943.pdf.

Sinclair, Philip A. (2007). "A Representation for the Mexican Political Networks," *Social Networks* 29(1) 81–92.

Sinclair, Philip A. (2011). "The Political Networks of Mexico and Measuring Centralization," *Procedia-Social and Behavioral Sciences* 10, 26–35.

Singh, Manmohan and James Aitken (2010). *The (Sizable) Role of Rehypothecation in the Shadow Banking System.* International Monetary Fund Working Papers 10/172. http://EconPapers.repec.org/RePEc:imf:imfwpa:10/172. http://www.imf.org/external/pubs/ft/wp/2010/wp10172.pdf.

Sinn, Hans-Werner (2014). *The Euro Trap: On Bursting Bubbles, Budgets, and Beliefs.* Oxford University Press.

Slesman, Ly, Ahmad Zubaidi Baharumshah, and Mark E. Wohar (2015). "Capital Inflows and Economic Growth: Does the Role of Institutions Matter?" *International Journal of Finance & Economics* 20(3) 191–290.

Smith, Adam (1759). *Theory of Moral Sentiments.* New York: Prometheus Books.

Smith, Adam (1999). *The Wealth of Nations (Book I–III).* London: Penguin.

Snowdon, Brian and Howard R. Vane (1998). "Transforming Macroeconomics: An interview with Robert E. Lucas, Jr," *Journal of Economic Methodology* 5(1) 115–46.

Soll, Jacob (2014). *The Reckoning: Financial Accountability and the Rise and Fall of Nations.* Basic Books.

Solomon, Steven Davidoff (2017). "Decade After Crisis, No Resolution for Fannie and Freddie," *New York Times*, February 7.

Solow, Robert (2008). "The State of Macroeconomics," *Journal of Economic Perspectives* 22(1) 243–6. http://pubs.aeaweb.org/doi/pdfplus/10.1257/jep.22.1.243.

Sorkin, Andrew Ross (2010). *Too Big to Fail: The Inside Story of how Wall Street and Washington Fought to Save the Financial System—and Themselves.* Penguin.

Spoerry, Lorenzo and Rabia Arif (2014). *Performance Link Questioned in Bank CEO Pay Debate*. SNL. https://www.snl.com/InteractiveX/Article.aspx?cdid=A-29599304-12071.

Steil, Benn (2013). *The Battle of Bretton Woods: John Maynard Keynes, Harry Dexter White, and the Making of a New World Order*. Princeton University Press.

Stein, Jeremy C. (2010). "Securitization, Shadow Banking and Financial Fragility," *Daedalus* 139 41–51. http://scholar.harvard.edu/files/stein/files/daedalus-sept-2010-final.pdf.

Stein, Judith (2010). *Pivotal Decade: How the United States Traded Factories for Finance in the Seventies*. Yale University Press.

Stenfors, Alexis (2014). "LIBOR as a Keynesian Beauty Contest: A Process of Endogenous Deception," *Review of Political Economy* 26(3) 392–407.

Stephens-Davidowitz, Seth (2015). "Just How Nepotistic Are We?" *New York Times*, March 22. http://www.nytimes.com/2015/03/22/opinion/sunday/seth-stephens-davidowitz-just-how-nepotistic-arewe.html.

Stevens, John (2014). "£41k a Month and 2% on Top: Blair's Deal with Saudis Leads to Questions over Former PM's Lucrative Contract," *Daily Mail*, November 9. http://www.dailymail.co.uk/news/article-2827263/Blairsigned-secret-contract-Saudi-oil-firm-promising-41-000month-slice-deals-helped-broker.html.

Stewart, Heather (2009). "This is how we let the credit crunch happen, Ma'am," *The Guardian*, July 26. http://www.theguardian.com/uk/2009/jul/26/monarchy-credit-crunch.

Stigler, George J. (1971). "The Theory of Economic Regulation," *The Bell Journal of Economics and Management Science* 2 3–21.

Stiglitz, Joseph (2002). "Globalism's Discontents," *American Prospect*. http://prospect.org/article/globalisms-discontents.

Stiglitz, Joseph (2003). *Globalization and Its Discontents*. WW Norton.

Stiglitz, Joseph (2010). *Freefall: America, Free Markets, and the Sinking of the World Economy*. WW Norton.

Stock, James H. and Mark W. Watson (2003). "Has the Business Cycle Changed and Why?" in *NBER Macroeconomics Annual 2002, Vol 17*. Edited by Mark Gertler and Kenneth S. Rogoff. MIT Press, pp. 159–230. http://www.nber.org/chapters/c11075.pdf.

Stockhammer, Engelbert (2004). "Financialisation and the Slowdown of Accumulation," *Cambridge Journal of Economics* 28(5) 719–41.

Stockhammer, Engelbert (2008). "Some Stylized Facts on the Finance-dominated Accumulation Regime," *Competition & Change* 12(2) 184–202.

Streeck, Wolfgang (2014). *Buying Time: The Delayed Crisis of Democratic Capitalism*. Verso.

Stryker, Robin (1990). "Science, Class, and the Welfare State: A Class-centered Functional Account," *American Journal of Sociology* 96(3) 684–726.

Summers, Lawrence H. (1986). "Does the Stock Market Rationally Reflect Fundamental Values?" *Journal of Finance* 41(3) 591–601.

Summers, Lawrence H. (2000). *Remarks of Treasury Secretary Lawrence H. Summers to the Securities Industry Association*. US Department of the Treasury. http://www.treasury.gov/press-center/press-releases/Pages/ls1005.aspx.

Summers, Lawrence H. (2013). "Speech on Secular Stagnation," IMF Fourteenth Annual Research Conference in Honor of Stanley Fischer. http://www.imf.org/external/mmedia/view.aspx?vid=2821294542001.

Summers, Lawrence H. (2014a). "Reflections on the 'New Secular Stagnation Hypothesis,'" in *Secular Stagnation: Facts, Causes and Cures*. Edited by Coen Teulings and Richard Baldwin. Centre for Economic Policy Research, pp. 27–38. https://voxeu.org/content/secular-stagnation-facts-causes-and-cures.

Summers, Lawrence H. (2014b). "US Economic Prospects: Secular Stagnation, Hysteresis, and the Zero Lower Bound," *Business Economics* 49(2) 65–73.

Summers, Lawrence H. (2015). "The Global Economy is in Serious Danger," *The Washington Post*. https://www.washingtonpost.com/opinions/the-global-economy-is-in-serious-danger/2015/10/07/85e81666-6c5d-11e5-b31c-d80d62b53e28_story.html.

Suskind, Ron (2011). *Confidence Men: Wall Street, Washington, and the Education of a President*. New York: Harper Collins.

Sveriges Riksbank (2013). *Eugene F. Fama—Facts*. The Sveriges Riksbank Prize in Economic Sciences in Memory of Alfred Nobel 2013. http://www.nobelprize.org/nobel_prizes/economic-sciences/laureates/2013/fama-facts.html.

Swissinfo (2016). *"Bahamas Leaks" puts spotlight on UBS and Credit Suisse*. http://www.swissinfo.ch/eng/offshore-files_-bahamasleaks–puts-spotlight-on-ubs-and-credit-suisse/42465208.

Szwarcberg, Mariela (2012). "Revisiting Clientelism: A Network Analysis of Problem-solving Networks in Argentina," *Social Networks* 34(2) 230–40.

Taibbi, Matt (2010a). *Griftopia: Bubble Machines, Vampire Squids, and the Long Con that is Breaking America*. Spiegel & Grau.

Taibbi, Matt (2010b). "The Great American Bubble Machine: From Tech Stocks to High Gas Prices, Goldman Sachs Has Engineered Every Major Market Manipulation since the Great Depression—and They're About to Do it Again," *Rolling Stone Magazine*, April 5. http://www.rollingstone.com/politics/news/the-great-american-bubble-machine-20100405.

Taleb, Nassim Nicholas (2007). *The Black Swan: The Impact of the Highly Improbable*. New York: Random House.

Tarullo, Daniel K. (2012). *Shadow Banking After the Financial Crisis*. Federal Reserve Bank of San Francisco Conference on Challenges in Global Finance: The Role of Asia, San Francisco, California. http://www. federalreserve.gov/newsevents/speech/tarullo20120612a.htm.

Taub, Jennifer (2009). "Recommendations for Reality-Based Regulatory Reform for Hedge Funds and Other Private Pools of Capital," *SAFER Policy Brief* 9. http://www.peri.umass.edu/fileadmin/pdf/other_publication_types/SAFERbriefs/SAFER_note6.pdf.

Taub, Jennifer (2010a). "A Whiff of Repo 105," *The Baseline Scenario* 16. http://baselinescenario.com/2010/03/16/a-whiff-of-repo-105/.

Taub, Jennifer (2010b). "Lehman Bros and Repo 105: A powerful case of addiction," *Journal of Regulation and Risk, North Asia* 2(2/3) (Summer/Autumn) 185–9.

Taub, Jennifer (2011). "The Sophisticated Investor and the Global Financial Crisis," *Corporate Governance Failures: The Role of Institutional Investors in the Global Financial Crisis*. Edited by James P. Hawley, Shyam J. Kamath, and Andrew T. Williams. University of Pennsylvania Press, pp. 188–216.

Taub, Jennifer (2013). "What We Don't Talk About When We Talk About Banking," in *Oxford Handbook of the Political Economy of Financial Crises*. Edited by Gerald A. Epstein and Martin H. Wolfson. Oxford University Press, pp. 447–66.

Taub, Jennifer (2014). *Other People's Houses: How Decades of Bailouts, Captive Regulators, and Toxic Bankers Made Home Mortgages a Thrilling Business*. Yale University Press.

Teichman, Judith A. (2001). *The Politics of Freeing Markets in Latin America: Chile, Argentina, and Mexico*. University of North Carolina Press.

The Telegraph (2010). "Stephen Byers: I'm like a cab for hire" March 22. http://www.telegraph.co.uk/news/newsvideo/uk-politics-video/7495978/Stephen-Byers-Im-like-a-cab-for-hire.html.

Teulings, Coen N. and Richard Baldwin (2014). *Secular Stagnation: Facts, Causes and Cures*. Centre for Economic Policy Research.

Thiemann, Matthias (2014). "In the Shadow of Basel: How competitive politics bred the crisis," *Review of International Political Economy* 21(6) 1203–39.

Thomas, Landon, Jr. (2016). "Hard-to-Sell Assets Complicate European Banks' 'Brexit' Risks," New York Times, June 28. http://www.nytimes.com/2016/06/29/business/dealbook/hard-to-sell-assetscomplicate-european-banks-brexit-risks.html.

Tian, Yuan (Gloria) (2006). *Three Essays on Corporate Control in Canada* (University of Alberta Ph.D. dissertation). Library and Archives Canada (Bibliothèque et Archives Canada).

Toporowski, Jan (2002). *The End of Finance: Capital Market Inflation, Financial Derivatives and Pension Fund Capitalism*. London: Routledge.

Tor, Maria and Rabia Arif (2014). *Top Paid US Bank CEOs*. SNL. https://www.snl.com/InteractiveX/Article.aspx?cdid=A-2820215213365.

Tribe, Keith (2009). "Liberalism and Neoliberalism in Britain," *The Road from Mont Pèlerin. The Making of the Neoliberal Thought Collective*. Edited by Philip Mirowski and Dieter Plehwe. Harvard University Press.

Trowbridge, Shannon O'Neil (2001). "The Role of Ideas in Neoliberal Economic Reform: The Case of Argentina," Latin American Studies Association Conference. Washington, DC.

Trump, Donald J. (2017). *Remarks by President Trump in Strategy and Policy Forum*. https://www.whitehouse.gov/briefings-statements/remarks-President-trump-strategy-policy-forum/.

Tsingou, Eleni (2015). "Club Governance and the Making of Global Financial Rules," *Review of International Political Economy* 22(2) 225–56.

Tucker, Paul (2010). "Shadow Banking, Capital Markets and Financial Stability," in Remarks, Bernie Gerald Cantor (BGC) Partners Seminar, Bank of England, London, pp. 1–8. http://www.bis.org/review/r100126d.pdf.

Turner, Adair (2012). *Shadow Banking and Financial Instability*. Cass Business School. http://www.cass.city.ac.uk/__data/assets/pdf_file/0013/120307/004-CASS-LECTURE-20120308.pdf.

United Nations General Assembly (2015). *Basic Principles on Sovereign Debt Restructuring Processes*. Resolution. http://unctad.org/en/pages/newshttp://details.http://aspx?OriginalVersionID=1074.

Urrutia, Miguel (1994). "Colombia," in *The Political Economy of Policy Reform*. Edited by J. Williamson. Washington DC: Institute for International Economics, pp. 285–315.

US Census Bureau (2016). *Health Insurance Coverage in the United States: 2015*. Current Population Reports. https://www.census.gov/content/dam/Census/library/publications/2016/demo/p60-257.pdf.

US Department of Justice (2015). *Settlement Agreement*. United States v. McGraw-Hill Companies, Inc. and Standard & Poor's Financial Services LLC, No. CV 13-00779-DOC. https://www.justice.gov/file/338701/download.

US Department of State (1948). *Proceedings and Documents of the United Nations Monetary and Financial Conference, Bretton Woods, New Hampshire, July 1–22, 1944*. Department of State, Publication 2866, International Organization and Conference Series 1,3. https://fraser.stlouisfed. org/files/docs/publications/books/1948_state_bwood_v1.pdf.

US Department of the Treasury (2014). *Ramin Toloui Confirmed as Treasury Assistant Secretary for International Finance*. Press Release. https://www.treasury.gov/press-center/press-releases/Pages/jl9706.aspx.

US Financial Crisis Inquiry Commission (2011). *The Financial Crisis Inquiry Report: Final Report of the National Commission on the Causes of the Financial and Economic Crisis in the United States*. Government Printing Office. http://fcic-static.law.stanford.edu/cdn_media/fcic-reports/fcic_final_report_full.pdf.

US House of Representatives, Committee on Banking and Financial Services (1998). *Hedge Fund Operations*. http://commdocs.house.gov/committees/bank/hba51526.000/hba51526_0f.htm.

US Securities and Exchange Commission v. Goldman Sachs & Co. and Fabrice Tourre (2010). *The SEC Charges Goldman Sachs With Fraud In Connection With The Structuring And Marketing of A Synthetic CDO*. 10 Civ. 3229, Litigation Release No. 21489. United States District Court Southern District of New York. http://www.sec.gov/litigation/

complaints/2010/comppr2010-59.pdf. https://www.sec.gov/litigation/litreleases/2010/lr21489.htm.

US Senate (2004). *Money Laundering and Foreign Corruption: Enforcement and Effectiveness of the Patriot Act. Case Study Involving Riggs Bank.* Minority Staff of the Permanent Subcommittee on Investigations. https://www.hsgac.senate.gov/imo/media/doc/ACF5F8.pdf.

US Senate Committee on the Budget (2011). *The Chorus Grows: Obama's Budget Represents Failure Of Leadership.* https://www.budget.senate.gov/newsroom/budget-background/the-chorus-growsobamas-budget-represents-failure-of-leadership.

Valdés, Juan Gabriel (1989). *La escuela de Chicago: operación Chile.* Vol. 11. Grupo Editorial Zeta.

Vélez, A. M. (2011). *Los expolíticos ganan peso en las grandes empresas.* Público. http://www.publico.es/actualidad/expoliticosganan-peso-grandes-empresas.html.

Vickers, John (2011). Independent Commission on Banking Final Report: Recommendations. The Stationery Office. https://www.gov.uk/government/news/independent-commission-on-banking-finalreport.

Waggoner, John (2008). "Reserve Primary Money Market Fund Breaks a Buck," *USA TODAY.* http://usatoday30.usatoday.com/money/perfi/basics/2008-09-16-damage_N.htm.

Walne, Toby (2012). "Barings Rogue Trader Nick Leeson: 'Money is not my motivation,'" *The Telegraph,* August 19. http://www.telegraph.co.uk/finance/personalfinance/fameandfortune/9483379/Baringsrogue-trader-Nick-Leeson-Money-is-not-my-motivation.html.

Walsh, Ben (2014). "Bizarre Trial Accuses Government Of Illegally Bailing Out AIG," *Huffington Post* September 29. http://www.huffingtonpost.com/2014/09/29/hank-greenberg-aig_n_5900082.html.

Weber, Bruce (2008). "Henry B. R. Brown, Who Opened Money Markets to Masses, Dies at 82," *New York Times* August 15. http://www.nytimes. com/2008/08/15/business/15brown.html.

Weck, Joseph de (2013). *Steinbrueck Hits Reset in German Election Campaign After Gaffes.* http://www.bloomberg.com/news/articles/201301-29/steinbrueck-hits-reset-in-german-election-campaignafter-gaffes.

West, Darrell M (2014). *Billionaires: Reflections on the Upper Crust.* Brookings Institution Press.

Williamson, John (1994). "In Search of a Manual for Technopols," in *The Political Economy of Policy Reform.* Edited by J. Williamson. Washington DC: Institute for International Economics, pp. 11–28.

Wise, Peter (2011). "A Degree of Influence," *Financial Times,* September 18. https://www.ft.com/content/ef25c728-de3a-11e0-9fb7-00144feabdc0.

Wolf, Martin (2014). *The Shifts and the Shocks: What We've Learned—and Have Still to Learn—From the Financial Crisis.* Penguin.

Woodford, Michael (2011). "Simple Analytics of the Government Expenditure Multiplier," *American Economic Journal: Macroeconomics* 3(1) 1–35.

World Bank (2017a). *DataBank.* http://databank.worldbank.org.

World Bank (2017b). *Informal Labor Markets in Transition Economies: Measuring the Size of the Informal Sector.* http://lnweb90.worldbank.org/eca/eca.nsf/Sectors/ECSPE/0E1CFCAE7D9EFA4185256A940073F4E5?OpenDocument.

World Bank and International Monetary Fund (2009). *Global Monitoring Report 2009: A Development Emergency.* World Bank. http://siteresources.worldbank.org/INTGLOMONREP2009/Resources/5924349-1239742507025/GMR09_book.pdf.

World Economic and Financial Surveys (2006a). *Global Financial Stability Report: Global Financial System Resilience in the Face of Cyclical Challenges.* International Monetary Fund. https://www.imf.org/External/Pubs/FT/GFSR/2006/02/index.htm.

World Economic and Financial Surveys (2006b). *Global Financial Stability Report: Market Developments and Issues.* International Monetary Fund. https://www.imf.org/External/Pubs/FT/GFSR/2006/02/index.htm.

World Economic and Financial Surveys (2009). *Global Financial Stability Report: Responding to the Financial Crisis and Measuring Systemic Risks.* International Monetary Fund. https://www.imf.org/External/Pubs/FT/GFSR/2009/01/index.htm.

World Economic and Financial Surveys (2014). "Global Financial Stability Report (GFSR): Risk Taking, Liquidity, and Shadow Banking: Curbing Excess While Promoting Growth," in *Shadow Banking around the Globe: How Large, and How Risky?* International Monetary Fund, pp. 65–104. https://www.imf.org/external/pubs/ft/gfsr/2014/02/pdf/c2.pdf.

Xafa, Miranda (2014). *Lessons from the 2012 Greek Debt Restructuring. VoxEU.org.* http://voxeu.org/article/greek-debt-restructuringlessons-learned.

Young, Kevin, Lasse Folke Henriksen, and Leonard Seabrooke (2016). "Neoliberal Grandfathers and the Success of Their Progeny: A Genealogical Analysis of Economists' Professional Networks," 28th Annual Meeting. SASE.

Young, Kevin, Tim Marple, and James Heilman (2017). "Beyond the Revolving Door: Advocacy behavior and social distance to financial regulators," *Business and Politics* 19(2) 327–64.

Zhu, Andong, Michael Ash, and Robert Pollin (2004). "Stock Market Liquidity and Economic Growth: A critical appraisal of the Levine/Zervos model," *International Review of Applied Economics* 18(1) 63–71.

Zucman, Gabriel (2014). "Taxing across Borders: Tracking personal wealth and corporate profits," *Journal of Economic Perspectives* 28(4) 121–48.

Zucman, Gabriel (2015). *The Hidden Wealth of Nations: The Scourge of Tax Havens.* University of Chicago Press.

Index

Tables and figures are indicated by an italic *t* and *f* following the page number. Notes are indicated by an n following the page number.